Financial Reporting for American Cities and Counties 1986

Financial Reporting for American Cities and Counties 1986

Formerly Governmental Accounting Procedures and Practices

Cornelius E. Tierney
Chairman, Government Services Group

Philip T. Calder
Director, Governmental Accounting and Auditing

Arthur Young & Company

Elsevier

New York • Amsterdam • Oxford

Elsevier Science Publishing Co., Inc.
52 Vanderbilt Avenue, New York, New York 10017

Distributors outside the United States and Canada:

Elsevier Science Publishers B.V.
P.O. Box 211, 1000 AE Amsterdam, The Netherlands

© 1986 by Arthur Young & Company

⚠ ARTHUR YOUNG

277 Park Avenue, New York, New York 10172

This book has been registered with the Copyright Clearance
Center, Inc. For further information please contact the Copyright
Clearance Center, Salem, Massachusetts.

ISBN 0-444-00993-0 (cloth)
ISBN 0-444-01002-5 (paper)
ISSN 0883-6779

This book reflects the observations and views of the authors and
is not an official statement of policy of Arthur Young &
Company.

Formerly published under the title
Governmental Accounting Procedures and Practices
(1983: ISBN 0-444-00792-X;
1985: ISBN 0-444-00878-0; ISSN 0748-0105).

Current printing (last digit):
10 9 8 7 6 5 4 3 2 1

Manufactured in the United States of America

Contents

Preface

Financial Reporting for American Cities and Counties, formerly entitled *Governmental Accounting Procedures and Practices*, was developed to meet a perceived need for a single reference on the accounting and financial reporting practices of local governmental units. That perception was confirmed by the financial media and by the professional acknowledgments received by Arthur Young & Company in the years following publication of that initial edition in 1983.

Like past editions, this edition contains observations from hundreds of governmental financial statements and still constitutes the largest and most comprehensive study of accounting and financial reporting practices. Arthur Young is truly appreciative of the support received from the U.S. Conference of Mayors and the National Association of Counties. Without the voluntary participation of their constituent members—the cities and counties—this study could not have been made.

Like the material in the first edition, the contents of this volume reflect the broad range of financial statements published by cities and counties, but the coverage is expanded in other ways. This edition contains the accounting principles declared to be appropriate for state and local governmental units by the National Council on Governmental Accounting and that have also been recognized by the American Institute of Certified Public Accountants as being in conformity with generally accepted accounting principles. Numerous tables present quantitative analyses of terms and formats of accounting and reporting practices. Hundreds of extracts from the annual financial reports of many governments illustrate contemporary accounting and reporting practices. Special analyses have been included to demonstrate compliance by governmental units with several new accounting requirements that will significantly affect the reported balances of governmental units during the next year and in all future years. For this edition we have expanded the summary description of generally accepted accounting principles for government, devoting more coverage to significant events in the last year affecting those principles. Also, a separate section has been included to illustrate how the study data might be used by professionals interested in or affected by the accounting and reporting by governmental units. All involved in any way with governments—elected officials, appointed officials, finance officers, treasurers, budget officers, accountants, auditors, underwriters, attorneys, rating agencies, and bankers—will find this expanded survey of accounting and reporting to be even more useful to them.

Having received no objection to earlier editions, we have continued certain practices to enhance readability. Capitalization in extracts has occasionally been altered to facilitate comparisons, a few obvious typographical errors in the original financial reports have been silently corrected, identifying headings have been inserted in square brackets, and formats may be ever so slightly altered to provide the maximum data as concisely as possible. Nevertheless, the overriding concern continues to be the preservation of variations in accounting and reporting practices actually observed.

This third edition was improved as a result of comments and suggestions received concerning the past editions. The authors would appreciate receiving similar thoughts and ideas concerning this edition.

Acknowledgments

For the third year, *Financial Reporting for American Cities and Counties* was made possible only with the professional efforts of the many students of accounting at Georgetown University's School of Business Administration. Their diligence and dedication once again permitted the completion of this study of governmental accounting and reporting practices in a timely manner:

William Ackerman	Neil Kinney
John Allario	Tara A. Leskanic
Bob Carnathan	Michael R. McDonnell
Andy Crnkovich	William P. McLaughlin
Edward DiGeronimo	Marcie M. Matthews
German Dominguez	Paul C. Opie
Linda DiRe	Mark Overdyk
David P. Doyal	Anayansie Perez
Kevin Egan	Philip Pettway
William Ficca	Timothy J. Scanlon
Chris Garagusi	Louis D. Schwartz
Sheila Gibbs	Mark Shutello
Alan Gilbert	Sally M. Sinton
Craig D. Grear	Mary A. St.Cyr
Michael J. Grisius	Robert E. Stenson
Claudia Hayes	Michael E. Tadie
Susan Hillery	Kelly A. Trybus

A special thanks is also due to Dr. Mortimer A. Dittenhofer, Associate Professor of Accounting at Georgetown University, whose continued assistance and expert advice are greatly appreciated.

Three students deserve special recognition: Kevin C. Gelston, Amy M. Graham, and Patrick J. Tadie. They provided project leadership and invaluable support with this edition. They were student participants for the previous edition.

Guidance and advice were volunteered by the many partners of Arthur Young who serve its numerous government clients.

Particular recognition is due John F. Ferraro, whose contributions to this and last year's editions are greatly appreciated.

Financial Reporting for American Cities and Counties 1986

Chapter 1
Introduction

This chapter has three main sections. The first is an overview of governmental accounting procedures and practices. The second section, on governmental accounting standards, describes the events leading to the formation of the Governmental Accounting Standards Board and describes the several regulating or standard-setting bodies now involved with the accounting and reporting practices of governmental units. A summary is also provided of the accounting and reporting procedures that are the substance of the generally accepted accounting principles of government. The third section describes the format of this book and suggests how its contents might be used.

GOVERNMENTAL ACCOUNTING PROCEDURES AND PRACTICES: AN OVERVIEW

This section discusses the extent and significance of public sector finances, particularly those of cities and counties, and describes the scope and methodology of this study. The succeeding chapters provide details and observations of specific elements of the study.

The Governmental Sector

The economic impact of governmental units is impressive, if not overwhelming. The annual-expenditure budgets of state and local governments exceed one-sixth of the country's estimated gross national product. The governmental services provided by cities and counties are practically limitless, reaching every household and family.

Even the number of governmental units is impressive. There are over 80,000 nonfederal governmental units, including states, counties, cities, towns, and numerous school and special districts. The 1982 census observed the array of local governmental organizations shown in table A.

The Census Bureau has defined *special districts* as limited-purpose governmental units (other than school districts) existing as separate entities with substantial fiscal and administrative independence from general-purpose local governments. Typically, special districts perform a single function or provide a single service, such as fire protection, sewerage, hospital operations, housing, or community development. The 1982 census of governmental units included the special districts shown in the following table.

A. LOCAL GOVERNMENTAL UNITS

Type of Government	1982	1972	1962
County	3,041	3,044	3,043
Municipal	19,076	18,517	18,000
Township	16,734	16,991	17,142
School district	14,851	15,781	34,678
Special district	28,588	23,885	18,323
Total local governments	82,290	78,218	91,186

Source: 1982 Census of Governments (Final), Governmental Organization, Vol. 1, U.S. Department of Commerce, Bureau of the Census, Washington, D. C., August 1983.

SPECIAL DISTRICT GOVERNMENTS BY FUNCTION: 1982

Function	Number	Percent
Single-function districts:		
Education	960	3.3
Libraries	638	2.2
Hospitals	775	2.7
Health	451	1.5
Highways	598	2.0
Airports	357	1.2
Fire protection	4,560	15.9
Natural resources	6,232	21.7
Parks and recreation	924	3.2
Housing and community development	3,296	11.5
Sewerage	1,631	5.6
Sanitation other than sewerage	101	0.3
Water supply	2,637	9.2
Cemeteries	1,577	5.3
Other	1,543	5.4
Multiple-function districts	2,597	9.0
Total	28,588	100.0

Source: 1982 Census of Governments (Final), Governmental Organization, Vol. 1, U.S. Department of Commerce, Bureau of the Census, Washington, D.C., August 1983.

Of the 80,000 governmental units, almost 50,000 have issued debt securities to the general public. The current outstanding value of these issues exceeds $400 billion.

The Analysis of Financial Statements of Governmental Units

Scope

For this third edition of *Financial Reporting for American Cities and Counties* (formerly entitled *Governmental Accounting Procedures and Practices*) over 550 financial statements of cities and counties were analyzed.

A microcomputer database has been constructed that is similar to the tables and other arrays of information in this book, although in greater detail. The data have been stratified by size of city and county (small, medium, or large), as defined in the accompanying table. This material will permit the construction of more specific accounting and reporting information should the need or interest arise.

GOVERNMENTAL UNITS INCLUDED IN THIS STUDY

Type of Local Governmental Unit	Population	Number of Units in This Study
Cities:		
Small cities	Under 50,000	130
Medium cities	50,001 to 500,000	182
Large cities	Over 500,000	14
Subtotal		326
Counties		
Small counties	Under 50,000	54
Medium counties	50,001 to 500,000	141
Large counties	Over 500,000	30
Subtotal		225
Total cities and counties in the study		551

Space limitations permit presentation in this book of only selected summary data for these governmental units. However, detailed data files are available by each of the above kinds of government.

In this edition, as in 1983 and 1984, all the financial reports were furnished voluntarily by governmental units among the members of the U.S. Conference of Mayors and the National Association of Counties. The reports analyzed for this study were prepared by the governmental units for fiscal years ended no later than September 30, 1984.

While their distribution was not planned, the governments submitting financial statements were well dispersed geographically and appear to be representative. The governments participating in this year's study are listed in the Appendix.

Approach

The study consisted of several specific analytical tasks. First, an inventory was made of accounting principles and auditing standards applicable to governmental units, and a review or protocol document was designed, pilot tested, and refined. The objective of this effort was to develop an extensive survey guide for use in the analysis of the individual financial statements. Initially an inventory of the types of funds and the accounts appearing in the combined financial statements—the general purpose financial statements—was compiled. A second study phase was directed toward gathering data related to several important subjects, such as the type and content of transmittal letters, the type of certificate issued by the auditor, the fiscal year used and other report submission data, footnote disclosures, detailed information on combining statements, and many other reporting practices. Third, special analyses were made to discern the new accounting and reporting practices related to governmental entities, compensated absences, leases, and pensions. The results of these analyses are reported in separate chapters.

Consistent with prior years, the overall objective of this study was to construct a profile of the accounting and reporting practices of a wide spectrum of local governmental units. The study results are thus a compilation and summary of the accounting and reporting practices of the surveyed units. They enable a comparative profile of the financial practices of individual governmental units, although the study itself did not include such a comparison.

Financial Reports Analyzed

Statement 1 of the National Council on Governmental Accounting (NCGA) indicates that each governmental unit should prepare and publish a comprehensive annual financial report (CAFR) that includes information on all funds and account groups. The NCGA states that the CAFR should contain (1) the general purpose financial statements (GPFS) by fund type and account group (these statements are the combined statements), (2) the combining statements by fund type, and (3) the individual fund statements.

The CAFR is the governmental unit's official annual report, although the unit may also issue the GPFS separately. The GPFS is, in effect, the separable portion of the CAFR statements. It is the GPFS data that are most often included in the prospectus for bond offerings or for distribution to users of financial statements that require less than the detailed information appearing in the CAFR.

Overview of This Book

The study data were largely obtained from the five combined statements in the GPFS, although reviews were also made of the combining and individual fund statements and of supplemental information to obtain certain detailed information thought to be of interest to governmental units, practitioners, and other users of these types of financial statements. In this edition the material has been arranged to parallel to a degree the several accounting principles of NCGA Statement 1 and the subject matter of possible significance to users of the study findings.

Chapter 2, Accounting and Reporting by Governmental Units, provides information concerning NCGA Statement 1, the basis of accounting, fund accounting systems, and types of funds. This chapter also includes a summary identification of those activities for which governments have established separate special revenue, capital projects, special assessment, enterprise, and internal service funds.

Chapter 3, Fixed Assets, Valuations, Depreciation, Noncancellable Leases, and Infrastructure Assets, reviews the compliance of the surveyed government units with Principles 5, 6, and 7 of Statement 1. Information is provided on the valuation practices applied to governmental and proprietary-type fixed assets, depreciation practices, and noncancellable leases. Information is also included on public domain or infrastructure fixed assets.

Chapter 4, Long-Term Liabilities, contains information reported by the government units surveyed relating to the accounting and reporting of long-term liabilities, both fund and general long-term debt. Since noncancellable leases for general fixed assets may in substance be acquisitions of assets with related long-term debt, illustrations have been included in this chapter of the manner in which several governments reported the long-term obligations resulting from those leases.

Chapter 5, Basis of Accounting and Budgetary Accounting, contains information on accounting and reporting under the modified accrual basis and the accrual basis. Also described are disclosure practices relating to the reporting of budget data.

Chapter 6, Interfund Transactions, Transfers, and Bond Proceeds, essentially relates to Principle 10 of Statement 1. This chapter contains examples and illustrations relating to several subjects: quasi-external transactions, reimbursement transactions, residual equity transfers, operating transfers, and proceeds from long-term debt.

Chapter 7, Revenues, Expenditures, and Changes in Fund Balances: Governmental Funds, summarizes selected survey observations relating to Principle 10 of NCGA Statement 1. This principle requires that, with respect to governmental funds, revenues be classified by fund and source and that expenditures be classified by several additional categories. Chapter 8 provides information similar to that contained in Chapter 7 but for proprietary funds that reflect revenues, expenses, and changes in retained earnings.

The next four chapters are devoted to the accounting and reporting procedures and practices used by governments in their balance sheet to report assets, liabilities, and fund equity. Chapter 9, The Balance Sheet: Accounting for Assets; Chapter 10, The Balance Sheet: Accounting for Liabilities; and Chapter 11, The Balance Sheet: Governmental Equities, precede a chapter devoted to the reporting made by the surveyed units of changes in the financial position of proprietary funds and similar trust funds.

Chapter 13, The Auditor's Report, has been expanded beyond last year's analysis. The types of opinions provided by independent auditors have been analyzed in detail, and illustrations of opinions where dependence was placed on the work of other auditors have been highlighted. As in earlier editions, the chapter contains data related to the auditor's certificate as well as illustrations of different kinds of auditors' opinions.

Chapter 14, Governmental Financial Statements, as in the 1983 and 1985 editions of this book, summarizes the hierarchy of accounting and reporting in the public sector. This edition also provides information on the accounting for "component units" of governmental entities. Consolidated reporting is not in accord with generally accepted governmental accounting principles, but some governmental units have found such reports to be of benefit in explaining to the general public the financial results of their operations. This type of reporting is illustrated in this chapter as well.

Chapter 15, Accounting and Reporting Practices for Selected Topics, contains expanded information on illustrations of accounting, reporting, and disclosures for such subjects and issues as capitalization of interest; commitments; contingencies; compliance, stewardship, and accountability; encumbrances; joint ventures; investments; new funds; operating leases; self-insurance; related-party transactions; special assessment accounting; and events subsequent to the balance sheet date.

Chapter 16, General Study Observations and Other Matters, contains observations on other reporting topics, such as letters of transmittal included in the annual reports of governments and data on the various fiscal years used by governments.

Chapter 17, Special Analyses of Recent Governmental Accounting Standards, summarizes the results of specific analyses of governmental financial reports for compliance with NCGA Statements 3 to 5 pertaining to governmental entities; claims, judgments, and compensated absences; and leases, respectively.

Chapter 18, Pension Accounting and Reporting for Public Employee Retirement Systems, is a summary of the results of a special analysis of governmental financial reports to assess the information provided on pension plans. Although the NCGA had adopted Statement 6, "Pension Accounting and Financial Reporting: Public Employee Retirement Systems and State and Local Government Employers," in April 1983, the effective date for implementation has been repeatedly deferred. Most recently, the NCGA deferred the effective date of this statement until an "unspecified future date."

Chapter 19, Status of Governmental Accounting Standards, provides information on the accounting pronouncements made by the NCGA over the years, as well as the various statements of position relating to governmental accounting issued by the American Institute of Certified Public Accountants and the Governmental Accounting Standards Board.

GOVERNMENTAL ACCOUNTING STANDARDS

In July 1984 the Governmental Accounting Standards Board (GASB) published its Statement 1, which continued in force the issuances of the NCGA and those of the American Institute of Certified Public Accountants (AICPA) relating to governmental accounting. This action culminated five years of intensive work by professional associations, public interest groups, and governmental organizations toward the creation of a governmental accounting standard-setting body. The five years of formal activity had been preceded by a substantial period of informal discussions among the same participants.

Standard-Setting Organizations: An Overview

Since the enactment of the Securities Acts of 1933 and 1934, the Securities and Exchange Commission (SEC) has played an important role in monitoring the accounting and reporting practices of corporate organizations selling securities to the public. In addition, over these years the primary standard-setting organizations for the accounting, auditing, and reporting practices of business organizations have been the

AICPA and, since 1973, the Financial Accounting Standards Board (FASB). In contrast, the securities of governmental units have been specifically excluded from SEC oversight. Thus, there has long been effort on the part of governmental executives, public interest groups, professional associations, and members of the accounting profession to establish uniform and consistent accounting and reporting practices for governmental units, particularly those with publicly sold securities.

Many of the pronouncements of the AICPA and FASB are equally applicable to government. Probably more important to governmental accounting, however, has been guidance provided by the National Committee on Governmental Accounting and its successor, the National Council on Governmental Accounting. As stated by the AICPA in its Statement of Position 80-2 (June 30, 1980), financial statements presented in accordance with NCGA Statement 1 are considered to be in conformity with generally accepted accounting principles.

The functions of the NCGA were assumed by the GASB, which became operational in 1984.

The GASB's responsibilities will include the issuance of pronouncements on governmental accounting standards, using the same due process procedure as that of the Financial Accounting Standards Board so as to provide broad public participation in all stages of the standard-setting process. In its first formal action, GASB Statement 1, "Authoritative Status of NCGA Pronouncements and AICPA Industry Audit Guide," the Board continued in force the current issuances of the NCGA and those of the AICPA relating to local government and state accounting, until specifically altered, amended, supplemented, revoked, or superseded by the GASB.

The GASB will establish accounting and financial reporting standards for activities and transactions of state and local governmental entities. The FASB will do the same for all other entities. Thus pronouncements of the GASB will supersede those of the FASB in the hierarchy of governmental accounting procedures and practices for state and local government entities.

The Need for the GASB

Prior to establishment of the GASB, there was a body of generally accepted accounting principles for governments, consisting of the publications of the National Council on Governmental Accounting, the publications of various committees of the AICPA, and the accounting practices followed by a large number of governments. The GASB was established to alleviate several concerns about the development of these principles. These concerns included the following:

1. Both standard-setting groups were part-time operations and thus were not able to react promptly to current problems or to develop substantial new projects.
2. The reporting formats were cumbersome and did not completely describe overall financial conditions.
3. Standard-setting activities were hampered by a lack of adequate funding.

These conditions, along with the financial distress of such major cities such as New York, Cleveland, and Detroit, prompted a series of informal discussions and several formal talks among knowledgeable officials. These officials concluded that timely action could eliminate the problems. Congressional interest, as shown in committee hearings on prospective bills affecting accounting practices, also lent impetus to the proposal.

The Concept of Generally Accepted Accounting Principles

Generally accepted accounting principles are those accounting principles that are considered essential if an organization is to report fairly and to fully disclose the economic results of operations for a given period and the economic and financial condition of the organization at a specific date. (Formerly, the words "accurately" and "correctly" were used in place of the word "fairly." The former adjectives gave the appearance of a precision that cannot be attained, primarily because of the substantial degree of subjectivity in the accounting process.)

The AICPA has continuously stated that the opinions of its Accounting Principles Board and, later, of the Financial Accounting Standards Board constitute the primary source of generally accepted accounting principles. General acceptance implies common agreement based on such considerations as experience, custom, reason, and most important, practical necessity. The AICPA defines them as "the conventions, rules, and procedures necessary to define accepted accounting practices at a particular time."

These principles have both primary and secondary sources. A primary source is one that is itself authoritative. Secondary sources can, in combination, also result in the identification of generally accepted principles.

The primary sources are

the Financial Accounting Standards Board,

the Governmental Accounting Standards Board,

the various standard-setting units of the American Institute of Certified Public Accountants, and

the National Council of Governmental Accounting.

Secondary sources include

industry usage,

directives of regulatory agencies,

the writings of recognized scholars and professionals,

pronouncements of industry associations,

textbooks, and

talks and addresses by accounting specialists.

Generally Accepted Accounting Principles for Government

The 1968 edition of *General Accounting, Auditing, and Financial Reporting* (GAAFR) described 13 basic accounting and financial reporting principles that were to be used by governmental units. As described in the 1968 publication, these principles, because they were found to be reasonable and generally accepted by public administrators, accountants, and others, were generally recognized as essential to the fair presentation and analysis of financial operations and to the proper preparation and presentation of required financial statements and reports. In 1974 the AICPA's Committee on Governmental Accounting and Auditing issued an industry guide for the audit of state and local governmental units. This guide set forth the following position with respect to the GAAFR principles:

> GAAFR's principles do not represent a complete and separate body of accounting principles, but rather are a part of the whole body of generally accepted accounting principles which deal specifically with governmental units. Except as modified in this guide, they constitute generally accepted accounting principles.

Subsequent to the issuance of NCGA Statement 1, in 1979, the AICPA published Statement of Position 80-2 (June 30, 1980), "Accounting and Financial Reporting by Governmental Units." This is an amendment to the industry audit guide and recognizes that Statement 1 updates, clarifies, and amplifies the 1968 GAAFR. The statement of position thus held that, because the AICPA audit guide had earlier recognized the 1968 GAAFR, it was now necessary to amend the audit guide to recognize Statement 1.

Statement 1 consists of 12 principles of governmental accounting and reporting. It is the authoritative modification to GAAFR. As described above, Statement 1 replaced the principles of governmental accounting, auditing, and reporting that were first published in 1968 by The National Committee on

Governmental Accounting, in the "Blue Book" (formally titled *Governmental Accounting, Auditing, and Financial Reporting*) and became effective for fiscal years ending after June 30, 1980. A summary of Statement 1 appears in Exhibit 1–1 at the end of this chapter.

In 1980 the Municipal Finance Officers Association republished GAAFR, but noted in the foreword that

> unlike 1968 GAAFR, this text neither establishes nor authoritatively interprets GAAP for governments. This edition of Governmental Accounting, Auditing, and Financial Reporting is intended to provide government finance officers, elected officials, independent auditors, and others with detailed guidance to the effective application of NCGA Statement 1 principles.

Municipal securities credit-rating organizations, while not prescribers of accounting principles, also influence the setting of governmental accounting and reporting principles. For example, in 1980, Standard & Poor's stated that an important factor in its governmental or municipal ratings was the timely receipt and analysis of financial statements certified by independent public accountants or by appropriate state or local auditing agencies and prepared in accordance with generally accepted accounting principles. Further, Standard & Poor's declared the accrual basis of accounting to be the superior method of accounting for the economic resources of any government organization; the cash basis was not considered appropriate. That same policy statement concluded that

> in the absence of financial reports prepared in accordance with the aforementioned guidelines, S&P will specifically reflect such absence in its rating process as a negative factor and, where the report is not timely or is substantially deficient in terms of reporting, will not rate at all.*

Methodology of the GASB

The methodology of the GASB conforms to that of the FASB. The steps are these:

1. An agenda is prepared. The items to be considered are those issues that are believed to be most pressing by statement preparers, attestors and users.
2. Items are assigned to staff members or to ad hoc task forces to be researched and developed.
3. Drafts are prepared and, after internal review and modification, an exposure draft is prepared and distributed for comment.
4. Comments are received and public hearings are

conducted to obtain the consideration of the position of those affected and to explore alternatives.
5. The standard is finalized and issued.
6. Communications are maintained with constituents to determine that the standards are properly understood and that the objective of the issuance is being served.

The GASB has identified five factors that will probably influence its early technical work:

1. *The models:* Either an accounting model or a financial reporting model may predominate. The former is concerned with flow of funds or spending; the latter is the traditional multicolumn fund-type report.
2. *The written record:* Consideration must be given to the public reaction to governments that have had acute financial trauma and alleged accounting and reporting failures, as well as to possible similarities and differences noted by students of accounting between the interests, needs, and methods of business and government.
3. *Recommendations:* A recently completed project offers recommendations for state accounting methods.
4. *The needs of users:* These include governmental managers, government oversight bodies, the securities industry, and the citizenry.
5. *Current events:* Emerging issues of particular importance include the infrastructure crisis, the increasing costs of operations, recent financial disasters in governments, and the increasing use of innovative financial practices.

Accomplishments of the GASB

Thus far, the GASB has issued its first statement. This statement continued in force the publications of the NCGA and AICPA. The NCGA had issued seven statements, 11 interpretations, and one concepts statement; the AICPA had issued an industry audit guide for governments and several amendments, interpretations, and other publications on governmental accounting.

The GASB has developed an agenda for future attention. This agenda includes

issues pertaining to financial reporting;

the basis of accounting and measurement objectives for governmental-type funds;

pension accounting and financial reporting;

deferred compensation;

codification of governments' generally accepted accounting principles;

---

* Standard & Poor's *Perspective*, "Who's Watching the Books," and attached policy statement, "Municipal Accounting and Financial Reporting," Standard and Poor's Corporation, New York, 1980.

elimination of the separate reporting of special assessment activities;

fixed assets and infrastructure accounting and reporting;

financial reporting standards for public authorities; and

the handling of demand bonds issued by state and local governmental entities.

The work will be performed by the GASB staff and by task forces now being formed. Target dates have been set. Due process is planned for all of these activities.

HOW TO USE THIS BOOK

It is important that the reader be aware of the potential uses of the material in this book. One might well believe that a complete analysis such as that contained in this reference work is in no need of explicit directions to the reader. Yet ultimately the potential uses of this material are so extensive that they require some formal attention together with an explanation of the methodology that would best serve the user.

Potential Uses

The information in this book combines descriptive and narrative data that have been assembled from an analysis of some 550 local governmental financial statements. The material is presented exactly as it was assembled by the analysts, without further analysis or opinion.

One objective of this study was to provide a profile of the accounting and reporting practices of hundreds of governmental units that could be of value to individual governments as a check on their own financial disclosure. Concurrently, it was believed that the results of the study would disclose the extent of adherence to generally accepted accounting principles. The study would show how governments for varying reasons—such as compliance with legislation, practical necessities, and differing theories of accounting and reporting—have modified and in many cases simplified their accounting and reporting. Further improvements may have to wait for legislative approval of the pronouncements of the GASB, for independent public accountants to accept what will be identified as generally accepted accounting principles, and for analysts to view these changes as normal and progressive evolutionary improvements.

This book thus can be used to

1. determine actual practices in accounting and reporting methods, so as to serve as guidance in evaluating financial statements being reviewed and preparing financial statements;

2. observe the methods and language used in account titles and in footnotes to financial statements;

3. compare the accounting and reporting methodologies of similar governments;

4. determine what constitutes general acceptability in terms of substantial usage;

5. observe current practices in audit exceptions and recommendations, so as to serve as authority and basis for individual audit reporting;

6. determine the degree of compliance of the observed reports with GAAP and with the legal requirements of state regulations; and

7. observe the compliance of local governments with new GAAP requirements and with those that are not yet effective.

Format

To enhance the book's usefulness, each topic is presented in a three-part format. First, the material is introduced by an outline of accounting principles from authoritative sources. Second, quantitative analyses are presented of important elements of the subject. Finally, selected extracts from the analyzed financial statements illustrate variations in the statement presentations. This format may be described more completely as follows.

First, an outline of accounting principles is given based on the pronouncements of the National Council on Governmental Accounting or by the Financial Accounting Standards Board and the American Institute of Certified Public Accountants for state and local governmental accounting and financial statement presentation.

Second, quantitative analyses, including tables, show how often important accounting terms, accounts, formats, procedures, and practices are actually used. The percentage of governmental units employing particular accounting and reporting methods accompanies the appropriate narrative section. The tables include

accounting practices cited in footnotes in the summary of significant accounting policies;

examples of individual special revenue funds reported;

examples of individual enterprise funds reported;

account titles used to report fund and general fixed assets;

statistical data relative to long-term liabilities;

sources of revenues and expenses for proprietary funds;

account titles used to report cash, receivables, inventories, restricted assets, payables, accruals, and deferrals;

type of auditors examining governmental financial statements;

auditing standards used;

analysis of qualifications with reference to departures from GAAP;

nature of the auditor's opinion;

information included in supplementary data;

reporting of commitments and contingencies;

fiscal years of governmental units;

topics discussed in footnotes;

reasons cited for excluding governmental entities from reporting; and

information disclosed in footnotes concerning pension plans.

Third, selected extracts from governmental financial reports—including specific report statements, footnotes, and schedules—illustrate the procedures and practices employed in reporting on the activities of more than 550 local governmental units. Participating local governments ranged from towns with populations of less than 50,000 to most of the country's largest units. A partial listing of these illustrations includes the following:

illustrations of combined balance sheets;

illustrations of combined statements of revenues and expenditures, statements of revenues and expenses, and statements of changes in financial position;

excerpts of footnote disclosures related to capitalized leases;

excerpts of footnote disclosures relating to the bases of accounting and budgeting;

excerpts from combined balance sheets relating to the reporting of cash and investments, receivables, inventories, prepaid expenses, payables, accrued liabilities, and deposits and deferred items;

examples of auditors' opinions;

excerpts from qualified audit opinions;

illustrations of reports under OMB Circular A-102, Attachment P;

excerpts of footnotes relating to commitments and contingencies, operating leases, related-party transactions, self-insurance, events subsequent to the balance sheet date, functions and organizations, and liabilities for compensated absences; and

excerpts of pension plan footnotes.

The material is presented in an objective, descriptive style. No subjective analysis or comment is included, so that users of the information can draw their own inferences free of suggestion.

Who Can Use the Material

The material is especially important for individuals who are engaged in preparing, interpreting, analyzing, comparing, or auditing local governmental financial reports. The material will also be useful in teaching governmental accounting in colleges and universities and in classes conducted by local governments for their own staffs. Thus the list of those who could profitably use the information would include

government finance officers, treasurers, controllers, and accountants preparing financial reports or using them for management purposes;

attorneys, rating agencies, underwriters, and bankers working with government securities;

independent public accountants and government auditors who audit government financial statements; and

governmental accounting scholars, writers, and researchers.

The material should be in the library of every business firm serving local governments and of every business school, law school, law firm, accounting firm, underwriting concern, and brokerage house.

Examples of Usage

This section offers several simplified examples of situations in which the material in earlier editions of this book has been of assistance to practitioners, managers, auditors, and others. (For convenience, chapter numbers have been altered to indicate topics in the present edition.)

Case 1

Since its inception, a city has used cash accounting. At a recent meeting the city council asked the finance director to report on the advantages and disadvantages of the modified accrual basis. It asked that the report also contain some examples of footnote descriptions from governments using the modified accrual method. The finance director referred to Chapter 5 of this book, selected appropriate footnotes, and prepared the report requested.

Case 2

A recent ordinance empowered a city to develop a series of enterprise funds. Management and fund maintenance were expected to be important considerations, so the city's finance director wanted to determine an appropriate set of expense descriptions that would provide the needed information for expense control. He turned to the exhibits in Chapter 8 to observe what a number of other governments were using. He made his selection from the many expense descriptors disclosed in the examples.

Case 3

A certified public accounting firm was conducting the annual audit of a county. During the audit several items were disclosed that the practice partner believed would result in a qualified report. These items were

the recording of the liability for compensated absences,

litigation in which the county was the defendant and in which the potential liability was material, and

a deficiency in the funding of the county's pension plan for policemen and firemen.

Reference to Chapter 13 provided examples of how other accounting firms had described similar conditions in their audit opinions.

Case 4

The new finance director of a city was preparing her first comprehensive annual financial report. Earlier reports had had very sparse comments in the footnotes and very little supplementary data. She wondered what other published reports were including. She referred to Chapter 2 for information on the footnotes on accounting practices cited under "significant accounting policies," to Chapter 14 for tabular and illustrative information on the supplementary data in published reports, and to Chapters 15 and 17 for footnotes on specific areas of interest.

Case 5

The chief accountant for a county was informed by the finance director of complaints that interfund transfers were not shown in sufficient detail. The accountant had no idea how this information could be shown so as to identify the receivables and payables for each fund type and by individual fund within a given fund type. He turned to Chapter 6 to find several illustrations that displayed "due to" payables and "due from" receivables—precisely the information his director asked for.

Case 6

A county board had consistent trouble in passing its budget ordinance by June 30 of each year. One board member suggested that the fiscal year closing be changed to September 30. The board chairman said that very few municipalities closed their books on a date other than June 30 or December 31. The finance director asked for a ten-minute recess, referred to

Chapter 16, and found that September 30 was being used by a substantial number of municipalities. He so reported to the board.

Case 7

A city had instituted monthly town meetings. A meeting held September 20 was scheduled to include a discussion of the prior year's financial statement. The audited statement has just been received, and copies were given to attendees at the meeting. The financial vice president of the city's largest employer asked to be recognized and questioned the unqualified audit opinion that the city had received, citing particularly the treatment of fixed assets. First, he said, the fixed assets were not in the fund financial statements. Second, they were not depreciated, except in some proprietary funds, whatever they were. Third, he said, some assets identified as infrastructure assets were not recorded at all.

The city finance director, who also attended the meeting, explained to the vice president that this treatment was in compliance with generally accepted accounting for municipal governments. He cited Statement 1 of the National Council on Governmental Accounting and then turned to Chapter 3 of this book and read examples to prove his point.

Case 8

A city had submitted its financial reports for a bond rating. The reports had been certified by an independent public accountant. There were two qualifications in the accountant's certificate. The official who was rating the statements noted them as related to "other basis of accounting" and "recoverability of assets." He referred to texts and reference books but could not get a clear picture of the problem. He then referred to Chapter 13 of this book and noted that it contained several examples of the former qualification and lengthy qualifications on the latter subject.

Case 9

The recently appointed finance director of a county was reviewing her first quarterly finance statement. She became aware that elements of the county performed service functions for itself. There was some question whether the services were being efficiently conducted or whether contractors could perform them more efficiently. She wondered if she could develop internal service funds to isolate the costs of the funds and to provide information, on an accrual basis of accounting relative to the efficiency of operation. She needed information on areas or functions that in other communities were handled by internal service funds. She found the information in Chapter 10 of this book.

Case 10

A town was growing by leaps and bounds. It was becoming a very desirable residential community, and in addition its location made it an opportune place for light industry. Its finances were becoming substantial. The mayor raised the question of whether the town should have a regular budget and should make comparisons with actual figures. He asked the new finance director about the prevalence of budget-to-actual comparisons. The finance director referred to the applicable portions of NCGA Statement 1 relative to budgets and then turned to Chapter 5 to determine the percentage of governmental units whose general purpose financial statements included a budget-to-actual comparison.

Concluding Observations

Care should be taken when interpreting the study observations. This is especially true when assessing the degree of compliance of a unit's financial statement with the accounting principles contained in NCGA Statement 1. The NCGA principles are applicable to a specific governmental entity if certain conditions, circumstances, or activities existed in that unit during the fiscal year being reported.

The information in this book can help whether one prepares governmental financial reports, designs governmental accounting systems, evaluates public sector financial statements, audits governmental statements, or is passing an opinion on the creditworthiness of financial statements.

EXHIBITS FOR CHAPTER 1

Exhibit 1-1. Summary of NCGA Statement 1: Governmental Accounting and Financial Reporting Principles

EXHIBIT 1-1. SUMMARY OF NCGA STATEMENT 1: GOVERNMENTAL ACCOUNTING AND FINANCIAL REPORTING PRINCIPLES

ACCOUNTING AND REPORTING CAPABILITIES

1. A governmental accounting system must make it possible to both: (a) present fairly and with full disclosure the financial position and results of financial operations of the funds and account groups of the governmental unit in conformity with generally accepted accounting principles; and (b) determine and demonstrate compliance with finance-related legal and contractual provisions.

FUND ACCOUNTING SYSTEMS

2. Governmental accounting systems should be organized and operated on a fund basis. A fund is defined as a fiscal and accounting entity with a self-balancing set of accounts recording cash and other financial resources, together with all related liabilities and residual equities or balances, and changes therein, which are segregated for the purpose of carrying on specific activities or attaining certain objectives in accordance with special regulations, restrictions, or limitations.

TYPES OF FUNDS

3. The following types of funds should be used by state and local governments:

Governmental Funds

(1) *The general fund* accounts for all financial resources except those required to be accounted for in another fund.
(2) *Special revenue funds* account for the proceeds of specific revenue sources (other than special assessments, expendable trusts, or major capital projects) that are legally restricted to expenditure for specified purposes.
(3) *Capital projects funds* account for financial resources to be used for the acquisition or construction of major capital facilities (other than those financed by proprietary funds, special assessment funds, and trust funds).
(4) *Debt service funds* account for the accumulation of resources for, and the payment of, general long-term debt principal and interest.
(5) *Special assessment funds* account for the financing of public improvements or services deemed to benefit the properties against which special assessments are levied.

Proprietary Funds

(6) *Enterprise funds* account for operations (a) that are financed and operated in a manner similar to private business enterprises—where the intent of the governing body is that the costs (expenses, including depreciation) of providing goods or services to the general public on a continuing basis be financed or recovered primarily through user charges; or (b) where the governing body has decided that periodic determination of revenues earned, expenses incurred, and/or net income is appropriate for capital maintenance, public policy, management control, accountability, or other purposes.

(7) *Internal service funds* account for the financing of goods or services provided by one department or agency to other departments or agencies of the governmental unit, or to other governmental units on a cost-reimbursement basis.

Fiduciary Funds

(8) *Trust and agency funds* account for assets held by a governmental unit in a trustee capacity or as an agent for individuals, private organizations, other governmental units, and/or other funds. These include (a) expendable trust funds, (b) nonexpendable trust funds, (c) pension trust funds, and (d) agency funds.

NUMBER OF FUNDS

4. Governmental units should establish and maintain those funds required by law and sound financial administration. Only the minimum number of funds consistent with legal and operating requirements should be established, since unnecessary funds result in inflexibility, undue complexity, and inefficient financial administration.

ACCOUNTING FOR FIXED ASSETS AND LONG-TERM LIABILITIES

5. A clear distinction should be made between (a) fund fixed assets and general fixed assets and (b) fund long-term liabilities and general long-term debt.
   a. Fixed assets related to specific proprietary funds or trust funds should be accounted for through those funds. All other fixed assets of a governmental unit should be accounted for through the general fixed assets account group.
   b. Long-term liabilities of proprietary funds, special assessment funds, and trust funds should be accounted for through those funds. All other unmatured general long-term liabilities of the governmental unit should be accounted for through the general long-term debt account group.

VALUATION OF FIXED ASSETS

6. Fixed assets should be accounted for at cost or, if the cost is not practicably determinable, at estimated cost. Donated fixed assets should be recorded at their estimated fair value at the time received.

DEPRECIATION OF FIXED ASSETS

7. a. Depreciation of general fixed assets should not be recorded in the accounts of governmental funds. Depreciation of general fixed assets may be recorded in cost accounting systems or calculated for cost finding analyses, and accumulated depreciation may be recorded in the general fixed assets account group.
   b. Depreciation of fixed assets accounted for in a proprietary fund should be recorded in the accounts of that fund. Depreciation is also recognized in those trust funds where expenses, net income, and/or capital maintenance are measured.

ACCRUAL BASIS IN GOVERNMENTAL ACCOUNTING

8. The modified accrual or accrual basis of accounting, as appropriate, should be utilized in measuring financial position and operating results.
   a. Governmental fund revenues and expenditures should be recognized on the modified accrual basis. Revenues should be recognized in the accounting period in which they become available and measurable. Expenditures should be recognized in the accounting period in which the fund liability is incurred, if measurable, except for unmatured interest on general long-term debt and on special assessment indebtedness secured by interest-bearing special assessment levies, which should be recognized when due.
   b. Proprietary fund revenues and expenses should be recognized on the accrual basis. Revenues should be recognized in the accounting period in which they are earned and become measurable; expenses, if measurable, should be recognized in the period incurred.
   c. Fiduciary fund revenues and expenses or expenditures (as appropriate) should be recognized on the basis consistent with the fund's accounting measurement objective. Nonexpendable trust and pension trust funds should be accounted for on the accrual basis; expendable trust funds should be accounted for on the modified accrual basis. Agency fund assets and liabilities should be accounted for on the modified accrual basis.
   d. Transfers should be recognized in the accounting period in which the interfund receivable and payable arise.

BUDGETING, BUDGETARY CONTROL, AND BUDGETARY REPORTING

9. a. An annual budget(s) should be adopted by every governmental unit.

b. The accounting system should provide the basis for appropriate budgetary control.

c. Budgetary comparisons should be included in the appropriate financial statements and schedules for governmental funds for which an annual budget has been adopted.

TRANSFER, REVENUE, EXPENDITURE, AND EXPENSE ACCOUNT CLASSIFICATIONS

10. a. Interfund transfers and proceeds of general long-term debt issues should be classified separately from fund revenues and expenditures or expenses.

b. Governmental fund revenues should be classified by fund and source. Expenditures should be classified by fund, function (or program), organization unit, activity, character, and principal classes of objects.

c. Proprietary fund revenues and expenses should be classified in essentially the same manner as those of similar business organizations, functions, or activities.

COMMON TERMINOLOGY AND CLASSIFICATION

11. A common terminology and classification should be used consistently throughout the budget, the accounts, and the financial reports of each fund.

INTERIM AND ANNUAL FINANCIAL REPORTS

12. a. Appropriate interim financial statements and reports of financial position, operating results, and other pertinent information should be prepared to facilitate management control of financial operations, legislative oversight, and, where necessary or desired, external reporting.

b. A comprehensive annual financial report covering all funds and account groups of the governmental unit—including appropriate combined, combining, and individual fund statements; notes to the financial statements; schedules; narrative explanations; and statistical tables—should be prepared and published.

c. General purpose financial statements may be issued separately from the comprehensive annual financial report. Such statements should include the basic financial statements and notes to the financial statements that are essential to fair presentation of financial position and operating results (and changes in financial position of proprietary funds and similar trust funds).

Chapter 2
Accounting and Reporting by Governmental Units

GENERALLY ACCEPTED ACCOUNTING PRINCIPLES AND LEGAL COMPLIANCE

The first principle of NCGA Statement 1 prescribes a principle for governmental units that states:

1. A governmental accounting system must make it possible to both: (a) present fairly and with full disclosure the financial position and results of financial operations of the funds and account groups of the governmental unit in conformity with generally accepted accounting principles; and (b) determine and demonstrate compliance with finance-related legal and contractual provisions.

Statement 1 provides additional discussion of this principle:

Generally accepted accounting principles are uniform minimum standards of and guidelines for financial accounting and reporting.

Adherence to GAAP is essential to ensuring a reasonable degree of comparability among the financial reports of state, provincial, and local governmental units.

Governmental accounting systems thus must provide data that permit reporting on the financial status and operations of a government in conformity with GAAP.

Where financial statements prepared in conformity with GAAP do not demonstrate finance-related legal and contractual compliance, the governmental unit should present such additional schedules and narrative explanations in the comprehensive annual financial report as may be necessary to report its legal compliance responsibilities and accountability.

Conflicts between legal provisions and GAAP do not require maintaining two accounting systems. Rather the accounting system may be maintained on a legal-compliance basis but should include sufficient additional records to permit GAAP-based reporting.

FUND ACCOUNTING SYSTEMS

The second principle of NCGA Statement 1 states that the accounting systems of governmental units should be on a fund accounting basis:

2. Governmental accounting systems should be organized and operated on a fund basis. A fund is defined as a fiscal and accounting entity with a self-balancing set of accounts recording cash and other financial resources, together with all related liabilities and residual equities or balances, and changes therein, which are segregated for the purpose of carrying on specific activities or attaining certain objectives in accordance with special regulations, restrictions, or limitations.

The third principle of Statement 1 views a governmental unit as a combination of several distinctly independent and varied fiscal and accounting entities, each having a separate set of accounts and functions. Nine types of funds and the two account groups are prescribed for governmental accounting:

five governmental fund types—general, special revenue, capital projects, debt service, and special assessment funds;

two proprietary fund types—enterprise and internal service funds;

two fiduciary fund types—trust and agency funds; and

two account groups—general fixed assets and general long-term debt account groups.

Principle 4 of NCGA Statement 1 recognizes that not all fund types are appropriate for use every year by all governments. Whereas Statement 1 points out that some units often need several funds of a single type, other governments have no requirement for such funds. The general rule, however, is that the smaller the number of individual funds used the better. This is described in Principle 4:

4. Governmental units should establish and maintain those funds required by law and sound financial administration. Only the minimum number of funds consistent with legal and operating requirements should be established, since unnecessary funds result in in-

flexibility, undue complexity, and inefficient financial administration.

Study observations with respect to selected aspects of the reported accounting practices are described in the next section and in the tables and exhibits at the end of this chapter.

SUMMARY OF ACCOUNTING POLICIES

The NCGA, in its Statement 1, requires that published financial reports contain a summary of the entities' significant accounting policies. This requirement is consistent with the Accounting Principle Board Opinion 22 of the American Institute of Certified Public Accountants, "Disclosure of Accounting Policies," which requires that there be information in the financial statements about the accounting policies adopted by a reporting entity. Accounting policies are defined by Opinion 22 as the specific accounting principles and methods of applying those principles that are judged by management to be most appropriate in the circumstances to present fairly the financial position, changes in financial position, and results of operations in accordance with generally accepted accounting principles.

In the case of the governmental units surveyed, most of the financial statements analyzed contained a section, in the footnotes, relating to the accounting policies of that particular governmental unit.

STUDY OBSERVATIONS

The footnote summarizing the governmental units' significant accounting policies described subjects such as "fund accounting," "basis of accounting," and "budgets and budgetary accounting." While the information reported under these captions varied somewhat by governmental entity, the footnotes to many financial statements described the unit's compliance with the first four NCGA principles described above.

Table 2-1 summarizes the accounting practices of the surveyed governments covered in their disclosure of accounting policies. Exhibit 2-1 contains excerpts from footnotes summarizing significant accounting policies, taken from various units' financial statements.

With respect to the number of funds and fund types, the financial statements of most governmental units used a clearly identified general fund category. In addition, there seemed to be a high level of usage of the other major fund types and recommended account groups. As mentioned, not all fund types would be appropriate for use by all governmental units. The application of a particular fund type would be dependent on the conditions, circumstances, or activities of an individual government. Table 2-2 indicates the number of governmental units using each of the prescribed fund types and account groups.

The reporting by individual fund type for the surveyed financial statements varied widely, reflecting the diversity of activities, functions, and characteristics of the separate governmental units. Examples of the reported fund types, extracted from the appropriate combining statement, appear in Tables 2-3 to 2-10.

EXHIBITS AND TABLES FOR CHAPTER 2

Table 2-1. Accounting Practices Cited in Footnotes in the Summary of Significant Accounting Policies

Exhibit 2-1. Selected Excerpts: Summary of Significant Accounting Policies—Fund Accounting

Table 2-2. Fund Types and Account Groups Reported by Governmental Units in the Combined Balance Sheet

Table 2-3. Examples of Individual Special Revenue Funds Reported by Governmental Units

Table 2-4. Examples of Individual Capital Projects Funds Reported by Governmental Units

Table 2-5. Examples of Individual Debt Service Funds Reported by Governmental Units

Table 2-6. Examples of Individual Special Assessment Funds Reported by Governmental Units

Table 2-7. Examples of Individual Enterprise Funds Reported by Governmental Units

Table 2-8. Examples of Individual Internal Service Funds Reported by Governmental Units

Table 2-9. Examples of Individual Trust Funds Reported by Governmental Units

Table 2-10. Examples of Individual Agency Funds Reported by Governmental Units

TABLE 2-1. ACCOUNTING PRACTICES CITED IN FOOTNOTES IN THE SUMMARY OF SIGNIFICANT ACCOUNTING POLICIES*

Accounting Practices Reported	Instances Observed (%)
Basis of accounting	94
Description of fund accounting	56
Accounting policies specifically described for	
inventory	70
general funds	63
encumbrances	61
investment	58
total columns	57
special revenue funds	52
fixed assets	51
capital projects funds	51
debt service funds	44
enterprise funds	43
special assessment funds	32
trust and agency funds	31
long-term liabilities	31
internal service funds	28
budget process	22
reporting entity	18
compensated absences	16
advances to other funds	10
pension plans	9
depreciation	4
leases	3
property accounting	2
change in accounting method	2
changes in accounting principles	1

* Observations for the 87% of the units having this footnote.

EXHIBIT 2-1. SELECTED EXCERPTS: SUMMARY OF SIGNIFICANT ACCOUNTING POLICIES—FUND ACCOUNTING

[MUNICIPALITY OF ANCHORAGE, ALASKA (DECEMBER 31, 1983 AND 1982), NOTE 1 (IN PART)]

Fund Accounting

The accounts of the Municipality of Anchorage are organized on the basis of funds and account groups, each of which is considered a separate accounting entity. The operations of each fund are accounted for with a separate set of self-balancing accounts that comprise its assets, liabilities, fund equity, revenues, and expenditures, or expenses, as appropriate. Government resources are allocated to and accounted for in individual funds based upon the purposes for which they are to be spent and the means by which spending activities are controlled. The various funds are grouped in the financial statements in this report into eight generic funds types and three broad fund categories as follows:

Governmental Fund Types

General Funds. To account for all financial resources except those required to be accounted for in another fund. Service Areas are accounted for as individual general funds as their revenues are unrestricted; but they are not considered subsidiary to the Areawide General Fund.

Special Revenue Funds. To account for the proceeds of specific revenue sources that are restricted by law or administrative action to expenditures for specified purposes.

Debt Service Funds. To account for the accumulation of resources for, and the payment of, general long-term principal and interest.

Capital Projects Funds. To account for financial resources to be used for the acquisition or construction of major capital facilities other than those financed by proprietary funds, special assessment funds, and trust funds.

Special Assessment Funds. To account for the financing of public improvements or services deemed to benefit the properties against which special assessments are levied.

Proprietary Fund Types

Enterprise Funds. To account for operations for which it is the stated intent that costs of providing services to the general public on a continuing basis be financed or recovered primarily through user charges; or where the governing body has decided that periodic determination of revenues earned, expenses incurred, and/or net income is appropriate for capital maintenance, public policy, management control, accountability, or other purposes.

Internal Service Funds. To account for the financing of goods or services provided by one department to other departments of the Municipality on a cost-reimbursement basis.

Fiduciary Fund Types

Trust Funds. To account for assets and activities restricted to a specific purpose in accordance with a trust agreement.

Agency Funds. To account for assets held by the Municipality as an agent for individuals, private organizations, and other governmental units.

Account Groups

General Fixed Assets. To maintain control and cost information on capital assets owned by the Municipality, other than those of the proprietary fund types.

General Long-Term Debt. To account for the unmatured general long-term indebtedness of the Municipality to be financed from governmental funds, except for General Obligation Bonds serviced by Special Assessment Funds and Enterprise Funds.

[CITY OF CLEVELAND, OHIO (DECEMBER 31, 1983), NOTE A (IN PART)]

Basis of Presentation. The accounts of the City are organized on the basis of funds or account groups, each of which is considered a separate accounting entity. The operations of each fund are accounted for with a separate set of self-balancing accounts that comprise its assets, liabilities, fund equity, revenues and expenditures (expense). The various funds are summarized by type in the general purpose financial statements.

Amounts in the "totals—memorandum only" columns in the preceding financial statements represent a summation of the general purpose financial statement line items of the fund types and account groups and are presented only for analytical purposes. The summation includes fund types and account groups that use different bases of accounting, both restricted and unrestricted amounts, interfund transactions that have not been eliminated and the caption "amounts to be provided," which is not an asset in the usual sense. Consequently, amounts shown in the "totals—memorandum only" columns are not comparable to a consolidation and do not represent the total resources available or total revenues and expenditures/expenses of the City.

The following fund types and account groups are used by the City:

Governmental Funds

General Fund. This fund, which is the major operating fund of the City, accounts for the general operating revenues and expenditures of the City not recorded elsewhere. Revenues are derived primarily from property and income taxes.

Special Revenue Funds. These funds are used to account for specific governmental revenues (other than major capital projects) requiring separate accounting because of legal or regulatory provisions or administrative action. These funds include all major federal and state grants.

Debt Service Funds. These funds are used to account for the resources received and used to pay principal and interest on debt reported in the General Long-Term Obligations Account Group and certain enterprise funds. Revenues and financing resources are derived primarily from property taxes and reimbursements by enterprise funds.

Capital Projects Funds. These funds are used to account for the acquisition or construction of capital assets other than those financed by special revenue, enterprise and internal service fund operations. Revenues and financing resources are derived primarily from the issuance of bonds and receipt of grants.

Proprietary Funds

Enterprise Funds. These funds are used to account for operations that provide services which are financed primarily by user charges, or activities where periodic measurement of income is appropriate for capital maintenance, public policy, management control or other purposes.

Internal Service Funds. These funds are used to account for the goods or services provided to certain City departments and funds or to other governments on a cost reimbursement basis.

Fiduciary Funds

Agency Funds. These funds are used to account for assets held by the City as an agency for others and include the Central Collection Agency and payroll deductions withheld and awaiting payment.

Account Groups

General Fixed Assets Account Group. This account group is used to present the general fixed assets of the City utilized in its general operations, exclusive of those used in enterprise and internal service funds. General fixed assets include land, buildings, betterments and equipment owned by the City and the City's investment in the Justice Center Building.

General Long-Term Obligations Account Group. This account group is used to account for all long-term obligations of the City except those accounted for in the enterprise funds.

[CITY OF DALLAS, TEXAS (SEPTEMBER 30, 1983), NOTE 1A (IN PART)]

Basis of Presentation

The accounts of the City are organized on the basis of funds and account groups, each of which is considered a separate accounting entity. The operations of each fund are accounted for with a separate set of self-balancing accounts that comprise its assets, liabilities, fund equity, revenues, and expenditures, or expenses as appropriate. Government resources are allocated to and accounted for in individual funds based upon the purposes for which they are to be spent and the means by which spending activities are controlled. The following fund types and account groups are maintained by the City:

Governmental Funds

General Fund. The General Fund is the general operating fund of the City. It is used to account for all financial resources except those required to be accounted for in another fund.

Special Revenue Funds. Special Revenue Funds are used to account for the proceeds of specific revenue sources (other than special assessments, expendable trusts, or major capital projects) that are legally restricted to expenditures for specified purposes.

Debt Service Funds. Debt Service Funds are used to account for the accumulation of resources for, and the payment of, general long-term debt principal, interest, and related costs.

Capital Project Funds. Capital Project Funds are used to account for financial resources to be used for the acquisition or construction of major capital facilities (other than those financed by proprietary funds and trust funds).

Proprietary Funds

Enterprise Funds. Enterprise Funds are used to account for operations (a) that are financed and operated in a manner similar to private business enterprises—where the intent of the governing body is that the costs (expenses, including depreciation) of providing goods or services to the general public on a continuing basis be financed or recovered primarily through user charges; or (b) where the governing body has decided that periodic determination of revenues earned, expenses incurred, and/or net income is appropriate for capital maintenance, public policy, management control, accountability, or other purposes.

Internal Service Funds. Internal Service Funds are used to account for the financing of goods or services provided by one department or agency to other departments or agencies of the City, or to other governments, on a cost-reimbursement basis.

Fiduciary Funds

Trust and Agency Funds. Trust and Agency Funds are used to account for assets held by the City in a trustee capacity or as an agent for individuals, private organizations, other governments, and/or other funds. These include Expendable Trust, Nonexpendable Trust, and Agency Funds. Nonexpendable Trust Funds are accounted for in essentially the same manner as proprietary funds since capital maintenance is critical. Expendable Trust Funds are accounted for in essentially the same manner as governmental funds. Agency Funds are custodial in nature (assets equal liabilities) and do not involve measurement of results of operations.

Account Groups

Account groups are used to establish accounting control and accountability for the City's general fixed assets and general long-term debt. The following are the City's account groups:

General Fixed Asset Group. This group of accounts is established to account for all fixed assets of the City, except those accounted for in the proprietary and trust funds.

General Long-Term Debt Group. This group of accounts is established to account for all long-term debt including general obligation bonds, warrants and certificates of the City, except those accounted for in the proprietary funds.

[CITY OF KANSAS CITY, MISSOURI (APRIL 30, 1984), NOTE 1 (IN PART)]

(b) Fund Accounting. The accounts of the City are organized on the basis of funds and account groups, each of which is considered a separate accounting entity. The operations of each fund are accounted for with a separate set of accounts that comprise its assets, liabilities, fund equity, revenues and expenditures or expenses as appropriate. Account groups are used to establish accounting control and accountability for the City's general fixed assets, the unmatured principal of its general long-term debt and long-term obligations of the City for certain employee benefits. Governmental resources are allocated to and accounted for in individual funds based upon the purposes for which they are spent. The various funds are grouped in the accompanying statements into eight generic fund types and three broad fund categories as follows:

Governmental Funds

General Fund. Accounts for all financial resources of the City not required to be accounted for in another fund. The General Fund is the general operating fund of the City.

Special Revenue Funds. Account for the proceeds of specific revenue sources (other than special assessments, certain capital projects or expendable trusts) that are legally restricted to expenditures for specified purposes. Certain of these funds, the Government Grants Funds, account for the activities carried out by the City under the terms of certain intergovernmental grants. Various other funds also reflect grant activity to a lesser extent. Also included in this fund type is the General Revenue Sharing Fund, which accounts for the receipt and disbursement of federal revenue sharing monies.

Debt Service Fund. Accounts for the accumulation of resources for, and the payment of, general long-term debt principal and interest.

Capital Projects Funds. Account for financial resources to be used for the acquisition of major capital facilities other than those accounted for in Enterprise, Internal Service and Special Assessment Funds.

Special Assessment Funds. Account for the financing and construction of public improvements deemed to benefit the properties against which special assessments are levied.

Proprietary Funds

Enterprise Funds. Account for the operations of enterprise for which the cost of providing the goods or services to the public on a continuing basis is designed to be financed or recovered through user charges.

Internal Service Funds. Account for the financing of goods or services provided by one department to other City departments on a cost-reimbursement basis.

Fiduciary Funds

Trust and Agency Funds. Account for assets held by the City in a trustee capacity or as an agent for individuals, private organizations, other governmental units or other City funds. These include Expendable Trust, Nonexpendable Trust, Pension Trust and Agency Funds.

Account Groups

General Fixed Assets. Accounts for fixed assets required for general City purposes, excluding fixed assets of the Enterprise and Internal Service Funds.

General Long-Term Debt. Accounts for unmatured long-term indebtedness which is backed by the full faith and credit of the City except general obligation bonds reported in the Special Assessment Funds. This also includes the long-term obligations of the City for certain employee benefits.

[COUNTY OF MILWAUKEE, WISCONSIN (DECEMBER 31, 1983), NOTE 1 (IN PART)]

(b) Basis of Presentation

The accounts of the County are maintained on the basis of funds and account groups. Each fund is a separate fiscal and accounting entity with a self-balancing set of accounts including assets, liabilities, equities, revenues and expenditures or expenses, which are segregated for the purpose of carrying on specific activities or attaining certain objectives. Account groups are used to establish accounting control and accountability for the County's general fixed assets and general long-term obligations. The various funds are grouped in the accompanying financial statements into six generic types and three broad fund categories as follows:

Government Funds

General Fund. The General Fund is used to account for all financial resources, except those required to be accounted for in another fund.

Debt Service Fund. The Debt Service Fund is used to account for the accumulation of resources and the payment of principal and interest on long-term general obligation debt.

Capital Projects Fund. The Capital Projects Fund is used to account for financial resources segregated for the acquisition or construction of major capital facilities other than those financed by proprietary funds.

Proprietary Funds

Enterprise Funds. The Enterprise Funds are used to account for operations that provide services which are financed primarily by user charges, or activities where periodic measurement of net income is appropriate for capital maintenance, public policy, management control or other purposes.

Internal Service Funds. The Internal Service Funds are used to account for the financing of goods and services provided by one department to other departments of the County, or to other governmental entities, on a cost reimbursement basis.

Fiduciary Funds

Trust and Agency Funds. Trust and Agency Funds are used to account for assets held in trust or as an agent by the County for others. The expendable trust fund is accounted for and reported in essentially the same manner as governmental funds. The Pension Trust Fund of the Employee's Retirement System is accounted for and reported in the same manner as proprietary funds. Agency funds are custodial in nature and are used to account for assets held by the County as an agent for individuals, private organizations and other governmental units.

Prior to 1983, amounts received from the State of Wisconsin and paid to third party providers of social services were recorded as revenues and expenditures in the General Fund. Effective in 1983, these social service activities are reported in the expendable trust fund.

Account Groups

General Fixed Assets Account Group. The General Fixed Assets Account Group is used to account for all general fixed assets of the County, other than those fixed assets accounted for in the proprietary funds.

General Long-Term Obligations Account Group. The General Long-Term Obligations Account Group is used to account for all long-term debt and certain unfunded claims and judgments of the County, except those accounted for in the proprietary funds.

[CITY OF OVERLAND PARK, KANSAS (DECEMBER 31, 1983), NOTE 1 (IN PART)]

Description of Funds

The accounts of the City are organized on the basis of funds and account groups, each of which is considered a separate accounting entity. The operations of each fund are accounted for with a separate set of self-balancing accounts that comprise its assets, liabilities, fund equity, revenues, and expenditures. Governmental resources are allocated to and accounted for in individual funds based upon the purpose for which they are to be spent and the means by which spending activities are controlled. The various funds are grouped, in the financial statements in this report, into five generic fund types and two broad fund categories as follows:

Governmental Funds

General Fund. The General Fund is the general operating fund of the City. It is used to account for all

financial resources except those required to be accounted for in another fund.

Special Revenue Funds. Special Revenue Funds are used to account for the proceeds of specific revenue sources (other than expendable trusts or major capital projects) that are legally restricted to expenditures for specified purposes.

Debt Service Fund. Debt Service Fund is used to account for the accumulation of resources for, and the payment of, general obligation bond principal, interest, and related costs.

Capital Projects Funds. Capital Projects Funds are used to account for financial resources to be used for the acquisition or construction of major capital facilities.

Fiduciary Funds

Trust and Agency Funds. Trust and Agency Funds are used to account for assets held by the City in trustee capacity or as an agent for individuals, private organizations, other governments, and/or other funds. The City's Expendable Trust Funds are accounted for in essentially the same manner as governmental funds. The City's pension trust funds are accounted for in a manner similar to private business enterprises.

Account Groups

Fixed assets used in governmental fund type operations (general fixed assets) are accounted for in the General Fixed Assets Account Group, rather than in governmental funds. Public domain assets ("infrastructure" assets consisting of certain improvements including roads, bridges, curbs and gutters, streets and sidewalks, drainage systems, and lighting systems) are not capitalized with other general fixed assets. No depreciation has been provided on general fixed assets.

All fixed assets are valued at historical cost or estimated historical cost if actual historical cost is not available. Donated fixed assets are valued at their estimated fair value on the date donated.

Long-term liabilities expected to be financed from governmental funds are accounted for in the General Long-Term Debt Account Group, not in the governmental funds. The long-term liabilities of the city include temporary notes payable, general obligation bonds, the long-term portion of accrued vacation, and accrued sick leave. The temporary notes will be refinanced by general obligation bonds. The general obligation bonds will be repaid solely by the Debt Service

Fund. The accrued vacation and sick leave will be paid from the applicable governmental funds, primarily the General Fund. The two account groups are not "funds." They are concerned only with the measurement of financial position. They are not involved with measurement of results of operations.

[ST. LOUIS COUNTY, MISSOURI (DECEMBER 31, 1983), NOTE 1 (IN PART)]

Fund Accounting

The accounts of the county are organized on the basis of generic fund types and account groups, each of which is considered a separate entity with self-balancing accounts that comprise its assets, liabilities, equity, revenues and expenditures or expenses. The various funds are grouped, in the financial statements in this report, into three broad fund categories and six generic fund types as follows:

Governmental Fund Types

General Operating. The General Operating Funds of the County are used to account for all financial resources except those required to be accounted for in another fund. The overall goal of the County's financial reporting is to provide financial information useful for making economic decisions, demonstrating accountability and evaluating managerial and organizational performance. While most governmental reporting entities use a single general fund, the County has established, under the caption General Operating Funds, four separate funds: the General Fund, the Road and Bridge Fund, the Health Fund and the Parks Fund. The four General Operating Funds reflect the County's financial administration and organization and are currently required by ordinance.

Special Revenue Funds. Special Revenue Funds are used to account for the proceeds of specific revenue sources (other than expendable trusts or major capital projects) that are legally restricted to expenditures for specified purposes.

Debt Service Fund. The Debt Service Fund is used to account for the accumulation of resources for, and the payment of, general long-term debt principal, interest and related costs.

Capital Projects Funds. Capital Projects Funds are used to account for financial resources to be used for the acquisition or construction of major capital facilities (other than those financed by Proprietary Funds and Trust Funds).

Proprietary Fund Type

Enterprise Funds. Enterprise Funds are used to account for operations that are financed and operated in a manner similar to commercial enterprises where the intent of the governing body is that the costs (expenses, including depreciation) of providing goods or services to the general public on a continuing basis be financed or recovered primarily through user charges.

Fiduciary Fund Types

Trust and Agency Funds. Trust and Agency Funds are used to account for assets held by the County in a trustee capacity or as an agent for individuals, private organizations, other governments and/or other funds. These include the Retirement Trust Fund and the Agency Funds. The Retirement Trust Fund is accounted for in essentially the same manner as proprietary funds since capital maintenance is critical. Agency Funds are custodial in nature (assets equal liabilities) and do not involve measurement of result of operations.

Account Groups

Unmatured long-term indebtedness backed by the full faith and credit of the County is accounted for in the General Long-Term Debt Account Group. The General Fixed Assets Account Group includes all fixed assets of the County not recorded in Enterprise Funds, except for streets, sidewalks, curbs and gutters, storm sewers, lighting systems and other infrastructure, which, because of their nature, are not reflected as assets in the accompanying financial statements.

[CITY OF ST. PETERSBURG, FLORIDA (SEPTEMBER 30, 1983), NOTE A (IN PART)]

Fund Accounting

A governmental accounting system must make it possible (1) to show that all applicable legal provisions have been complied with and (2) to determine fairly, and with full disclosure, the financial position and results of financial operations of the funds and account groups of the City. In order to accomplish these objectives, the City's accounting records are organized and operated on a fund basis. A fund is a fiscal and accounting entity, with a self-balancing set of accounts recording cash and other financial resources, together with all related liabilities and residual equities, or balances, and changes therein, which are segregated for the purpose of carrying on the specific activities, or attaining certain objectives, in accordance with special regulations, restrictions, or limitations.

The following types of funds and account groups are used in accounting for the financial operations of the City.

Governmental Funds

The General Fund. To account for all financial resources except those accounted for in another fund.

Special Revenue Funds. To account for the proceeds of specific revenue sources (other than special assessments, expendable trusts, or for major capital projects) that are restricted by law or administrative action to expenditure for specified purposes.

Debt Service Funds. To account for the accumulation of resources for, and the payment of, general long-term debt principal and interest.

Capital Projects Funds. To account for financial resources to be used for the acquisition or construction of major capital facilities (other than those financed by Proprietary Funds, Special Assessment Funds, and Trust Funds).

Special Assessment Funds. To account for the financing of public improvements or services deemed to benefit the properties against which special assessments are levied.

Proprietary Funds

Enterprise Funds. To account for operations (a) that are financed and operated in a manner similar to private business enterprises, where the intent of the governing body is that the costs (expenses, including depreciation) of providing goods or services to the general public on a continuing basis be financed or recovered primarily through user charges; or (b) where the governing body has decided that periodic determination of revenues earned, expenses incurred, and/or net income is appropriate for capital maintenance, public policy, management control, accountability, or other purposes.

Internal Service Funds. To account for the financing of goods or services provided by one department or agency to other departments or agencies of the governmental unit, or to other governmental units, on a cost reimbursement basis.

Fiduciary Funds

General Fixed Assets Account Group. To account for general fixed assets acquired principally for general City purposes and excludes fixed assets of the Enterprise and Internal Service Funds.

General Long-Term Debt Account Group. To account for the outstanding principal balances of General Obligation Bonds and limited obligation bonds and certificates not supported by Proprietary Funds.

[CITY OF SAVANNAH, GEORGIA (DECEMBER 31, 1983), NOTE 1 (IN PART)]

(A) Description of Funds

Each fund and account group is considered a separate accounting activity with a separate set of self-balancing accounts. Funds are classified into three basic fund types: governmental funds, proprietary funds, and fiduciary funds. The following is a description of the funds and account groups used by the City:

(1) Governmental Funds

These funds are often called "source and disposition," "expendable," or "governmental-type" funds, and most governmental functions are typically financed through them. The acquisition, use, and balances of the City's expendable financial resources and the related current liabilities are accounted for through governmental funds. The measurement focus is upon determination of changes in financial position, rather than upon net income determination. The following are the governmental fund types of the City:

(a) General Fund. The General Fund accounts for all financial resources except those to be accounted for in another fund.

(b) Special Revenue Funds. Special Revenue Funds account for the proceeds of specific revenue sources (other than special assessments, expendable trusts, or major capital projects) that are legally restricted to expenditures for specified purposes.

The Special Revenue Funds maintained by the City follow:

(i) *Grant Fund.* The Grant Fund accounts for all grants not properly accounted for in another fund. The major grant revenues are received from the Department of Labor as Prime Sponsor and subgrantee under the Comprehensive Employment and Training Act of 1973, as amended, and from the State of Georgia as Prime Sponsor and subgrantee under the Jobs Training Partnership Act.

(ii) *Federal Revenue Sharing Fund.* The Federal Revenue Sharing Fund accounts for revenues received under the Federal Revenue Sharing Program.

(iii) *Community Development Fund.* The Community Development Fund accounts for revenues received from the Department of Housing and Urban Development under the Community Development Block Grant Program. This fund also accounts for revenues received from the Georgia Department of Human Resources under the Title XX program. All revenues received by this fund are used in implementing the Community Development program.

(c) Capital Projects Fund. The Capital Projects Fund accounts for financial resources to be used for the acquisition or construction of major capital facilities.

(d) Debt Service Fund. The Debt Service Fund accounts for the accumulation of resources for, and the payment of, general long-term debt principal, interest, and related costs.

(e) Special Assessment Fund. The Special Assessment Fund accounts for the financing of public improvements or services deemed to benefit the properties against which special assessments are levied.

(2) Proprietary Funds

These funds are often called "income determination," "nonexpendable," or "commercial-type" funds and are used to account for the ongoing activities of the City which are similar to those often found in the private sector. All assets, liabilities, equities, revenues, expenses, and transfers relating to the City's business and quasi-business activities are accounted for through proprietary funds. The measurement focus is upon determination of net income, financial position, and changes in financial position. The following are the Proprietary Fund types of the City.

(a) Enterprise Funds. Enterprise Funds are used to account for operations (1) that are financed and operated in a manner similar to private business enterprises—where the intent of the governing body is that the costs (expenses, including depreciation) of providing goods or services to the general public on a continuing basis be financed or recovered primarily through user charges; or (2) where the governing body has decided that periodic determination of revenues earned, expenses incurred, and/or net income is appropriate for capital maintenance, public policy, management control, accountability, or other purposes.

The Enterprise Funds maintained by the City follow:

(i) *Water and Sewer Fund.* The Water and Sewer Fund accounts for the operations of the water and sewer system of the City. The system supplies water and sewerage to area residents.

(ii) *Industrial and Domestic Water Supply Fund.* The Industrial and Domestic Water Supply Fund accounts for the operation of the Savannah River Water System. The system supplies water to industrial contract users and certain other commercial users.

(iii) *Golf Course Fund.* The Golf Course Fund accounts for the operation of the Bacon Park Golf Course.

(iv) *Civic Center Fund.* The Civic Center Fund accounts for the operation of the Savannah Civic Center.

(v) *Parking Garage Fund.* The Parking Garage Fund accounts for the operation of the City of Savannah Parking Garage.

(b) Internal Service Fund. The Internal Service Fund accounts for goods and services, including the repair, maintenance, and replacement of City-owned vehicles, provided by one department to other departments on a cost-reimbursement basis. In addition, certain services are supplied to outside agencies at a fee.

(3) Fiduciary Funds

These funds include expendable trust funds, nonexpendable trust funds, agency funds, and pension trust funds, and are used to account for assets held by the City in a trustee capacity or as an agent for individuals, private organizations, other governmental units, and/or other funds. The measurement focus of expendable trust funds is the same as for governmental funds. The measurement focus of the nonexpendable trust funds and pension trust funds is similar to that of proprietary funds since capital maintenance is critical. The City does not have any expendable trust funds. The following are the fiduciary funds of the City:

(a) Cemetery Perpetuity Fund. The Cemetery Perpetuity Fund accounts for the revenues received for the upkeep of cemetery lots located in Greenwich, Bonaventure, and Laurel Grove perpetual care cemeteries. Interest earned on investments held by this is transferred to the General Fund to defray a portion of the cost of the upkeep.

(b) Employees Retirement Plan Fund. The Employees Retirement Fund accounts for the assets and the liabilities of the Employees Retirement Plan.

(c) Old Pension Fund. The Old Pension Fund accounts for the assets and the liabilities of the Old Pension Plan.

(d) Investment Fund. The Investment Fund accounts for the pooled cash and investments of the City, except for those funds whose cash and investments must remain segregated because of bond requirements or federal regulations.

(4) Account Groups

Account groups are not funds—they do not reflect available financial resources and related liabilities—but are accounting records of the general fixed assets and general long-term debt and certain associated information. Account groups are used to establish accounting control and accountability for the general fixed assets and general long-term debt of the City. The following are the account groups of the City:

(a) General Fixed Assets Account Group. This group of accounts is established to account for all fixed assets of the City, other than those accounted for in the Proprietary Funds.

(b) General Long-Term Debt Group. This group of accounts is established to account for all long-term liabilities of the City, other than those accounted for in the Proprietary Funds and the Special Assessment Fund.

TABLE 2-2. FUND TYPES AND ACCOUNT GROUPS REPORTED BY GOVERNMENTAL UNITS IN THE COMBINED BALANCE SHEET

Fund Types Reported*	Instances Observed (%)
Governmental funds:	
General fund	98
Special revenue funds	93
Capital projects funds	85
Debt service funds	78
Special assessment funds	54
Proprietary funds:	
Enterprise funds	76
Internal service funds	51
Fiduciary funds:	
Trust and agency funds	62
Agency funds	14
Trust funds	5
Account groups:	
General fixed assets account group	81
Long-term debt account group	90

* Observations for the 88% of the units having this statement.

TABLE 2-3. EXAMPLES OF INDIVIDUAL SPECIAL REVENUE FUNDS REPORTED BY GOVERNMENTAL UNITS

Descriptors of Special Revenue Funds*	Instances Observed (%)
Revenue sharing	52
Library	25
Community development	23
Community development block grant	19
Parks/recreation	13
Gas (tax)	12
CETA	11
Grants	11
Roads/streets/highways	11
Fire	8
Parks	8
Transportation/transit	8
Health	7
Schools	6
Sewer/sewage/storm drainage	6
Traffic (safety)	5
Retirement	5
Social services	5
Economic development	5
Revaluation	4
Health, mental	4
Parking	4
All other descriptors	<1

* Observations for the 74% of the units having a combining statement for special revenue funds.

TABLE 2-4. EXAMPLES OF INDIVIDUAL CAPITAL PROJECTS FUNDS REPORTED BY GOVERNMENTAL UNITS

Descriptors of Capital Projects Funds*	Instances Observed (%)
Roads/streets/highways	16
Sewer/sewage/storm drainage	13
Parks	13
Library	8
Parks/recreation	7
Improvements	7
Redevelopment agency	7
Fire	6
Schools/school construction	6
Drainage	5
Capital outlay	5
Buildings	5
Civic center	5
Community development	5
Airports	5
Courthouse/corrections/jails	4
Public works	4
Transportation/transit	4
Water	3
Parking	3
Bridges	3
Police	3
Recreation	2
Hospital	2
Sanitation	2
All other descriptors	<2

* Observations for the 54% of the units having a combining statement for capital projects funds.

TABLE 2-5. EXAMPLES OF INDIVIDUAL DEBT SERVICE FUNDS REPORTED BY GOVERNMENTAL UNITS

Descriptors of Debt Service Funds*	Instances Observed (%)
Bonds/general obligation	14
Parks	7
Improvements	6
Schools	6
Library	5
Roads/streets/highways	5
Courthouse/correction	4
Airports	4
Civic center	4
Parking	3
Redevelopment agency	3
Sewer/sewage/storm drainage	3
Hospital	2
Parks/recreation	2
Drainage	2
Public benefit	2
Buildings	2
Motor vehicle	2
Sanitation	2
Golf courses	2
Water	1
Other descriptors	<1

* Observations for the 33% of the units having a combining statement for debt service funds.

TABLE 2-6. EXAMPLES OF INDIVIDUAL SPECIAL ASSESSMENT FUNDS REPORTED BY GOVERNMENTAL UNITS

Descriptors of Special Assessment Funds*	Instances Observed (%)
Sewer/sewage/storm drainage	20
Roads/streets/highways	14
Improvements	13
Street lighting	8
Sidewalks	8
Paving	5
Other descriptors	<1

* Observations for the 25% of the units having a combining statement for special assessment funds.

TABLE 2-7. EXAMPLES OF INDIVIDUAL ENTERPRISE FUNDS REPORTED BY GOVERNMENTAL UNITS

Descriptors of Enterprise Funds*	Instances Observed (%)
Water	36
Airports	29
Sewer/sewage/storm drainage	27
Parking	23
Golf course	20
Water and sewer	19
Transportation/transit	16
Solid waste	12
Sanitation	11
Civic center	7
Electric	6
Utilities	6
Cemetery	5
Hospital	5
Waste	4
Harbor/dock/marina	3
Parks/recreation	3
Garbage	3
Mental health	2
Parks	2
Recreation	2
Housing	2
Gas	1
Bridges	1
Other descriptors	<1

* Observations for the 53% of the units having a combining statement for enterprise funds.

TABLE 2-8. EXAMPLES OF INDIVIDUAL INTERNAL SERVICE FUNDS REPORTED BY GOVERNMENTAL UNITS

Descriptors of Internal Service Funds*	Instances Observed (%)
Computer/data processing	19
Self-insurance	18
Garage	15
Workers compensation	11
Motor pool/vehicles	10
Stores	9
Equipment maintenance	8
Duplicating and printing	8
Equipment	8
Risk management	7
Insurance	7
Services (general)	6
Communications	4
Public works	3
Maintenance	3
Drainage	3
Transportation/transit	2
Roads/street/highways	2
Buildings	1
Garbage	1
Other descriptors	<1

* Observations for the 32% of the units having a combining statement for internal service funds.

TABLE 2-9. EXAMPLES OF INDIVIDUAL TRUST FUNDS REPORTED BY GOVERNMENTAL UNITS

Descriptors of Trust Funds*	Instances Observed (%)
Firemen's pension/retirement	46
Police	19
Pension	18
Cemetery (perpetual)	13
Expendable trust	12
Employee retirement	12
Deferred compensation	11
Nonexpendable trust	10
Library	9
Police and fire pension/retirement	6
Community development	3
Law library	2
Other descriptors	<2

* Observations for the 30% of the units having a combining statement for trust funds.

TABLE 2-10. EXAMPLES OF INDIVIDUAL AGENCY FUNDS REPORTED BY GOVERNMENTAL UNITS

Descriptors of Agency Funds*	Instances Observed (%)
Clerk of courts	17
Sheriff	13
Payroll	12
Deferred compensation	10
Courts	8
Tax collection	8
Tax commissioner	5
Special welfare	4
Game and fish	4
Other agency	3
CETA	2
Other descriptors	<1

* Observations for the 40% of the units having a combining statement for agency funds.

Chapter 3
Fixed Assets, Valuations, Depreciation, Noncancellable Leases, and Infrastructure Assets

FIXED ASSETS

The fifth principle of NCGA Statement 1 prescribes generally accepted accounting principles related to fixed assets and long-term liabilities:

5. A clear distinction should be made between (a) fund fixed assets and general fixed assets and (b) fund long-term liabilities and general long-term debt.

With respect to fixed assets, the principle states:

a. Fixed assets related to specific proprietary funds or trust funds should be accounted for through those funds. All other fixed assets of a governmental unit should be accounted for through the general fixed assets account group.

In addition, Statement 1 provides the following guidance with respect to fixed assets:

Enterprise fund fixed assets are capitalized in the fund accounts to facilitate reporting of all costs of providing the goods or services that require the use of the fixed assets and to include among the assets of the enterprise funds all fixed assets that may have been used to secure fund debt.

Similarly, internal service fund fixed assets are recorded in internal service fund accounts.

Fixed assets associated with trust funds are accounted for through the appropriate trust fund: fixed assets of nonexpendable trusts are accounted for in the same manner as the fixed assets of proprietary funds. Expendable trust funds account for fixed assets in the same way as do the government funds for their general fixed assets.

Fixed assets other than those accounted for in the proprietary funds or trust funds are general fixed assets, which are accounted for in the general fixed asset account group rather than in the governmental funds.

Table 3-1 lists the more frequently observed account titles used to identify the fund and general fixed assets of the surveyed governments.

Exhibit 3-1 gives examples from governmental financial statements relating to accounting and reporting for proprietary-fund-type fixed assets and general fixed assets. Selected footnote disclosures related to these fixed assets are also included in this exhibit.

The sixth principle of NCGA Statement 1 establishes the valuation basis for fund fixed assets as well as general fixed assets:

6. Fixed assets should be accounted for at cost or, if the cost is not practicably determinable, at estimated cost. Donated fixed assets should be recorded at their estimated fair value at the time received.

Cost has been defined by the NCGA as consideration given or received, whichever is more objectively determinable. According to the NCGA, cost includes not only the purchase price or construction cost, but also ancillary charges to put the asset in its intended location and condition for use. The NCGA further states that ancillary charges include such items as freight, transportation, site preparation, professional fees, and legal claims directly attributable to asset acquisition. If there is capitalization of the interest cost incurred during construction, Statement 1 requires that the adopted accounting policy be disclosed and consistently applied.

In many instances, as shown in Table 2-1, the footnotes to the surveyed financial statements do describe accounting practices for fixed assets.

DEPRECIATION OF FIXED ASSETS

The seventh principle of NCGA Statement 1 contains the following guidance on the depreciation of fixed assets:

7.a. Depreciation of general fixed assets should not be recorded in the accounts of governmental funds. Depreciation of general fixed assets may be recorded in cost accounting systems or calculated for cost finding analyses, and accumulated depreciation may be recorded in the general fixed assets account group.

b. Depreciation of fixed assets accounted for in a proprietary fund should be recorded in the accounts of that fund. Depreciation is also recognized in those trust funds where expenses, net income, and/or capital maintenance are measured.

The NCGA states that depreciation expense is determined by allocating in a systematic manner the net asset cost (original cost less estimated salvage value) or assigned value over the estimated service life of the asset. Depreciation expense is recognized in proprietary funds and those trust funds where expense, net income, and/or capital maintenance are measured.

For general fixed assets, the recording of depreciation is optional, but the accounting should not be done in the accounts of the governmental funds. Rather, the depreciation entry is recorded in the general fixed assets account group through an increase in accumulated depreciation and a decrease to the investment in general fixed assets accounts.

No instances were noted of depreciation of general fixed assets being recorded in the accounts of a governmental fund. A few governmental units elected to record depreciation of general fixed assets in the general fixed assets account group. Table 3-2 lists several of the more frequent descriptors used in the financial statements examined for reporting accumulated depreciation.

NONCANCELLABLE OR CAPITALIZED LEASES

Statement 1 also provides that the fixed assets classification should include assets that are, in substance, acquired under noncancellable leases. The related lease obligation should be recorded as a long-term debt. Statement 1 requires also that significant noncapitalized lease commitments also be disclosed in the notes to the financial statements.

With respect to these leases for general fixed assets, the asset is recorded in the general fixed asset account group, the related lease (debt) in the general long-term debt account group. Proprietary-fund-type leased fixed assets and the related lease (debt) are recorded within the appropriate proprietary fund.

Exhibit 3-2 illustrates excerpts from notes in financial statements relating to capitalized leases.

INFRASTRUCTURE FIXED ASSETS

Certain governmental fixed assets are referred to as *public domain* or *infrastructure* fixed assets. These assets include roads, bridges, curbs and gutters, streets and sidewalks, drainage systems, lighting systems, and similar assets. Such assets are generally immovable and of value only to a governmental unit. The NCGA states that reporting of such assets is optional. Typi-

cally, depreciation is not recorded for these types of assets. However, the NCGA provides that the accounting policy should be consistently applied and be disclosed in the summary of significant accounting policies.

Exhibit 3-3 illustrates selected examples of footnote disclosures related to infrastructure assets that the governmental unit has elected to record.

EXHIBITS AND TABLES FOR CHAPTER 3

Table 3-1. Account Titles Used by Governmental Units to Report Fund and General Fixed Assets

Exhibit 3-1. Selected Excerpts Illustrating Reporting of Proprietary Fund and General Fixed Assets

Table 3-2. Account Titles Used by Governmental Units to Report Fixed Assets—Accumulated Depreciation Accounts

Exhibit 3-2. Excerpts of Footnote Disclosures Related to Capitalized Leases

Exhibit 3-3. Excerpts of Footnote Disclosures Related to Infrasructure Assets

TABLE 3-1. ACCOUNT TITLES USED BY GOVERNMENTAL UNITS TO REPORT FUND AND GENERAL FIXED ASSETS

Account Title Used*	Instances Observed (%)
Construction in progress	24
Land	20
Buildings	13
Fixed assets	12
Machinery and equipment	12
Improvements other than buildings	11
Equipment	7
Other	5
Property, plant, and equipment	5
General fixed assets	5
Buildings and improvements	4
Buildings and structures	2
Land and buildings	2
Property and equipment	2
Furniture, fixtures, and equipment	2
Furniture and fixtures	2
Furniture and equipment	2
Utility plant (in service)	2
Improvements	1
Vehicles	1
Land improvements	1
Other descriptors:	<1
Land, buildings, and equipment	
Structures and improvements	
Work in process	
Capitalized leases	
Vehicles and equipment	
Land held for resale	

* Observations for the 88% of the units having a combined balance sheet.

EXHIBIT 3-1. SELECTED EXCERPTS ILLUSTRATING REPORTING OF PROPRIETARY FUND AND GENERAL FIXED ASSETS

[DEKALB COUNTY, GEORGIA]

Combined Balance Sheet [in part]—All Fund Types and Account Groups, December 31, 1983

	Proprietary Fund Types		Account Groups
	Enterprise	Internal Service	General Fixed Assets
ASSETS AND OTHER DEBITS			
	* * *		
PROPERTY, PLANT AND EQUIPMENT, net of accumulated depreciation and amortization (Note F)	$262,223,765	15,831,101	$63,639,272
	* * *		
LIABILITIES			
	* * *		
FUND EQUITY INVESTMENT IN GENERAL FIXED ASSETS			63,639,272
	* * *		

Note A [in part]

(7) Fixed Assets, Depreciation, and Amortization. Fixed assets of the Proprietary Funds are recorded at cost except for contributed water and sewer lines, which are recorded at fair market value (which approximate cost). Depreciation and amortization is computed on the straight-line basis over the estimated useful lives of the respective assets. Depreciation and amortization of contributed assets is closed to contributed capital. Indirect costs of the Water and Sewage System Fund, such as administration, planning, engineering, and construction management, are capitalized as a percentage of direct labor costs incurred in construction.

Fixed assets in the General Fixed Assets Account Group are recorded at cost where applicable. For various older assets, fair market value at the time of recording was utilized when the original costs could not be determined. "Public domain" fixed assets (streets, bridges, etc.) are not recorded in the General Fixed Assets Account Group. No depreciation has been recorded on General Fixed Assets.

Interest during construction is capitalized if material. During the current year, no interest was capitalized.

Normal maintenance and repairs are charged to expense as incurred. Major improvements to existing facilities are capitalized.

Note F. Property, Plant, and Equipment

A summary of changes in property, plant and equipment follows:

	Estimated Life (in Years)	Balance 1-1-83	Additions	Deletions	Transfers	Balance 12-31-83	Accumulated Depreciation and Amortization 12-31-83	Book Value 12-31-83
Enterprise Funds								
Land	—	$ 3,571,513	$	$	$ 28,000	$ 3,599,513	$	$ 3,599,513
Land improvements	25–40	5,720,382			4,620,908	10,341,290	2,164,998	8,176,292
Buildings	40	4,004,862	88,000	(59,647)		4,033,215	1,607,542	2,425,673
Plants	50	32,714,017			63,202,109	95,916,126	7,363,397	88,552,729
Lines	50	170,131,994	3,499,729		6,846,351	180,478,074	44,685,512	135,792,562
Water meters	15	6,796,316			848,246	7,644,562	2,876,548	4,768,014
Other equipment	5–10	2,689,926	67,146	(374,974)	167,338	2,544,436	1,554,553	989,883
Leaseholds	50	14,671,150				14,671,150	2,417,703	12,253,447
Construction in progress	—	70,871,921	10,501,683		(75,707,952)	5,665,652		5,665,652
		$311,172,081	$14,156,558	$ (434,621)	$ —	$324,894,018	$62,670,253	$262,223,765
Internal Service Funds								
Buildings	5–25	$ 1,498,035	$	$ (7,374)		$ 1,490,661	$ 165,555	$ 1,325,106
Vehicles and portable equipment	1–10	25,886,129	5,931,267	(2,689,680)		29,127,716	14,746,183	14,381,533
Other equipment	5	736,543	34,157	(567,153)		203,547	79,085	124,462
		$28,120,707	$5,965,424	$(3,264,207)		$ 30,821,924	$14,990,823	$15,831,101
General Fixed Assets								
Land		$ 7,718,782	$ 202,050	$ (5,000)	$ 897,514	$ 8,813,346		
Land improvements		5,148,363	884,868		194,299	6,227,530		
Buildings		39,002,332	796,518	(400,000)	1,046,078	40,444,928		
Other equipment		6,491,947	1,685,099	(2,002,370)		6,174,676		
Construction in progress		1,371,029	2,745,654		(2,137,891)	1,978,792		
		$ 59,732,453	$ 6,314,189	$(2,407,370)	$ —	$ 63,639,272		

[DISTRICT OF COLUMBIA]

Combined Balance Sheet [in part]—All Fund Types and Account Groups, September 30, 1983 [in thousands]

	Proprietary Fund Types			Account Groups
	University	Enterprise (Note 9)	Internal Service	General Fixed Assets
ASSETS		* * *		
Fixed Assets (Note 4):				
Property and equipment, at cost	$109,741	706,445	3,793	2,717,996
Less—Accumulated depreciation	26,022	141,508	2,237	929,292
Net fixed assets	$ 83,719	564,937	1,556	1,788,704
		* * *		
LIABILITIES AND FUND EQUITY				
		* * *		
Fund Equity				
Contributed capital (Note 4)	$ 83,396	373,669	3,159	—
Investment in general fixed assets (Note 4)	$ —	—	—	1,788,704
		* * *		

Note (4) Fixed Assets

A. General Fixed Assets. A summary of changes in general fixed assets and investment in general fixed assets follows ($000s):

Asset Class	Balance October 1, 1982	Acquisitions	Transfers/ Retirements	Balance September 30, 1983
Land	$ 102,436	1,599	3,371	107,406
Streets and bridges	793,509	—	34,920	828,429
Storm drains	121,425	—	202	121,627
Buildings and fixtures	1,019,823	—	63,225	1,083,048
Furniture and equipment	113,163	27,391	(2,212)	138,342
Construction in progress	56,823	155,037	(154,340)	57,520
Transit system investment	344,198	—	37,426	381,624
Total	2,551,377	184,027	(17,408)	2,717,996
Less—Accumulated depreciation	865,855	67,640	(4,203)	929,292
Net general fixed assets	$1,685,522	116,387	(13,205)	1,788,704
Federal capital grants	$ 483,064	45,194	(27,682)	500,576
District resources	1,202,458	138,833	(53,163)	1,288,128
Total investment in general fixed assets	$1,685,522	184,027	(80,845)	1,788,704

Acquisitions consist of expenditures ($000s) from the General Fund ($29,990) for land, furniture and fixtures and from the Capital Projects Fund ($152,903) plus capitalized interest ($2,134) for construction in progress. When a project is completed, costs in the construction in progress account are transferred to one or more of the other asset classes or are retired. The foregoing net cost of buildings and fixtures includes $212 million at September 30, 1983 and 1982, for buildings which were constructed on land owned by the Federal government.

A schedule of changes in general fixed assets by function follows ($000s):

Function	Balance October 1, 1982	Acquisitions	Transfers/ Retirements	Balance September 30, 1983
Governmental direction and support	$ 75,335	7,952	(20,174)	63,113
Economic development and regulation	209,460	2,783	29,439	241,682
Public safety and justice	219,476	3,131	20,870	243,477
Public education system	542,544	11,926	19,358	573,828
Human support services	98,149	667	19,675	118,491
Transportation services and assistance	807,330	1,324	35,597	844,251
Environmental services and supply	198,062	1,207	(5,259)	194,010
Construction in progress	56,823	155,037	(154,340)	57,520
Transit system investment	344,198	—	37,426	381,624
Total	$2,551,377	184,027	(17,408)	2,717,996

B. Proprietary Fixed Assets. A summary of proprietary fixed assets and contributed capital at September 30, 1983 follows ($000s):

Asset Class	University	Enterprise	Internal Service
Land	$ 8,729	23,243	8
Water and sewer facilities	—	472,650	—
Buildings and fixtures	81,620	156,529	719
Furniture and equipment	19,392	24,870	3,066
Construction in progress	—	29,153	—
Total	109,741	706,445	3,793
Less—Accumulated depreciation	26,022	141,508	2,237
Net proprietary fixed assets	$ 83,719	564,937	1,556

A summary of changes in contributed capital during 1983 follows ($000s):

Asset Class	University	Enterprise	Internal Service
Federal capital grants:			
Balance at beginning of year	$ —	123,626	—
Additional grants	—	3,687	—
Less—			
Depreciation	—	2,287	—
Balance at end of year	$ —	125,026	—
District resources:			
Balance at beginning of year	$83,777	199,694	3,159
Additional resources	3,370	48,949	—
Less—			
Depreciation	3,751	—	—
Balance at end of year	$83,396	248,643	3,159

D. Depreciation and Interest. The depreciation recorded on fixed assets and the interest costs capitalized during construction of fixed assets, by fund or account group, for 1983 follow ($000s):

Fund or Account Group	Depreciation Recorded	Interest Capitalized
Water and sewer	$ 6,159	1,700
General hospital	3,168	4
Starplex	889	—
Convention center	1,510	1,847
Lottery and games	37	—
General services	90	—
Correctional industries	77	—
Motor vehicle maintenance	3	—
Housing finance	7	—
General fixed assets	67,640	2,134
Total	$79,580	5,685

Additional depreciation in the amount ($000s) of $2,287 on fixed assets acquired through Federal capital grants was charged directly to Contributed Capital in the Water and Sewer Fund. Depreciation in the amount ($000s) of $3,751 was charged directly to Contributed Capital in the University Funds.

[CITY OF INDIANAPOLIS, INDIANA]

Combined Balance Sheet [in part]—All Fund Types and Account Groups, December 31, 1983

	Proprietary Fund Type	Fiduciary Fund Type	Account Groups
	Enterprise	Trust and Agency	General Fixed Assets
ASSETS AND OTHER DEBITS	* * *		
Land, buildings and other fixed assets (Note 1B and 7)	$18,586,356	$85,155	$368,973,287
Land held for redevelopment			7,033,976
	* * *		
LIABILITIES AND FUND EQUITY			
Liabilities:			
	* * *		
Fund equity:			
Investment in general fixed assets (Notes 1B and 7)			$376,007,263

Note 1B [in part] Fixed Assets and Long-Term Liabilities

Fixed assets used in governmental fund type operations (general fixed assets) are accounted for in the General Fixed Assets Account Group, rather than in governmental funds. Public domain ("infrastructure") general fixed assets, consisting of certain improvements other than buildings (e.g., streets, sewers, bridges), are not capitalized. Net interest cost related to debt financing during construction is capitalized. No depreciation has been provided on general fixed assets.

All fixed assets are valued at historical cost or estimated historical cost if actual historical cost is not available. Donated fixed assets are valued at their estimated fair value on the date donated.

* * *

Depreciation of all exhaustible fixed assets used by proprietary funds is charged as an expense against their operations. Accumulated depreciation is reported on proprietary fund balance sheets. Depreciation has been provided on the straight-line method using estimated useful lives as follows:

City Market buildings	50 years
City Market equipment	10 years
Off Street Parking buildings	50 years
Off Street Parking equipment	10 years
Housing Authority buildings	15 years
Housing Authority equipment	3 years

Note 7 Changes in General Fixed Assets

A summary of changes in general fixed assets:

	Balance January 1, 1983	Additions	Transfers and Reclassifications	Reductions	Balance December 31, 1983
General fixed assets used in operations:					
Land	$ 13,905,432	$ 554,428	$	$	$ 14,459,860
Buildings	51,070,846	577,005	84,861,575	136,127	136,373,299
Improvements	50,851,674	583,395	1,319,492		52,754,561
Equipment	38,912,118	6,659,071		1,481,001	44,090,188
Land held for redevelopment	4,292,305	4,851,325		2,109,654	7,033,976
Construction in progress	188,305,321	11,884,421	(86,181,067)		114,008,675
Total fixed assets used in operations	347,337,696	25,109,645		3,726,782	368,720,559
Fixed assets held for investment (note 1B and 7):					
Leased sports arena and land	16,717,144			16,717,144	
Multi-purpose stadium	4,000,000				4,000,000
Leased land	3,286,704				3,286,704

(continued)

[CITY OF INDIANAPOLIS, INDIANA] (Continued)

	Balance January 1, 1983	Additions	Transfers and Reclassifications	Reductions	Balance December 31, 1983
Total fixed assets held for investment	24,003,848			16,717,144	7,286,704
Total general fixed assets	$371,341,544	$25,109,645	$	$20,443,926	$376,007,263
Investment in general fixed assets:					
From capital projects funds	$ 54,146,320	$11,849,745	$ (4,184,430)	$12,317,144	$ 49,494,491
From federal funds	180,034,105		10,036,851	6,285,456	183,785,500
From general funds	130,296,760	13,231,191	(5,856,191)	1,841,326	135,830,434
From special revenue funds	6,579,903	28,709			6,608,612
Donations	284,456		3,770		288,226
Total	$371,341,544	$25,109,645	$	$20,443,926	$376,007,263
Capital outlay expenditures not capitalized		9,209,596			
Total capital outlay expenditures		$34,319,241			

* * *

Construction in progress is composed of the following:

* * *

A summary of proprietary fund type property, plant and equipment at December 31, 1983 follows:

	Enterprise Funds				Trust and Agency
	City Market	Off Street Parking	Housing Authority	Total	
Land	$ 102,676	$549,740	$ 9,599,338	$10,251,754	$
Buildings	4,858,962		46,872,247	51,731,209	
Equipment	29,787		1,577,316	1,607,103	95,155
Total	4,991,425	549,740	58,048,901	63,590,066	95,155
Less accumulated depreciation	605,575		44,398,135	45,003,710	10,000
Net	$4,385,850	$549,740	$13,650,766	$18,586,356	$85,155

[CITY OF JACKSONVILLE, FLORIDA]

Combined Balance Sheet (in part)—All Fund Types and Account Groups, September 30, 1983 [in thousands]

	Proprietary Fund Types		Account Group
	Enterprise	Internal Service	General Fixed Assets
ASSETS			
	* * *		
Property and equipment, at cost:			
Land	$ 10,315	$ 124	$ 28,251
Buildings and improvements	359,576	4,045	82,164
Improvements other than buildings	24,478	93	
Furniture and equipment	2,246	40,058	14,855
Construction in progress	56,240		33
Less accumulated depreciation	(83,725)	(28,069)	
	* * *		
LIABILITIES AND FUND EQUITY			
Fund equity:			
	* * *		
Investment in general fixed assets			$125,303

Note A [in part] Summary of Significant Accounting Policies

Fixed Assets and Long-Term Liabilities. The accounting and reporting treatment applied to the fixed assets and long-term liabilities associated with each fund are determined by that fund's measurement focus. Financial statement measurement focus objectives for Governmental and Expendable Trust Funds vary significantly from the objectives of the statements for Proprietary, Nonexpendable Trust and Pension Trust Funds.

Governmental and Expendable Trust Funds—In these funds the measurement focus objective is to determine financial flow and availability of financial resources. The operating statements present the "expendable available financial resources" by reporting changes (revenue and expenditures) in those resources. The balance sheets of these funds identify those amounts and their availability for appropriation as fund balance. Fund Balance is the remainder when current liabilities are deducted from current assets. Only current assets and liabilities are reported in Governmental and Expendable Trust Funds.

General Fixed Assets—Fixed Assets used in governmental fund type operations (general fixed assets) are accounted for in the General Fixed Assets Account Group, rather than in the governmental funds. General fixed assets purchased, including land, are initially reported as expenditures in the general, special revenue, capital projects and expendable trust funds. Such assets are capitalized at cost in the general fixed assets group of accounts except for improvements other than buildings, which include streets, alleys, sidewalks, drainage and lighting systems. Gifts and contributions

are recorded in general fixed assets at fair market value as of the date of receipt. Depreciation is not required and has not been provided on general fixed assets.

* * *

Property and Depreciation—Property, plant and equipment in the enterprise and internal service funds is accounted for in essentially the same manner as the general fixed assets, except that depreciation is provided, and improvements other than buildings are recognized as assets. Depreciation is computed using the straight-line method over the estimated useful lives of the assets, which are as follows:

	Years
Buildings and improvement	12–45
Furnishings and equipment	2–10
Vehicles, light	3– 5
Vehicles, heavy	10–15
Scales and improvements	7
Water and Sewer Distribution System	20–75

Upon disposal of property, the related cost and accumulated depreciation are removed from the accounts with gains or losses on disposal reported within income. Expenditures for maintenance, repairs and minor renewals and betterments are charged to income. Renewals and betterments of a major character are capitalized.

Note J General Fixed Assets

During the fiscal year ended September 30, 1983, the following changes in general fixed assets occurred:

	Balance September 30, 1982	Transfers in	Additions	Transfers out and Disposals	Balance September 30, 1983
Cost:					
Land	$ 20,906,083		$7,448,102	$ 103,391	$ 28,250,794
Buildings	84,232,382			2,068,639	82,163,743
Furniture and equipment	14,259,566	$1,425,539	1,234,023	2,064,170	14,854,958
Construction work in progress	33,365				33,365
	$119,431,396	$1,425,539	$8,682,125	$4,236,200	$125,302,860
Net investment in general fixed assets:					
Current revenue	$ 19,903,403	$1,355,395	$1,239,611	$1,961,401	$ 20,537,008
Bond proceeds	34,508,747	212	5,924	425	34,514,458
Federal grants	63,160,102	69,404	7,433,442	2,219,513	68,443,435
Gifts	1,859,144	528	3,148	54,861	1,807,959
	$119,431,396	$1,425,539	$8,682,125	$4,236,200	$125,302,860

[JEFFERSON COUNTY, COLORADO]

Combined Balance Sheet [in part]—All Fund Types and Account Groups, December 31, 1983

	Account Groups
	General Fixed Assets
Assets:	
* * *	
Fixed assets—Notes 1 and 3	$59,307,651
* * *	
Liabilities and Fund Equity:	
Liabilities:	
* * *	
Fund equity:	
Investment in general fixed assets	$59,307,651
* * *	

Note 1

B. [in part] Fixed Assets and Long-Term Liabilities

* * *

	Balance January 1, 1983	Additions	Deletions	Balance December 31, 1983
Land	$24,338,751	$ 8,837,710	$1,567,527	$31,608,934
Building	7,211,625	580,344	12,489	7,779,480
Vehicles, furniture and equipment	18,398,252	2,449,451	928,466	19,919,237
Total	$49,948,628	$11,867,505	$2,508,482	$59,307,651

Fixed assets used in governmental fund type operations (general fixed assets) are accounted for in the General Fixed Assets Account Group, rather than in governmental funds. Public domain ("infrastructure") general fixed assets consisting of certain improvements other than buildings, including roads, bridges, curbs and gutters, streets and sidewalks, drainage systems and lighting systems are not capitalized along with other general fixed assets. No depreciation has been provided on general fixed assets.

All fixed assets are valued at historical cost or estimated historical cost if actual historical cost is not available. Donated fixed assets are valued at their estimated fair value on the date donated.

* * *

Note 3: Changes in General Fixed Assets

A summary of changes in general fixed assets follows:

[ST. LOUIS COUNTY, MISSOURI]

Combined Balance Sheet [in part]—All Fund Types and Account Groups, December 31, 1983

Assets	Proprietary Fund Type — Enterprise	Account Groups — General Fixed Assets
* * *		
Capital assets:		
Land and improvements	$ 8,906,440	$ 41,667,572
Buildings and other structures	10,321,414	50,974,653
Airport runways and aprons	1,863,695	—
Communication equipment	7,731	4,510,153
Medical equipment and other	2,288,548	967,754
Motor vehicle equipment	38,538	9,434,836
Office furniture and fixtures	2,747	5,682,972
Other equipment	63,180	12,099,814
	23,492,293	125,137,754
Less accumulated depreciation	8,333,705	34,525,211
Net capital assets	15,158,588	90,612,543
* * *		

Note 1 [in part] Capital Assets and Depreciation

Enterprise Funds. Capital assets are recorded generally at cost. Contributed assets are carried at estimated fair market value at the date of contribution, except assets contributed by other funds, which are recorded at the contributing fund's costs. For retirements or other dispositions of assets, the asset and related accumulated depreciation accounts are eliminated and the difference between the net carrying value and any proceeds received is included in income.

Depreciation is provided on the straight-line basis over the following estimated useful lives:

Buildings and other structures	16 to 50 years
Airport runways and aprons	10 to 30 years
Communication equipment	10 years
Medical equipment	8 to 15 years
Motor vehicle equipment	4 to 6 years
Office furniture and fixtures	10 to 20 years
Other equipment	3 to 20 years

Depreciation provided on donated assets is reflected in operating statements and closed to retained earnings without affecting the contributed capital account.

The costs of normal maintenance and repairs are charged to operations as incurred. Renewals and betterments are capitalized and depreciated over the remaining useful lives of the related assets.

General Fixed Assets Account Group. General fixed assets are recorded as expenditures in the Governmental Fund Types and, except for streets, sidewalks, curbs and gutters, storm sewers, lighting systems and similar immovable County improvements, are capitalized in the General Fixed Assets Group of Accounts.

Assets in this account group are recorded at cost, estimated historical cost where original historical cost is not available, or, in the case of contributed assets, at estimated fair market value at the time of acquisition.

Accumulated depreciation is recorded on general fixed assets by reducing the appropriate investment in the general fixed assets account. Such depreciation is computed on the straight-line basis over estimated useful lives comparable to those used for Enterprise Funds fixed assets.

[CITY OF ALLENTOWN, PENNSYLVANIA]

Combined Balance Sheet [in part]—All Fund Types and Account Groups, December 31, 1983

Assets	Proprietary Funds	Account Groups
	Enterprise Funds	General Fixed Assets
	* * *	
Land	$ 3,465,209	$ 6,943,099
Property held for development		2,545,858
Building	21,653,271	14,895,180
Land and building improvements	1,929,182	3,100,675
Machinery and equipment	4,505,641	5,812,740
Vehicles	1,170,287	4,298,422
Distribution and collection systems	13,008,445	
Construction in progress	4,115,461	220,282
	$49,847,496	$37,816,256
Accumulated depreciation	(14,128,152)	(12,107,872)
	$37,719,344	$25,708,384
	* * *	

Note B [in part]

Property and Equipment. During 1979, the City conducted, through an independent appraiser, an inventory of all fixed assets of the water and sewer utility systems and general fixed assets. All assets have been stated at cost or estimated historical cost if cost records were not readily available. Estimated cost was determined by reverse trending the current cost of the asset back to the estimated acquisition date. Certain governmental improvements, including streets, curbs and gutters, are not capitalized. Substantially all items which were capitalized initially are stated at estimated historical cost. Donated fixed assets are valued at their estimated fair market value as of the date donated.

Depreciation is computed on a straight-line basis over an asset's estimated useful life (vehicles 2–10 years; equipment 5–25 years; buildings and improvements 35–80 years; and reservoirs and water and sewer distribution and collection systems 99 years). Depreciation in the enterprise funds is charged to operations. Depreciation on general fixed assets is treated as a reduction in the investment.

Note F—Changes in Fixed Assets

General fixed assets changed during the year as follows:

	Beginning of Year (Restated)	Additions	Transfers and Disposals	End of Year
Land	$ 6,890,106	$ 52,993	$ —	$ 6,943,099
Property held for development	2,239,704	591,550	(285,396)	2,545,858
Building	14,658,836	236,344		14,895,180
Land and building improvements	3,032,826	36,887	30,962	3,100,675
Machinery and equipment	5,154,817	722,771	(64,848)	5,812,740
Vehicles	4,035,689	404,135	(141,402)	4,298,422
Construction in progress	87,832	157,595	(25,145)	220,282
	$36,099,810	$2,202,275	$(485,829)	$37,816,256

[WASHTENAW COUNTY, MICHIGAN]

Combined Balance Sheet [in part]—All Fund Types and Account Groups, December 31, 1983

Assets	Proprietary Fund Types Internal Service	Account Groups General Fixed Assets
	* * *	
Land		$ 2,099,310
Buildings		24,934,478
Improvements other than buildings		1,236,579
Equipment	361,416	10,606,198
Accumulated depreciation	(159,054)	(4,302,370)
Equipment under capital lease (Note 3)	333,124	
Accumulated amortization	(108,968)	
	* * *	

Note 1 [in part]

General Fixed Assets. Fixed assets acquired or constructed for general governmental services are recorded as expenditures in the fund making the expenditure and capitalized in the general fixed asset group at cost, or estimated cost if original cost was not available. Donated fixed assets are recorded at estimated fair value at the time of acquisition. No provision for depreciation is made for general fixed assets except for property equipment of the County Road Commission.

Property, Plant and Equipment. Fixed assets of internal service funds and County Road Commission are stated at cost or estimated cost if original cost was not available. Donated fixed assets are recorded at estimated fair value at the time of acquisition. Depreciation is computed on the straight-line method, based on the estimated useful lives of the assets except for road equipment, which utilizes sum-of-the-years-digits method.

Note 5. Property and Equipment

A summary of changes in general fixed assets follows:

	Balance January 1, 1983	Additions	Deletions	Balance December 31, 1983
Land	$ 1,940,195	$ 159,115		$ 2,099,310
Buildings	24,599,320	342,358	$ 7,200	24,934,478
Improvements other than buildings	1,156,043	80,536		1,236,579
Equipment	10,280,875	923,502	598,179	10,606,198
	37,976,433	1,505,511	605,379	38,876,565
Allowances for depreciation	4,040,902	354,004	92,536	4,302,370
	$33,935,531	$1,151,507	$512,843	$34,574,195

Major sources of general fixed assets at December 31, 1983 include:

County Road Commission, net of allowances for depreciation of $4,302,370	$ 2,628,534
General County	32,307,077
	$34,935,611

TABLE 3-2. ACCOUNT TITLES USED BY GOVERNMENTAL UNITS TO REPORT FIXED ASSETS—ACCUMULATED DEPRECIATION ACCOUNTS

Account Title Used*	Instances Observed (%)	Account Title Used*	Instances Observed (%)
Accumulated depreciation	24	Other descriptors:	<1
Fixed assets, net of accumulated depreciation	15	Accumulated depreciation—equipment	
Property, plant, and equipment,net	12	Accumulated depreciation and amortization	
Property and equipment, net	4	Accumulated amortization of lease hold improvements	
Accumulated depreciation—machinery and equipment	1	Machinery and equipment—net	
Accumulated depreciation—buildings	<1		

* Observation for the 88% of the units having a combined balance sheet.

EXHIBIT 3-2. EXCERPTS OF FOOTNOTE DISCLOSURES RELATED TO CAPITALIZED LEASES

[GWINNETT COUNTY, GEORGIA (DECEMBER 31, 1983), NOTES TO FINANCIAL STATEMENTS (IN PART)]

Note 7 [in part]

Leases

Capital Leases and Direct Financing Leases. Fire stations, fire fighting vehicles and equipment, and property for recreation purposes are used under capital lease agreements with the Financing Authorities. Equipment for road construction and certain property for recreation purposes are used under capital leases with other lessors.

The following is a summary of changes in obligations under capital leases for the year ended December 31, 1983:

Obligations under capital leases at January 1, 1983	$ 6,087,080
Obligations incurred	824,389
Principal payments	(1,366,095)
Obligations under capital leases at December 31, 1983	$ 5,545,374

The following is a schedule by years of future lease payments under capital leases together with the present value of the net lease payments as of December 31, 1983:

	Financing Authorities	Other Lessors	Total
1984	$1,000,858	$ 733,174	$1,734,032
1985	947,075	616,075	1,563,150
1986	892,764	117,129	1,009,893
1987	757,537	26,056	783,593
1988	706,984	25,113	732,097
1989–1992	1,051,784	67,324	1,119,108
Total lease payments	$5,357,002	$1,584,871	$6,941,873
Imputed interest	(1,266,536)	(129,963)	(1,396,499)
Present value of lease payments	$4,090,466	$1,454,908	$5,545,374

The Financing Authorities account for their leases as direct financing leases and classify the present value of payments due within one year, $670,000, as current assets and the present value of payments due after one year, $3,420,466, as noncurrent assets.

[CITY OF KALAMAZOO, MICHIGAN (DECEMBER 31, 1983), NOTES TO FINANCIAL STATEMENTS (IN PART)]

Note I

Lease Obligations

The Kalamazoo Center Fund (an enterprise fund) leases certain land underlying a portion of the Kalamazoo Center under a noncancellable lease which expires in 2033 and is renewable for two additional successive fifteen-year periods. The City is required to pay all taxes and assessments levied against the property. Rental rates are to be reviewed in the year 2003 and at five-year intervals thereafter with rentals being adjusted for changes in the Consumer Price Index.

Under the terms of the agreement, Kalamazoo Center Fund operations have been charged with rent expense of $12,031 in 1983.

At December 31, 1983, the approximate future base rental payments under the noncancellable lease are as follows:

1984	$ 10,500
1985	10,500
1986	10,500
1987	10,500
1988	10,500
Thereafter	464,625
	$517,125

[CITY OF OMAHA, NEBRASKA (DECEMBER 31, 1983), NOTES TO FINANCIAL STATEMENTS (IN PART)]

Note 6

Lease Agreements

General Fund. The City is leasing the Orpheum Theatre, a waste disposal facility, and several libraries and other buildings under non-cancellable lease-purchase agreements expiring from 1983 to 1996, at which time title will be conveyed to the City. The rental payments are designed to equal the debt service requirements of certain non-profit organizations that financed the construction of the facilities. The City has an option to purchase the facilities at any time by paying an amount equal to the total of all remaining unpaid obligations of the owner at that time.

The following is a schedule by years of future minimum lease payments under the lease-purchase agreements together with the present value of the net minimum lease payments as of December 31, 1983:

Fiscal Year Ending:	
1984	$ 1,059,911
1985	1,053,696
1986	1,048,436
1987	1,045,789
1988	1,045,115
Later years	7,306,030
Total minimum lease payments	$12,558,977
Less amount representing interest	4,102,058
Total obligation under capital leases, with interest rates from 3.25% to 7.75%	$ 8,456,919

The City leases space in the Omaha-Douglas Civic Center and the adjoining Hall of Justice under a noncancellable operating lease that expires only upon payment of all outstanding bonds (1997) of the Omaha-Douglas Public Building Commission. The annual rental payments are determined based upon actual space occupied by the City plus an additional amount for operation and maintenance. At the expiration of the lease term, title will be conveyed to the City for that portion of the building occupied during the immediately preceeding twelve months. Minimum rental payments for 1983 were $442,277.

Enterprise Funds. The City is a party to a non-cancellable lease-purchase agreement with the Omaha Pollution Control Corporation involving the use of a packing house waste treatment facility. The agreement expires in 1997, at which time the City can purchase the facility for $1. The agreement provides for annual rentals of $360,000 and is accounted for as a capital lease. The City has subcontracted the operation of this facility to a group of meatpackers.

The following is a schedule by years of future minimum lease payments under this capital lease together with the present value of the net minimum lease payments as of December 31, 1983:

Fiscal Year Ending:	
1984	$ 360,000
1985	360,000
1986	360,000
1987	360,000
1988	360,000
Later years	3,240,000
Total minimum lease payments	$5,040,000
Less amount representing interest	1,536,680
Total obligation under the capital lease	$3,503,320
Less current portion of obligation under capital lease	172,880
Long-term obligation under the capital lease, with an interest rate implicit in the agreement of 5.4%	$3,330,440

Expendable Trust Fiduciary Funds. The City has entered into an agreement with the State of Nebraska whereby the City has issued revenue bonds to construct from the proceeds thereof and certain contributions a public facility, the Downtown Education Center, to be leased to the State. The lease agreement provides, among other things, that rental payments to the City will be established in amounts sufficient to reimburse the City for all costs incurred including the debt service on all bonds issued and any refunding thereof. In addition the State may acquire the public facility at any time the lease agreement is outstanding for a price resulting in no gain or loss to the City, with such amount being computed giving effect to any amounts required by the City to retire the then outstanding bonds.

This lease became effective July 1, 1981, and extends to June 30, 1986. Rentals received in 1983 totaled $1,285,000.

[CITY OF PHOENIX, ARIZONA (JUNE 30, 1984), NOTES TO FINANCIAL STATEMENTS (IN PART)]
Note 21 [in part]
Leases

Capital Leases. The City has entered into certain agreements with the Phoenix Civic Plaza Building Corporation and the City of Phoenix Civic Improvement Corporation, affiliated nonprofit corporations, to lease certain facilities. Such agreements are, in substance, lease-purchase agreements, and are included as contracts payable in the accompanying financial statements and preceding Note 17.

A summary of capitalized leases under these agreements follows:

	June 30	
	1984	**1983**
Enterprise Funds		
Phoenix Civic Plaza	$22,134,491	$22,134,491
Airport Terminal	30,130,093	30,130,093
Less: Accumulated Amortization	(10,535,200)	(8,866,771)
	$41,729,384	$43,397,813
General Government		
Public Parking Facility	6,697,343	6,307,165
Total	$48,426,727	$49,704,978

Not included in the above is $32,996,421 for the expansion of the Phoenix Civic Plaza, which is still under construction.

The land underlying each facility is owned by the City and is leased to the nonprofit corporations. Upon normal termination of the lease agreements, titles to the facilities will pass to the City.

The following is a schedule of the future minimum lease payments under the above capital leases, including the Phoenix Civic Plaza expansion, and the present value of net minimum lease payments at June 30, 1984:

Year Ending June 30,	
1985	$ 10,010,415
1986	10,617,783
1987	10,592,884
1988	11,537,958
1989	13,153,793
Later years	69,831,098
Total minimum lease payments	$125,743,931
Less: Amount representing interest	(44,973,931)
Present value of net minimum lease payments at June 30, 1984	$ 80,770,000

The City has pledged excise taxes for payments of these installments. The City also pays all expenses of operating and maintaining the facilities in addition to the lease obligations.

During the fiscal year ending June 30, 1978, the City acquired the lease-hold interest in a City-owned Plaza Municipal Building for $1,160,000. Under the terms of the purchase agreement, the City paid $116,000 cash and issued a note payable in ten annual installments for the balance. The balance payable at June 30, 1984 was $488,404. The City has pledged excise taxes for payments of these installments, which are subordinate to the excise taxes pledged for the aforementioned capital lease.

[PINELLAS COUNTY, FLORIDA (SEPTEMBER 30, 1983), NOTES TO FINANCIAL STATEMENTS (IN PART)]

Note O—Obligations Under Capital Lease

Obligations under capital lease at September 30, 1983, consist of a lease obligation on the Park Boulevard Bridge Facility with the State of Florida which matches all the terms of the State of Florida Full Faith and Credit, Pinellas County Road and Bridge Bonds, Series 1979 Bond issue (dollars in thousands):

State of Florida, Full Faith and Credit, Pinellas County Road and Bridge Bonds, Series 1979 Serial bonds due annually at varying amounts ($320 to $1,470) commencing June 1, 1982, with interest at 7.00% to

7.25%, payable semiannually

Bonds payable 10/1/82	$19,700
Bonds retired	(320)
Bonds payable 9/30/83	$19,380
Less current maturities	340
	$19,040

The principal and interest due on the Series 1979 bonds are payable from and secured by the net tolls derived from the project, and to the extent required, the eighty percent Second Gas Tax Funds allocated for use in Pinellas County under the provisions of Article XII, Section 9(c), of the Florida Constitution. The payment of principal and interest are further secured by a pledge by Full Faith and Credit of the State of Florida, and the State is unconditionally and irrevocably obligated to make all such payments to the extent that the net tolls and pledged County Gasoline Tax Funds are insufficient for the full payment of principal and interest on the bonds at the stated maturity dates. The ad valorem taxing power of the County is not pledged to the payment of the 1979 Series. However, after all covenants and agreements related to bond payments have been satisfied, the State of Florida will convey fee simple title and ownership of the Facility to the County.

Bond Indenture Requirements. The amount required to be accumulated in the Debt Service Reserve Account is an amount equal to the maximum future annual debt service—$1.7 million.

The monies in the Construction Account or any of the Debt Service Accounts may be invested in direct obligations of the United States Government or in securities authorized by Section 215.47, Florida Statutes. All income earned on such investments is deposited in the respective trust accounts.

Total interest costs incurred in 1983 were $1,390,178. A schedule of maturities for the years indicated is as follows (dollars in thousands):

Year Ended June 1	Debt Service Cash Required		
	Principal	Interest	Total
1984	$ 340	$ 1,375	$ 1,715
1985	360	1,351	1,711
1986	385	1,326	1,711
1987	410	1,299	1,709
1988	435	1,270	1,705
Thereafter	17,450	15,554	33,004
	$19,380	$22,175	$41,555

[CITY OF SARASOTA, FLORIDA (SEPTEMBER 30, 1983), NOTES TO FINANCIAL STATEMENTS (IN PART)]

Note 13—Commitments

(a) Capitalized Leases

The following is a schedule by years of future minimum lease payments under capitalized leases together with the present value of the net minimum lease payments as of September 30, 1983:

1984	$ 75,912
1985	37,956
Total minimum lease payments	$113,868
Less amount representing interest	6,675
Present value of net minimum lease payments	$107,193

(b) Operating Leases

Commitments under operating lease agreements for equipment provide for minimum annual rental payments as follows:

1984	$13,446
1985	13,446
1986	13,446
1987	2,241

1983 Rental Expense was $13,446.

[SALT LAKE CITY CORPORATION, UTAH (JUNE 30, 1984), NOTES TO FINANCIAL STATEMENTS (IN PART)]

Note 7. Capitalized Leases

The City is obligated under certain leases accounted for as capital leases. The leased assets and related obligations are accounted for in the funds or account groups to which they apply. Assets under capital leases totalled $4,624,848 at June 30, 1984, and accumulated amortization on those assets totalled $483,603.

The following is a schedule of future minimum lease payments under capital leases, together with the net present value of the minimum lease payments, as of June 30, 1984:

	Internal Service Funds		General Long-Term Obligations Account Group
Year Ending June 30	Fleet Management Fund	Data Processing Fund	
1985	$156,175	$ 778,526	$120,339
1986	155,213	912,136	29,788
1987	97,386	910,288	6,216
1988	13,495	769,160	1,023
1989 and thereafter	—	608,513	—
Total minimum lease payments	422,269	3,978,623	157,366
Less amount representing interest	62,213	571,189	15,330
Net present value of minimum lease payments	$360,056	$3,407,434	$142,036

[CITY OF ALLENTOWN, PENNSYLVANIA (DECEMBER 31, 1983), NOTES TO FINANCIAL STATEMENTS (IN PART)]

Note I [in part]—Long Term Obligation

Capitalized Leases

1978 lease payable to the Allentown Authority with variable semi-annual payments through 1999.	$13,573,383	$ (894,110)	$12,679,273
Vacation	519,358	15,891	535,249
Unfunded pension	4,494,592	1,029,793	5,524,385
	22,619,598	(141,398)	22,478,200

The equipment notes are secured by computer equipment with a net book value of $272,907. The capitalized leases cover facilities financed through various prior debt obligations which have been refinanced. The City has pledged its full faith, credit and taxing power to payment of principal and interest on bonds of the Allentown Authority and guarantees the obligations of the AEDC parking revenue bonds and bond anticipations. In March 1984, the City contributed $125,000 to the debt service reserve fund for the AEDC parking revenue bonds.

Future minimum payments under capitalized leases consist of the following at December 31, 1983:

	General Long-Term Obligations
1984	$ 1,544,458
1985	1,526,543
1986	1,512,493
1987	1,499,110
1988	1,499,950
Thereafter	9,054,717
Total minimum lease payments	16,637,271
Amounts representing interest	3,957,998
Present value of minimum lease payments	$12,679,273

The annual requirements to pay principal and interest on all debt and capitalized lease obligations outstanding at December 31, 1983, are as follows:

	General Long-Term Obligations	Enterprise Funds	Expendable Trust Funds
1984	$ 1,975,461	$ 1,449,727	$ 77,053
1985	4,888,535	8,509,512	77,053
1986	1,503,868	966,292	77,053
1987	1,517,035	962,971	77,053
1988	1,517,425	966,569	77,053
1989–1993	6,613,230	4,810,221	385,266
1994–1998	2,399,756	4,777,520	377,767
1999–2003	122,358	4,755,187	377,767
2004–2006		5,382,100	
	$20,564,668	$32,580,099	$1,434,369

Bonds payable, notes payable and the capitalized lease obligations of the General Long-Term Obligations Group are serviced through general revenue. Notes payable are serviced through Enterprise Fund revenues of the Water, Sewer, Municipal Airport and AEDC Parking Funds. Funds are provided for the revenue bonds in the Enterprise Funds by the Sewer Fund and the AEDC Parking Fund. Notes payable in the Expendable Trust Fund are serviced through payments of notes receivable from various AEDC borrowers under the SBA 503 Urban Revitalization Loan Program.

The City's debt margin on net non-electoral including lease rental debts was approximately $88,477,000 at December 31, 1983.

[COUNTY OF CONTRA COSTA, CALIFORNIA (JUNE 30, 1984), NOTES TO FINANCIAL STATEMENTS (IN PART)]

Note (7) Lease Commitments

The County has leasing arrangements covering various County land, buildings and equipment as follows:

Capital Leases

Lease payments (principal and interest) under capital lease agreements included in expenditures for the year amounted to $2,446,432 for the General Fund, $6,084 for the Hospital Enterprise Fund and $379,320 for Special Districts under control of the Board of Supervisors.

Real property under capital leases, included in fixed assets at June 30, 1984, is $24,345,779. Real property under capital leases for Special Districts under control of the Board of Supervisors at June 30, 1984 approximated $3,354,000.

Interest rates on capital lease obligations range from 5 percent to 12.4 percent.

Included in fixed assets are various County buildings, under lease/purchase agreements with the Employee's Retirement Association. The County has an option to purchase each of the properties at any time during the term of each lease for the remaining amount of the capital lease obligation, subject in some cases to a premium ranging from 5.0 percent to 9.5 percent. In the event the County does not exercise its option to purchase a building, the Retirement Association has the option to purchase the County land on which the building is located at its fair market value at the time the lease terminates.

The County has also lease/purchase agreements with non-profit Public Facilities Corporations. The buildings under these lease agreements are included in fixed assets. The related obligations are more fully described in note 8.

The following is a summary of changes in general County capital lease obligations for the year ended June 30, 1984:

Balance at July 1, 1983	$8,285,028
Additional obligations	478,191
Current maturities or cancellations	(2,176,289)
Balance at June 30, 1984	$6,586,930

Future minimum lease payments under capital leases together with the related present value of the capital lease obligations at June 30, 1984, are as follows:

	Fiscal Year Ending June 30,	Equipment Leases	Lease/Purchase Agreement with Employees Retirement Association	Other Building Leases	Total
General County	1985	$ 604,095	283,456	398,652	1,286,203
	1986	567,451	283,456	420,222	1,271,129
	1987	412,927	439,723	441,792	1,294,442
	1988	212,534	85,452	441,792	739,778
	1989	75,382	108,484	441,792	625,658
	1990–2003	—	—	6,176,910	6,176,910
Total minimum capital lease payments		1,872,389	1,200,571	8,321,160	11,394,120
Less amount representing interest		(298,457)	(147,570)	(4,361,163)	(4,807,190)
Present value of capital lease obligations		$1,573,932	1,053,001	3,959,997	6,586,930
Enterprise Funds	1985	248,288	—	—	248,288
	1986	232,285	—	—	232,285
	1987	187,159	—	—	187,159
	1988	51,267	—	—	51,267
	1989	24,138	—	—	24,138
Total minimum capital lease payments		743,137	—	—	743,137
Less amount representing interest		(112,302)	—	—	(112,302)
Present value of capital lease obligations		$ 630,835	—	—	630,835

The present value of the future minimum capital lease payments for Special Districts under control of the Board of Supervisors approximated $1,532,582 at June 30, 1984.

[DANE COUNTY, WISCONSIN (DECEMBER 31, 1983), NOTES TO FINANCIAL STATEMENTS (IN PART)]

Note 10. Airport Leases

The County is a lessor of certain airport facilities such as terminal concession space, warehouses, and hangars under various operating leases. Lease terms vary; lease expiration dates range from 1984 through 2082. Revenues and related expenses for these leases are recorded in the Airport Enterprise fund.

The County's cost of buildings leased under operating leases at December 31, 1983, is not determinable since many leases are for partial buildings.

Future minimum lease payments to be received under noncancellable operating leases as of December 31, 1983, are as follows:

Year ending December 31,	
1984	$ 680,000
1985	506,000
1986	408,000
1987	350,000
1988	302,000
Thereafter	10,224,000
Total future minimum rentals	$12,470,000

The amounts above do not include contingent rentals which may be received under certain leases, based on usage or sales dollars. Contingent rentals approximated $204,000 for the year ended December 31, 1983.

[ORLANDO, FLORIDA (SEPTEMBER 30, 1983), NOTES TO FINANCIAL STATEMENTS (IN PART)]

Note 5. Lease Obligations:

a. Capitalized

The noncurrent liability for general fixed assets acquired under capitalized leases is recorded in the General Long-Term Obligations Account Group. The total liability for capital leases to be funded by the General Fund amounts to $677,565, of which $512,235 represents the noncurrent portion. The liability for property, plant and equipment acquired under capitalized leases is recorded in the appropriate Proprietary Fund.

The following is a description of the leased property under capital leases within the General and Internal Service Funds as of September 30, 1983:

	General	Internal Service
Equipment	$966,296	$384,546
Less: Accumulated Depreciation	—	219,960
	$966,296	$164,586

b. Operating

On April 2, 1983, the City entered into a long-term lease agreement with the Orange County Civic Facilities Authority (CFA) for the Tinker Field and the Tangerine Bowl facilities. The lease is for an initial term of 30 years and is accounted for as an operating lease. The lease also includes a 20 year renewal option.

[KANE COUNTY, ILLINOIS (NOVEMBER 30, 1983), NOTES TO FINANCIAL STATEMENTS (IN PART)]

Note 4 [in part]. Long-Term Debt

Capital Leases with Related Party

The County has entered into four noncancelable capital lease agreements with the Kane County Public Building Commission (Commission), a related party through common control. The Commission issues $750,000, $3,200,000 and $1,040,000 of revenue bonds to finance the cost of constructing improvements to the courthouse, the courthouse project and public safety building, and jail addition and courthouse annex, respectively.

The County is responsible for maintenance, operation, upkeep and safekeeping of the public safety building, jail addition, courthouse project and the courthouse annex. The County signed an agreement with the Commission whereby the Commission pays the County to operate and maintain the Courthouse through October 31, 1984.

The following is a schedule by years of future minimum lease payments under the capital leases together with the present value of the net minimum lease payments as of November 30, 1983:

	Annual Lease Payments
Year ending November 30:	
1984	$ 1,537,500
1985	1,572,500
1986	1,535,000
1987	1,541,000
1988	520,000
Later years	3,370,000
Total annual lease payments	$10,076,000
Less amount representing estimated executory costs (operating, maintenance and payments to bond reserve accounts)	4,970,000
Net minimum lease payments	5,106,000
Less amount representing interest	1,266,000
Present value of net minimum lease payments	$ 3,840,000

The present value of net minimum lease payments is recorded in the General Long-Term Debt Account Group.

Under provisions of the lease agreements, the County is entitled to reimbursement from the Commission at the expiration of each lease for any amounts not required to pay outstanding bonds and expenses of the Commission for the related project. It is management's policy to record the reimbursement at the time the lease expires and funds are received in that actual reimbursement is contingent upon future events.

At November 30, 1983, the estimated amounts that would be reimbursable, by fiscal year, are as follows:

Fiscal Year	
1984	$ 855,000
1987	3,000
1988	9,000
1995	1,317,000

Under the agreements, the County transferred the deed for land and facilities of the courthouse, public safety building jail addition, and courthouse annex to the Commission. Ownership will revert to the County upon termination of the leases. Accordingly, the original cost of the assets transferred and the $4,990,000 cost of the additions and improvements are included in the General Fixed Assets Account Group.

[ELGIN, ILLINOIS (DECEMBER 31, 1983), NOTES TO FINANCIAL STATEMENTS (IN PART)]

Note 7 [in part]

Lease Agreement—Buses

Under a lease agreement with the Regional Transportation Authority approved October 27, 1976, the City has acquired the use of buses at an annual rent of one dollar per bus. This lease is considered an operating lease and, hence, these buses are not recorded as assets in the Transit Fund.

At the inception of the lease, the City gave eleven older buses, with a net book value at date of disposition of $198,884, to the Regional Transportation Authority in exchange for use of the new buses.

* * *

Lease Agreement—Sears Building

The City entered into a 5 year lease agreement with Elgin Community College on August 16, 1982. Under the terms of the lease ECC will lease the Sears Building from the City for the purpose of providing a downtown campus. The lease may be renewed annually after its expiration with increases based on the consumer price index.

The following is a schedule by years of the revenue the City will recognize on the lease:

1984	$ 85,000
1985	110,000
1986	110,000
1987	110,000

[CITY OF GLENDALE, CALIFORNIA (JUNE 30, 1984), NOTES TO FINANCIAL STATEMENTS (IN PART)]

Note (5) [in part]

Bonds Payable, Notes Payable, Changes in Long-Term Debt and Contingent Liabilities

* * *

The Agency's outstanding long-term debts carry certain provisions unique to each debt. A summary of these provisions follow:

Parking Lease Revenue Bonds, Series A

Original issue—$6,200,000

Interest rate—6.00%–7.00%

Amount outstanding at June 30, 1984—$5,365,000

The bonds, issued in 1974, mature in regularly increasing amounts ranging from $150,000 to $4,430,000 annually from 1983 to 2003. Bonds maturing on or after

May 1, 1986, are subject to redemption at the option of the Agency at a price ranging from 102.5% to 100% of principal value. The bond indebtedness is secured by a lease to the City of Glendale and is payable from rentals received under terms of the lease agreement dated May 1, 1974.

The Agency is required to contribute to the Bond Service Fund amounts sufficient to provide for payment of interest on the outstanding bonds on the next interest payment date and to pay 50% of the principal amount of serial bonds maturing on the succeeding May 1. Commencing October 15, 1989, the Agency will be required to make contributions to a sinking fund in amounts equal to 50% of the amount sufficient to call and redeem the principal amount of term bonds for which minimum payment is due on the succeeding May 1.

Parking Lease Revenue Bonds, Series B. (See refunding parking lease revenue bonds, Series 1976 below.)

Original issue—$14,300,000

Interest rate—7.20%–8.00%

Amount outstanding at June 30, 1984—$12,675,000

The bonds, issued in 1974, mature in amounts from $300,000 to $350,000 annually from 1983 to 1985. Bonds maturing on or after May 1, 1986, are scheduled to be called and redeemed on May 1, 1985 (the earliest call date), at a price of 102.5% of principal value. The call premium, aggregating $308,125, associated with the early extinguishment of debt, has previously been provided in the Agency's financial statements. The call premium will be paid from monies currently held in an irrevocable escrow account, established via the proceeds of sale of the refunding parking lease revenue bonds, Series 1976.

Refunding Parking Lease Revenue Bonds, Series 1976

Original issue—$13,725,000

Interest rate—5.50%–7.00%

Amount outstanding at June 30, 1984—$11,900,000

The bonds, issued in 1976, mature in regularly increasing annual installments ranging from $325,000 to $1,025,000 annually from 1983 to 2003. Bonds maturing on or before May 1, 1987, are not subject to call and redemption prior to maturity. Refunding bonds due on or after May 1988 are subject to redemption at the option of the Agency from any source of funds, as a whole or in part, in inverse order of maturity and by lot within a maturity, on any interest payment date on and after May 1, 1987, at prices ranging from 102.5% to 100% of principal value. The bond indebtedness is secured by a lease to the City and is payable from rentals received under terms of the lease agreement dated May 1, 1974.

Terms of the refunding bond indenture provide for the establishment of a bond service fund of escrowed cash and investments in Federal securities. The Agency is required to maintain the bond service fund at an amount sufficient to pay interest on the outstanding bonds on the next interest payment date and to pay 50% of the principal amount of the bonds maturing on the next succeeding May 1.

An insurance reserve of at least $386,000 is required to be maintained by the Agency under terms of the bond indenture for the refunded parking revenue bonds, Series B. This amount is shown as reserved fund balance on the combined balance sheet. No modification of this requirement will be made as a result of the refunding transaction. The Insurance Reserve Fund may be used for: (a) repairing or rebuilding the parking facility in the event of loss or damage not covered by the Agency's insurance, (b) redemption of bonds in the event the parking facility is not to be rebuilt or repaired, or (c) payment of debt service on the bonds in the event sufficient monies are not available in the Bond Service Fund or Sinking fund.

Tax Allocation Bonds, Series A

Original issue—$6,750,000

Interest rate—$7.25%–8.00%

Amount outstanding at June 30, 1984—$5,500,000

The bonds, issued in 1976, mature in regularly increasing annual installments ranging from $80,000 to $4,100,000 from 1983 to 2003. Bonds maturing on or after May 1, 1987, are subject to redemption at the option of the Agency on any interest payment date after May 1, 1986, at a price ranging from 102.5% to 100% of principal value. The bond indebtedness is secured by a first pledge of all increment property taxes allocated to and received by the Agency commencing November 1, 1975.

Terms of the bond indenture agreement provide for the establishment of a special fund in an amount sufficient to equal at least 125% of the total principal and interest due on the next following May 1 and November 1. Property tax increment funds in excess of the 125% requirement, if any, may be used for other Agency purposes.

The Agency's long-term debt decreased by $7,965,000 from $43,405,000 to $35,440,000 from payment of bond principal. In June 1983, the Agency entered into an agreement with the Glendale Unified School District to allocate approximately 10% of its actual tax increment received for the next two fiscal years. This debt decreased from $980,900 to $400,000 at June 30, 1984.

Capitalized Lease Obligations

In May 1974, the City entered into a noncancelable lease agreement with the Glendale Redevelopment Agency, a separately empowered entity, to lease the multistory parking facility constructed adjacent to the Glendale Galleria Regional Shopping Center. This facility was substantially completed at June 30, 1986. The term of the lease began in June 1976. Commencing August 15, 1978, base rentals become due semiannually on February 15 and August 15 over the term of the lease. The lease will terminate on the earlier of May 1, 2008, or upon payment of all principal and interest due on the outstanding bond indebtedness attributable to the leased premises. Annual base rentals are to be at a rate sufficient to meet debt service requirements of the outstanding bond indebtedness on the leased premises. Such base rental is approximately $1,630,000 annually. The City is also required to pay, as additional rent, all administrative costs incurred by the Agency which are related to the leased premises.

The lease payment has not been shown in these statements due to the inclusion of the Agency operations in accordance with "Statement 3" (note 2).

EXHIBIT 3-3. EXCERPTS OF FOOTNOTE DISCLOSURES RELATED TO INFRASTRUCTURE ASSETS

[CITY OF EVANSTON, ILLINOIS (FEBRUARY 29, 1984), NOTES TO FINANCIAL STATEMENTS (IN PART)]

Note 1 [in part]

E. Assets, Liabilities, and Fund Equity

* * *

Fixed assets used in governmental fund type operations (general fixed assets) are accounted for in the General Fixed Assets Account Group, rather than in governmental funds. Public domain ("infrastructure") general fixed assets consisting of certain improvements other than buildings, including roads, bridges, curbs and gutters, streets and sidewalks, drainage systems, and lighting systems, are not capitalized along with other general fixed assets. No depreciation has been provided on general fixed assets.

All fixed assets are valued at historical cost or estimated historical cost if actual historical cost is not available. Donated fixed assets are valued at their estimated fair value on the date donated.

[GRAND FORKS, NORTH DAKOTA (DECEMBER 31, 1983), NOTES TO FINANCIAL STATEMENTS (IN PART)]

Note 1.B [in part]

Fixed Assets and Long-Term Liabilities

The accounting and reporting treatment applied to the fixed assets and long-term liabilities associated with a fund are determined by its measurement focus. All governmental funds and Expendable Trust Funds are accounted for on a spending or "financial flow" measurement focus. This means that only current assets and current liabilities are generally included on their balance sheets. Their reported fund balance (net current assets) is considered a measure of "available spendable resources." Governmental fund operating statements present increases (revenues and other financing sources) and decreases (expenditures and other financing uses) in net current assets. Accordingly, they are said to present a summary of sources and uses of "available spendable resources" during a period.

Fixed assets used in governmental fund type operations (general fixed assets) are accounted for in the General Fixed Assets Account Group, rather than in governmental funds. Public domain ("infrastructure") general fixed assets consisting of certain improvements other than buildings, including roads, bridges, curbs and gutters, streets and sidewalks, drainage systems, and lighting systems, are capitalized along with other general fixed assets. No depreciation has been provided on general fixed assets.

All fixed assets are valued at historical cost or estimated historical cost if actual historical cost is not available. Donated fixed assets are valued at their estimated fair value on the date donated.

* * *

All property funds and Nonexpendable Trust and Pension Trust Funds are accounted for on a cost of services or "capital maintenance" measurement focus. This means that all assets and all liabilities (whether current or noncurrent) associated with their activity are included on their balance sheets. Their reported fund activity (net total assets) is segregated into contributed capital and retained earnings components. Proprietary fund type operating statements present increases (revenues) and decreases (expenses) in net total assets.

Depreciation of all exhaustible fixed assets used by proprietary funds is charged as an expense against their operations. Accumulated depreciation is reported on proprietary fund balance sheets. Depreciation has been provided over the estimated useful lives using the straight line method. The estimated useful lives are as follows:

Buildings	10–75 years
Improvements	10–100 years
Equipment	5–33 years

[CITY OF GRAND PRAIRIE, TEXAS (SEPTEMBER 30, 1983), NOTES TO FINANCIAL STATEMENTS (IN PART)]

Note A [in part]

Fixed Assets and Depreciation

General Fixed Assets Account Group. Fixed assets are recorded at cost or, if cost is not practically determinable, at estimated cost. The costs of purchasing or constructing fixed assets are recorded as expenditures in the governmental funds and are capitalized in the General Fixed Assets Account Group. General fixed assets are not depreciated, and upon disposal, the original cost is removed from the accounts. Maintenance and repairs are recorded as expenditures in the governmental funds as incurred and are not capitalized. The City has chosen the option provided by generally accepted accounting principles of not reporting the value of improvements other than buildings (roads, bridges, curbs and gutters, streets and sidewalks, and similar assets) which are immovable and of value only to the City.

The estimated useful lives are as follows:

Buildings	10–30 years
Equipment	5–10 years
Water meters	33 years

[CITY OF IRVING, TEXAS (SEPTEMBER 30, 1983), NOTES TO FINANCIAL STATEMENTS (IN PART)]

Note 1 [in part]

General Fixed Assets

General fixed assets purchased for general governmental purposes are recorded as expenditures in the governmental funds and capitalized at cost in the general fixed assets account group. Contributed assets are recorded in general fixed assets at estimated fair market value at the time received. No depreciation has been provided on general fixed assets, nor has interest been capitalized.

Public domain (infrastructure) fixed assets consisting of certain improvements other than buildings, including roads, bridges, curbs and gutters, streets and sidewalks, drainage systems, and lighting systems, have been capitalized as general fixed assets.

Utility plant in service	50–80 years
Buildings and improvements	20–50 years
Motor vehicles and motorized equipment	6–15 years
Furniture, machinery, and equipment	10–15 years

[CITY OF KETTERING, OHIO (DECEMBER 31, 1983), NOTES TO FINANCIAL STATEMENTS (IN PART)]

Note H [in part]

Fixed Assets

General Fixed Assets. Fixed assets used in governmental fund type operations (general fixed assets) are accounted for in the general fixed assets account group, rather than in governmental funds. No depreciation has been provided on general fixed assets. Interest on constructed fixed assets is capitalized. All fixed assets are valued at historical cost, or estimated historical cost if actual historical cost is not available. Donated fixed assets are valued at their estimated fair market value at the time received.

Public domain (infrastructure) general fixed assets consisting of certain improvements other than buildings including roads, bridges, curbs and gutters, streets and sidewalks, and drainage systems are not capitalized.

[CITY OF LAKEWOOD, OHIO (JUNE 30, 1984), NOTES TO FINANCIAL STATEMENTS (IN PART)]

Note A [in part]

Fixed Assets

Fixed assets include land, utility plant in service, buildings, improvements, and equipment owned by the City. Infrastructure including streets, bridges, and sidewalks is not included.

Fixed assets acquired or constructed for general governmental purposes are reported as expenditures in the fund that finances the asset acquisition and capitalized in the General Fixed Assets Account Group. Property and equipment acquired by proprietary funds are reported in those funds. All fixed assets are recorded at cost or at estimated fair market value at time of donation.

* * *

Depreciation

No depreciation is provided on general fixed assets. Depreciation is charged to operations of proprietary funds over the fixed assets' estimated useful lives using the straight-line method. The following lives are used:

[LUBBOCK, TEXAS, (SEPTEMBER 30, 1983), NOTES TO FINANCIAL STATEMENTS (IN PART)]

Note 1 [in part]

B. Fixed Assets and Long-Term Liabilities

The accounting and reporting treatment applied to the fixed assets and long-term liabilities associated with a fund are determined by its measurement focus. All governmental funds and Expendable Trust Funds are accounted for on a spending or "financial flow" measurement focus. This means that only current assets and current liabilities are generally included on their balance sheets. Their reported fund balance (net current assets) is considered a measure of "available spendable resources." Governmental fund operating statements present increases (revenue and other financing sources) and decreases (expenditures and other financing uses) in net current assets. Accordingly, they are said to present a summary of sources and uses of "available spendable resources" during a period.

Fixed assets used in governmental fund type operations (general fixed assets) are accounted for in the General Fixed Assets Account Group, rather than in governmental funds. Public domain ("infrastructure") general fixed assets consisting of certain improvements other than buildings, including roads, bridges, curbs and gutters, streets and sidewalks, drainage systems, and lighting systems, are capitalized along with other general fixed assets. No depreciation has been provided on general fixed assets.

All fixed assets are valued at historical cost or estimated historical cost if actual historical cost is not available. Donated fixed assets are valued at their estimated fair value on the date donated.

* * *

All proprietary funds are accounted for on a cost of services or "capital maintenance" measurement focus. This means that all assets and all liabilities (whether current or noncurrent) associated with their activities are included on their balance sheet. Their reported fund equity (net total assets) is segregated into contributed capital and retained earnings components. Proprietary fund type operating statements present increases (revenues) and decreases (expenses) in net total assets.

Depreciation of all exhaustible fixed assets used by proprietary funds is charged as an expense against their operations. Accumulated depreciation is reported on proprietary fund balance sheets. Depreciation has been provided over the estimated useful lives using the straight line method. The estimated useful lives are as follows:

Water pipelines	50 years
Sewer pipelines	20 years
Runways and related improvements	10–20 years
Terminals, hangars and other airport buildings	50 years
Water and sewer buildings and other structures	50 years
Motor buses	10 years
Automobiles, vans, etc.	5 years
Machinery and other equipment	1–15 years

[MESA, ARIZONA (JUNE 30, 1984), NOTES TO FINANCIAL STATEMENTS (IN PART)]

Note 1 [in part]

Property, Plant and Equipment—General Fixed Assets

General Fixed Assets purchased are recorded as expenditures in the General Capital Projects or Special Revenue Funds at the time of purchase. Such assets are capitalized at cost in the General Fixed Asset Account Group with the exception of certain assets acquired prior to June 30, 1978, which have been valued as described below. Gifts or contributions are recorded in the General Fixed Asset Account Group at fair market value at the time received.

Prior to June 30, 1978, the City did not maintain detailed property cost records of its general fixed assets other than for rolling stock. A physical inventory was performed during the fiscal year ended June 30, 1978, and detailed property records were prepared. Generally, the assets were recorded at cost. Where historical cost information was not available, the assets were valued at estimated cost using engineering estimates, appraisals or current replacement cost, adjusted to the year of acquisition.

Certain improvements other than buildings which are immovable assets of value only to the governmental unit, such as roads, bridges, streets and sidewalks, are not recorded in the accounting records. Therefore, the purpose of stewardship for capital expenditures is satisfied without recording these assets.

No depreciation is provided on general fixed assets. General fixed assets sold or otherwise disposed of are eliminated from the accounts.

A summary of changes in General Fixed Assets follows:

	Balance July 1, 1983	Additions	Retirements and Transfers	Balance June 30, 1984
Land	$ 8,611,766	$ 1,442,971	$ (285,011)	$ 9,769,726
Buildings	17,501,321	1,458,980	—	18,960,301
Other Improvements	6,754,859	104,892	—	6,859,751
Machinery and Equipment	11,348,334	3,049,684	(1,209,545)	13,188,473
Construction in Progress	14,645,972	27,362,844	(22,975,709)	19,033,107
Total	$58,862,252	$33,419,371	$(24,470,265)	$67,811,358

[SAGINAW COUNTY, MICHIGAN (DECEMBER 31, 1983), NOTES TO FINANCIAL STATEMENTS (IN PART)]

Note 1 [in part]

B. Fixed Assets and Long-Term Liabilities

The accounting and reporting treatment applied to the fixed assets and long-term liabilities associated with a fund are determined by its measurement focus. All governmental funds and Expendable Trust Funds are accounted for on a spending or "financial flow" measurement focus. This means that only current assets and current liabilities are generally included on their balance sheets. Their reported fund balance (net current assets) is considered a measure of "available spendable resources." Governmental fund operating statements present increases (revenues and other financing sources) and decreases (expenditures and other financing uses) in net current assets. Accordingly, they are said to present a summary of sources and uses of "available spendable resources" during a period.

Fixed assets used in governmental fund type operations (general fixed assets) are accounted for in the General Fixed Assets Account Group, rather than in governmental funds. Public domain ("infrastructure") general fixed assets consisting of certain improvements other than buildings, including roads, bridges, curbs and gutters, streets and sidewalks, drainage systems, and lighting systems are capitalized along with other general fixed assets. No depreciation has been provided on general fixed assets.

All fixed assets are valued at historical cost or estimated historical cost if actual historical cost is not available. Donated fixed assets are valued at their estimated fair value on the date donated.

* * *

All proprietary funds and Nonexpendable Trust Funds are accounted for on a cost of services or "capital maintenance" measurement focus. This means that all assets and all liabilities (whether current or noncurrent) associated with their activity are included on their balance sheets. Their reported fund equity (net total assets) is segregated into contributed capital and retained earnings components. Proprietary fund type operating statements present increases (revenues) and decreases (expenses) in net total assets.

Depreciation of all exhaustible fixed assets used by proprietary funds is charged as an expense against their operations. Accumulated depreciation is reported on proprietary fund balance sheets. Depreciation has been provided over the estimated useful lives using the straight line method.

[SEDGWICK COUNTY, KANSAS (DECEMBER 31, 1983), NOTES TO FINANCIAL STATEMENTS (IN PART)]

Note 2 [in part]

Property and Equipment

Property and equipment is recorded at cost or estimates of original cost and gifts at fair value at the date of the gift. The general fixed assets account group does not include infrastructure fixed assets—roads, bridges, curbs and gutters, streets and sidewalks, drainage systems, etc. Depreciation is not provided on general fixed assets. Depreciation of property and

equipment of the proprietary fund types, except for the Central Motor Pool, is provided by the straight-line method over the following estimated useful lives:

Buildings and structures	15 to 40 years
Utility plant and laterals	50 years
Machinery and equipment	4 to 10 years

Depreciation on equipment of the Central Motor Pool is provided by the units-of-production method based generally on estimated useful lives of 60,000 miles on motor vehicles and 20,000 hours on heavy machinery. Depreciation on Kansas Coliseum assets acquired or constructed with contributed equity is closed to the contributed capital equity account.

[CITY OF TUSCALOOSA, ALABAMA (SEPTEMBER 30, 1983), NOTES TO FINANCIAL STATEMENTS (IN PART)]

Note 1 [in part]

B. Fixed Assets and Long-Term Liabilities

* * *

Fixed assets used in governmental fund type operations (general fixed assets) are accounted for in the General Fixed Assets Account Group, rather than in governmental funds. Public domain ("infrastructure") general fixed assets consisting of certain improvements other than buildings, including roads, bridges, curbs and gutters, streets and sidewalks, drainage systems, and lighting systems, are capitalized along with other general fixed assets. No depreciation has been provided on general fixed assets.

All fixed assets are valued at historical cost or estimated historical cost if actual historical cost is not available. Donated fixed assets are valued at their estimated fair market value on the date donated.

Chapter 4
Long-Term Liabilities

LONG-TERM LIABILITIES

The fifth principle of NCGA Statement 1 (previously discussed in Chapter 3) also prescribes the generally accepted accounting principles related to fixed assets and long-term liabilities:

> 5. A clear distinction should be made between (a) fund fixed assets and general fixed assets and (b) fund long-term liabilities and general long-term debt.

With respect to long-term liabilities, the principle states:

> b. Long-term liabilities of proprietary funds, special assessment funds, and trust funds should be accounted for through those funds. All other unmatured general long-term liabilities of the governmental unit should be accounted for through the general long-term debt account group.

Statement 1 provides the following additional guidance concerning long-term liabilities:

Fund long-term liabilities. Bonds, notes, and other long-term liabilities (e.g., for capital leases, pensions, judgments, and similar commitments) directly related to and expected to be paid from proprietary funds, special assessment funds, and trust funds should be included in the accounts of such funds.

General long-term debt. All other unmatured long-term debt of the government is general long-term debt and should be accounted for in the general long-term debt account group.

General long-term debt is the unmatured principal of bonds, warrants, notes, or other forms of noncurrent or long-term general obligation indebtedness.

General long-term debt is not limited to liabilities related to debt issuances, but may also include noncurrent liabilities on lease-purchase agreements and other commitments that are not current liabilities properly recorded in governmental funds.

Table 4-1 lists the accounts used by the surveyed governments to report general long-term debt. Table 4-2 lists the contra accounts related to the general long-term debt of these governments.

In many instances, the footnotes to the surveyed financial statements described accounting policies and contained other information concerning fund long-term liabilities and general long-term debt; examples are noted in the accompanying table.

Information on Accounting for Long-Term Liabilities	Instances Observed (%)
Significant accounting policies:*	
Debt service	44
Long-term liabilities	31
Other footnotes:	
General long-term debt	65
Long-term debt	38
Statistical data:**	
Ratio of net general bonded debt to assessed value/net bonded debt per capita	42
Computation of legal debt margin	34
Changes in long-term debt	19
Computation of overlapping debt	16
Revenue bond coverage	15
Computation of direct and overlapping debt	14
Debt service requirements to maturity	7

 * Observations for the 87% of the units having this footnote.
** Observations for the 72% of the units with this section.

Exhibit 4-1 contains selected excerpts from governmental financial statements relating to the accounting and reporting of fund long-term liabilities and general long-term debt, including the matured portions of this long-term debt. Selected footnote disclosures related to these long-term obligations have also been included in this exhibit.

NONCANCELLABLE OR CAPITALIZED LEASE AGREEMENTS

Noncancellable leases for general fixed assets may, in substance, be contracts for the acquisition of assets that would be properly recordable as general fixed assets of the government. Under these circumstances, the related lease obligations should be recorded as part of the government's general long-term debt. Exhibit 3-2, relating to fixed assets, illustrates excerpts from footnotes to financial statements resulting from these types of leases.

In December 1982, the NCGA adopted Statement 5, "Accounting and Financial Reporting Principles for Lease Agreements of State and Local Governments." The earlier Statement 1 did not provide specific accounting and reporting requirements for lease agreements. The intent of Statement 5 was to promote uniformity in accounting for those types of leases covered in FASB Statement of Financial Accounting Standards 13, "Accounting for Leases." Statement 5 was effective for fiscal years beginning after June 30, 1983.

EXHIBITS AND TABLES FOR CHAPTER 4

Table 4-1. Examples of Account Titles Used to Report Fund Long-Term Liabilities and General Long-Term Debt

Table 4-2. Examples of Contra Accounts to General Long-Term Debt

Exhibit 4-1. Excerpts Illustrating Reporting of Fund Long-Term Liabilities and General Long-Term Debt

TABLE 4-1. EXAMPLES OF ACCOUNT TITLES USED TO REPORT FUND LONG-TERM LIABILITIES AND GENERAL LONG-TERM DEBT

Account Titles Used*	Instances Observed (%)
General obligation bonds payable	25
Revenue bond payable	18
Bonds payable	14
Notes payable	13
Special assessment bonds payable	10
Long-term debt	8
Compensated absences	7
Obligations under capitalized leases	6
General obligation bonds	6
General long-term debt	4
Bond anticipation notes payable	3
Other long-term liabilities	3
Lease obligations payable	3
Capitalized lease obligations	3
General obligation bonds payable and notes payable	3
Others	3
General obligation debt payable	2
General obligation notes payable	2
Long-term debt (net of current portion)	1
Leases payable	1
Loans payable	1
Contracts payable	1
Bonds and notes payable	1
Noncurrent portion of long-term debt	1
Other long-term debt payables:	<1
Long term debt payable	
Lease purchase agreements	
Bond anticipation notes	
Advances from other funds	

* Observations for the 88% of the units having a combined balance sheet.

TABLE 4-2. EXAMPLES OF CONTRA ACCOUNTS TO GENERAL LONG-TERM DEBT

Account Titles Used*	Instances Observed (%)
Amount to be provided for payment (or retirement) of general long-term debt	63
Amount available (in debt service funds)	50
Amount available for retirement of general long-term debt	2
Amount to be provided for retirement of bonds	2
Amount to be provided for debt service	1
Amount available for retirement of debt	1
Amount available for retirement of long-term debt	1
Amount to be provided for retirement of general long-term debt	1
Amount to be provided from future tax levies and other sources	1

* For the 81% of the units having a general long-term debt account group.

EXHIBIT 4-1. EXCERPTS ILLUSTRATING REPORTING OF FUND LONG-TERM LIABILITIES AND GENERAL LONG-TERM DEBT

[CITY OF BLOOMINGTON, MINNESOTA]

Combined Balance Sheet [in part]—All Fund Types and Account Groups, December 31, 1983

	Proprietary Fund Types	Account Groups
	Enterprise	General Long Term Debt
Assets		
	* * *	
Amount available in debt service funds		$18,115,490
Resources to be provided		28,250,510
Liabilities and Fund Equity		
Liabilities:		
	* * *	
Long-term debt payable:		
Future maturities (Note 5)	$3,355,000	$46,366,000
Bond discount	(17,042)	
	* * *	

Note 5

5. Long-Term Debt. The long-term debt obligations outstanding at year-end are summarized as follows:

Bonds	Maturities	Rates	December 31, 1983
Water and sewer bonds	1984–1996	4.5%–5.2%	$ 2,725,000
Recreational facility bonds	1984–1990	6.0%–6.75%	630,000
Improvement bonds	1984–2004	3.7%–9.5%	30,765,000
State aid bonds	1984–1985	3.6%–8.0%	850,000
Tax increment revenue bonds	1985–1992	10.9%	540,000
General long-term debt	1984–1996	3.75%–8.3%	14,211,000
Total			$49,721,000

Changes in long-term debt during 1983 are summarized as follows:

	Balance January 1, 1983	Issued	Retired	Balance December 31, 1983
Enterprise bonds	$ 3,720,000		$ 365,000	$ 3,355,000
Improvement bonds	32,919,000	$ 4,600,000	6,754,000	30,765,000
State aid bonds	1,310,000		460,000	850,000
Tax increment revenue bonds	540,000			540,000
General long-term debt	9,123,000	6,275,000	1,187,000	14,211,000
Total	$47,612,000	$10,875,000	$8,766,000	$49,721,000

Long-term debt maturities (including interest) are as follows:

	Enterprise Bonds	Improvement Bonds	State Aid Bonds	Tax Increment Revenue Bonds	General Long-Term Debt	Total
1984	$ 536,833	$ 7,777,201	$521,850	$ 58,500	$ 2,387,515	$11,281,899
1985	469,250	6,376,762	390,000	82,219	2,217,073	9,535,304
1986	452,540	5,862,732		108,050	2,161,172	8,584,494
1987	413,062	4,132,888		107,013	2,148,033	6,800,966
1988	397,188	3,366,357		105,369	1,929,157	5,798,071
1989 and thereafter	2,163,950	12,176,940		411,274	8,370,855	23,123,019
Total	$4,432,823	$39,692,880	$911,850	$872,425	$19,213,775	$65,123,753

General Obligation Water and Sewer Bonds are serviced by the Utility Funds and are carried as debt of those funds. The Recreational Facilities Fund also supports its limited General Obligation Gross Revenue Bonds. These bonds are payable from gross revenues of the recreation facilities and are backed by a limited tax (⅔ mill) pledge. City Improvement Bonds and other general bonds are backed by the full faith, credit and taxing power of the City, and are supported by various debt service funds. State Aid Bonds are general obligations principally payable from Minnesota State Aid allotments.

The bond indenture for the enterprise fund bonds contain various restrictive covenants and requirements for reserve accounts and sinking funds. The City is in compliance with all requirements of the indentures.

[GUILFORD COUNTY, NORTH CAROLINA]

Combined Balance Sheet [in part]—All Fund Types and Account Groups, June 30, 1984

	Proprietary Fund Type	Account Groups
	Internal Service	General Long-Term Obligations
Assets		
* * *		
Amount available in debt service funds	—	$ 3,240,778
Amount to be provided for retirement of general long-term obligations	—	60,933,802
* * *		
Liabilities		
* * *		
Long-term obligations (notes 5 and 9)	$1,838,468	$64,174,580
* * *		

Note 1(g)

Vacation Benefits. It is the County's policy to permit employees to accumulate a limited amount of earned vacation benefits, which, if not used, will be paid to employees upon separation from County service at the rates of pay then in effect. The current portion of such accumulated vacation benefits at June 30, 1984, is recorded as accrued vacation in the governmental funds. The remainder of such accumulated vacation benefits is recorded in the General Long-term Obligations Account Group since the County must fund such benefits from future available financial resources (see note 3 concerning change in accounting principle).

Accumulated vacation benefits are accrued when earned in the Internal Service Fund.

Note 1(h)

Long-term Obligations. Long-term obligations that will be financed through the governmental funds are accounted for in the General Long-term Obligations Account Group. Long-term obligations of the Internal Service Fund are included in that fund because they will be financed by billings to other departments and users.

Note 3

Change in Accounting Principle. During the year ended June 30, 1984, the County adopted the provisions of the National Council on Governmental Accounting's Statement 4, "Accounting and Financial Reporting Principles for Claims and Judgments and Compensated Absences," by recording the County's liability for accumulated vacation benefits earned by employees whose payroll costs are accounted for in the governmental funds (see note 1-g). The cumulative effect of adopting this change in accounting principle has been reported as a restatement of the June 30, 1983, fund balance with respect to the current portion and by inclusion of the long-term portion in the General Long-term Obligations Account Group.

Note 5

Long-term Obligations. The following is a summary of transactions affecting long-term obligations of the County for the year ended June 30, 1984:

	General Obligation Bonds	Obligations Under Capital Leases (note 9)	Purchase Money Installment Contract	Liability for Accumulated Vacation Benefits (note 3)	Total
Long-term obligations at July 1, 1983	$68,215,000	342,514	—	—	68,557,514
Additions during the fiscal year:					
Purchase money installment contract	—	—	1,838,468	—	1,838,468
Liability for accumulated vacation benefits	—	—	—	718,399	718,399
Retirements during the fiscal year:					
Bonds	(4,920,000)	—	—	—	(4,920,000)
Obligations under capital leases	—	(181,333)	—	—	(181,333)
Long-term obligations at June 30, 1984	$63,295,000	161,181	1,838,468	718,399	66,013,048

Long-term obligations at June 30, 1984 are comprised of the following:

General Obligation Bonds:	
1961 School Building serial bonds due in annual installments of $395,000 to $475,000 through May 1, 1986; interest at .25% to 3.5%	$ 870,000
1967 School Building serial bonds due in annual installments of $250,000 to $625,000 through May 1, 1987; interest at 3.4%	1,875,000
1968 School Building serial bonds due in annual installments of $50,000 to $500,000 through June 1, 1988; interest at 4% to 4.3%	2,150,000
1971 County Courthouse serial bonds due in annual installments of $325,000 to $675,000 through May 1, 1994; interest at 4% to 4.5%	6,150,000
1971 County Building serial bonds due in annual installments of $25,000 through May 1, 1992; interest at 4% to 4.5%	200,000
1974 School Building serial bonds due in annual installments of $450,000 to $1,800,000 through June 1, 1996; interest at 4.5% to 6.5%	13,950,000
1974 Guilford Technical Community College serial bonds due in annual installments of $75,000 to $250,000 through June 1, 1995; interest at 4.5% to 6.5%	2,225,000
1974 County Building serial bonds due in annual installments of $75,000 to $250,000 through June 1, 1995; interest at 4.5% to 6.5%	2,125,000
1977 Public Improvements serial bonds due in annual installments of $325,000 to $1,300,000 through June 1, 1998; interest at 4% to 6%	7,350,000
1977 Water and Sewer serial bonds due in annual installments of $175,000 to $700,000 through June 1, 1998; interest at 4% to 6%	3,950,000
1982 Public Improvements serial bonds due in annual installments of $1,250,000 to $2,775,000 through June 1, 1999; interest at 10.5% to 10.6%	22,450,000
Total general obligation bonds	63,295,000
Obligations under capital leases (note 9):	
$698,974 capitalized landfill equipment lease obligation due in monthly installments of $14,006 through May 1985, including imputed interest at 7.5%	148,442
$91,615 capitalized landfill equipment lease obligation due in monthly installments of $1,906 through September 1984, including imputed interest at 9.1%	5,631
$42,683 capitalized office equipment lease obligations due in various monthly installments through May 1985, including imputed interest at 7.5% to 28.5%	7,108
Total obligations under capital leases	161,181
Purchase money installment contract (see below)	1,838,468
Liability for accumulated vacation benefits (note 3)	718,399
	$66,013,048

During the year ended June 30, 1984, the County and the City of Greensboro jointly purchased a new telecommunications system, financed through a purchase money installment contract with a bank. The contract requires that payments be made in various monthly installments, including interest at 8.25% through June 1988. The County's portion of the payments to be made during the year ending June 30, 1985, is $610,025 (including interest of $142,672), which is included in Internal Service Fund accounts payable in Exhibit 1. The long-term portion of the County's obligation under the contract, $1,838,468, is included in Internal Service Fund long-term obligations. The cost of the County's portion of the telecommunication system is included in Internal Service Fund fixed assets as part of construction work in progress at June 30, 1984 (see note 4).

Of the total long-term obligations of $66,013,048, the long-term portion of the purchase money installment contract, $1,838,468, has been recorded in the Internal Service Fund. The remainder of $64,174,580 has been recorded in the General Long-term Obligations Account Group.

The annual requirements to amortize all long-term obligations outstanding other than the liability for accumulated vacation benefits as of June 30, 1984, including interest payments of $36,163,751, are as follows:

Year Ending June 30	General Obligation Bonds	Obligations Under Capital Leases	Purchase Money Installment Contract	Total
1985	$ 8,791,862	167,548	—	8,959,410
1986	8,508,413	—	693,896	9,202,309
1987	8,249,175	—	693,896	8,943,071
1988	7,971,925	—	693,835	8,665,760
1989	7,674,050	—	—	7,674,050
1990–1994	33,894,250	—	—	33,894,250
1995–1999	24,119,550	—	—	24,119,550
	$99,209,225	167,548	2,081,627	101,458,400

$3,240,778 is available in the Debt Service Funds to service the general obligation bonds.

The County is subject to the Local Government Bond Act of North Carolina, which limits the amount of net bonded debt (exclusive of funding and refunding bonds, bonds issued for water, gas, or electric power purposes, and bonds issued for certain other specified purposes) the County may have outstanding to 8% of the appraised value of property subject to taxation. At June 30, 1984, such statutory limit for the County was $758,819,428, providing a debt margin of approximately $688 million.

Authorized, unissued debt at June 30, 1984 was as follows:

For Additions and/or Improvements to	Amount
School buildings and facilities	$ 8,700,000
Guilford Technical Community College facilities	2,050,000
Solid waste disposal system	1,155,000
Sheltered workshop facilities	50,000
	$11,955,000

On October 30, 1984, the County is scheduled to sell the remaining $8,700,000 of school buildings and facilities general obligation bonds and the $2,050,000 of Guilford Technical Community College facilities general obligation bonds.

Note 9

Lease Commitments. The County leases certain equipment under lease agreements which are classified as capital leases under the provisions of the Financial Accounting Standards Board Statement No. 13, "Accounting for Leases." For governmental fund types the net present value of obligations under these lease agreements at inception, $833,272, is included in Exhibit 1 in the General Fixed Assets and General Long-term Obligations Account Groups.

At June 30, 1984, future minimum lease payments due under capital leases and operating leases with initial or remaining noncancellable lease terms in excess of one year are as follows:

Year Ending June 30	Capital Leases	Operating Leases
1985	$167,548	$1,253,699
1986	—	1,251,580
1987	—	1,185,992
1988	—	717,313
1989	—	61,033
Total minimum lease payments	167,548	$4,469,617
Less amount representing interest	6,367	
Present value of net minimum lease payments	$161,181	

There were no contingent rentals or sublease rentals associated with leases in effect at June 30, 1984. The total rental expense for all operating leases amounted to $1,715,248 for the year ended June 30, 1984.

[MADISON COUNTY, ILLINOIS]

Combined Balance Sheet [in part]—All Fund Types and General Long-Term Debt Account Group, November 30, 1983

	Governmental Fund Types	General Long-Term Debt Account Group
	Debt Service	
Assets and Other Debits		
* * *		
Amount available in debt service funds	$ —	134,260
Amount to be provided for payment of long-term debt	—	6,965,740
Amount to be provided for payment of accrued vacation and sick leave		2,133,258
* * *		
Liabilities and Fund Equity		
Liabilities:		
* * *		
Accrued vacation and sick leave	—	2,133,258
Bonds payable	$475,000	7,100,000
Interest payable	254,744	—
* * *		

Note 1

(i) Vacation and Sick Pay. Under the terms of the County's labor contracts, County employees are granted vacation based on continuous service. Upon leaving the employ of the County, an employee is entitled to payment for accrued vacation. Accrued expenditures for unused vacation of $398,638 at November 30, 1983, have been recorded in the General Long-Term Debt Account Group.

Through November 30, 1975, and October 31, 1978, respectively, two groups of employees were allowed to accumulate sick pay up to a maximum number of days. Certain portions of this accumulated unused sick pay are due these employees upon termination of employment. For years subsequent to those previously described, County employees continue to be allowed to accumulate sick pay up to a maximum number of days. However, the accumulated unused amounts related to such years are due to employees only upon specific types of termination from employment (i.e., retirement, death, or disability). Accrued expenditures for accumulated sick pay have been recorded in the General Long-Term Debt Account Group and amount to $1,734,620 at November 30, 1983.

Note 4

General Long-Term Debt. At November 30, 1983, the County has the following two bond issues outstanding:

Jail Construction Bonds—December 1, 1974

Special Service Area No. 1 Bonds—April 1, 1978

The Jail Construction Bonds are general obligation bonds and are supported by a pledge of the County's full faith and credit. The Special Service Area No. 1 Bonds are limited obligation bonds of the County and are payable from ad valorem taxes levied against all taxable property in the special service area.

The following is a summary of bond transactions of the County for the year ended November 30, 1983:

	Balance November 30,		Principal Payments
	1983	1982	
Jail Construction Bonds of December 1, 1974, 6.3%–7.0%, payable in varying amounts through 1994	$2,925,000	3,100,000	175,000
Special Service Area No. 1 Bonds of April 1, 1978, 6.25%–7.75%, payable in varying amounts through 1993	4,175,000	4,475,000	300,000
	$7,100,000	7,575,000	475,000

Following are summaries of the debt service requirements through maturity for each of the bond issues:

Due in fiscal year	Jail Construction Bonds		
	Principal	Interest	Total
1984	$ 175,000	196,288	371,288
	* * *		
1993	350,000	50,750	400,750
1994	375,000	26,250	401,250
	$2,925,000	1,347,263	4,272,263

Due in fiscal year	Special Service Area No. 1 Bonds		
	Principal	Interest	Total
1984	$ 325,000	278,573	603,573
	* * *		
1992	500,000	68,250	568,250
1993	550,000	35,750	585,750
	$4,175,000	1,632,378	5,807,378

Note 5

Employee Retirement Plan. The County provides retirement benefits to all regular full-time employees through participation in the Illinois Municipal Retirement Fund (IMRF). Pension expenditures during the year ended November 30, 1983, were $1,343,744, which includes amortization of prior service costs over 40 years. Expenditures for pensions are funded as accrued. The unfunded prior service cost as of December 31, 1983, the date of the latest actuarial valuation, was $5,355,828. Net assets available for benefits as of December 31, 1983, amounted to $7,522,138. The present value of vested and nonvested benefits as they relate to individual governmental units participating in the plan was not determined in connection with the actuarial valuation of the plan.

[MESA, ARIZONA]

Combined Balance Sheet [in part]—All Fund Types and Account Groups, June 30, 1984

	Governmental Fund Types		Proprietary Fund Types	Account Groups
	Debt Service	**Special Assessment**	**Enterprise**	**General Long-Term Obligations**
ASSETS				
	* * *			
Amounts to be provided for retirement of general long-term obligations				$21,035,568
	* * *			
LIABILITY AND FUND EQUITY				
Liabilities:				
Accrued Payroll Payable				$ 1,091,164
	* * *			
Restricted Liabilities				
Current Portion of Bonds Payable			$ 5,438,984	
	* * *			
Revenue Bonds			74,085,000	
General Obligation Bonds	$441,016		53,320,596	18,444,404
Municipal Development Corporation Bonds				1,500,000
Special Assessment Bonds		$2,211,000		
Refunded Bonds in Excess of Escrow Assets				
Unamortized Bond Premium			743,654	
	* * *			

Note 3 [in part]

Compensated Absence. In order to conform with the reporting requirements of the National Council of Governmental Accounting pronouncement *Accounting and Financial Reporting Principles for Claims and Judgments and Compensated Absences* (Statement 4) certain changes as compared with prior years were made in the accompanying financial statements. Th₂ new pronouncement requires that a liability be accrued for those leave benefits that are vested and payment is probable.

For the City, vacation leave meets the above criteria. Accordingly, a change in accounting principle for accrued liabilities was made in the June 30, 1984, financial statements. The current portion of the vacation benefits payable is shown as a liability in the Payroll Trust & Agency Fund and the remainder appears in the General Long-Term Obligation account group. The effect of this change on prior years was not material. This change affects only the governmental funds as the vacation leave was accrued in the proprietary funds in prior years.

Note 5 [in part]

Bonds Payable. At June 30, 1984, bonds payable were comprised of:

	Average Interest Rate	Amount
General Obligation Bonds:		
Limited to 6% of Assessed Valuation	3.02% to 11.95%	$ 8,130,000
Limited to 20% of Assessed Valuation	3.02% to 11.95%	65,640,000
Total General Obligation Bonds		73,770,000
Non-Profit Corporation Bonds:		
1984 City of Mesa Municipal Development Corporation Bonds	8.35	1,500,000
Revenue Bonds:		
1976 Utility System Revenue Refunding Bonds	6.20%	11,505,000
1971 Utility System Revenue Bonds	5.30%	4,000,000
1962 Water, Electric and Gas System Revenue Bonds	4.50%	2,500,000
1971 Utility System Revenue Bonds	5.13%	7,750,000
1979 Utility System Revenue Bonds	6.44%	9,700,000
1983 Utility System Revenue Refunding Bonds	8.71%	8,340,000
1983 Utility System Revenue Bonds	9.52%	34,165,000
Total Revenue Bonds		77,960,000
Special Assessment Bonds:		
Issued 1961 thru 1983	4.50% to 9.00%	2,211,000
Total Bonds		$155,441,000

The annual requirements to amortize all debt outstanding as of June 30, 1984, including interest payments of $93,604,376 are as follows:

Fiscal Year Ending June 30,	General Obligation	Municipal Development Corporation	Revenue	Special Assessments	Total
1985	$ 10,111,918	$ 272,335	$ 10,043,176	$ 591,220	$ 21,018,649
1986	10,104,830	264,725	10,053,070	478,530	20,901,155
1987	10,075,418	250,850	10,047,044	387,735	20,761,047
1988	10,059,005	263,850	10,043,426	369,350	20,735,631
1989	10,072,043	274,850	10,045,342	324,020	20,716,255
1990 and later	68,615,272	820,750	68,834,292	750,325	139,020,639
Total	$119,038,486	$2,147,360	$119,066,350	$2,901,180	$243,153,376

$5,892,000 is available in cash with Paying Agent to service the current principal portion of outstanding bonds.

The following is a summary of bond transactions of the City for the fiscal year ended June 30, 1984:

	General Obligation	Municipal Development Corporation	Revenue	Special Assessments	Total
Bonds Payable at June 30, 1983	$44,570,000	$	$46,990,000	$2,385,846	$ 93,945,846
New Bonds Issued:					
1983 Utility System			34,165,000		34,165,000
1983 General Obligation	30,315,000				30,315,000
1984 Municipal Development		1,500,000			1,500,000
Improvement District #220				279,641	279,641
Bonds Retired	(1,115,000)		(3,195,000)	(454,487)	(4,764,487)
Bonds Payable at June 30, 1984	$73,770,000	$1,500,000	$77,960,000	$2,211,000	$155,441,000

The City of Mesa Municipal Development Corporation ("Corporation") is an Arizona non-profit corporation formed for the purpose of acquiring land and performing construction on various municipal facilities to be used by and eventually sold to the City of Mesa. During fiscal 1984, the corporation issued bonds aggregating $1,500,000 for the construction of a parking facility. Concurrently, the City entered into a contract with the Corporation whereby the City will pay to the Corporation amounts sufficient to retire the Corporation's bonds and related interest.

The City has a relationship of trustee for special assessment districts whereby it collects the assessments levied against owners of property within established districts and disburses the amounts so collected to retire the bonds issued to finance the improvements. The City was contingently liable for $2,211,000 of special

assessment bonds at June 30, 1984. At June 30, 1984, the special assessments receivable, together with amounts paid in advance and interest to be received over the life of the assessment period, are adequate to meet the scheduled maturities of the bonds payable and the related interest. Improvement bonds are collateralized by properties within the districts. In the event of default by the property owner, the City may auction the property to satisfy the debt service requirements.

The General Obligation Bonds are backed by the ultimate taxing power and general revenues of the City; however, $54,884,580 of these bonds at June 30, 1984, are carried as a liability of the Enterprise Fund to reflect the intention of retirement out of resources of that fund.

The bonds are callable by the City at various dates and at various premiums.

Reserves For Bond Indentures. Pursuant to the indenture ordinances of the City of Mesa Utility System Revenue Refunding Bonds, the City of Mesa Utility System Revenue Bonds, and the City of Mesa Water, Electric and Gas System Revenue Bonds, the City is required to establish reserve funds and make annual deposits totaling $844,044, in order to accumulate and maintain the appropriate Reserve Funds. The total Reserve Fund requirement to be accumulated by the end of fiscal year 1990–91 is $10,022,980. There is $4,114,669 in the Reserve Funds as of June 30, 1984.

In addition, Replacement and Extension Reserve Funds are required to be established for each issue, into which a sum equal to two percent of the gross revenues must be deposited until a sum equal to two percent of all tangible assets of the Utility System is accumulated. As of June 30, 1984, the amount provided in the Replacement and Extension Funds equaled $4,033,955.

Note 6

Liabilities to Be Paid from Assets Held in Escrow. Liabilities to be paid from assets held in escrow include bonded debt of the City that has been provided for through an Advanced Refunding Bond Issue. Under an Advanced Refunding Arrangement, Refunding Bonds are issued and the net proceeds, plus additional resources that may be required, are used to purchase securities issued or guaranteed by the United States Government. These securities are then deposited in an irrevocable trust under an escrow agreement which provides that all proceeds from the trust will be used to fund the principal and interest payments of the previously issued bonded debt being refunded. The trust deposits have been computed so that the securities in the trust, along with future cash flow generated by the securities, will be sufficient to service the previously issued bonds.

In accordance with Statement of Financial Accounting Standards #76, *Extinguishment of Debt,* the refunded debt outstanding as reflected below is not included on the City's financial statements.

Refunded debt outstanding of the City at June 30, 1984 is as follows:

1962 Water, Electric and Gas Revenue Bonds, 1971 City of Mesa Utility Systems Revenue Bonds and 1965 Water, Electric and Gas Systems Revenue Refunding Bonds	$16,125,000
General Obligation Bonds issue dated April 1, 1982	16,975,000
Utility System Revenue Bonds issue dated April 1, 1982	7,425,000
Total refunded bonds outstanding	$40,525,000

Note 7

Extraordinary Loss on Advance Refunding. During the 1983 fiscal year, in order to take advantage of lower interest rates, the City provided for the advance refunding of a portion of its General Obligation debt of 1981, Series A (1982), and a full refunding of the Enterprise Fund Utility System Revenue Bonds Project of 1981, Series A (1982). The proceeds of the refunding issues, together with other available City funds, have been placed in irrevocable escrow accounts and invested in U.S. Treasury obligations that, together with interest earned thereon, will provide amounts sufficient for future payment of interest and principal on the issues, which totalled in principle $26,090,000 at the date of refunding. Accordingly, the escrow accounts and the refunded bonds are not reflected in the financial statements of the City. This refunding results in an extraordinary loss, including refunding expenses, being recognized of $2,923,876.

The 1983 General Obligation Refunding and Utility System Revenue Refunding Bonds were issued to refund the above described bonds. These refunding bonds are expected to create a net reduction of debt service requirements of approximately $1,000,000 over the term of the bonds, as compared to the refunded bonds.

[CITY OF NORWALK, CONNECTICUT]

Combined Balance Sheet [in part]—All Fund Types and Account Groups, June 30, 1984

	Governmental Fund Types	Account Groups
	Capital Project	**General Long-Term Debt**
ASSETS		
* * *		
Amounts to be provided in future years for retirement of general long-term obligations:		
From future tax levies		$94,493,318
From other governments		1,325,066
* * *		
LIABILITIES AND FUND EQUITY (DEFICIT)		
* * *		
Accrued Pension Costs		$ 4,923,384
Accrued Compensated Absences		6,240,000
Notes and Bonds Payable	$3,700,000	84,655,000
* * *		

Note 2

Accounting Changes. The accounting practices of the City were changed in the current year to conform with the requirements of Statement 4, ''Accounting and Financial Reporting Principles for Claims, Judgments, and for Compensated Absences,'' issued by the National Council on Governmental Accounting. Under the statement, the City is required to accrue a liability for its obligation relating to an employees' vested right to receive compensation for future absences that is attributable to services already rendered by such employee. The liability for these compensated absences is recorded in the General Long-Term Debt Account Group as of June 30, 1984, since the ultimate liquidation of these benefits will not require the utilization of financial resources available at the balance sheet date.

Note 4

Debt. At June 30, 1984, bond anticipation notes are outstanding as temporary financing of the Clear Water capital project in the amount of $3,700,000 at interest rates of 5.82–5.87%. These notes will not be refinanced on a long-term basis and are therefore recorded in the Capital Projects Fund at June 30, 1984.

The following is a summary of long-term notes and bonds outstanding at June 30, 1984:

	Interest Rates	Maturity	Amount
General obligation bonds	3.05–10.75%	5/85– 4/01	$82,455,000
Bond anticipation notes	5.79– 5.87%	8/84–10/84	$ 2,200,000

The notes in the long-term debt account group will be reduced when (a) the projects are permanently financed through the issuance of general obligation bonds or (b) legally required payments are made.

A summary of long-term notes and bond principal maturities and amounts available from the State of Connecticut for repayment of long term debt is as follows:

Year ended June 30,	Principal Amount	Available from State of Connecticut
1985	$ 9,810,000	$ 256,778
1986	7,365,000	248,614
1987	7,115,000	244,793
1988	7,115,000	163,504
1989	7,110,000	157,707
1990–1994	28,425,000	253,670
1995–1999	16,690,000	
2000–2001	1,025,000	
Total	$84,655,000	$1,325,066

Note 6 [in part]

Pension Plans. Four separate contributory pension plans cover substantially all City employees except those employees (principally teachers) in the public schools who are eligible to participate in the Connecticut Teachers' Retirement System.

Prior to fiscal 1979, the City was funding pension costs based upon a plan which was not calculated under an acceptable actuarial method. This policy resulted in a substantial underfunding of pension costs.

During fiscal 1979, the City adopted a program to fund these accumulated, prior years' deficiencies in the Employees', Police and Firemen's pension plans (A definitive funding plan for the Food Service Employees' pension plan has not been established.) In order to avoid immediate, substantial increases in property tax levies, yet fulfill its aforementioned funding commitment, the City adopted a forty year funding program commencing in fiscal 1979 involving increased levels of annual contributions through fiscal 1987 followed by a constant level through fiscal 2019. Under GAAP, the City is required to adopt an acceptable actuarial method and accrue pension costs in accordance therewith, regardless of the funding program. Thus, the funding program will result in a planned shortfall of contributions through 1987 as compared to pension costs accrued under GAAP. The shortfall will be reduced through contributions from 1988 forward and eliminated in 2019.

During fiscal 1982, the City began recording this shortfall in contributions in the long-term obligations group of accounts. The amount transferred to the long-term obligations account group represents the total amount of estimated underfunded accumulated plan benefits as of June 30, 1984, as follows:

Excess of pension costs calculated in accordance with GAAP over amounts funded in:	
Prior fiscal years	$4,256,459
1984	666,925
	$4,923,384

[CITY OF SPRINGFIELD, ILLINOIS]

Combined Balance Sheet [in part]—All Fund Types and Account Groups, February 29, 1984

| | Governmental Fund Types | | Proprietary Fund Types | Account Groups |
| | | | | |
	Special Revenue	Special Assessment	Enterprise	General Long-Term Debt
ASSETS				
	* * *			
Amount available in Debt Service Funds				$ 66,181
Amount to be provided for:				
Retirement of debt				3,443,486
Claims and judgments				234,000
Compensated absences				5,641,000
	* * *			
LIABILITIES AND FUND EQUITY LIABILITIES:				
	* * *			
Special assessment bonds payable (Note 5)		$2,160,985		
Revenue bonds and notes payable (Note 5)			$157,005,247	
General obligation bonds and notes payable (Note 5)				$3,509,667
Other liabilities (Note 2)	$10,997		554,973	5,875,000
	* * *			

Note 1B [in part]

Long-Term Liabilities. Long-term liabilities expected to be financed from governmental funds are accounted for in the General Long-Term Debt Account Group, not in the governmental funds. The single exception to this general rule is for special assessment bonds, which are accounted for in Special Assessment Funds.

Because of their spending measurement focus, expenditure recognition for governmental fund types is limited to exclude amounts represented by liabilities not currently payable. Since they do not affect net assets, such long-term amounts are not recognized as governmental fund type expenditures or fund liabilities. They are instead reported as liabilities in the General Long-Term Debt Account Group. The General Long-Term Debt Account Group currently accounts for General Obligation Street Lighting Bonds, Lincoln Square Redevelopment Bond Anticipation Notes, and General Obligation Interim Notes, to be paid from future revenues of the General Fund, Special Allocation Debt Service Fund, and Recreation Fund, respectively.

Note 1H [in part]

Debt Issuance Expense and Debt Discount. Debt issue expense and debt discount on long-term debt are amortized over the lives of the related issues.

Note 2

Compensated Absences and Claims and Judgments. To conform with Statement 4 of the National Council on Governmental Accounting, effective for fiscal years beginning after December 31, 1982, the accumulated unpaid vacation, sick pay, and other employee benefit amounts at February 29, 1984, are recorded on the Combined Balance Sheet—All Fund Types and Account Groups. In addition, the amount of claims and judgments against the City which would normally be expected to result in liabilities of the City are also recorded on the Combined Balance Sheet—All Fund Types and Account Groups at February 29, 1984. Corresponding amounts shown at February 28, 1983, in the accompanying financial statements have been restated to give effect to the adoption of Statement 4 as follows:

	As Previously Reported	Adjustment	As Restated
Amount to be provided for:			
Compensated absences	None	$5,058,000	$5,058,000
Claims and judgments	None	285,430	$ 285,430
Other liabilities	$471,645	$5,343,430	$5,815,075

Note 5

Bonds and Notes Payable and Restricted Investment Accounts: Changes in Long-Term Debt. Following is a summary of bond and note transactions of the City for the year ended February 29, 1984 (in thousands of dollars):

	Special Assessment Bonds	Revenue Bonds and Notes	General Obligation Bonds and Notes	Total
Bonds and note payable at March 1, 1983	$2,321	$161,391	$ 557	$164,269
Bonds and notes issued:				
Street improvements	250			250
General Obligation Bond Anticipation Note			3,100	3,100
7.88% Subordinate Revenue Notes, due serially from 1984 to 1987		207		207
Bonds retired	(434)	(4,630)	(147)	(5,211)
Amortization of debt discount	24	37		61
Bonds and notes payable at February 29, 1984	$2,161	$157,005	$3,510	$162,676

Debt at February 29, 1984, consists of (in thousands of dollars):

Description	Interest Rate (%)	Date Issued	Date Matures	Outstanding
Special Assessment Bonds	5.75–10.0	Various	1993	$ 2,161
Reenue Bonds and Notes Payable:				
Electric Revenue Bonds	4.4–5.35	1977	2004	27,580
Electric Revenue Bonds	5.0–6.0	1976	2003	16,650
Electric Revenue Bonds	5.25–6.0	1974	2002	29,445
Electric Revenue Bonds	5.0–6.5	1970	1999	10,500
Electric Revenue Bonds	5.0	1969	1999	11,680
Electric Revenue Bonds	3.25–3.5	1967	1998	2,200
Electric Revenue Bonds	3.6–3.75	1966	1998	12,905
Electric Revenue Bonds	3.1–3.2	1963	1992	2,640
Electric Revenue Bonds	3.5–3.8	1958	1992	2,545
Electric Revenue Bonds	3.0	1956	1985	150
General Obligation Demand Notes	5.25	1982	1986	25,000
Subordinate Revenue Notes	7.88	1984	1987	207
Water Revenue Bonds	5.5–7.0	1975	1994	10,430
Sewerage Refunding Revenue Bonds	7.7–9.2	1980	2001	4,160
Motor Vehicle Parking Revenue Bonds	4.75–4.875	1966	1996	850
Motor Vehicle Parking Revenue Bonds	6.0	1969	1989	530
Total				157,472
Unamortized Debt Discount (deduct)				(467)
Revenue Bonds and Notes Payable—net				157,005
General Obligation Bonds and Notes:				
Lincoln Redevelopment Bond Anticipation Notes	7.0	1983	1986	3,100
Street Lighting Bonds	3.6–3.7	1967	1987	200
Interim Note	60% of prime	1981	1988	170
Interim Note	6.75	1982	1985	40
Total				3,510
TOTAL				$162,676

Special Assessment Bonds. Substantially all bonds are collaterialized by the City's pledge of future motor fuel tax allotments and special assessment collections. The bonds are callable at any time. Special assessment bonds scheduled to be paid during the next year approximate $394,000 (see Note 6).

Revenue Bonds and Note. Revenue bonds scheduled to be paid in the next year approximate $4,917,000.

Electric revenue bonds maturing in the years 2004, 2003, 2002, and 1999 may be called beginning 1988, 1987, 1984, and 1980, respectively, and all other electric revenue bonds are callable upon demand. Water revenue bonds maturing in 1994 and 1984 are callable beginning 1985, 1980, and upon demand, respectively. Motor Vehicle Parking revenue bonds maturing in 1996 are redeemable prior to maturity, through the use of general City funds or operating revenues of the system, at the principal amount plus accrued interest and any redemption premium; bonds maturing in 1989 are redeemable on any interest payment date at the principal amount plus accrued interest. Sewerage Refunding Revenue Bonds maturing in 1991 and thereafter are redeemable, at the option of the City, on or after September 1, 1990, at the principal amount plus accrued interest and any redemption premium.

In November 1982, the City issued General Obligation Demand Notes totalling $25,000,000. A portion of the proceeds were used to retire the 1980 Construction Certificate Note of the Electric Light and Power Fund and meet certain bond ordinance sinking fund requirements. The remaining funds will be used to finance future capital projects of the Electric Light and Power Fund.

Principal and interest on the notes is to be paid by the Electric Light and Power Fund, and the principal is recorded as a liability of that fund.

General Obligation Bonds and Notes. General obligation bonds and notes scheduled to be paid in the next year total $152,000.

Debt Service Requirements. General obligation bonds and notes and related interest are paid from general revenues of the City. Revenue bonds and notes and related interest are paid from user charges from the respective enterprise funds. General obligation demand notes classified with revenue bonds and notes are paid from user charges of the Electric Light and Power Fund. Special assessment bonds and related interest are paid from the special revenue gas tax fund transfers and from assessments to property owners.

The annual requirements to amortize all debt outstanding as of February 29, 1984, including interest payments of $83,538,000, are as follows (in thousands):

Year Ending February 28	General Obligation Bonds and Notes	Revenue Bonds and Notes	Special Assessment Bonds	Total
1985	$ 393	$ 13,272	$ 587	$ 14,252
1986	390	13,274	531	14,195
1987	3,273	37,914	407	41,594
1988	46	11,884	371	12,301
1989		11,875	311	12,186
1990–94		58,646	751	59,397
1995–99		51,313		51,313
2000–2004		41,443		41,443
Total	$4,102	$239,621	$2,958	$246,681

Revenue Bond Ordinance Requirements. Under the terms of certain revenue bond ordinances, additional revenue bonds cannot be issued unless net revenues (all revenues of the systems after deduction of the reasonable and necessary expenses of operation and maintenance but before depreciation, interest, and amortization) for the last preceding completed fiscal year prior to the issuance of such bonds are equal to at least an amount ranging from 120% and 135% of the combined maximum annual principal and interest payment on the bonds then outstanding and the additional bonds to be issued.

Also under the terms of the bond ordinances, the Springfield City Council is to establish and maintain rates sufficient at all times to pay all operating and maintenance expenses, to pay principal and interest on bonds, and to make all other payments to the accounts established by the various revenue bond ordinances. No free service is allowed, except that the City of Springfield may be given credit against charges made by the Electric Light and Power Fund for amounts that would be due the City if the electric properties were taxable.

Certain revenue bond ordinances also require the segregation of cash, receivables, payables, and investments. The following items were so segregated at February 29, 1984, and February 28, 1983:

	1984	1983
Cash	$ 69,085	$ 15,801
Investments (at cost, which approximates market)	33,697,263	32,592,650
Interest receivable	843,657	636,952
Intra-fund receivable (payable)	(910)	27,959
Total	$34,609,095	$33,273,362

The preceding were allocated to the following accounts:

	1984	1983
Construction Accounts	$ 8,200,650	$10,780,892
Bond Principal and Interest Accounts	24,700,657	20,948,928
Depreciation Accounts	1,401,805	1,370,308
Surplus Accounts	305,983	173,234
Total	$34,609,095	$33,273,362

The funding requirements of accounts are established by the revenues bond ordinances and are outlined as follows:

The Operations and Maintenance Account (classified with non-restricted cash and investments) is required to receive monthly deposits sufficient to pay the subsequent month's operating expenses. In addition, the account for the Sewer Fund and the Electric Light and Power Fund is required to pay the current month's operating expense. At February 29, 1984, the accounts were funded as required.

The Construction Accounts represent unexpended proceeds from related revenue bond issues and are to be used principally for completion of Dallman Power Station No. 3 and related construction by the Electric Light and Power Fund and land acquisition by the Water Fund.

The Bond Principal and Interest Accounts, established to pay bond principal and interest, are required to be funded monthly at various amounts and rates as specified in the ordinances. At February 29, 1984, the accounts were funded as required.

The Depreciation Accounts, established to pay for certain repairs and replacements when other funds are not available, are funded monthly at specified rates related primarily to depreciation. At February 29, 1984, the accounts were funded as required.

The Surplus Accounts represent amounts in excess of the requirements outlined above and are to be used as specified in the related bond ordinances.

Chapter 5
Basis of Accounting and Budgetary Accounting

BASIS OF ACCOUNTING

Principle 8 of NCGA Statement 1 requires that the modified accrual or accrual basis of accounting, as appropriate, should be used in measuring financial position and operating results. The specific NCGA accounting principles are as follows:

8.a. Governmental fund revenues and expenditures should be recognized on the modified accrual basis. Revenues should be recognized in the accounting period in which they become available and measurable. Expenditures should be recognized in the accounting period in which the fund liability is incurred, if measurable, except for unmatured interest on general long-term debt and on special assessment indebtedness secured by interest-bearing special assessment levies, which should be recognized when due.

b. Proprietary fund revenues and expenses should be recognized on the accrual basis. Revenues should be recognized in the accounting period in which they are earned and become measurable; expenses, if measurable, should be recognized in the period incurred.

c. Fiduciary fund revenues and expenses or expenditures (as appropriate) should be recognized on the basis consistent with the fund's accounting measurement objective. Nonexpendable trust and pension trust funds should be accounted for on the accrual basis; expendable trust funds should be accounted for on the modified accrual basis. Agency fund assets and liabilities should be accounted for on the modified accrual basis.

d. Transfers should be recognized in the accounting period in which the interfund receivable and payable arise.

Statement 1 also provides that property taxes collected in advance of the year to which they applied are not to be recognized as revenues until the fiscal period to which they applied. Revenues collected in advance are to be shown as deferred revenues.

Subsequent to the issuance of Statement 1, the NCGA published Interpretation 3, "Revenue Recognition—Property Taxes," in June 1981. In the interpretation, the NCGA concluded as follows:

Property tax revenue should be recognized in the fiscal year for which levied, provided that the criteria of availability, defined below, are met.

When property taxes receivable are recognized, or when property taxes are collected in advance of the year for which they are levied, they should be recorded as deferred revenue and recognized as revenue in the year for which they are levied.

Property tax revenues should be recognized when they become available. "Available" means (1) then due, or (2) past due and receivable within the current period, or (3) expected to be collected soon enough thereafter to be used to pay liabilities of the current period. Except under unusual circumstances, the time by which the revenues in (3) may be expected shall not exceed 60 days, and the government should disclose the period being used and the justifying conditions.

Interpretation 3 is effective for the fiscal years beginning after September 30, 1981.

BUDGETARY ACCOUNTING

Principle 9 of NCGA Statement 1 sets forth the principles relating to budgeting, budgetary control, and budgetary reporting by governmental units:

9.a. An annual budget(s) should be adopted by every governmental unit.

b. The accounting system should provide the basis for appropriate budgetary control.

c. Budgetary comparisons should be included in the appropriate financial statements and schedules for governmental funds for which an annual budget has been adopted.

The NCGA recommends that the basis upon which the budget is prepared should be consistent with the basis of accounting used.

Statement 1 further recommends that one of the five combined statements contained in the general purpose financial statement be a comparison of budget data and and actual financial results. This financial statement is titled revenues, expenditures, and changes in fund balance—budget and actual; it should include the budgeted and actual data for governmental fund types for which annual budgets have been adopted. Such a statement is recommended for all governmental funds, although in practice budgets typically exist only for a government's general fund and special revenue funds.

When the budget is prepared on a basis consistent with generally accepted accounting principles, the budgetary data are on the same basis as the actual data included in the statement of revenues, expenditures, and changes in fund balance for all governmental fund types. When the legally prescribed budgetary basis differs from generally accepted accounting principles then the budgetary data cannot be compared to *actual* financial statements prepared according to GAAP. In such instances, the actual data in the financial statement should be prepared on, or converted by statement adjustments to, the same basis as the budgetary data (e.g., a cash basis, or with all encumbrances recorded as expenditures). Any differences between GAAP and the budgetary basis should then be explained in the notes to financial statements.

As noted in Table 5-1, most of the financial statements of the surveyed governments included a statement of revenues, expenditures, and changes in fund balances—budget and actual. Table 5-1 also indicates that usage of the budget-to-actual statement has been consistently high among the surveyed governments. Budgets existed most often for the general fund and for special revenue funds.

Exhibit 5-1 contains excerpts of footnotes of governmental units related to the reported bases of accounting and budgeting.

TABLE 5-1. OBSERVATIONS RELATING TO THE COMBINED STATEMENT OF REVENUES, EXPENDITURES, AND CHANGES IN FUND BALANCES—BUDGET AND ACTUAL—FOR GOVERNMENTAL FUNDS

Fund Comparisons—Budget and Actual	Instances Observed (%)
Governmental units whose general purpose financial statement included a combined statement of revenues, expenditures, and changes in fund balances—budget and actual—for governmental funds	83
Governmental fund types:*	
General fund	98
Special revenue funds	87
Debt service funds	39
Capital projects funds	29
Special assessment funds	11
Expendable trusts	2

* Observations for those units having the budget-to-actual statement.

EXHIBITS AND TABLES FOR CHAPTER 5

Table 5-1. Observations Relating to the Combined Statement of Revenues, Expenditures, and Changes in Fund Balances—Budget and Actual—for Governmental Funds

Exhibit 5-1. Excerpts of Footnote Disclosures Related to the Bases of Accounting and Budgeting

EXHIBIT 5-1. EXCERPTS OF FOOTNOTE DISCLOSURES RELATED TO THE BASES OF ACCOUNTING AND BUDGETING

[ARVADA, COLORADO (DECEMBER 31, 1983), NOTES TO FINANCIAL STATEMENTS (IN PART)]

Note 1 [in part]

C. Basis of Accounting

Basis of accounting refers to when revenues and expenditures or expenses are recognized in the accounts and reported in the financial statements. Basis of accounting relates to the timing of the measurements made, regardless of the measurement focus applied.

All governmental funds and expendable trust funds are accounted for using the modified accrual basis of accounting. Their revenues are recognized when they become measurable and available as net current assets. Taxpayer-assessed income, gross receipts, and sales taxes are considered "measurable" when in the hands of intermediary collecting governments and are recognized as revenue at that time.

Expenditures are generally recognized under the modified accrual basis of accounting when the related fund liability is incurred. Exceptions to this general rule include: (1) accumulated unpaid vacation, sick pay, and other employee amounts which are not accrued; and (2) principal and interest on general long-term debt, which is recognized when due.

All proprietary funds and Nonexpendable Trust and Pension Trust Funds are accounted for using the accrual basis of accounting. Their revenues are recognized when they are earned, and their expenses are recognized when they are incurred.

D. Budgets and Budgetary Accounting

Formal budgetary integration is employed as a management control device during the year for the General Fund, Special Revenue Funds, Debt Service Fund, Capital Projects Funds, Proprietary Funds, Fiduciary Funds, and Special Assessment Funds. Formal budgetary integration is also employed to comply with the State of Colorado Budget Law.

Budgets for the governmental funds are adopted on a basis which differs from generally accepted accounting principles (GAAP) in so far as encumbrances are included with expenditures. Reconciliation of expenditures reported in accordance with GAAP and those presented in accordance with the non-GAAP budgetary basis can be found on separate schedules in the budgetary section of this report. Budgets for Enterprise Fund are adopted on a basis which differs from GAAP in so far as accumulated unpaid vacation, sick pay, and other employee amounts are not included with expenses in each fund. The amounts not included in non-GAAP budgetary basis schedules are reflected on the schedules in the budget section of this report.

The budget column in these financial statements has been adjusted for supplemental appropriations and intra-fund transfers.

[CITY OF DES PLAINES, ILLINOIS (DECEMBER 31, 1983), NOTES TO FINANCIAL STATEMENTS (IN PART)]

Note 1 [in part]

C. Basis of Accounting

Basis of accounting refers to when revenues and expenditures or expenses are recognized in the accounts and reported in the financial statements. Basis of accounting relates to the timing of the measurements made, regardless of the measurement focus applied.

All Governmental Funds and Expendable Trust Funds are accounted for using the modified accrual basis of accounting. Their revenues are recognized when they become measurable and available as net current assets. Taxpayer-assessed income, gross receipts, and sales taxes are considered "measurable" when in the hands of the collecting government and are recognized as revenue at that time.

Expenditures are generally recognized under the modified accrual basis of accounting when the related fund liability is incurred. Exceptions to this general rule include: (1) accumulated unpaid vacation and sick pay; and (2) principal and interest on general long-term debt, which is recognized when due.

All Proprietary Funds and Nonexpendable Trust and Pension Trust Funds are accounted for using the accrual basis of accounting. Their revenues are recognized when they are earned, and their expenses are recognized when they are incurred. Unbilled water utility service receivables are recorded at year-end.

D. Budgets and Budgetary Accounting

The City follows these procedures in establishing the budgetary data reflected in the financial statements:

1. Prior to the end of the fiscal year, the Mayor submits to the City Council a proposed operating budget for the fiscal year commencing January 1. The operating budget includes proposed expenditures and estimated revenues.

2. The City Council Finance Committee holds public hearings to discuss the proposed budget.

3. After approval of the budget by the City Council, an ordinance is drafted and enacted by the City Council. By state statute, this ordinance must be enacted within the first quarter of the year.

4. At the end of the fiscal year, a transfer ordinance is approved by the City Council to transfer budgeted amounts between line items within any fund.

5. Formal budgetary integration is employed as a management control device during the year for the General Fund, Special Revenue Funds (except Paramedic Fund), Debt Service Funds, and Enterprise Funds. Budgets are not adopted for the Capital Project Funds and Special Assessment Fund. The level of control is on a line item basis.

6. Budgets for General, Special Revenue (except for the Paramedic Fund), Enterprise, and Debt Service Funds are adopted on a basis consistent with generally accepted accounting principles (GAAP).

[CITY OF GREELEY, COLORADO (DECEMBER 31, 1983), NOTES TO FINANCIAL STATEMENTS (IN PART)]

Note 1 [in part]

Basis of Accounting

Basis of accounting refers to when revenues and expenditures or expenses are recognized in the accounts and reported in the financial statements. Basis of accounting relates to the timing of the measurements made, regardless of the measurement focus applied.

All governmental funds and Expendable Trust Funds utilize the modified accrual basis of accounting. Under this method revenues are recognized in the accounting period when they become both measurable and available as net current assets.

Revenues susceptible to accrual under the modified accrual basis of accounting consist primarily of the following: (1) property taxes assessed in 1982 and payable in 1983; (2) cigarette taxes; (3) auto use taxes; (4) highway users tax; (5) franchise taxes; (6) revenue sharing entitlements and other grants that are established on a reimbursable basis.

Expenditures are generally recognized when the related fund liability is incurred except for unmatured interest on general long-term debt and accumulated unpaid vacation and sick pay, which are not accrued but reported in the General Long-Term Debt Account Group.

Proprietary Funds and Nonexpendable Trust Funds utilize the accrual basis of accounting. Revenues are recognized in the accounting period in which they are earned and become measurable. Expenses are recognized when liabilities are incurred.

Budgets and Budgetary Accounting

An annual budget and appropriation ordinance is adopted by the City Council in accordance with the Colorado State Budget Act and City of Greeley Home Rule Charter. The budget is prepared on a basis consistent with generally accepted accounting principles for all governmental, proprietary, Expendable and Nonexpendable Trust Funds.

On or before the fifteenth of September of each year the City Manager is required to submit to the City Council a recommended budget covering the next fiscal year including the following information: (1) proposed expenditures for each agency of the City; (2) debt service requirements; (3) an estimate of the amount of anticipated revenues from all sources other than property taxes; (4) an estimate of the balance or deficit for the end of the current fiscal year; (5) an estimate of the amount of money to be raised from property taxes and bond issues and (6) other supporting information as the City Council may request.

Prior to October 31 of each year, the City Council is required to set a tax levy and certify same to the County Commissioners. Upon completion of a public hearing and the tax levy certification, City Council must adopt the budget and make the necessary appropriations by ordinance no later than December 15.

The accounting system is employed as a budgetary management control device during the year to monitor the individual departments or divisions within departments (level of classification which expenditures may not legally exceed appropriations). All unexpended or unencumbered appropriations lapse at the end of the budget year except for capital projects, which lapse at the end of the second full year after the budget year.

After the adoption of the Annual Appropriation Ordinance, the City Council may, by ordinance, make the following changes: (1) after July first of each budget year, transfer any uncommitted appropriations balance from one department to another and (2) make additional appropriations during the fiscal year for unanticipated expenditures to the extent that actual or anticipated revenues of the year exceed the estimated revenues in the budget, unless the appropriations are necessary to relieve an emergency situation. The City Manager may, without Council action, approve the

transfer of budgeted expenditures between programs within departments or divisions. During 1983, supplemental appropriations were made for outstanding encumbrances at December 31, 1982, and for other unanticipated expenditures or expenses.

[GREENWOOD COUNTY, SOUTH CAROLINA (JUNE 30, 1984), NOTES TO FINANCIAL STATEMENTS (IN PART)]

Note 1 [in part]

Basis of Accounting

The accompanying financial statements have been prepared on the accrual or modified accrual basis of accounting as recommended by the National Committee on Governmental Accounting and the American Institute of Certified Public Accountants. Basis of accounting refers to when revenues and expenditures are recorded and reported in the financial statements. Under the modified accrual basis of accounting, revenues are recorded when received in cash, except for measurable and available revenues which are accrued to reflect properly the taxes levied and revenue sharing contributions received in the accounting period allocated by the federal government. Expenditures, other than principal and interest on long-term indebtedness, which is recorded when due, are recorded at the time the liabilities are incurred.

The basis of accounting used for each fund in the preparation of the accompanying financial statements is as follows:

Fund	Basis of Accounting
General	Modified accrual
Revenue sharing	Modified accrual
Capital projects	Modified accrual
Debt service	Modified accrual
Trust and agency	Accrual

Budgets and Budgetary Accounting

The accompanying financial statements and the County records reflect no adjustments for differences between the amount appropriated for expenditures and amounts actually expended, or in estimated revenues and actual revenues. The differences between appropriations and actual expenditures are approved after the end of the year by action of County Council. In the opinion of counsel for the County, this procedure meets statutory requirements relating to over-expenditure of line items within the budget.

[INGHAM COUNTY, MICHIGAN (DECEMBER 31, 1983), NOTES TO FINANCIAL STATEMENTS (IN PART)]

Note 2 [in part]

Basis of Accounting

The Governmental Funds are maintained on the modified accrual basis of accounting. Modifications in such methods from the accrual basis are as follows:

(a) Revenues are recorded as received in cash, except for revenues susceptible to accrual and material revenues that are not received at their normal time. Revenues for 1983 include property taxes levied principally on December 1, 1982, and substantially collected in early 1983. The "1983 property taxes" become a lien on December 1, 1983, and are to be collected principally by March 1, 1984. These taxes have been recorded as a receivable and as deferred revenue at December 31, 1983, since they are not available to fund expenditures until 1984.

(b) Expenditures are recorded when the liability is incurred, except for interest on long-term liabilities which is recorded when paid.

The Proprietary Funds are maintained on the accrual basis.

The Agency Funds are maintained on the basis of cash receipts and disbursements, which approximates the modified accrual method for these Funds.

Budgetary Accounting Controls

The General, substantially all Special Revenue and all Debt Service Funds are subject to budgetary control. Formal budgets are adopted (as required by law) and budgetary transfers, additional appropriations from additional revenues received or from unexpended funds appropriated but not spent in prior years, etc., are made as and when required. Under the County's budget procedures amounts appropriated by functional classification as revenues and expenditures of the General Fund and Special Revenue Funds include interfund transfers. Since such transfers represent internal transactions within the County government, they are reported separately in the financial statements of the various Funds. The comparative statement of revenues and expenditures—amended budget and actual—General Fund (page 5) reflects the adjustments for such internal transfers.

[CITY OF MIAMI, FLORIDA (SEPTEMBER 30, 1983), NOTES TO FINANCIAL STATEMENTS (IN PART)]

Note 2 [in part]

(C) Basis of Accounting

Basis of accounting refers to when revenues and expenditures or expenses are recognized in the accounts and reported in the financial statements. Basis of accounting relates to the timing of the measurements made, regardless of the measurement focus applied.

All Governmental Funds and Expendable Trust Funds are accounted for using the modified accrual basis of accounting. Their revenues are recognized in the period in which they become susceptible to accrual—that is, when they become measurable and available to pay liabilities of the current period. Ad valorem taxes, utility and franchise taxes, licenses and permits, fines and forfeitures, and charges for services are susceptible to accrual when collected in the current year or within 60 days subsequent to September 30, provided that amounts received pertained to billings through the fiscal year just ended. Occupational license revenues collected in advance of periods to which they relate are recorded as deferred revenues. Investment earnings are recorded as revenue when earned since they are measurable and available. Where grants revenue is dependent upon expenditures by the City, revenue is accrued as obligations are incurred.

Special assessments are considered susceptible to accrual when collected in the current year or within 60 days subsequent to September 30, provided that amounts received pertain to liens assessed prior to the end of the current fiscal year. The special assessment receivables at year-end of $7,782,469, of which $652,000 are delinquent, are shown net of deferred revenues of $7,479,000. Special assessments are recorded in the general obligation bonds debt service fund since they represent only a partial reimbursement of costs incurred in certain capital projects financed with general obligation bonds.

Expenditures under the modified accrual basis of accounting are generally recognized when the related fund liability is incurred and expected to be liquidated with available resources. Exceptions to this general rule include accumulated unpaid vacation, sick pay and other employee benefits which are not accrued, and principal and interest on general long-term debt, which are recognized when due.

All Proprietary Funds are accounted for using the accrual basis of accounting. Their revenues are recognized when they are earned, and their expenses are recognized when they are incurred.

(D) Budgets and Budgetary Accounting

The City follows these procedures in establishing the budgetary data reflected in the financial statements:

1. Prior to August 31, the City Manager submits to the City Commission a proposed operating budget for the fiscal year commencing the following October 1. The operating budget includes proposed expenditures and the means of financing them.
2. Public hearings are conducted to obtain taxpayer comments.
3. Prior to October 1, the budget is legally enacted through passage of an ordinance.
4. Encumbrance accounting, under which purchase orders, contracts, and other commitments for the expenditure of monies are recorded in order to reserve that portion of the applicable appropriation, is employed in the General and Capital Projects Funds. On a non-GAAP budgetary basis, encumbrances are recorded as expenditures of the current year. On a GAAP basis, encumbrances outstanding at year-end are reported as reservations of fund balance since they do not constitute expenditures or liabilities.
5. Annual operating budgets for the General, Special Revenue, and Debt Service Funds are adopted on a basis substantially consistent with generally accepted accounting principles (GAAP) except that budgetary comparisons for the General Fund include encumbrances as expenditures.

   Adjustments necessary to compare the results of operations in the General Fund on a GAAP basis to that on a non-GAAP budgetary basis for the year ended September 30, 1983, are as follows:

Excess of revenues and other financing sources over expenditures and other uses (GAAP basis)	$2,225,117
Less encumbrances at September 30, 1983	(1,493,805)
Plus encumbrances at September 30, 1982	2,057,724
Excess of revenues and other financing sources over expenditures and other uses (Non-GAAP budgetary basis)	$2,789,036

For 1983, annual operating budgets were not adopted for the following Special Revenue Funds: Community Development, Cable T.V., and other miscellaneous special revenue funds. In addition, budgets were not adopted for the inactive Debt Service Funds for the Orange Bowl and the Incinerator Bonds. Subsequent to September 30, 1983, the out-

standing fund balances of the inactive Debt Service Funds totaling $836,893 were appropriated into the Capital Improvements Fund. Budgeted amounts are as originally adopted, or as amended by the City Commission through the year.

6. Upon request of the City Manager, the Commission may transfer any part of an unencumbered balance of an appropriation to a purpose or object for which an appropriation for the current year has proved insufficient, or may authorize a transfer to be made between items appropriated to the same office, department or division. At the close of each fiscal year, the unencumbered balance of each appropriation reverts to the fund from which it was appropriated and shall be subject to future appropriations.

[MILWAUKEE COUNTY, WISCONSIN (DECEMBER 31, 1983), NOTES TO FINANCIAL STATEMENTS (IN PART)]

Note 1 [in part]

(d) Basis of Accounting

All governmental and expendable trust funds utilize the modified accrual basis of accounting. Under this method, revenues are recognized in the accounting period in which they become susceptible to accrual, that is, when they become both measurable and available to finance expenditures and commitments of the current period. Significant revenues susceptible to accrual include most governmental revenues and charges for services. Licenses and permits, fines and forfeits generally are recorded as revenues when received in cash because they are not measurable until actually received.

Under the modified accrual basis of accounting, expenditures are recognized when the related liability is incurred, if measurable, except for interest on general long-term debt and unfunded claims and judgments.

The accrual basis of accounting is followed by the proprietary funds and the Pension Trust Fund. Under the accrual basis of accounting, revenues are recognized in the accounting period in which they are earned and expenses are recognized in the period they are incurred.

Budgets and Budgetary Accounting

All County departments are required to submit their annual budget requests for the ensuing year to the County Executive by July 15. The Department of Administration, acting as staff for the County Executive, reviews the requests in detail with the departments during July, August and September. After all of the requests have been reviewed, the County Executive submits his proposed Executive Budget to the Board of Supervisors. The County ordinances require that this be done on or before October 1. The Board of Supervisors must complete its review and adopt the budget on or before November 15th. Annual budgets are legally adopted by the Board of Supervisors for all governmental funds.

All adopted budgets for the governmental funds are prepared in accordance with the modified accrual basis of accounting except for the treatment of the fund balance–Reserved for 1984 and 1985 Appropriations. For budget purposes, the fund balance–Reserved for 1984 and 1985 Appropriations is reflected as other financing sources whereas for accounting purposes, it is reflected as part of fund balance.

The legal level of control for each budget is by department, as defined. Once the budget is adopted, transfers of appropriations among departments require approval by the Board of Supervisors and are permitted only during the last three months of the year. Supplemental appropriations for the purpose of public emergencies may be made from unanticipated revenues received or surplus, as defined, by resolution adopted by a vote of two-thirds of the members of the Board of Supervisors. Supplemental appropriations from the issuance of tax anticipation notes require an affirmative vote of three-fourths of the members of the Board of Supervisors.

[CITY OF PINE BLUFF, ARKANSAS (DECEMBER 31, 1983), NOTES TO FINANCIAL STATEMENTS (IN PART)]

Note 1 [in part]

C. Basis of Accounting

Basis of accounting refers to when revenue and expenditures or expenses are recognized in the accounts and reported in the financial statements. Basis of accounting relates to the timing of the measurements made.

All governmental funds are accounted for using the modified accrual basis of accounting. Revenue is recognized when it becomes measurable and available. Revenue subject to accrual included property taxes, state turnbacks, utility franchises, federal revenue sharing entitlements, and interest earned on investments. License and permit revenue is accounted for when received.

Expenditures are generally recognized under the modified accrual basis of accounting when the related liability is incurred. The major exception to this general rule is the accounting for principal and interest on general long-term debt, which is recognized when due.

The Proprietary Fund is accounted for using the accrual basis of accounting. Its revenue is recognized when earned and its expenses are recognized when incurred. The Pension Trust Funds are accounted for using the cash basis of accounting. Its revenue is recognized when received and its expenses are recognized when paid.

D. Budgets and Budgetary Accounting

The City follows these procedures in establishing the budgetary data reflected in the financial statements:

1. Prior to December 1, the Mayor submits to the City Council a proposed operating budget for the fiscal year commencing the following January 1. The operating budget includes proposed expenditures and the means of financing them.
2. The budget is taken under advisement by the Council for study and comments.
3. Prior to February 1, the budget is legally enacted by action of the Council.
4. Revisions and amendments to the budget must be approved by the Council.
5. Formal budgetary integration is employed as a management control device during the year for the General Fund, Special Revenue Funds, and the Proprietary Fund.
6. Budgets for the General Fund, Special Revenue Funds, and the Proprietary Fund are adopted on a basis consistent with generally accepted accounting principles (GAAP).

[RICHMOND, VIRGINIA (JUNE 30, 1984), NOTES TO FINANCIAL STATEMENTS (IN PART)]

D. Basis of Accounting

Basis of accounting refers to when revenues and expenditures or expenses are recognized in the accounts and reported in the financial statements. Basis of accounting relates to the timing of the measurements made, regardless of the measurement focus applied.

All governmental funds, Expendable Trust Funds and Agency Funds utilize the modified accrual basis of accounting. Under the modified accrual basis of accounting, revenues are recognized when they become susceptible to accrual, that is, when they become both "measurable" and "available" to finance expenditures of the current period. Accordingly, real and personal property tax revenues are recorded as revenues principally on the cash basis until year end, at which time current property tax receipts received within 60 days of year end are accrued. Property taxes not collected within 60 days after year end are reflected as receivables net of allowances for uncollectible accounts and deferred revenues. Licenses, permits and fines are recorded as revenues when received. Intergovernmental revenues, consisting principally of categorical aid from federal and state agencies, are recognized when earned or at the time of the specific expenditure. Revenues from general purpose grants are recognized in the period to which the grant applies.

Sales and public utility taxes, which are collected by the Commonwealth and public utilities, respectively, and subsequently remitted to the City, are recognized as revenues and receivables when collected by authorized agents.

Expenditures in governmental funds and Expendable Trust Funds are generally recognized under the modified accrual basis of accounting when the related fund liability is incurred. An exception to this general rule is principal and interest on general long-term debt, which is recognized when due, and prepaid expenses, which are not recorded.

All proprietary funds, Nonexpendable Trust Funds and Pension Trust Funds are accounted for using the accrual basis of accounting. Revenues are recognized when earned, including unbilled utility receivables, and expenses are recognized when the related liabilities are incurred.

It is the policy of the public utility Enterprise Fund to capitalize during the period of construction only, the interest costs associated with the acquisition or construction of major additions to utilities plant in service. During fiscal 1984 the public utility Enterprise Funds incurred interest costs associated with debt of $9,078,641, of which $318,937 was capitalized.

E. Budgets and Budgetary Accounting

The City follows these procedures in establishing the budgetary data reflected in the financial statements.

1. On or before April 7, the City Manager submits to the City Council a proposed operating budget for the fiscal year commencing the following July 1. The operating budget including a transfer to the Schools Special Revenue Fund includes proposed expenditures and the means of financing them.
2. Public hearings are conducted to obtain taxpayer comments.
3. Prior to May 31, the budget is legally enacted through passage of an ordinance.
4. The City Manager is authorized to transfer budgeted amounts within departments; however, any revisions that alter the total expenditures of any department or agency must be approved by the City Council.
5. Formal budgetary integration is employed as a management control device during the year for all funds.

6. Budgets for the General Fund, Special Revenue Funds and Capital Projects Funds are principally prepared on the modified accrual basis of accounting except that encumbrances, which do not lapse at the end of a fiscal year, are included as budgetary expenditures. Accordingly, the actual data presented in Exhibit C for the General Fund and for the Special Revenue Fund is presented on a basis consistent with the budget, which includes in expenditures encumbrances at June 30, 1984, and excludes encumbrances at June 30, 1983. Project budgets are utilized in the Capital Projects Funds. The General Fund actual expenditures presented in Exhibit C include workers' compensation expenses, which have been treated as a prior period adjustment in Exhibit B. These expenditures are presented in this manner in Exhibit C because the budget data presented therein also includes these expenditures (see Note 11). All appropriations not encumbered lapse at year end for the General Fund. Appropriations for the Capital Projects Funds and certain Special Revenue Funds are continued until completion of applicable projects, even when projects extend more than one fiscal year, or until repealed.

The City Charter (the "Charter") requires that the General Fund budget be prepared in accordance with accepted principles of municipal accounting and budgetary procedures and techniques. City management has interpreted the intent of the Charter to mean that the budget be prepared in the manner described in subparagraph 6 above.

Budgeted amounts are as originally adopted or as amended by the City Council. The General Fund budget presented in Exhibit C gives effect to certain transfers between departments for which the ordinance approving these transfers is pending before City Council. Expenditures may not exceed appropriations on a departmental level in the General Fund and at a functional level in the Schools Special Revenue Fund.

The Combined Statement of Revenues, Expenditures and Changes in Fund Balances—Budget and Actual—General and Special Revenue Fund Types reflects the budgeted and actual amounts for the General Fund and the annually budgeted Special Revenue Fund (Schools). Other Special Revenue Funds do not have annual budgets since grant awards and revenues received under other contractual requirements recorded in these funds span more than a single fiscal year.

Following is a reconciliation of actual data presented on a generally accepted accounting principle basis to the budgetary basis.

	General Fund	Special Revenue Fund
Excess of revenues and other financing sources over expenditures and other financing uses in accordance with generally accepted accounting principles	$1,058,283	$2,145,738
Increase (decrease) due to:		
Encumbrances at June 30, 1983, expended in fiscal 1984	2,831,052	761,261
Encumbrances at June 30, 1984, recognized as expenditures for budget purposes	(3,108,184)	(1,982,473)
Excess of revenues and other financing sources over expenditures and other financing uses—budget basis	$ 781,151	$ 924,526

[SPARTANBURG COUNTY, SOUTH CAROLINA (JUNE 30, 1984), NOTES TO FINANCIAL STATEMENTS (IN PART)]

Note 1 [in part]

C. Basis of Accounting

Basis of accounting refers to when revenues and expenditures or expenses are recognized in the accounts and reported in the financial statements. Basis of accounting relates to the timing of the measurements made, regardless of the measurement focus applied.

All governmental funds are accounted for using the modified accrual basis of accounting. Their revenues are recognized when they become measurable and available as net current assets. Property tax assessments are considered "measurable" when in the hands of the County Treasurer and are recognized as revenue at that time.

Expenditures are generally recognized under the modified accrual basis of accounting when the related fund liability is incurred. Exceptions to this general rule include: (1) accumulated unpaid vacation, sick pay, and other employee amounts which are not accrued; and (2) principal and interest on general long-term debt, which is recognized when due.

All proprietary funds are accounted for using the accrual basis of accounting. Their revenues are recognized when they are earned, and their expenses are recognized when they are incurred.

D. Budgets and Budgetary Accounting

The County follows these procedures in establishing the budgetary data reflected in the financial statements.

1. Prior to July 1, the County Administrator submits to the County Council a proposed budget for the fiscal year commencing on that date. The operating budget includes proposed expenditures and the means of financing them.
2. The proposed budget is discussed at regular meetings of County Council.
3. After three (3) readings before County Council, the budget ordinance is legally enacted.
4. The County Administrator is authorized to transfer budgeted amounts within departments in any fund. During the year, as additional resources become available and/or additional services and programs are approved by County Council, the revenue and expenditures exceed the original budgeted amounts.
5. Formal budgetary integration is employed as a management control device during the year for the General Fund, Special Revenue Funds, and Capital Projects Funds. Formal budgetary integration is not employed for Debt Service Funds because effective budgetary control is alternatively achieved through general obligation bond indenture provisions.
6. Budgets for the General, Special Revenue, and Capital Projects Funds are adopted on a basis primarily consistent with generally accepted accounting principles (GAAP). Appropriations for the General and Special Revenue Funds lapse at the end of the fiscal year unless approved for carryforward as supplemental appropriations. Appropriations for Capital Projects continue until the project is complete.

[CITY OF TOLEDO, OHIO (DECEMBER 31, 1983), NOTES TO FINANCIAL STATEMENTS (IN PART)]

Note 1 [in part]

B. Basis of Accounting

The modified accrual basis of accounting is utilized by the Governmental and Expendable Trust Funds. Under this method of accounting, the City recognizes revenue when it becomes both measurable and available to finance current City operations. Revenues accrued at the end of the year include individual income taxes arising from payroll withholdings in December that are received within 60 days after year-end and amounts due under the Federal General Revenue Sharing Program. Property taxes are recognized in the year they are remitted to the City by the County Auditor as such amounts usually are not received within a timely enough period after the City's year-end to be considered available to finance current operations.

Expenditures other than interest on general obligation long-term debt are recorded when the related liabilities are incurred.

The accrual basis of accounting is utilized by the Proprietary and Nonexpendable Trust Funds. Their revenues are recognized when they are earned, and their expenses are recognized when they are incurred. Unbilled Water and Sewer Funds' utility service receivables are recorded at year-end.

Since Agency Funds are custodial in nature and do not involve measurement of results of operations, Agency Fund assets and liabilities are recognized on the modified accrual basis of accounting.

(2) Budgetary Process

The City follows these procedures in establishing the budgetary data reported in the combined financial statements:

(a) *Budget:* A tax budget of estimated revenue and expenditures is submitted to the County Auditor, as Secretary of the County Budget Commission, by July 20 of each year, for the period January 1 to December 31 of the following year. A proposed budget of estimated revenues and expenditures is submitted to the Mayor and members of City Council of the City of Toledo by November 15 of each year, for the year January 1 to December 31 of the following year.

(b) *Estimated Resources:* The County Budget Commission certifies its actions to the City by September 1. As part of this certification, Toledo receives the official certificate of estimated resources, which states the projected revenue of each fund. On or about January 1, the certificate is amended to include any unencumbered balances from the preceding year. Prior to December 31, Toledo must revise its budget so that the total contemplated expenditure from any fund during the ensuing fiscal year will not exceed the amount stated in the Certificate of Estimated Resources.

(c) *Appropriations:* A temporary appropriation measure to control disbursements may be passed on or about January 1 of each year for the period of Jan-

uary 1 to March 31. The annual appropriation ordinance must be passed by April of each year for the period January 1 to December 31. The Appropriation Ordinance is amended or supplemented during the year as new information becomes available. Appropriations may not exceed the estimated resources.

Amounts shown in the financial statements represent the original budgeted amounts and all supplemental appropriations. Supplemental appropriation measures were enacted during 1983 as follows:

	Original Budget	Total Revisions	Revised Budget
General Fund	$111,904	$ 1,040	$112,944
Special Revenue	19,060	18,810	37,870
Debt Service	7,035	6,418	13,453
Capital Projects	7,870	14,238	22,108
Special Assessments	22,554	2,253	24,807

(d) *Budgeted Level of Expenditure:* Administrative control is maintained through the establishment of detailed line-item budgets. Funds appropriated may not be expended for purposes other than those designated in the Appropriation Ordinance without authority from Council. Expenditures may not legally exceed budgeted appropriations at the fund level.

(e) *Encumbrances:* Encumbrance accounting, under which pressure orders, contracts and other commitments for the expenditure of monies are recorded in order to reserve that portion of the applicable appropriation, is employed as an extension of the formal budgetary control.

(f) *Lapsing of Appropriations:* At the close of each year, the unencumbered balance of each appropriation reverts to the respective fund from which it was appropriated and becomes subject to future appropriations. The encumbered appropriation balance is carried foward to the succeeding fiscal year and need not be reappropriated.

Chapter 6
Interfund Transactions, Transfers, and Bond Proceeds

INTERFUND TRANSACTIONS

Principle 10.a of NCGA Statement 1 and its accompanying explanatory material deal with the appropriate accounting and reporting for interfund transactions, transfers, and bond proceeds. The principle states:

> 10.a. Interfund transfers and proceeds of general long-term debt issues should be classified separately from fund revenues and expenditures or expenses.

The explanatory material notes the potential confusion that can arise because interfund transfers constitute elements of revenues and expenditures or expense only for the particular funds, not for the governmental unit as a whole. Statement 1 also notes that when the proceeds of borrowings are not recorded as liabilities of specific funds, such proceeds normally are reflected as "other financing sources" in the operating statement of the appropriate fund. This chapter contains examples and illustrations relating to the following interfund transactions and transfers:

quasi-external transactions,

reimbursement transactions,

residual equity transfers,

operating transfers, and

proceeds from long-term debt.

QUASI-EXTERNAL TRANSACTIONS

Quasi-external transactions are interfund transactions that would be treated as revenues and expenditures or expenses if these same transactions involved organizations external to the governmental unit. Statement 1 of the NCGA provides the following examples of quasi-external transactions:

payments in lieu of taxes (e.g., from an enterprise fund to the general fund);

billings from an internal service fund to other departments of the government that purchased goods or services from the internal service fund;

routine contributions by the employer government (from the general fund) to a pension trust fund; and

routine service charges for governmental inspections, engineering, utilities, or similar services provided by the fund financing the servicing or selling department to the fund of the receiving or buying department.

In all such cases of quasi-external transactions, it is correct to recognize the interfund transactions as revenues and expenditures or expenses in the affected funds. At the end of the fiscal period, the unpaid or unsettled amounts of these types of interfund transactions are reported as interfund receivables ("due from. . .") and interfund payables ("due to. . .") balances.

Tables 6-1 and 6-2 illustrate the variety of descriptors used by the surveyed governmental units to identify the end-of-period interfund receivables and payables, respectively, resulting from quasi-external transactions. Exhibit 6-1 contains examples from several governmental financial statements illustrating the reporting of these receivables and payables, along with selected excerpts from footnote disclosures.

REIMBURSEMENT TRANSACTIONS

Reimbursement transactions are repayments to one fund for expenditures or expenses initially made by that fund but that are properly applicable to another fund. In Principle 10, the NCGA states that proper accounting is to record the expenditure or expense in the reimbursing fund and reflect a reduction of an expenditure or expense in the fund reimbursed. The reporting of balances resulting from reimbursement transactions is similar to those illustrated in Tables 6-1 and 6-2 and Exhibit 6-1.

INTERFUND TRANSFERS

The NCGA, in Principle 10, also recognizes two categories of interfund transfers: *Residual equity trans-*

fers, or "capital contributions," are the nonrecurring or nonroutine transfers of equity between funds, e.g., contributions of proprietary fund capital by the general fund, subsequent returns of part of the contribution to the general fund, and transfers of residual balances of discontinued funds to the general fund or a debt service fund. *Operating transfers* are all other interfund transfers, such as the following:

legally authorized transfers from a fund receiving revenue to the fund through which the resources are to be expended;

transfers of tax revenues from a special revenue fund to a debt service fund;

transfers from the general fund to a special revenue or capital projects fund;

operating subsidy transfers from the general or special revenue fund to an enterprise fund; and

transfers from an enterprise fund other than payments in lieu of taxes to finance general fund expenditures.

Interfund transfers, according to the NCGA, must be segregated from revenues and expenditures or expenses in the governmental unit's financial statements. The following accounting practices apply to transfer transactions:

Residual equity transfers are additions to or deductions from the beginning fund balance of governmental funds.

Residual equity transfers to proprietary funds are additions to contributed capital; such transfers from proprietary funds are reductions of retained earnings or contributed capital, as appropriate in the circumstances.

Operating transfers are "other financing sources (uses)" in the statement of revenues, expenditures, and changes in fund balance (for governmental funds) and are "operating transfers in (out)" in the statement of revenues, expenses, and changes in retained earnings (for proprietary funds).

Tables 6-3 and 6-4 illustrate the variety of descriptors used by the surveyed governmental units to identify the types of transfers in and out shown in the revenue and expenditure or expense statements. Exhibits 6-2 and 6-3 contain excerpts from several governmental financial statements illustrating the accounting for other sources and uses of funds and transfers in and out of governmental funds.

BOND PROCEEDS

The liabilities from borrowings of proprietary, special assessment, and trust funds are recorded as fund liabilities of those funds. Liabilities from borrowings of other funds are reflected as liabilities of the general long-term debt account group, and bond proceeds are shown in the operating statement of the recipient fund among the "other financing sources."

Some summary observations relating to the accounting for borrowings follow:

Accounting for Debt Proceeds	Instances Observed (%)
Statements of revenues, expenditures, and changes in fund balances—governmental funds—with bond proceeds activities*	41
Bond proceeds reported as	
other financing sources (uses)	70
revenues	9
other financing sources	8
Statement of revenues, expenditures, and changes in fund balances—governmental funds—with debt payment*	47
Debt payments reported as	
expenditures	82
other financing (uses)	<1
other captions	<1

* Observations for the 85% of the units having a statement of revenues, expenditures, and changes in fund balance.

OTHER OBSERVATIONS

Most of the governments utilized the revenue and expenditure statements recommended by NCGA Statement 1, as shown in the following table:

Financial Statements	Instances Observed (%)
Revenue, expenditures, and changes in fund balances—governmental funds	85
Revenue, expenditures, and changes in fund balances—budget and actual	83

Additional details and specific observations relating to the "other financing" section of these statements appear in the tables and exhibits that follow.

EXHIBITS AND TABLES FOR CHAPTER 6

Table 6-1. Account Titles Used by Governmental Units to Report "Due from. . ." Receivables

Table 6-2. Account Titles Used by Governmental Units to Report "Due to. . ." Payables

Exhibit 6-1. Excerpts from Governmental Balance Sheets of "Due from" Receivables and "Due to" Payables

Table 6-3. Account Titles Used by Governmental Units to Report Other Financing Sources and Uses

Table **6-4.** Account Titles Used by Governmental Units to Report Operating Transfers in (out)

Exhibit **6-2.** Excerpts from Governmental Revenue and Expenditure Statements—Other Financing Sources and Uses and Interfund Transactions

Exhibit **6-3.** Excerpts from Governmental Revenue and Expense Statements—Operating Transfers in and out and Interfund Transactions

TABLE 6-1. ACCOUNT TITLES USED BY GOVERNMENTAL UNITS TO REPORT "DUE FROM. . ." RECEIVABLES

Account Title*	Instances Observed (%)
Due from other funds	83
Due from other governments	40
Due from other governmental units	12
Advances to other funds	11
Due from other government agencies	6
Due from federal government	3
Due from other agencies	2
Due from state	2
Due from general fund	1
Due from city funds	1
Other descriptors:	<2
Due from other funds and agencies	
Advances to other government units	
Advances to other funds and agencies	
Due from other county funds	
Due from other county units	

* Observations for the 88% of the units having a combined balance sheet.

TABLE 6-2. ACCOUNT TITLES USED BY GOVERNMENTAL UNITS TO REPORT "DUE TO. . ." PAYABLES

Account Title*	Instances Observed (%)
Due to other funds	83
Due to other governments	26
Due to other governmental units	9
Due to other taxing authorities	6
Due to other governmental agencies	4
Due to others	4
Due to other agencies	2
Due to general fund	1
Due to other city funds	1
Due to school district	<1
Other descriptors:	<1
Due to state	
Due to restricted funds	
Due to other county funds	
Due to municipalities	

* Observations for the 88% of the units having a combined balance sheet.

EXHIBIT 6-1. EXCERPTS FROM GOVERNMENTAL BALANCE SHEETS OF "DUE FROM" RECEIVABLES AND "DUE TO" PAYABLES.

[CITY OF COLUMBUS, OHIO]

Combined Balance Sheet [in part]—All Fund Types and Account Groups, December 31, 1983

	Governmental Fund Types					Proprietary Fund Types		Fiduciary Fund Types
	General	Special Revenue	Debt Service	Capital Projects	Special Assessment	Enterprise (note 17)	Internal Service	Expendable Trust and Agency
Assets				* * *				
Due from other governments	$ —	9,836,535	—	749,403	—	2,701,567	—	548,314
Due from other funds (note 6)	990,590	2,972,574	147,782	1,643,441	15,120	4,809,012	2,321,126	36,258
Liabilities				* * *				
Due to other:								
Governments	$ —	17,104,093	—	—	17,870	—	—	6,149,217
Funds (note 6)	256,624	2,906,335	1,872,391	2,153,623	128,708	3,452,208	497,727	1,668,287
Others	—	—	—	—	—	—	—	5,188,881

Note (6) Interfund Receivables and Payables

Interfund balances at December 31, 1983, consists of the following individual fund receivables and payables:

	Receivable	Payable		Receivable	Payable
	(in thousands)			(in thousands)	
General	$ 990	257	General Expressway Improvement		
Special Revenue:			and Construction	105	—
Cable Communication Fund	32	1	G.S.C. Project R163 Mt. Vernon		
CETA I Grant	—	8	Plaza	—	312
CETA III—SYEP	—	2	Mt. Vernon Plaza Project Section A		
CETA VII—PSIP	—	59	City	—	2
Community Development Act Years			Parks, Recreation and Zoo		
1–3	107	1	Improvement	9	1
Community Development Act Year 4	1	1	Parks, Recreation and Improvement	13	11
Community Development Act Year 6	171	—	Recreation and Parks Improvement	—	15
Community Development Act Years			Riverfront Park Note	15	—
7–10	78	34	Street and Highway Improvement	—	15
Community Services Grants	—	7	Streets—Highways—81	400	136
Development Department Grants	—	57		1,644	2,154
Energy and Telecommunications			Special Assessment:		
Grants	—	22	Bond Fund	—	129
Federal Shared Revenue	105	37	Lynn–Pearl Street Improvement	15	—
General Government Grants	3	2		15	129
Health Department Grants	26	311	Enterprise:		
Health Special Revenue	935	64	Water	2,320	946
Recreation and Parks—Grants	—	26	Sewer	2,057	1,320
Recreation and Parks—Operations	26	13	Electricity	422	112
Social Services Title 20	—	73	Airport	10	1,074
Special Income Tax	1,364	—		4,809	3,452
Street Construction Maintenance &			Internal Service:		
Repair	81	2,188	Construction Inspection	1,766	26
Treasury Investment Earnings	44	—	Data Processing Services	360	367
	2,973	2,906	Land Acquisition Service	86	—
Debt Service—General Bond			Municipal Garage Services	70	105
Retirement	148	1,872	Purchasing Stores	39	—
Capital Projects:				2,321	498
CDA Capital Projects	$ —	$ 17	Trust and Agency:		
CDA Park Development	—	5	Auditor's Suspense	—	19
CDA Street Improvement	25	26	City Auditor's Deposit	—	8
Express, Streets and Traffic Control	626	23	Community Health Care Service	—	591
Expressways, Streets and Traffic			Construction Inspection Deposits	—	1,050
Control	451	—	Unemployment Compensation	36	—
Federal State Highway Engineering	—	1,591		36	1,668
				$12,936	12,936

[CITY OF FORT COLLINS, COLORADO]

Combined Balance Sheet [in part]—For All Fund Types and Account Groups, December 31, 1983

	Government Fund Types					Proprietary Fund Types		Fiduciary Fund Types
	General Fund	Special Revenue	Debt Service	Capital Projects	Special Assessment	Enterprise	Internal Service	Trust
ASSETS								
Current Assets:								
			* * *					
Due from Other Funds	$2,051,103	$325,835	$149,972	$517,570	$ —	$1,389,067	$1,652,993	$273,000
			* * *					
Advance to Other Funds	—	—		—	—	53,273	—	—
			* * *					
LIABILITIES AND FUND EQUITY								
Current Liabilities:								
			* * *					
Due to Other Funds	$813,507	$2,297,285	$ —	$136,370	$10,791	$1,907,674	$1,193,913	$ —
			* * *					

[Summary of Significant Accounting Policies (in part)]

Interfund Transfers. Transfers between funds of the City, unless they are capital in nature, are reflected on the operating statements of the funds involved.

Note 16. Interfund Advances To/From

Advance from Water Fund to Golf Fund. This account represents monies advanced for the acquisition and construction of the Collindale Golf Course by the Water Fund. A repayment schedule has been adopted to repay the balance due in equal annual principal and interest installments of $26,234 through 1998 bearing interest at 4%.

Advance from Perpetual Care Fund to Cemeteries Fund. This account represents monies advanced for the construction of the cemetery maintenance building by the Perpetual Care Fund. A repayment schedule has been adopted to repay the balance due with principal payments of $19,500 and interest payments of $4,598 through 1984. The non-current portion of the Advance to Cemeteries in Perpetual Care Fund for 1982 of $19,500 has been offset by a fund balance reserve which indicates that it does not constitute "available spendable resources," since it is not a component of net current assets.

Loan Payable—Downtown Development Authority. An intergovernmental agreement was entered into August 18, 1981, between the Downtown Development Authority and the City of Fort Collins, whereby the City would provide funds not to exceed $27,000 for use by the Authority to pay operating expenses incurred during calendar year 1981. An addendum to this agreement dated December 30, 1982, was initiated, which expanded the scope of monies to be lent to include expenses also obligated and committed during calendar year 1981, not to exceed the same $27,000 amount. The outstanding amount loaned of $19,293 is reflected in Downtown Development Authority General Long-Term Debt. Repayments began in 1983 for $2,500.

Advance from Water Fund to Parkland Fund. This account represents water certificates issued in lieu of cash for land purchased by the Parkland Fund for the Huntington Hills–Portner Reservoir Parksite. A repayment schedule has been formulated to repay the amount due to equal installments of $60,905 through 1987 bearing interest at 12%.

Advance from General Fund to Transportation Fund. This account represents monies advanced for the construction of the Jefferson Street Parking Lot by the Capital Projects Fund, which is being financed by the Transportation Fund. A repayment schedule has been drafted to repay the balance due with principal payments of $21,300 and interest payments of 8.55% on the outstanding balance through 1987.

Note 17. Interfund Receivables/Payables

Interfund Receivables (Due From)/Payables (Due To)
at December 31, 1983, are as follows:

Fund	Due from	Due to	Fund	Due from	Due to
General	$2,051,103	$ 813,507	Improvement Districts	—	10,791
Equipment	16,116	10,438	Federal Revenue Sharing	—	34,091
Warehouse	1,330,236	1,182,436	Community Development Block		
Communications	232,840	424	Grant	—	2,707
Self Insurance	73,801	—	Perpetual Care	25,023	16,662
Energy Conservation	—	615	Downtown Development		
Seven-Year Capital	—	125,676	Authority Debt Service	149,972	—
Capital Projects	517,570	10,509	Downtown Development		
Employees' Retirement	227,000	—	Authority	—	149,973
Policemen's Pension	46,000	—	Parkland	—	185
Light and Power	1,263,596	897,632	Community Services	13,087	329
Water	28,202	587,597	Larimer County Library Services	147	478
Sewer	31	306,865	Sales and Use Tax	—	1,862,706
Golf	—	30,528	Street Oversizing	—	195,847
Transportation Services	55,614	16,991	Rockwell Ranch	—	1,324
Cultural Services and Facilities	103,636	7,567	Federal Aid Urban Systems	—	97
Recreation	128,328	8,513	Grand Total	$6,359,540	$6,359,540
Cemeteries	97,238	27,373			
Storm Drainage	—	57,679			

[CITY OF NEWPORT NEWS, VIRGINIA]

Combined Balance Sheet [in part]—All Fund Types and Account Groups, June 30, 1984

	Governmental Fund Types			Proprietary Fund Types	Fiduciary Fund Types
	General	Special Revenue	Capital Projects	Enterprise	Trust and Agency
ASSETS					
		* * *			
Due from other governments	$2,744,259	$2,789,219	$1,336,690	$ —	$ 58,051
Due from other funds	879,416	537,712	—	—	—
		* * *			
LIABILITIES AND FUND EQUITY					
		* * *			
Due to other funds	$ —	$25,319	$680,276	$140,000	$571,533
Due to other governments	—	—	—	—	199,585
* * *					

Note 5. Interfund Receivables and Payables

Details of interfund receivables and payables as of June 30, 1984, are as follows:

Receivable Fund	Payable Fund	Amount
General Fund	Special Revenue—Revenue Sharing	$ 24,906
General Fund	Trust & Agency—General Workers' Compensation	33,821
General Fund	Special Revenue—Community Development	413
General Fund	Capital Projects—Other Federal & State Grants	680,276
General Fund	Enterprise—Oyster Point Development Corp.	140,000
Special Revenue—School Operating	Trust & Agency—School Worker's Compensation	302,040
Special Revenue—School Operating	Trust & Agency—Other Agency Funds	235,672
		$1,417,128

In addition, the following interfund receivables and payables were eliminated in the preparation of the combined financial statements:

Receivable Fund	Payable Fund	Amount
Special Revenue Funds: School Operating	School Titles	$ 566,000
Capital Projects Funds: Revenue Sharing	EDA Grant	$ 328,600
Revenue Sharing	General Capital Improvements	2,470,203
		$2,798,803

[CITY OF RALEIGH, NORTH CAROLINA]

Combined Balance Sheet [in part]—All Fund Types and Account Groups, June 30, 1984

	Governmental Fund Types			Proprietary Fund Types
	General	Special Revenue	General Capital Projects	Enterprise
ASSETS				
	* * *			
Due from Other Governmental Agencies	$ —	231,451	223,602	2,073,996
	* * *			
Due from Other Funds	140,140	—	—	16,274
	* * *			
LIABILITIES AND FUND EQUITY Liabilities:				
	* * *			
Due to Other Governmental Agencies	$ —	31,813	—	116,507
	* * *			
Due to Other Funds	16,274	14,061	—	126,079
	* * *			

Note C. Interfund Receivables and Payables

Individual fund interfund receivable and payable balances at June 30, 1984, are as follows:

Fund	Interfund Receivables	Interfund Payables	Fund	Interfund Receivables	Interfund Payables
General Fund	$140,140	$ 16,274	Enterprise Funds:		
Special Revenue Funds:			Mass Transit Fund	—	126,079
Grants Fund	—	13,086	Parking Deck Fund	16,274	—
Community Development Fund	—	508		16,274	126,079
Manpower Fund	—	467		$156,414	$156,414
	—	14,061			

[CITY OF SAN ANTONIO, TEXAS]

Combined Balanced Sheet [in part]—All Fund Types and Account Groups, September 30, 1983 [in thousands]

	Governmental Fund Types				Proprietary Fund Types		Fiduciary Fund Types
	General	Special Revenue	Debt Service	Capital Projects	Enterprise	Internal Service	Trust and Agency
ASSETS							
			*	*	*		
Due from Other Funds	$2,278	496	2,958	7,348	174		
Due from Other Governmental Agencies	151	7,481				291	16
Restricted Assets:							
Due from Other Funds					337		
			*	*	*		
LIABILITIES							
			*	*	*		
Due to Other Governmental Agencies					590	560	
Other Funds	$3,281	4,766		5,318	217		9
			*	*	*		

Note 3. Interfund Receivables and Payables

The following is a summary of interfund receivables and payables as of September 30, 1983:

	Interfund Receivables	Interfund Payables		Interfund Receivables	Interfund Payables
General Fund	$ 2,278	$ 3,281	Capital Projects Funds:		
Special Revenue Funds:			General Obligation Bonds	6	5,230
Convention Center Arena Revenue Fund	—	25	Improvement Projects	7,342	88
Traffic Signals Revolving Fund	—	39	Enterprise Funds:		
Special Revenue Reserve Fund	88	1,575	Sewer System Fund	337	—
Federal Revenue Sharing Fund	—	2,216	Airport System Fund	172	217
Community Development Program Fund	—	350	Parking Facilities Fund	2	—
Categorical Grants-in-Aid Funds	408	561	Fiduciary Funds:		
Debt Service Funds	2,958	—	Agency Funds	—	9
				$13,591	$13,591

(Amounts are expressed in thousands.)

[CITY OF SANTA BARBARA, CALIFORNIA]

Combined Balance Sheet [in part]—All Fund Types and Account Groups, June 30, 1984

	Governmental Fund Types				Proprietary Fund Types	Fiduciary Fund Types
	General	Special Revenue	Debt Service	Capital Projects	Enterprise (Note 9)	Trust and Agency
ASSETS						
		* * *				
Due from other funds (note 10)	$ 33,112	—	205,830	4,299,779	4,235	—
Due from other agencies (note 4)	523,436	385,969	—	—	619,072	36,241
		* * *				
LIABILITIES AND FUND EQUITY						
		* * *				
Due to other funds (note 10)	$3,259,348	1,283,608	—	—	—	—
		* * *				

Note (4) Due from Other Agencies

The City has receivables from governmental agencies.
This balance is made up of the following:

Fund	Federal	State	Local	Total
General Fund:	$ 8,074	$149,282	$366,080	$ 523,436
Special Revenue Funds:				
Special Gas Tax	82,251	—	—	82,251
CDBG Jobs Bill	2,834	—	—	2,834
Redevelopment Agency	—	—	34,763	34,763
Revenue Sharing	266,121	—	—	266,121
Subtotal	351,206	—	34,763	385,969
Enterprise Funds:				
Water	55,147	—	—	55,147
Wastewater	96,505	16,083	—	112,588
Airport	451,337	—	—	451,337
Subtotal	602,989	16,083	—	619,072
Nonexpendable Trust Funds:				
Harbor	—	36,241	—	36,241
TOTAL	$962,269	$201,606	$400,843	$1,564,718

Note (10) Interfund Receivables and Payables

Individual fund interfund receivable and payable balances. Such balances at June 30, 1984 were:

Fund	Interfund Receivables	Interfund Payables	Fund	Interfund Receivables	Interfund Payables
General Fund	$ 33,112	$3,259,348	Capital Project Funds:		
Special Revenue Funds:			Capital Outlays	3,049,283	—
Redevelopment Agency	—	1,250,496	Redevelopment Agency	1,250,496	—
Community Development Block			Enterprise Funds:		
Grant	—	33,112	Consolidated Parking	4,235	—
Debt Service Fund:			TOTAL	$4,542,956	$4,542,956
1966 Parks	205,830	—			

[CITY OF TEMPE, ARIZONA]

Combined Balance Sheet [in part]—All Fund Types and Account Groups, June 30, 1984

	Governmental Fund Types				Proprietary Fund Type
	General	Special Revenue	Debt Service	Capital Projects	Enterprise
Assets					
		* * *			
Due from other governments	$ —	1,618,187	—	19,368	—
Due from Special Revenue Funds	227,098	—	645,726	—	—
Due from Enterprise Funds	5,403	—	—	—	—
		* * *			
Liabilities					
		* * *			
Due to Debt Service Fund	$ —	645,726	—	—	—
Due to General Fund	—	227,098	—	—	5,403
		* * *			

Note 1 [in part]

(j) Interfund Transactions. Interfund transactions consisting of identified services performed for other funds or costs billed to other funds are treated as expenditures in the fund receiving the services and as a reimbursement, reducing expenditures, in the fund performing the service except for the following:

Sales of water, sewer and refuse services to other City departments are recorded as revenue.

Operating transfers are made in certain funds to shift resources from a fund legally authorized to receive revenue to a fund authorized to expend the revenue.

[COUNTY OF ROCKINGHAM, VIRGINIA]

Combined Balance Sheet [in part]—All Fund Types and Account Groups, June 30, 1984

	Governmental Fund	
	General	Special Revenue
Assets		
	* * *	
Due from other governmental units (Note 3)	$307,377	$491,903
Advances to other school districts		518,917
	* * *	
Liabilities		
	* * *	
Due to School Textbook Fund		25,000
	* * *	

Note 3—Due from Other Governmental Units:

	1984	1983
Commonwealth of Virginia:		
State sales taxes	$262,430	$238,904
Local sales taxes	112,390	106,282
Shared expenses	129,202	127,738
Total from Commonwealth of Virginia	505,022	472,924
Federal Government:		
School Funds	145,017	298,905
Shared expenses	65,785	37,692
Revenue sharing entitlements	77,023	133,805
Total from Federal Government	287,825	470,402
City of Harrisonburg:		
School Funds	6,433	38,237
Total	$799,280	$981,563

Note 9—Transfers to the School Board:

Operating transfers from the General Fund to the School Fund totaled $9,469,540 and $9,459,983 for the years ended June 30, 1984 and 1983, respectively. It is the practice of the Board of Supervisors to transfer cash at the time disbursements are made.

[CHARLOTTE COUNTY, FLORIDA]

Combined Balance Sheet [in part]—All Fund Types and Account Groups, September 30, 1983

	Governmental Fund Types				Fiduciary Fund Type
	General	Special Revenue	Capital Projects	Special Assessments	Agency
Assets					
	* * *				
Due from other funds—Note 13	$125,520	$168,430	$7,107	$13,848	$264,002
Due from other governmental agencies	347,904	306,069	900	—	—
	* * *				
Liabilities					
	* * *				
Due to other funds—Note 13	$346,835	$ 41,500	$ —	$ 37	$190,535
Due to other governmental agencies	30,473	6,094	—	102	813,006
Due to individuals	1,263	—	—	—	81,082
	* * *				

Note 13—Interfund Receivable and Payable Balances

Interfund receivable and payable balances at September 30, 1983, consist of:

Fund	Interfund Receivables	Interfund Payables	Fund	Interfund Receivables	Interfund Payables
General	$125,520	$346,835	Special Assessments	13,848	37
Special Revenue	168,430	41,500	Agency	264,002	190,535
Capital Projects	7,107	—		$578,907	$578,907

[CITY OF CHICAGO, ILLINOIS]

Combined Balance Sheet [in part]—All Fund Types and Account Groups, December 31, 1983 [in thousands]

	Governmental Fund Types					Proprietary Fund Type	Fiduciary Fund Types
	General	Special Revenue	Debt Service	Capital Projects	Special Assessment (Unaudited)	Enterprise	Trust and Agency (Partially Unaudited)
Assets							
			* * *				
Due from other funds	$ 58,968	$ 2,471	$ 360	$16,090	$79	$ 7,970	$218,582
Due from other governments	55,974	35,947	4,271	8,711	—	6	81,127
			* * *				
Liabilities							
			* * *				
Due to other funds	$115,870	$30,297	$3,865	$ 6,113	$83	$36,502	$111,790
			* * *				

Note (1) [in part]

(g) *Interfund Transactions.* The General Fund provides services to the Enterprise Funds and various Special Revenue Funds. The amounts charged to the Enterprise Funds and Special Revenue Funds for these services are treated as internal service revenue in the General Fund and as operating expenses in the Enterprise Funds and current expenditures in the Special Revenue Funds.

[BOISE CITY, IDAHO]

Combined Balance Sheet [in part]—All Fund Types and Account Groups, September 30, 1983

	Governmental Fund Types				Proprietary Fund Types		Fiduciary Fund Type
	General	Special Revenue	Capital Projects	Special Assessments	Enterprise	Internal Service	Trust and Agency
Assets							
			*	*	*		
Due from other funds	$815,862	$102,093	$59,198	$ 4,736	$140,075	$69,736	$ 34,396
			*	*	*		
Liabilities							
			*	*	*		
Due to other funds	$121,418	$211,941	$ 9,279	$46,717	$249,559	$ 4,661	$582,521
			*	*	*		

Note A [in part]

Interfund Transactions. During the course of normal operations the City has numerous transactions between funds, including expenditures and transfers of resources to provide services and construct assets. The accompanying financial statements generally reflect such transactions as operating transfers. Operating subsidies are also recorded as operating transfers.

Internal service funds are used to record charges for services to all City departments and funds as operating revenue. All City funds record these payments to the internal service funds as operating expenditures/expenses.

The General Fund provides administrative services to enterprise funds. Amounts charged to a fund for these services are based on the City's central service cost allocation plan and are treated as other revenue in the General Fund and as operating expenses in enterprise funds.

TABLE 6-3. ACCOUNT TITLES USED BY GOVERNMENTAL UNITS TO REPORT OTHER FINANCING SOURCES AND USES*

Account Titles/Descriptions*	Instances Observed (%)
Other financing sources/uses	74
Other financing sources	8
Other financing uses	4
Other uses	4
Other sources	2
Other sources/uses	1
Operating transfers to/out	11
Operating transfers from/in	11
Operating transfers to/from	2
Statements with no "other financing" or "operating transfer" sections	18

* Observations for the 85% of the units having the statement of revenue, expenditures, and changes in fund balance.

TABLE 6-4. ACCOUNT TITLES USED BY GOVERNMENTAL UNITS TO REPORT OPERATING TRANSFERS IN (OUT)

Account Titles/Descriptions*	Instances Observed (%)
Operating transfers in (from)	18
Operating transfers to (out)	15
Operating transfers to/from (in/out)	11
Operating transfers	6
Transfers to/out	2
Transfer from/in	2
Transfers to/from (in/out)	1
Other financing sources (uses)	5
Other financing sources	2
Other financing uses	1
Other sources	0
Other uses	<1
Other sources/uses	<1
Statements with no "other financing" or "operating transfers" section	46

* Observations for the 72% of the units having a statement of revenues, expenses, and changes in retained earnings/fund balances—all proprietary fund types and similar trust funds.

EXHIBIT 6-2. EXCERPTS FROM GOVERNMENTAL REVENUE AND EXPENDITURE STATEMENTS—OTHER FINANCING SOURCES AND USES AND INTERFUND TRANSACTIONS

[CITY OF COLUMBUS, OHIO]

Combined Statement of Revenues, Expenditures and Changes in Fund Balances [in part]—All Governmental Fund Types and Trust Funds, Year Ended December 31, 1983

	Governmental Fund Types					Fiduciary Fund Type
	General	Special Revenue	Debt Service	Capital Projects	Special Assessment	Expendable Trust
Revenues:	$	* * *				
Expenditures:		* * *				
Other financing sources (uses):						
Proceeds of general obligation bonds and notes	—	—	49,215,000	17,580,000	—	—
Operating transfers in (note 16)	$11,237,499	18,953,268	5,703,671	2,906,614	—	—
Operating transfers out (note 16)	(15,983,044)	(12,377,028)	(7,587,192)	(2,853,788)	—	—
Total other financing sources (uses)	(4,745,545)	6,576,240	47,331,479	17,632,826	—	—
Excess (deficiency) of revenues and other financing sources over expenditures and other uses before cumulative effect of changes in accounting principles	$ 3,942,629	2,137,842	(3,925,067)	8,694,230	237,155	44,498
Cumulative effect on prior years (to December 31, 1982) of changing method of accounting for:						
Income tax revenue (note 2)	—	6,041,000	—	—	—	—
Special assessment revenue (note 3)	—	—	—	—	(2,018,725)	—
Excess (deficiency) of revenues and other sources over expenditures and other uses	3,942,629	8,178,842	(3,925,067)	8,694,230	(1,781,570)	44,498
Fund balances at beginning of year	290,639	30,396,491	8,542,410	8,822,130	508,413	482,688
Fund balances (deficit) at end of year	$ 4,233,268	38,575,333	4,617,343	17,516,360	(1,273,157)	527,186

Note (16) Operating Transfers

For the year ended December 31, 1983, operating transfers presented in accordance with generally accepted accounting principles (GAAP) and on the City's budgetary basis (Budget) consisted of the following:

	Transfers in (in thousands)					Transfers in (in thousands)			
	General		Special Revenue			General		Special Revenue	
	GAAP	Budget	GAAP	Budget		GAAP	Budget	GAAP	Budget
Income taxes	$ —	98,924	815	815	Income taxes	$ —	—	815	125,735
Investment earnings	6,486	13,140	—	—	Investment earnings	—	—	6,674	19,445
Recreation	—	—	10,279	10,279	Recreation	10,279	10,279	—	—
Health	—	—	5,464	7,110	Health	5,489	5,489	—	—
Property taxes	2,826	2,826	—	—	Property tax	—	—	2,826	2,826
Refunds	—	—	1,161	—	Hotel/motel taxes	—	—	998	998
Hotel/motel taxes	998	998	—	—	Other	215	215	1,064	534
Rent expense	740	—	—	—		$15,983	15,983	12,377	149,538
Other	187	4	1,234	606					
	$11,237	115,892	18,953	18,810					

[CITY OF NEWPORT NEWS, VIRGINIA]

Combined Statement of Revenues, Expenditures and Changes in Fund Balances [in part]—All Governmental Fund Types, for the Year Ended June 30, 1984

	General	Special Revenue	Debt Service	Capital Projects
Revenues:	$	$	$	$
	* * *			
Other sources:				
Transfer from General Fund	—	29,491,774	8,804,447	445,070
Transfer from Special Revenue Funds	1,368,652	—	—	1,235,208
Transfer from Enterprise Fund	2,802,323	—	—	—
Transfer from Capital Projects Funds	—	674,718	—	—
Total revenues and other sources	104,314,098	84,272,088	9,433,148	3,086,220
Expenditures:				
	* * *			
Other uses:				
Transfer to General Funds	—	1,368,652	—	—
Transfer to Special Revenue Funds	29,491,774	—	—	674,718
Transfer to Debt Service Fund	8,804,447	—	—	—
Transfer to Capital Projects Funds	445,070	1,235,208	—	—
Transfer to Enterprise Funds	107,099	—	—	—
Total expenditures and other uses	98,264,435	84,855,303	10,196,068	15,701,857
Excess of revenues and other sources over (under) expenditures and other uses	6,049,663	(583,215)	(762,920)	(12,615,637)
Fund balances, July 1, 1983	10,677,280	5,504,151	1,017,610	11,827,173
Increase in reserve for inventory	—	167,646		
Equity transfer	(410,644)	(189,356)	—	—
Fund balances—June 30, 1984	$16,316,299	$4,899,226	$ 254,690	$ (788,464)

[CITY OF OKLAHOMA CITY, OKLAHOMA]

Combined Statement of Revenues, Expenditures, and Changes in Fund Balances [in part]—All Governmental Fund Types and Expendable Trust Funds, Year Ended June 30, 1984

	General	Special Revenue	Debt Service	Capital Projects	Special Assessment	Expendable Trust
			Governmental Fund Types			Fiduciary Fund Types
REVENUES	$		* * *			
EXPENDITURES			* * *			
OTHER FINANCING SOURCES (USES)						
Operating transfers in	1,594,433	12,578,182	241,585	13,172,730	—	—
Operating transfers out	(26,453,744)	(10,822,396)	—	(568,188)	(28)	—
Total other financing sources (uses)	(24,859,311)	1,755,786	241,585	12,604,542	(28)	—
Excess (deficiency) of revenues and other sources over expenditures and other uses	(3,842,713)	1,053,042	103,440	(6,549,009)	410,757	(854,570)
Fund balance, beginning, as related	28,955,994	29,241,586	39,808,032	33,565,200	(1,654,364)	1,464,387
Residual equity transfer	—	(60,358)	—	—	—	—
Increase (decrease) in reserve for receivables	(49,384)	—	(3,471,851)	—	—	—
Fund balance, ending	$25,063,897	30,234,270	36,439,621	27,016,191	(1,243,607)	609,817

Note D [in part]. Interfund Transactions

1. Interfund transfers. Interfund transfers for the year ended June 30, 1984, consisted of the following:

Transfer out/from	General	Special Revenue	Debt Service	Capital Projects	Enterprise	Internal Service	Total Transfers out
			Transfers in/to				
Operating:							
General	$ —	12,578,154	235,851	3,316,305	10,323,434	—	$26,453,744
Special Revenue	1,314,047	—	—	9,508,349	—	—	10,822,396
Capital Projects	—	—	5,733	348,076	178,211	36,168	568,188
Special Assessments	—	28	—	—	—	—	28
Enterprise	109,335	—	—	—	—	—	109,335
Internal Service	171,051	—	—	—	—	—	171,051
Total transfers in	$1,594,433	12,578,182	241,584	13,172,730	10,501,645	36,168	$38,124,742
Residual equity:							
Special Revenue	$ —	—	—	—	60,358	—	$ 60,358

[CITY OF RALEIGH, NORTH CAROLINA]

Combined Statement of Revenues, Expenditures and Changes in Fund Balances [in part], All Governmental Fund Types for the Fiscal Year Ended June 30, 1984

	Governmental Fund Types			
	General	Special Revenue	Debt Service	General Capital Projects
Revenues:	$	$	$	$
	*	* *		
Other Financing Sources:				
Operating Transfers from Other Funds	1,859,352	120,802	4,563,210	2,899,112
In-Kind Contribution from City	—	26,910	—	—
Proceeds of General Obligation Bonds	3,750,000	—	—	—
Total Other Financing Sources	5,609,352	147,712	4,563,210	2,899,112
Total Revenues and Other Financing Sources	59,952,152	9,748,825	4,717,258	7,640,806
Expenditures:				
	*	* *		
Other Uses:				
Operating Transfers to Other Funds	4,187,110	3,919,097	—	2,126,718
Refinancing of Long-Term Obligations	4,187,287	—	—	—
Total Other Uses	8,374,397	3,919,097	—	2,126,718
Total Expenditures and Other Uses	57,053,152	13,435,756	4,112,617	7,862,712
Excess of Revenues and Other Financing Sources Over (Under) Expenditures and Other Uses	2,899,000	(3,686,931)	604,641	(221,906)
Fund Balances—Beginning of Year	16,821,512	8,161,265	1,366,604	21,346,549
Residual Transfer of Equity	4,388	(4,388)	—	—
Fund Balances—End of Year	$19,724,900	$4,469,946	$1,971,245	$21,124,643

[CITY OF ROANOKE, VIRGINIA]

Combined Statement of Revenues, Expenditures and Changes in Fund Balances [in part]—All Governmental Fund Types, Year Ended June 30, 1984

	Governmental Fund Types				Governmental Fund Types		
	General	Debt Service	Capital Projects		General	Debt Service	Capital Projects
Sources of Financial Resources				Other Uses:			
Revenues:	$	$	$	Transfers to Governmental Fund Types	9,795,903	—	—
	*	* *		Transfers to Proprietary Fund Types	949,194	—	—
Other Sources:				Total Uses of Financial Resources	101,938,991	7,744,355	14,031,957
Bond Proceeds	—	—	—	Net Increase (Decrease) in Fund Balances	1,231,700	53,687	(2,180,247)
Transfers from General Fund	—	7,331,935	2,463,968	Fund Balances—July 1 (Note 2)	5,095,343	5,750,167	17,957,007
Total Sources of Financial Resources	103,170,691	7,798,042	11,851,710	Fund Balances—June 30	$ 6,327,043	$5,803,854	$15,776,760
Uses of Financial Resources							
Expenditures:							
	*	* *					

[CITY OF SANTA ANA, CALIFORNIA]

Combined Statement of Revenues, Expenditures and Changes in Fund Balances [in part]—All Governmental Fund Types For the Fiscal Year Ended June 30, 1984

	Governmental Fund Types			
	General	Special Revenue	Capital Project	Debt Service
Revenues:				
	* * *			
Expenditures:				
	* * *			
Other Financing Sources (Uses):				
Proceeds of sale of bonds	—	—	—	—
Operating transfers in	$7,262,272	255,672	15,160,274	33,902
Operating transfers out	(2,802,333)	(8,406,244)	(4,402,738)	(2,569,879)
Contribution to proprietary funds	(353,238)	—	—	—
Net Other Financing Sources (Uses)	4,106,701	(8,150,572)	10,757,536	(2,535,977)
Excess of Revenues and Other Sources Over (Under) Expenditures and Other Uses	$2,591,973	(244,297)	1,769,222	326,133
Fund Balance—Beginning of Period	5,379,378	15,668,285	18,501,372	4,158,170
Equity Transfers In (Out)	(7,339)	7,339	—	—
Fund Balance—End of Period	$7,964,012	$15,451,327	$20,270,594	$4,484,303

[SPARTANBURG COUNTY, SOUTH CAROLINA]

Combined Statement of Revenues, Expenditures and Changes in Fund Balances [in part]—All Governmental Fund Types and Expendable Trust Fund, for the Year Ended June 30, 1984

	Governmental Fund Types				Fiduciary Fund Type
	General	Special Revenue	Debt Service	Capital Projects	Real Property Expendable Trust
REVENUES:	$				
		* * *			
EXPENDITURES:					
		* * *			
OTHER FINANCING SOURCES (USES):					
Transfers in	$1,909,734	289,097	1,549,630	28	
Bond proceeds				5,025,000	
Transfers out		(202,797)			
Capital outlay		(119,733)			
Revenue sharing		(1,909,734)			
Total Other Financing Sources (Uses)	$1,909,734	(1,943,167)	1,549,630	5,025,028	
Excess (Deficiency) of Revenues and Other Financing Sources over Expenditures and Other Uses	$ 631,614	459,336	(953,055)	28	
FUND BALANCES, July 1, 1983	1,804,033	687,885	1,459,989	(28)	67,168
Prior Period Adjustment for Delinquent Taxes (Note 8)	(188,854)				
FUND BALANCES, June 30, 1984	$2,246,793	1,147,221	516,934		67,168

[CITY OF TEMPE, ARIZONA]

Combined Statement of Revenues, Expenditures and Change in Fund Balances [in part]—All Governmental Fund Types, Year Ended June 30, 1984

	Governmental Fund Types				
	General	Special Revenue	Debt Service	Capital Projects	Special Assessment
Revenues:	$				
	* * *				
Expenditures:					
	* * *				
Other financing sources (uses):					
Operating transfers in:					
General Fund	—	—	—	1,047,459	—
Special Revenue Funds	$25,615,074	—	1,155,804	6,500,000	—
Capital Projects Funds	—	—	—	116,144	—
Operating transfers out:					
General Fund	—	(25,615,074)	—	—	—
Debt Service Fund	—	(1,155,804)	—	—	—
Capital Projects Funds	(1,047,459)	(6,500,000)	—	(116,144)	—
Enterprise Funds	(20,721)	—	—	—	—
Bonds proceeds, net	—	—	—	—	—
	$24,546,894	(33,270,878)	1,155,804	7,547,459	—
Excess (deficiency) of revenues and other sources over expenditures and other uses	$ 7,986,448	(2,523,490)	155	2,351,764	(136,622)
Fund balances at beginning of year	12,585,583	2,743,200	3,944,359	15,337,201	(5,634,951)
Fund balances at end of year	$20,572,031	219,710	3,944,514	17,688,965	(5,771,573)

[CITY OF WAUKESHA, WISCONSIN]

Combined Statement of Revenues, Expenditures and Changes in Fund Balances [in part]—All Governmental Fund Types, Year Ended December 31, 1983

	General Fund	Special Revenue Funds	Debt Service Fund	Capital Projects Funds
Revenues				
	* * *			
Expenditures				
	* * *			
Other Financing Sources (Uses):				
Proceeds from sale of general obligation bonds or notes	$6,162,938		$ 31,350	
Payment of short-term note payable	(230,000)			
General obligation bonds serviced through Enterprise Fund				
Operating transfers in	751,344	$ 14,878	2,271,744	$5,168,960
Operating transfers out	(7,024,284)	(938,840)		(1,085,471)
Total other financing sources (uses)	(340,002)	(923,962)	2,303,094	4,083,489
Excess (deficiency) of revenues and other sources over (under) expenditures and other uses	1,574,994	22,942	614,375	504,559
Fund Balance—Beginning of year, as originally reported	1,513,278	2,007,718	128,919	5,856,054
Cumulative effect of change in method of accounting for vacation pay—Note B	(253,890)			
January 1, 1983, as restated	1,259,388	2,007,718	128,919	5,856,054
Fund Balance—End of year	$2,834,382	$2,030,660	$ 743,294	$6,360,613

Note H—Operating and Nonoperating Transfers in and out

Operating and nonoperating transfers in and out other funds for the year ended December 31, 1983, were:

Fund	Transfer in	Transfer out
General	$ 751,344	$7,024,284
Special Revenue	14,878	938,840
Debt Service	2,271,744	
Capital Projects	5,168,960	1,085,471
Enterprise:		
Water Utility	93,212[2]	
Parking Utility	300,000[3]	11,199
Prairie Home Cemetery	83,125	14,206
Transit System Utility	459,656[1]	
Trust and Agency	14,206	83,125

[1] Includes $334,344 of contributed capital and $49,175 for charges not requiring current outlay of funds.
[2] Transfer contributed capital.
[3] Transfer of general obligation note proceeds.

[CITY OF FORT LAUDERDALE, FLORIDA]

Combined Statement of Revenues, Expenditures and Changes in Fund Balances [in part]—All Governmental Fund Types and Expendable Trust Funds for the Fiscal Year Ended September 30, 1983

	Governmental Funds					Fiduciary Funds
	General	Special Revenue	Debt Service	Capital Projects	Special Assessment	Expendable Trust
Revenues			* * *			
Expenditures			* * *			
Other Financing Sources (Uses)						
Operating Transfers in	$1,015,952	$ 33,000	$2,996,295	$3,639,401	$118,909	$ —
Operating Transfers out	(5,784,616)	(1,633,564)	—	(774,310)	(148,559)	—
Total Other Financing Sources (Uses)	(4,768,664)	(1,600,564)	2,996,295	2,865,091	(148,559)	—
Excess Revenues and Other Sources Over (Under) Expenditures and Other Uses	(2,947,326)	1,975,573	78,381	1,501,928	159,052	3,886
Fund Balances— Beginning of Period—As Restated	9,311,714	3,395,375	4,033,764	11,854,057	238,448	537,218
Equity Transfers to Other Funds	(141,142)	(78,000)	—	—	—	—
Fund Balances—End of Year	$6,223,246	5,292,948	4,112,145	13,355,985	397,500	541,104

EXHIBIT 6-3. EXCERPTS FROM GOVERNMENTAL REVENUE AND EXPENSE STATEMENTS—OPERATING TRANSFERS IN AND OUT AND INTERFUND TRANSACTIONS

[CITY OF AURORA, COLORADO]

Combined Statement of Revenues, Expenses and Changes in Retained Earnings/Fund Balances [in part]—All Proprietary Fund Types and Pension Trust Funds, for the Year Ended December 31, 1983

	Proprietary Fund Types		Fiduciary Fund Types			Proprietary Fund Types		Fiduciary Fund Types
	Enterprise	Internal Service	Pension Trust			Enterprise	Internal Service	Pension Trust
Operating revenues	* * *				Retained earnings/fund balances—January 1			
Operating expenses	* * *				As previously reported	48,051,230	503,611	14,066,023
Nonoperating revenues (expenses)	* * *				Adjustment for Equity contributed from other funds (note A12)	—	(654,808)	—
Income (loss) before operating transfers and extraordinary item	$ 6,871,200	$(796,522)	$ 6,582,913		As restated	48,051,230	(151,197)	14,066,023
Operating transfers from (to) other funds	(137,388)	885,951	—		Residual equity transfers (to) from other funds	(241,363)	(74,644)	—
Income before extraordinary item	6,733,812	89,429	6,582,913		Retained earnings/fund balance—December 31	$52,824,897	$(136,412)	$20,648,936
Extraordinary item—loss on issuance of refunding bonds	(1,718,782)	—	—					
NET INCOME	5,015,030	89,429	6,582,913					

[CITY OF BROWNSVILLE, TEXAS]

Combined Statement of Revenues, Expenses and Changes in Retained Earnings [in part]—All Proprietary Fund Types, Year Ended September 30, 1983

	Proprietary Fund Types
	Enterprise
Operating revenues	
	* * *
Operating expenses	
	* * *
Nonoperating income (expenses)	
	* * *
Operating transfers	
Transfers from other funds	$ 457,486
Transfers to other funds	(202,981)
Total operating transfers	254,505
NET LOSS	(1,513,998)
Add amortization of contributed capital (note A13)	424,622
NET DECREASE IN RETAINED EARNINGS	(1,089,376)
Retained earnings at beginning of year	24,470,706
Retained earnings at end of year (note H)	$23,381,330

[CITY OF MOBILE, ALABAMA]

All Proprietary Fund Types and Similar Trust Funds, Combined Statement of Revenue, Expenses and Changes in Retained Earnings/Fund Balance [in part]—Year Ended September 30, 1983

	Proprietary Fund Types	Fiduciary Fund Types
	Enterprise and Internal Service	Pension Trust
Revenue and other additions		
	* * *	
Other additions:		
Annuities awarded	$	$ 6,615
Transfers	323,981	358,205
Total other additions	323,981	364,820
Total revenue and other additions	2,377,715	379,287
Expenditures and other deductions		
	* * *	
Other deductions:		
Transfers	550,000	
Total expenditures and other deductions	3,000,996	372,623
Excess of revenue and other additions over (under) expenditures and other deductions	(623,281)	6,664
Retained earnings (deficit)/ fund balance (deficit) at beginning of year	(3,218,461)	—
Decrease in pension member reserves		(6,664)
Retained earnings (deficit)/ fund balance (deficit) at end of year	$(3,841,742)	$ —

[CITY OF OKLAHOMA CITY, OKLAHOMA]

Combined Statement of Revenues, Expenses, and Changes in Retained Earnings/Fund Balances [in part]—Proprietary Fund Types and Pension Trust Funds, Year Ended June 30, 1984

	Proprietary Fund Types		Fiduciary Fund Types
	Enterprise	Internal Service	Pension Trusts
OPERATING REVENUES			
	* * *		
OPERATING EXPENSES			
	* * *		
NON-OPERATING REVENUES (EXPENSES)			
	* * *		
Income (loss) before operating transfers	$(7,539,340)	482,504	7,516,623
Operating transfers in	10,501,644	36,168	—
Operating transfers out	(109,335)	(171,051)	—
Net operating transfers	10,392,309	(134,883)	—
Net income before extraordinary charge	2,852,969	347,621	7,516,623
Extraordinary charge for advance refunding	—	—	—
Net income	$ 2,852,969	347,621	7,516,623

Note D. Interfund Transactions [in part]

1. Interfund Transfers. Interfund transfers for the year ended June 30, 1984, consisted of the following:

		Transfers in/to					
Transfer out/from	General	Special Revenue	Debt Service	Capital Projects	Enterprise	Internal Service	Total Transfers out
Operating:							
General	$ —	12,578,154	235,851	3,316,305	10,323,434	—	$26,453,744
Special Revenue	1,314,047	—	—	9,508,349	—	—	10,822,396
Capital Projects	—	—	5,733	348,076	178,211	36,168	568,188
Special Assessments	—	28	—	—	—	—	28
Enterprise	109,335	—	—	—	—	—	109,335
Internal Service	171,051	—	—	—	—	—	171,051
Total transfers in	$1,594,433	12,578,182	241,584	13,172,730	10,501,645	36,168	$38,124,742
Residual equity:							
Special Revenue	$ —	—	—	—	60,358	—	$ 60,358

[CITY OF PITTSBURGH, PENNSYLVANIA]

Combined Statement of Revenues, Expenses and Changes in Retained Earnings/Fund Balance [in part]—Proprietary Fund Type and Similar Trust Funds, for the Year Ended December 31, 1983

	Proprietary Fund Types	Fiduciary Fund Type	
	Enterprise	Nonexpendable Trust	Pension Trust
Operating revenues:			
	* * *		
Operating expenses:			
	* * *		
Nonoperating revenues and (expenses):			
	* * *		
Income before operating transfer	$ 2,060,025	12,496	4,610,715
Operating transfers to other funds	(1,837,303)	—	—
Net income	222,722	12,496	4,610,715
Retained earnings, beginning of year	42,097,214	221,294	18,214,502
Equity transfers between funds	(156,243)	—	1,645,000
Retained earnings, end of year	$42,163,693	233,790	24,470,217

Note 1.L. [in part]

Enterprise Fund Operating Transfers. An annual operating transfer is made from the Enterprise Fund to the General Fund to assist in servicing the City's general obligation indebtedness.

Chapter 7
Revenues, Expenditures, and Changes in Fund Balances: Governmental Funds

REVENUES AND EXPENDITURES

Principle 10 of NCGA Statement 1 provides guidance for the classification and reporting of revenues and expenditures of governmental funds:

> 10.b. Governmental fund revenues should be classified by fund and source. Expenditures should be classified by fund, function (or program), organization unit, activity, character, and principal classes of objects.

CLASSIFICATION OF REVENUES AND EXPENDITURES

Revenues

As provided by Statement 1, revenues should be classified by fund and source. The funds are those outlined in earlier chapters. Classification by source gives recognition to the activity generating the revenues—taxes, licenses and permits, intergovernmental revenues, charges for services, fines and forfeits, and miscellaneous sources.

In the case of intergovernmental revenues—e.g., grants, entitlements, and shared revenue—the NCGA (in its Statement 2) states that the basis of accounting for such revenues will be determined according to the procedures common to each fund type in which the grant, entitlement, or shared revenues are recorded. For those grants, entitlements, and shared revenues received earlier than the time established by the applicable revenue recognition criteria set forth in Statement 2, those monies should be reported as deferred revenues. The deferred revenues should remain a liability of the governmental unit until such time as those monies meet the revenue recognition criteria.

Also, resources due from grants and entitlements but not received when the appropriate revenue recognition criteria have been met should be reported as a receivable in the financial statement. Where such resources have not met the revenue recognition criteria, any receipts should not be reported on the financial statements, although a disclosure in a footnote to the financial statement would be proper.

Several accounts were used by each governmental unit to record its revenues. The most frequently used descriptors conformed to the NCGA's suggested categories.

Expenditures

In addition to the fund classification, Statement 1 suggests that expenditures be further categorized by function (or program), organization unit, activity, character, and principal classes of objects:

The *function* or *program* classification (e.g., safety, health, or recreation) provides financial data relating to the overall purpose of the expenditure. That is, the functional groupings of cost are related to activities aimed at accomplishing a major governmental or administrative service.

Classification of expenditures by *organization* (e.g., police or fire department) is primarily to account for the varying financial responsibilities of governmental units. This classification corresponds to the organizational structure of the governmental units. Note that the same activity, function, or program is sometimes a part of the work of several organizational units.

Classification of expenditures by *character* identifies them on the basis of the fiscal period benefited. For example, one character classification is *current expenditures*. In this category are those expenditures benefiting the current fiscal period. In contrast, a second classification of the character grouping, *capital outlays*, benefits both the present and future periods. The third grouping of expenditures, *debt service*, benefits prior fiscal periods and the current fiscal period, as well as future fiscal periods. Some governmental units have used a fourth, *intergovernmental*, character classification for situations in which a governmental unit transfer funds to another level of government.

The basic or primary classification of expenditures is by *object class*. This designation of expenditures relates to the types of products or services received. Examples of this category include expenditures for personal services (salaries and wages), supplies, utilities, capital outlays, contractual services, and debt service.

Many classifications were used by the surveyed governmental units to report expenditures. Probably the most common, although not the majority, format of reporting classifications was a combined function–character–object class presentation.

CHANGES IN FUNDS BALANCES: THE ALL-INCLUSIVE CONCEPT

The operating statements for governmental units should reflect all revenues, all expenditures, and all other changes in fund balances. That portion of the statement relating to other changes in fund balances should have a format that provides a useful identification of the changes and a reconciliation between the beginning and ending balances. The components of a surplus or deficit should be clearly identified.

Further, the revenues and expenditures statements should adhere to the all-inclusive concept, thus eliminating the need for a separate statement of the changes in fund balances. In this way all changes in fund balances will be clearly set forth. This approach eliminates questions as to whether unusual changes in the individual fund balance accounts should be separately reported in a statement of changes in the fund balance or shown in the operating statements along with uses and transfers and all other revenues, expenditures, and financing sources.

REPORTING REVENUES AND EXPENDITURES

The NCGA prescribes two combined statements for reporting governmental revenues and expenditures:

a combined statement of revenues, expenditures, and changes in fund balances—all governmental fund types and expendable trust funds; and

a combined statement of budgeted and actual revenues, expenditures, and changes in fund balances for general and special revenue fund types.

These two combined operating statements are sufficient for general purpose financial statements. However, the comprehensive annual financial report of a governmental unit also includes combining statements and individual fund statements of revenues and expenditures, as well as schedules to demonstrate compliance with finance-related legal provisions.

For complete disclosure, the combined statement of revenues and expenditures for all governmental fund types typically comprises the following sections:

revenues,

expenditures,

other financing sources and uses,

the fund balance at the beginning of the year, and

the fund balance at the end of the year

Revenues should be classified by the various funds and sources from which they are derived. Expenditures should also be displayed by fund and should also reflect a higher-level classification of expenditures, such as by function or program. Many of the surveyed governmental units, however, used a more detailed classification, such as by the character and object class of expenditures.

Table 7-1 summarizes several characteristics of the reporting observed with respect to revenues, expenditures, and other financing sources as reported on this revenue statement.

Exhibits 7-1 to 7-3 contain several examples of financial statements showing revenues, expenditures, and changes in fund balances.

EXHIBITS AND TABLES FOR CHAPTER 7

Table 7-1. Format Observations Relating to the Combined Statement of Revenues, Expenditures, and Changes in Fund Balances for All Governmental Fund Types and Expendable Trust Funds

Exhibit 7-1. Examples of Reporting by Governmental Units of Revenues, Expenditures, Changes in Fund Balances

Exhibit 7-2. Examples of Reporting by Governmental Units of Revenues, Expenditures, and Changes in Fund Balances—Budget (GAAP Basis) and Actual

Exhibit 7-3. Examples of Reporting by Governmental Units of Revenues, Expenditures, and Changes in Fund Balances—Budget and Actual (Budgetary Basis)

TABLE 7-1. FORMAT OBSERVATIONS RELATING TO THE COMBINED STATEMENT OF REVENUES, EXPENDITURES, AND CHANGES IN FUND BALANCES FOR ALL GOVERNMENTAL FUND TYPES AND EXPENDABLE TRUST FUNDS

	Instances Observed (%)
Governmental units whose general-purpose financial statement included a combined statement of revenues, expenditures, and changes in fund balances	85
Governmental fund types identified:*	
General fund	98
Special revenue funds	95
Capital projects funds	87
Debt service funds	81
Special assessment funds	53
Expendable trust funds	50
Memorandum totals:*	92
Current and prior year	65
Current year only	35
Expenditures,* grouped by	
program/function	95
character (current, capital, debt)	64
organization/department	38
Other financing sources (uses) separately identified*	82

*Observations for the units having this statement.

EXHIBIT 7-1. EXAMPLES OF REPORTING BY GOVERNMENTAL UNITS OF REVENUES, EXPENDITURES, AND CHANGES IN FUND BALANCES

[CITY OF FORT WORTH, TEXAS]

Combined Statement of Revenues, Expenditures and Changes in Fund Balances—All Governmental Fund Types and Expendable Trust Funds, December 31, 1983

	Governmental Fund Types					Fiduciary Fund Type	Total (Memorandum Only)	
	General	Special Revenue	Debt Service	Capital Projects	Special Assessments	Expendable Trust	1983	1982
Revenues:								
General Property Taxes	$ 59,808,153	$ 0	$ 0	$ 0	$ 0	$ 0	$ 59,808,153	$52,692,395
Other Local Taxes	31,220,257	0	0	0	0	0	31,220,257	29,541,360
Special Assessments	0	0	0	0	2,370,358	0	2,370,358	1,567,560
Charges for Services	7,896,249	0	0	0		0	7,896,249	13,349,332
Licenses and Permits	14,896,907	0	0	0		0	14,896,907	13,013,297
Revenue Sharing	6,043,347	0	0	0	0	0	6,043,347	5,893,841
Fines and Forfeitures	5,685,843	0	0	0	0	0	5,685,843	4,412,196
Revenue from the Use of Money and Property	6,697,771	0	0	419,103	278,217	590,864	7,985,955	6,097,672
Intergovernmental	1,892,252	24,617,368	0	0	0	0	26,509,620	25,498,196
Other	314,284	0	0	0	6,312	6,312	320,596	1,357,085
Contributions	0	0	0	3,756,895	0	9,966,962	13,723,857	9,606,575
Total Revenues	$134,455,063	$24,617,368	$ 0	$ 4,175,998	$ 2,648,575	$10,564,138	$176,461,142	$163,029,509
Expenditures:								
General Administration	$ 9,236,689	$ 1,048,164	$ 0	$ 0	$ 27,226	$ 8,300,009	$ 18,612,088	$ 17,753,323
Public Safety	56,169,087	435,334	0	0	0	0	56,604,421	51,988,392
Public Works	17,509,305	664,656	0	0	0	0	18,173,961	25,116,598
Park and Recreation	8,436,265	23,311	0	0	0	50,748	8,510,324	8,055,443

Public Libraries	3,633,180	410,870	0	0	0	0	4,044,050	3,778,025
Public Health	3,000,630	469,636	0	0	0	0	3,470,266	3,265,864
Public Events and Facilities	3,050,112	0	0	0	0	0	3,050,112	2,673,524
Other	2,394,165	1,800	0	0	0	70,534	2,466,499	2,693,740
Planning	2,343,749	31,210	0	0	0	0	2,374,959	2,493,660
Finance	2,527,014	0	0	0	0	0	2,527,014	2,358,980
Housing and Human Services	1,356,556	15,410,395	0	0	0	0	16,766,951	16,254,967
Debt Service								
Principal Retirement	0	0	7,028,000	0	0	0	7,028,000	7,191,000
Interest and Service Charges	0	0	15,249,095	0	0	0	15,249,095	10,920,693
Capital Outlay	0	$ 7,611,592	0	0	$47,043,289	55,611	54,710,492	33,905,372
Total Expenditures	$109,656,752	$26,106,968	$22,277,095	$ 27,226	$47,043,289	$ 8,476,902	$213,588,232	$188,449,581
Excess of Revenues Over (Under) Expenditures	24,798,311	(1,489,600)	(22,277,095)	2,621,349	(42,867,291)	2,087,236	(37,127,090)	(25,420,072)
Other Financing Sources (Uses):								
Operating Transfers In	580,484	1,730,413	20,403,774	0	2,615,178	85,000	25,414,849	20,416,293
Operating Transfers Out	(23,142,761)	(416,436)	0	(882,988)	(3,224,222)	(13,372)	(27,679,779)	(22,609,556)
Bond Sales	0	0	0	0	40,000,000	0	40,000,000	40,000,000
Total Other Financing Sources (Uses):	(22,562,277)	1,313,977	20,403,774	(882,988)	39,390,956	71,628	37,735,070	37,806,737
Excess of Revenues and Other Sources Over (Under) Expenditures and Other Uses	2,236,034	(175,623)	(1,873,321)	1,738,361	(3,476,335)	2,158,864	607,980	12,386,665
Fund Balances (Deficit), Beginning of Year	7,727,154	75,005	11,505,176	(6,393,916)	30,125,799	1,534,588	44,573,806	36,589,498
Equity Transfer in (out)	(363,700)	0	0	0	0	115,232	(248,468)	(4,402,357)
Fund Balances (Deficits), Ending of Year	$ 9,599,488	$ (100,618)	$ 9,631,855	$(4,655,555)	$26,649,464	$ 3,808,684	$ 44,933,318	$ 44,573,806

[CITY OF LUBBOCK, TEXAS]

Combined Statement of Revenues, Expenditures and Changes in Fund Balances—All Governmental Fund Types and Expendable Trust Funds, September 30, 1983

	Governmental Fund Types					Fiduciary Fund Type	Total (Memorandum Only)	
	General	Special Revenue	Debt Service	Capital Projects	Special Assessments	Expendable Trust	1983	1982
Revenues:								
Taxes and special assessments (note 4)	$25,219,089	$ 1,091,977	$ 9,009,898	$ —	$ 204,339	$ —	$35,525,303	$33,367,936
Licenses and permits	864,448	—	—	—	—	—	864,448	555,496
Intergovernmental (notes 5 and 15)	1,015,231	2,836,765	—	3,491,998	—	5,058,176	12,402,170	9,956,740
Charges for services	1,830,953	270,143	—	—	—	—	2,101,096	2,026,009
Fines and forfeits	1,236,545	—	—	—	—	—	1,236,545	1,292,728
Contributions	—	75,000	—	726,885	—	—	801,885	135,933
Miscellaneous	3,408,194	143,958	496,961	153,065	—	670,479	4,872,657	4,018,524
Total revenue	$33,574,460	$ 4,417,843	$ 9,506,859	$ 4,371,948	$ 204,339	$5,728,655	$57,804,104	$51,353,366
Expenditures:								
General government	$ 2,188,747	$ 329,820	$	$	$	$5,776,415	$ 8,294,982	$ 7,340,717
Financial services	1,379,512	30,395	—	—	—	—	1,409,907	1,532,364
Management services	1,584,996	127,786	—	—	—	—	1,712,782	1,987,008
Management information	—	—	—	—	—	—	—	296,086
Development services	5,127,150	(162,231)	—	—	—	—	4,964,919	5,100,184
Public safety and services	28,673,646	191,225	—	—	—	—	28,864,871	28,199,162
Non-departmental	96,645	—	—	—	—	—	95,645	195,835

Public utilities	591,922	68,230	—	—	—	—	68,230	—
Capital projects	3,031,566	9,363,342	—	129,862	9,233,480	—	—	—
Civic Lubbock, Inc.	169,194	251,176	—	—	—	—	251,176	—
Lubbock Board of City Development	777,873	845,481	—	—	—	—	845,481	—
Debt service:								
Principal retirement	4,760,000	5,182,997	—	—	—	5,182,997	—	—
Interest and fiscal charges	4,176,088	4,979,353	—	—	—	4,979,353	—	—
Total expenditures	$58,157,999	$66,033,685	$5,776,415	$ 129,862	$ 9,233,480	$10,162,350	$ 1,681,882	$39,049,696
Excess (deficiency) of revenues over expenditures	$(6,804,633)	$(8,229,581)	$ (47,760)	$ 74,477	$(4,861,532)	$ (655,491)	$ 2,735,961	$(5,475,236)
Other financing sources (uses):								
Proceeds of general obligation bonds	$ 9,048,000	$ 2,025,000	$ —	$ —	$ 2,025,000	$ —	$ —	$ —
Proceeds of note	—	1,751,000	—	—	1,751,000	—	—	—
Operating transfers in	9,910,528	9,359,968	—	—	—	2,004,000	—	7,625,696
Operating transfers out	(2,820,804)	(7,335,045)	—	—	(269,728)	—	(6,107,907)	(1,227,138)
Total other financing sources (uses)	$16,137,724	$ 5,800,923	$ —	$ —	$ 3,506,272	$ 2,004,000	$(6,107,907)	$ 6,398,558
Excess (deficiency) of revenues and other financing sources over expenditures and other uses	$ 9,333,091	$ (2,428,658)	$ (47,760)	$ 74,477	$ (1,355,260)	$ 1,348,509	$(3,371,946)	$ 923,322
Fund balances at beginning of year	24,178,025	27,863,218	77,571	1,169,202	14,522,628	1,734,496	4,326,028	6,033,293
Fund balance at end of year	$33,511,116	$25,434,560	$ 29,811	$1,243,679	$13,167,368	$ 3,083,005	$ 954,082	$ 6,956,615

[COUNTY OF MONROE, STATE OF NEW YORK]

Combined Statement of Revenues, Expenditures and Changes in Fund Balances—All Governmental Fund Types and Expendable Trust Funds, December 31, 1983 [in thousands]

| | Governmental Fund Types | | | | | Fiduciary | Totals (Memorandum Only) |
	General	Special Revenue	Debt Service	Capital Projects	Special Assessment	Trust and Agency	
Fund Equity—January 1, 1983:							
Reserved for Encumbrances	$ 1,766	$ 359	$ —	$ 3,520	$ 1,123	$ —	$ 6,768
Reserved for Bonded Debt	—	—	5,313	—	—	—	5,313
Reserved for Self-Insurance	—	—	—	—	—	443	443
Fund Balance:							
Appropriated for Subsequent Year's Expenditures	(7,000)	—	—	3,002	1,132	—	(2,866)
Undesignated	218	271	—	—	13	—	502
Total Fund Equity—January 1, 1983	(5,016)	630	5,313	6,522	2,268	443	10,160
Revenues:							
Taxes	157,097	—	—	—	—	—	157,097
Special Assessment Levied	—	—	—	—	15,275	—	15,275
Intergovernmental Revenues	132,597	10,386	—	51,352	5,910	—	200,245
Charges for Services	18,426	1,537	—	—	10,328	—	30,291
Fines and Forfeits	687	—	—	—	—	—	687
Miscellaneous Revenues	16,419	311	519	—	15,630	749	33,628
Total Revenues	325,226	12,234	519	51,352	47,143	749	437,223
Total Revenues and Fund Equity	320,210	12,864	5,832	57,874	49,411	1,192	447,383
Expenditures:							
General Government	28,873	—	—	1,434	—	550	30,857
Public Safety	28,773	—	—	1,284	—	—	30,057
Transportation	1,297	12,511	—	12,083	32,779	—	58,057
Health	22,588	—	—	—	—	—	22,588
Economic Assistance & Opportunity	165,554	—	—	—	—	—	165,554
Culture and Recreation	9,384	5,100	—	2,729	—	—	17,213
Education	16,984	—	—	523	—	—	17,507
Home and Community Services	11,873	1,842	—	56,221	—	—	69,936
Debt Service:							
Principal Retirement	6,008	6,717	—	—	3,085	—	15,810
Interest and Fiscal Charges	6,941	4,377	—	—	8,610	—	19,928
Total Expenditures	$298,275	30,547	—	74,274	44,474	550	448,120
Other Financing Sources (Uses):							
Proceeds of General Obligation Notes and Bonds	—	—	—	79,507	—	—	79,507
Operating Transfers in	5,552	23,096	—	3,474	411	—	32,533
Operating Transfers out	(24,449)	(4,780)	(593)	(318)	(2,610)	—	(32,750)
Total Other Financing Sources (Uses)	(18,897)	18,316	(593)	82,663	(2,199)	—	79,290
Total Fund Equity December 31, 1983	$ 3,038	$ 633	$5,239	$66,263	$ 2,738	$ 642	$ 78,553
Fund Equity—December 31, 1983:							
Reserved for Encumbrances	$ 1,514	288	—	5,202	858	—	7,862
Reserved for Debt Service	—	—	5,239	—	—	—	5,239
Reserved for Self-Insurance	—	—	—	—	—	642	642
Fund Balance:							
Appropriated	—	—	—	61,061	1,184	—	62,245
Undesignated	1,524	345	—	—	696	—	2,565
Total Fund Equity December 31, 1983	$ 3,038	$ 633	$5,239	$66,263	$ 2,738	$ 642	$ 78,553

[RICHMOND COUNTY, GEORGIA]

Combined Statement of Revenues, Expenditures, and Changes in Fund Balances—All Governmental Fund Types, December 31, 1983

	General	Special Revenue	Debt Service	Capital Projects	Special Assessments	Totals (Memorandum Only) 1983	1982
REVENUES							
Real and personal property taxes	$ 4,124,062	$ 2,381,798	$1,232,554	$	$	$ 7,738,414	$ 7,021,040
Other taxes	2,246,460	659,909			1,005,075	3,911,444	3,061,588
Licenses and permits	741,422					741,422	767,603
Use of money and property	495,338					495,338	476,912
Charges for services	766,060				475,405	1,241,465	1,323,468
Fines and fees	2,485,721					2,485,721	1,829,532
From other agencies	104,247					104,247	235,591
Other revenue and cost:							
Reimbursement	866,987		26,029			893,016	622,669
Federal appropriations		2,619,950				2,619,950	2,609,694
Sales taxes		13,140,689				13,140,689	11,895,051
Interest		211,087	39,500	1,154,311	15,900	1,420,798	803,699
Other		71,715		70,380		142,095	7,915
Rental				12,757		12,757	11,467
1981 HUD Grant				395,000		395,000	595,000
1982 HUD Grant				151,900		151,900	
1983 HUD Grant				21,689		21,689	
General obligation bonds							8,000,000
TOTAL REVENUES	11,830,297	19,085,148	1,298,083	1,806,037	1,496,380	35,515,945	39,261,229
EXPENDITURES:							
Administration	285,634	33,725				319,359	271,894
Personnel	89,605					89,605	84,888
Finance and tax administration	3,494,689	141,076				3,635,765	3,159,703
Judicial	2,500,166	31,248				2,531,414	2,410,480
Public safety	6,334,771	2,931,231				9,266,004	8,344,580
Traffic, road, and drainage	2,105,319	746,139			441,825	3,293,283	3,158,954
Health and welfare	4,783,340	77,570				4,860,910	4,241,171
Recreation and education	2,653,555	119,531				2,773,086	2,557,529
Miscellaneous appropriation and other	676,907	93,765			1,006,240	1,776,912	2,071,685
Bonds principal			529,000			529,000	517,000
Bond interest			724,372			724,372	498,990
Paying agents fee			2,717			2,717	2,852
Law enforcement facility				3,106,127	3,106,127		
1976 Local Public Work HUD Grant				802,569		802,569	387,723
Columbia Nitrogen Overpass				223,115		223,115	707,959
TOTAL EXPENDITURES	22,923,986	4,174,285	1,256,089	4,131,811	1,448,065	33,934,238	28,415,408
EXCESS (DEFICIENCY) OF REVENUES OVER EXPENDITURES	(11,093,689)	14,910,863	41,994	(2,325,774)	48,315	1,581,709	10,845,821
OTHER FINANCING SOURCES (USES)							
Operating transfers in	12,285,193	26,536		775,000		13,086,729	16,941,942
Operating transfers out		(13,011,993)			(53,636)	(13,065,629)	(16,927,263)
TOTAL OTHER FINANCING SOURCES (USES)	12,285,193	(12,985,457)		775,000	(53,636)	21,100	14,679
EXCESS (DEFICIENCY) OF REVENUES OVER EXPENDITURES AND OTHER SOURCES	1,191,504	1,925,406	41,994	(1,550,774)	(5,321)	1,602,809	10,860,500
FUND BALANCE AT BEGINNING OF YEAR	2,825,488	3,948,589	40,363	14,037,679	30,680	20,882,799	10,022,299
FUND BALANCE AT END OF YEAR	$ 4,016,992	$ 5,873,995	$ 82,357	$12,486,905	$ 25,359	$ 22,485,608	$ 20,882,799

[COUNTY OF VOLUSIA, FLORIDA]

Combined Statement of Revenues, Expenditures and Changes in Fund Balances, All Governmental Fund Types, for the Year Ended September 30, 1983

	General	Special Revenue	Debt Service	Capital Projects	Special Assessments	Totals (Memorandum Only) 1983	1982
REVENUES							
Taxes	$20,314,380	$12,638,625	$ —	$ —	$ —	$32,953,005	$32,088,063
Licenses and Permits	—	983,351	—	—	—	983,351	745,253
Intergovernmental Revenues	451,652	22,253,803	92,409	229,906	—	23,027,770	15,251,060
Charges for Services	2,131,703	2,264,981	—	—	—	4,396,684	3,601,779
Fines and Forfeitures	896,497	769,122	—	—	—	1,665,619	1,468,622
Miscellaneous Revenues	1,919,839	1,052,603	205,513	1,302,268	40,442	4,520,665	3,482,831
Special Assessments Levied	—	—	—	—	119,094	119,094	119,734
TOTAL REVENUES	$25,714,071	$39,962,485	$ 297,922	$ 1,532,174	$159,536	$67,666,188	$56,757,342
EXPENDITURES							
Current:							
General Government	$ 8,009,598	$ 2,441,434	$ —	$ 31,449	$100,000	$10,582,481	$10,466,169
Public Safety	12,870,922	6,642,050	—	10,834	—	19,523,806	17,260,882
Physical Environment	308,156	598,631	—	—	—	906,787	741,019
Transportation	—	6,155,298	—	15,595	19,527	6,190,420	5,764,871
Economic Environment	349,026	4,307,132	—	—	—	4,656,158	3,908,964
Human Services	2,172,142	2,329,040	—	12,599	—	4,513,781	4,423,518
Culture/Recreation	590,452	1,988,213	—	12,085	—	2,590,750	3,845,116
Capital Outlay	229,209	5,190,851	—	3,337,172	—	8,757,232	5,893,011
Debt Service:							
Principal Retirement	—	46,659	640,000	—	—	686,659	642,030
Interest and Fiscal Charges	—	3,265	61,477	—	—	64,742	145,660
TOTAL EXPENDITURES	$24,529,505	$29,702,573	$ 701,477	$ 3,419,734	$119,527	$58,472,816	$53,091,240
EXCESS OF REVENUES OVER (UNDER) EXPENDITURES	$ 1,184,566	$10,259,912	$ (403,555)	$(1,887,560)	$ 40,009	$ 9,193,372	$ 3,666,102
OTHER FINANCING SOURCES (USES)							
Proceeds from Notes Payable (Note 8)	$ —	$ 7,829	$ —	$ —	$ —	$ 7,829	$ 95,557
Proceeds from Bond Sale	—	—	—	49,633,956	—	49,633,956	—
Operating Transfers in	1,354,037	2,721,070	6,623,460	4,764,764	—	15,463,331	5,645,933
Operating Transfers out	(1,618,131)	(8,769,686)	—	(5,446,576)	—	(15,834,393)	(6,492,200)
TOTAL OTHER FINANCING SOURCES (USES)	$ (264,094)	$(6,040,787)	$6,623,460	$48,952,144	$ —	$49,270,723	$ (750,710)
EXCESS OF REVENUES AND OTHER SOURCES OVER (UNDER) EXPENDITURES AND OTHER USES	$ 920,472	$ 4,219,125	$6,219,905	$47,064,584	$ 40,009	$58,464,095	$ 2,915,392
FUND BALANCES AT BEGINNING OF YEAR (Note 23)	2,302,993	7,943,901	1,266,802	2,517,085	653,099	14,683,880	11,768,488
Residual Equity Transfers in (out) (Note 19)	(161,289)	162,289	—	—	—	—	—
FUND BALANCES AT END OF YEAR	$ 3,062,176	$12,324,315	$7,486,707	$49,581,669	$693,108	$73,147,975	$14,683,880

[CITY OF WESTMINSTER, COLORADO]

Combined Statement of Revenues, Expenditures and Changes in Fund Balances, All Governmental Fund Types and Expendable Trust Funds, Year Ended December 31, 1983

	Governmental Fund Types					Fiduciary Fund Type	Totals (Memorandum Only)	
	General	Special Revenue	Debt Service	Capital Projects	Special Assessments	Expendable Trust	December 31, 1983	December 31, 1982
Revenues:								
Taxes	$13,103,659	$ 124,521	$ —	$ —	$ —	$ —	$13,228,180	$11,782,077
Assessments	—	—	—	—	69,757	—	69,757	69,758
Licenses and permits	873,620	—	—	—	—	—	873,620	483,017
Intergovernmental	1,525,499	1,266,037	—	251,923	—	—	3,043,459	1,919,456
Recreation	677,103	—	—	—	—	—	677,103	744,453
Rental and service fees	—	522,256	—	—	—	—	522,256	472,738
Fines and forfeits	354,253	—	—	—	—	—	354,253	282,042
Fees and surcharges	436,113	3,200	—	—	—	—	439,313	
Interest	977,132	31,427	24,536	26,656	15,144	5,847	1,080,742	1,034,511
Contributions	422,000	—	—	—	—	107,331	529,331	—
Miscellaneous	366,518	661	—	—	—	—	367,179	269,661
Total revenues	18,735,897	1,948,102	24,536	278,579	84,901	113,178	21,185,193	17,057,693
Expenditures:								
City Council	70,546	—	—	—	—	—	70,546	54,582
City Attorney	57,377	—	—	—	—	—	57,377	—
City Manager's Office	545,087	—	—	—	—	—	545,087	451,993
Non-departmental	2,279,245	76,312	—	—	—	52,881	2,408,438	3,085,927
Finance	253,940	—	—	—	—	—	253,940	234,186
Police	3,581,794	120,916	—	—	—	—	3,702,710	2,937,511
Fire	1,607,058	51,422	—	—	—	—	1,658,480	1,350,860
Community development	1,420,099	9,529	—	—	—	—	1,429,628	1,241,996
Public works	1,812,922	168,187	—	—	—	—	1,981,109	2,501,446
Parks & recreation	2,054,399	33,791	—	—	—	—	2,088,190	1,792,624
Library	344,398	95,762	—	—	—	—	440,160	336,223
Housing	—	232,774	—	—	—	—	232,774	162,988
Capital construction	—	—	—	5,822,036	—	—	5,822,036	2,930,888
Plan payments	—	—	—	—	—	328,823	328,823	—
Debt service	—	494,301	632,560	—	34,831	—	1,161,692	947,398
Amortization	—	34,482	—	—	—	—	34,482	34,482
Total expenditures	14,026,865	1,317,476	632,560	5,822,036	34,831	381,704	22,215,472	18,073,104
Revenues over (under) expenditures	4,709,032	630,626	(608,024)	(5,543,457)	50,070	(268,526)	(1,030,279)	(1,015,411)
Other financing sources (uses):								
Proceeds from bonds	—	—	—	815,000	—	—	815,000	2,800,000
Lease purchase agreement	—	—	—	—	—	—	—	5,870
Operating transfers out	(3,766,866)	—	—	—	—	—	(3,766,866)	(3,437,452)
Operating transfers in	719,442	—	724,512	2,594,566	—	344,917	4,383,437	4,196,767
Total other sources (uses)	(3,047,424)	—	724,512	3,409,566	—	344,917	1,431,571	3,565,185
Revenue and other sources over (under) expenditures and other uses	1,661,608	630,626	116,488	(2,133,891)	50,070	76,391	401,292	2,549,774
Fund balance, beginning	3,155,531	588,229	—	7,678,701	(455,563)	—	10,966,898	8,985,425
Prior period adjustment	—	—	—	—	—	—	—	(568,301)
Fund balance, adjusted beginning	3,155,531	588,229	—	7,678,701	(455,563)	—	10,966,898	8,417,124
Fund balance, ending	$ 4,817,139	$1,218,855	$116,488	$5,544,810	$(405,493)	$ 76,391	$11,368,190	$10,966,898

[COUNTY OF LANCASTER, PENNSYLVANIA]

Combined Statement of Revenues, Expenditures and Changes in Fund Balances—All Governmental Fund Types, Year Ended December 31, 1983

	Governmental Fund Types				(Memorandum Only)
	General	Special Revenue	Capital Projects	Debt Service	1983
Revenues					
Real estate taxes (Note 3)	$ 8,142,731	$	$	$	$ 8,142,731
Personal property taxes	1,755,249				1,755,249
Intergovernmental revenues (Note 10)	1,385,204	16,591,496			17,976,700
Departmental revenues	2,149,904	381,023			2,530,927
Fines and costs	1,101,162				1,101,162
Interest revenue	824,419	244,880		126,811	1,196,110
Indirect revenue	904,544				904,544
County support		2,141,982			2,141,982
Other revenue	136,304	71,048			207,352
Total revenue	16,399,517	19,430,429		126,811	35,956,757
Expenditures					
Current					
General government	4,958,218	178,092	3,497		5,139,807
Public safety	1,254,562	106,716			1,361,278
Roads and bridges	4,066	751,762			755,828
Health, education and welfare					
Employment and training	28,680	2,447,457			2,476,137
County nursing home	526,921				526,921
MH/MR, drug and alcohol	333,166	6,560,346			6,893,512
Office of aging	112,494	2,315,024			2,427,518
Children and youth	1,574,376	2,729,729	449,886		4,753,991
Other	522,982	103,000			625,982
Judicial	5,370,311	871,738			6,242,049
Corrections	2,801,312	2,966,142			5,767,454
Cultural and recreation	578,739	529,500			1,108,239
Other programs supported	98,424	287,362			385,786
Total current expenditures	18,164,251	19,846,868	453,383		38,464,502
Debt service					
Principal retirement				2,985,139	2,985,139
Interest and fiscal charges (Note 5)				937,044	937,044
Total expenditures	18,164,251	19,846,868	453,383	3,922,183	42,396,685
Excess of revenues over (under) expenditures	(1,764,734)	(416,439)	(453,383)	(3,795,372)	(6,429,928)
Other financing sources (uses)					
Transfer in	158,341	71,155	453,383	1,572,489	2,255,368
Transfer out	(2,097,027)	(158,341)			(2,255,368)
Total other financial sources (uses)	(1,938,686)	(87,186)	453,383	1,572,489	
Excess of revenues and other sources over (under) expenditures and other uses	(3,703,420)	(503,625)		(2,222,883)	(6,429,928)
Fund balances at beginning of year	7,892,940	1,571,779		2,222,883	11,687,602
Prior period adjustments					
Fund balances transferred to establish separate funds	(615,393)	615,393			
Funding of prior years accrued vacation and sick pay for Enterprise Fund	(217,488)				(217,488)
Fund balances at beginning of year, as restated	7,060,059	2,187,172		2,222,883	11,470,114
Fund balances at end of year	$ 3,356,639	$ 1,683,547	$	$	$ 5,040,186

[CITY OF TALLAHASSEE, FLORIDA]

Combined Statement of Revenues, Expenditures, and Changes in Fund Balances, All Governmental Fund Types and Expendable Trust Funds, for the Fiscal Year Ended September 30, 1983

| | Governmental Fund Types | | | | | Fiduciary Fund Type | Totals (Memorandum Only) | |
	General	Special Revenue	Debt Service	Capital Projects	Special Assessment	Expendable Trust	September 30, 1983	September 30, 1982
Fund Balances—								
October 1	$ 1,929,200	$18,888,700	$ 8,238,900	$19,711,800	$507,700	$231,600	$49,507,900	$50,674,100
Revenues:								
Taxes	8,595,100	—	—	—	—	52,500	8,647,600	8,259,200
Licenses and permits	1,719,800	—	—	—	—	—	1,719,800	1,050,300
Intergovernmental revenues	8,298,900	—	—	3,223,000	—	44,300	11,566,200	7,531,400
Charges for services	3,540,200	612,200	—	—	—	139,600	4,292,000	3,515,600
Fines and forfeits	389,500	—	—	—	—	—	389,500	274,200
Interest earned	665,800	2,860,200	350,700	2,684,500	233,900	41,300	6,836,400	8,193,500
Miscellaneous revenues	129,900	12,300	46,300	41,300	300	—	230,100	226,200
Total Revenues	23,339,200	3,484,700	397,000	5,948,800	234,200	277,700	33,681,600	29,050,400
Expenditures:								
Current:								
General government	5,274,600	—	—	1,444,400	94,700	208,600	7,022,300	7,054,200
Public safety	11,589,300	—	—	—	—	—	11,589,300	10,803,700
Highways and streets	4,362,200	—	—	1,762,400	355,200	—	6,443,800	3,186,000
Sanitation	4,043,000	—	—	—	—	—	4,043,000	3,314,400
Health	247,200	—	—	15,100	—	—	262,300	1,060,200
Welfare	799,900	—	—	1,024,300	—	—	1,824,200	1,135,800
Culture and recreation	3,686,700	—	—	—	—	—	3,686,700	3,205,200
Education	—	—	—	86,600	—	—	86,600	104,100
Capital outlay	—	18,800	—	7,178,100	—	—	7,196,900	11,911,000
Debt service:								
Principal retirement	—	—	20,000,000	—	—	—	20,000,000	—
Interest and fiscal charges	—	—	3,320,400	—	—	—	3,320,400	4,195,600
Total Expenditures	29,966,900	18,800	23,320,400	11,510,900	449,900	208,600	65,475,500	45,970,200
Excess of Revenues over (under) Expenditures	(6,627,700)	3,465,900	(22,923,400)	(5,562,100)	(215,700)	69,100	(31,793,900)	(16,919,800)
Other Financing Sources (Uses):								
Proceeds from sale of property	—	—	—	40,000	—	25,000	65,000	150,000
Proceeds from capital bonds	—	—	—	24,613,400	—	—	24,613,400	—
Operating transfers in	21,754,800	2,000,000	27,539,500	8,278,700	—	—	59,573,000	29,889,400
Operating transfers out	(14,812,300)	(2,143,300)	—	(25,086,900)	—	(76,200)	(42,118,700)	(14,285,800)
Total Other Financing Sources (Uses)	6,942,500	(143,300)	27,539,500	7,845,200	—	(51,200)	42,132,700	15,753,600
Excess of Revenues and Other Sources over (under) Expenditures and Other Uses	314,800	3,322,600	4,616,100	2,283,100	(215,700)	17,900	10,338,800	(1,166,200)
Fund Balances—								
September 30	$ 2,244,400	$22,211,300	$12,855,000	$21,994,900	$292,000	$249,500	$59,846,700	$49,507,900

[Statements included for illustrative purposes. For brevity the footnotes accompanying the statements have not been included.]

EXHIBIT 7-2. EXAMPLES OF REPORTING BY GOVERNMENTAL UNITS OF REVENUES, EXPENDITURES, AND CHANGES IN FUND BALANCES—BUDGET (GAAP BASIS) AND ACTUAL

[CITY OF WESTMINSTER, COLORADO]

Combined Statement of Revenues, Expenditures, and Changes in Fund Balances—Budget (GAAP Basis) and Actual—General, Special Revenue, Debt Service, and Capital Project Fund Types, Year Ended December 31, 1983

	General Fund			Special Revenue Funds			Debt Service Fund			Capital Project Funds		
	Final Budget	Actual	Variance—Favorable (Unfavorable)	Final Budget	Actual	Variance—Favorable (Unfavorable)	Final Budget	Actual	Variance—Favorable (Unfavorable)	Final Budget	Actual	Variance—Favorable (Unfavorable)
Revenues:												
Taxes	$12,072,000	$13,103,659	$1,031,659	$112,619	$124,521	$11,902	$ —	$ —	$ —	$ —	$ —	$ —
Licenses and permits	341,000	873,620	532,620	—	—	—	—	—	—	—	—	—
Intergovernmental	1,270,936	1,525,499	254,563	685,600	1,266,037	580,437	—	—	—	450,000	251,923	(198,077)
Recreation	778,950	677,103	(101,847)	—	—	—	—	—	—	—	—	—
Rental and service fees	—	—	—	502,764	522,256	19,492	—	—	—	—	—	—
Fines and forfeits	265,500	354,253	88,753	—	—	—	—	—	—	—	—	—
Fees and surcharges	118,000	436,113	318,113	500	3,200	2,700	—	—	—	—	—	—
Interest	801,589	977,132	175,543	25,200	31,427	6,227	—	24,536	24,536	—	26,656	26,656
Contributions	250,000	422,000	172,000	—	—	—	—	—	—	—	—	—
Miscellaneous	129,500	366,518	237,018	—	661	661	—	—	—	—	—	—
Total revenues	16,027,475	18,735,897	2,708,422	1,326,683	1,948,102	621,419	—	24,536	24,536	450,000	278,579	(171,421)
Expenditures:												
City Council	75,955	70,546	5,409	—	—	—	—	—	—	—	—	—
City Attorney	67,803	57,377	10,426	—	—	—	—	—	—	—	—	—

	General Fund (Budget)	General Fund (Actual)	General Fund (Variance)	Special Revenue (Budget)	Special Revenue (Actual)	Special Revenue (Variance)	Debt Service (Budget)	Debt Service (Actual)	Debt Service (Variance)	Capital Projects (Budget)	Capital Projects (Actual)	Capital Projects (Variance)
City Manager's Office	541,281	545,087	(3,806)	—	—	—	—	—	—	—	—	—
Non-departmental	2,340,257	2,279,245	61,012	92,274	76,312	15,962	—	—	—	—	—	—
Finance	254,197	253,940	257	—	—	—	—	—	—	—	—	—
Police	3,614,853	3,581,794	33,059	124,711	120,916	3,795	—	—	—	—	—	—
Fire	1,664,869	1,607,058	57,811	54,671	51,422	3,249	—	—	—	—	—	—
Community development	1,486,300	1,420,099	66,201	11,959	9,529	2,430	—	—	—	—	—	—
Public works	1,929,061	1,812,922	116,139	168,383	168,187	196	—	—	—	—	—	—
Parks and recreation	2,235,335	2,054,399	180,936	36,776	33,791	2,985	—	—	—	—	—	—
Library	344,812	344,398	414	90,000	95,762	(5,762)	—	—	—	—	—	—
Housing	—	—	—	236,542	232,774	3,768	—	—	—	—	—	—
Capital construction	—	—	—	494,405	494,301	104	—	—	—	11,503,513	5,822,036	5,681,477
Debt service	—	—	—	—	—	—	724,512	632,560	91,952	—	—	—
Amortization	—	—	—	34,500	34,482	18	—	—	—	—	—	—
Total expenditures	14,554,723	14,026,865	527,858	1,344,221	1,317,476	26,745	724,512	632,560	91,952	11,503,513	5,822,036	5,681,477
Revenues Over (Under) Expenditures	1,472,752	4,709,032	3,236,280	(17,538)	630,626	648,164	(724,512)	(608,024)	116,488	(11,053,513)	(5,543,457)	5,510,056
Other Financing Sources (Uses):												
Proceeds from bonds	—	—	—	—	—	—	—	—	—	815,000	815,000	—
Operating transfers out	(3,766,866)	(3,766,866)	—	—	—	—	—	—	—	—	—	—
Operating transfers in	719,442	719,442	—	—	—	—	724,512	724,512	—	2,594,566	2,594,566	—
Total other sources (uses)	(3,047,424)	(3,047,424)	—	—	—	—	724,512	724,512	—	3,409,566	3,409,566	—
Revenues and Other Sources Over (Under) Expenditures	(1,574,672)	1,661,608	3,236,280	(17,538)	630,626	648,164	—	116,488	116,488	(7,643,947)	(2,133,891)	5,510,056
Fund Balances, Beginning	3,155,531	3,155,531	—	541,362	588,229	46,867	—	—	—	7,678,701	7,678,701	—
Fund Balances, Ending	$1,580,859	$4,817,139	$3,236,280	$523,824	$1,218,855	$695,031	$—	$116,488	$116,488	$34,754	$5,544,810	$5,510,056

[CITY OF LUBBOCK, TEXAS]

Combined Statement of Revenues, Expenditures, and Changes in Fund Balances—Budget (GAAP Basis) and Actual—General, Special Revenue, and Capital Projects Fund Types, Year Ended September 30, 1983

	General Fund			Special Revenue Fund Types			Capital Projects Fund Types		
	Budget	Actual	Variance— Favorable (Unfavorable)	Budget	Actual	Variance— Favorable (Unfavorable)	Budget	Actual	Variance— Favorable (Unfavorable)
Revenues:									
Taxes (note 4)	$24,963,439	$25,219,089	$ 255,650	$ 910,868	$ 1,091,977	$ 181,109	$ —	$ —	$ —
Licenses and permits	769,694	864,448	94,754	—	—	—	—	—	—
Intergovernmental (notes 5 and 15)	937,654	1,015,231	77,577	2,834,243	2,836,765	2,522	3,492,068	3,491,998	(70)
Charges for services	1,808,064	1,830,953	22,889	—	270,143	270,143	—	—	—
Fines and forfeits	1,316,000	1,236,545	(79,455)	—	—	—	—	—	—
Contributions	—	—	—	50,000	75,000	25,000	726,885	726,885	—
Miscellaneous	3,160,872	3,408,194	247,322	124,097	143,958	19,861	153,065	153,065	—
Total revenue	$32,955,723	$33,574,460	$ 618,737	$3,919,208	$ 4,417,843	$ 498,635	$ 4,372,018	$ 4,371,948	$ (70)
Expenditures:									
General government	$ 1,883,442	$ 2,188,747	$ (305,305)	$ 251,000	$ 329,820	$ (78,820)	$ —	$ —	$ —
Financial services	1,397,930	1,379,512	18,418	246,619	30,395	216,224	—	—	—
Management services	1,608,857	1,584,996	23,861	811,690	127,786	683,904	—	—	—
Management information	—	—	—	—	—	—	—	—	—
Development services	5,482,744	5,127,150	355,594	348,160	(162,231)	510,391	—	—	—
Public safety and services	29,013,243	28,673,646	339,597	895,634	191,225	704,409	—	—	—
Non-departmental	294,000	95,645	198,355	—	—	—	—	—	—

Public utilities	—	—	—	1,357,597	68,230	1,425,827	—	—
Capital projects	2,200,291	9,233,480	11,433,771	—	—	—	—	—
Civic Lubbock, Inc.	—	—	—	(251,176)	251,176	—	—	—
Lubbock Board of City Development	—	—	—	12,569	845,481	858,050	—	—
Total expenditures	$2,200,291	$ 9,233,480	$11,433,771	$3,155,098	$ 1,681,882	$ 4,836,980	$ 630,520	$39,049,696	$39,680,216
Excess (deficiency) of revenue over expenditures	$2,200,221	$(4,861,532)	$(7,061,753)	$3,653,733	$ 2,735,961	$ (917,772)	$1,249,257	$(5,475,236)	$(6,724,493)
Other financing sources (uses):									
Proceeds of general obligation bond issues	$ —	$ 2,025,000	$ 2,025,000	$ —	$ —	$ —	$ —	$ —	$ —
Proceeds of note	—	1,751,000	1,751,000	—	—	—	—	—	—
Operating transfers in	—	565,888	565,888	—	—	—	(205,548)	7,625,696	7,831,244
Operating transfers out	—	(835,616)	(835,616)	(137,406)	(6,107,907)	(5,970,501)	(751,453)	(1,227,138)	(475,685)
Total other financing sources (uses)	$ —	$ 3,506,272	$ 3,506,272	$ (137,406)	$(6,107,907)	$(5,970,501)	$ (957,001)	$ 6,398,558	$ 7,355,559
Excess (deficiency) of revenue and other sources over expenditures and other uses	$2,200,221	$ (1,355,260)	$(3,555,481)	$3,516,327	$(3,371,946)	$(6,888,273)	$ 292,256	$ 923,322	$ 631,066
Fund balances at beginning of year	—	14,522,628	14,522,628	—	4,326,028	4,326,028	—	6,033,293	6,033,293
Fund balances at end of year	$2,200,221	$13,167,368	$10,967,147	$3,516,327	$ 954,082	$(2,562,245)	$ 292,256	$ 6,956,615	$ 6,664,359

[COUNTY OF OTTAWA, MICHIGAN]

Combined Statement of Revenues, Expenditures, and Changes in Fund Balances—Budget and Actual—General and Special Revenue Fund Types, Year Ended December 31, 1983

	General Fund			Special Revenue Fund Types			Totals (Memorandum Only)		
	Amended Budget	Actual	Actual Over (Under) Amended Budget	Amended Budget	Actual	Actual Over (Under) Amended Budget	Amended Budget	Actual	Actual Over (Under) Amended Budget
Revenues:									
Taxes	$ 7,721,498	$ 7,690,453	$ (31,045)				$ 7,721,498	$ 7,690,453	$ (31,045)
Intergovernmental revenues	2,374,617	2,537,898	163,281	$15,048,089	$16,276,647	$1,228,558	17,422,706	18,814,545	1,391,839
Charges for services	724,000	965,523	241,523	188,900	356,231	167,331	912,900	1,321,754	408,854
Fines and forfeits	132,200	161,600	27,400				134,200	161,600	27,400
Interest on investments	770,000	870,195	100,195	395,009	527,271	132,262	1,165,009	1,397,466	232,457
Rental income	242,970	292,981	50,011				242,970	292,981	50,011
Licenses and permits	78,800	74,373	(4,427)				78,800	74,373	(4,427)
Other	22,000	34,561	12,561	614,526	645,708	31,182	636,526	680,269	43,743
TOTAL REVENUES	12,068,085	12,627,584	559,499	16,246,524	17,805,857	1,559,333	28,314,609	30,433,441	2,118,832
Expenditures:									
Legislative	157,494	141,033	(16,461)				157,494	141,033	(16,461)
Judicial	1,986,719	2,018,843	32,124	186,638	163,530	(23,108)	2,173,357	2,182,373	9,016
General government	2,471,757	2,360,476	(11,281)	1,186,358	838,490	(347,868)	3,658,115	3,198,966	(459,149)
Public safety	2,499,512	2,443,272	(56,240)	923,865	847,420	(76,445)	3,423,377	3,290,692	(132,685)

Highways and streets	33,149	24,330	(8,819)	8,773,142	8,493,134	(280,008)	8,806,291	8,517,464	(288,827)
Health	40,025	38,668	(1,357)	5,525,735	5,028,501	(497,234)	5,565,760	5,067,169	(498,591)
Welfare	41,800	26,946	(14,854)	3,876,143	4,692,760	816,617	3,917,943	4,719,706	801,763
Culture and recreation	2,760	2,239	(521)	269,729	406,034	136,305	272,489	408,273	135,784
Other governmental functions	1,708,491	1,061,342	(647,149)				1,708,491	1,061,342	(647,149)
TOTAL EXPENDITURES	8,941,707	8,117,149	(824,558)	20,741,610	20,469,869	(271,741)	29,683,317	28,587,018	(1,096,299)
REVENUES OVER (UNDER) EXPENDITURES	3,126,378	4,510,435	1,384,057	(4,495,086)	(2,664,012)	1,831,074	(1,368,708)	1,846,423	3,215,131
Other financing sources (uses): Bond proceeds					2,650,000	2,650,000		2,650,000	2,650,000
Operating transfers in (out)	(3,736,079)	(3,742,692)	(6,613)	2,175,014	3,042,692	867,678	(1,561,065)	(700,000)	861,065
REVENUES AND OTHER SOURCES OVER (UNDER) EXPENDITURES AND OTHER USES	(609,701)	767,743	1,377,444	(2,320,072)	3,028,680	5,348,752	(2,929,773)	3,796,423	6,726,196
Fund balances at beginning of year	2,226,000	2,226,000		6,997,699	6,997,699		9,223,699	9,223,699	
Contributions of capital to Self-Insurance Fund		(400,000)	(400,000)					(400,000)	(400,000)
FUND BALANCE AT END OF YEAR	$ 1,616,299	$ 2,593,743	$ 977,444	$ 4,677,627	$10,026,379	$5,348,752	$ 6,293,926	$12,620,122	$6,326,196

[MONTGOMERY COUNTY, MARYLAND]

Combined Statement of Revenues, Expenditures and Changes in Fund Balances, Budget and Actual, General, Special Revenue, Debt Service, and Capital Projects Fund Types, for the Fiscal Year Ended June 20, 1984

	General Fund			Special Revenue Funds		
	Budget	Actual	Variance Favorable (Unfavorable)	Budget	Actual	Variance Favorable (Unfavorable)
Revenues:						
Taxes (Note III)	$468,735,000	$484,692,904	$15,957,904	$ 88,346,296	$ 90,379,700	$2,033,404
Licenses and permits	4,009,000	3,731,426	(277,574)	903,000	866,720	(36,280)
Intergovernmental	58,810,954	58,553,605	(257,349)	71,558,151	70,809,506	(748,645)
Charges for services	2,305,000	3,714,592	1,409,592	12,726,214	10,448,575	(2,277,639)
Fines and forfeits	1,025,000	1,209,973	184,973	—	—	—
Miscellaneous	14,007,527	13,535,180	(472,347)	3,588,369	5,800,572	2,212,203
Total Revenues (Note I)	548,892,481	565,437,680	16,545,199	177,122,030	178,305,073	1,183,043
Expenditures and Encumbrances:						
Current:						
General government	47,270,151	45,041,073	2,229,078	2,041,831	2,026,672	15,159
Public safety	71,990,357	71,186,273	804,084	30,889,050	30,653,560	235,490
Transportation	19,764,482	19,510,834	253,648	42,506,677	42,161,229	345,448
Health	24,763,539	24,306,658	456,881	—	—	—
Welfare	29,643,172	25,082,098	4,561,074	5,224,932	4,154,932	1,070,654
Culture and recreation	11,183,862	11,155,298	28,564	33,038,315	31,635,613	1,402,702
Education	—	—	—	360,006,756	358,755,653	1,251,103
Capital Projects	—	—	—			
Debt Service:						
Principal retirement	—	—	—	—	—	—
Interest and fiscal charges	—	—	—	—	—	—
Participation in State school loans	—	—	—	—	—	—
Total Expenditures and Encumbrances (Note I)	204,615,563	196,282,234	8,333,329	473,707,561	469,387,005	4,320,556
Excess of Revenues Over (Under) Expenditures and Encumbrances	344,276,918	369,155,446	24,878,528	(296,585,531)	(291,081,932)	5,503,599
Other Financing Sources (Uses):						
Operating transfers in (out) net	(345,918,600)	(345,160,012)	758,588	288,920,118	289,761,323	841,205
Sale of land	—	—	—	—	—	—
Proceeds of general obligation bonds	—	—	—	—	—	—
Total Other Financing Sources (Uses) (Note I)	(345,918,600)	(345,160,012)	758,588	288,910,118	289,761,323	841,205
Excess of Revenues and Other Sources Over (Under) Expenditures, Encumbrances and Other Sources (Uses)	(1,641,682)	23,995,434	25,637,116	(7,665,413)	(1,320,609)	6,344,804
Fund Balances—July 1, 1983 (Note I)	13,393,533	13,393,533	—	15,292,464	15,292,464	—
Fund Balances—June 30, 1984 (Note I)	$ 11,751,851	$ 37,388,967	$25,637,116	$ 7,627,051	$ 13,971,855	$6,344,804

	Debt Service Funds			Capital Projects Funds			Totals (Memorandum Only)	
Budget	Actual	Variance Favorable (Unfavorable)	Budget	Actual	Variance Favorable (Unfavorable)	Budget	Actual	Variance Favorable (Unfavorable)
$ —	$ 14,010	$ 14,010	$ —	$ —	$ —	$557,081,296	$575,086,614	$ 18,005,318
—	—	—	—	—	—	4,912,000	4,598,146	(313,854)
4,231,130	4,171,539	(59,591)	32,716,195	8,748,772	(23,967,423)	167,316,430	142,283,422	(25,033,008)
500,000	668,571	168,571	—	—	—	15,531,214	14,831,738	(699,476)
—	—	—	—	—	—	1,025,000	1,209,973	184,973
3,475,000	1,009,888	(2,465,112)	1,501,323	4,397,718	2,896,395	22,572,219	24,743,358	2,171,139
8,206,130	5,684,008	(2,342,122)	34,217,518	13,146,490	(21,071,028)	768,438,159	762,753,251	(5,684,908)
—	—	—	—	—	—	49,311,982	47,067,745	2,244,237
—	—	—	—	—	—	102,879,407	101,839,833	1,039,574
—	—	—	—	—	—	62,271,159	61,672,063	599,096
—	—	—	—	—	—	24,763,539	24,306,658	456,881
—	—	—	—	—	—	34,868,104	29,236,376	5,631,728
—	—	—	—	—	—	44,222,177	42,790,911	1,431,266
—	—	—	—	—	—	360,006,756	358,755,653	1,251,103
—	—	—	181,782,472	70,750,093	111,032,379	181,782,472	70,750,093	111,032,379
40,157,514	40,062,000	95,514	—	—	—	40,157,514	40,062,000	95,514
32,926,745	32,541,201	385,544	—	—	—	32,926,745	32,541,201	385,544
—	—	—	—	—	—	890,501	890,501	—
73,974,760	73,493,702	481,058	181,782,472	70,750,093	111,032,379	934,080,356	809,913,034	124,167,322
(65,768,630)	(67,629,694)	(1,861,064)	(147,564,954)	(57,603,603)	89,961,351	(165,642,197)	(47,159,783)	118,482,414
64,992,680	67,437,466	2,444,786	14,128,692	4,809,935	(9,318,757)	22,122,890	16,848,712	(5,274,178)
—	—	—	770,143	363,339	(406,804)	770,143	363,339	(406,804)
—	—	—	86,067,754	41,651,323	(44,416,431)	86,067,754	41,651,323	(44,416,431)
64,992,680	67,437,466	2,444,786	100,966,589	46,824,597	(54,141,992)	108,960,787	58,863,374	(50,097,413)
(775,950)	(192,228)	583,722	(46,598,365)	(10,779,006)	35,819,359	(56,681,410)	11,703,591	68,385,001
290,941	290,941	—	75,121,087	75,121,087	—	104,098,025	104,098,025	—
$ (485,009)	$ 98,713	$ 583,722	$ 28,522,722	$64,342,081	$ 35,819,359	$ 47,416,615	$115,801,616	$ 68,385,001

[CITY OF BIRMINGHAM, ALABAMA]

General Fund, Statement of Revenues, Expenditures and Changes in Fund Balance—Budget and Actual, for the Year Ended June 30, 1984

	Budget	Actual	Over (Under) Budget
Fund balance at beginning of year		$ 9,102,677	
Revenues:			
Taxes	$49,281,500	52,349,286	$3,067,786
Licenses and permits	24,438,750	24,723,112	284,362
Fines and forfeitures	2,724,000	2,617,649	(106,369)
Intergovernmental revenues	10,192,000	11,757,777	1,565,777
Charges for services	6,947,000	7,324,658	377,658
Other operating revenues	2,582,514	4,417,778	1,835,264
Total revenues	96,165,764	103,190,251	7,024,487
Expenditures:			
Current operations:			
Public safety	55,531,346	55,270,132	(261,214)
Streets and sanitation	14,849,608	14,811,288	(38,320)
Cultural and recreational	16,711,371	16,467,496	(243,875)
General government	11,035,967	10,762,616	(273,351)
Total current operations	98,128,292	97,311,532	(816,760)
Excess revenues over (under) expenditures	(1,962,528)	5,878,719	7,841,247
Other financing sources (uses):			
Operating transfers in	409,000	517,457	108,457
Operating transfers out	(6,266,764)	(6,266,764)	—
Excess of revenues and other sources over expenditures and other uses (Note 1E)		129,412	
Fund balance at end of year		$ 9,232,089	

[SUFFOLK COUNTY, NEW YORK]

Combined Statement of Revenues and Expenditures—Budget and Actual—General and Special Revenue Funds, for the Year Ended December 31, 1983

	General Fund on a Budget Basis			Special Revenue Fund on a Budget Basis		
	Actual	**Budget**	**Variance Favorable (Unfavorable)**	**Actual**	**Budget**	**Variance Favorable (Unfavorable)**
REVENUES:						
Real property taxes	$ 89,607,869	$ 91,161,204	$(1,553,335)	$165,068,050	$164,002,079	$ 1,065,971
Non-property taxes:						
Sales and use tax	210,778,737	195,412,000	15,366,737			
OTB pari-mutuel tax	7,268,234	9,225,000	(1,956,766)			
State aid	106,554,856	108,763,001	(2,208,145)	19,856,064	21,269,226	(1,413,162)
Federal aid	77,810,679	76,341,954	1,468,725	58,868,157	68,836,366	(9,968,209)
Licenses, permits, fines, fees, etc.	41,490,957	37,376,367	4,114,590	4,589,561	7,381,167	(2,791,606)
Interest on investments	4,310,016	6,829,985	(2,519,969)	2,530,272	1,087,000	1,443,272
Student revenue				15,089,608	13,798,347	1,291,261
Miscellaneous	6,997,595	7,471,329	(473,734)	6,297,395	5,032,208	1,265,187
Total revenues	544,818,943	532,580,840	12,238,103	272,299,107	281,406,393	(9,107,286)
EXPENDITURES:						
Current:						
General government support	79,659,476	78,838,278	(821,198)	3,670,534	3,057,417	(613,117)
Economic assistance and opportunity	201,810,366	220,729,941	18,919,575	11,394,386	16,491,608	5,097,222
Health	46,810,362	51,935,272	5,773,910		15,197	15,197
Public safety	5,386,780	58,074,519	2,687,739	99,677,927	111,396,992	11,719,065
Culture and recreation	9,423,532	10,112,870	689,338			
Education	13,421,692	15,550,415	2,128,723	48,123,003	48,226,422	103,419
Home and community services	3,885,335	3,855,260	(30,075)	41,698,836	50,109,987	8,411,151
Transportation	27,231,920	30,229,681	2,997,761	1,197,765	1,510,790	313,025
Employee benefits	50,172,201	50,427,630	255,429	47,593,241	48,215,566	622,325
Debt service—principal and interest	42,443,082	50,133,416	7,690,334	63,519,360	69,350,229	5,830,869
Total expenditures	525,595,746	569,887,282	40,291,536	316,875,052	348,374,208	31,499,156
Excess (deficiency) of revenues over expenditures	15,223,197	(37,306,442)	52,529,639	(44,575,945)	(66,967,815)	22,391,870
OTHER FINANCING SOURCES (USES):						
Interfund transfers in	15,134,778	22,400,011	(7,265,233)	74,396,013	78,865,838	(4,469,825)
Interfund transfers out	(16,940,125)	(15,695,309)	(1,244,816)	(15,856,407)	(17,960,401)	2,103,994
Total other financing sources (uses)	(1,805,347)	6,704,702	(8,510,049)	58,539,606	60,905,437	(2,365,831)
Excess (deficiency) of revenues and other sources over expenditures and other uses	$ 13,417,850	$(30,601,740)	$ 44,019,590	$ 13,963,661	$ (6,062,378)	$20,026,039

[Statements included for illustrative purposes. For brevity the footnotes accompanying the statements have not been included.]

EXHIBIT 7-3. EXAMPLES OF REPORTING BY GOVERNMENTAL UNITS OF REVENUES, EXPENDITURES, AND CHANGES IN FUND BALANCES—BUDGET AND ACTUAL (BUDGETARY BASIS)

[CITY OF ORLANDO, FLORIDA]

Combined Statement of Revenues, Expenditures, Encumbrances, and Changes in Fund Balances [in part]—Budgetary Basis, General and Special Revenue Funds, Year Ended September 30, 1983

	General Fund					Special Revenue Funds					Debt Service Funds		
	Actual	Adjustments to Budgetary Basis	Budgetary Basis	Budget	Variance Favorable (Unfavorable)	Actual	Adjustments to Budgetary Basis	Budgetary Basis	Budget	Variance Favorable (Unfavorable)	Actual and Budgetary Basis	Budget	Variance Favorable (Unfavorable)
Revenues													
Property Taxes	$12,491,330	$ —	$12,491,330	$12,725,000	$ (233,670)	$ 187,961	$ —	$ 187,961	$ 186,415	$ 1,546	$ —	$ —	$ —
Occupational Licenses and Franchise Fees	8,372,360	—	8,372,360	7,955,000	417,360	—	—	—	—	—	—	—	—
Intergovernmental	20,313,428	—	20,313,428	19,614,940	698,488	5,470,293	627,897	6,098,190	8,156,385	(2,058,195)	480,000	480,000	—
Other Licenses, Permits, and Fees	5,286,225		5,286,225	4,319,281	966,944	—	—	—	—	—	—	—	—
Fines and Forfeitures	934,241	—	934,241	636,510	297,731	—	—	—	—	—	—	—	—
Other	4,411,394	—	4,411,394	3,524,565	886,829	126,995	—	126,995	185,040	(58,045)	255,533	—	255,533
Total Revenues	51,808,978	—	51,808,978	48,775,296	3,033,682	5,785,249	627,897	6,413,146	8,527,840	(2,114,694)	735,533	480,000	255,533
Expenditures													
Current Operating:													
General Administration	1,954,633	9,022	1,963,655	2,029,021	65,366	101,392	64	101,456	90,642	(10,814)	—	—	—
Planning and Development	2,024,025	64,872	2,088,897	2,127,065	38,168	966,798	41,209	1,008,007	1,398,423	390,416	—	—	—
Finance	1,290,264	69,652	1,359,916	1,443,158	83,242	678,585	239,443	918,028	2,557,706	1,639,678	—	—	—
Public Works	6,725,536	391,028	7,116,564	7,508,062	391,498	1,081,218	348,261	1,429,479	1,695,693	266,214	—	—	—
Parks and Recreation	5,663,867	185,204	5,849,071	6,068,154	219,083						—		—

Centroplex	380,544	9,459	390,003	414,231	24,228	—	—	—	—	—	—	—
												—
Police	18,768,725	642,961	19,411,686	20,012,515	600,829	—	—	—	—	—	—	—
												—
Administrative Support	3,477,661	305,910	3,783,571	3,824,228	40,657	—	—	—	—	—	—	—
												—
Personnel	877,261	12,979	890,240	894,088	3,848	—	—	—	—	—	—	—
												—
Fire	12,247,964	549,875	12,797,839	13,329,303	531,464	—	—	—	—	—	—	—
												—
Other Expenditures	2,620,547	—	2,620,547	3,694,013	1,073,466	—	—	—	—	—	—	—
												—
Downtown Development Board	—	—	—	—	—	—	—	—	—	—	—	—
												—
Debt Service	—	—	—	—	—	332,212	35,870	368,082	426,332	58,250	442,245	480,000
												37,755
Total Expenditures	56,031,027	2,240,962	58,271,989	61,343,838	3,071,849	3,160,205	664,847	3,825,052	6,168,796	2,343,744	442,245	480,000
												37,755
Excess (Deficiency) of Revenues Over Expenditures	(4,222,049)	(2,240,962)	(6,463,011)	(12,568,542)	6,105,531	2,588,094	(36,950)	2,588,094	2,359,044	229,050	293,288	—
												293,288
Other Sources and (Uses)												
Operating Transfers in	12,859,205	—	12,859,205	12,795,211	63,994	233,008	—	233,008	219,292	13,716	—	—
												—
Operating Transfers (out)	(3,990,326)	1,227,813	(2,762,513)	(2,902,529)	140,016	(2,793,149)	1,337	(2,791,812)	(2,791,812)	—	(61,348)	—
												(61,348)
Total Other Sources and (Uses)	8,868,879	1,227,813	10,096,692	9,892,682	204,010	(2,560,141)	1,337	(2,558,804)	(2,572,520)	13,716	(61,348)	—
												(61,348)
Excess (Deficiency) of Revenues and Other Sources Over Expenditures and Other (Uses)	4,646,830	(1,013,149)	3,633,681	(2,675,860)	6,309,541	64,903	(35,613)	29,290	(213,476)	242,766	231,940	—
												231,940
Fund Balance Allocation	—	—	—	2,675,860	(2,675,860)	—	—	—	213,476	(213,476)	—	—
												—
Excess (Deficiency) of Revenues and Other Sources Over Expenditures and Other (Uses)	$4,646,830	$(1,013,149)	$3,633,681	$—	$3,633,681	$64,903	$(35,613)	$29,290	$—	$29,290	$231,940	—
												$231,940

[TOWN OF EAST HARTFORD, CONNECTICUT]

Combined Statement of Revenues, Expenditures, and Changes in Fund Balances [in part]—Budget and Actual—General and Special Revenue Funds, Year Ended June 30, 1984

	General Fund					Special Revenue Funds			Totals (Note 1) (Memorandum Only)		
	Actual	Adjustment to Budgetary Basis	Actual on Budgetary Basis (Note 1)	Amended Budget	Variance Favorable (Unfavorable)	Actual	Amended Budget	Variance Favorable (Unfavorable)	Actual on Budgetary Basis	Amended Budget	Variance Favorable (Unfavorable)
REVENUES:											
General property taxes (Note 2)	$34,258,027	$ —	$34,258,027	$34,311,183	$ (53,156)	$ —	$ —	$ —	$34,258,027	$34,311,183	$ (53,156)
Licenses and permits	260,315	—	260,315	154,153	106,162	—	—	—	260,315	154,153	106,162
Intergovernmental revenues	10,764,880	—	10,764,880	10,726,865	38,015	2,756,681	3,125,011	(368,330)	13,521,561	13,851,876	(330,315)
Charges for services	1,035,848	—	1,035,848	861,100	174,748	660,994	654,610	6,384	1,696,842	1,515,710	181,132
Fines and forfeits	67,745	—	67,745	65,000	2,745	—	—	—	67,745	65,000	2,745
Miscellaneous	1,101,170	—	1,101,170	848,580	252,590	39,796	35,000	4,796	1,140,966	883,580	257,386
Total revenues	47,487,985	—	47,487,985	46,966,881	521,104	3,457,471	3,814,621	(357,150)	50,945,456	50,781,502	163,954
EXPENDITURES:											
General government	6,773,149	(19,621)	6,753,528	7,022,088	268,560	16,459	16,800	341	6,769,987	7,038,888	268,901
Public safety	7,256,491	4,317	7,260,808	7,340,628	79,820	—	51,000	51,000	7,260,808	7,391,628	130,820
Inspection and permits	285,769	(2,633)	285,769	297,608	11,839	—	—	—	285,769	297,608	11,839
Public works	4,472,653	(2,633)	4,470,020	4,483,399	13,379	274,088	451,832	177,744	4,744,108	4,935,231	191,123
Parks and recreation	1,244,154	8,613	1,252,767	1,265,501	12,734	11,560	44,000	32,440	1,264,327	1,309,501	45,174
Health and social services	913,438	—	913,438	916,206	2,768	105,439	108,379	2,940	1,018,877	1,024,585	5,708
Education	26,238,654	71,254	26,309,908	26,309,905	(3)	1,754,532	1,759,610	5,078	28,064,440	28,069,515	5,075
Total expenditures	47,184,308	61,930	47,246,238	47,635,335	389,097	2,162,078	2,431,621	269,543	49,408,316	50,066,956	658,640
Excess of revenues over (under) expenditures	303,677	(61,930)	241,747	(668,454)	910,201	1,295,393	1,383,000	(87,607)	1,537,140	714,546	822,594
OTHER FINANCING SOURCES (USES):											
Operating transfers in	1,436,518	—	1,436,518	1,288,900	147,618	—	—	—	1,436,518	1,288,900	147,618
Operating transfers out	(1,161,479)	—	(1,161,479)	(1,161,492)	13	(1,260,000)	(1,260,000)	—	(2,421,479)	(2,421,492)	13
Total other financing sources (uses)	275,039	—	275,039	127,408	147,631	(1,260,000)	(1,260,000)	—	(984,961)	(1,132,592)	147,631
Excess of revenues and other sources over (under) expenditures and other uses	578,716	(61,930)	516,786	(541,046)	1,057,832	35,393	123,000	(87,607)	552,179	(418,046)	970,225
FUND BALANCE, July 1, 1983	978,018	(414,214)	563,804	(2,070,043)	2,633,847	78,480	62,090	16,390	642,284	(2,007,953)	2,650,237
FUND BALANCE, June 30, 1984	$ 1,556,734	$(476,144)	$ 1,080,590	$(2,611,089)	$3,691,679	$ 113,873	$ 185,090	$ (71,217)	$ 1,194,463	$(2,425,999)	$3,620,462

[CITY OF TALLAHASSEE, FLORIDA]

Combined Statement of Revenues and Expenditures [in part]—Budget and Actual—General and Special Revenue Fund Types, for the Fiscal Year Ended September 30, 1983

	General Fund					Special Revenue Funds		
	Actual	Encumbrances	Budgetary Basis	Budget	Variance Favorable (Unfavorable)	Actual	Budget	Variance Favorable (Unfavorable)
Revenues:								
Taxes	$ 8,595,100	$ —	$ 8,595,100	$ 8,442,100	$ 153,000	$ —	$ —	$ —
Licenses and permits	1,719,800	—	1,719,800	1,553,600	166,200	—	—	—
Intergovernmental revenues	8,298,900	—	8,298,900	6,226,000	2,072,900	612,200	612,200	—
Charges for services	3,540,200	—	3,540,200	3,234,100	306,100	—	—	—
Fines and forfeits	389,500	—	389,500	273,000	116,500	—	—	—
Interest earned	665,800	—	665,800	727,600	(61,800)	2,860,200	2,840,200	20,000
Miscellaneous revenues	129,900	33,200	163,100	63,300	99,800	12,300	12,300	—
Total Revenues	23,339,200	33,200	23,372,400	20,519,700	2,852,700	3,484,700	3,464,700	20,000
Expenditures:								
Current:								
General government	5,274,600	43,500	5,318,100	6,259,100	941,000		500,000	500,000
Public safety	11,598,300	159,500	11,748,800	12,095,400	346,600	—	—	—
Highways and streets	4,326,200	34,600	4,360,800	4,592,700	231,900	—	—	—
Sanitation	4,043,000	6,600	4,049,600	3,984,300	(65,300)	—	—	—
Health	247,200	1,000	248,200	223,800	(24,400)	—	—	—
Welfare	799,900	3,400	803,300	825,700	22,400	—	—	—
Culture and recreation	3,686,700	18,600	3,705,300	3,604,000	(101,300)	—	—	—
Capital Outlay						18,800	18,800	—
Total Expenditures	29,966,900	267,200	30,234,100	31,585,000	1,350,900	18,800	518,800	500,000
Excess of Revenues over (under) Expenditures	(6,627,700)	(234,000)	(6,861,700)	(11,065,300)	4,203,600	3,465,900	2,965,900	500,000
Other Financing Sources (Uses):								
Operating transfers in	21,754,800	—	21,754,800	19,529,600	2,225,200	2,000,000	2,000,000	—
Operating transfers out	(14,812,300)	—	(14,812,300)	(8,464,300)	(6,348,000)	(2,143,300)	(2,143,300)	—
Total Other Financing Sources (Uses)	6,942,500	—	6,942,500	11,065,300	(4,122,800)	(143,300)	(143,300)	—
Excess of Revenues and Other Sources over Expenditures and Other Uses	$ 314,800	$(234,000)	$ 80,800	$ —	$ 80,800	$ 3,322,600	$ 2,802,600	$520,000

[RAMSEY COUNTY, MINNESOTA]

Combined Statement of Revenues, Expenditures, and Changes in Fund Balances [in part]—Budgetary Comparisons (Non GAAP Budgetary Basis)—General, Special Revenue, and Debt Service Fund Types, Year Ended December 31, 1983

	General Fund			Special Revenue Funds			Debt Service Fund			Totals (Memorandum Only)		
	Budget	Actual	Variance Favorable (Unfavorable)	Budget	Actual	Variance Favorable (Unfavorable)	Budget	Actual	Variance Favorable (Unfavorable)	Budget	Actual	Variance Favorable (Unfavorable)
Revenues:												
Taxes	$61,934,998	$62,193,921	$ 258,923	$ 1,867,153	$ 1,906,782	$ 39,629	$2,963,879	$3,081,192	$117,313	$ 66,766,030	$ 67,181,895	$ 415,865
Licenses and Permits	79,600	94,561	14,961	—	—	—			—	79,600	94,561	14,961
Intergovernmental	98,024,012	93,370,538	(4,653,474)	12,678,065	12,686,133	8,068	813,499	819,471	5,972	111,515,576	106,876,142	(4,639,434)
Private Grants and Donations	13,044	15,791	2,747	—	—	—			—	13,044	15,791	2,747
Charges for Services	9,804,294	9,960,683	156,389	22,225	23,339	1,114			—	9,826,519	9,984,022	157,503
Fines and Forfeitures	2,074,800	2,293,585	218,785	27,730	24,243	(3,487)			—	2,102,530	2,317,828	215,298
Sales	396,949	377,202	(19,747)	35,700	48,615	12,915			—	432,649	425,817	(6,832)
Use of Money and Property	3,971,412	5,679,917	1,708,505	157,800	157,743	(57)	—	375,000	375,000	4,129,212	6,212,660	2,083,448
Community Human Services—Program Recoveries	10,168,683	9,039,435	(1,129,248)	—	—	—	—	—	—	10,168,683	9,039,435	(1,129,248)
Miscellaneous	565,919	467,262	(98,657)	484,049	492,733	8,684	—	237,617	237,617	1,049,968	1,197,613	147,645
Total Revenues	187,033,711	183,492,895	(3,540,816)	15,272,722	15,339,588	66,866	3,777,378	4,513,280	735,902	206,083,811	203,345,764	(2,738,047)
Expenditures: (Includes Encumbrances)												
General Government	26,719,383	24,819,326	1,900,057	14,269	14,269	—	—	—	—	26,733,652	24,833,595	1,900,057
Public Safety	23,112,922	22,529,211	583,711	3,000,776	2,769,190	231,586	—	—	—	26,113,698	25,298,401	815,297
Highways and Streets	13,009,773	12,729,944	279,829	—	—	—	—	—	—	13,009,773	12,729,944	279,829
Health	11,672,228	11,374,022	298,206	13,220	13,220	—	—	—	—	11,685,448	11,387,242	298,206
Welfare	117,859,918	109,100,166	8,759,752	3,622,378	3,622,378	—	—	—	—	121,482,296	112,722,544	8,759,752

Culture and Recreation	323,981	7,161,658	7,485,639	—	—	—	35,515	2,587,089	2,622,604	288,466	4,574,569	4,863,035
Conservation of Natural Resources	10,568	539,117	549,685	—	—	—	—	330,779	330,779	10,568	208,338	218,906
Economic Development and Assistance	—	1,649,455	1,649,455	—	—	—	—	1,649,455	1,649,455	—	—	—
Debt Service:												
Principal Retirement	—	3,195,000	3,195,000	—	3,195,000	3,195,000	—	—	—	—	—	—
Interest	2	1,230,539	1,230,541	2	1,230,539	1,230,541	—	—	—	—	—	—
Total Expenditures	12,387,692	200,747,495	213,135,187	2	4,425,539	4,425,541	267,101	10,986,380	11,253,481	12,120,589	185,335,576	197,456,165
Excess (Deficiency) of Revenues over Expenditures	9,649,645	2,598,269	(7,051,376)	735,904	87,741	(648,163)	333,967	4,353,208	4,019,241	8,579,773	(1,842,681)	(10,422,454)
Other Financing Sources (Uses):												
Operating Transfers in	24,860	4,949,568	4,924,708	163,343	163,343	—	22,606	99,873	77,267	2,255	4,849,696	4,847,441
Operating Transfers out	130,845	(4,581,096)	(4,711,941)	—	—	—	—	(4,540,941)	(4,540,941)	(32,498)	(203,498)	(171,000)
Total Other Financing Sources (Uses)	155,705	368,472	212,767	163,343	163,343	—	22,606	(4,441,068)	(4,463,674)	(30,243)	4,646,198	4,676,441
Excess (Deficiency) of Revenues and Other Sources over Expenditures and Other Uses	9,805,350	2,966,741	(6,838,609)	899,247	251,084	(648,163)	356,573	(87,860)	(444,433)	8,549,530	2,803,517	(5,746,013)
Adjustment (Note 1)	8,058,492	8,058,492	—	—	—	—	197,260	197,260	—	7,861,232	7,861,232	—
Fund Balances at Beginning of Year	—	42,567,889	42,567,889	—	3,612,804	3,612,804	—	2,152,104	2,152,104	—	36,802,981	36,802,981
Increase (Decrease) in Reserve for Inventories	87,532	87,532	—	—	—	—	(4,199)	(4,199)	—	91,731	91,731	—
Fund Balances at End of Year	$17,951,374	$53,680,654	$35,729,280	$899,247	$3,863,888	$2,964,641	$549,634	$2,257,305	$1,707,671	$16,502,493	$47,559,461	$31,056,968

[CITY OF PORTLAND, OREGON]

Combined Statement of Revenues, Expenditures and Changes in Fund Balances—Budget and Actual, All Governmental Fund Types, Year Ended June 30, 1984

	Governmental Fund Types								
	General Fund			Special Revenue Funds			Debt Service Funds		
	Budget	Actual	Variance Favorable (Unfavorable)	Budget	Actual	Variance Favorable (Unfavorable)	Budget	Actual	Variance Favorable (Unfavorable)
REVENUES:									
Taxes	$52,145,164	$ 52,472,079	$ 326,915	$ 3,993,600	$ 3,972,877	$ (20,723)	$ 11,812,158	$ 11,943,180	$ 131,022
Special assessments									
Licenses and permits	26,560,702	26,301,648	(259,054)						
Intergovernmental revenues	8,870,684	7,277,818	(1,502,866)	58,288,067	45,591,578	(12,696,489)			
Charges for services	18,751,448	17,149,638	(1,601,810)	4,623,320	4,962,579	339,259			
Miscellaneous	28,289,243	27,351,093	(938,150)	5,370,100	3,619,689	(1,750,411)	3,312,000	3,102,207	(209,793)
Total revenues	134,527,241	130,552,276	(3,974,965)	72,275,087	58,146,723	(14,128,364)	15,124,158	15,045,387	(78,771)
EXPENDITURES:									
Current:									
General government	32,143,339	27,013,684	5,129,655	20,611,525	15,548,856	5,062,669	37,545	37,545	
Public safety	68,576,523	66,155,073	2,421,450	2,008,000		2,008,000			
Highways and streets	27,823,839	22,560,207	5,263,632	12,409,111	7,326,291	5,082,820			
Sanitation	2,114,884	2,064,677	50,207	64,717	53,006	11,711			
Health	815,530	759,378	56,152						
Culture and recreation	14,350,599	14,068,472	282,127	977,315	769,658	207,657			
Capital outlay	4,669,903	2,116,693	2,553,210	14,600	10,380	4,220			
Debt service:									
Principal							26,990,000	26,365,000	625,000
Interest							9,192,612	9,066,530	126,082
Total expenditures	150,494,617	134,738,184	15,756,433	36,085,268	23,708,191	12,377,077	36,220,157	35,469,075	751,082
Revenues over (under) expenditures	(15,967,376)	(4,185,908)	11,781,468	36,189,819	34,438,532	(1,751,287)	(21,095,999)	(20,423,688)	672,311
OTHER FINANCING SOURCES (USES):									
Temporary loans, net of repayments and other									
Warrant and bond sale proceeds									
Operating transfers in	40,263,438	32,824,089	(7,439,349)	131,173	116,957	(14,216)	25,950,000	24,375,000	(1,575,000)
Operating transfers out	(29,296,062)	(26,740,649)	2,555,413	(39,366,415)	(33,527,013)	5,839,402	(1,725,000)	(355,000)	1,369,700
Total other financing sources (uses)	10,967,376	6,083,440	(4,883,936)	(39,235,242)	(33,410,056)	5,825,186	24,225,000	24,019,700	(205,300)
Revenues and other sources over (under) expenditures and other uses	(5,000,000)	1,897,532	6,897,532	(3,045,423)	1,028,476	4,073,899	3,129,001	3,596,012	467,011
FUND BALANCES—BUDGETARY BASIS, June 30, 1983	5,000,000	5,099,943	99,943	16,573,669	16,536,546	(37,123)	18,729,908	18,813,555	83,647
FUND BALANCES—BUDGETARY BASIS, June 30, 1984	$ —		$ 6,997,475	$ 13,528,246	17,565,022	$ 4,036,776	$ 21,858,909	22,409,567	$ 550,658
Adjustments to generally accepted accounting principles basis:									
Encumbrances		1,522,179			711,076				
Assets net of liabilities budgeted as revenues and expenditures									
Items reflected on the cash basis for budget purposes:									
Federal revenue sharing entitlement receivable					2,411,189				
Inventories		921,383			66,678				
Increase in petty cash		14,110			(169)				
Assessment collection									
Assessment revenues earned not recognized as revenues on the budgetary basis									
Debt redemption principal									
Proceeds from improvement warrant and bond sales not recognized as other financing sources on the generally accepted accounting principles basis									
Short-Term Debt Interest and Sinking Fund budgeted as a debt service fund but included as part of the General Fund for generally accepted accounting principles purposes		207						(207)	
Cumulative differences between budgetary and generally accepted accounting principles basis—June 30, 1983									
FUND BALANCES (DEFICIT)—GENERALLY ACCEPTED ACCOUNTING PRINCIPLES BASIS, June 30, 1984		$ 9,455,354			$ 20,753,796			$ 22,409,360	

	Governmental Fund Types								
	Capital Projects Funds			Special Assessment Funds			Total (Memorandum Only)		
	Budget	Actual	Variance Favorable (Unfavorable)	Budget	Actual	Variance Favorable (Unfavorable)	Budget	Actual	Variance Favorable (Unfavorable)
				$ 3,812,416	$ 3,821,267	$ (8,851)	$ 67,950,922	$ 68,388,136	$ 437,214
							3,821,416	3,821,267	(8,851)
							26,560,702	26,301,648	(259,054)
	$ 9,151,476	$ 8,445,544	$ (705,932)				76,220,227	61,314,940	(14,905,287)
	404,000	1,100,183	696,183				23,778,768	23,212,400	(566,368)
	9,085,941	5,436,035	(3,649,906)	1,984,507	1,755,242	(229,265)	48,041,791	41,264,266	(6,777,525)
	18,641,417	14,981,762	(3,659,655)	5,805,774	5,567,658	(238,116)	246,373,677	224,293,806	(22,079,871)
	5,825,262	5,085,956	739,306				58,617,671	47,686,041	10,931,630
							70,584,523	66,155,073	4,429,450
				9,176,121	2,043,850	7,132,271	49,409,071	31,930,348	17,478,723
							2,179,601	2,117,683	61,918
							815,530	759,378	56,152
	19,178,798	12,796,395	6,382,403	6,159,400	2,310,202	3,849,198	15,327,914	14,838,130	489,784
							30,022,198	17,233,670	12,789,031
				1,700,417	1,700,416	1	28,690,417	28,065,416	625,001
				1,412,719	1,348,496	64,223	10,605,331	10,415,026	190,305
	25,004,060	17,882,351	7,121,709	18,448,657	7,402,964	11,045,693	266,252,759	219,200,765	47,051,994
	(6,362,643)	(2,900,589)	3,462,054	(12,642,883)	(1,835,306)	10,807,577	(19,879,082)	5,093,041	24,972,123
	(8,193,267)	(3,418,306)	4,774,961				(8,193,267)	(3,418,306)	4,774,961
				11,000,000	57,200	(10,942,800)	11,000,000	57,200	(10,942,800)
	1,481,655	15,000	(1,466,655)				67,826,266	57,331,046	(10,495,220)
	(1,481,655)	(15,000)	1,466,655				(71,869,132)	(60,637,962)	11,231,170
	(8,193,267)	(3,418,306)	4,774,961	11,000,000	57,200	(10,942,800)	(1,236,133)	(6,668,022)	(5,431,889)
	(14,555,910)	(6,318,895)	8,237,015	(1,642,883)	(1,778,106)	(135,106)	(21,115,215)	(1,574,981)	19,540,234
	22,283,000	23,952,766	1,669,766	7,892,366	9,571,394	1,679,028	70,478,943	73,974,204	3,495,261
	$ 7,727,090	17,633,871	$ 9,906,781	$ 6,249,483	7,793,288	$ 1,432,805	$ 49,363,728	72,399,233	$ 23,035,495
					16,953			2,250,208	
		6,396,697						6,396,697	
								2,411,189	
								988,061	
								13,941	
					(89,487)			(89,487)	
					8,164			8,164	
					1,700,416			1,700,416	
					(57,200)			(57,200)	
					(20,342,609)			(20,342,609)	
		$24,030,568			$(20,970,475)			$ 65,678,603	

Note 4. Reconciliation of Generally Accepted Accounting Principles Basis to Budgetary Basis

The budget of the City is prepared differently from generally accepted accounting principles. Therefore, the Combined Statement of Revenues, Expenditures and Changes in Fund Balances—Budget and Actual—All Governmental Fund Types is presented on the budgetary basis and is adjusted to the Combined Statement of Revenues, Expenditures and Changes in Fund Balances—All Governmental Fund Types and Expendable Trust Funds presented on the generally accepted accounting principles basis.

The following is a reconciliation of the differences between the budgetary basis and generally accepted accounting basis for revenues and other sources over (under) expenditures and other uses for the governmental funds in the aforementioned combined financial statements:

	General Fund	Special Revenue	Debt Service	Capital Projects	Special Assessments	Total
Revenues and other sources over (under) expenditures and other uses—generally accepted accounting principles basis	$ 937,573	$ 1,149,505	$ 3,595,805	$(5,888,820)	$ (199,260)	$ (405,197)
Revenues:						
Assessment collections budgeted as revenues					89,487	89,487
Assessment revenues earned not budgeted as revenues					(8,164)	(8,164)
Grant revenues accrued as earned on the budgetary basis based on encumbrances recognized as expenditures for grants		892,262*				892,262
Decrease in federal sharing entitlement receivable		206,991				206,991
Proceeds from sale of property and other fixed assets deferred for reinvestment in grant project				366,310		366,310
Grant revenues recognized on the budgetary basis in excess of amounts recognized on a generally accepted accounting principles basis				3,324,902		3,324,902
Revenues recognized as operating transfers in for budget purposes	(158,807)					(158,807)
Proceeds of tax anticipation notes budgeted as revenues	24,375,000					24,375,000
Short-Term Debt Interest and Sinking Fund budgeted as a debt service fund but included as part of the General Fund for generally accepted accounting principles purposes	(1,179,428)		1,179,428			
Miscellaneous other adjustments				(6,423)		(6,423)
	23,036,765	1,099,253	1,179,428	3,684,789	81,323	29,081,558

(continued)

[CITY OF PORTLAND, OREGON] (Continued)

	General Fund	Special Revenue	Debt Service	Capital Projects	Special Assessments	Total
Expenditures:						
Decrease (increase) in encumbrances during fiscal 1984	827,451	(1,230,721)*			(16,953)	(420,223)
Inventories recognized as expenditures when purchased for budgetary purposes	132,675	4,270				136,945
Debt principal payments budgeted as expenditures					(1,700,416)	(1,700,416)
Capital leases not recognized as expenditures for budget purposes	3,534,896					3,534,896
Short-Term Debt Interest and Sinking Fund budgeted as a debt service fund but included as part of the General Fund for generally accepted accounting principles purposes	823,921		(25,198,921)			(24,375,000)
Expenditures recognized on the budgetary basis in excess of amounts recognized on the generally accepted accounting principles basis				(766,056)		(766,056)
Miscellaneous other adjustments	40	6,169				6,209
Operating transfer out for budget purposes recognized as expenditures for generally accepted accounting principles purposes	2,066,911	520,621				2,587,532
	7,385,894	(699,661)	(25,198,921)	(766,056)	(1,717,369)	(20,996,113)
Other financing sources (uses):						
Revenues recognized as operating transfers in for budget purposes	158,807					158,807
Operating transfers out recognized as expenditures for generally accepted accounting principles purposes	(2,066,911)	(520,621)				(2,587,532)
Temporary loans, mortgage loan collections, repayments and other budgeted as other financing uses				(3,348,808)		(3,348,808)
Proceeds from improvement warrant and bond sales not recognized as other financing sources on the generally accepted accounting principles basis					57,200	57,200
Short-Term Debt Interest and Sinking Fund budgeted as a debt service fund but included as part of the General Fund for generally accepted accounting principles purposes	(24,019,700)		24,019,700			
Capital lease obligations not recognized as other financing source for budget purposes	(3,534,896)					(3,534,896)
	(29,462,700)	(520,621)	24,019,700	(3,348,808)	57,200	(9,255,229)
Revenues and other sources over (under) expenditures and other uses—budgetary basis	$ 1,897,532	$ 1,028,476	$ 3,596,012	$(6,318,895)	$(1,778,106)	$(1,574,981)

* Includes encumbrances for grant programs at June 30, 1984, which are not revenues or expenditures on a generally accepted accounting principles basis.

[WESTMORELAND COUNTY, PENNSYLVANIA]

Combined Statement of Revenues, Expenditures, and Changes in Fund Balances, Amended Budget and Actual—Cash Basis, Certain Governmental Fund Types (Note 1), for the Year Ended December 31, 1983

	General Fund			Institutional District Fund			Special Revenue Funds		
	Actual	Budget	Actual Over (Under) Budget	Actual	Budget	Actual Over (Under) Budget	Actual	Budget	Actual Over (Under) Budget
REVENUES:									
Real estate taxes	$17,433,638	$15,800,000	$ 1,633,638	$ 11,350	$ 705,040	$ (693,690)	$ 720,000	$ —	$ 720,000
Personal property taxes	702,018	606,000	96,018	—	—	—	—	—	—
Federal grants	214,293	100,000	114,293	—	—	—	1,840,949	1,803,510	37,439
State grants	1,595,886	1,703,358	(107,472)	—	—	—	9,800,934	9,364,569	436,365
Other grants	—	—	—	—	—	—	3,461,179	2,626,919	834,260
Social rehabilitation services	—	—	—	—	—	—	—	—	—
Reimbursements and departmental charges	2,479,886	2,004,926	474,960	—	—	—	—	—	—
Interest income	1,422,667	375,000	1,047,667	295,469	100,000	195,469	557,611	475,000	82,611
Joint projects	1,877,166	1,900,520	(23,354)	—	—	—	—	—	—
Redemption of investments	—	—	—	—	—	—	—	—	—
Proceeds from tax anticipation loans	3,000,000	3,000,000	—	—	—	—	—	—	—
Other revenue	1,453,260	928,490	524,770	350,592	291,047	59,545	118,574	85,000	33,574
Total revenues	$30,178,814	$26,418,294	$ 3,760,520	$ 657,411	$1,096,087	$ (438,676)	$16,499,247	$14,354,998	$ 2,144,249
EXPENDITURES:									
Current—									
General government	$ 6,857,539	$ 7,376,747	$ (519,208)	$ 139,414	$ 197,308	$ (57,894)	$ 1,953,664	$ 7,234,977	$(5,281,313)
Judicial	7,408,203	7,813,865	(405,662)	—	—	—	—	—	—
Corrections	3,687,473	4,058,021	(370,548)	—	—	—	—	—	—
Social and welfare	594,537	76,745	517,792	—	—	—	13,569,514	7,323,424	6,246,090
Joint projects	4,573,902	4,498,641	75,261	—	—	—	—	—	—
Public works	—	—	—	—	—	—	—	—	—
Other	2,634,459	4,486,793	(1,852,334)	—	—	—	253,124	128,862	124,262
Capital outlay	—	—	—	—	—	—	52,457	309,039	(256,582)
Repayment of loans	—	—	—	—	—	—	—	—	—
Debt service—									
Principal	—	—	—	—	—	—	—	—	—
Interest	—	—	—	—	—	—	—	—	—
Total expenditures	$25,756,113	$28,310,812	$ (2,554,699)	$ 139,414	$ 197,308	$ (57,894)	$15,828,759	$14,996,302	$ 832,457
Revenues over (under) expenditures	$ 4,422,701	$(1,892,518)	$ 6,315,219	$ 517,997	$ 898,779	$ (380,782)	$ 670,488	$ (641,304)	$ 1,311,792
Transfers—in	$ 4,012,658	$ 2,743,654	$ 1,269,004	$3,966,000	$4,130,000	$ (164,000)	$ 1,619,960	$ 2,297,062	$ (677,102)
Transfers—out	5,524,097	4,650,189	873,908	4,789,679	3,924,594	865,085	3,000,000	2,420,000	580,000
Net transfers—in (out)	$(1,511,439)	$(1,906,535)	$ 395,096	$ (823,679)	$ 205,406	$(1,029,085)	$(1,380,040)	$ (122,938)	$(1,257,102)
Revenues over (under) expenditures and transfers	$ 2,911,262	$(3,799,053)	$ 6,710,315	$ (305,682)	$1,104,185	$(1,409,867)	$ (709,552)	$ (764,242)	$ 54,690
FUND BALANCES (CASH BASIS), BEGINNING OF YEAR	12,791,605	—	12,791,605	965,442	—	953,442	5,769,332	—	5,769,332
FUND BALANCES (CASH BASIS), END OF YEAR	$15,702,867	$(3,799,053)	$19,501,920	$ 647,760	$1,104,185	$ (456,425)	$ 5,059,780	$ (764,242)	$ 5,824,022

	Debt Service Funds			Capital Projects Funds			Total (Memorandum Only)		
	Actual	Budget	Actual Over (Under) Budget	Actual	Budget	Actual Over (Under) Budget	Actual	Budget	Actual Over (Under) Budget
	$ —	$ —	$ —	$ —	$ —	$ —	$18,164,988	$16,505,040	$ 1,659,948
	—	—	—	—	—	—	702,018	606,000	96,018
	—	—	—	2,684,667	5,531,220	(2,846,553)	4,739,909	7,434,730	(2,694,821)
	—	—	—	—	—	—	11,396,820	11,067,927	328,893
	—	—	—	—	—	—	3,461,179	2,626,919	834,260
	—	—	—	—	—	—	—	—	—
	—	—	—	—	—	—	2,479,886	2,004,926	474,960
	731,783	—	731,783	112,674	70,000	42,674	3,120,204	1,020,000	2,100,204
	—	—	—	—	—	—	1,877,166	1,900,520	(23,354)
	691,782	—	691,782	—	—	—	691,782	—	691,782
	—	—	—	—	—	—	3,000,000	3,000,000	—
	—	—	—	68,468	—	68,468	1,990,894	1,304,537	686,357
	$ 1,423,565	$ —	$1,423,565	$2,865,809	$5,601,220	$(2,735,411)	$51,624,846	$47,470,599	$ 4,154,247
	$ —	$ —	$ —	$ —	$ —	$ —	$ 8,950,617	$14,809,032	$(5,858,415)
	—	—	—	—	—	—	7,408,203	7,813,865	(405,662)
	—	—	—	—	—	—	3,687,473	4,058,021	(370,548)
	—	—	—	—	—	—	14,164,051	7,400,169	6,763,882
	—	—	—	—	—	—	4,573,902	4,498,641	75,261
	—	—	—	2,473,795	4,461,220	(1,987,425)	2,473,795	4,461,220	(1,987,425)
	—	—	—	—	—	—	2,887,583	4,615,655	(1,728,072)
	—	—	—	869,426	1,400,000	(530,574)	921,883	1,709,039	(787,156)
	—	—	—	—	—	—	—	—	—
	4,175,000	3,680,000	495,000	—	—	—	4,175,000	3,680,000	495,000
	2,441,310	1,918,575	522,735	—	—	—	2,441,310	1,918,575	522,735
	$ 6,616,310	$ 5,598,575	$1,017,735	$3,343,221	$5,861,220	$(2,517,999)	$51,683,817	$54,964,217	$(3,280,400)
	$(5,192,745)	$(5,598,575)	$ 405,830	$ (477,412)	$ (260,000)	$ (217,412)	$ (58,971)	$(7,493,619)	$ 7,434,647
	$ 5,959,519	$ 5,598,575	$ 360,944	$ —	$ —	$ —	$15,558,137	$14,769,291	$ 788,846
	731,783	—	731,783	499,811	70,000	429,811	14,545,370	11,064,783	3,480,587
	$ 5,227,736	$ 5,598,575	$ (370,839)	$ (499,811)	$ (70,000)	$ (429,811)	$ 1,012,767	$ 3,704,508	$(2,691,741)
	$ 34,991	$ —	$ 34,991	$ (977,223)	$ (330,000)	$ (647,223)	$ 953,796	$(3,789,110)	$ 4,742,906
	14,655	—	14,655	2,366,362	—	2,366,362	21,895,396	—	21,895,396
	$ 49,646	$ —	$ 49,646	$1,389,139	$ (300,000)	$ 1,719,139	$22,849,192	$(3,789,110)	$26,638,302

Note A [in part]

(8) Budgets. The County Board of Commissioners approves, at the beginning of each year, an annual budget on a cash basis for all general governmental activities. The County Code allows the Board of Commissioners to authorize budget amendments during the year. The budget data reflected in the combined financial statements includes the effect of such approved budget amendments and, for comparative purposes, the actual amounts have also been presented on a cash basis.

[FULTON COUNTY, GEORGIA]

Combined Statement of Revenues and Expenditures—Budget (Cash Basis) and Actual—General and Special Revenue Fund Types, Year Ended December 31, 1983

	General Fund					Special Revenue Funds (Special Services District Fund)					Totals (Memorandum Only)		
	Modified Accrual Basis	Adjustment to Actual	Actual	Budget	Variance Favorable (Unfavorable)	Modified Accrual Basis	Adjustment to Actual	Actual	Budget	Variance Favorable (Unfavorable)	Actual	Budget	Variance Favorable (Unfavorable)
REVENUES:													
Taxes	$117,538,636	$ (101,601)	$117,437,035	$108,393,245	$ 9,043,790	$ 9,426,130	$(575,860)	$ 8,850,270	$ 9,236,916	$ (386,646)	$126,287,305	$117,630,161	$ 8,657,144
Licenses and permits	13,335		13,335	6,030	7,305	3,745,113	19,757	3,764,870	2,758,781	1,006,089	3,778,205	2,764,811	1,013,394
Federal Revenue Sharing	10,215,576	(6,432,512)	3,783,064	13,403,851	(9,620,787)						3,783,064	13,403,851	(9,620,787)
Intergovernmental	14,400,787	92,146	14,492,933	12,961,146	1,531,787	159,400	(54,071)	105,329		105,329	14,598,262	12,961,146	1,637,116
Charges for services	7,936,369	167,999	8,104,368	6,375,971	1,728,397						8,104,368	6,375,971	1,728,397
Courts and law enforcement	7,407,438	659,949	8,067,387	7,456,275	611,112						8,067,387	7,456,275	611,112
Use of money and property	2,870,506		2,870,506	3,121,206	(250,700)	434,835		434,835	339,629	95,206	3,305,341	3,460,835	(155,494)
Miscellaneous	894,404	92,889	987,293	935,837	51,456	369,625	482,889	852,514	84,264	768,250	1,839,807	1,020,101	819,706
Total Revenues	161,277,051	(5,521,130)	155,755,921	152,653,561	3,102,360	14,135,103	(127,285)	14,007,818	12,419,590	1,588,228	169,763,739	165,073,151	4,690,588
EXPENDITURES:													
Current:													
General government	25,390,138	353,008	25,743,146	27,659,159	1,916,013	1,354,087	(94,000)	1,260,087	1,858,134	598,047	27,003,233	29,517,293	2,514,060
Public safety	30,055,934	(83,726)	29,972,208	31,305,030	1,332,822	12,097,984	12,907	12,110,891	15,102,843	2,991,952	42,083,099	46,407,873	4,324,774
Roads, highways and bridges	8,164,062	(116,250)	8,047,812	8,785,189	737,377						8,047,812	8,785,189	737,377
Sanitation	2,235,718	(9,046)	2,226,672	2,554,360	327,688						2,226,672	2,554,360	327,688
Education	148,232		148,232	171,892	23,660						148,232	171,892	23,660
Health	58,875,769	(2,793,336)	56,082,433	61,423,974	5,341,541						56,082,433	61,423,974	5,341,541
Welfare	6,368,571	23,425	6,391,996	6,698,443	306,447						6,391,996	6,698,443	306,447
Culture and recreation	7,957,690	(211,321)	7,746,369	9,326,300	1,579,931						7,746,369	9,326,300	1,579,931
Capital outlay	2,747,243		2,747,243	2,747,243							2,747,243	2,747,243	
Debt service: Principal and interest retirement	1,743,500		1,743,500	1,915,000	171,500						1,743,500	1,915,000	171,500
Total Expenditures	143,686,857	(2,837,246)	140,849,611	152,586,590	11,736,979	13,452,071	(81,093)	13,370,978	16,960,977	3,589,999	154,200,589	169,547,567	15,326,978
EXCESS (DEFICIENCY) OF REVENUES OVER EXPENDITURES	17,590,194	(2,683,884)	14,906,310	66,971	14,839,339	683,032	(46,192)	636,840	(4,541,387)	5,178,227	15,543,150	(4,474,416)	20,017,566

OTHER FINANCING SOURCES (USES):													
Sale of property	128,814	128,814	126,147	2,667									
Operating transfers out	(5,065,200)	(5,097,111)	(6,145,050)	1,047,939	(31,911)								
	(4,936,386)	(4,968,297)	(6,018,903)	1,050,606	(31,911)								
EXCESS (DEFICIENCY) OF REVENUES AND OTHER SOURCES OVER EXPENDITURES AND OTHER USES	$ 12,653,808	$ 9,938,013	$(5,951,932)	$15,889,945	$(2,715,795)	$ 683,032	$ (46,192)	$ 636,840	$(4,541,387)	$5,178,227	$ 10,574,853	$(10,493,319)	$21,068,172

Note A. Summary of Significant Accounting Policies [in part]

4) Budgets and Budgetary Accounting

	General Fund	Special Services District
Revenues and Other Sources:		
GAAP basis	$161,405,865	$14,135,103
Add: prior year accrual adjustments	6,309,825	426,347
Less: current year accrual adjustments	(11,830,955)	(553,633)
Cash Basis	$155,884,735	$14,007,817
Expenditures and Other Uses:		
GAAP basis	$148,752,057	$13,358,071
Add: prior year accrual adjustments	(1,151,926)	98,622
Less: prior year accrual adjustments current year accrual adjustments	(1,653,409)	(85,714)
Cash Basis	$145,946,722	$13,370,979

[CITY OF SANTA ANA, CALIFORNIA]

Combined Statement of Revenues, Expenditures, and Changes in Fund Balances—Budget (Budgetary Basis) and Actual General, Special Revenue, and Capital Project Fund Types, for the Fiscal Year Ended June 30, 1984

	General Fund				
	Actual	Adjustment to Budgetary Basis (See Note 1)	Actual on Budgetary Basis	Budget	Variance Favorable (Unfavorable)
Revenues:					
Taxes	$41,665,355	$ —	$41,665,355	$39,902,685	$ 1,762,670
Licenses and permits	2,400,649	—	2,400,649	1,368,475	1,032,174
Intergovernmental	3,557,961	—	3,557,961	3,294,315	263,646
Charges for services	3,198,691	—	3,198,691	2,912,610	286,081
Fines and forfeits	783,263	—	783,263	731,000	52,263
Special assessments	—	—	—	—	—
Use of money and property	1,551,805	—	1,551,805	1,540,000	11,805
Miscellaneous	1,070,435	—	1,070,435	601,750	468,685
Total Revenues	54,228,159	—	54,228,159	50,350,835	3,877,324
Expenditures:					
Current:					
General government	2,431,357	88,810	2,520,167	2,517,475	(2,692)
Police services	22,062,174	(7,116)	22,055,058	22,286,515	231,457
Fire services	11,658,107	(43,517)	11,614,590	11,654,080	39,490
Recreation and cultural services	6,847,298	44,833	6,892,131	6,931,485	39,354
Personnel services and manpower	757,159	4,260	761,419	783,155	21,736
Finance Department	1,233,883	(17,638)	1,216,245	1,219,260	3,015
Development services	9,825,212	(106,808)	9,718,404	9,979,970	261,566
Redevelopment and housing services	—	—	—	—	—
Total Current	54,815,190	(37,176)	54,778,014	55,371,940	593,926
Capital	463,397	(463,397)	—	—	—
Debt Service:					
City Hall lease payment	464,300	(38,692)	425,608	465,000	39,392
Total Expenditures	55,742,887	(539,265)	55,203,622	55,836,940	633,318
Excess of Revenues Over (Under) Expenditures	(1,514,728)	539,265	(975,463)	(5,486,105)	4,510,642
Other Financing Sources (Uses):					
Proceeds of sales of bonds	—	—	—	—	—
Operating transfers in	7,262,272	(1,890,834)	5,371,438	6,840,375	(1,468,937)
Operating transfers out	(2,802,333)	2,017,635	(784,698)	(1,812,135)	1,027,437
Contribution to proprietary funds	(353,238)	—	(353,238)	(353,240)	2
Net Other Financing Sources (Uses)	4,106,701	126,801	4,233,502	4,675,000	(441,498)
Excess of Revenues and Other Sources Over (Under) Expenditures and Other Uses	2,591,973	$ 666,066	$ 3,258,039	$ (811,105)	$ 4,069,144
Fund Balance—Beginning of Period	5,379,378				
Equity Transfers in (out)	(7,339)				
Fund Balance—End of Period	$ 7,964,012				

Note: Budgets are adopted for the General, Special Revenue, and Capital Project Funds on the modified accrual basis (see summary of significant accounting policies) except that encumbrances are treated as budgeted expenditures in the year of the commitment to purchase. For the purpose of this statement, actual GAAP expenditures have been adjusted to also include encumbrances outstanding at year end.

The notes to the financial statements are an integral part of this statement.

	Special Revenue Funds				Capital Project Fund				
Actual	Adjustment to Budgetary Basis (See Note 1)	Actual on Budgetary Basis	Budget	Variance Favorable (Unfavorable)	Actual	Adjustment to Budgetary Basis (See Note 1)	Actual on Budgetary Basis	Budget	Variance Favorable (Unfavorable)
$ 300,000	$ —	$ 300,000	$ 300,000	$ —	$ —	$ —	$ —	$ 1,267,810	$ (1,267,810)
—	—	—	—	—	—	—	—	—	—
16,573,565	—	16,573,565	18,655,960	(2,082,395)	3,961,983	—	3,961,983	15,947,180	(11,985,197)
468,643	—	468,643	469,500	(857)	55,205	—	55,205	10,000	45,205
1,604,230	—	1,604,230	1,925,000	(320,770)	—	—	—	—	—
—	—	—	—	—	1,107,698	—	1,107,698	545,575	562,123
1,708,415	—	1,708,415	766,470	941,945	4,822,107	—	4,822,107	4,862,220	(40,113)
23,537	—	23,537	210,255	(186,718)	354,889	—	354,889	694,200	(339,311)
20,678,390	—	20,678,390	22,327,185	(1,648,795)	10,301,882	—	10,301,882	23,326,985	(13,025,103)
54,168	1,019	55,187	313,084	257,897	—	—	—	—	—
155,941	814	156,755	414,500	257,745	—	—	—	—	—
11,864	—	11,864	11,870	6	—	—	—	—	—
788,438	14,363	802,801	1,235,770	432,969	—	—	—	—	—
1,045,362	81,164	1,126,526	1,936,990	810,464	—	—	—	—	—
20,320	11,172	31,492	45,978	14,486	—	—	—	—	—
130,583	3,116	133,699	160,587	26,888	—	—	—	—	—
5,559,689	1,420,799	6,980,488	8,952,199	1,971,711	—	—	—	—	—
7,766,365	1,532,447	9,298,812	13,070,978	3,772,166	—	—	—	—	—
4,985,750	3,861,223	8,846,973	13,721,580	4,874,607	19,290,196	(530,457)	18,759,739	28,563,916	9,804,177
—	—	—	—	—	—	—	—	—	—
12,752,115	5,393,670	18,145,785	26,792,558	8,646,773	19,920,196	(530,457)	18,759,739	28,563,916	9,804,177
7,926,275	(5,393,670)	2,532,605	(4,465,373)	6,997,978	(8,988,314)	530,457	(8,457,857)	(5,236,931)	(3,220,926)
—	—	—	—	—	—	—	—	6,200,000	(6,200,000)
255,672	(5,000)	250,672	251,760	(1,088)	15,160,724	(9,369,365)	5,790,909	4,401,715	1,389,194
(8,406,244)	2,859,398	(5,546,846)	(9,395,295)	3,848,449	(4,402,738)	2,992,983	(1,409,755)	(7,357,885)	5,948,130
—					—				
(8,150,572)	2,854,398	(5,296,174)	(9,143,535)	3,847,361	10,757,536	(6,376,382)	4,381,154	3,243,830	1,137,324
(224,297)	$(2,539,272)	$(2,763,569)	$(13,608,908)	$10,845,339	1,769,222	$(5,845,925)	$(4,076,703)	$(1,993,101)	$ (2,083,602)
15,668,285					18,501,372				
7,339					—				
$15,451,327					$20,270,594				

Chapter 8
Revenues, Expenses, and Changes in Retained Earnings: Proprietary Funds and Similar Trust Funds

REVENUES AND EXPENSES

Principle 10 of NCGA Statement 1 also provides guidance for the classification and reporting of revenues and expenses of proprietary funds and trust funds of similar type:

> 10.c. Proprietary fund revenues and expenses should be classified in essentially the same manner as those of similar business organizations, functions, or activities.

The choice of revenue and expense account nomenclature in these combined statements appears directly related to the nature of the enterprise or internal service activities operated by the governmental unit. Also, the number and types of trust funds established by the governmental unit caused the revenue and expense account classifications to differ among the units.

CHANGES IN RETAINED EARNINGS

The NCGA states that the section of the operations statement concerning changes in retained earnings or equity balances should be in a format that provides a meaningful summary of the changes and a reconciliation between the beginning and ending balances. As for governmental funds, the NCGA has prescribed the all-inclusive concept of retained earnings reporting for proprietary funds. Adherence to this concept eliminates the need to reflect changes in retained earnings in a separate statement of changes. Thus, the statement of revenues and expenses should contain all revenues, expenses, and transfers and other changes related to the retained earnings of all proprietary funds.

REPORTING PRACTICES

The reporting practices of proprietary funds and similar trust funds closely parallel comparable commercial financial reporting. The guidance published for business operations in the private sector applies to similar governmental activity. The NCGA has prescribed a combined statement (the statement of revenues, expenses, and changes in fund balances) for use by governments with proprietary-type fund activities. About 72% of the surveyed governmental units utilized such a financial statement. The surveyed governments' financial statements for proprietary funds typically included the following major sections:

operating and nonoperating revenues,

operating and nonoperating expenses,

operating transfers in (out),

net income (loss),

retained earnings or fund balances at the beginning of the year,

reconciling items in retained earnings or fund balances, and

retained earnings or fund balances at the end of the year.

A selection of reported revenue and expense accounts is given in Tables 8-1 and 8-2, respectively. It should be noted that revenues and expenses were not always uniformly categorized as operating or nonoperating. Exhibit 8-1 contains examples of governmental financial statements reporting revenues, expenses, and changes in retained earnings or fund balances for proprietary funds and similar trust fund types.

SEGMENT REPORTING

In its Statement 1, the NCGA calls segment information "essential" for enterprise funds with bonds and other debt securities outstanding. It also states that the reporting may be accomplished either in the combined statements or in similar combining statements of revenues, expenses, and changes in retained earnings for proprietary funds and in the statement of changes in financial position. A *segment*, as used in Statement 1, is an individual enterprise fund of a governmental unit. (This differs from the use of the term "segment" in Statement 14 issued by the Financial Accounting Standards Board, "Financial Reporting for Segments of a Business Enterprise." There a segment is a particular line of business endeavor.)

In 1980 the NCGA issued Interpretation 2, "Segment Information for Enterprise Funds," which stated that segment disclosures are required for all enterprise funds with any type of material long-term liabilities outstanding. Further, segment disclosures are required by this interpretation if such disclosures are necessary to prevent the general purpose financial statements from being misleading. Such disclosures may relate to

material intergovernmental operating subsidies to an enterprise fund,

material intragovernmental operating subsidies to or from an enterprise fund

material enterprise fund tax revenues, or

material enterprise fund net income or loss.

For qualifying enterprise funds, those with material long-term liabilities, Interpretation 2 states that the following segment information should be the minimum presented:

the types of goods or services provided;

operating revenues (sales to other funds being separately disclosed);

depreciation, depletion, and amortization expenses;

operating income or loss (operating revenues less operating expenses);

operating grants, entitlements, and shared revenues;

operating interfund transfers in and out;

tax revenues;

net income or loss (total revenues less total expenses);

current capital contributions and transfers;

plant, property, and equipment additions and deletions;

net working capital (current assets less current liabilities);

total assets;

bonds and other material long-term liabilities outstanding; and

total equity.

The presentation of segment information in footnotes to the general-purpose financial statement is preferable, although reporting may be made in columns of enterprise fund statements. Interpretation 2 was ef-

fective for fiscal years ending after September 30, 1980.

Exhibit 8-2 contains examples of the segment data reported and some financial statements.

EXHIBITS AND TABLES FOR CHAPTER 8

Table 8-1. Account Titles Used by Governmental Units to Report Revenues for Proprietary Fund Types

Table 8-2. Descriptors Used by Governmental Units to Report Expenses for Proprietary Fund Types

Exhibit 8-1. Examples of Reporting by Governmental Units of Statements of Revenues, Expenses, and Changes in Retained Earnings for Proprietary Fund Types and Similar Trust Funds

Exhibit 8-2. Examples of Segment Reporting by Governmental Units

TABLE 8-1. ACCOUNT TITLES USED BY GOVERNMENTAL UNITS TO REPORT REVENUES FOR PROPRIETARY FUND TYPES

Account Title*	Instances Observed (%)
Charges for services	68
Contributions	30
Other	30
Miscellaneous	26
Interest Income	20
Interest	18
Investment income	11
Other revenues	9
Taxes	8
Rentals	7
Intergovernmental revenue	6
Gains on investment disposal	6
Water sales	6
Interest earned	6
Operating revenues	5
Property taxes	5
Interest and dividend income	5
Interest on investments	5
Contributions from employees	4
Connection charges	4
Rents	4
Sewer charges	3
Use of money and property	3
User charges	3
Intragovernmental revenues	3
Parking (fees)	2
Concessions	2
Sewer service charges	2
Sales	2
Dividends	2
All other descriptors	<2

* Observations for the 60% of the units having this statement.

TABLE 8-2. DESCRIPTORS USED BY GOVERNMENTAL UNITS TO REPORT EXPENSES FOR PROPRIETARY FUND TYPES

Descriptors	Instances Observed (%)	Descriptors	Instances Observed (%)
Governmental units whose general purpose financial statement included a revenue, expense, and changes in retained earnings statement	72	Operating transfers to/out (or from/in)	12
		Operating transfers	6
		Other financing sources (uses)	6
		Other financing sources	2
Expense descriptors noted:*		Other financing uses	<1
Operating expenses	91	Net income (loss)	35
Nonoperating expenses	25	Net income	32
Operating expenses, before depreciation	<1	Net loss	3
Operating transfers from (or in)	20	Other descriptors	<1
Operating transfers to (or out)	17		

* Observations for those governments having this statement.

EXHIBIT 8-1. EXAMPLES OF REPORTING BY GOVERNMENTAL UNITS OF REVENUES, EXPENSES, AND CHANGES IN RETAINED EARNINGS FOR PROPRIETARY FUND TYPES AND SIMILAR TRUST FUNDS

[CITY OF ALBUQUERQUE, NEW MEXICO]

Combined Statement of Revenues, Expenses, and Changes in Retained Earnings/Fund Balances—All Proprietary Fund Types and Similar Trust Funds, Year Ended June 30, 1984 (in thousands of dollars)

	Enterprise	Internal Service	Non-expendable Trust Fund	Pension Trust Fund	June 30, 1984	June 30, 1983 as restated
Operating revenues:						
Charges for services	$70,467	$11,160	—	—	$ 81,627	$66,270
Loss recoveries	—	336	—	—	336	122
Interest on investments	—	—	1,596	46	1,642	272
Gross receipts tax	—	—	16,755	—	16,755	7,352
Total operating revenues	70,467	11,496	18,351	46	100,360	74,016
Operating expenses:						
Salaries and fringe benefits	23,161	3,965	—	—	27,126	21,938
Professional services	154	—	5	—	159	50
Utilities	7,091	15	—	—	7,106	7,119
Supplies	4,034	2,068	1	—	6,103	3,016
Travel	60	4	—	—	64	71
Repairs and maintenance	10,148	243	—	—	10,391	7,434
Contractual services	2,990	943	77	—	4,010	3,645
Claims and judgments	—	7,400	—	—	7,400	4,176
Insurance premiums	—	613	—	—	613	251
Other operating expenses	3,749	619	—	—	4,368	3,648
Payments in lieu of taxes	1,586	—	—	—	1,586	2,584
Payments to retirees	—	—	—	44	44	55
Depreciation	15,233	95	—	—	15,328	15,899
Amortization	525	—	—	—	525	420
Bad debt expense	2	—	—	—	2	1
Total operating expenses	68,733	15,965	83	44	84,825	70,307
Operating income (loss)	1,734	(4,469)	18,268	2	15,535	3,709

(continued)

[CITY OF ALBUQUERQUE, NEW MEXICO] (Continued)

	Proprietary Funds		Fiduciary Funds		Totals (Memorandum Only) Year Ended	
	Enterprise	Internal Service	Non-expendable Trust Fund	Pension Trust Fund	June 30, 1984	June 30, 1983 as restated
Non-operating revenues (expense):						
Interest on investments	6,340	577	—	—	6,917	4,781
Cash discounts earned	—	15	—	—	15	9
Operating grants	—	—	—	—	—	1,000
Gain on disposition of property and equipment	12	—	9	—	21	335
Interest expense	(9,769)	—	(1,186)	—	(10,955)	(8,761)
City water service expansion charges	3,114	—	—	—	3,114	2,227
Other	51	14	—	—	65	58
Refund of payments in lieu of taxes	46	—	—	—	46	—
Total non-operating revenues (expenses)	(206)	606	(1,177)	—	(777)	(351)
Income (loss) before operating transfers and extraordinary item	1,528	(3,863)	17,091	2	14,758	3,358
Operating transfers in (Note 14)	7,437	—	—	—	7,437	7,731
Operating transfers out (Note 14)	(336)	—	(1,181)	—	(1,517)	(492)
Income (loss) before extraordinary item	8,629	(3,863)	15,910	2	20,678	10,597
Gain on refunding of bonds	11,041	—	—	—	11,041	6,506
Net income (loss)	19,670	(3,863)	15,910	2	31,719	17,103
Decrease in contributed capital for depreciation on assets acquired with federal grants	1,286	—	—	—	1,286	893
Other changes in unreserved retained earnings/fund balance:						
Decrease (increase) in reserves:						
Employees retirement system	—	—	—	(2)	(2)	17
Bond debt service and retirement	4,056	—	—	—	4,056	(1,449)
Acquisition and management of open space land	—	—	(9,327)	—	(9,327)	(1,147)
Urban enhancement	—	—	(6,583)	—	(6,583)	—
Transfer of land to General Fixed Assets	—	—	—	—	—	(5,642)
Unreserved retained earnings/fund balance (deficit), July 1	14,924	(1,649)	—	—	13,275	3,500
Unreserved retained earnings/fund balance (deficit), June 30	$39,936	$(5,512)	$ —	$ —	$ 34,424	$13,275

[COUNTY OF ALLEGHENY, PENNSYLVANIA]

Combined Statement of Revenues, Expenses and Changes in Retained Earnings/Fund Balances—Proprietary Fund Types and Similar Trust Funds, Year Ended December 31, 1983

	Proprietary Fund Types		Fiduciary Fund Type	Totals (Memorandum Only)
	Enterprise	Internal Service	Pension Trust	
Operating revenues:				
Aviation—principally landing fees	$11,990,100	—	—	11,990,100
Charges for services	—	4,116,207	—	4,116,207
Contributions—employee	—	—	10,153,141	10,153,141
Contributions—employer	—	—	10,095,049	10,095,049
Investment income	—	—	13,545,237	13,545,237
Concession and parking fees	10,789,171	—	—	10,789,171
Utility sales	2,137,021	—	—	2,137,021
Rentals	6,703,052	—	—	6,703,052
Maintenance services	32,761	—	—	32,761
Interim terminal expansion revenue (note 1)	2,405,257	—	—	2,405,257
Miscellaneous income	89,470	—	54,862	144,332
	34,146,832	4,116,207	33,848,289	72,111,328
Operating expenses:				
Salaries, wages, and related expenses	7,415,043	2,179,670	117,954	9,712,667
Materials and supplies	944,872	771,794	—	1,716,666
Repair and replacement of equipment	108,923	132,004	—	240,927
Cleaning and maintenance	1,241,577	—	—	1,241,577
Cost allocations from General Fund	3,349,699	—	—	3,349,699
Equipment rental	30,080	263,798	—	293,878
Utilities	4,813,730	—	—	4,813,730
Depreciation	10,060,248	239,900	—	10,300,148
Postage	—	535,118	—	535,118
Professional services	547,988	—	443,920	991,908
Benefit payments	—	—	13,275,246	13,275,246
Refunds of contributions	—	—	2,002,749	2,002,749
Other	485,869	—	38,038	523,907
	28,998,029	4,122,284	15,877,907	48,998,220
Income (loss) from operations	5,148,803	(6,077)	17,970,382	23,113,108
Non-operating income (expense):				
Interest expense	(4,175,430)	—	—	(4,175,430)
Interest income	301,606	—	—	301,606
	(3,873,824)	—	—	(3,873,824)
Net income (loss)	1,274,979	(6,077)	17,970,382	19,239,284
Add depreciation on fixed assets acquired by grants	2,530,344	—	—	2,530,344
Increase (decrease) in retained earnings/fund balance from operations	3,805,323	(6,077)	17,970,382	21,769,628
Retained earnings/fund balance at December 31, 1982, as previously reported	9,413,020	807,138	80,498,797	90,718,955
Effect of restatements (note 13)	(149,154)	—	—	(149,154)
Retained earnings/fund balance at December 31, 1982, as restated	9,263,866	807,138	80,498,797	90,569,801
Transfer of long-term debt (note 7)	(3,289,147)	—	—	(3,289,147)
Equity transfers	12,000	—	—	12,000
Retained earnings/fund balances at December 31, 1983	$ 9,792,042	801,061	98,469,179	109,062,282

[CITY OF ATLANTA, GEORGIA]

Combined Statement of Revenues, Expenses and Changes in Contributed Capital and Retained Earnings/Fund Balances—All Proprietary Fund Types and Similar Trust Funds for the Year Ended December 31, 1983 with Comparative Totals for 1982 (in Thousands)

	Proprietary Fund Types		Fiduciary Fund Types		Totals (Memorandum Only)	
	Enterprise Funds	Internal Service Fund	Nonexpendable Trust Fund	Pension Trust Fund	1983	1982
OPERATING REVENUES:						
Charges for services	$ 86,068	$20,193	$ —	$ —	$106,261	$104,796
Rentals and concessions	72,839	—	—	—	72,839	66,166
Employer and employee contributions	—	—	—	36,772	36,772	33,717
Tax on fire insurance premiums	—	—	—	2,875	2,875	2,529
Refunds and other	7,528	35	—	34	7,597	6,835
Total operating revenues	166,435	20,228	—	39,681	226,344	214,043
OPERATING EXPENSES:						
Salaries and employee benefits (Note 4)	39,617	8,671	—	—	48,288	46,930
Utilities	11,818	382	—	—	12,200	11,478
Repairs and maintenance	2,656	382	—	—	3,607	3,593
Materials and supplies	4,470	7,594	—	—	12,064	12,252
Janitorial and other contractual services	4,676	1,273	—	—	5,949	5,183
Motor equipment service	1,666	—	—	—	1,666	1,398
Engineering and consultant fees	1,138	—	—	—	1,138	1,213
General services	3,790	—	—	—	3,790	3,639
Benefit payments	—	—	—	19,002	19,002	16,874
Refunds	—	—	—	4,416	4,416	2,022
Provision for alleged noise disturbance and other claims (Note 7)	—	—	—	—	—	2,300
Depreciation	37,435	1,140	—	—	38,575	34,525
Other	8,577	61	3	275	8,916	4,111
Total operating expenses	115,843	20,972	3	23,693	159,611	145,518
OPERATING INCOME (LOSS)	50,592	156	(3)	15,988	66,733	68,525
NONOPERATING REVENUES (EXPENSES), net (Note 7)	(42,213)	67	12	21,393	(20,741)	7,458
INCOME BEFORE CUMULATIVE EFFECT OF THE CHANGE IN METHOD OF RECORDING REVENUES, OPERATING TRANSFERS AND MINORITY INTEREST	8,379	223	9	37,381	45,992	75,983
CUMULATIVE EFFECT OF ACCRUING UNBILLED REVENUES (Note 1)	5,376	—	—	—	5,376	—
INCOME BEFORE OPERATING TRANSFERS AND MINORITY INTEREST	13,755	223	9	37,381	51,368	75,983
OPERATING TRANSFERS TO EXPENDABLE TRUST FUND	—	—	(5)	—	(5)	(6)
NET INCOME BEFORE MINORITY INTEREST	13,755	223	4	37,381	51,363	75,977
MINORITY INTEREST (Note 8)	(557)	—	—	—	(557)	(265)
NET INCOME	13,198	223	4	37,381	50,806	75,712

(continued)

[CITY OF ATLANTA, GEORGIA] (Continued)

	Proprietary Fund Types		Fiduciary Fund Types		Totals (Memorandum Only)	
	Enterprise Funds	Internal Service Fund	Nonexpendable Trust Fund	Pension Trust Fund	1983	1982
CONTRIBUTED CAPITAL AND RETAINED EARNINGS/ FUND BALANCES, beginning of year	621,662	4,638	161	159,763	786,224	677,568
CONTRIBUTIONS FROM:						
U.S. Government (Note 5)	32,886	—	—	—	32,886	33,536
Other	304	41	—	—	345	33
RESIDUAL TRANSFERS TO DEBT SERVICE FUNDS (Note 3)	(748)	—	—	—	(748)	(625)
CONTRIBUTED CAPITAL AND RETAINED EARNINGS/ FUND BALANCES, end of year	$667,302	$ 4,902	$ 165	$197,144	$869,513	$786,224

[CITY OF BEAUMONT, TEXAS]

Combined Statement of Revenues, Expenses, and Changes in Fund Equity—All Proprietary Fund Types and Similar Trust Funds for the Year Ending September 30, 1983

	Proprietary Fund Types		Fiduciary Fund Type	Totals (Memorandum Only)	
	Enterprise	Internal Service	Nonexpendable Trust	1983	1982
Operating revenues:					
Charges for services	$13,961,509	$3,782,009	$ —	$17,743,518	$16,127,001
Interest	—	67,991	—	67,991	219,197
Disposal of assets	—	67,182	—	67,182	1,506
Other revenues	30,672	2,637	—	33,309	43,787
Total operating revenues	13,992,181	3,919,819	—	17,912,000	16,391,491
Operating expenses:					
Personnel services	7,243,698	82,235	—	7,325,933	7,885,173
Other operating expenses	4,703,158	2,269,805	—	6,972,963	6,213,957
Depreciation	1,645,462	1,588,102	—	3,233,564	2,969,545
Loss on uncollected accounts	126,571	—	—	126,571	72,816
Total operating expenses	13,718,889	3,940,142	—	17,659,031	17,141,491
Operating income (loss)	273,292	(20,323)	—	252,969	(750,000)
Non-operating revenues (expenses):					
Intergovernmental	4,349,984	—	—	4,349,984	7,835,702
Gain on sale of assets	4,008	—	—	4,008	—
Gain on service installations	14,541	—	—	14,541	36,529
Interest income	783,259	—	—	783,259	1,340,935
Interest expense and fiscal charges	(1,741,141)	—	—	(1,741,141)	(1,470,639)
Operating grants	504,226	—	—	504,226	394,169
Payments to the General Fund in lieu of taxes	(2,050,000)	—	—	(2,050,000)	(1,000,000)
Gain (loss) on refunding long-term debt	(3,110,000)	—	—	(3,110,000)	760,000
Net non-operating revenues (expenses)	(1,245,123)	—	—	(1,245,123)	7,896,696
Income (loss) before operating transfer	(971,831)	(20,323)	—	(992,154)	7,146,696
Operating transfers in	494,195	—	—	494,195	373,545
Net income (loss) (as restated in 1982)	(477,636)	(20,323)	—	(497,959)	7,520,241

(continued)

[CITY OF BEAUMONT, TEXAS] (Continued)

	Proprietary Fund Types		Fiduciary Fund Type	Totals (Memorandum Only)	
	Enterprise	Internal Service	Nonexpendable Trust	1983	1982
Fund equity, beginning of year as previously reported	53,508,716	3,165,981	19,243	56,693,940	49,256,117
Prior period adjustment—revenue correction	—	—	—	—	(278,445)
Fixed asset inventory correction	5,915,866	500,342	—	6,416,208	6,623,318
Fund equity, beginning of year—as restated	59,424,582	3,666,323	19,243	63,110,148	55,600,990
Decrease in reserve for injuries and damages	(4,454)	—	—	(4,454)	(7,608)
Contributed capital:					
Property owners	43,314	—	—	43,314	—
Governmental agencies	123,187	—	—	123,187	—
Equity transfers out	—	—	—	—	(3,475)
Prior period adjustment—Equity correction	—	—	(19,243)	(19,243)	—
Fund equity (deficit) end of year	$59,108,993	$3,646,000	$ —	$62,754,993	$63,110,148

[CITY OF BIRMINGHAM, ALABAMA]

Combined Statement of Revenues, Expenses and Changes in Retained Deficit/Fund Balances, All Proprietary Fund Types and Similar Trust Funds, for the Year Ended June 30, 1984

	Proprietary Fund Type	Fiduciary Fund Type	Total (Memorandum Only)	
	Enterprise	Pension Trust	1984	1983
Operating revenues:				
Facility charges	$ 7,247,746	$	$ 7,247,746	$ 6,735,199
Contributions		13,219,932	13,219,932	12,871,310
Taxes		311,717	311,717	361,062
Interest and gain on sale of investments		18,754,660	18,754,660	15,673,277
Total operating revenues	7,247,746	32,286,309	39,534,055	35,640,848
Operating expenses:				
Current operations:				
Public safety	1,261,311		1,261,311	1,222,499
Depreciation	1,034,678		1,034,678	1,002,088
Repairs and maintenance	727,062		727,062	420,332
General and administration	2,196,337	371,804	2,568,141	2,343,097
Annuities		8,222,648	8,222,648	7,367,937
Refunds		802,234	802,234	551,280
Loss on sale of investments		279,165	279,165	
Total operating expenses	5,219,388	9,675,851	14,895,239	12,907,233
Operating income	2,028,358	22,610,458	24,638,816	22,733,615
Nonoperating revenues (expenses):				
Interest earned	486,809		486,809	568,737
Gain on sale of investments	21,750		21,750	61,875
Interest expense	(1,207,308)		(1,207,308)	(1,332,561)
Net nonoperating revenues (expenses)	(698,749)		(698,749)	(701,949)
Net income	1,329,609	22,610,458	23,940,067	22,031,666
Retained earnings (deficit)/fund balances, beginning of the year	(10,352,301)	167,842,306	157,490,005	135,458,339
Residual equity transfer	(356,566)		(356,566)	
Retained earnings (deficit)/fund balances, end of the year	$ (9,379,258)	$190,452,764	$181,073,506	$157,490,005

[CITY OF TOPEKA, KANSAS]

Combined Statement of Revenue, Expenses and Changes in Retained Earnings—All Proprietary Fund Types, Year Ended December 31, 1983, with Comparative Totals for the Year Ended December 31, 1982

	Enterprise Funds	Internal Service Funds	Totals (Memorandum Only) 1983	Totals (Memorandum Only) 1982
Operating revenues:				
Charges for services	$12,082,269	2,501,874	14,584,053	13,059,622
Concession sales, net	99,336	—	99,336	44,400
Employee contributions	—	656,539	656,539	616,813
Other	660,010	5,590	665,600	632,558
	12,841,615	3,163,913	16,005,528	14,353,393
Operating expenses other than depreciation and payments in lieu of taxes:				
Salaries, wages and benefits	4,497,543	481,445	4,978,988	4,798,873
Materials, supplies and chemicals	1,271,498	452,277	1,723,775	1,215,081
Contractual services	497,053	60,817	557,870	681,537
Utilities	1,349,737	72,278	1,422,015	1,121,460
Insurance premiums	215,129	1,611,306	1,826,435	1,563,119
Insurance claims	—	431,803	431,803	207,194
Repairs and maintenance	1,155,627	119,645	1,275,272	908,984
Other	372,371	134,346	506,717	651,075
	9,358,958	3,363,917	12,722,875	11,147,323
Operating income (loss) before depreciation and payments in lieu of taxes	3,482,657	(200,004)	3,282,653	3,206,070
Depreciation	1,871,460	49,743	1,921,203	1,890,379
Payments in lieu of taxes	700,313	—	700,313	579,998
Operating income (loss)	910,884	(249,747)	661,137	735,693
Nonoperating revenues (expenses):				
Intergovernmental revenue (note 3)	47,980	—	47,980	285,641
Interest income	2,437,845	245,912	2,683,757	3,453,430
Interest expense	(1,661,363)	—	(1,661,363)	(1,574,676)
Other income (expense)	27,421	—	27,421	(22,238)
	851,883	245,912	1,097,795	2,142,157
Net income (loss) before operating transfers	1,762,767	(3,835)	1,758,932	2,877,850
Other financing sources (uses):				
Operating transfers in	—	339,013	339,013	200,555
Operating transfers out	—	(157,450)	(157,450)	(127,728)
Net income	1,762,767	177,728	1,940,495	2,950,677
Retained earnings, beginning of year	30,936,027	2,248,529	33,184,556	30,233,879
Retained earnings, end of year	$32,698,794	2,426,257	35,125,051	33,184,556

[CITY OF COLORADO SPRINGS, COLORADO]

All Proprietary Fund Types and Similar Trust Funds, Combined Statement of Revenues, Expenses and Changes in Retained Earnings/Fund Balance, for the year Ended December 31, 1983

	Proprietary Fund Types		Fiduciary Fund Types		Memorandum Only
	Enterprise	Internal Service	Non-expendable Trust	Pension Trust	Totals
Operating revenues:					
Charges for services	$ 4,142,349	457	34,970	—	4,177,776
Sale of lots	175,124	—	—	—	175,124
Interest transfer from Endowment Fund	131,107	—	—	—	131,107
Concessions	183,658	—	—	—	183,658
Miscellaneous	72,747	13,839	188,270	1,465,567	1,740,423
Interdepartmental charges	—	3,051,787	—	—	3,051,787
Total operating revenues	4,704,985	3,066,083	223,240	1,465,567	9,459,875
Operating expenses:					
Salaries, wages and fringe benefits	1,702,232	191,484	—	—	1,893,716
Repairs and maintenance	184,936	1,738,406	—	—	1,923,342
Professional services	495,640	140	—	—	495,780
Utilities	385,586	—	—	—	385,586
Insurance	51,550	33,152	—	—	84,702
Supplies	244,155	107,360	—	—	351,515
Administration	84,996	33,175	—	—	118,171
Miscellaneous	43,509	10,710	8,822	89,749	152,790
Total operating expenses	3,192,604	2,114,427	8,822	89,749	5,405,602
Operating income before depreciation	1,512,381	951,656	214,418	1,375,818	4,054,273
Less provision for depreciation—Note 2	977,937	428,465	—	—	1,406,402
Operating income	534,444	523,191	214,418	1,375,818	2,647,871
Add non-operating income:					
Interest on investments	923,214	77,111	—	—	1,000,325
	1,457,658	600,302	214,418	1,375,818	3,648,196
Deduct non-operating transfers					
Interest expense	188,673	—	—	—	188,673
Income before operating transfers	1,268,985	600,302	214,418	1,375,818	3,459,523
Operating transfers (out)	—	—	(131,108)	—	(131,108)
Net income	1,268,985	600,302	83,310	1,375,818	3,328,415
Retained earnings at beginning of year—Note 11	10,392,702	4,229,807	1,785,454	2,347,615	18,755,578
Retained earnings at end of year	$11,661,687	4,830,109	1,868,764	3,723,433	22,083,993

[CITY OF LAKEWOOD, COLORADO]

Combined Statement of Revenues, Expenses and Changes in Retained Earnings/Fund Balances—All Proprietary Fund Types and Similar Trust Funds, Year Ended December 31, 1983

	Proprietary	Fiduciary	Total
	Enterprise Water & Sewer	Pension Trust	(Memorandum Only)
Operating revenues:			
Charges for service	$1,727,839	$ —	$1,727,839
Contributions:			
Employee	—	455,295	455,295
City	26,821	532,993	559,814
State of Colorado	—	81,854	81,854
Investment income	—	716,803	716,803
Other income	160,129	—	160,129
Total operating revenues	1,914,789	1,786,945	3,701,734
Operating expenses:			
Administration fees	—	38,896	38,896
Personnel services	194,108	—	194,108
Board expense	4,995	—	4,995
Operating supplies and expense	19,069	—	19,069
Professional services	39,504	—	39,504
Communications	5,728	—	5,728
Transportation	15,354	—	15,354
Advertising and printing	448	—	448
Sanitation treatment	991,621	—	991,621
Water purchased	204,686	—	204,686
Utilities	12,960	—	12,960
Repairs and maintenance	122,040	—	122,040
Depreciation	95,995	—	95,995
Refund on employee contributions	—	311,478	311,478
Other expenses	52,022	896	52,918
Benefit payments	—	36,129	36,129
Legal service	18,324	—	18,324
Total operating expenses	1,776,854	387,399	2,164,253
Net income from operation	137,935	1,399,546	1,537,481
Investment income	69,121	—	69,121
Depreciation reclassified to contributions (note 1)	94,870	—	94,870
Net income	301,926	1,399,546	1,701,472
Retained earnings/fund balances at beginning of year	299,155	5,789,410	6,088,565
Retained earnings/fund balances at end of year	$ 601,081	$7,188,956	$7,790,037

[HOWARD COUNTY, MARYLAND]

Combined Statement of Revenues, Expenses and Changes in Retained Earnings—Proprietary Fund Types, for the Year Ended June 30, 1984

	Enterprise Fund	Internal Service Funds	Total Memorandum Only
Operating revenues:			
User charges	$ 7,974,582	$1,258,226	$ 9,232,808
Insurance recoveries	—	35,694	35,694
Miscellaneous sales and service	93,045	—	93,045
Total operating revenues	8,067,627	1,293,920	9,361,547
Operating expenses:			
Salaries and employee benefits	2,826,210	17,965	2,844,175
Contractual services	1,275,789	318,966	1,594,755
Supplies and materials	748,867	175,735	924,602
Business and travel	58,806	48,971	107,777
Purchased water, capacity and transmission charges	1,657,069	—	1,657,069
Sewage treatment charges	325,224	—	325,224
Share of County administrative expense	783,450	—	783,450
Other	4,252	—	4,252
Insurance claims	—	206,286	206,286
Less:			
House connection expense	(276,219)	—	(276,219)
Capitalized overhead costs	(128,482)	—	(128,482)
Total operating expenses except depreciation	7,274,966	767,923	8,042,889
Operating income before depreciation	792,661	525,997	1,318,658
Depreciation expense:			
Applicable to contributed assets	(1,098,073)	—	(1,098,073)
Applicable to assets financed with bonds	(2,056,502)	—	(2,056,502)
Other	(100,976)	(14,756)	(115,732)
Operating income (loss)	(2,462,890)	511,241	(1,951,649)
Nonoperating revenues (expenses):			
Interest on investments	3,291,776	300,598	3,592,374
Local taxes	6,214,975	—	6,214,975
Charges for services	805,996	—	805,996
Interest expense	(5,940,784)	—	(5,940,784)
Net income before operating transfers	1,909,073	811,839	2,720,912
Operating Transfers (out)	—	(50,000)	(50,000)
Net income	1,909,073	761,839	2,670,912
Add: Depreciation on assets acquired from contributions	1,098,098	—	1,098,098
Increase transferred to retained earnings	3,007,171	761,839	3,769,010
Retained earnings, July 1, 1983, as restated	18,208,907	2,727,972	20,936,879
Retained earnings, June 30, 1984	$21,216,078	$3,489,811	$24,705,889
Sources of Financial Resources:			
Operations:			
Net Income	$ 1,909,073	$ 761,839	$ 2,670,912
Items not requiring financial resources			
Depreciation	3,255,551	14,756	3,270,307
Total sources of financial resources provided by operations	5,164,624	776,595	5,941,219
Federal and state grants	3,131,064	—	3,131,064
In aid of construction charges	3,744,236	—	3,744,236
Developers' contributions	407,182	—	186,182
Major water agreements issued	186,700	—	186,700
Increase in accounts payable and accrued expenses	—	16,878	16,878

(continued)

[HOWARD COUNTY, MARYLAND] (Continued)

	Enterprise Fund	Internal Service Funds	Total Memorandum Only
Increase in deposits and connection fees	6,544	—	6,544
Increase in deferred revenue	15,986	—	15,986
Net decrease in restricted assets	3,109,277	—	3,109,277
Net increase in payables from restricted assets	460,406	—	460,406
Total sources of working capital	16,226,019	793,382	17,019,401
Uses of Financial Resources:			
Construction of water and sewer system	12,866,204	—	12,866,204
Acquisition of equipment	141,303	10,690	151,993
Retirement of metropolitan district bonds	2,280,000	—	2,280,000
Retirement of major water agreements	127,455	—	127,455
Increase in service billing receivables	398,903	—	398,903
Increase in property taxes receivable	87,378	—	87,378
Increase in materials and supplies	61,443	3,502	64,945
Decrease in accounts payable and accrued expenses	521,536	77,282	598,818
Total uses of financial resources	16,484,222	91,474	16,575,696
Net increase (decrease) in equity in pooled cash and cash equivalents	$ (258,203)	$ 701,908	$ 443,705

[CITY OF COLUMBUS, OHIO]

Combined Statement of Revenues, Expenses and Changes in Retained Earnings—All Proprietary Fund Types, Year Ended December 31, 1983, with Comparative Totals for 1982

	Enterprise (Note 17)	Internal Service	1983	1982
Operating revenues:				
Charges for services	$124,537,794	16,653,610	141,191,404	132,950,934
Other	1,651,502	22,460	1,673,962	1,480,849
	126,189,296	16,676,070	142,865,366	134,431,783
Operating expenses:				
Personal services	31,739,083	6,554,044	38,293,127	33,635,809
Contractual services	24,448,102	2,366,630	26,814,732	24,780,415
Materials and supplies	8,289,875	5,513,590	13,803,465	12,758,051
Purchased power	11,921,110	—	11,921,110	13,501,050
Depreciation	14,743,607	1,036,710	15,780,317	13,042,335
Other	1,764,719	50,983	1,815,702	1,670,389
	92,906,496	15,521,957	108,428,453	99,388,049
Operating income	33,282,800	1,154,113	34,436,913	35,043,734
Nonoperating revenues (expenses):				
Interest income	6,003,422	—	6,003,422	4,392,422
Interest expense	(26,227,956)	(187,648)	(26,415,604)	(26,370,647)
Net income	13,058,266	966,465	14,024,731	13,065,509
Retained earnings at beginning of year	123,258,813	735,152	123,996,965	110,931,456
Retained earnings at end of year	$136,317,079	1,704,617	138,021,696	123,996,965

[CITY OF ST. PETERSBURG, FLORIDA]

Combined Statement of Revenues, Expenses and Changes in Retained Earnings, All Proprietary Fund Types, Fiscal Year Ended September 30, 1983

	Proprietary Fund Types		Totals (Memorandum Only)	
	Enterprise	Internal Service	1983	1982
OPERATING REVENUES				
Sales	$14,023,145	$ 99,011	$14,122,156	$13,284,719
Service Charges and Fees	31,806,497	16,511,607	48,318,104	50,385,006
Rentals	2,591,579	2,262,082	4,853,661	5,938,047
Other	458,187	—	458,187	282,425
Total Operating Revenues	48,879,408	18,872,700	67,752,108	69,890,197
OPERATING EXPENSES				
Personal Services and Benefits	17,177,315	6,771,937	23,949,252	22,565,451
Supplies and Services	19,514,736	10,673,886	30,188,622	32,026,970
General Administrative Charges	3,992,060	—	3,992,060	3,433,725
Payment in Lieu of Taxes	2,528,000	—	2,528,000	2,418,900
Depreciation	7,149,991	1,824,982	8,974,973	8,055,519
Total Operating Expenses	50,362,102	19,270,805	69,632,907	68,500,565
OPERATING INCOME (LOSS)	(1,482,694)	(398,105)	(1,880,799)	1,389,632
NON-OPERATING REVENUES (EXPENSES)				
Intergovernmental Revenue	1,840,068	—	1,840,068	1,541,387
Interest on Pooled Investments	3,876,711	478,610	4,355,321	4,063,965
Other Interest Revenue	1,814,927	—	1,814,927	1,471,271
Interest Expense	(4,041,325)	(46,591)	(4,087,916)	(4,746,587)
Amortized Bond Discount, Fees and Issue Expense	(219,774)	(10,285)	(230,059)	(230,728)
Gain (Loss) on Disposition of Fixed Assets	482,851	(26,038)	456,813	126,598
Other	201,731	1,854	203,585	275,712
Total Non-Operating Revenues (Expenses)	3,955,189	397,550	4,352,739	2,501,618
INCOME BEFORE OPERATING TRANSFERS	2,472,495	(555)	2,471,940	3,891,250
OPERATING TRANSFERS IN				
General Fund	1,117,000	220,000	1,337,000	1,516,500
Special Revenue Funds	944,000	—	944,000	766,000
Total Operating Transfers in	2,061,000	220,000	2,281,000	2,282,500
NET INCOME BEFORE CUMULATIVE EFFECT OF A CHANGE IN ACCOUNTING PRINCIPLE	4,533,495	219,445	4,752,940	6,173,750
CUMULATIVE EFFECT OF A CHANGE IN ACCOUNTING PRINCIPLE	(1,306,319)	(511,988)	(1,818,307)	—
NET INCOME	3,227,176	(292,543)	2,934,633	6,173,750
DEPRECIATION ON ASSETS CONTRIBUTED BY GRANTS, ENTITLEMENTS AND SHARED REVENUE	625,902	—	625,902	420,886
INCREASE TO RETAINED EARNINGS	3,853,078	(292,543)	3,560,535	6,594,636
RETAINED EARNINGS— OCTOBER 1	84,872,265	8,188,255	93,060,520	86,465,884
RETAINED EARNINGS— SEPTEMBER 30	$88,725,343	$ 7,895,712	$96,621,055	$93,060,520

[Statements included for illustrative purposes. For brevity the footnotes accompanying the statements have not been included.]

EXHIBIT 8-2. EXAMPLES OF SEGMENT REPORTING BY GOVERNMENTAL UNITS

[BLOOMINGTON, MINNESOTA (DECEMBER 31, 1983), NOTES TO FINANCIAL STATEMENTS (IN PART)]

Note 8. Segment Information

The City maintains three enterprise funds, which account for water and wastewater utilities and recreation facilities, which include golf and ice arena services. Segment information for the year ended December 31, 1983, was as follows:

	Utility Funds		Recreational Facilities Fund	Total Enterprise Funds
	Water	Wastewater		
Operating revenues	$ 3,796,464	$ 3,000,895	$1,051,374	$ 7,848,733
Depreciation expense	499,934	672,000	85,379	1,257,313
Operating income (loss)	652,172	(893,216)	142,516	(98,528)
Net income (loss)	471,667	(689,963)	166,668	(51,628)
Current capital contributions	652,152	789,589	41,507	1,483,248
Property, plant, and equipment additions	774,694	935,669	52,333	1,762,696
Net working capital	1,522,878	1,312,789	786,584	3,622,251
Total equity	20,746,668	26,446,056	3,816,356	51,009,080

[CITY OF BROWNSVILLE, TEXAS (SEPTEMBER 30, 1983), NOTES TO FINANCIAL STATEMENTS (IN PART)]

Note L—Segment Information for Enterprise Funds

The City maintains four Enterprise Funds. Segment information for the year ended September 30, 1983, is as follows:

	Airport	Parking Revenue	Public Transit	Public Utilities Board	Total
Operating revenues	$ 584,814	$260,154	$ 752,645	$ 38,290,545	$ 39,888,158
Depreciation	279,070	7,842	298,293	3,119,393	3,704,598
Amortization	—	—	—	482,449	482,449
Operating income (loss)	(237,184)	33,568	(1,310,883)	1,238,831	(275,668)
Operating grants	—	—	553,728	—	553,728
Operating transfers					
In	—	—	457,486	—	457,486
(Out)	—	—	—	(202,981)	(202,981)
Net income (loss)	(192,309)	20,326	(298,099)	(1,043,916)	(1,513,998)
Current capital contributions	1,159,973	—	1,513	2,925,389	4,086,875
Amortization on contributed capital	147,209	—	277,413	—	424,622
Property, plant and equipment					
Net additions	1,326,726	588	—	7,377,320	8,704,634
Net deletions	—	—	—	—	—
Net working capital (deficit)	359,210	(43,316)	68,308	5,491,352	5,875,554
Restricted assets	—	—	—	9,636,387	9,636,387
Total assets	7,553,095	658,567	3,490,298	106,412,443	118,114,403
Long-term liabilities	578,419	155,988	—	46,054,281	46,788,688
Payable from operating revenue	—	155,988	—	46,054,281	46,210,269
Contributed capital	11,916,924	—	3,742,797	27,532,346	43,192,067
Accumulated amortization	(3,491,952)	—	(616,087)	—	(4,108,039)
Contributed capital—net	8,424,972	—	3,126,710	27,532,346	39,084,028
Retained earnings (deficit)	(2,091,084)	435,633	140,747	24,896,034	23,381,330

[CITY OF LAKEWOOD, OHIO (DECEMBER 31, 1983), NOTES TO FINANCIAL STATEMENTS (IN PART)]

Note L—Segment Information for Enterprise Funds

The City maintains five enterprise funds, which provide hospital, water, sewer, parking and housing services. Information for the year ended December 31, 1983, for the five major enterprise funds is summarized as follows:

	Lakewood Hospital	Water	Sewer and Wastewater	Parking Facilities	Congregational Living Facility	Total Enterprise Funds
Operating revenues	$46,111,755	$2,556,243	$ 2,608,022	$1,301,279	$ 8,065	$ 52,585,364
Depreciation and amortization expense	1,313,924	42,724	207,704	143,038	488	1,707,878
Operating income (loss)	2,002,903	(117,368)	464,928	421,075	3,476	2,775,014
Tax revenues			890,743			890,743
Extraordinary loss	(1,208,491)					(1,208,491)
Net income (loss)	3,398,732	(171,460)	656,179	202,338	3,476	4,089,265
Current capital contributions		160,000	2,601,302			2,761,302
Net additions to property, plant and equipment	20,861,044	541,012	4,663,966	5,539		26,071,561
Net working capital (deficit)	5,396,159	285,168	696,527	(15,834)	12,516	6,374,536
Total identifiable assets	73,019,470	2,504,266	28,191,946	6,034,658	46,152	109,796,492
Bonds and other long-term liabilities payable from operating revenues	36,725,108	84,000	1,280,000	2,765,000		40,854,108
Total equity	29,251,131	439,849	20,655,003	2,363,943	45,479	52,755,405

[CITY OF MESA, ARIZONA (JUNE 30, 1984), NOTES TO FINANCIAL STATEMENTS (IN PART)]

Note 9. Segment Information Enterprise Activities

The Enterprise fund included operations of electricity, gas, water, sewer, sanitation, irrigation, swimming pools, airport, golf course and community center.

These services provided by the City of Mesa are financed by user charges and are of such significance as to warrant disclosure as segment functions of the Enterprise Fund. Operating revenue, expenses and operating income for the year ended June 30, 1984, for these services are as follows:

Functions	Operating Revenue	Operating Expenses		Operating Income (Loss)
		Depreciation	Other	
Electric	$15,043,427	$ 672,721	$ 9,078,940	$ 5,291,766
Gas	14,050,953	542,348	12,292,916	1,215,689
Water	13,361,653	1,938,113	6,851,711	4,571,829
Sewer	8,177,377	837,426	3,017,069	4,322,882
Sanitation	7,649,283	487,184	6,458,015	704,084
Irrigation	85,888	2,406	160,485	(77,003)
Swimming Pools	184,252	99,683	790,062	(705,493)
Airport	834,249	231,620	976,738	(374,109)
Golf Course	766,068	86,262	797,173	(117,367)
Community Center	380,001	182,713	881,438	(684,150)
Total	$60,533,151	$5,080,476	$41,304,547	$14,148,128

Net Income, Assets, Bonds Payable, Fund Equity and Capital Expenditures for all Enterprise Functions are listed below; however, amounts are not readily allocable to the respective segments since amounts are accounted for within a single fund.

Net Income	$ 24,176,625
Assets	336,529,929
Bonds Payable	132,844,580
Fund Equity	192,265,091
Capital Expenditures	31,621,608

[ROANOKE, VIRGINIA (JUNE 30, 1984), NOTES TO FINANCIAL STATEMENTS (IN PART)]

Note (11) Segment Information for Enterprise Funds

The City maintains five Enterprise Funds, which provide transit, water, sewage, airport and civic center services. Key financial data for the year ended June 30, 1984, for those services are as follows:

	Transit Company	Water	Sewage Treatment	Airport	Civic Center	Total
Operating Revenues	$ 807,707	$ 3,531,855	$ 6,397,330	$ 1,660,008	$ 802,983	$13,199,883
Operating Expenses:						
Depreciation	247,289	563,977	763,668	581,396	310,823	2,467,153
Other	2,079,607	3,135,358	4,359,312	1,375,205	1,256,527	12,206,009
	2,326,896	3,699,335	5,122,980	1,956,601	1,567,350	14,673,162
Operating Income (Loss)	$(1,519,189)	$ (167,480)	$ 1,274,350	$ (296,593)	$ (764,367)	$(1,473,279)
Operating Grants	1,001,989	—	—	—	—	1,001,989
Operating Transfers	261,793	918	2,808	432	626,872	892,823
Non Operating Income (Expense)	19,921	219,616	(37,251)	175,385	30,677	408,348
Net Income (Loss)	$ (235,486)	$ 53,054	$ 1,239,907	$ (120,776)	$ (106,818)	$ 829,881
Current Capital Contributions	$ 1,544,667	$ 11,428	$ 29,054	$ 2,646,136	$ —	$ 4,231,285
Bonds Payable	$ —	$ 1,400,000	$ 3,345,000	$ 564,510	$ —	$ 5,309,510
Net Working Capital	$ 236,600	$ 2,330,390	$ 3,010,001	$ 2,936,910	$ 527,397	$ 9,086,298
Acquisition of Fixed Assets	$ 1,434,583	$ 523,994	$ 186,784	$ 2,765,046	$ 50,376	$ 4,960,783
Total Assets	$ 4,521,491	$15,393,392	$40,271,003	$20,644,738	$11,567,433	$92,398,057
Total Liabilities	$ 188,586	$ 1,854,547	$ 3,692,810	$ 837,460	$ 129,885	$ 6,703,288
Total Equity	$ 4,332,905	$13,538,845	$36,578,193	$19,807,278	$11,437,548	$85,694,769

[SAN LEANDRO, CALIFORNIA (JUNE 30, 1984), NOTES TO FINANCIAL STATEMENTS (IN PART)]

Note 8. Segment Information for Enterprise Funds

The City maintains Enterprise Funds which provide sewage treatment, refuse, golf course and marina services. Segment information for the year ended June 30, 1984, follows:

	Sewage Treatment	Refuse	Golf Course	Marina	Total
Operating revenues	$3,093,161	1,830,623	656,037	785,078	6,364,899
Operating income (loss)	1,291,164	166,349	(20,264)	275,863	1,713,112
Net income (loss)	1,190,184	184,203	(20,264)	377,836	1,731,959
Fixed assets					
Balance, 7/1/83	2,999,329*	26,772	2,850,356*	19,444	5,895,901
Additions, net of disposals	85,558	71	9,339	150	95,118
Balance, 6/30/84	3,084,887	26,843	2,859,695	19,594	5,991,019
Net working capital	2,531,801	734,006	(11,068)	1,655,794	4,910,533
Total assets	5,717,453	792,826	2,864,476	1,706,202	11,080,957
Long-term obligations	2,771,055	104,450	2,806,016	680,566	6,362,087
Equity:					
Retained earnings	$2,845,634	656,399	42,611	994,823	4,539,467

*Restated to include construction costs incurred for the Water Pollution Control Plant and Golf Course of $2,720,878 and $2,804,030, respectively.

[SIOUX FALLS, SOUTH DAKOTA (DECEMBER 31, 1983), NOTES TO FINANCIAL STATEMENTS (IN PART)]

Note 15—Segments of Enterprise Activities

There are eight services provided by the City of Sioux Falls which are financed primarily through user charges or which the governing body has decided that periodic determination of revenues earned, expenses incurred, and/or net income is appropriate for capital maintenance, public policy, management control accountability, or other purposes. The significant financial data for the year ended December 31, 1983, for these services are as follows:

	Airport	Electric Light	Block 11A Ramp Parking	Parking Lot and Area	Sanitary Landfill	Water	Water Reclamation	Transit System
Revenues:								
Operating	$ 1,294,371	$1,660,163	$ 109,424	$ 762,682	$387,589	$ 4,037,625	$ 3,535,318	$ 196,614
Other	177,198	63,001	15,186	196,895	21,150	115,039	249,674	575,722
Total	1,471,569	1,723,164	124,610	959,577	408,739	4,152,664	3,784,992	772,336
Expenses:								
Depreciation	811,993	208,616	40,590	44,231	46,162	601,668	659,849	233,939
Other	1,140,505	1,392,151	159,281	523,655	306,696	3,018,921	2,469,260	788,683
Total	1,952,498	1,600,767	199,871	567,886	352,858	3,620,589	3,129,109	1,022,622
Net income (loss)	$ (480,929)	$ 122,397	$ (75,261)	$ 391,691	$ 55,881	$ 532,075	$ 655,883	$ (250,286)
Assets	$15,580,791	$5,817,155	$2,380,808	$5,348,142	$684,495	$26,478,318	$56,820,365	$4,497,970
Bonds payable	$ 1,250,000		$1,000,000	$1,459,000		$ 315,000	$13,290,000	
Fund equity:								
Contributed capital	$14,885,936	$1,704,795	$1,388,498	$ 303,706	$540,374	$18,236,264	$40,382,419	$4,784,474
Retained earnings (deficit):								
Reserved			121,173	23,268			5,549,022	45,294
Unreserved	(714,794)	3,818,265	(143,390)	4,466,647	97,202	7,149,799	(4,260,191)	(657,453)
Total	$14,171,142	$5,523,060	$1,366,281	$3,793,621	$637,576	$25,386,063	$41,671,250	$4,172,315

[CITY OF TOPEKA, KANSAS (DECEMBER 31, 1983), NOTES TO FINANCIAL STATEMENTS (IN PART)]

Note (8) Segments of Enterprise Activities

The City maintains nine enterprise funds, the operations of which are financed primarily by user charges. Additional financial data for these funds as of December 31, 1983, is as follows (the funds have been combined by type of activity for more concise presentation):

	Water Utility Fund	Water Pollution Control Fund	Combined Public Parking	Recreation	Total
Assets					
Current assets	$14,496,135	(761,023)	455,604	51,998	14,242,714
Restricted assets	10,581,026	2,693,200	468,740	—	13,742,966
Property, plant and equipment, net	35,932,719	36,704,841	4,571,076	194,125	77,402,761
	$61,009,880	38,637,018	5,495,420	246,123	105,388,441
Liabilities and Equity					
Current liabilities	$ 287,683	355,208	44,426	1,843	689,160
Liabilities payable from restricted assets	1,195,345	1,232,398	104,063	—	2,531,806
Long-term liabilities	21,190,000	3,801,230	477,000	—	25,468,230
Equity	38,336,852	33,248,182	4,869,931	244,280	76,699,245
	$61,009,880	38,637,018	5,495,420	246,123	105,388,441
Operating revenues	$ 7,928,015	3,568,060	1,047,139	298,401	12,841,615
Operating expenses:					
Depreciation	995,167	752,837	100,025	23,431	1,871,460
Other	5,580,256	3,415,836	769,577	293,606	10,059,275
Operating income (loss)	$ 1,352,592	(600,613)	177,537	(18,636)	910,880
Net income (loss)	$ 2,126,750	(620,723)	232,648	24,092	1,762,767
Working capital	$14,208,452	(1,116,231)	411,178	50,155	13,553,554
Acquisition of property, plant and equipment	$ 1,353,249	7,302,111	118,557	34,656	8,808,573
Capital contributions:					
Federal	$ —	4,082,365	—	—	4,082,365
City	—	402,096	4,244	12,326	418,666
Developers	—	156,953	—	—	156,953
Customers	1,251,692	—	—	—	1,251,692
	$ 1,251,692	4,641,414	4,244	12,326	5,909,676

[CITY OF FULLERTON, CALIFORNIA (JUNE 30, 1984), NOTES TO FINANCIAL STATEMENTS (IN PART)]

Note (19) Segment Information for Enterprise Funds

The City maintains four enterprise funds, which provide water, airport, parking, and golf/tennis services and facilities. Segment information summarized in dollars, for the year ended June 30, 1984, is as follows:

	Water Utility Fund	Airport Fund	Parking Facilities Fund	Brea Dam Recreational Facilities Fund	Total Enterprise Funds
Operating revenues	8,309,618	477,846	25,609	88,511	8,901,584
Depreciation expense	414,318	30,922	46,942	10,460	502,822
Operating income (loss)	2,862,182	91,075	(37,665)	22,559	2,938,151
Operating grants					
Operating transfers:					
In (Out)	(483,376)	(330,905)	1,364		(812,917)
Net income (loss)	2,361,823	(271,953)	61,992	(18,268)	2,133,594
Current capital:					
Contributions	293,900			13,268	307,168
Property, plant and equipment:					
Additions	558,054	16,660			574,714
Deletions					
Net working capital	3,928,779	121,557	171,112	(1,784,083)	2,437,365
Bonds and other long-term liabilities:					
Payable from operating revenues	581,822	551,914	630,000		1,763,736
Total equity	19,578,965	969,787	952,007	(346,682)	21,154,077

[CITY OF WESTMINSTER, COLORADO (DECEMBER 31, 1983), NOTES TO FINANCIAL STATEMENTS (IN PART)]

Note 9. Segment Information

The Enterprise Fund provides water and wastewater services to the citizens of the City of Westminster, Colorado, as well as certain other users. Operations accounted for in the Enterprise Fund are financed and operated in a manner similar to private business enterprises. It is generally intended that the costs of providing goods or services to the general public on a continuing basis be financed or recovered primarily through user charges. Significant financial data for the year ended December 31, 1983, follows:

	Water	Wastewater	Total
Operating Revenues	$ 3,785,744	$ 2,429,936	$ 6,215,680
Operating expenses before depreciation	2,551,415	2,448,614	5,000,029
Depreciation	842,548	907,021	1,749,569
Operating income (loss)	391,781	(925,699)	(533,918)
Net non-operating revenue	160,124	356,872	516,996
Operating transfers in (out)	(238,808)	(377,763)	(616,571)
Net income (loss)	(313,097)	(946,590)	(633,493)
Current capital contributions	873,354	10,245,627	11,118,981
Plant, property and equipment:			
Additions	2,023,874	8,215,156	10,239,030
(Deletions)	(378,873)	(16,006)	(394,879)
Net working capital	4,113,156	17,234,365	5,837,521
Total assets	61,056,996	31,224,690	92,281,686
Long-term liabilities	12,750,715	3,316,510	16,067,225
Total equity	45,813,119	26,913,471	72,726,590
Operating transfers in (out)	(238,808)	(377,763)	(616,571)
Depreciation on contributed assets	(1,715,736)	1,444,204	(271,532)
Current ratio	2.6 to 1	2.7 to 1	2.7 to 1

[CARROLL COUNTY, MARYLAND (JUNE 30, 1984), NOTES TO FINANCIAL STATEMENTS (IN PART)]

Note 11—Segment Information for Enterprise Funds

The County maintains two Enterprise Funds, which provide water, sewer and economic development services. Water and sewer services are provided through the Carroll County Bureau of Utilities and economic development services are accounted for by the Industrial Development Authority of Carroll County. Segment information for the year ended June 30, 1984, was as follows:

	Bureau of Utilities	Industrial Development Authority	Total Enterprise Funds
Operating revenues	$ 992,516	$ —	$ 992,516
Operating loss	(567,198)	(12,581)	(579,779)
Net income	112,222	3,461	115,683
Depreciation	430,631	—	430,631
Current capital contributions	484,932	—	484,932
Plant, property and equipment additions	227,050	154,006	381,056
Net working capital	1,154,251	61,286	1,215,537
Total assets	35,910,761	573,021	36,483,782
Bonds and Other Long-Term Liabilities			
Payable from nonoperating revenues	10,320,000	—	10,320,000
Payable from other sources	—	530,000	530,000
Total equity	22,313,265	20,029	22,333,294

Chapter 9
The Balance Sheet: Accounting for Assets

The objective of this chapter is to present information on the manner in which governmental units account for and report on assets used in their operations. Examples of combined balance sheet presentations are included for several types of assets, such as

cash and short-term investments;

accounts, notes, taxes, and special assessments receivable;

receivables due from other funds, governments, and employees;

restricted assets;

investments;

inventories; and

prepaid expenses.

Additional information is provided on the prevalence of particular accounting practices and formats.

CASH AND INVESTMENTS

A variety of accounts are used by governmental units to report on unrestricted cash, investments, and cash with various fiscal agents. Table 9-1 shows that fewer than half the surveyed governmental units presented cash as a single item in their balance sheets. Many units elected to combine cash with investments or other cash equivalents. Exhibit 9-1 presents excerpts relating to the presentation of cash and investments from the combined balance sheets of several governmental units.

ACCOUNTS, NOTES, TAXES, AND SPECIAL ASSESSMENTS RECEIVABLE

The receivables of the surveyed governmental units were presented in many different formats. In some instances, receivables were shown in total, and an allowance for uncollectible accounts receivable was shown as a separate deduction. In other instances, accounts receivable were shown as a net balance; that is, the allowance for uncollectible receivables had been deducted from the total accounts receivable, and only the net amount due to the government was reflected

in the financial statement. Generally, receivables are amounts due—on open account or from notes, loans, or the provision of materials and services. Receivables may also be special amounts due from private citizens and organizations, taxes due, and the current portion of special assessments due.

Table 9-2 shows the diversity of accounts used by governmental units to report receivables due. Exhibit 9-2 contains excerpts from several combined balance sheets showing the manner in which some governmental units accounted for and reported various types of receivables.

RECEIVABLES DUE FROM OTHER FUNDS, GOVERNMENTS, AND EMPLOYEES

Another category of receivables uses a descriptor common in the public sector to report amounts due from another fund or from another level of government. These receivable accounts contain the preface, "due from . . . ." Generally, the "due from. . ." receivables represent amounts owed by the governmental units within its family of funds, amounts anticipated from other levels of government, or amounts due from employees resulting from loans or advances to those individuals.

Government interfund receivables and payables are also discussed in Chapters 6 and 10. Intergovernmental receivables in the form "due from. . ." are identified in Table 6-1. Exhibit 9-2 also illustrates excerpts from several governmental combined balance sheets on the manner of reporting these assets.

RESTRICTED ASSETS

Generally, governmental units clearly identified as a separate grouping of assets those assets whose use is restricted for some specific purpose. A variety of accounts were used by the surveyed units to account for these limited purpose assets. The combined balance sheet often also provided detailed accounting for liabilities that were to be paid from the restricted funds or from revenues derived from their employment.

Table 9-3 is a list of the account titles used to report restricted assets. Exhibit 9-3 contains examples from combined balance sheets showing the manner in which some governmental units accounted for restricted assets and examples of liabilities that could be paid only from the above-defined restricted funds.

LONG-TERM INVESTMENTS

Permanent or long-term investments, according to the NCGA, should be recorded at cost or, if there has been a permanent impairment of the asset value involved, at the lower market value. The difference between the par value of an investment security and its cost is a premium or a discount that must be amortized.

Table 9-4 illustrates several titles of accounts used by governmental units to report investments. Exhibit 9-4 contains examples extracted from combined balance sheets to show the manner in which selected governments have accounted for investments. Footnotes related to the investments have been included in some instances.

INVENTORY

An alternative accounting method of recording expenditures is permitted by the NCGA for certain relatively minor items. One of the permissible alternatives relates to inventory. In discussing inventories, Principle 8 of NCGA Statement 1 provides that

> inventory items (e.g., materials and supplies) may be considered expenditures either when purchased (purchased method) or when used (consumption method), but significant amounts of inventory should be reported in the balance sheet.

With the purchase method of inventory accounting, a contra amount should be provided as a reservation of fund balance, indicating that this portion of fund balance is not available for appropriation and expenditure.

Table 9-5 illustrates several kinds of accounts used to report inventories. Exhibit 9-5 contains examples from governmental financial statements related to the reporting of year-end inventory balances.

PREPAID AND DEFERRED EXPENSES

There is no requirement that governmental units record or account for advances, prepayments, or deferrals of certain expenditures that can be allocated to the benefited periods. However, the NCGA recognizes that accounting for prepaid expenditures might be an alternative recognition method in governmental fund accounting. Although prepaid items are usually relatively minor, accounting for them was described by the NCGA Principle 8:

> Expenditures for insurance and similar services extending over more than one accounting period need not be allocated between or among accounting periods, but may be accounted for as expenditures of the period of acquisition.

Many governmental units reported prepaid expenses as assets in the combined balance sheet. Generally, the governments elected to show a single account title such as "prepaid expenses," "prepaid items," or "prepaid expenses and other items." Prepaid amounts were reflected as assets in both governmental funds and proprietary funds.

Table 9-6 lists additional details on these prepaid and deferred items. Exhibit 9-6 contains examples from governmental financial statements related to the reporting of prepaid expenses.

EXHIBITS AND TABLES FOR CHAPTER 9

Table 9-1. Account Titles Used by Governmental Units to Report Cash, Cash Equivalents, and Investments

Exhibit 9-1. Excerpts from Combined Balance Sheets Relating to the Reporting of Cash and Investments

Table 9-2. Account Titles Used by Governmental Units to Report Accounts, Notes, Taxes, and Special Assessments Receivable

Exhibit 9-2. Excerpts from Combined Balance Sheets Relating to the Reporting of Receivables

Table 9-3. Account Titles Used by Governmental Units to Report Restricted Assets

Exhibit 9-3. Excerpts from Combined Balance Sheets Relating to the Reporting of Restricted Assets and Liabilities Payable from Restricted Assets

Table 9-4. Account Titles Used by Governmental Units to Report Investments

Exhibit 9-4. Excerpts from Combined Balance Sheets Relating to Investments

Table 9-5. Account Titles Used by Governmental Units to Report Inventories

Exhibit 9-5. Excerpts from Combined Balance Sheets Relating to the Reporting of Inventories

Table 9-6. Account Titles Used by Governmental Units to Report Prepayments and Deferrals

Exhibit 9-6. Excerpts from Combined Balance Sheets Relating to the Reporting of Prepaid Expenses

TABLE 9-1. ACCOUNT TITLES USED BY GOVERNMENTAL UNITS TO REPORT CASH, CASH EQUIVALENTS, AND INVESTMENTS

Account Title*	Instances Observed (%)	Account Title*	Instances Observed (%)
Cash	45	Cash and certificates of deposit	2
Cash and investments	18	Equity in pooled cash and investments	2
Cash/investments with a fiscal agent (escrow)	16	Cash held in trust	1
Petty cash/imprest fund	5	Cash on hand and in bank	1
Cash and short-term investments	5	Cash and cash investments	1
Cash—cash equivalents	4	Cash with treasurer (in treasury)	1
Cash and temporary cash investments	4	Departmental cash	1
Cash (with an) agent (fiscal, etc.)	4	Other descriptors:	<1
Cash and temporary investments	4	Deposits	
Cash on hand	3	Cash and savings	
Cash in bank	3	Savings account	
Certificates of deposit	2	Equity in cash accounts (pooled)	
Equity in cash accounts (pooled) and investments	2	Cash and time deposits	
Cash escrow	2	Other current assets	
Cash and investments—at cost	2	Cash and investments (including CDs)	

* Observations for the 88% of the units having a combined balance sheet.

EXHIBIT 9-1. EXCERPTS FROM COMBINED BALANCE SHEETS RELATING TO THE REPORTING OF CASH AND INVESTMENTS

[CITY OF LUBBOCK, TEXAS]

Combined Balance Sheet [in part]—All Fund Types and Account Groups, September 30, 1983

Assets	General	Special Revenue	Debt Service	Capital Projects	Special Assessment	Enterprise	Internal Service	Trust and Agency
Cash and investments	$937,127	$1,328,286	$2,731,883	$11,998,627	$1,243,679	$4,387,732	$320,891	$87,933
Cash restricted for potential tax refund obligation	572,951	—	—	—	—	—	—	—

* * *

Note 2—F. Cash and Investments

Cash balances of most City funds are pooled and invested. Interest earned from investments purchased with pooled cash is allocated to each of the funds based on the fund's average equity balance. Investments are carried at cost or amortized cost. The City contract with the Depository Bank requires that an average monthly balance be maintained in "demand" accounts to compensate for services rendered. This compensating balance is based on a formula which assumes bank earnings at the average 30 day Treasury Bill Yield rate to allow $150,000 annual earnings on these uninvested funds. During this fiscal year, the average "demand" account balances averaged $2,459,763.

[CITY OF ALLENTOWN, PENNSYLVANIA]

Combined Balance Sheet [in part]—All Fund Types and Account Groups, December 31, 1983

	Governmental Funds				Proprietary Funds	Fiduciary Funds
	General	Special Revenue	Debt Service	Capital Projects	Enterprise Funds	Trust and Agency Funds
ASSETS						
Cash and investments	$4,022,510	$1,551,155	$20,514	$969,875	$7,292,968	$25,082,690

* * *

Note E—Pooled Cash and Investment

The City, during 1983, began to pool cash for all funds. Interest earnings are allocated to funds based upon the average daily balance of funds invested in the pool. The balance recorded as cash and investments, restricted and unrestricted, in each fund type is principally the allocation of the pooled investment.

Included in AEDC parking fund is cash and investments totalling $1,782,865, which is restricted for retirement of the Lehigh County Industrial Development Authority Revenue Bond Series and for the construction of a new parking facility funded by issuance of bond anticipation notes.

[CITY OF TYLER, TEXAS]

Combined Balance Sheet [in part]—All Fund Types and Account Groups, September 30, 1983

	Governmental Fund Types				Proprietary Fund Types		Fiduciary Fund Types
Assets	General (Exh. "B-1")	Special Revenue (Exh. "C-1")	Debt Service (Exh. "D-1")	Capital Projects (Exh. "E-1")	Enterprise (Exh. "F-1")	Central Garage Fund (Exh. "G-1")	Trust and Agency (Exh. "H-1")
Cash—demand deposits and on hand	$ 7,132	$279,079	$ 91,927	$ 925,614	$ 571,870	$119,883	$ 747,006
Cash—time deposits	800,000	451,000	3,539,000	17,435,000	18,104,000	—	1,140,000

* * *

[CITY OF LAKEWOOD, COLORADO]

Combined Balance Sheet [in part]—All Fund Types and Account Groups, December 31, 1983

	Governmental Fund Types					Proprietary Fund Type	Fiduciary Fund Type
	General	Special Revenue	Debt Service	Capital Project	Special Assessment	Enterprise	Trust
ASSETS							
Cash:							
Petty cash	$ 6,020	$ —	$ —	$ —	$ —	$ —	$ —
Savings	858,092	751	—	—	—	—	60,085
Certificates of deposit	6,775,000	465,630	—	—	2,418,407	—	—
Investments, at cost (note 1)	—	—	—	9,701,845	—	—	7,565,988

* * *

[CITY AND COUNTY OF SAN FRANCISCO]

Combined Balance Sheet [in part]—All Fund Types and Account Groups, June 30, 1984 [in thousands]

	Governmental Fund Types				Proprietary Fund Types		Fiduciary Fund Type
	General	**Special Revenue**	**Capital Projects**	**Debt Service**	**Enterprise (Note 10)**	**Internal Service**	**Trust and Agency**
Cash and investments (note 5)	$154,790	$82,514	$60,225	$(1,007)	$305,837	$(1,394)	$ 96,245
Investments with trustee (note 5)	—	—	6,596	17,946	13,502	—	1,769,889

* * *

Note 5. Cash and Investments

The City's pooled cash and investments are invested pursuant to investment policy guidelines established by the City Treasurer. The objectives of the policy are, in order of priority, preservation of capital, liquidity, and yield. The policy addresses soundness of financial institutions in which the City will deposit funds, types of investment instruments as permitted by the California State Government Code, and the percentage of the portfolio which may be invested in certain instruments with longer terms to maturity.

At June 30, 1984, cash and investments included the following (in thousands):

Type of Investment	Weighted Average Interest Rate	Cost	Market Value
Cash and demand deposit accounts net of warrants outstanding	—	$ (2,856)	$ —
Investments in City Treasury:			
Overnight commercial paper	10.75%	145,000	145,000
U.S. Treasury bills	10.14	199	197
U.S. Treasury notes	11.00	632,340	573,579
U.S. Treasury bonds	12.19	45,271	39,688
U.S. agency instruments	11.23	93,082	84,913
Certificates of deposit	10.41	22,598	22,598
Negotiable certificates of deposit	10.87	54,703	52,027
	11.02%	993,193	918,002
Investments with Redevelopment Agency:			
Repurchase agreements	10.16	5,900	5,900
U.S. agency instruments	9.48	1,554	1,554
	10.39	7,454	7,454
Total investments	11.01%	1,000,647	$925,456
Less Enterprise Fund restricted amounts		$ 300,581	
Cash and Investments		697,210	

At June 30, 1984, maturity dates were as follows:

Maturity	Weighted Average Interest Rate	Cost	Market Value
Overnight commercial paper and repurchase agreements	10.33%	$ 150,900	$150,900
Less than one year	11.18	123,702	123,473
One to five years	10.98	334,778	310,791
Five to ten years	11.12	345,996	300,604
More than ten years	12.19	45,271	39,688
	11.01%	$1,000,647	$925,456

The Treasurer's investments have a market value of $75.2 million (7.6%) below book value at June 30, 1984. City management believes the liquidity of its investment portfolio is more than adequate to meet cash flow requirements; consequently, it will not be necessary to sell its investments for amounts that are below cost for this purpose.

The earned interest yield on all investments held by the City Treasurer for fiscal 1984 was 11.48%.

Investments with trustee included in the Trust and Agency fund type, which represent investments in securities and bonds owned by the Employee's Retirement System, have a market value $227.6 million (15.7%) below amortized cost at June 30, 1984, due to long-term bonds which are expected to be held to maturity. The market value of other investments with trustees, including restricted amounts in the Enterprise Funds, is at amortized cost, which approximates market value.

TABLE 9-2. ACCOUNT TITLES USED BY GOVERNMENTAL UNITS TO REPORT ACCOUNTS, NOTES, TAXES, AND SPECIAL ASSESSMENTS RECEIVABLE

Account Title*	Instances Observed (%)	Account Title*	Instances Observed (%)
Accounts and notes:		Taxes:	
Accounts receivable	41	Taxes	17
Accrued interest	31	Property taxes	13
Other	19	Taxes receivable	13
Special assessments	14	Taxes receivable, net	10
Accounts receivable, net	12	Delinquent property taxes receivable	3
Receivables, net of allowance for uncollectibles	12	Taxes receivable—allowance for uncollectible taxes	3
Notes receivable	12	Delinquent tax receivable	3
Interest receivable	10	Taxes receivable, delinquent	2
Accounts receivable (net of allowance for uncollectibles)	8	Tax liens receivable	1
Other (net)	6	Other taxes receivable:	1
Grants receivable	5	Taxes receivable, current	1
Loans receivable	5	Tax sale certificates receivable	1
Receivables	3	Tax foreclosure	1
Miscellaneous—other	3	Taxes receivable—general property	1
Allowance for uncollectible accounts (receivables)	3	Interest and penalties receivable on taxes	1
Contracts receivable	2	Taxes receivable delinquent, net	1
Accrued revenue	2	Allowance for uncollectible taxes	1
Allowance for doubtful accounts	4	Taxes and special assessments receivable	1
Accounts (receivable) and notes (receivable)	2	Special assessments:	
Contracts receivable	2	Special assessments receivable	6
Mortgages	2	Special assessments	6
Notes receivable, net	2	Assessments receivable	5
Federal government	2	Assessments	3
Interest and dividends	1	Special assessments receivable, deferred	2
Other descriptors:	<1	Special assessments receivable, delinquent	1
		Special assessments receivable, net	1
		Special assessments receivable, current	1
		Accrued interest	1
		Special assessments, less allowance for uncollectibles	1

* For the 88% of the units having a combined balance sheet.

EXHIBIT 9-2. EXCERPTS FROM COMBINED BALANCE SHEETS RELATING TO THE REPORTING OF RECEIVABLES

[CITY OF FORT WORTH, TEXAS]
Combined Balance Sheet [in part]—All Fund Types and Account Groups, September 30, 1983

| | Governmental Fund Types | | | | | Proprietary Fund Types | | Fiduciary Fund Types |
	General	Special Revenue	Debt Service	Capital Projects	Special Assessments	Enterprise	Internal Service	Trust and Agency
Assets:			* * *					
Receivables from:								
Taxes	$ 2,128,514	$ 0	$ 0	$ 0	$ 0	$ 0	$ 0	$2,029,195
Grants and Other Governments	2,935,592	7,927,773	0	2,768,405	0	395,798	0	0
[Dallas–Fort Worth] Regional Airport	0	0	0	10,000,000	0	0	0	0
Assessments	0	0	0	0	4,488,603	0	0	0
Unbilled Assessments on Work-in-Process	0	0	0	0	5,372,140	0	0	0
Sale of Land	0	0	0	0	0	13,204,143	0	0
Loans	0	744,132	0	0	0	0	0	629,772
Accounts and Other (Billed & Unbilled)	1,187,407	0	0	14,348	51,444	7,588,613	14,288	14,345
Allowance for Doubtful Accounts	(2,075,225)	0	0	0	0	0	0	0

[CITY OF SAVANNAH, GEORGIA]

Combined Balance Sheet [in part]—All Fund Types and Account Groups, December 31, 1983

	Governmental Fund Types					Proprietary Fund Types	
	General	Special Revenue	Debt Service	Capital Projects	Special Assessments	Enterprise (Note 17)	Internal Service
Assets			* * *				
Receivables:							
Taxes (Note 1)	$ 676,101						
Special assessments					$1,931,046		
Accounts	580,870			$41,655		$1,553,201	$103,394
Savannah Transit Authority	100,000						
Less allowance for doubtful accounts	(100,000)				(269,269)		
			* * *				

Note 1 [in part]

(I) **Property Taxes.** Property taxes are levied on all taxable real, public utility, and personal property (including vehicles) located within the City. Assessed values for property tax purposes are determined by the Chatham County Board of Tax Assessors for all property except public utility. Assessed value is set at 40% of market value. Public utility assessed value is set by the State of Georgia.

[CITY OF GREEN BAY, WISCONSIN]

Combined Balance Sheet [in part]—All Fund Types and Account Groups, December 31, 1983

	Governmental Fund Types					Proprietary Fund Types
	General	Special Revenue	Debt Service	Capital Projects	Special Assessments	Enterprise
ASSETS			* * *			
Receivables (*net*):						
Taxes (Note F)	$8,332,804	$	$6,223,568	$1,342,648	$	$
Accounts	98,607	609,277		365,788		1,381,184
Special assessment					5,385,903	
Interest	161,841		42,227	129,170	74,645	
			* * *			
Due from other governments						334,986
			* * *			

Note F—Property Tax

The City bills and collects its own property taxes and also taxes for the Green Bay Area Public Schools, Brown County, Northeast Wisconsin VTAE District, and the State of Wisconsin. Collections and remittances of taxes for other entities are accounted for in the Property Tax Agency Fund. City property taxes are recorded in the year levied as taxes receivable and deferred revenue. They are recognized as revenue in the succeeding year when services financed by the levy are being provided.

[CITY OF HUNTSVILLE, ALABAMA]

Combined Balance Sheet [in part]—All Fund Types and Account Groups, September 30, 1983

	Governmental Funds				Proprietary Funds
	General	Special Revenue	Debt Service	Capital Projects	Enterprise
ASSETS					
		* * *			
Receivables (net of allowances for estimated uncollectibles):					
Taxes	$2,613,859	$5,279,201	$ —	$ —	$ —
Accounts	26,305	73,047	—	—	609,922
Notes	2,896,300	3,558,785	—	—	—
Accrued interest	100,930	9,886	455	—	699
Travel advances	6,002	—	—	—	—
Advances to sub-recipients	—	24,084	—	—	—
		* * *			
Due from other governmental entities	907,558	221,601	—	—	—
		* * *			

Note 7—Note Receivable

The City of Huntsville loaned the Huntsville–Madison County Airport Authority $7,212,777 for the construction of the new jetport. During the fiscal year 1967–68 the City of Huntsville purchased the old airport property for $3,355,000, giving the Authority credit on their note for this amount. Interest was accrued on the note during that period. The above-mentioned interest is included on the financial statements in "Due from Other Government Entities" in the amount of $188,989. The Authority has been reducing the amount of the note with proceeds from the sale of parts of the land. The City anticipates that the balance of the note will be paid by the Authority from proceeds received by it from the issuance of its own long-term debt. The note amounted to $2,896,300 and $2,950,000 at September 30, 1983, and September 30, 1982, respectively. Accrued interest on this note amounted to $71,804 and $125,498 at September 30, 1983, and September 30, 1982, respectively.

Note 8 [in part]—Due from Other Governmental Entities

Amounts receivable from federal, state and county governments are reflected in these accounts along with amounts receivable from independent boards and agencies which constitute governmental entities.

[COUNTY OF MILWAUKEE, WISCONSIN]

Combined Balance Sheet [in part]—All Fund Types and Account Groups, December 31, 1983

Assets	Governmental Fund Types			Proprietary Fund Types		Fiduciary Fund Types
	General	Debt Service	Capital Projects	Enterprise	Internal Service	Trust and Agency
			* * *			
Due from Other Funds	$18,015,492	$ —	$ —	$ 2,698,334	$1,144,094	$ —
Receivables						
Accounts (Net of Allowances for Uncollectibles)	—	—	—	29,971,294	3,124,626	—
Property taxes:						
Current Levy	—	—	—	—	—	115,231,982
Delinquent	10,421,590	—	—	—	—	—
Pension Trust Contribution	—	—	—	—	—	27,860,512
Accrued Interest and Dividends	4,756,070	—	—	—	—	4,343,286
Other	3,481,711	—	—	6,701,219	—	7,521,097
Due from Other Governments	9,627,667	—	977,046	3,334,273	—	2,566,537
		* * *				

Note (3) [In Part]

Accounts Receivable. At December 31, 1983, accounts receivable and the allowance for uncollectible accounts of the Enterprise Funds are as follows:

	Accounts Receivable	Allowance for Uncollectible Accounts	Net Accounts Receivable
Medical Complex—Patient Receivables	$22,556,839	$ 6,000,000	$16,556,839
Mental Health Complex	23,093,969	11,498,000	11,595,969
Other Funds	1,818,486	—	1,818,486
	$47,469,294	$17,498,000	$29,971,294

The Medical Complex allowance for uncollectible accounts is based on management's overall estimate of ultimate collectibility using historic collection experience.

[VILLAGE OF OAK PARK, ILLINOIS]
Combined Balance Sheet [in part]—All Fund Types and Account Groups, December 31, 1983

| | Governmental Fund Types | | | | | Proprietary Fund Types | | Fiduciary Fund Types |
| | | | | | | | | Pension and Insurance Trust and Expendable Trust |
Assets	General	Special Revenue	Debt Service	Capital Project	Special Assessment	Enterprise	Internal Service	
Receivables, net of allowances for uncollectibles:								
Accrued interest	$ 56,538	$ 15,735	$ 2,615	* * *	$ 409	$ 70,225		$388,666
Property taxes	5,874,226	1,243,478	1,202,078					
Accounts and special assessments	693,974	1,141			1,433	1,017,388		28,681
Due from Federal, State and other governmental units	972,737	1,068,102		* * *				
Notes receivable		1,177,045				2,397,384		

Note 5. Notes receivable

The Village has several programs pursuant to which loans are made to Village residents and certain housing development agencies for the rehabilitation of single-family and multi-family housing. Funding for such loans is from community development grants, the proceeds of general obligation bonds, and the Equity Assurance Fund. In addition, the Equity Assurance Fund is used to finance housing downpayment loans for qualifying Village employees. The community develop-ment single-family program and single-family emergency loan programs provide 29-year deferred payment loans. The housing bond multi-family loan program makes loans for 10 to 20-year terms. The equity assurance rehabilitation loans have 6 to 15-year repayment terms. The equity assurance employee downpayment loans are 13-year loans with payments deferred for the first 3 years and a balloon payment in the thirteenth year.

The following table summarizes the loan activity during 1983 under the Village's various loan programs.

Fund Name	Interest Rates	Due Dates	Balance at January 1, 1983	Loans Made	Repayments	Balance at December 31, 1983
Community Development Loan	0%–8%	1986 through 2012	$1,187,439	205,200	39,605	1,353,034
1973 Housing Bond Loan	6%–10.5%	1985 through 1994	1,207,287		162,937	1,044,350
1982 Housing Bond	7.75%–11%	1986 through 2003	13,059	680,148	4,226	688,981
Equity Assurance	6.875%–9.25%	1989 through 1997		510,679	22,615	488,064

[CITY OF PEORIA, ILLINOIS]

Combined Balance Sheet [in part]—All Fund Types and Account Groups, December 31, 1983

	Governmental Funds					Fiduciary Funds
Assets	Corporate Fund	Special Revenue Funds	Debt Service Funds	Capital Projects Funds	Special Assessment Fund	Trust and Agency Funds
		* * *				
Taxes and grants receivable—						
General property taxes, net, restricted in the amount of $12,174,400 (Notes 7 and 10)	$12,385,510	$3,522,125	$ 22,991	$448,984	$ —	$1,220,787
State of Illinois	2,899,957	—	—	—	—	—
Governmental grants	—	1,193,969	—	16,318	—	—
Hotel, restaurant and amusement taxes (Note 15(b))	157,629	—	—	—	—	—
Personal property replacement taxes	180,791	—	35,388	—	—	—
Other	292,450	145,995	—	—	—	24,500
Loans receivable	—	1,318,295	—	276,483	—	—
Accrued interest	177,376	228,860	157,878	402,219	—	63,607
Assessments receivable	—	—	—	—	2,778,483	—
		* * *				

Note (5) Property Tax Revenue Recognition

The City prepares its annual budget and makes expenditures on the basis of the current-year property tax levy. Accordingly, it is the City's policy to recognize property tax revenues in the year of levy. Since property tax payments for the current-year levy are due and collected in the following year, the City finances current-year expenditures through short-term borrowings secured by and repaid from receipts of the current-year levy (see Note 10).

NCGA Interpretation 3—"Revenue Recognition—Property Taxes" requires the recognition of current-year tax levies as revenue only to the extent they are available to pay liabilities of the current period. In general, NCGA Interpretation 3 defines "available" as being "due and collected" within the fiscal year. The previously noted City accounting policy does not conform to the provisions of NCGA Interpretation 3.

In general, had the City adopted the provisions of NCGA Interpretation 3, 1983 property tax levies would not have been recognized as revenue but would have been deferred on the balance sheet until they became available for payment of liabilities. As a result, the fund equity balance at December 31, 1983, is overstated by the approximate amount of the 1983 general property tax levy. In addition, current-year revenues are overstated (understated) to the extent they are greater (less) than the amount of revenues, primarily the 1982 property tax levy, which would have been recognized

had the City adopted the provisions of NCGA Interpretation 3.

The following indicates the differences in revenue and fund equity (deficit) between the amounts included in the financial statements and those required under generally accepted accounting principles (GAAP).

	General Property Tax Revenues		Fund Equity (Deficit)	
	As Reported	GAAP	As Reported	GAAP
Corporate	$12,252,380	$12,114,434	$ 8,614,001	$(3,757,325)
Civil Defense	$ 64,127	$ 68,492	$ 81,127	$ 16,227
Public Benefit	1,432,629	1,406,210	5,009,610	3,576,920
Municipal Band	80,972	89,616	156,783	75,363
Public Library	1,845,726	1,558,916	2,367,486	504,804
Tuberculosis	76,126	74,745	163,813	87,140
Total Special Revenue Funds	$ 3,499,580	$ 3,197,979	$ 7,778,819	$ 4,260,454
Southtown Tax Increment Project	$ 410,392	$ 251,047	$ 3,630,631	$ 3,192,447
Bond and Interest	$ 46,661	$ 348,268	$ 905,817	$ 883,176
Illinois Municipal Retirement	$ 1,211,614	$ 1,013,692	$ 3,162,010	$ 1,942,396
	$17,420,627	$16,925,420	$24,091,278	$ 6,521,148

TABLE 9-3. ACCOUNT TITLES USED BY GOVERNMENTAL UNITS TO REPORT RESTRICTED ASSETS

Account Title*	Instances Observed (%)
Cash	14
Restricted assets	10
Cash and investments	8
Investments	8
Accrued interest receivables	7
Investment at cost	5
Due from other funds	5
Cash with fiscal (paying, etc.) agent	4
Accounts receivable	4
Interest receivables	2
Other	2
Cash and investments at cost or amortized cost	2
Restricted cash and investments	2
Receivables	2
Other receivables	2
Cash and short-term investments	1
Cash/certificate of deposit	1
Construction account	1
Deposits	1
Equity in pooled cash and investments	1
Restricted assets—cash and investments	1
Cash, investments, and accrued interest	1
Intrafund receivables	1
Other descriptors:	<1
Grants receivable	
Federal grants receivable	
Cash, investments, and receivables	
Cash deposits	
Certificates of deposit	
Cash and investments held by fiscal agent for bond redemption	

* For the 88% of the units having a combined balance sheet.

EXHIBIT 9-3. EXCERPTS FROM COMBINED BALANCE SHEETS RELATING TO THE REPORTING OF RESTRICTED ASSETS AND LIABILITIES PAYABLE FROM RESTRICTED ASSETS

[CITY OF BROWNSVILLE, TEXAS]

Combined Balance Sheet [in part]—All Fund Types and Account Groups, September 30, 1983

	Proprietary Fund Type Enterprise
ASSETS * * *	
Restricted assets (note D)	
Cash and certificates of deposit	$ 314,375
Investments (note A6)	9,321,310
Investment income receivable	702
* * * LIABILITIES AND FUND EQUITY * * *	
Liabilities of restricted assets	
Current maturities of long-term debt (note F2)	$ 475,000
Accounts payable and other liabilities	1,364,471
Customer deposits	798,982
* * *	

Note D—Restricted Assets

The revenue bond indenture of trust requires that during the period over which the bonds are outstanding, the Public Utilities Board (a component unit of the reporting entity) must maintain certain separate accounts and funds to account (1) for the proceeds from the issuance of the revenue bonds and (2) for the debt service deposits made from the net revenues (as defined by the indenture of trust) of the Public Utilities Board (note F2). These restricted assets can then only be used in accordance with the revenue bond indenture of trust to pay (1) the capital costs of enlarging, extending, or improving utility facilities, (2) the costs of emergency repairs or of extraordinary operating and

maintenance expenses, or (3) the debt service payments on such revenue bonds.

The Public Utilities Board's policy restricts the use of customer utility deposits held by the Public Utilities Board.

The separate accounts and funds maintained for the restricted assets at September 30, 1983, are as follows:

	Cash and Certificates of Deposit	Investments	Investment Income Receivable	Total
Construction Fund				
Special construction account	$ 70	$ 102,000	$ 25	$ 102,095
Construction account	995	43,000	11	44,006
Construction account special No. 1	120	436,000	627	436,747
Utilities Plant Improvement Fund				
Repair and contingency account	132,906	1,000,000	—	1,132,906
Improvement account	175,248	—	39	175,287
Debt Service Fund				
Interest account (1978 series)	1,092	921,663	—	922,755
Interest account (1980 series)	1,405	368,665	—	370,070
Reserve account (1978 series)	469	4,436,000	—	4,436,469
Reserve account (1980 series)	70	1,217,000	—	1,217,070
Customers' Deposits	2,000	796,982	—	798,982
Overall total	$314,375	$9,321,310	$702	$9,636,387

[CITY OF CLEARWATER, FLORIDA]

Combined Balance Sheet [in part]—All Fund Types and Account Groups, September 30, 1983

	Proprietary Fund Types
	Enterprise
ASSETS AND OTHER DEBTS	
* * *	
Restricted Assets:	
Equity in Pooled Cash and Investments	$14,101,098
Due from Other Funds	4,462,958
Federal Grants Receivable	358,144
Investments, at Cost or Amortized Cost	3,917,520
Interest Receivable	118,769
Receivable from Property Owners	2,000
Receivable from Escrow Agent	1,402
* * *	
LIABILITIES	
* * *	
Payable from Restricted Assets	$ 2,182,095
* * *	

Note (3D) Current Liabilities Payable from Restricted Assets

As of September 30, 1983, with comparative figures for 1982, the current liabilities payable from restricted assets of the Enterprise Funds were as follows:

	September 30	
	1983	1982
Construction Contracts Payable	$ 24,104	175,142
Due to Other Funds	4,872	
Accrued Interest Payable	632,414	612,364
Current Portion of Long-Term Debt (Revenue Bonds)	81,250	55,000
Customer Deposits	1,439,455	1,231,213
	$2,182,095	2,073,719

[DEKALB COUNTY, GEORGIA]

Combined Balance Sheet [in part]—All Fund Types and Account Groups, December 31, 1983

	Proprietary Fund Types
	Enterprise
ASSETS AND OTHER DEBITS	
* * *	
RESTRICTED ASSETS (Note E):	
Cash and investments	$57,893,500
Accounts receivable, net of allowance for uncollectibles of $36,483	109,448
Due from other governments (Note D), net of allowance for uncollectibles of $1,514	513,792
Net investment in direct financing lease, current portion (Note I)	66,240
* * *	
LIABILITIES	
* * *	
PAYABLE FROM RESTRICTED ASSETS (Note E)	
Construction contracts payable	$ 565,649
Accrued interest on bonds	1,262,226
Advance payments and deposits	98,993
Revenue bonds payable, current portion (Note G)	2,260,000
Obligations under capital lease, current portion (Note I)	150,468
* * *	

E. Restricted Assets of Enterprise Funds

Proceeds from the sale of revenue bonds plus interest earned on the investment of these funds are restricted to the construction of new capital facilities and other improvements to the Water and Sewerage System. Also, any reimbursements from outside sources (such as EPA) that are reimbursing bond related expenditures are similarly restricted.

All monies in excess of those required to maintain the working capital of the Water and Sewerage System's operations are transferred to a separate account and restricted to the construction of new capital facilities and other expenditures as allowed by the System's bond resolutions. Any reimbursements from outside sources for these projects are restricted accordingly.

Sinking fund monies are restricted to the payment of bond principal and interest requirements as they become due as well as the maintenance of required services.

Liabilities payable from these restricted assets are reported separately to indicate that the source of payment is the restricted assets.

[CITY OF FORT LAUDERDALE, FLORIDA]

Combined Balance Sheet [in part]—All Fund Types and Account Groups, September 30, 1983

	Proprietary Funds	
	Enterprise	Internal Service
ASSETS		
* * *		
Restricted Assets		
Cash	$ —	
Equity in Pooled Investments	24,014,822	3,591,935
Investments	7,559,558	
Receivables		
Accounts	132,758	
Unbilled Service	162,260	
Accrued Interest	325,050	
Due from Other Governments	7,144,537	
* * *		
LIABILITIES AND FUND EQUITY		
LIABILITIES		
* * *		
Payable from Restricted Assets		
Vouchers Payable	$ 2,782,184	
Contracts Payable	2,700,772	
Accrued Interest	330,683	
Due to Other Governments	3,826	
Deposits	1,210,799	
* * *		

[HOUSTONA COUNTY, GEORGIA]

Combined Balance Sheet [in part]—All Fund Types and Account Groups, June 30, 1984

	Proprietary Fund Type
	Enterprise
Assets and Other Debits	
* * *	
Restricted Assets:	
Cash with Fiscal Agent	$ 4,998
Debt Service Account:	
Investments, at Cost	518,243
Renewal and Extension Account:	
Investments, at Cost	103,308
Construction Account: Cash	192,421
Customer Deposits:	
Cash	5,699
Investments, at Cost	43,000
* * *	
Liabilities and Fund Equity	
Liabilities:	
* * *	
Payable from Restricted Assets:	
Construction Contracts	$132,005
Bond Interest and Call Premiums on Series 1963 and 1964 Bonds	4,998
Accrued Revenue Bond Interest	184,144
Revenue Bonds	50,000
Customer Deposits	48,699
* * *	

[CITY OF LARGO, FLORIDA]

Combined Balance Sheet [in part]—All Fund Types and Account Groups, September 30, 1983

	Proprietary Fund Types
	Enterprise
ASSETS	
* * *	
Restricted assets (Note D):	
Equity in pooled cash and investments	$ 6,879,108
Accrued revenues receivable	66,441
Due from other governmental agencies (Note C)	273,826
Impact fees receivable	46,852
Construction-in-progress (net of depreciation)	14,135,768
* * *	
LIABILITIES:	
* * *	
Current liabilities payable from restricted assets	$ 677,855
* * *	

Note D—Restricted Assets

The sewer utility and sanitation utility funds are required by certain ordinances and resolutions to set up restricted funds for the purpose of servicing the utility debt, maintenance and repairs, and capital outlays of the systems. These funds can only be used for the purposes specified in the ordinances and resolutions. Amounts equal to the restricted assets, less the liabilities payable from such assets, are reflected in the equity section of enterprise funds' balance sheets as either contributed capital or reservations of retained earnings.

[CITY OF MONROE, LOUISIANA]

Combined Balance Sheet [in part]—All Fund Types and Account Groups, April 30, 1984

	Proprietary Fund Types
	Enterprise
ASSETS	
* * *	
Restricted Assets:	
Customer Deposits	$ 990,655
Bond and Interest Redemption Funds	715,727
Bond Reserve Funds	3,868,268
Capital Additions and Improvement Funds	720,910
Unexpended Bond Proceeds	3,897,668
* * *	
LIABILITIES AND FUND EQUITY	
Liabilities	
* * *	
Payable From Restricted Assets:	
Customers' Deposits	$ 990,655
Revenue Bonds Payable	1,765,000
Accrued Interest Payable	271,479
* * *	

Note 7—Restricted Assets and Related Reserves

Under terms of the various bond indentures, the Utilities Department is required to establish and maintain a bond reserve equal to the highest annual maturity of interest and principal in any single future year. At April 30, 1984, the amounts on hand exceed the required amount by $998,803. In addition, an amount equal to 5% of gross revenues must be set aside for capital improvements and one-twelfth of the current year's principal and interest must be put monthly in a bond and interest redemption fund. All bonds are secured by the revenue earned or derived from operations of the Utilities Department.

	Total	Cash	Certificates of Deposits	Receivable
Bond and Interest Redemption Funds	$ 715,727	$ 303	$ 135,500	$579,924
Bond Reserve Funds	3,868,268	337	3,786,826	81,105
Capital Additions & Improvements Funds	720,910	30,945	684,967	4,998
Unexpended Bond Proceeds	3,897,668	283,582	3,578,109	35,977
Customer's Deposits	990,655	—	990,655	—
TOTAL	$10,193,228	$315,167	$9,176,057	$702,004

[CITY OF OMAHA, NEBRASKA]

Combined Balance Sheet [in part]—All Fund Types and Account Groups, December 31, 1983

	Proprietary Fund Types	Fiduciary Fund Types
	Enterprise (Note 8)	Trust and Agency
ASSETS		
* * *		
Restricted assets (Note 4)	$20,852,063	$ (104)
* * *		
LIABILITIES AND RESERVES AND FUND EQUITY		
Liabilities and Reserves:		
* * *		
Payable from restricted assets:		
Warrants payable	$ 75,082	
Contracts payable	494,615	
Bonds payable (Note 5)	1,075,000	
Accrued expenses	1,196,760	
Retained percentages payable, construction	445,937	
* * *		

Note 4. Restricted Assets:

Restricted assets at December 31, 1983, comprised the following (See Note 5):

	Bond Improvement Account	Bond Account	Bond Reserve Account	Construction Account	Total
Enterprise Funds:					
Sewer Revenue Fund:					
Cash and cash with paying agent	$1,801,172	$1,913,480	$ —	$2,144,158	$ 5,858,810
Investments*	6,553,397	—	2,521,115	1,657,780	10,732,292
Accrued interest receivable	269,402	—	—	32,339	301,741
Federal and state grants receivable	—	—	—	2,957,557	2,957,557
	8,623,971	1,913,480	2,521,115	6,791,834	19,850,400
Dodge Park Marina Fund:					
Cash	—	—	(7,128)	—	(7,128)
Investments*	—	11,100	128,931	—	140,031
Accrued interest receivable	—	—	2,832	—	2,832
	—	11,100	124,635	—	135,735
Downtown Redevelopment Project No. 1 Fund:					
Cash	(36,122)	188,930	(138,614)	—	14,194
Investments*	318,710	—	503,624	—	822,334
Accrued interest receivable	10,857	—	18,543	—	29,400
	293,445	188,930	383,553	—	865,928
Total Enterprise Funds	8,917,416	2,113,510	3,029,303	6,791,834	20,852,063
Expendable Trust Fiduciary Fund:					
Downtown Education Center Fund:					
Cash	—	(104)	—	—	(104)
Total Expendable Trust Fund	—	(104)	—	—	(104)
Total all funds, 1982	$8,917,416	$2,113,406	$3,029,303	$6,791,834	$20,851,959

*United States Government securities—at cost; market values were as follows:

Sewer Revenue Fund	$11,072,076
Dodge Park Marina Fund	139,731
Downtown Redevelopment Project No. 1 Fund	849,507
	$12,061,314

TABLE 9-4. ACCOUNT TITLES USED BY GOVERNMENTAL UNITS TO REPORT INVESTMENTS

Account Title*	Instances Observed (%)	Account Title*	Instances Observed (%)
Investments	29	Other investments	1
Investments (at cost)	12	Other descriptors:	<1
Investments, at cost or amortized costs	2	Unamortized premiums on investments	
Bond issue costs	1	Marketable securities	
Investments, at cost, which approximates market	1	Investments including accrued interest	
		Investments in internal service	
Investments in deferred compensation plans	1	Temporary investments	
Investments, at amortized costs	1		

* For the 88% of the units having a combined balance sheet.

EXHIBIT 9-4. EXCERPTS FROM COMBINED BALANCE SHEETS RELATING TO INVESTMENTS

[CITY OF BELLEVUE, WASHINGTON]

Combined Balance Sheet [in part]—All Fund Types and Account Groups, December 31, 1983

	Governmental Fund Types					Proprietary Fund Types		Fiduciary Trust and Agency
	General	Special Revenue	Debt Service	Capital Projects	Special Assessment	Enterprise	Internal Service	
ASSETS				* *ˡ* *				
Investments	$28,392	2,400,000	400,000	4,300,000	—	7,674,533	3,640,000	1,267,880
				* * *				

Note 6. Investments

All investments are stated at cost, which approximates market. Investments of City funds (except as noted below) are in the form of BA's and TCD's or passbook accounts with banks and savings and loan associations or direct obligations of the U.S. Government pursuant to the requirements of Washington State law in Chapter 39.58 RCW. At December 31, 1983, investments held for all City funds amounted to $44,025,852, of which $14,900,019 related to proprietary funds. Management intends to hold these until maturity. Interest receipted during 1983 for all funds amounted to $3,919,958, of which $2,478,463 was receipted to pro-

prietary funds. For reporting purposes interest earnings for all funds are recognized in the accounting period in which they become available and measurable.

It is the City's policy to invest all surplus cash. To facilitate the investment process an agency fund (Undesignated Investment Control Fund) has been established as a control conduit for the investment of undesignated money over weekends and holidays in short-term instruments. Interest earned from such is allocated to funds based on cash participation. At December 31, 1983, the City was holding $20,729,562 in short-term investments in this City Fund.

[COUNTY OF OAKLAND, MICHIGAN]

Combined Balance Sheet [in part]—All Fund Types and Account Groups, December 31, 1983

	Governmental Funds					Proprietary Funds		Fiduciary Funds
	General	Special Revenue	Debt Services	Capital Projects	Special Assessments	Internal Service	Enterprise	
ASSETS				* * *				
Cash and Short-Term Investments	$21,645,824	$16,715,009	$3,829,687	$8,718,344	$53,088,104	$113,379,757	$22,877,155	$ 31,119,523
Investments at Cost (Note E)								129,922,399
				* * *				

E. Investments

Cost and Related Market Value of Investments at December 31, 1983, are:

	Cost	Market Value
Oakland County Employees' Retirement System:		
U.S. Government securities	$ 15,993,460	$ 15,535,024
Foreign Government securities	994,875	920,390
Corporate and public utility bonds	51,207,523	49,993,311
Common stock	33,624,134	38,819,683
FHA mortgages and other	840,201	840,201
	$102,660,193	$106,108,609
Road Commission Retirement Plan:		
Bonds and U.S. Government securities	$ 16,422,000	$ 13,638,205
Common stock	611,167	601,562
Guaranteed payment contract	5,208,200	5,208,200
	$ 22,241,367	$ 19,447,967
Deferred Compensation Fund:		
Corporate and public utilities bonds	$ 4,820,839	$ 4,916,414
U.S. Government securities	200,000	200,000
	$ 5,020,839	$ 5,116,414
Total	$129,922,399	$130,672,990

[GENESEE COUNTY, MICHIGAN]

Combined Balance Sheet [in part]—All Fund Types and Account Groups, December 31, 1983

	Governmental Funds Debt Service	Fiduciary Funds
ASSETS		
	* * *	
Investments—Note C	$1,867,529	$77,164,358
	* * *	

Note C—Investments

The cost and market value of fiduciary fund investments by fund and type at December 31, 1983, are as follows:

	Cost	Market Value
Retirement Fund:		
U.S. Government securities	$21,090,619	$20,400,085
Corporate bonds	19,042,721	16,505,674
Common stock	28,369,050	36,201,611
Other investments	4,533,000	4,053,116
	73,035,390	77,160,486
Agency Fund:		
Corporate bonds	3,872	3,872
	$73,039,262	$77,164,358

Retirement investments are subject to a number of restrictions as to the type, quality, and concentration of investments made, including limiting common stock to less than 60% of the portfolio.

[CITY OF ROCKFORD, ILLINOIS]

Combined Balance Sheet [in part]—All Fund Types and Account Groups, December 31, 1983

| | Governmental Fund Types | | | | | Proprietary Fund Types | | Fiduciary Fund Types |
	General	Special Revenue	Debt Services	Capital Projects	Special Assessment	Enterprise	Internal Service	Trust and Agency
ASSETS				* * *				
Cash and investments due from the General Fund	$ —	$3,269,233	$6,206,062	$6,866,521	$127,086	$8,037,866	$124,749	$ 1,124,186
Investments	31,742,000	3,539,926	1,111,116	37,700	—	367,498	—	51,827,007
				* * *				

Note 1 [in part] Investments

Investments are stated at cost or amortized cost, which approximates market. Substantially all City investment activity is carried on by the City in an investment pool, except for those funds required to maintain their investments separately. Cost or amortized cost of investments approximates market.

Many of the City's funds combine their cash in a common cash account included in the general fund where available cash is invested. The funds included in the pool participate in the earnings of the pool in proportion to their average balance therein. Should any of these funds have an average deficit in the pool, they are charged interest accordingly.

[ST. CLAIR COUNTY, MICHIGAN]

Combined Balance Sheet [in part]—All Fund Types and Account Groups, December 31, 1983

| | Governmental Fund Types | | | | | Proprietary Fund Types | | Fiduciary Fund Types |
	General	Special Revenue	Debt Service	Capital Projects	Special Assessments	Enterprise	Internal Service	Trust and Agency
ASSETS								
Cash and temporary investments	$1,161,027	$7,017,083	$1,115,971	$2,137,444	$265,329	$943,399	$17,790,153	$ 5,163,961
Investments	—	—	—	—	—	—	—	24,130,633
				* * *				

Note 2 [in part]—Summary of Significant Accounting Policies

Temporary Investments. Temporary investments consist of certificates of deposit, repurchase agreements, and time certificates and are recorded at cost, which approximates market value.

Investments. Investments are recorded at cost, which approximates market. Adjustments are made to cost for any premium or discount and amortized over the life of the investment.

TABLE 9-5. ACCOUNT TITLES USED BY GOVERNMENTAL UNITS TO REPORT INVENTORIES

Account Title*	Instances Observed (%)
Inventory	47
Inventory at cost	14
Inventories of supplies	4
Inventory of supplies at cost	3
Inventory of materials and supplies	2
Inventories of materials and supplies at cost	1
Other descriptors:	<1
Inventory and prepaid expenses	
Inventory material	
Inventory at average cost	
Inventory of material, supplies, and other	
Materials and supplies	
Merchandise inventory	
Inventory, supplies	
Supplies	

* For the 88% of the units having a combined balance sheet.

EXHIBIT 9-5. EXCERPTS FROM COMBINED BALANCE SHEETS RELATING TO THE REPORTING OF INVENTORIES

[COUNTY OF ALBEMARLE, VIRGINIA]

Combined Balance Sheet [in part]—All Fund Types and Account Groups, June 30, 1984

	Governmental Fund Types	
	General	Special Revenue
ASSETS		
* * *		
Inventory (Notes 1 and 6)	$68,712	$121,610
* * *		
LIABILITIES AND FUND BALANCE		
* * *		
Fund Balance: Reserved for:		
* * *		
Inventory (Notes 1 and 6)	$68,712	$121,610
* * *		

Note 1 [in part]

Inventories. Inventories, consisting of office and operating supplies, are accounted for under the consumption method where purchases of goods are recorded as expenditures when the goods are used.

Note 6—Change in Accounting Method

Inventories of materials and supplies for the year ended June 30, 1984, have been recorded using the consumption method of accounting for inventory, whereby inventory is considered to be an expenditure as it is used. In prior years inventory was recorded using the purchases method, which recognizes inventory as an expenditure when it is purchased. The new method of recording inventory was adopted to recognize inventory on hand at the end of the fiscal year which has not yet been used but is available for use in subsequent fiscal years. The cumulative effect of the change in the methods for prior years was to increase the General and School Fund balances at July 1, 1983, by $130,538 and is reflected in the Statement of Revenues, Expenditures, and Changes in Fund Balances (Exhibit 2) as an adjustment to beginning fund balance.

[CITY OF BELLEVUE, WASHINGTON]

Combined Balance Sheet [in part]—All Fund Types and Account Groups, December 31, 1983

	Proprietary Fund Types	
	Enterprise	Internal Service
Assets		
	* * *	
Inventory	$165,866	$147,329
	* * *	

Note 7. Inventory and Inventory Pricing

Governmental funds in the City use the purchase method, whereby inventory items are considered expenditures when purchased. They are not included in the balance sheet of the non-proprietary funds because the amounts outstanding at year end are immaterial.

The inventory in the internal service fund consists principally of expendable items held for consumption (use or repair) and it is valued at cost. In 1983 a physical inventory was taken and adjustments made accordingly in the Mechanical Equipment Rental Fund. Other internal service funds do not maintain an inventory.

Utility enterprise inventory was also valued at cost and the average cost method of inventory costing was used for 1983. Average cost was also used for the last 6 months of 1981, though previous to this the first-in–first-out method was used.

[CITY OF HUNTSVILLE, ALABAMA]

Combined Balance Sheet [in part]—All Fund Types and Account Groups, September 30, 1983

	Governmental Funds
	General
ASSETS	
	* * *
Inventories, at cost	$123,256
	* * *
FUND EQUITY	
	* * *
Fund balance:	
	* * *
Reserved for inventory	$123,256
	* * *

Note 1-G—Inventory

Inventory is valued at the lower of cost (first-in, first-out) or market. Inventory in the General Fund consists of expendable supplies held for consumption. The cost is recorded as an expenditure at the time individual inventory items are purchased. Reported inventories are equally offset by a fund balance reserve, which indicates that they do not constitute "available spendable resources" even though they are a component of net current assets.

[MONTGOMERY COUNTY, MARYLAND]

Combined Balance Sheet [in part]—All Fund Types and Account Groups, June 30, 1984

	Governmental Fund Types			Proprietary Fund Types		Fiduciary Fund Types
	General	Special Revenue	Capital Projects	Enterprise (Note IV)	Internal Service	Trust and Agency
ASSETS						
			* * *			
Inventory, at cost (Note I)	$991,031	$2,006,954	$570,597	$9,289,322	$1,070,289	$225,687
			* * *			
LIABILITIES AND FUND EQUITIES						
			* * *			
Fund Equities:						
			* * *			
Fund Balances:						
			* * *			
Reserved for inventory (Note III)	$991,031	$2,006,954	$570,597	—	—	—
			* * *			

Note 1 E) [in part] Assets, Liabilities and Fund Equity

Inventories. Montgomery County Government—Inventories are valued at lower of cost (principally first-in, first-out) or market in the Enterprise Fund (Liquor) and consist of goods held for resale. Inventories valued at cost (principally moving-average) are carried in the Internal Service Fund (Motor Pool) and the governmental type funds. All inventories are maintained by perpetual records and adjusted by an annual physical count.

Inventories in the government funds and motor pool fund consist of items held for consumption. The cost is recorded as an expenditure at the time individual items are withdrawn for use. In governmental funds, the reserve for inventory is equal to the amount of inventory to indicate that portion of fund balance which is not available for funding other expenditures.

Montgomery County Public Schools—Inventories are valued at the lower of cost or market. For maintenance supplies, textbooks, and instructional materials, the average cost method is used; for transportation supplies, cost is determined by the first-in, first-out method. The cost of inventories is recorded as an expenditure at the time the individual inventory items are consumed. A minimum level of textbooks and instructional supply inventories is maintained to meet current demands. The reserve for inventory in the MCPS special revenue fund is equal to the amount of inventory to indicate that portion of fund balance which is not available for funding other expenditures.

Maryland–National Capital Park and Planning Commission—Inventories are valued at the lower of cost (first-in, first-out) or market. Inventories in the Special Revenue Funds are offset by corresponding reservations of fund balance. Inventories are reflected as an expenditure at the time of sale or use.

Montgomery Community College—Inventories are valued at the lower of cost (first-in, first-out) or market, and consist of supplies, bookstore, and food service items.

Montgomery County Revenue Authority—The Montgomery County Revenue Authority does not maintain significant inventories of supplies. Fertilizers, grass seed, and similar maintenance materials are expensed when purchased and are consumed on a current basis.

Note 3 E) [in part] Reservation of Fund Balance

Reserves segregate a portion of fund balance to indicate that these resources are for a specific purpose and not available for appropriation for other purposes:

* * *

Reserved for inventories. This amount represents the portion of fund balance that is not available for expenditures because the asset is in the form of commodities, and the County anticipates utilizing them in the normal course of future operations.

* * *

General Fund	$ 991,031	
Special Revenue	2,006,954	
Capital Projects	570,597	$3,568,582

[PALM BEACH COUNTY, FLORIDA]

Combined Balance Sheet [in part]—All Fund Types and Account Groups, September 30, 1983

	Governmental Fund Types		Proprietary Fund Types	
	General	Special Revenue	Enterprise	Internal Service
ASSETS AND OTHER DEBITS				
	* * *			
Inventory of materials, supplies and other	$1,374,815	$826,275	$940,684	$423,841
	* * *			
LIABILITIES				
	* * *			
FUND EQUITY				
	* * *			
Fund balances:				
	* * *			
Reserved for inventory	$1,374,815	$826,275		
	* * *			

Note 1 [in part] Inventories

Inventories, consisting primarily of materials and supplies, are stated at the lower of cost or net realizable value determined on a first-in, first-out basis. Governmental fund type inventories are recorded as expenditures when they are purchased (purchases method). Year-end inventories are recorded as assets and are offset by a reserve of fund balance, indicating that such amounts do not represent "available spendable resources."

[CITY OF SAN BUENAVENTURA, CALIFORNIA]

Combined Balance Sheet [in part]—All Fund Types and Account Groups, June 30, 1984

	Governmental Fund Types
	General
ASSETS	
* * *	
Inventory, at cost	$314,355
* * *	

Note 1 G. Inventories

Inventories are valued at average cost on a first in, first out basis. Inventories recorded in the general fund consist of expendable supplies earmarked for consumption. Land inventory in the Redevelopment Agency (capital projects fund type) shows no amount due to the fact all parcels have been disposed of. Inventory amounts are fully reserved in the applicable funds since they do not represent available, spendable resources.

TABLE 9-6. ACCOUNT TITLES USED BY GOVERNMENTAL UNITS TO REPORT PREPAYMENTS AND DEFERRALS

Account Title	Instances Observed (%)
Prepaid expenses	35
Other assets	12
Deferred charges	7
Deposits	5
Prepaid expenses and other assets	2
Prepaid insurance	1
Prepaid expenses and deposits	1
Prepaid expenses and expenditures	1
Other	1
Other descriptors:	<1
Prepaid items	
Prepaid interest	
Prepaid expenditures	
Prepayments and other assets	
Deferred debts	
Deposits with others	

* Observations for the 88% of those units having a combined balance sheet.

EXHIBIT 9-6. EXCERPTS FROM COMBINED BALANCE SHEETS RELATING TO THE REPORTING OF PREPAID EXPENSES

[CITY OF CLEARWATER, FLORIDA]

Combined Balance Sheet [in part]—All Fund Types and Account Groups, September 30, 1983

	Governmental Fund Types				Proprietary Fund Types		Fiduciary Fund Type
	General	**Special Revenue**	**Capital Projects**	**Special Assessment**	**Enterprise**	**Internal Service**	**Trust and Agency**
ASSETS AND OTHER DEBITS							
			* * *				
Prepaid Expenses and Other Assets	$25,728	$291	$504	$2,080	$19,284	$184,002	$156,212
			* * *				

[FORT COLLINS, COLORADO]

Combined Balance Sheet [in part]—All Fund Types and Account Groups, December 31, 1983

	Governmental Fund Types		Proprietary Fund Types	
	General Fund	Special Revenue	Enterprise	Internal Service
ASSETS				
Current Assets				
	*	*	*	
Prepaid Expenses	$23,015	$1,050	$7,588	$2,840
	*	*	*	

Summary of Significant Accounting Policies [in part]

Prepaid Expenses. The City accounts for all prepaid expenses on an accrual basis. A prepaid expense is recognized when a cash expenditure is made for goods or services that were purchased for consumption but are unconsumed as of December 31.

[OUTAGAMIE COUNTY, WISCONSIN]

Combined Balance Sheet [in part]—All Fund Types and Account Groups, December 31, 1983

	Governmental Fund Types	Proprietary Fund Types	
	General	Enterprise	Internal Service
ASSETS			
	* * *		
Prepaid expenses	$116,072	$76,756	$497,226
	* * *		
LIABILITIES AND FUND EQUITY			
Liabilities:			
	* * *		
Fund Equity:			
	* * *		
Fund balances:			
	* * *		
Unreserved:			
	* * *		
Designated for prepaid expenses	$116,072	—	—
	* * *		

Note 1 [in part]. Nature and Purpose of Reservations and Designations of Fund Equity

Amounts equal to inventories and prepaid expenses of governmental fund types are reserved from fund balances because they do not constitute available spendable resources.

[PINELLAS COUNTY, FLORIDA]

Combined Balance Sheet [in part]—All Fund Types and Account Groups, September 30, 1983 [in thousands]

		Governmental Fund Types		Proprietary Fund Types
		General	Special Revenue	Enterprise
ASSETS				
	* * *			
Prepaid expenses and other assets		$145	$66	$2,215
	* * *			
FUND EQUITY				
	* * *			
Fund Balances				
Reserved for prepaid rent		$139		
	* * *			

Note I—Prepaid Rent

On April 13, 1976, the County approved a 20-year operating land lease with the St. Petersburg-Clearwater International Airport for the jail complex. The General Fund balance sheet shows prepaid rent to the Airport of $150,000, which represents the balance of the advance lease payment that is being amortized over 20 years. Details of the amortization are as follows (dollars in thousands):

Advance lease payment	$220
Amortization through September 30, 1983	81
Prepaid rent to Airport, September 30, 1983	$139

In addition to the advance lease payment, the County has agreed to pay $7,750 a year to the Airport as an additional rent expense for the term of the lease.

[CITY OF SEATTLE, WASHINGTON]

Combined Balance Sheet [in part]—All Fund Types and Account Groups, December 31, 1983

		Governmental Fund Types	Proprietary Fund Types	
		Special Assessment	Enterprise	Internal Service
ASSETS				
	* * *			
Prepaid and other current assets		$36,901	$487,038	$34,099
	* * *			

Chapter 10
The Balance Sheet: Accounting for Liabilities

The objective of this chapter is to present general information on the manner in which an accounting and reporting is made by governmental units of the liabilities incurred by their operations. Examples of balance sheet presentations are included illustrating several types of liabilities:

short-term liabilities;

liabilities due to other funds, governments, and employees;

accrued liabilities;

deposits, advances, and deferred items;

payables from restricted assets; and

long-term obligations.

Additional information is also provided on the prevalence of particular accounting practices and the formats used.

SHORT-TERM LIABILITIES

While not required to do so by NCGA Statement 1, some governments in their combined balance sheets distinguish between current liabilities and other types of obligations. Generally, these current liabilities are those debts owed for which payment must be made by the government in the relatively near term, i.e., within the year.

As noted in Table 10-1, although some of the accounts used to signify current governmental liabilities are unique, most of the accounts are the same as those used by corporate organizations and other institutions. Exhibit 10-1 illustrates excerpts from the combined balance sheet of several governmental units showing the presentation of current liabilities.

LIABILITIES DUE TO OTHER FUNDS, GOVERNMENTS, AND EMPLOYEES

Another category of current liabilities uses a descriptor common to the public sector to report amounts owed between one fund and another or to another level of government. These liability accounts usually contain the prefix "due to. . ." In most instances, the "due to" liability account represents amounts owed by the governmental unit within its family of funds, to another level of government, or to governmental employees.

Government interfund receivables and payables were discussed in Chapters 6 and 9. Other liabilities in the "due to. . ." account were identified in Table 6-2. Exhibit 10-2 illustrates excerpts from several governmental combined balance sheets on the type of reporting made for these liabilities.

ACCRUED LIABILITIES

Governmental units practice two types of accrual accounting: (1) the modified accrual method of accounting, used for their governmental-type funds, and (2) full accrual (corporate-type) accounting, used for their proprietary-type funds and nonexpendable trust funds. Under the modified accrual basis of accounting, expenditures are recognized in the accounting period in which the fund liability is incurred, if such liability is measurable. Modified accrual accounting makes certain exceptions to this general rule. These exceptions have been listed by the NCGA in its Statement 1 and include the following:

When interest expenditures on special assessments indebtedness are approximately offset by interest earnings or special assessment levies, both the interest expenditure and the interest earnings may be recorded when due rather than be accrued.

As a general rule, expenditures related to the unmatured principle and interest on general long-term debt are not accrued. The financial statements do not reflect such interest expenditures until the year of payment.

On the other hand, under the full accrual basis, expenses incurred in a government's proprietary fund and the related liability are recognized in the same manner as would be done for a commercial organization, i.e., when the services have been rendered or the products provided.

The accounts used to reflect several accrued- or accrual-type liabilities in governmental balance sheets are listed in Table 10-2. Exhibit 10-3 illustrates the manner in which some governmental units presented accrued liabilities in their combined balance sheets.

DEPOSITS, ADVANCES, AND DEFERRED ITEMS

Many governmental units require deposits for certain types of utility services; further, they can withhold amounts due contractors performing services for the government (contract retention), they may collect revenues in advance, and they may be holding amounts due to fiscal agents. All these funds of others are liabilities that must be reflected in the financial statements of the governmental unit.

Table 10-3 identifies several of these types of liabilities reported by governmental units. Exhibit 10-4 illustrates how some governmental units reported in their combined balance sheet the liability for these types of funds due to others.

PAYABLES FROM RESTRICTED ASSETS

Several financial statements for governmental units separately accounted for or reported those liabilities that were payable from specific or restricted assets. The manner in which governmental units reported these types of liabilities was discussed and illustrated in Chapter 9, along with restricted assets.

REPORTING OF LONG-TERM OBLIGATIONS

The reporting of long-term obligations for public sector organizations must be reflected in two parts: the current portion of the long-term obligation and related interest, and the unmatured portion of the long-term obligation. As mentioned earlier in this chapter, there is a major exception to accrual accounting with respect to interest on long-term debt. In this connection, the AICPA, in its Statement of Position 75-3, "Accrual of Revenues and Expenditures by State and Local Governmental Units," tried to clarify this exception with the following example:

> This principle applies whether or not the date for payments to bondholders coincides with the date for collection from property owners; for example, if interest from property owners is due on March 1, and the corresponding payment to bondholder is payable on June 1, the entity will report as interest receivable on June 30 only the amount still uncollected from property owners for the preceding March 1 and prior interest dates. Interest payable reported at June 30 should be

only the amount still payable to bondholders from the preceding June 1 and prior interest dates.

With respect to this principle, NCGA Statement 1 requires that bonds, notes, and other long-term liabilities (such as captial leases, obligations related to pensions, and judgments) and interest directly related to and expected to be paid from proprietary funds, special assessment funds, and trust funds should be included in the accounts of those funds. Thus, these debts are specific liabilities of those funds. The other unmatured long-term debts of the government are general long-term debts and must be accounted for in the general long-term debt account group. This long-term debt may comprise the unmatured principal of several types of obligations: bonds, capital leases, notes, and other forms of noncurrent or long-term obligations that are not a specific liability of any proprietary fund or any special assessment or trust fund.

Several accounts used for reporting the current portion of long-term obligations were observed. These have been identified in Table 10-4.

Chapter 4 contains a detailed discussion of long-term liabilities. Formats for reporting the unmatured portion of long-term obligations were illustrated in Exhibit 4-1. Table 4-1 lists several accounts used by governmental units to report the unmatured portion of long-term obligations.

EXHIBITS AND TABLES FOR CHAPTER 10

Table 10-1. Account Titles Used by Governmental Units to Report Short-Term Liabilities

Exhibit 10-1. Examples of Reporting by Governmental Units of Short-Term Liabilities

Exhibit 10-2. Examples of Reporting by Governmental Units of Obligations Due to Other Funds, Governments, and Third Parties

Table 10-2. Account Titles Used by Governmental Units to Report Accrued Liabilities

Exhibit 10-3. Examples of Reporting by Governmental Units of Selected Accrued Liabilities

Table 10-3. Account Titles Used by Governmental Units to Report Deposits, Advances, and Deferrals

Exhibit 10-4. Examples of Reporting by Governmental Units of Deposits, Advances, Retainages and Deferred Items

Table 10-4. Account Titles Used by Governmental Units to Report Long-Term Obligations—Current Portion

TABLE 10-1. ACCOUNT TITLES USED BY GOVERNMENTAL UNITS TO REPORT SHORT-TERM LIABILITIES

Account Title*	Instances Observed (%)	Account Title*	Instances Observed (%)
Accounts payable	63	Accounts payable and accrued expenses	3
Contracts payable	22	Revenue bonds payable	3
Notes payable	13	Salaries payable	3
Claims payable	13	Loans payable	2
Other liabilities	12	Other current liabilities	2
Vouchers payable	9	Capital lease obligations	1
Cash overdraft	9	Interfund payables	1
Accounts payable and accrued liabilities	6	Payroll withholdings	1
Deposits payable	6	Payroll taxes payable	1
Interest payable	5	Salaries and wages payable	1
Others	5	Matured interest payable	1
Wages payable	5	Warrants outstanding	1
Accounts and contracts payable	5	Other descriptors:	<1
Retainage payable	5	Payroll deductions payable	
Miscellaneous (liabilities)	4	Sales tax payable	
Bank overdraft	4	Notes payable: tax anticipation	
Vouchers and accounts payable	4		

*Observations for the 88% of the units having a combined balance sheet.

EXHIBIT 10-1. EXAMPLES OF REPORTING BY GOVERNMENTAL UNITS OF SHORT-TERM LIABILITIES

[CITY OF CHICAGO, ILLINOIS]

Combined Balance Sheet [in part]—All Fund Types and Account Groups, December 31, 1983 [in thousands]

	Governmental Fund Types					Proprietary Fund Type	Fiduciary Fund Types
	General	Special Revenue	Debt Service	Capital Projects	Special Assessment (Unaudited)	Enterprise	Trust and Agency (Paritally Unaudited)
LIABILITIES							
Voucher warrants payable	$65,116	$ 8,400	$	$4,211	$63	$30,475	$132,689
Tax anticipation notes	76,850	42,275					
Bonds, notes and capitalized lease obligations payable— current			28,165			31,534	
			* * *				

[CITY OF ROCKFORD, ILLINOIS]

Combined Balance Sheet [in part]—All Fund Types and Account Groups, December 31, 1983

| | Governmental Fund Types | | | | | Proprietary Fund Types | | Fiduciary Fund Types |
| | | | | | | | | |
	General	Special Revenue	Debt Service	Capital Project	Special Assessment	Enterprise	Internal Service	Trust and Agency
LIABILITIES AND MUNICIPAL EQUITY								
Liabilities								
Bank overdraft	$ 855,266	$ —	$ —	$ —	$ —	$ —	$ —	$213,723
Cash and investments due to other funds	25,755,703	—	—	—	—	—	—	—
Accounts and contracts payable	597,666	568,437	1,358	1,830,781	—	957,319	40,560	179,679
			* * *					
Property taxes payable	—	—	—	—	—	393,176	—	—
			* * *					
Other liabilities	362,565	188,395	—	—	732	86,128	—	5,378
			* * *					

[CITY OF LARGO, FLORIDA]

Combined Balance Sheet [in part]—All Fund Types and Account Groups, September 30, 1983

Liabilities	Governmental Fund Types				Proprietary Fund Types		Fiduciary Fund Types
	General	Special Revenue	Debt Service	Capital Projects	Enterprise	Internal Service	Trust and Agency
Current portion of long-term debt	$ —	$ —	$ —	$ —	$444,964	$ —	$ —
Accounts and refunds payable	162,992	18,947	—	20,587	47,978	23,059	3,547
			* * *				
Other liabilities	16,375	—	78,600	—	—	—	—
			* * *				

[CITY OF LAWRENCE, KANSAS]

Combined Balance Sheet [in part]—All Fund Types and Account Groups, December 31, 1983

	Governmental Fund Types				Proprietary Fund Types		Fiduciary Fund Types
	General	Special Revenue	Debt Service	Capital Projects	Enterprise	Internal Service	Trust and Agency
Liabilities and Fund Equity Liabilities							
Bank overdraft	$	$	$	$37,212	$	$	$20,423
Accounts payable	1,348	9,586			40,750		13,108
Sales tax payable					2,098		
Court bonds payable							2,508
Contracts payable				83,510			2,582
			* * *				
Matured bonds payable			7,000				
Matured interest payable			9,384				
			* * *				

[CITY OF ORLANDO, FLORIDA]

Combined Balance Sheet [in part]—All Fund Types and Account Groups, September 30, 1983

	Governmental Fund Types				Proprietary Fund Types	
	General	Special Revenue	Debt Service	Capital Projects	Enterprise	Internal Service
Liabilities and Fund Equity Current Liabilities (Payable from Current Assets)						
Accounts Payable	$1,375,310	$174,086	$ —	$334,013	$629,980	$151,425
			* * *			
Compensated Absences	172,389	—	—	—	404,032	74,309
			* * *			
Other Current Liabilities	144,185	—	—	—	39,700	57,986
			* * *			

[CITY OF STAMFORD, CONNECTICUT]

Combined Statement of Financial Position [in part]—All Fund Types and Account Groups, June 30, 1984

	Governmental Fund Types			Fiduciary Fund Types	
Liabilities and Fund Equities	General	Special Revenue	Capital	Trust and Agency	Pension Trust
Liabilities:					
Bank overdrafts	$ 2,677,834		$ 624,418		$142,049
Bond anticipation notes (Note 7)	14,000,000				
Accounts payable and accrued liabilities	12,257,871	$1,983,169	3,068,912	$150,371	31,659
		* * *			

[CITY OF WHITTIER, CALIFORNIA]

Combined Balance Sheet [in part]—All Fund Types and Account Groups, June 30, 1984 [in thousands]

	Governmental Fund Types				Proprietary Fund Types		Fiduciary Fund Type
	General	Special Revenue	Debt Service	Capital Projects	Enterprise	Internal Service	Trust and Agency
LIABILITIES AND FUND EQUITY							
Liabilities							
Accounts payable	$112	$174	$ —	$37	$75	$ 15	$10
Other liabilities	183	—	—	—	—	—	—
			* * *				
Employee benefits payable—short-term	—	—	—	—	—	475	—
			* * *				
Matured bonds and interest payable	—	—	1	—	—	—	—
			* * *				

[Statements included for illustrative purposes. For brevity the footnotes accompanying the statements have not been included.]

EXHIBIT 10-2. EXAMPLES OF REPORTING BY GOVERNMENTAL UNITS OF OBLIGATIONS DUE TO OTHER FUNDS, GOVERNMENTS, AND THIRD PARTIES

[CITY OF APPLETON, WISCONSIN]

Combined Balance Sheet [in part]—All Fund Types and Account Groups, December 31, 1983

	Governmental Fund Types		Proprietary Fund Types		Fiduciary Fund Type
	Special Revenue	Special Assessment	Enterprise	Internal Service	Trust and Agency
LIABILITIES AND FUND EQUITY LIABILITIES:		* * *			
Due to Federal government	$70,298	$ —	$148,386	$ —	$ —
Due to other governmental units	—	—	165,321	—	—
Due to other taxing units	—	—	—	—	2,614,314
Due to other funds	—	441,005	936,466	5,430	1,474,907
Advance from General Fund	—	—	75,706	—	—
		* * *			

[FREDERICK COUNTY, MARYLAND]

Combined Balance Sheet [in part]—All Fund Types and Account Groups, June 30, 1984

	Governmental Fund Types			Proprietary Fund Types		Fiduciary Fund Type
	General	Special Revenue	Capital Projects	Enterprise	Internal Service	Agency
LIABILITIES		* * *				
Due to Other Government	$ 399,430	$ 15,617	$ —	$ —	$ —	$ —
Due to Other Funds	6,495,049	2,734,949	315,258	216,348	103,796	183
Due to Board of Education	—	—	—	—	—	—
Due to Employees Deferred Compensation	320,180	—	—	—	—	—
Due to Third Parties	—	—	—	36,392	—	278,782
		* * *				

[CITY OF GREENVILLE, SOUTH CAROLINA]

Combined Balance Sheet [in part]—All Fund Types and Account Groups, December 31, 1983

	Governmental Fund Types			Fiduciary Fund Type	Proprietary Fund Type
	General	Special Revenue	Capital Projects	Trust and Agency	Enterprise Fund
Liabilities					
		* * *			
Due to other funds:					
General	$ —	$140,254	$86,156	$25,629	$217,390
Special Revenue	2,751	—	—	—	—
Capital projects	534,995	—	—	—	—
Enterprise	175,763	—	—	—	—
		* * *			

[CITY OF SANTA MONICA, CALIFORNIA]

Combined Balance Sheet [in part]—All Fund Types and Account Groups, June 30, 1984

	Governmental Fund Types	Proprietary Fund Types	Fiduciary Fund Type
	Capital Projects	Enterprise	Trust
Liabilities			
	* * *		
Due to:			
Participants	$ —	$ —	$2,678,393
Other governmental units	—	13,156	—
Other funds (note 8)	—	107,465	—
	* * *		
Advances from other funds	11,572,617	1,617,133	—
	* * *		

[CITY OF VIRGINIA BEACH, VIRGINIA]

Combined Balance Sheet [in part]—All Fund Types and Account Groups, June 30, 1984

	Governmental Fund Types		Proprietary Fund Types	Fiduciary Fund Type
	General	Special Revenue	Enterprise	Trust and Agency
LIABILITIES				
		* * *		
Due to:				
Other Funds	$2,099	$ —	$456,809	$256,229
Federal Government	—	10,454	—	—
		* * *		

[CITY OF WICHITA FALLS, TEXAS]

Combined Balance Sheet [in part]—All Fund Types and Account Groups, September 30, 1983

	Governmental Fund Types			Proprietary Fund Types	Fiduciary Fund Type
	General	Special Revenue	Capital Projects	Enterprise	Agency
LIABILITIES AND FUND EQUITY					
Liabilities:					
		* * *			
Payable to other City funds	$ 9,470	$173,892	$1,811	$239,285	$ 13,281
Payable to government agencies	24,110	—	—	—	2,115,553
		* * *			

[Statements included for illustrative purposes. For brevity the footnotes accompanying the statements have not been included.]

TABLE 10-2. ACCOUNT TITLES USED BY GOVERNMENTAL UNITS TO REPORT ACCRUED LIABILITIES

Account Titles*	Instances Observed (%)
Accrued liabilities	22
Accrued interest payable	13
Accrued payroll	9
Accrued expenses	7
Accrued vacation and sick leave payable	6
Accrued vacation pay	6
Accrued interest	5
Other accrued liabilities	3
Other accrued expenses	2
Accrued wages payable	2
Accrued salary and wages	1
Accrued payroll and payroll taxes	1
Accrued salary	1
Matured interest payable	1
Compensatory time accrued	1
Accrued payroll, payroll taxes, and withholdings	1
Accrued payroll and payroll deductions	1
Accrued expenses and other liabilities	1
Other descriptors:	<1
Accrued bond interest payable	
Accrued expenses payable	
Accrued payroll deductions	
Accrued taxes payable	
Accrued leave	
Accrued self-insurance claims	
Accrued expenses and claims payable	
Accrued salaries and benefits	

* Observations for the 88% of the units having a combined balance sheet.

EXHIBIT 10-3. EXAMPLES OF REPORTING BY GOVERNMENTAL UNITS OF SELECTED ACCRUED LIABILITIES

[CITY OF ALBUQUERQUE, NEW MEXICO]

Combined Balance Sheet [in part]—All Fund Types and Account Groups, June 30, 1984 [in thousands]

| | Governmental Funds | | Proprietary Funds | | Fiduciary Funds |
	General	Special Revenue	Enterprise	Internal Service	Trust and Agency
LIABILITIES AND FUND EQUITY					
Liabilities:					
		* * *			
Accrued employee compensation and vacation (Note 2)	$5,151	$190	$1,737	$281	$ 57
Accrued interest payable	—	—	708	—	250
		* * *			
Payable from restricted assets:					
		* * *			
Matured bonds and interest payable	—	—	1,426	—	—
Accrued interest	—	—	1,517	—	—
		* * *			

[CITY OF WEST COVINA, CALIFORNIA]

Combined Balance Sheet [in part]—All Fund Types and Account Groups, June 30, 1984

| | Governmental Fund Types | | | | Proprietary Fund Types | |
Liabilities and Municipal Equity	General	Special Revenue	Capital Projects	Special Assessment	Enterprise	Internal Service
LIABILITIES						
		* * *				
Accrued self-insured claims	$ —	$ —	$ —	$ —	$ —	$590,329
Other accrued liabilities	811,104	15,009	768	19,791	12,377	2,152
		* * *				

[CITY OF DURHAM, NORTH CAROLINA]

Combined Balance Sheet [in part]—All Fund Types and Account Groups, June 30, 1984

| | Governmental Fund Types | | | Proprietary Fund Types | Account Groups |
Liabilities and Fund Equity (Deficit)	General	Special Revenue	Special Assessment	Enterprise	General Long-Term Debt
		* * *			
Accrued payroll	$342,922	$81,840	$ —	$ 61,821	$ —
Accrued interest	—	—	—	199,938	—
		* * *			
Accrued compensated absences	—	—	—	208,689	1,286,355
		* * *			

[GENESEE COUNTY, MICHIGAN]

Combined Balance Sheet [in part]—All Fund Types and Account Groups, December 31, 1983

| | Governmental Funds | | | | Proprietary Funds | | |
Liabilities	General	Special Revenue	Debt Service	Special Assessment	Internal Service	Enterprise	Fiduciary Funds
			* * *				
Accrued payroll	$236,183	$450,417	$ —	$ —	$ 55,239	$107,867	$987,465
Accrued vacation and other employee benefits	954,579	381,042	—	—	—	265,718	—
Other accrued liabilities and deposits	5,884	443,687	—	870	412,176	12,406	308,459
			* * *				
Accrued interest payable	—	—	—	—	666,030		
Payable from restricted assets Accrued interest payable	—	—	—	—	—	130,806	
			* * *				

[FREDERICK COUNTY, MARYLAND]

Combined Balance Sheet [in part]—All Fund Types and Account Groups, June 30, 1984

| | Governmental Fund Types | | Proprietary Fund Types | Fiduciary Fund Type | Account Groups |
Liabilities	General	Special Revenue	Enterprise	Agency	General Long-Term Obligation
		* * *			
Accrued and Other Liabilities	$1,054,402	$394,864	$97,357	$1,118	$ —
		* * *			
Accrued Liability— Unfunded Vested Accumulated Annual Leave	—	—	—	—	590,837
		* * *			

[CITY OF JACKSONVILLE, FLORIDA]

Combined Balance Sheet [in part]—All Fund Types and Account Groups, September 30, 1983 [in thousands]

| | Governmental Fund Types | | | | Proprietary Fund Types | | Fiduciary Fund Types |
	General	Special Revenue	Debt Service	Capital Projects	Enterprise	Internal Service	Trust and Agency
LIABILITIES AND FUND EQUITY							
Liabilities:							
Accounts payable and accrued expenses	$3,201	$378	$115	$ —	$ 759	$ 336	$544
Accrued interest	—	—	—	—	1,789	2,192	444
			* * *				
Payable from restricted assets:							
Accounts payable and accrued expenses	—	—	—	—	—	—	—
Contracts payable	—	—	—	—	523	—	—
Accrued interest payable	—	—	—	—	2,175	—	—
Due to other funds	—	—	—	—	102	—	—
			* * *				

[CITY OF PUEBLO, COLORADO]

Combined Balance Sheet [in part]—All Fund Types and Account Groups, December 31, 1983

	Governmental Fund Types	Proprietary Fund Types	
Liabilities and Fund Equity	General	Enterprise	Internal Service
LIABILITIES			
	* * *		
Accrued compensated absences (Note 12)	$150,000	$137,520	$25,989
Accrued expenses	179,008	12,583	—
	* * *		
Accrued payroll	766,080	—	—
	* * *		

[CITY OF TAMPA, FLORIDA]

Combined Balance Sheet [in part]—All Fund Types and Account Groups, September 30, 1983 [in thousands]

	Governmental Fund Types			Proprietary Fund Types	
	General	Special Revenue	Debt Service	Enterprise	Internal Service
LIABILITIES AND FUND EQUITY					
		* * *			
Accrued liabilities	$2,023	$258	$1,700	$545	$ 165
Accrued claims payable	—	—	—	—	7,627

[Statements included for illustrative purposes. For brevity the footnotes accompanying the statements have not been included.]

TABLE 10-3. ACCOUNT TITLES USED BY GOVERNMENTAL UNITS TO REPORT DEPOSITS, ADVANCES, AND DEFERRALS

Account Title*	Instances Observed (%)	Account Title*	Instances Observed (%)
Deferred revenue	70	Funds held in escrow	1
Deposits	13	Advances and deposits	1
Advances from other funds	10	Performance deposits	1
Customer deposits	7	Other	1
Deferred compensation payable	4	Deposits held in trust	1
Advances from general fund	3	Taxes collected in advance	1
Deferred property tax revenue	3	Other descriptors:	<1
Revenue collected in advance	3	Deferred tax revenue	
Deferred income	2	Refundable deposits	
Deferred credit	2	Advances from other agencies	
Deferred revenue—other	1	Security deposits	
Escrow deposits	1	Advances from municipality	
Deferred revenue—property taxes	1	Unearned revenue	
Deferred property taxes	1		

* Observations for the 88% of the units having a combined balance sheet.

EXHIBIT 10-4. EXAMPLES OF REPORTING BY GOVERNMENTAL UNITS OF DEPOSITS, ADVANCES, RETAINAGES, AND DEFERRED ITEMS

[CITY OF ALBUQUERQUE, NEW MEXICO]

Combined Balance Sheet [in part]—All Fund Types and Account Groups, June 30, 1984 [in thousands]

	Governmental Funds				Proprietary Funds	Fiduciary Funds
	General	Special Revenue	Capital Projects	Special Assessments	Enterprise	Trust and Agency
LIABILITIES AND FUND EQUITY						
Liabilities:						
		* * *				
Retainage payable	$ —	$ —	$ 390	$ 230	$ —	$ —
		* * *				
Advances from other governments	1,001	29	—	6,462	3,951	280
Deferred revenue (Note 1)	136	—	1,419	6,462	71	—
Fare tokens outstanding	—	—	—	—	50	—
Deposits	6	661	—	—	—	—
		* * *				

[CITY OF DALY CITY, CALIFORNIA]

Combined Balance Sheet [in part]—All Fund Types and Account Groups, June 30, 1984

	Governmental Fund Types				Fiduciary Fund Types
	General	Special Revenue	Capital Projects	Special Assessments	Trust and Agency
LIABILITIES					
		* * *			
Advances from Other Funds	$ —	$ —	$ —	$176,748	$60,459
Deferred Revenue (Note 18)	207,924	360,000	72,694	—	—

[COUNTY OF OAKLAND, MICHIGAN]

Combined Balance Sheet [in part]—All Fund Types and Account Groups, December 31, 1983

	Governmental Funds		Proprietary Funds	
	General	Special Revenue	Internal Service	Fiduciary Funds
LIABILITIES				
	* * *			
Deposits Held	$ —	$ —	$ —	$3,478,002
	* * *			
Long-Term Advance	—	—	875,000	—
Deferred Revenue	64,998,581	6,159,125	—	169,322
	* * *			

[CITY OF SIOUX FALLS, SOUTH DAKOTA]

Combined Balance Sheet [in part]—All Fund Types and Account Groups, December 31, 1983

| | Governmental Fund Types | | | | Proprietary Fund Types | | Fiduciary Fund Type |
	General	Special Revenue	Debt Service	Special Assessment	Enterprise	Internal Service	Trust and Agency
LIABILITIES:							
			* * *				
Deposits	$ —	$ 21,930	$ —	$ —	$ —	$ —	$26,285
			* * *				
Deferred revenues	10,871,566	3,680,423	217,765	2,108,201	—	—	—
			* * *				
Advances from other funds	—	—	—	—	120,000	80,000	5,000
			* * *				

[CITY OF FULLERTON, CALIFORNIA]

Combined Balance Sheet [in part]—All Fund Types and Account Groups, June 30, 1984

| | Governmental Fund Types | | Proprietary Fund Type | Fiduciary Fund Type |
	Special Revenue	Capital Projects	Enterprise	Agency
LIABILITIES AND FUND EQUITY				
Liabilities:				
	* * *			
Deposits	$ —	$ 7,500	$152,055	$1,509,834
Deferred revenue	170,269	1,492,962	—	—

[Statements included for illustrative purposes. For brevity the footnotes accompanying the statements have not been included.]

[CITY OF SAN MATEO, CALIFORNIA]

Combined Balance Sheet [in part]—All Fund Types and Account Groups, June 30, 1984

| | Governmental Fund Types | | Fiduciary Fund Type |
	General	Special Revenue	Expendable Trust
LIABILITIES:			
	* * *		
Advance fees, deposits, deferred revenue, and other liabilities	$278,566	$98,719	$365
	* * *		

TABLE 10-4. ACCOUNT TITLES USED BY GOVERNMENTAL UNITS TO REPORT LONG-TERM OBLIGATIONS—CURRENT PORTION

Account Title*	Instances Observed (%)
Current portion of long-term debt	9
Revenue bonds payable	4
Current maturity of long-term debt	2
Obligations under capital lease	2
Capital lease obligations, current	1
Lease purchase agreements	1
Special assessments bonds payable	1
Matured bonds payable	1
Serial bonds payable	1
Current portion of general obligation bonds	1
Other descriptors:	<1
Bonds payable within one year	
Amounts held under state lease agreements	
Capital leases payable (one year)	
Current maturities of bonds payable	
Installment purchase contracts payable	

* Observations for the 88% of the units having combined balance sheet.

Chapter 11
The Balance Sheet: Governmental Equities

The fund equity section of the combined balance sheet for a governmental unit comprises two separate elements. The equity portion of the balance sheet related to governmental-type funds is referred to as the fund balance. The equity portion of the balance sheet of a governmental unit for its proprietary-type funds is referred to as retained earnings and, where applicable, contributed capital. In both cases these sections are residual balances, the difference between assets and liabilities. Several subordinate accounts or groups of accounts may appear in the fund equity section of governmental units, such as reservations, designations, contributions, or investments in fixed assets, depending on the circumstances of the reporting government.

RESERVES

In governmental fund accounting the term "reserve" identifies that portion of either of the two fund equity balances that is not appropriable or available for expenditure. For example, the reserve for inventories is an example of resources already expended (but not consumed), so that there is a portion of fund balance that is not available for expenditure in a future fiscal period. The term "reserve" may also refer to that portion of the fund balance that is legally separated for a specific future use. An example is the reserve for encumbrances. This reserve indicates that portion of the fund balance that has been segregated for expenditure under executory contracts. Thus, this portion of the fund balance is reserved, or set aside, to meet the future obligations of these outstanding encumbrances. A third example of a reserve is the reserve for debt service. This segregation ensures the maintenance of a liquid condition for debt requirements.

Reservations of fund balances are appropriate in the case of both governmental funds and certain proprietary funds.

DESIGNATIONS

Another group of equity accounts carries the descriptive title "designations." A designated account is one in which the amounts have been designated and labeled by governmental executives to indicate tentative plans or commitments for those resources in a future period.

Designated accounts are allocations of fund balances at the discretion of the government, reflecting a management intent to expend the resources in the designated manner. In contrast, reserves, as discussed in the preceding section, often are statutory requirements or reflect decisions and commitments already made.

REPORTING RESERVES AND DESIGNATIONS

Designated funds are reported as part of the unreserved or free fund balance but are shown as designated for a specific purpose. Reserves, on the other hand, while part of the fund balance section, are segregated from the free or designated portions of the fund balance amount.

According to the NCGA, reserves should be reported in the fund balance section of the governmental fund balance sheet and should not be included as liabilities or placed as a group of accounts between liabilities and the fund balance in the financial statements. If the fund balance section of the balance sheet is subdivided into the reserved and unreserved amounts, the designated accounts are included among the unreserved fund balance accounts.

In the case of enterprise funds, the reserve accounts are accounted for and reported in the same manner as in commercial accounting and reporting.

CONTRIBUTED EQUITY

Statement 2 of the NCGA, "Grant, Entitlement, and Shared Revenue Accounting and Reporting by State and Local Governments," sets forth the accounting principles and procedures related to grants, contributions, gifts, and other donations received by a governmental unit. In that statement the NCGA indicates that proprietary-type fund grant receipts whose use is restricted to the acquisition or construction of capital assets should be accounted for as additions to contributed equity. (All other receipts of this kind by a proprietary-type fund should be recognized as nonoperating revenues in the accounting period when earned and measurable.)

INVESTMENT IN GENERAL FIXED ASSETS

A segregation in the combined fund equity section of a governmental unit relates to the investments in general fixed assets—i.e., fixed assets other than those authorized to be recorded in certain fund accounts (proprietary and designated trust funds). These are fixed assets for which resources were expended by governmental-type funds in past periods and do not represent resources available for current or future uses. However, the value of general fixed assets should be accounted for in the combined financial statements of the governmental unit. This investment in general fixed assets may also be segregated and accounted for as a contra account and equity-type item but separate from the unreserved or free fund balance of a governmental unit.

The fixed asset accounts in the general fixed assets account group and the proprietary funds and trust funds should include the cost of capitalized fixed assets acquired from grants, entitlements, or shared revenues. Accumulated depreciation accounts, optional in the case of general governmental fixed assets, should include the depreciation recognized on the contributed proprietary fixed assets.

STUDY OBSERVATIONS

Tables 11-1 to 11-3 indicate account titles used by the surveyed governmental units to describe reservations of fund balances, retained earnings, and designations of unreserved fund balances, respectively. Contributions for capital expenditures, if material, should also be identified and segregated in the fund equity accounts. Several examples of account titles used to report contributed capital are listed in Table 11-4.

As noted in Table 11-5, investments in general fixed assets are segregated and identified as a separate item in the governmental section of the combined balance sheet, although the presentation varied slightly among the governmental units surveyed. As discussed in Chapter 3, in some cases general fixed assets were reported with no indication as to whether depreciation was a factor in the accounting reflected. In other instances the gross investment in general fixed assets was reported along with the credit amount of the accumulated depreciation.

Exhibit 11-1 contains excerpts from the combined balance sheets of several governmental units, illustrating the type of reporting made of governmental equity and certain other components of the equity balances. Exhibit 11-2 illustrates footnote disclosures relating to the reservation or designation of governmental equity balances.

EXHIBITS AND TABLES FOR CHAPTER 11

Table 11-1. Account Titles Used by Governmental Units to Report Governmental-Type Fund Balance Reserves

Table 11-2. Account Titles Used by Governmental Units to Report Retained Earnings Reserved

Table 11-3. Account Titles Used by Governmental Units to Report Unreserved but Designated Fund Balances

Table 11-4. Account Titles Used by Governmental Units to Report Capital Contributions to Fund Equity

Table 11-5. Account Titles Used by Governmental Units to Report Investment in General Fixed Assets

Exhibit 11-1. Examples of Reporting of Governmental Equities—Fund Balances and Retained Earnings

Exhibit 11-2. Excerpts of Footnote Disclosures Related to Governmental Equity—Reserves and Designations

TABLE 11-1. ACCOUNT TITLES USED BY GOVERNMENTAL UNITS TO REPORT GOVERNMENTAL-TYPE FUND BALANCE RESERVES

Account Title:* "Fund balance reserved for . . ."	Instances Observed (%)	Account Title:* "Fund balance reserved for . . ."	Instances Observed (%)
Encumbrances	60	Commitments and contingencies	2
Debt service	30	Other	2
Inventories	28	Petty cash	2
Reserved (unspecified)	11	Special purposes	2
Employee retirement system	9	Long-term receivables	2
Advance to other funds	6	Prepaid items	2
Prepaid expenses	6	Pension payments	1
State statute	6	Advances	1
Inventory of supplies	4	Restricted purposes	1
Self-insurance	4	Subsequent years' appropriation	1
Capital projects	4	Deferred compensation	1
Employee retirement	4	Special assessments	1
Endowments	3	Inventory and prepaid expenses	1
Loans	3	Receivables	1
Employee benefits	3	Imprest cash	1
Trust purposes	3	Unemployment insurance	1
Retirement benefits	3	Other descriptors	<1
Capital improvements	2		

* Observations for the 88% of the units having a combined balance sheet.

TABLE 11-2. ACCOUNT TITLES USED BY GOVERNMENTAL UNITS TO REPORT RETAINED EARNINGS RESERVED

Account Title:* "Retained earnings reserved for . . ."	Instances Observed (%)	Account Title:* "Retained earnings reserved for . . ."	Instances Observed (%)
Reserved (unspecified)	11	Bond indentures	1
Revenue bond retirement	6	Equipment replacement	1
Debt service	5	Other descriptors:	<1
Construction	3	Replacement and improvements	
Bond retirement	3	Improvements	
Revenue bond debt service	3	Claims	
Self-insurance	2	Operations and maintenance	
Revenue bond indenture	2	Authorized construction	
Revenue bond requirement	2	Bond and interest redemption	
Debt retirement	1	Depreciation	
Contingencies	1	Replacements	
Capital improvements	1	Reserve accounts	
Equipment renewal and replacement	1	Reserve bond contingency (renewal and	
Bond debt service	1	replacement) account	
Other purposes	1	Surplus fund	
Revenue bonds	1		

* Observations for the 88% of the units having a combined balance sheet.

TABLE 11-3. ACCOUNT TITLES USED BY GOVERNMENTAL UNITS TO REPORT UNRESERVED BUT DESIGNATED FUND BALANCES

Account Title:* "Fund balance designated for"	Instances Observed (%)	Account Title:* "Fund balance designated for"	Instances Observed (%)
Subsequent/future years' expenditures	22	Contingencies	1
Debt service	17	Trust purposes	1
Unreserved but designated (unspecified)	9	Programs and debt service	1
Capital projects	5	Other descriptors:	<1
Unappropriated	3	Capital outlay	
Appropriated	3	Next year's budget	
Self-insurance	3	Future contingencies	
Capital improvements	2	Operations	
Special purpose	1	Public library	
Construction	1	Capital expenditure	
Working capital	1	Subsequent expenditures	
Future expenditures	1	Authorized expenditure	
Deferred compensation	1	Specific capital project	
Subsequent years' budget	1	Landfill equipment	
Special projects	1		

* Observations for the 88% having a combined balance sheet.

TABLE 11-4. ACCOUNT TITLES USED BY GOVERNMENTAL UNITS TO REPORT CAPITAL CONTRIBUTIONS TO FUND EQUITY

Account Title*	Instances Observed (%)
Contributed capital	61
Contributions	5
Contribution in aid of construction	2
Contributed capital—general fund	1
Contributions—net	1
Contributed capital by	
city	1
federal	1
developers	1
subdividers	1
others	1
Other descriptors:	<1
Other governments	
Municipality	
Contributed capital—other sources	
Contributions from developers	

* Observations for the 88% of the units having a combined balance sheet.

TABLE 11-5. ACCOUNT TITLES USED BY GOVERNMENTAL UNITS TO REPORT INVESTMENT IN GENERAL FIXED ASSETS

Account Title*	Instances Observed (%)
Investment in general fixed assets	77
Investment in property, plant, and equipment	30
Invested in fixed assets	5
Investments in general fixed assets and capital leases	2

* Observations for the 88% of the units having a combined balance sheet.

EXHIBIT 11-1. EXAMPLES OF REPORTING OF GOVERNMENTAL EQUITIES—FUND BALANCES AND RETAINED EARNINGS

[CITY OF CHESAPEAKE, VIRGINIA]

Combined Balance Sheet [in part]—All Funds and Account Groups (June 30, 1984)

| | Governmental Fund Types | | | | Proprietary Fund Types | | Fiduciary Fund Types | Account Groups | |
	General	Special Revenue	Debt Service	Capital Projects	Enterprise	Internal Service	Trust and Agency	General Fixed Assets	General Long-Term Debt
Liabilities and Fund Equity									
Liabilities:					* * * *				
Fund Equity:									
Investment in general fixed assets	$ —	$ —	$ —	$ —	$ —	$ —	$ —	$114,655,651	$ —
Contributed capital:									
from the City	—	—	—	—	18,740,609	31,170	—	—	—
from others	—	—	—	—	21,309,057	—	—	—	—
from grants	—	—	—	—	3,043,030	—	—	—	—
Retained earnings:									
Reserved for:									
Textbooks	—	—	—	—	1,388,457	—	—	—	—
Bus replacement	—	—	—	—	—	6,366	—	—	—
Construction projects	—	—	—	—	1,595,915	—	—	—	—
Unreserved	—	—	—	—	12,461,678	672,092	—	—	—
Fund balances:									
Reserved (note 10)	10,680,828	1,551,614	—	4,951,937	—	—	12,795	—	—
Unreserved:									
Designated for debt service	—	—	3,309,498	—	—	—	—	—	—
Designated for construction projects	—	—	—	7,912,831	—	—	—	—	—
Undesignated	16,511,012	7,721,842	—	—	—	—	37,893	—	—
Total fund equity	27,191,840	9,273,456	3,309,498	12,864,768	58,538,746	709,628	50,688	114,655,651	—
Commitments and contingent liabilities (notes 9, 11 and 12)									
	$31,812,266	$13,076,525	$3,346,425	$13,463,340	$104,541,701	$1,463,933	$943,429	$114,655,651	$44,777,612

[CITY OF DAYTONA BEACH, FLORIDA]

Combined Balance Sheet [in part]—All Funds and Account Groups (September 30, 1983)

	Governmental Fund Types					Proprietary Fund Types		Fiduciary Fund Types	Account Groups	
	General	Special Revenue	Debt Service	Capital Projects	Special Assessments	Enterprise	Internal Service	Trust and Agency	General Fixed Assets	General Long-Term Debt
LIABILITIES & FUND EQUITY										
LIABILITIES				* * * *						
COMMITMENTS & CONTINGENCIES (Note 26)										
FUND EQUITY										
Investment in general fixed assets	$ —	$ —	$ —	$ —	$ —	$ —	$ —	$ —	$21,469,418	$ —
Contributions—net	—	—	—	—	—	26,391,784	169,481	—	—	—
Retained earnings:										
Reserved for bond retirement	—	—	—	—	—	5,664,799	—	—	—	—
Reserved for unemployment compensation	—	—	—	—	—	—	371,818	—	—	—
Reserved for general liability claims	—	—	—	—	—	—	21,098	—	—	—
Reserved for specific capital projects	—	—	—	—	—	3,702,289	—	—	—	—
Reserved for Workers' Compensation claims	—	—	—	—	—	—	447,864	—	—	—
Unreserved	—	—	—	—	—	21,408,022	418,752	—	—	—
Fund balances:										
Reserved for specific capital projects	—	1,967,505	—	61,353	—	—	—	—	—	—
Reserved for encumbrances	138,805	14,750	—	—	—	—	—	—	—	—
Reserved for inventories	300,804	—	—	—	—	—	—	—	—	—
Reserved for police education	155,157	—	—	—	—	—	—	—	—	—
Reserved for advance to other funds (Note 7)	572,029	—	—	—	—	—	—	—	—	—
Reserved for debt service	—	—	660,257	—	—	—	—	—	—	—
Unreserved:										
Designated for program expenditures	—	496,670	—	—	—	—	—	—	—	—
Designated for law enforcement	—	41,921	—	—	—	—	—	—	—	—
Designated for police & fire pension	—	—	—	—	—	—	—	10,709,103	—	—
Designated for employer contribution actuarial deficiency (Note 22)	—	—	—	—	—	—	—	—	—	—
Designated for deferred compensation	—	—	—	—	—	—	—	3,917,464	—	—
Undesignated—(deficit)	2,956,377	(896,896)	—	46,907	32,366	—	—	160,941 / (3,917,464)	—	—
TOTAL FUND EQUITY	$4,123,172	$1,623,950	$660,257	$108,260	$32,366	$57,166,894	$1,429,013	$10,870,044	$21,469,418	$ —
TOTAL LIABILITIES & FUND EQUITY	$5,270,965	$2,529,628	$664,391	$135,245	$33,304	$86,306,666	$2,329,902	$10,921,082	$21,469,418	$3,076,950

[CITY OF COLORADO SPRINGS, COLORADO]

Combined Balance Sheet [in part]—All Funds and Account Groups (December 31, 1983)

	Governmental Fund Types				Proprietary Fund Types		Fiduciary Fund Types	Account Groups	
	General	Special Revenue	Capital Projects	Special Assessment	Enterprise	Internal Service	Trust and Agency	General Fixed Assets	General Long-Term and Other Debt
LIABILITY AND FUND EQUITY									
Liabilities:				* * *					
Fund Equity:									
Contributions	$ —	$ —	$ —	$ —	$29,104,160	$2,265,888	$ —	$ —	$ —
Investment in General Fixed Assets, Note 2	—	—	—	—	—	—	—	57,187,072	—
Retained earnings: Unreserved	—	—	—	—	11,661,687	4,830,109	—	—	—
Fund balances:									
Reserved for encumbrances, Note 2	4,032,423	1,161,441	52,818	270,983	—	—	34,610	—	—
Reserve for legal defense, Note 2	48,586	—	—	—	—	—	—	—	—
Reserve for general obligation bond interest, Note 2	94,863	—	—	—	—	—	—	—	—
Reserve for museum endowments	—	—	—	—	—	—	1,000	—	—
Reserve for City contribution	—	—	—	—	—	—	815,921	—	—
Reserve for perpetual care endowment, Note 7	—	—	—	—	—	—	1,868,764	—	—
Reserve for members' contributions, Note 2	—	—	—	—	—	—	1,311,333	—	—
Reserve for incurred but unreported claims	—	—	—	—	—	—	774,497	—	—
Unreserved: Appropriated, Note 2	2,368,006	—	2,433,391	510,400	—	—	5,787,409	—	—
Unappropriated	7,991,948	1,663,197	—	—	—	—	—	—	—
Total fund equity	14,535,826	2,824,638	2,486,209	781,383	40,765,847	7,095,997	10,593,534	57,187,072	—
Total liabilities and fund equity	$29,285,653	$3,030,605	$2,560,118	$2,286,618	$43,376,456	$7,383,720	$11,567,485	$57,187,072	$24,958,370

[CITY OF EVANSTON, ILLINOIS]

Combined Balance Sheet [in part]—All Funds and Account Groups (February 29, 1984)

	Governmental Fund Types					Proprietary Fund Types		Fiduciary Fund Types	Account Groups	
	General	Special Revenue	Debt Service	Capital Projects	Special Assessment	Enterprise	Internal Service	Trust and Agency	General Fixed Assets	General Long-Term Debt
Liabilities and Fund Equity										
Liabilities				* * *						
				* * *	* * *					
Fund Equity										
Contributed Capital						$ 4,793,965	$2,591,712	$ 345,000		
Investment in General Fixed Assets Assets									$30,752,739	
Retained Earnings										
Reserved—Restricted Accounts						$ 2,834,531				
Reserved for Construction						6,785,897				
Unreserved						17,369,572	204,756			
						$26,990,000	$ 204,756			
Fund Balances										
Reserved for Encumbrances	$ 213,135									
Reserved for Debt Service			$3,062,848							
Reserved for Arts Council	13,201									
Reserved for Cable Communications	26,771									
Reserved for Private Trees	19,147									
Reserved for Scholarship Contributions	33,147									
Reserved for Library Acquisition	203,212									
Reserved For Employees' Retirement System								$48,521,391		
Reserved for Payment of Claims								254,979		
Unreserved	4,224,542	$2,518,509		$8,615,448	$ 584,734			(33,044,016)		
	$ 4,733,155	$2,518,509	$3,062,848	$8,615,448	$ 584,734			$15,732,354		
Total Retained Earnings/ Fund Balances	$ 4,733,155	$2,518,509	$3,062,848	$8,615,448	$ 584,734	$26,990,000	$ 204,756	$15,732,354		
Total Fund Equity	$ 4,733,155	$2,518,509	$3,062,848	$8,615,448	$ 584,734	$31,783,965	$2,796,468	$16,077,354	$30,752,739	
Total Liabilities and Fund Equity	$16,984,763	$3,500,716	$6,007,752	$9,079,861	$3,204,646	$54,104,672	$3,242,009	$16,693,544	$30,752,739	$47,723,132

[DEKALB COUNTY, GEORGIA]

Combined Balance Sheet [in part]—All Funds and Account Groups (December 31, 1983)

	Governmental Fund Types				Proprietary Fund Types		Fiduciary Fund Types	Account Groups	
	General	Special Revenue	Debt Service	Capital Projects	Enterprise	Internal Service	Trust and Agency	General Fixed Assets	General Long-Term Obligation
FUND EQUITY									
INVESTMENT IN GENERAL FIXED ASSETS	$	$	$	$	$	$	$	$63,639,272	$
CONTRIBUTED CAPITAL (NOTE K)					124,100,332	1,325,106			
RETAINED EARNINGS:									
Reserved for restricted assets					54,245,644				
Unreserved					53,853,821	29,126,387			
TOTAL RETAINED EARNINGS					108,099,465	29,126,387			
FUND BALANCE:									
Reserved for:									
Encumbrances	1,224,300	223,577		4,440,293					
Inventories	80,921								
Prepaids	57,800	17,994							
Retirement benefits							99,258,872		
Unreserved:									
Designated							60,719		
Undesignated	6,297,130	6,657,952	2,194,218	11,985,695					
TOTAL FUND BALANCE	7,660,151	6,899,523	2,194,218	16,425,988			99,319,591		
TOTAL FUND EQUITY	7,660,151	6,899,523	2,194,218	16,425,988	232,199,797	30,451,493	99,319,591	63,639,272	
TOTAL LIABILITIES AND FUND EQUITY	$9,799,273	$10,075,181	$2,194,218	$16,480,024	$338,471,681	$31,318,742	$114,256,894	$63,639,272	$46,770,611

[CITY OF GLENDALE, CALIFORNIA]

Combined Balance Sheet [in part]—All Funds and Account Groups (June 30, 1984)

	Governmental Fund Types			Proprietary Fund Types		Fiduciary Fund Types	Account Groups	
	General Fund	Special Revenue Fund	Capital Projects Funds	Enterprise Funds	Internal Service Funds	Expendable Trust Funds	General Fixed Assets	General Long-Term Debt
Liabilities and Fund Equity								
Current liabilities:				* * *				
Other liabilities:				* * *				
Fund equity:								
Contributions	$ —	—	—	17,044,339	—	—	—	—
Investment in general fixed assets	—	—	—	—	—	—	105,808,044	—
Retained earnings:								
Reserved for principal and interest	—	—	—	5,000,684	—	—	—	—
Reserved for Insurance (note 6)	—	—	—	—	12,243,936	—	—	—
Reserved for bond construction	—	—	—	2,259,201	—	—	—	—
Unreserved	—	—	—	72,380,513	4,602,064	—	—	—
Fund balances:								
Reserved:								
Principal and interest	—	—	—	—	—	14,289,601	—	—
Insurance	—	—	—	—	—	386,000	—	—
Encumbrances	144,177	1,615,530	2,587,531	—	—	75,146	—	—
Contingencies (notes 1 and 4)	24,384,603	—	—	—	—	—	—	—
Unreserved:								
Appropriated	—	3,749,639	9,776,655	—	—	3,332,062	—	—
Unappropriated (note 7)	10,118,737	2,251,349	23,371,345	—	—	(6,180,976)	—	—
Total fund equity	34,647,517	7,616,518	35,735,531	96,684,737	16,846,000	11,901,833	105,808,044	—
Total liabilities and fund equity	$38,185,591	7,992,377	35,850,531	147,078,780	16,847,884	30,628,194	105,808,044	38,085,751

[HOWARD COUNTY, MARYLAND]

Combined Balance Sheet [in part]—All Funds and Account Groups (June 30, 1984)

	Governmental Fund Types				Proprietary Fund Types		Fiduciary Fund Type	College Fund Type	Account Groups	
	General	Special Revenue	Debt Service	Capital Projects	Enterprise	Internal Service	Agency	Community College	General Fixed Assets	Long-Term Obligations
FUND EQUITY										
Investment in fixed assets	$ —	$ —	$ —	$ —	$ —	$ —	$ —	$15,053,536	$237,096,886	$ —
Contributed capital	—	—	—	—	105,570,330	80,452	—	—	—	—
Retained earnings (deficit):										
Designated for insurance claims	—	—	—	—	—	3,203,868	—	—	—	—
Designated for depreciation	—	—	—	—	17,063,387	—	—	—	—	—
Designated for construction	—	—	—	—	5,815,007	—	—	—	—	—
Undesignated	—	—	—	—	(1,662,316)	285,943	—	—	—	—
Fund balance:										
Reserved for encumbrances	1,183,065	1,564,494	—	17,031,737	—	—	—	—	—	—
Reserved for college programs	—	—	—	—	—	—	—	129,726	—	—
Unreserved:										
Designated for subsequent years' expenditures	7,473,891	598,434	—	301,400	—	—	—	126,077	—	—
Undesignated (deficit)	1,612,997	6,066,062	—	12,925,634	—	—	—	(134,683)	—	—
Total fund equity	10,269,953	8,228,990	—	30,258,771	126,786,408	3,570,263	—	15,174,656	237,096,886	—
Total liabilities and fund equity	$14,043,163	$17,614,697	$135,751	$32,035,282	$226,271,198	$3,931,467	$3,947,467	$15,932,226	$237,096,886	$103,724,583

[CITY OF SAN BUENAVENTURE, CALIFORNIA]

Combined Balance Sheet [in part]—All Funds and Account Groups (June 30, 1984)

	Governmental Fund Types				Proprietary Fund Types		Fiduciary Fund Types	Account Groups	
	General	Special Revenue	Debt Service	Capital Projects	Enterprise	Internal Service	Agency	General Fixed Assets	General Long-Term Obligation
Liabilities and Fund Equity									
Liabilities:									
				* * *					
Fund Equity:									
Contributed capital	$ —	$ —	$ —	$ —	$38,724,712	$1,834,997	$ —	$ —	$ —
Investment in general fixed assets (Note 6)	—	—	—	—	—	—	—	32,452,370	—
Retained earnings:									
Reserved (Note 15)	—	—	—	—	7,852,558	851,835	—	—	—
Unreserved	—	—	—	—	16,643,929	2,241,662	—	—	—
Fund Balance (Note 15):									
Reserved	11,182,776	2,225,502	19,247,072	16,731,076	—	—	—	—	—
Unreserved:									
Designated	9,735,197	—	—	—	—	—	—	—	—
Undesignated	—	1,347,915	—	2,245,936	—	—	—	—	—
Total Fund Equity	20,917,973	3,573,417	19,247,072	18,977,012	63,221,199	4,928,494	—	32,452,370	—
Commitments and contingencies (Note 12)									
Total Liabilities and Fund Equity	$22,008,490	$4,234,047	$20,266,658	$19,042,390	$78,082,485	$9,116,477	$2,624,635	$32,452,370	$45,824,694

[SHREVEPORT, LOUISIANA]

Combined Balance Sheet [in part]—All Funds and Account Groups (December 31, 1983)

	Governmental Fund Types					Proprietary Fund Types	Fiduciary Fund Types	Account Groups	
	General	Special Revenue	Debt Service	Capital Projects	Special Assessment	Enterprise	Pension Trust Funds	General Fixed Assets	General Long-Term Obligation
LIABILITIES AND FUND EQUITY									
Liabilities (Note 6):				* * *					
Fund equity (notes 2 and 8):									
Contributed capital	—	—	—	—	—	$ 87,079,681	—	—	—
Investment in general fixed assets	—	—	—	—	—	—	—	$83,140,292	—
Retained earnings:									
Reserved for debt service (note 6)	—	—	—	—	—	9,250,674	—	—	—
Unreserved	—	—	—	—	—	37,879,285	—	—	—
Fund balances:									
Reserved for:									
Endowments	$ 39,719	—	—	—	—	—	—	—	—
Encumbrances	789,737	$ 5,148,189	—	$ 4,717,036	—	—	—	—	—
Inventories	385,379	65,916	—	—	—	—	—	—	—
Debt service	—	—	$12,814,643	—	$ (536,547)	—	—	—	—
Employees retirement systems	—	—	—	—	—	—	$32,113,514	—	—
Unreserved—Designated for subsequent years' expenditures	$5,537,874	(1,182,795)	—	38,320,429	—	—	—	—	—
Total retained earnings/ fund balances	$6,752,709	4,031,310	12,814,643	43,037,465	(536,547)	47,129,959	32,113,514	—	—
Total fund equity	$6,752,709	4,031,310	12,814,643	43,037,465	(536,547)	134,209,640	32,113,514	83,140,292	—
	$9,106,928	$ 6,673,807	$12,814,643	$44,661,842	$2,694,728	$185,787,959	$32,831,375	$83,140,292	$152,927,294

[CITY OF WESTMINSTER, COLORADO]
Combined Balance Sheet [in part]—All Funds and Account Groups (December 31, 1983)

	Governmental Fund Types					Proprietary Fund Type	Fiduciary Fund Types	Account Groups	
	General	Special Revenue	Debt Service	Capital Projects	Special Assessment	Enterprise	Trust and Agency	General Fixed Assets	General Long-Term Debt
LIABILITIES AND FUND EQUITY									
Liabilities:	$ —	$ —	$ —	* * * *	$ —	$ —	$ —	$ —	$ —
Equity:									
Contributed capital	—	—	—	—	—	59,806,639	—	—	—
Investment in general fixed assets	—	—	—	—	—	—	—	27,256,970	—
Retained earnings:									
Reserved for debt service	—	—	—	—	—	950,000	—	—	—
Unreserved:									
Designated for:									
Subsequent years	—	—	—	—	—	3,984,149	—	—	—
Continuing appropriations	—	—	—	—	—	2,916,425	—	—	—
Undesignated	—	—	—	—	—	5,069,377	—	—	—
Fund balance:									
Reserved for:									
Encumbrances	2,628,707	—	—	932,196	—	—	—	—	—
Prepaid expenses	2,067	23,704	—	—	—	—	—	—	—
Inventories	217,934	—	—	—	—	—	—	—	—
Future benefits	—	—	—	—	—	—	7,141,014	—	—
Unreserved:									
Designated for:									
Subsequent years	—	558,068	—	—	699	—	—	—	—
Continuing appropriations	—	—	—	4,896,204	—	—	—	—	—
Debt service	678,563	95,000	116,488	—	—	—	—	—	—
Undesignated	1,289,868	542,083	—	(283,590)	(406,192)	—	—	—	—
Total retained earnings/fund balance	4,817,139	1,218,855	116,488	5,544,810	(405,493)	12,919,951	7,141,014	—	—
Total fund equity	4,817,139	1,218,855	116,488	5,544,810	(405,493)	72,726,590	7,141,014	27,256,970	—
Commitments and contingent liabilities									
Total liabilities and fund equity	$6,072,144	$1,934,963	$127,663	$6,757,939	$ 511,162	$92,281,686	$7,293,686	$27,256,970	$9,611,198

[Statements included for illustrative purposes. For brevity the footnotes accompanying the statements have not been included.]

EXHIBIT 11-2. EXCERPTS OF FOOTNOTE DISCLOSURES RELATED TO GOVERNMENTAL EQUITY—RESERVES AND DESIGNATIONS

[CITY OF FULLERTON, CALIFORNIA (JUNE 30, 1984), NOTES TO FINANCIAL STATEMENTS (IN PART)]

Note (18) Retained Earnings/Fund Balance Reserves and Designations

Reserves

The various reserves established as of June 30, 1984, are described below and tabulated as follows:

Reserve	General Fund	Special Revenue Funds	Debt Service Funds	Capital Projects Funds	Enterprise Funds
Encumbrances	$ 90,756	$557,280		$ 54,121	
Advance to Brea Dam recreational facilities	1,771,480				
Restricted revenues		108,970		40,089	
Restricted cash			$1,016,197		$172,549
Inventory	541,375			390,908	
Notes receivable				286,656	
Totals	$2,403,611	$666,250	$1,016,197	$771,774	$172,549

Reserve for Encumbrances. These reserves represent the portion of purchase orders and contracts awarded for which the goods or services had not yet been received at June 30, 1984.

Reserve for Advance to Brea Dam Recreational Facilities. Due to the uncertainty of collection of the amount advanced to the Brea Dam Recreational Area Fund, a reserve has been set up in the amount corresponding to the advance.

Reserve for Restricted Revenues. Certain revenues received by the General, Library, and Capital Projects Funds are restricted by the grantor for specific uses. The revenues restricted represent private gifts and donations to the Library and interest income earned on State grants received but not yet expended by the Capital Projects Fund.

Reserve for Restricted Cash. The fiscal agent for the revenue bonds holds cash restricted solely for paying debt service on the bonds. Reserves have been established in the Library Building Authority and Redevelopment Agency debt service funds and in the Airport and Parking Facilities enterprise funds.

Reserve for Inventory. Reserves have been established for inventory held by the General Fund (stationery and maintenance supplies) and Redevelopment Agency project funds (land and improvements held for resale).

Reserve for Notes Receivable (Noncurrent Portion). The Redevelopment Agency has loaned various amounts (evidenced by notes receivable) to commercial property owners to enable them to rehabilitate their property (see Note 22 and additional information). In addition, the Agency sold various real estate parcels and aided the buyers in financing the acquisitions by accepting installment notes receivable (having due dates in 1986 and 1992).

A reserve has been established for the amount of loan principal due more than one year from the end of the fiscal year. Included in the reserve are amounts for: commercial rehabilitation notes—$148,801; property sales notes—$137,855.

Designations

The unreserved fund balances of certain governmental funds have been designated for self-insurance, subsequent years expenditures, debt service, or management designations for emergencies and contractual obligations. The fund types affected as of June 30, 1984, are tabulated as follows:

Designation	General Fund	Special Revenue Fund	Debt Service Fund	Capital Projects Funds
Self-Insurance	$ 88,804			
Subsequent Year Expenditures		$1,305,069		$9,063,481
Debt Service			$990,104	
Contractual Obligations	2,252,000	126,000		
Emergencies	1,621,458			
Totals	$3,962,262	$1,431,069	$990,104	$9,063,481

[CITY OF SAINT PAUL, MINNESOTA (DECEMBER 31, 1983), NOTES TO FINANCIAL STATEMENTS (IN PART)]

Note VI.C. [in part]

ii) Reserved Fund Equities

These are reported as "Retained Earnings—Reserved" in the Proprietary Funds and "Fund Balance—Reserved" in the Governmental Funds.

Reserved Fund Equities are reported to meet legal requirements and/or to report that certain assets are not available for appropriation as follows:

	Legal	Legal and Not Available for Appropriation	Not Available for Appropriation		Legal	Legal and Not Available for Appropriation	Not Available for Appropriation
Retained Earnings:				Energy Improvement			
Reserved for Revenue Bonds	×			Program		×	
Reserved for Revenue Bond Sinking Fund	×			Mandatory 5% for Retirement of Debt		×	
Reserved for Special Ramp Maintenance			×	Tax Anticipation Note Interest		×	
Fund Balance:				Civic Center Lease Debt		×	
Reserved for—				Trust		×	
Encumbrances			×	Civic Center Project Deferred Payment			
Imprest Funds			×	Note Security		×	
Advance to Other Funds			×	Civic Center Project Demand Note			
Materials & Supplies Inventory			×	Security		×	
Shared Solar Bank Savings Program		×					

A more detailed note is included herein on "Reserved For Mandatory 5% for Retirement of Debt," as this could be considered unusual to Saint Paul and require a more detailed disclosure. (See Note VI.C. (iv).)

iii) Fund Balance—Reserved

As of December 31, 1983, reservations of fund balances were reported in the following fund types:

	General	Special Revenue	Debt Service	Capital Projects	Special Assessment	Trust and Agency
Reserved for:						
Encumbrances	$1,536,695	$553,324	$	$ 30,271	$	$107,609
Imprest Funds	30,190	725			50	
Advance to Other Funds	4,681,067					
Materials & Supplies Inventory	1,369,493				4,037	
Shared Solar Bank Saving Program		100,000				
Energy Improvement Program	64,000					
Mandatory 5% for Retirement of Debt			978,387			
Tax Anticipation Note Interest			1,191,750			
Civic Center Lease Debt						515,500
Trust						7,944
Civic Center Project Deferred Payment Note Security				8,103,251		
Civic Center Project Demand Note Security				2,140,000		
	$7,617,445	$718,049	$2,170,137	$10,273,522	$4,087	$631,053

iv) Fund Balance—Reserve for Mandatory 5% for Retirement of Debt

Minnesota State Law requires agencies issuing General Obligation Bonds to certify an irrevocable tax levy to the County Auditor covering annual principal and interest payments plus 5% at the time bonds are issued. The annual tax levy can be reduced if the issuing agency annually certifies to funds on hand; this reserve is established to allow Saint Paul to certify and reduce its annual property tax levy for debt.

v) Fund Balance—Unreserved—Designated

As of December 31, 1983, designations of unreserved fund balance were reported in the following fund types:

	General	Special Revenue	Debt Service	Capital Projects	Special Assessment
Unreserved—Designated for:					
Next Year's Appropriation	$1,979,534	$	$ 8,144,696	$	$2,795,217
Cash Flow and Revenue Estimates	2,938,000	144,312			
Homestead Credit Loss Council Action	533,850				
Charter Commission	12,818				
Tort Liability	410,778				
Employee Insurance	365,000				
Workers Compensation	250,000				
HRA Activities		2,390,971		16,440,000	
Specific Capital Projects				13,405,204	
Maximum Annual Debt Service			246,000		
1984 Bond Sale			181,290		
G.O. Bond Retirement			190,330		
1½ years Debt Service			2,679,258		
Debt Service			3,374,341		
Advance Sewer Collections					50,000
	$6,489,980	$2,535,283	$14,815,915	$29,845,204	$2,845,217

[WINNEBAGO COUNTY, WISCONSIN (DECEMBER 31, 1983), NOTES TO FINANCIAL STATEMENTS (IN PART)]

Note 1 [in part]

K. Nature and Purpose of Reservations and Designations of Fund Equity

The reserves for landfill maintenance and long-term care represent amounts legally required by the Department of Natural Resources to be in escrow for the closure of the present landfill site and future maintenance costs. The reserve for self-insurance represents funds restricted for use to pay for those risks which are funded internally, such as workmen's compensation, limited property and liability insurance, and health insurance. The reserve for capital outlay represents fully appropriated and legally authorized funds for future capital improvements. It is comprised of the ever-to-date excess of specific capital project revenues and other financing sources over associated project expenditures.

The designations for landfill, employee benefits, and economic development represent tentative plans by County Board resolution for financial resource utilization in future periods. The designation for employee benefits represents amounts to be used to pay employees for unused sick leave upon retirement or termination as provided by various labor contracts. The reserve for inventory and designation for debt service amounts have been previously discussed in Note 1.

The designated for subsequent year's expenditures amount represents a segregation of a portion of fund equity to be utilized in the 1984 budget, as well as carryovers of 1983 budget appropriations.

[ORANGE COUNTY, NORTH CAROLINA (JUNE 30, 1983), NOTES TO FINANCIAL STATEMENTS (IN PART)]

Note A [in part]

7. Fund Balances

Fund balances are segregated into the following classifications:

Reserved for encumbrances—represents commitments for the expenditure of funds under purchase orders and contracts.

Reserved by state statute—represents the amount of revenue that has been recognized on an accrual basis for financial statement purposes, but which is not available for appropriation in accordance with state statute.

Designated for subsequent year's expenditure—represents the amount of fund balance appropriated to the budget for the year ending June 30, 1985.

Undesignated—represents the amount of fund balance which is available for future appropriations.

[COUNTY OF LOUDOUN, VIRGINIA (JUNE 30, 1984), NOTES TO FINANCIAL STATEMENTS (IN PART)]

Note XIV—Fund Balances/Retained Earnings

A. Reserves

The term "reserve" indicates that a portion of the fund balance is not appropriable for expenditures or is legally segregated for a specific future use. The following reserves appear in these financial statements.

Reserve for:

Encumbrances

Advance to Central Services Fund

Noncurrent notes and loans receivable

Trust and Agency Funds

B. Designated

The term "designated" has been established to indicate tentative managerial plans for financial resource utilization in a future period, but is not a legal reservation of fund balance and may be appropriable for expenditures upon legislative action by the governing body of the County. The following are the items terms as designated:

Appropriations—(funds set aside for subsequent years appropriations).

Fiscal cash liquidity purposes—(funds set aside to protect cash liquidity).

Public official liability self-insurance—(funds set aside to self-insure the public officials of the County for liability claims).

Group health self-insurance—(funds set aside to self-insure part of the group health coverage of the County if liability claims are incurred beyond a prescribed dollar amount).

C. Fund Corpus

"Fund Corpus" represents the amount of endowment principal in the Peabody Trust Fund, which is nonexpendable. This portion of fund balance is used solely to generate revenue and cannot be expended.

D. Unreserved

Unreserved fund balances/retained earnings represent funds available for appropriation in future periods. At

June 30, 1984, the unreserved fund balance by fund is as follows:

General Fund		$4,214,652
Special Revenue Funds:		
School Fund		1,235,307
Capital Projects Fund:		
General Capital Projects Fund	$ 301	
School Capital Projects Fund	9,072	9,373
Total		$5,460,332

[FOUNTAIN VALLEY, CALIFORNIA (JUNE 30, 1984), NOTES TO FINANCIAL STATEMENTS (IN PART)]

Note 10. Reserves and Designations of Fund Equity

Under the provisions of NCGA Statement 1, a city may set up "reserves" of fund equity to segregate fund balances which are not appropriable for expenditure in future periods, or which are legally set aside for a specific future use. Fund "designations" also may be established to indicate tentative plans for financial resource utilization in a future period.

The City's reserves at June 30, 1984, are described below.

Reserve for Inventory. A reserve has been established for inventory held by the General Fund.

Reserve for Long-Term Receivable. A reserve has been established for a note receivable, the principal of which is due June 30, 1985.

Reserve for Capital Sinking Fund. The amount reserved represents the unexpected portion authorized by council for capital equipment replacement during 1983–84.

Reserve for Individual Fund Deficits. A reserve has been established to cover the individual fund deficits at June 30, 1984, as described in Note 7.

Reserve for Self-Insurance. This reserve has been established to provide for the general liability, workers' compensation and employee long-term disability insurance programs.

Reserve for Encumbrances. Amounts reserved for encumbrances are commitments for materials and services on purchase orders and contracts which are unperformed.

Reserve for Appropriations Carried Forward. Amounts reserved for appropriations carried forward represent unexpended appropriations on incomplete projects carried forward to fiscal year 1984–85.

Reserve for Revenue Bond Retirement. A reserve has been established in the Water Utility Fund for future debt service payments as required by the bond indenture.

[CITY OF WICHITA FALLS, TEXAS (SEPTEMBER 30, 1983), NOTES TO FINANCIAL STATEMENTS (IN PART)]

Note 1 [in part]

I. Reserves and Designations

Portions of fund equity are segregated for future use, and are therefore not available for future appropriation or expenditures. Amounts reserved for revenue bond debt service and retirement represent portions of fund equity which are required to be segregated in accordance with the City's bond ordinances.

Designations are unreserved fund balances in governmental funds which indicate City management's tentative plans for use of financial resources in a future period.

[IRVINE, CALIFORNIA (JUNE 30, 1984), NOTES TO FINANCIAL STATEMENTS (IN PART)]

Note 2—Reserved Governmental Fund Type Balances

The General Fund balance contains the following reserved and unreserved amounts:

Reserved for:	
Reimbursement agreements*	$ 396,700
Bond value reduction**	655,000
1984–85 budget appropriations***	3,394,000
1983–84 encumbrances carried forward	482,598
Street lighting	20,678
	4,948,976
Unreserved	
Designated for capital improvement appropriations	$ 276,576
Designated for inventory acquisition	200,000
Undesignated	865,513
	1,342,089
Total General Fund	$6,291,065

* Reimbursement agreements are agreements that are made between the City and property owners within the City for payments that are to be received when development starts. As to timing of receipts, the receivable is reserved.

** Bond value reduction reserve was set up because unfavorable bond markets reduced the value of certain City owned long term bonds below par. It is the City's intention to hold these bonds until maturity; however, this reserve was set up to offset any loss the City could incur if required to sell.

*** It is the policy of the City to budget any estimated fund surplus in the next fiscal year. This reserve was set aside for that purpose.

Designated fund balances in other governmental fund types include:

Special Revenue Funds	
Gas tax funded streets and roads	$ 190,078
Street lighting district carry forward	1,181,088
Capital project appropriations	689,880
Traffic signal and bridges	673,051
Refuse service	307,431
Drainage facilities	31,483
Total Service Revenue Funds	$3,073,011
Debt Service Fund	
Debt service	$1,547,114
Capital Projects Funds	
Assessment district bond proceeds for infrastructure	$ 883,199
Park bond proceeds for park projects	1,341,932
Trail bond proceeds for trail projects	677,402
Circulation and public facility projects	3,052,042
Undesignated	723,024
Total Capital Projects Funds	$6,677,599

[STOCKTON, CALIFORNIA (JUNE 30, 1984),
NOTES TO FINANCIAL STATEMENTS (IN PART)]

Note 8—Nature and Purpose of Reported Reserves

A summary of reported reserves (in thousands) by fund
follows:

| Account Title | Governmental Fund Types | | | | Proprietary Fund Types | | Fiduciary Fund Type | Total (Memorandum Only) |
	General	Special Revenue	Capital Projects	Special Assessments	Enterprise	Internal Service	Trust and Agency	
Encumbrance	$ 670	$1,741	$1,165	$1,132	$ —	$ —	$ —	$ 4,708
Inventory	441	—	—	—	—	—	—	441
Loans and advances	73	—	—	—	—	—	100	173
Authorized expenditures/ projects	2,394	3,763	8,494	1,275	14,588	—	—	30,514
Metro/Lincoln recreation	82	—	—	—	—	—	—	82
Endowment	—	—	—	—	—	—	87	87
Revolving Fund	7	—	—	—	—	—	—	7
Fixed assets replacements	—	—	—	—	201	—	—	201
Self-insurance	—	—	—	—	—	5,369	—	5,369
Debt service	—	—	—	—	194	—	—	194
Others	—	—	—	34	—	—	—	34
Total	$3,667	$5,504	$9,659	$2,441	$14,983	$5,369	$187	$41,810

Chapter 12
Changes in Financial Position

In addition to a combined balance sheet for all fund types and account groups, general purpose financial statements for governmental units include (1) two statements reporting on the operations for governmental fund types, one of which includes budget-to-actual comparisons; (2) a combined statement of revenues, expenses, and changes in retained earnings/fund balances for proprietary fund types and similar trust funds; and (3) a combined statement of changes in financial position for proprietary fund types and similar trust funds. This chapter focuses on the last statement.

STATEMENT OF CHANGES

Accounting Principles Board Opinion 19, "Reporting Changes in Financial Position," which requires a statement of changes or a funds statement for commercial enterprises, states:

> The objectives of a funds statement are (1) to summarize the financing and investing activities of the entity, including the extent to which the enterprise has generated funds from operations during the period, and (2) to complete the disclosure of changes in financial position during the period. The information shown in a funds statement is useful to a variety of users of financial statements in making economic decisions regarding the enterprise.

Opinion 19 also states:

> The concept of *funds* in funds statements has varied somewhat in practice, with resulting variations in the nature of the statements. For example, *funds* is sometimes interpreted to mean *cash* or its equivalent, and the resulting funds statement is a summary of cash provided and used. Another interpretation of *funds* is that of *working capital*, i.e., current assets less current liabilities, and the resulting funds statement is a summary of working capital provided and used.

These concepts have been embodied in NCGA Statement 1. The NCGA-suggested format has the usual three main sections: sources of funds, uses of funds, and the elements of net increase (or decrease) in funds. Reports of about 90% of the governments using this statement were on a working capital basis, 10% on a cash basis.

The combined statement of changes in financial position for proprietary and trust funds was included by many of the governmental units surveyed. When included as part of the unit's combined financial statements, the statements provided the data shown in the accompanying table.

Data in Changes in Financial Position Statement	Instances Observed (%)
Units whose report contained a change in financial position statement	70
Proprietary fund data:	
Enterprise funds	88
Internal service funds	62
Fiduciary fund data:*	
Pension trust funds	40
Nonexpendable trust funds	28
Reports with memo columns:*	78
Current and past years	69
Current year only	31

* Observations for those units having this statement.

Exhibits 12-1 and 12-2 contain examples of these changes in financial position statements.

EXHIBITS FOR CHAPTER 12

Exhibit 12-1. Examples of Governmental Statements of Changes in Financial Position—Working Capital Basis

Exhibit 12-2. Examples of Governmental Statements of Changes in Financial Position—Cash Basis

EXHIBIT 12-1. EXAMPLES OF GOVERNMENTAL STATEMENTS OF CHANGES IN FINANCIAL POSITION—WORKING CAPITAL BASIS

[CITY OF IRVINE, CALIFORNIA]

Combined Statement of Changes in Financial Position—All Proprietary Funds, Nonexpendable Trust Fund and Pension Trust Fund (Year Ended June 30, 1984)

	1984	1983
Sources of working capital:		
Operations:		
Income before extraordinary loss	$ 1,131,633	$ 1,213,314
Items not requiring working capital:		
Current year depreciation	416,934	268,607
Amortization of bond discount	11,962	10,371
Loss on disposal of equipment	2,640	59,491
Working capital provided by operations before extraordinary loss	1,563,169	1,551,783
Extraordinary loss	(1,103,002)	
Proceeds from bonds	7,011,393	6,792,583
Contributions	813,666	2,802,816
Total sources of working capital	8,285,226	11,147,242
Uses of working capital:		
Decrease in long-term claims payable	40,000	
Retirement of bonds	6,877,953	
Acquisition of fixed assets	4,028,067	5,997,253
Decrease in capitalized lease obligations	4,031	106,263
Repayment of loan from General Fund		1,095,159
Total uses of working capital	10,950,051	7,198,675
Net increase (decrease) in working capital	$(2,664,825)	$ 3,948,567
Elements of net increase (decrease) in working capital:		
Cash and investments	$(3,227,182)	$ 4,559,151
Accrued interest receivable	(21,229)	(19,722)
Prepaid expenses	(33,753)	1,268
Accounts receivable	16,850	
Due from other funds	27,327	
Due from other governments		157,584
Accounts payable	111,068	(299,517)
Claims payable	140,000	
Interest payable	22,660	(134,940)
Contract retentions payable	306,335	(315,257)
Due to other funds	(6,901)	
	$(2,664,825)	$ 3,948,567

[CITY OF MODESTO, CALIFORNIA]

Combined Statement of Changes in Financial Position—All Proprietary Funds, Nonexpendable Trust Fund and Pension Trust Fund (Year Ended June 30, 1983)

	Enterprise	Internal Service	Totals (Memorandum Only)
SOURCES OF WORKING CAPITAL:			
Operations:			
Net income (loss)	$1,053,427	$ (969,414)	$ 84,013
Add charges not requiring working capital:			
Depreciation	1,004,757	684,698	1,689,455
Loss on sale of land, buildings and equipment		2,753	2,753
Less: Items not providing working capital—			
Gain on sale of land, buildings and equipment		(12,360)	(12,360)
Working capital provided by operations	2,058,184	(294,323)	1,763,861
Contributed capital before depreciation	4,841,554		4,841,554
Loan proceeds		906,867	906,867
Disposal of land, buildings and equipment		193,137	193,137
Total sources of working capital	6,899,738	805,681	7,705,419
USES OF WORKING CAPITAL:			
Reductions of contributed capital		11,111	11,111
Purchase of land, buildings and equipment	4,811,905	1,328,068	6,139,973
Retirement of bonds payable	270,000		270,000
Total uses of working capital	5,081,905	1,339,179	6,421,084
INCREASE (DECREASE) IN WORKING CAPITAL	$1,817,833	$ (533,498)	$1,284,335
INCREASE (DECREASE) IN COMPONENTS OF WORKING CAPITAL:			
Cash	$1,409,511	$ 493,197	$1,902,708
Cash with fiscal agents	(22,885)		(22,885)
Receivables	513,459	6,046	519,505
Inventories	(15,549)	5,528	(10,021)
Prepaid expenses		(10,190)	(10,190)
Accounts payable	8,701	(992,016)	(983,315)
Interest payable		(41,966)	(41,966)
Matured bonds and interest payable	22,885		22,885
Due to other funds	(115,000)		(115,000)
Current portion long-term debt	(10,000)	10,467	467
Deferred revenue	61,806		61,806
Accrued vacation and sick leave	(35,095)	(4,564)	(39,659)
INCREASE (DECREASE) IN WORKING CAPITAL	$1,817,833	$ (533,498)	$1,284,335

Combined Statement of Changes in Financial Position—All Proprietary Fund Types and Similar Trust Funds (for the Year Ended June 30, 1984, with Comparative Totals for 1983)

	Enterprise Funds			Internal Service Funds				Total (Memorandum Only) (Note 11)	
	Water Fund	Waste Collection Fund	Total Enterprise Funds	Fleet Fund	Stores & Purchase Fund	Data Processing Fund	Total Internal Service Fund	1984	1983
SOURCES OF WORKING CAPITAL:									
Operations:									
Net income (loss)	$ 249,786	$63,891	$ 313,677	$133,210	$ 11,284	$(16,749)	$127,745	$ 441,422	$ 430,682
Items not requiring (providing) working capital:									
Depreciation	677,070		677,070	271,340		34,715	306,055	983,125	863,315
Gain on disposal of equipment	(222)		(222)	(7,022)			(7,022)	(7,244)	(10,460)
Total from operations	926,634	63,891	990,525	397,528	11,284	17,966	426,778	1,417,303	1,283,537
Connection fees collected	1,148,530		1,148,530					1,148,530	766,770
Contributions from subdividers	73,721		73,721	4,950			4,950	78,671	621,505
Contributions from other funds						80,046	80,046	80,046	80,046
Operating transfer						50,000	50,000	50,000	50,000
Proceeds from sale of assets	222		222	28,785			28,785	29,007	26,053
Increase in obligation under capital lease				99,558			99,558	99,558	
Total sources of working capital	2,149,107	63,891	2,212,998	530,821	11,284	148,012	690,117	2,903,115	2,697,865
USES OF WORKING CAPITAL:									
Purchases of water stock	2,845		2,845					2,845	14,035
Additions to utility plant in service	876,208		876,208					876,208	1,602,355
Increase in construction in progress	1,017,380		1,017,380					1,017,380	106,222
Additions to machinery and equipment				570,055		123,250	693,305	693,305	295,478
Payments and current maturities of bonds payable	113,000		113,000					113,000	108,000
Decrease in obligation under capital lease									17,182
Increase in restricted assets	4,250		4,250					4,250	30,000
Other									(1,800)
Total uses of working capital	2,013,683		2,013,683	570,055		123,250	693,305	2,706,988	2,171,472
NET INCREASE (DECREASE) IN WORKING CAPITAL	$ 135,424	$63,891	$ 199,315	$(39,234)	$ 11,284	$ 24,762	$ (3,188)	$ 196,127	$ 526,393
INCREASE (DECREASE) IN WORKING CAPITAL BY COMPONENTS:									
Cash and interest earning deposits	$ 314,674	$55,424	$ 370,098	$(18,115)	$(29,847)	$ 34,383	$(13,579)	$ 356,519	$ 563,528
Accrued interest receivable	22,935	2,557	25,492	1,673		145	1,818	27,310	(7,054)
Accounts receivable—Net	108,654	8,971	117,625	12,340	785		13,125	130,750	(14,300)
Other assets	(971)		(971)	9		104	113	(858)	1,002
Inventory					31,220		31,220	31,220	6,902
Accounts payable	(275,632)	(3,061)	(278,693)	(20,733)	9,126	(5,335)	(16,942)	(295,635)	(46,109)
Wages and salaries payable	(27,375)		(27,375)	(11,148)		(4,535)	(15,683)	(43,058)	(2,306)
Customer deposits	(1,861)		(1,861)					(1,861)	37,000
Obligation under capital lease—current portion				(3,260)			(3,260)	(3,260)	(1,270)
Bonds payable—current portion	(5,000)		(5,000)					(5,000)	(11,000)
INCREASE (DECREASE) IN WORKING CAPITAL	$ 135,424	$63,891	$ 199,315	$(39,234)	$ 11,284	$ 24,762	$ (3,188)	$ 196,127	$ 526,393

[CITY OF TYLER, TEXAS]

Combined Statement of Changes in Financial Position—All Proprietary Fund Types and Similar Trust Funds for the Fiscal Year Ended September 30, 1983

	Proprietary Fund Types		Fiduciary Fund Types	Totals (Memorandum Only)	
	Enterprise (Exh. "F-3")	Central Garage Fund (Exh. "G-3")	Non-expendable Trust (Exh. "H-6")	1983	1982
SOURCES OF WORKING CAPITAL					
Operations:					
Net income (loss) before extraordinary items	$ 2,234,519	$152,652	$714,001	$ 3,101,172	$ 3,399,600
Items not requiring (providing) working capital:					
Disposal of non-depreciated assets in current period	24,142	2,260	—	26,402	142,631
Forfeitures of refunds on water and sewer contracts	—	—	—	—	(174,254)
Amortization of bond issuance expense	3,052	—	—	3,052	—
Working Capital Provided by (Used in) Operations Exclusive of Extraordinary Item	2,261,713	154,912	714,001	3,130,626	3,367,977
Extraordinary item—gain on advance refunding of revenue bonds	—	—	—	—	3,039,436
Net proceeds from bond issue	15,698,947	—	—	15,698,947	—
Issuance of revenue refunding bonds	—	—	—	—	4,085,000
Decrease in deferred expenses	13,580	—	—	13,580	—
Increase in refundable water and sewer contracts	752,109	—	—	752,109	830,244
Increase in advances from other funds	—	—	—	—	100,000
Property, plant and equipment provided by other funds	635,631	—	—	635,631	552,736
Decrease in advances to other funds	100,000	—	—	100,000	230,000
Contributions from municipality	310,533	3,028	—	313,561	2,532,253
Total Sources of Working Capital	19,772,513	157,940	714,001	20,644,454	14,737,646
USES OF WORKING CAPITAL					
Construction-in-progress	130,000	—	—	130,000	—
Net advance refunding of revenue bonds	—	—	—	—	7,375,000
Long-term portion of revenue bonds becoming currently payable	370,000	—	—	370,000	70,000
Discount on revenue refunding bonds issued	—	—	—	—	102,125
Deferred expenses on refunding bonds issued	—	—	—	—	131,659
Acquisition of property, plant and equipment	2,772,800	23,931	—	2,796,731	4,269,550
Long-term portion of water supply and storage contract becoming currently payable	447,000	—	—	447,000	447,000
Purchase of U.S. Government bonds	—	—	—	—	551,597
Refunds on water and sewer contracts	—	—	—	—	271,738
Increase in completed water and sewer line stubouts	24,408	—	—	24,408	23,221
Decrease in advances from other funds	100,000	—	—	100,000	150,000
Total Uses of Working Capital	3,844,208	23,931	—	3,868,139	13,391,890
NET INCREASE (DECREASE) IN WORKING CAPITAL	$15,928,305	$134,009	$714,001	$16,776,315	$ 1,345,756
ELEMENTS OF NET INCREASE (DECREASE) IN WORKING CAPITAL					
Cash	$15,976,251	$256,643	$(87,617)	$16,145,277	$ (326,054)
Notes receivable—current portion	(5,520)	—	—	(5,520)	(4,019)
Accounts receivable	(15,710)	—	21,503	5,793	11,505
Accrued interest and dividends receivable	312,760	—	33,598	346,358	39,687
Due from other funds	(81,935)	(130,574)	(11,797)	(224,306)	344,143
Prepaid auto allowance	750	250	—	1,000	—
Inventory	—	5,554	—	5,554	50,584
Investments	—	—	758,314	758,314	1,248,687
Accounts and contracts payable	44,776	1,790	—	46,566	(132,145)
Due to other funds	76,678	346	—	77,024	(155,074)
Accrued interest payable	(79,495)	—	—	(79,495)	(36,808)
Current portion of revenue bond payable	(300,000)	—	—	(300,000)	305,000
Current portion of water supply and storage contract payable	(250)	—	—	(250)	250
NET INCREASE (DECREASE) IN WORKING CAPITAL	$15,928,305	$134,009	$714,001	$16,776,315	$ 1,345,756

[CITY OF TULSA, OKLAHOMA]

Combined Statement of Changes in Financial Position—All Proprietary Fund and Similar Trust Funds for the Year Ended June 30, 1984

	Proprietary Fund Types		Fiduciary Fund Types		Total (Memorandum Only)
	Enterprise	Internal Service	Pension Trust	Nonexpendable Trust	
Sources of working capital:					
Operations:					
Net income (loss) before extraordinary items	$ 3,315,137	$ (89,710)	$6,030,939	$ (81,206)	$ 9,175,160
Items not requiring current outlay of funds:					
Depreciation and amortization	15,106,983	570,792		199,533	15,877,308
Reduction of land costs to market value	2,112,980				2,112,980
Other	368,000				368,000
Working capital provided by operations before extraordinary item	20,903,100	481,082	6,030,939	118,327	27,533,448
Extraordinary gain on debt defeasance	2,140,752				2,140,752
Capital contributions	39,250,047			855,005	40,105,052
Proceeds from other debt	8,466,503				8,466,503
Decreases in restricted assets	18,514,036				18,514,036
Increase in restricted liabilities	17,141,435				17,141,435
Increase in water main extension contracts	2,049,176				2,049,176
Land sales	396,679				396,679
Residual equity transfers in	3,360,167	121,931		397,481	3,879,579
Proceeds from issuance of revenue bonds	78,102,583				78,102,583
Disposition of fixed assets	1,434,202			25,198	1,459,400
Other, net	1,535,507			21,008	1,556,515
Total sources of working capital	193,294,187	603,013	6,030,939	1,417,019	201,345,158
Uses of working capital:					
Additions to land held for resale	2,861,477				2,861,477
Additions to plant and equipment	69,882,359	285,918		1,718,633	71,886,910
Increase in restricted assets	26,932,574				26,932,574
Reduction of long-term debt	40,941,690	326,757			41,268,447
Decrease in restricted liabilities	1,171,771				1,171,771
Payments and reclassifications of water main extension contracts	2,706,196				2,706,196
Residual equity transfer out	3,906,276				3,906,276
Increases in loan receivables	8,903,455				8,903,455
Other	3,867				3,867
Total uses of working capital	157,309,665	612,675	—	1,718,633	159,640,973
Net increase (decrease) in working capital	$ 35,984,522	$ (9,662)	$6,030,939	$ (301,614)	$ 41,704,185
Elements of net increase (decrease) in working capital:					
Cash	$ 513,823	$ 401,282	$ 235	$ (215,313)	$ 700,027
Investments	39,232,541	302,743	6,170,512	399,229	46,105,025
Accounts receivable	407,136	207,739	(114,929)	(23,021)	476,925
Inventories	(428,899)				(428,899)
Other receivables	455,622			2,099	457,721
Other current assets	139,101			(27,747)	111,354
Due from other funds	(1,840,341)	283,976			(1,556,365)
Warrants payable	873,028	(601,998)		(219,075)	51,955
Due to pooled cash and investments	(119,994)			(30,497)	(150,491)
Accounts payable and accrued liabilities	(907,878)	138,734	(24,879)	(176,081)	(970,104)
Liability for incurred claims		(558,433)			(558,433)
Deposits subject to refund	(349,295)				(349,295)
Due to other funds	(2,473,785)	18			(2,473,767)
Current portion of long term debt	1,061,540	66,453			1,127,993
Other current liabilities	(418,723)	(919)			(419,642)
Deferred revenue	(159,354)	(249,257)			(408,611)
Loans payable				(11,208)	(11,208)
Net increase (decrease) in working capital	$ 35,984,522	$ (9,662)	$6,030,939	$ (301,614)	$ 41,704,185

[CITY OF ATLANTA, GEORGIA]

Combined Statement of Changes in Financial Position—All Proprietary Fund Types and Similar Funds for the Year Ended December 31, 1983, with Comparative Totals for 1982 [in thousands]

	Proprietary Fund Types		Fiduciary Fund Types		Totals (Memorandum Only)	
	Enterprise Funds	Internal Service Fund	Nonexpendable Trust Fund	Pension Trust Fund	1983	1982
SOURCES OF WORKING CAPITAL:						
From operations—						
Net income, before minority interest and cumulative effect of the change in method of recording revenues	$ 8,379	$ 223	$ 4	$37,381	$ 45,987	$ 75,977
Add—Expenses not requiring current outlay of working capital—						
Depreciation and amortization	37,435	1,140	—	—	38,575	34,525
Retirement of old airport terminal facilities	16,830	—	—	—	16,830	—
Amortization of net bond discount	719	—	—	—	719	711
Total from operations	63,363	1,363	4	37,381	102,111	111,213
Cumulative effect of accruing unbilled revenues	5,376	—	—	—	5,376	—
Contributions from—						
Other governmental units	32,886	—	—	—	32,886	33,536
Other	456	41	—	—	497	33
Increase in long-term debt, net of discount	82,652	—	—	—	82,652	63,312
Net decrease in restricted assets	413	—	—	—	413	899
Increase in long-term payable to other funds	—	—	—	—	—	355
Net decrease in deferred expenses	—	—	—	—	—	9
Net increase in liabilities payable from restricted assets	7,355	—	—	—	7,355	442
Net increase in deferred pension costs	869	221	—	—	1,090	1,208
Net increase in capital lease obligations	—	362	—	—	362	—
Increase in deferred revenues	125	—	—	—	125	—
	193,495	1,987	4	37,381	232,867	211,007
USES OF WORKING CAPITAL:						
Additions to property and equipment net of minor retirements	83,066	771	—	—	83,837	83,363
Net increase in other assets	289	—	—	—	289	440
Reduction of long-term debt	20,556	—	—	—	20,556	34,958
Reduction of long-term payable to Community Development Fund	9	—	—	—	9	—
Net increase in restricted assets	85,402	—	—	—	85,402	16,883
Net decrease in liabilities payable from restricted assets	558	—	—	—	558	39,461
Transfer to General Obligation Bond Sinking Fund	748	—	—	—	748	625
	190,628	771	—	—	191,399	175,730
INCREASE IN WORKING CAPITAL	$ 2,867	$1,216	$ 4	$37,381	$ 41,468	$ 35,277
CHANGES IN WORKING CAPITAL COMPONENTS						
Increase (decrease) in current assets—						
Cash	$ (254)	$ (81)	$—	$ 186	$ (149)	$ 895
Short-term investments	(14)	865	4	36,186	37,041	34,748
Receivables	6,409	6	—	1,009	7,424	(566)
Materials and supplies	(1,341)	321	—	—	(1,020)	636
Due from other funds	(45)	—	—	—	(45)	46
Prepaid expenses	5	—	—	—	5	(4)
	4,760	1,111	4	37,381	43,256	35,755
(Increase) decrease in current liabilities—						
Accounts payable	(1,619)	66	—	—	(1,553)	(30)
Accrued salaries and vacation pay	(202)	54	—	—	(148)	(387)
Deferred revenues	—	—	—	—	—	(65)
Due to other funds	(72)	(15)	—	—	(87)	4
	(1,893)	105	—	—	(1,788)	(478)
INCREASE IN WORKING CAPITAL	$ 2,867	$1,216	$ 4	$37,381	$ 41,468	$ 35,277

EXHIBIT 12-2. EXAMPLES OF GOVERNMENTAL STATEMENTS OF CHANGES IN FINANCIAL POSITION—CASH BASIS

[CITY OF BALTIMORE, MARYLAND]

Combined Statement of Changes in Financial Position—All Proprietary Fund Types and Similar Trust Funds (for the Year Ended June 30, 1984) [in thousands]

	Proprietary Fund Types		Fiduciary Fund Types		Total (Memorandum Only)
	Enterprise	Internal Service	Nonexpendable Trust	Pension Trust	
Sources of funds:					
Operations:					
Net income (loss)	$(19,487)	$ 5,208	$(33)	$ 81,375	$ 67,063
Items not requiring outlay of funds:					
Amortization of bond issuance cost	241				241
Depreciation	11,937	4,130			16,067
Funds provided by operations	(7,309)	9,338	(33)	81,375	83,371
Proceeds from issuance of debt	3,450				3,450
Increase in accounts payable and accrued liabilities		588		109	697
Increase in contributions, net	43,039	787			43,826
Decrease in property, plant and equipment	33,794				33,794
Decrease in investments	1,333	1,642	109	11,860	14,944
Residual equity transfer	9,647				9,647
Decrease in inventories		9			9
Decrease in accounts receivable		130		300	430
Increase in provision for compensated absences	285	133			418
Decrease in other assets	15,597		5	89	15,691
Increase in other liabilities	5,615				5,615
Increase in due to other funds	63				63
Decrease in restricted assets	4,172				4,172
Total sources of funds	109,686	12,627	81	93,773	216,127
Application of funds:					
Increase in investments	6,559		8	598	7,165
Increase in notes and mortgages receivable	19,307				19,307
Additions to property, plant and equipment, net	37,621	4,146			41,767
Decrease in general long-term debt payable	13,940				13,940
Decrease in notes payable	11,966				11,966
Decrease in revenue bonds payable	6,405				6,405
Decrease in deferred revenue	648	13			661
Decrease in due to other funds		25			25
Increase in other assets	5,343	618		21	5,982
Increase in restricted assets	43	274			317
Decrease in liabilities payable from restricted assets	5,905				5,905
Decrease in provision for compensated absences		8			8
Increase in inventories		35			35
Decrease in accounts payable and accrued liabilities	5,115	4,063		565	9,743
Decrease in contributions, net	10,146				10,146
Decrease in other liabilities	6,035	55			6,090
Total application of funds	129,033	9,237	8	1,184	139,462
Net increase in funds	(19,347)	3,390	73	92,549	76,665
Cash and cash equivalents, July 1, 1983	69,442	13,513	156	88,633	171,744
Cash and cash equivalents, June 30, 1984	$ 50,095	$16,903	$229	$181,182	$248,409

[COUNTY OF CONTRA COSTA, CALIFORNIA]

Combined Statement of Changes in Financial Position—All Proprietary Fund Types and Similar Trust Funds (for the Year Ended June 30, 1984)

	Proprietary Fund Types		Fiduciary Fund Types	Totals (Memorandum Only) Year ended	
	Enterprise	Internal Service	Pension Trust	June 30, 1984	June 30, 1983
Funds provided (used) by operations:					
Net income (loss) before operating transfers	$(20,365,003)	(2,094,681)	39,110,896	16,651,212	30,437,356
Items not requiring (providing) the use of funds:					
Depreciation	931,132	—	—	931,132	872,158
Transfer of assets	(1,267,429)	—	—	(1,267,429)	—
Total funds provided (used) by operations before operating transfers	(20,701,300)	(2,094,681)	39,110,896	16,314,915	31,309,514
Operating transfers (net)	23,022,781	—	—	23,022,781	14,301,883
Increase in accounts payable and accrued liabilities	—	2,832,263	171,517	3,003,780	5,388,671
Increase in Employee Benefits Payable	1,829,669	—	13,740	1,843,409	—
Increase in amounts due to other funds	—	171,647	—	171,647	8,530,433
Decrease in accounts receivable and accrued revenue	4,801,079	—	—	4,801,079	206,390
Decrease in inventories	103,198	—	—	103,198	—
Decrease in prepaid expenses and deposits	29,760	—	—	29,760	45,928
Decrease in amounts due from other funds	—	12,036,845	2,144,864	14,181,709	—
Increase in capital lease obligations	118,981	—	—	118,981	—
Net decrease in fixed assets	301,266	—	—	301,266	—
Total funds provided	9,505,434	12,946,074	41,441,017	63,892,525	59,782,819
Funds used for:					
Increase in accounts receivable and accrued revenue	—	249,666	1,053,993	1,303,659	2,275,108
Increase in amounts due from other funds	4,206,179	—	—	4,206,179	14,571,192
Increase in inventories	—	—	—	—	131,409
Increase in prepaid expenses and deposits	—	—	17,190	17,190	31,494
Net increase in fixed assets	—	—	—	—	553,410
Decrease in accounts payable and accrued liabilities	172,467	—	—	172,467	—
Decrease in other current liabilities	—	—	—	—	104,554
Decrease in amounts due to other funds	3,289,506	—	1,530,078	4,819,584	—
Decrease in capital lease obligations	—	—	—	—	31,078
Decrease in retained earnings/fund balance:					
Cumulative effect of change in accounting principle	1,852,020	—	13,582	1,865,602	—
Total funds used	9,520,172	249,666	2,614,843	12,384,681	17,698,245
Net increase (decrease) in cash and investments	(14,738)	12,696,408	38,826,174	51,507,844	42,084,574
Cash and investments at beginning of year	508,906	8,084,137	356,248,012	364,841,035	322,756,481
Cash and investments at end of year	$ 494,168	20,780,545	395,074,186	416,348,899	364,841,055

[CITY OF ELGIN, ILLINOIS]

Combined Statement of Changes in Financial Position—All Proprietary Fund Types and Similar Trust Funds (for the Year Ended December 31, 1983)

	Proprietary Fund Types		Fiduciary Fund Types		Totals (Memorandum Only)	
	Enterprise	Internal Service	Nonexpendable Trust	Pension Trust	December 31, 1983	December 31, 1982
Source of cash and investments						
Operations						
Net income (loss)	$ (214,594)	$ 31,499	$25,000	$2,638,859	$2,480,764	$ 4,500,209
Add (deduct) items not requiring or providing cash						
Depreciation	1,150,977	10,246	—	—	1,161,223	412,509
Gain on sale of assets	(707)	—	—	—	(707)	(2,149)
Contribution by developers	(93,775)	—	—	—	(93,775)	(3,400)
Total from operations	841,901	41,745	25,000	2,638,859	3,547,505	4,907,169
Decrease in deferred charges	266	—	—	—	266	3,213
Decrease (increase) in receivables	110,875	(15,405)	(1,293)	429,616	523,793	543,545
Decrease (increase) in prepaid expenses	—	4,332	—	—	4,332	(46,402)
Increase in accounts payable, accrued expenses and interest payable	26,324	188,315	—	—	214,639	505,257
Proceeds from sale of fixed assets	707	—	—	—	707	2,149
Total cash and investments provided	980,073	218,987	23,707	3,068,574	4,291,242	5,914,931
Use of cash and investments						
Decrease in deferred income	1,696	—	—	447,900	449,596	73,629
Decrease (increase) in due to other funds, net	152,082	(9,448)	621	4,184	147,399	(216,416)
Increase in deposits	—	20,000	—	—	20,000	5,000
Increase (decrease) in inventory	38,304	1,353	—	—	39,657	95,819
Acquisition of property and equipment	1,691,071	450	—	—	1,691,521	7,839,145
Payment of principal of general obligation bonds	475,000	—	—	—	475,000	375,000
Payment of principal of revenue bonds	150,000	—	—	—	150,000	150,000
Decrease in advance from General Fund	—	—	—	—	—	90,000
Increase (decrease) in due from other governmental units	5,087	—	—	(4,241)	846	(63,927)
Total cash and investments used	2,513,240	12,315	621	447,843	2,974,019	8,348,250
Net increase (decrease) in cash and investments	$(1,533,167)	$206,672	$23,086	$2,620,632	$1,317,223	$(2,433,319)

[CITY OF JOLIET, ILLINOIS]

Combined Statement of Changes in Financial Position—All Proprietary Fund Types and Pension Trust Funds (for the Year Ended December 31, 1983)

	Proprietary Fund Type	Fiduciary Fund Type	Total (Memorandum Only)
	Enterprise	Pension Trusts	
Funds were provided by			
Operations:			
Net income	$ 1,013,581	$4,441,369	$ 5,454,950
Charges and credits to operations not affecting funds:			
Depreciation	97,167	—	97,167
Amortization of bond discount	6,243	—	6,243
Amortization of imputed interest on long-term receivable	(4,085)	—	(4,085)
(Increase) in:			
Water and sewer receivable and connection fees	(328,044)	—	(328,044)
Estimated unbilled water and sewer usage	(77,000)	—	(77,000)
Accrued interest on investments	(1,007)	(291,097)	(292,104)
Increase (reduction) in:			
Property taxes receivable from other funds	—	1,180,938	1,180,938
Vouchers payable	(171,166)	—	(171,166)
Accrued interest payable	(4,135)	—	(4,135)
Deferred property tax revenue	—	115,153	115,153
Total	$ 531,554	$5,446,363	$ 5,977,917
Other sources:			
Collection of long-term receivable	30,368	—	30,368
Increase in due to other funds	8,661	—	8,661
Total funds provided	$ 570,583	$5,446,363	$ 6,016,946
Funds were applied to			
Restatement of property tax revenue	$ —	$1,282,592	$ 1,282,592
Property and equipment acquisition	636,339	—	636,339
Payment of bonds	658,939	—	658,939
Increase in customer deposits receivable	3,195	—	3,195
Increase in due from other funds	600	—	600
Decrease in due to other funds	209,541	—	209,541
Reduction in customer guaranteed deposits	100,525	—	100,525
Total funds applied	$ 1,609,139	$1,282,592	$ 2,891,731
Net increase in cash and investments as below	$(1,038,556)	$4,163,771	$ 3,125,215
Summary of net changes in cash and investments			
Increase in:			
Cash	$ (899,761)	$ (437,056)	$(1,336,817)
Investments	(138,795)	4,600,827	4,462,032
Total	$(1,038,556)	$4,163,771	$ 3,125,215

[CITY OF McALLEN, TEXAS]

Combined Statement of Changes in Financial Position—All Proprietary Fund Types and Similar Trust Funds (for the Year Ended September 30, 1983)

	Proprietary Fund Types		Fiduciary Fund Types	Total (Memorandum Only)
	Enterprise	Internal Service	Pension Trust	
Sources of cash				
Operations				
Net income (loss) for the year	$4,295,101	$(45,716)	$ 354,463	$4,603,848
Charges to operations not using cash				
Depreciation (note A3)	1,406,159	65,157	—	1,471,316
Cash provided by operations	5,701,260	19,441	354,463	6,075,164
Contributions of property, plant and equipment from private developers	1,168,224	—	—	1,168,224
Net increase in restricted assets (note C)	476,955	—	—	476,955
Decrease in receivables	25,702	—	—	25,702
Decrease in due from other funds	447,026	431,390	—	878,416
Decrease in inventories	22,824	11,826	—	34,650
Decrease in prepaid assets	9,709	—	—	9,709
Increase in accounts payable and other liabilities	45,885	—	—	45,885
Increase in due to other funds	83,765	—	—	83,765
Total sources of cash (totals forward)	7,981,350	462,657	354,463	8,798,470
Applications of cash				
Net acquisitions of property, plant and equipment	2,911,052	10,347	—	2,921,399
Reductions in long-term obligations	573,390	—	—	573,390
Reduction in deferred revenue	3,147	—	—	3,147
Net increase in restricted assets (note C)	835,201	—	—	835,201
Increase in receivables	284,553	2,244	5,345	292,142
Decrease in accounts payable and other liabilities	16,404	32,784	—	49,188
Decrease in due to other funds	707,002	264,073	—	971,075
Decrease in liabilities payable from restricted assets	24,170	—	—	24,170
Increase in due from other funds	11,852	—	—	11,852
Total applications of cash	5,366,771	309,448	5,345	5,681,564
INCREASE IN CASH	2,614,579	153,209	349,118	3,116,906
Cash at beginning of year	2,449,805	149,344	1,383,475	3,982,624
Cash at end of year	$5,064,384	$302,553	$1,732,593	$7,099,530

[PALM BEACH COUNTY, FLORIDA]

Combined Statement of Changes in Financial Position—All Proprietary Fund Types (for the Year Ended September 30, 1983)

	Enterprise	Internal Service	Totals (Memorandum Only)
Sources of funds:			
Operations:			
Net income	$ 4,798,484	$ 108,599	$ 4,907,083
(Loss) from discontinued operations	(3,932,334)	—	(3,932,334)
Items not requiring outlay of funds:			
Depreciation	5,892,937	982,138	6,875,075
Gain on sale of fixed assets	(78,568)	—	(78,568)
Loss on disposal of sanitary landfill	4,290,946	—	4,290,946
Other	134,826	54,076	188,902
Funds provided from operations	11,106,291	1,144,813	12,251,104
Capital contributions	10,821,005	452	10,821,457
Increase in liabilities payable from restricted assets	217,457	—	217,457
Decrease in inventory	19,282	—	19,282
Decrease in restricted assets	4,368,274	—	4,368,274
Deferred gain on sale of land	3,014,234	—	3,014,234
Increase in notes payable	—	775,367	775,367
Sale of land, net of gain	724,738	—	724,738
Increase in advances from other County funds	—	33,042	33,042
Decrease in accounts receivable	40,751	—	40,751
Decrease in accrued interest receivable	162,194	38,134	200,328
Decrease in due from other County funds	375,693	373,731	749,424
Decrease in due from other governments	109,715	18,523	128,238
Decrease in deferred charges	26,757	—	26,757
Increase in vouchers payable and accrued liabilities	739,649	141,540	881,189
Increase in due to other County funds	373,128	459,462	832,590
Increase in current deferred revenue	547,720	—	547,720
Increase in insurance claims payable	—	128,605	128,605
Increase in inventory of materials	—	71,288	71,288
Increase in current portion of notes payable	180,000	—	180,000
Increase in due to South Palm Beach Utilities Corporation	2,403,865	—	2,403,865
Increase in other current liabilities	220,388	—	220,388
Increase in due to other governments	103,550	—	103,550
Increase in other long-term liabilities	47,335	—	47,335
Costs of fixed assets transferred	561,648	—	561,648
Other	21,458	—	21,458
Total sources of funds	$36,185,132	$3,184,957	$39,370,089
Uses of funds:			
Plant, property and equipment purchased	$14,648,294	$1,190,893	$15,839,187
Plant, property and equipment contributed	8,462,446	—	8,462,446
Increase in restricted assets	6,129,143	—	6,129,143
Decrease in revenue bonds	180,000	—	180,000
Decrease in other long-term liabilities	2,719	7,065	9,784
Decrease in notes payable	—	229,154	229,154
Decrease in liabilities payable from restricted assets	1,132,557	—	1,132,557
Increase in accounts receivable	698,712	4,333	703,045
Increase in accrued interest receivable	100,580	9,476	110,056
Increase in due from other County funds	45,132	—	45,132
Increase in due from other governments	587,314	34,076	621,390
Increase in inventory of materials, supplies and other	170,138	—	170,138
Increase in deferred charges	55,207	—	55,207
Increase in other assets	11,273	—	11,273
Decrease in other liabilities	—	23,230	23,230
Decrease in deferred revenue	74,541	—	74,541
Decrease in vouchers payable and accrued liabilities	61,987	—	61,987

(continued)

[PALM BEACH COUNTY, FLORIDA] (Continued)

	Enterprise	Internal Service	Totals (Memorandum Only)
Decrease in due to other County funds	—	10,347	10,347
Decrease in insurance claims payable	—	480,618	480,618
Equity transfer of contributed assets	561,648	—	561,648
Funds transferred to Palm Beach County Solid Waste Authority	1,242,000	—	1,242,000
Other	—	3,904	3,904
Total uses of funds	$34,163,691	$1,993,096	$36,156,787
Increase (decrease) in cash and short-term investments	$ 2,021,441	$1,191,861	$ 3,213,302

[ST. LOUIS COUNTY, MISSOURI]

Combined Statement of Changes in Financial Position—Proprietary Fund Types and Retirement Trust Funds (for the Year Ended December 31, 1983)

	Proprietary Fund Type	Fiduciary Fund Type	Totals (Memorandum Only)
	Enterprise	Retirement Trust Fund	
Sources of cash and investments:			
Operations:			
Net income	$ 4,483,149	$ 9,438,686	$13,921,835
Add charges to operations not using cash and investments:			
Increase in accrued liabilities	692,113	496,889	1,189,002
Depreciation	543,561	—	543,561
Cash and investments provided from operations	5,718,823	9,935,575	15,654,398
Nonoperating:			
Proceeds from issuance of tax anticipation warrants	4,200,000	—	4,200,000
Contributed capital	949,519	—	949,519
	10,868,342	9,935,575	20,803,917
Applications of cash and investments:			
Increase in receivables	1,635,340	163,038	1,798,378
Increase in capital assets	1,135,666	—	1,135,666
Increase in prepaid expenses and inventories	35,032	—	35,032
Decrease in accrued liabilities	342	—	342
Retirement of tax anticipation warrants	5,500,000	—	5,500,000
	8,306,380	163,038	8,469,418
Increase in cash and investments for the year	2,561,962	9,772,537	12,334,499
Cash and investments, January 1	7,726,370	34,565,258	42,291,628
Cash and investments, December 31	$10,288,332	$44,337,795	$54,626,127

[CITY OF SCOTTSDALE, ARIZONA]

Combined Statement of Changes in Financial Position—All Proprietary Fund Types (for the Year Ended June 30, 1984)

	Enterprise	Internal Service	Totals (Memorandum Only) June 30, 1984	June 30, 1983
Sources of Funds				
From Operations				
Net Income	$ 6,152,367	$ 93,296	$ 6,245,663	$ 3,056,871
Noncash Charge—Depreciation & Amortization	2,146,109	780,219	2,926,328	2,749,338
Total from Operations	8,298,476	873,515	9,171,991	5,806,209
Contributions				
Water/Sewer Assets from Subdividers	12,167,538		12,167,538	4,845,708
From Government Units	434,850		434,850	1,032,143
From Municipality				455,566
Increase in				
Current Liabilities	1,352,749	221,953	1,574,702	694,405
Long-Term Debt	6,861,962		6,861,962	
Other Liabilities	20,610		20,610	285,669
Decrease in				
Receivables	31,415		31,415	20,686
Net Assets Held for Refunded Debt				150,664
Restricted Cash & Investments				470,318
Property, Plant, and Equipment		2,455	2,455	553,999
	29,167,600	1,097,923	30,265,523	14,315,367
Uses of Funds:				
Contributions of Water/Sewer Assets from Subdividers	12,167,538		12,167,538	4,845,708
Purchase of Other Property, Equipment, & Construction in Progress	5,351,373	1,045,519	6,396,892	6,961,459
Increase in Receivables	1,102,011	85,318	1,187,329	758,257
Increase in Restricted Cash and Investments	1,254,601		1,254,601	
Decrease in				
Refunded Debt				168,180
Other Liabilities	31,462		31,462	879
Long-Term Debt	350,573		350,573	1,285,790
Contributions from Government Units				142,847
Current Liabilities	30		30	69,177
	20,257,588	1,130,837	21,388,425	14,232,297
Increase (Decrease) in Cash and Short-Term Investments	8,910,012	(32,914)	8,877,098	83,070
Cash and Short-Term Investments				
July 1	5,847,093	2,319,939	8,167,032	8,083,962
June 30	$14,757,105	$2,287,025	$17,044,130	$ 8,167,032

[Statements included for illustrative purposes. For brevity the footnotes accompanying the statements have not been included.]

Chapter 13
The Auditor's Report

In most cases, the governmental units obtained independent audits of their financial statements. This chapter contains additional details on information related to the auditor and the nature of the report rendered.

AUDITOR OF GOVERNMENTS

This year's analysis of auditor's reports included some 489 financial statements. All large and medium-sized cities and counties in the study were included in this special analysis. In addition, a sample of approximately half of the smaller cities and counties were also reviewed in order to allow the smaller units to influence the results of the survey. Of these 489 financial statements, 413, or 84%, of the financial statements analyzed were audited. However, the type of auditor varied as noted in the following tabulation:

Type of Auditor Examining Governmental Financial Statements*	Instances Observed (%)
Certified public accountants	95
State audit agency	3
Municipal accountant or auditor	<1
More than one audit or organization:	
Two or more public accounting firms	2
Government auditor and CPA firm	<1
Other	<1

* Observations for the 84% of the units with audited financial statements.

Where the audits were performed jointly by more than one auditor, these joint audit efforts generally consisted of audits by two independent CPA firms or by a CPA firm and a governmental audit organization. In addition, where independent CPA firms were used by governments to audit their financial records, in 61% of the surveyed governments the audits were made by a firm other than a "Big 8" accounting firm.

NCGA RECOMMENDATIONS ON THE SCOPE OF GOVERNMENTAL AUDITS

The NCGA views an independent audit as an essential element of the financial control and accountability of a governmental unit. The Council therefore recommended that annual independent audits be made in accordance with the generally accepted auditing standards of the American Institute of Certified Public Accountants. Further, according to NCGA Statement 1, the general purpose financial statements comprise the minimum acceptable scope of annual audits. However, the Council, in Statement 1, makes the following recommendations relative to the scope of the annual audit:

The annual audit should encompass, in addition to the combined statements, the combining and individual financial statements of the funds and account groups.

While audit tests of individual funds are not necessary to a presentation in accordance with generally accepted accounting principles, individual funds should be subjected to such tests and to other audit procedures.

The auditor's opinion with respect to individual fund statements should, as a minimum, make reference to their fairness in all material respects in relation to the general-purpose financial statements.

It is important to highlight that the auditor can take a higher level of responsibility for the combining, individual, and account group fund statements by reporting on them not as accompanying (or supplemental) information, but rather as a part of the basic financial statements encompassed by the primary audit opinion. Tables 13-1 and 13-2 show how often the combined, combining individual, and account group fund statements were reported on as a part of the basic financial statements or, alternatively, as accompanying (supplemental) information.

Statement 1 excludes statistical tables from the recommended audit scope, for such tables cover several years and contain nonaccounting data.

REQUIREMENTS OF THE RATING AGENCY

In 1980 Standard & Poor's (S&P Perspective "Who's Watching the Books?") stated that the quality of financial reporting and accounting has long been considered in analyzing applications by governments for rating of their prospective bond offerings. At that same time, S&P policy requested that governmental financial statements

conform to generally accepted accounting principles;

be independently audited within six months of the end of the fiscal year;

be stated on a modified accrual rather than cash basis, so that revenues are reported when they become measurable and available to pay expenses; and

contain an auditor's opinion and disclosure notes, and cite any variance from generally accepted accounting principles that affect the results.

With respect to the basis of accounting, S&P stated that the accrual basis is the superior method of accounting for the economic resources of any organization.

THE AUDITOR'S OPINION

For the most part, the auditor's opinions conformed to the standards described in the literature of the American Institute of Certified Public Accountants. That is, the opinions stated that the audit was made in accordance with generally accepted auditing standards and that the financial statements presented fairly the financial position of the governmental unit in accordance with generally accepted accounting principles applied on a basis consistent with the preceding fiscal period.

As noted in the following tables, other standards and review criteria were also referred to in some of the audit opinions.

Auditing Standards Employed in Audits*	Instances Observed (%)
Generally accepted auditing standards (GAAS)	89
GAAS and State standards	6
GAAS and GAO standards	1
GAAS, GAO, and State standards	1
State standards	<1
Other audit criteria	<1
No audit performed	16

Accounting Principles Used in Financial Statement Presentation*	Instances Observed (%)
Generally accepted accounting principles (GAAP)	95
State government principles	2
GAAP and State principles	1
Some other combination of the above	<1
Other basis of presentation	<1

* Observations for governments with audited financial statements.

The survey obtained data concerning the differences in the opinions being rendered by the auditors of governmental financial statements and the level of audit responsibility being assumed by the auditor for supplemental information. Supplemental information can include, for example, the combining financial statements, the individual fund financial statements, the individual account group statements, various financial statements, and statistical information.

With respect to supplemental information, the auditor may take various responsibilities.

The auditor can disclaim an opinion on such data. (For example, "The statistical information was not subject to the auditing procedures applied in the examination of the financial statements and, accordingly, the auditor expressed no opinion.")

The auditor can state the opinion that the information is fairly stated in all material respects to the audited financial statements. (For example, "The statistical information is presented for purposes of additional analysis and is not a required part of the financial statements. This information has been subjected to the auditing procedures applied in the examination of the financial statements and, in the auditor's opinion, is fairly stated in all material respects in relation to the financial statements taken as a whole.")

The auditor can report using a combination of these. For example, the auditor could disclaim an opinion on the statistical data, but give an opinion on the individual fund financial statements in all material respects in relation to the audited financial statements.

In addition, the composition of the financial statements for which an audit opinion is expressed could vary. Generally, auditors stated that their examinations were made for the primary purposes of rendering an opinion on either

the combined financial statements (i.e., the general purpose financial statements) taken as a whole;

the combined, combining, and individual fund financial statements; or

the combined, combining, and individual fund financial statements and the account group statements.

Tables 13-1 and 13-2 summarize the variances of opinions supplemental reporting observed among the surveyed financial statements. Several examples of opinions relating to the audit of governmental units appear in Exhibits 13-1 to 13-8.

NATURE OF THE AUDITOR'S OPINION

Of the opinions observed during this year's analysis, 34% were qualified. Table 13-3 lists the more commonly cited reasons for a qualified audit opinion.

The nature of a qualified audit opinion requires the reader to research the reason for the qualification. Qualified audit opinions are not necessarily indicative of a "deficiency." For example, qualified opinions relating to consistency are, in fact, desired, if they are occasioned by changes to more acceptable accounting practices.

Audit opinions that contained the phrase "subject to" relate to qualifications that arise because of an uncertainty affecting the financial statements (e.g., "In our opinion, subject to the effect of any adjustments that might have been required had the outcome of the litigation mentioned in the preceding paragraph been known,. . ."). The phrase "except for" is used in all other qualifications (e.g., "In our opinion, except for the omission of a general fixed asset group of accounts as discussed in the preceding paragraph,. . ."). Table 13-4 summarizes the reasons given by independent auditors for issuing qualifications for departures from generally accepted accounting principles.

Exhibit 13-9 contains selected examples of the qualification paragraphs appearing in the audit reports of surveyed financial statements.

TIMELINESS OF REPORTS

The time that elapsed between the end of the fiscal year and the date of the auditor's report varied among the surveyed governments. Table 13-5 summarizes the time, on average, between these two dates.

EXHIBITS AND TABLES FOR CHAPTER 13

TABLE 13-1. FINANCIAL STATEMENTS COVERED BY THE BASIC AUDITOR'S OPINION

Level of Primary Audit Responsibility*	Instances Observed (%)
Combined financial statements (GPFS)	67
GPFS and, where applicable, combining, individual fund, and account group financial statements	28
GPFS and combining financial statements	3
Other	2

* As noted in the basic auditor's opinion; observations for units with audited statements.

TABLE 13-2. AUDIT OPINION ON SUPPLEMENTAL OR ACCOMPANYING INFORMATION REPORTING

Supplemental Opinions	Instances Observed (%)
Supplemental opinions on statements with audit opinion on supplemental or accompanying information	75
Opinion related to*	
combining statements	86
individual funds	79
account groups	63
statistical data	25

* Observations for units with audited financial statements that present supplemental information.

EXHIBIT 13-1. OPINIONS ON COMBINED STATEMENTS TAKE AS A WHOLE

Board of Commissioners
Catawba County
North Carolina

We have examined the combined financial statements of Catawba County, North Carolina, as of and for the year ended June 30, 1984, as listed in the table of contents. Our examination was made in accordance with generally accepted auditing standards and, accordingly, included such tests of the accounting records and such other auditing procedures as we considered necessary in the circumstances.

In our opinion, the combined financial statements referred to above present fairly the financial position of Catawba County, North Carolina, at June 30, 1984, and the results of its operations for the year then ended, in conformity with generally accepted accounting principles applied on a basis consistent with that of the preceding year.

Our examination was made for the purpose of forming an opinion on the combined financial statements taken as a whole. The combining, individual fund, and account group financial statements and schedules listed in the table of contents are presented for purposes of additional analysis and are not a required part of the combined financial statements of Catawba County, North Carolina. The information has been subjected to the auditing procedures applied in the examination of the combined financial statements and, in our opinion, is fairly stated in all material respects in relation to the combined financial statements taken as a whole.

[Certified Public Accountants]
October 25, 1984

Honorable City Council
City of Visalia, California

We have examined the combined financial statements of the City of Visalia at June 30, 1984, and for the year then ended, as listed in the accompanying table of contents. Our examination was made in accordance with generally accepted auditing standards and, accordingly, included such tests of the accounting records and such other auditing procedures as we considered necessary in the circumstances.

In our opinion, the combined financial statements mentioned above present fairly the financial position of the City of Visalia at June 30, 1984, and the results of operations for the year then ended and the changes in financial position of its proprietary fund types for the year then ended, in conformity with generally accepted accounting principles applied on a basis consistent with that of the preceding year.

Our examination was made for the purpose of forming an opinion on the basic combined financial statements taken as a whole. The combining, individual fund and account group financial statements listed as additional financial information in the table of contents are presented for purposes of additional analysis and are not a required part of the basic combined financial statements of the City of Visalia. Such additional financial information has been subjected to the auditing procedures applied in our examination of the basic combined financial statements and, in our opinion, is fairly stated in all material respects in relation to the basic combined financial statements taken as a whole.

The accompanying statistical exhibits are also presented for the purpose of additional analysis and are not a required part of the combined financial statements of the City of Visalia. These statistical exhibits were not audited by us and, accordingly, we do not express an opinion on them.

[Certified Public Accountants]
Fresno, California
October 29, 1984

To the Honorable Mayor and Members of the City
   Council
City of West Covina, California

We have examined the combined financial statements of the City of West Covina, California, as of and for the year ended June 30, 1984, as listed in the contents. Our examination was made in accordance with generally accepted auditing standards and, accordingly, included such tests of the accounting records and such other auditing procedures as we considered necessary in the circumstances.

In our opinion, the combined financial statements referred to above present fairly the financial position of the City of West Covina, California as of June 30, 1984, and the results of its operations and changes in financial position of its proprietary fund types for the year then ended, in conformity with generally accepted accounting principles applied on a basis consistent with that of the preceding year.

Our examination was made for the purpose of forming an opinion on the combined financial statements taken as a whole. The combining, individual fund and account group financial statements and schedules listed in the contents as supplementary information are presented for purposes of additional analysis and are not a required part of the combined financial statements of the City of West Covina, California. Such information has been subjected to the auditing procedures applied in the examination of the combined financial statements and, in our opinion, is fairly stated in all material respects in relation to the combined financial statements taken as a whole.

[Certified Public Accountants]
San Bernardino, California
October 26, 1984

EXHIBIT 13-2. OPINION ON COMBINED AND COMBINING STATEMENTS

To the Honorable County Commissioners and
   Constitutional Officers
Alachua County, Florida

We have examined the combined financial statements of Alachua County, Florida, and the combining financial statements of Alachua County as of and for the year ended September 30, 1983, as listed in the table of contents. Our examination was made in accordance with generally accepted auditing standards and, accordingly, included such tests of the accounting records and such other auditing procedures as we considered necessary in the circumstances.

In our opinion, the combined financial statements referred to above present fairly the financial position of Alachua County, Florida, at September 30, 1983, and the results of its operations and changes in financial position of its proprietary fund types and similar trust fund for the year then ended, in conformity with generally acepted accounting principles applied on a basis consistent with that of the preceding year. Also, in our opinion, the combining financial statements referred to above present fairly the financial position of the individual funds of Alachua County, Florida, at September 30, 1983, and the results of operations of such funds and the changes in financial position of individual proprietary funds and similar trust fund for the year then ended, in conformity with generally accepted accounting principles applied on a basis consistent with that of the preceding year.

Our examination was made for the purpose of forming an opinion on the combined financial statements taken as a whole and on the combining financial statements. The accompanying statistical section listed in the table of contents on Pages 158 through 171 is presented for purposes of additonal analysis and is not a required part of the combined financial statements of Alachua County, Florida. The information has not been subjected to the auditing procedures applied in the examination of the combined and combining financial statements and, accordingly, we express no opinion.

[Certified Public Accountants]
January 4, 1984

EXHIBIT 13-3. OPINIONS ON COMBINED, COMBINING, AND INDIVIDUAL FUND STATEMENTS

Honorable Mayor and City Commissioners
City of Largo, Florida

We have examined the combined financial statements of the City of Largo, Florida, and its combining and individual fund financial statements as of and for the year ended September 30, 1983, as listed in the table of contents. Our examination was made in accordance with generally accepted auditing standards and, accordingly, included such tests of the accounting records and such other auditing procedures as we considered necessary in the circumstances.

In our opinion, the combined financial statements referred to above present fairly the financial position of the City of Largo, Florida, at September 30, 1983, and the results of its operations and the changes in

financial position of its proprietary fund types and similar trust funds for the year then ended, in conformity with generally accepted accounting principles applied on a basis consistent with that of the preceding year. Also, in our opinion, the combining and individual fund financial statements referred to above present fairly the financial position of the individual funds of the City of Largo, Florida, at September 30, 1983, their results of operations, and the changes in financial position of individual proprietary funds and similar trust funds for the year then ended, in conformity with generally accepted accounting principles applied on a basis consistent with that of the preceding year.

Our examination was made for the purpose of forming an opinion on the combined financial statements taken as a whole and on the combining and individual fund financial statements. The accompanying financial information listed as Schedule 1 in the table of contents is presented for purposes of additional analysis and is not a required part of the combined financial statements of the City of Largo, Florida. The information has been subjected to the auditing procedures applied in the examination of the combined, combining, and individual fund financial statements and, in our opinion, is fairly stated in all material respects in relation to the combined financial statements taken as a whole.

[Certified Public Accountants]
St. Petersburg, Florida
January 6, 1984

The Honorable Mayor and Members of the City Council
Brigham City Corporation
Brigham City, Utah

We have examined the combined financial statements of the Brigham City Corporation and its combining and individual fund financial statements as of and for the year ended June 30, 1984, as listed in the table of contents. Our examination was made in accordance with generally accepted auditing standards and, accordingly included such tests of the accounting records and such other auditing procedures as we considered necessary in the circumstances.

In our opinion, the combined financial statements referred to above present fairly the financial position of Brigham City Corporation at June 30, 1984, and the results of its operations and the changes in financial position of its proprietary fund types and similar trust funds for the year then ended, in conformity with generally accepted accounting principles applied on a basis consistent with that of the preceding year. Also, in our opinion, the combining and individual fund financial statements referred to above present fairly the financial position of the individual funds of Brigham City Corporation at June 30, 1984, their results of operations, and the changes in financial position of individual proprietary funds for the year then ended, in conformity with generally accepted accounting principles applied on a basis consistent with that of the preceding year.

Our examination was made for the purpose of forming an opinion on the combined financial statements taken as a whole and on the combining and individual fund financial statements. The accompanying financial information listed under the statistical section in the table of contents is presented for purposes of additional analysis and is not a required part of the combined financial statements of Brigham City Corporation. The information has not been subjected to the auditing procedures applied in the examination of the combined, combining, and individual fund financial statements and, as such, we express no opinion on the statistical section.

[Certified Public Accountants]
August 30, 1984

Honorable District Judges of the 9th, Second 9th, 221st,
   and 248th Judicial Districts and Members of the
   Commissioners' Court
County of Montgomery, Texas
Conroe, Texas

We have examined the combined financial statements of Montgomery County, Texas, and its combining and individual fund financial statements as of the year ended September 30, 1983, as listed in the table of contents. Our examination was made in accordance with generally accepted auditing standards and, accordingly, included such tests of the accounting records and such other auditing procedures as we considered necessary in the circumstances.

In our opinion, the combined financial statements referred to above present fairly the financial position of Montgomery County, Texas, at September 30, 1983, and the results of its operations and the changes in financial position of its proprietary fund types and similar trust funds for the year then ended, in conformity with generally accepted accounting principles. Also, in our opinion, the combining and individual fund financial statements referred to above present fairly the financial position of the individual funds of Montgomery County, Texas at September 30, 1983, their results of operations, and the changes in financial position of individual proprietary funds for the year ended, in conformity with generally accepted accounting principles.

Our examination was made for the purpose of forming an opinion on the combined financial statements taken as a whole and on the combining and individual fund financial statements. Information contained in the statistical tables as listed in the tables of contents has not been subjected to the auditing procedures applied

in the examination of the combined, combining, and individual fund financial statements and therefore we do not express any opinion concerning them.

[Certified Public Accountants]
November 23, 1984

EXHIBIT 13-4. OPINIONS ON COMBINED, COMBINING, AND INDIVIDUAL FUND AND ACCOUNT GROUP STATEMENTS
REPORT OF INDEPENDENT CERTIFIED PUBLIC ACCOUNTANTS
March 23, 1984

The Honorable Mayor—Commissioner, City
   Commissioners and City Managers
City of Clearwater, Florida

We have examined the combined financial statements of the City of Clearwater, Florida, and the combining, individual fund and account group financial statements of the City as of and for the year ended September 30, 1983, as listed in the table of contents on pages iii thru v. Our examination was made in accordance with generally accepted auditing standards and accordingly included such tests of the accounting records and such other auditing procedures as we considered necessary in the circumstances.

In our opinion, the combined financial statements referred to above present fairly the financial position of the City of Clearwater, Florida, at September 30, 1983, and the results of its operations and the changes in financial position of its proprietary, nonexpendable and pension trust fund types for the year then ended, in conformity with generally accepted accounting principles applied on a basis consistent with that of the preceding year. Also, in our opinion, the combining, individual fund and account group financial statements referred to above present fairly the financial position of the individual funds and account groups of the City of Clearwater, Florida, at September 30, 1983, and the results of operations of such funds and the changes in financial position of individual proprietary, nonexpendable and pension trust funds for the year then ended, in conformity with generally accepted accounting principles applied on a basis consistent with that of the preceding year.

Our examination was made for the purpose of forming an opinion on the combined financial statements taken as a whole and on the combining, individual fund and account group financial statements. The accompanying financial information listed as supplemental schedules in the table of contents is presented for purposes of additional analysis and is not a required part of the combined financial statements of the City of Clearwater, Florida. Such information has been subjected to the auditing procedures applied in the examination of the combined, combining, individual fund and account group financial statements and, in our opinion, is fairly stated in all material respects in relation to the combined financial statements taken as a whole.

[Certified Public Accountants]

Honorable Mayor and Members of the City Commission
City of Sarasota, Florida

We have examined the combined financial statements of the City of Sarasota, Florida, and the combining, individual fund, and account group financial statements of the City as of and for the year ended September 30, 1983, as listed in the table of contents. Our examination was made in accordance with generally accepted auditing standards and, accordingly, included such tests of the accounting records and such other auditing procedures as we considered necessary in the circumstances.

In our opinion, the combined financial statements referred to above present fairly the financial position of the City of Sarasota, Florida, as of September 30, 1983 and the results of its operations and the changes in financial position of its proprietary fund types for the year then ended, in conformity with generally accepted accounting principles applied on a basis consistent with that of the preceding year. Also, in our opinion, the combining, individual fund, and account group financial statements referred to above present fairly the financial position of the individual funds and account groups of the City as of September 30, 1983, and the results of operations of such funds and the changes in financial position of individual propreitary funds for the year then ended, in conformity with generally accepted accounting principles applied on a basis consistent with that of the preceding year.

Our examination was made for the purpose of forming an opinion on the combined financial statements taken as a whole and on the combining, individual fund, and account group financial statements. The accompanying financial information listed as supporting schedules in the table of contents is presented for purposes of additional analysis and is not a required part of the combined financial statements of the City. The information has been subjected to the auditing procedures applied in the examination of the combined, combining, individual fund, and account group financial statements and, in our opinion, is fairly stated in all material respects in relation to the combined financial statements taken as a whole.

In connection with our examination, nothing came to our attention that caused us to believe that the City was not in compliance with any of the terms, covenants, provisions, or conditions of sections 701 to 715, inclusive of the 1977 Water and Sewer Utility Revenue Bond Resolutions. However, it should be noted that our examination was not directed primarily toward obtaining knowledge of such noncompliance.

[Certified Public Accountants]
Sarasota, Florida
December 28, 1983

The Honorable Members of the City Council
City of Tempe, Arizona

We have examined the combined financial statements of the City of Tempe, Arizona and the combining, individual fund, and account group financial statements of the City as of and for the year ended June 30, 1984, as identified in the Financial Section Table of Contents. Our examination was made in accordance with generally accepted auditing standards and, accordingly, included such tests of the accounting records and such other auditing procedures as we considered necessary in the circumstances.

In our opinion, the combined financial statements referred to above present fairly the financial position of the City of Tempe, Arizona, at June 30, 1984, and the results of its operations and the changes in financial position of its proprietary fund types and similar trust funds for the year then ended, in conformity with generally accepted accounting principles applied on a basis consistent with that of the preceding year. Also, in our opinion, the combining, individual fund, and account group financial statements referred to above present fairly the financial position of the individual funds and account groups of the City of Tempe, Arizona, at June 30, 1984, and the results of their operations and the changes in financial position of the proprietary fund types and similar trust funds for the year then ended, in conformity with generally accepted accounting principles applied on a basis consistent with that of the preceding year.

Our examination was made for the purpose of forming an opinion on the combined financial statements taken as a whole and on the combining, individual fund, and account group financial statements. The exhibits of supplemental information identified in the Financial Section Table of Contents are presented for purposes of additional analysis and are not a required part of the financial statements of the City of Tempe, Arizona. The information has been subjected to the auditing procedures applied in the examination of the combined, combining, and individual fund financial statements and, in our opinion, is fairly stated in all material respects in relation to the basic financial statements taken as a whole.

[Certified Public Accountants]
October 19, 1984

EXHIBIT 13-5. OPINIONS ON FINANCIAL STATEMENTS WITH REFERENCE TO RELIANCE ON OTHER AUDITORS

To the Board of Commissioners
St. Clair County
Port Huron, Michigan

We have examined the combined financial statements of St. Clair County, Michigan, for the year ended December 31, 1983, listed in the foregoing Table of Contents. Our examination was made in accordance with generally accepted auditing standards, and accordingly included such tests of the accounting records and such other auditing procedures as we considered necessary in the circumstances. We did not examine the financial statements of the St. Clair County Road Commission, Mental Health, Department of Public Works, and Building Authority. These financial statements reflect 71 percent of the assets and 70 percent of the revenue of the Special Revenue Funds, 100 percent of the assets and 100 percent of the revenues of the Debt Service Funds, 90 percent of the assets and 98 percent of the revenues of the Capital Project Funds, 96 percent of the assets and 58 percent of the revenues of the Enterprise Funds, .2 percent of the assets and .5 percent of the revenues of the Internal Service Funds, 32 percent of the General Fixed Assets, and 97 percent of the General Long-Term Debt. These financial statements were examined by other auditors whose reports thereon have been furnished to us and our opinion expressed herein, insofar as it relates to the amounts included for the aforementioned entities, is based solely upon the reports of other auditors.

In our opinion, based upon our examination and the reports of the other auditors, the combined financial statements referred to above present fairly the financial position of St. Clair County, Michigan, at December 31, 1983, and the results of its operations and changes in financial position of its proprietary and selected fiduciary fund types for the year then ended, in conformity with generally accepted accounting principles applied on a consistent basis after giving retroactive effect to the change, with which we concur, in the method of accounting for compensated absences as explained in Note 3.

Our examination was made for the purpose of forming an opinion on the combined financial statements taken as a whole. The combining, individual fund, and account group financial statements listed in the Table of Contents are presented for purposes of additional analysis and are not a required part of the combined financial statements of St. Clair County, Michigan. The information has been subjected to the auditing procedures applied in the examination of the combined financial statements and, in our opinion, is fairly stated

in all material respects in relation to the combined financial statements taken as a whole.

[Certified Public Accountants]
May 25, 1984

Honorable Mayor and Members of the City Council
City of Green Bay, Wisconsin

We have examined the combined financial statements of the City of Green Bay, Wisconsin, as of and for the year ended December 31, 1983, as listed in the table of contents. Our examination was made in accordance with generally accepted auditing standards and, accordingly, included such tests of the accounting records and such other auditing procedures as we considered necessary in the circumstances. We did not examine the financial statements of the Enterprise Funds, which statements reflect total assets and revenues constituting 18 percent and 8 percent, respectively, of the combined totals. These statements were examined by other auditors whose report thereon has been furnished to us and our opinion expressed herein, insofar as it relates to these funds, is based solely upon the report of the other auditors.

In our opinion, based upon our examination and the report of other auditors, the combined financial statements referred to above present fairly the financial position of the City of Green Bay, Wisconsin, at December 31, 1983, and the results of its operations and the changes in financial position of its proprietary fund types for the year then ended, in conformity with generally accepted accounting principles applied on a basis consistent with that of the preceding year.

Our examination was made for the purpose of forming an opinion on the combined financial statements taken as a whole. The combining, individual fund, and account group financial statements and schedules listed in the table of contents are presented for purposes of additional analysis and are not a required part of the combined financial statements of the City of Green Bay, Wisconsin. The information has been subjected to the auditing procedures applied in the examination of the combined financial statements and, in our opinion, is fairly stated in all material respects in relation to the combined financial statements taken as a whole.

[Certified Public Accountants]
March 23, 1984

The Honorable County Council
Montogomery County, Maryland

We have examined the combined financial statements of Montgomery County, Maryland, and the combining, individual fund and account group financial statements for the year ended June 30, 1984, identified as Exhibits A-1 to I-2, inclusive, in the table of contents. Our examination was made in accordance with generally accepted auditing standards and, accordingly, included such tests of the accounting records and such other auditing procedures as we considered necessary in the circumstances. We did not examine the financial statements of the Board of Education of Montgomery County, Montgomery Community College, Maryland–National Capital Park and Planning Commission and the Montgomery County Revenue Authority. These statements were examined by other auditors whose reports thereon have been furnished to us, and our opinion expressed herein, insofar, as it relates to the amounts included in the aforementioned component unit entities, is based solely upon the reports of the other auditors. The statements of these component entities reflect the following percent of total assets and revenues of the indicated fund types and account groups:

	Percent of Total Assets	Percent of Total Revenues
Special Revenue Fund types	41%	44%
Debt Service Fund types	9%	8%
Capital Project Fund types	15%	40%
Enterprise Fund types	10%	13%
Internal Service Fund types	10%	4%
Trust and Agency Fund types	29%	22%
General Fixed Assets Account Group	57%	—
General Long Term Debt Account Group	11%	—
Higher Education Fund types	100%	100%

In our opinion, based upon our examination and the reports of other auditors, the combined financial statements referred to above present fairly the financial position of Montgomery County, Maryland, at June 30, 1984, and the results of its operations and changes in financial position of its Proprietary Fund types for the year then ended, in conformity with generally accepted accounting principles applied on a basis consistent with that of the preceding year after restatement for the changes, with which we concur, in the method of accounting for compensated absences, claims and judgments and capital leases as described in Notes IG and IIIE, respectively, to the financial statements. Also, in our opinion, the combining, individual fund and account group financial statements referred to above present fairly the financial position of the individual funds and account groups in conformity with generally accepted accounting principles applied on a basis consistent with that of the preceding year after the restatements described in the preceding sentence.

The schedules identified as Exhibits J-1 to J-18 and the statistical section of this report identified as Table I to Table XVI have not been audited by us and, accordingly, we express no opinion of them.

[Certified Public Accountants]
November 9, 1984

The Honorable County Council
Howard County, Maryland

We have examined the combined financial statements of Howard County, Maryland, as of and for the year ended June 30, 1984, as listed in the foregoing table of contents. Our examination was made in accordance with generally accepted auditing standards and, accordingly, included such tests of the accounting records and such other auditing procedures as we considered necessary in the circumstances. We did not examine the financial statements of the Board of Education of Howard County and the Howard County Library, which account for the following percentages of the related amounts in the combined financial statements:

	Percentage of Assets	Percentage of Revenues
Special revenue funds	68%	77%
Capital projects funds	9	40
Agency funds	11	—
General fixed assets account group	56	—

The financial statements of these two entities were examined by other auditors whose reports thereon were furnished to us and our opinion herein, insofar as it relates to the amounts included for these two entities, is based solely upon the reports of the other auditors.

In our opinion, based upon our examination and the reports of other auditors, the aforementioned combined financial statements present fairly the financial position of Howard County, Maryland, at June 30, 1984, and the results of its operations and the changes in financial position of its proprietary funds for the year then ended, in conformity with generally accepted accounting principles applied on a basis consistent with that of the preceding year after giving retroactive effect to the changes, with which we concur, in the methods of accounting for compensated absences, accrued pension cost related to unfunded amortization of prior service costs and water and sewer activities as described in note 3 to the combined financial statements.

Our examination was made for the purpose of forming an opinion on the combined financial statements taken as a whole. The combined financial statements and schedules, as listed in the foregoing table of contents are presented for purposes of additional analysis and are not a required part of the combined financial statements of Howard County, Maryland. Such information has been subjected to the auditing procedures applied in the examination of the combined financial statements and, in our opinion, is fairly stated in all material respects in relation to the combined financial statements taken as a whole.

The supplementary information included in the Statistical Section in the foregoing table of contents has not been subjected to the auditing procedures applied in the examination of the combined financial statements and, accordingly, we express no opinion on it.

[Certified Public Accountants]
October 11, 1984

EXHIBIT 13-6. OPINIONS ON OTHER THAN GENERALLY ACCEPTED ACCOUNTING PRINCIPLES

INDEPENDENT AUDITOR'S REPORT   *March 3, 1984*

The Honorable Director and Board of Chosen Freeholders
County of Morris
Morristown, New Jersey

We have examined the financial statements of the various funds of the County of Morris for the year ended December 31, 1983, listed in the foregoing table of contents. Our examination was made in accordance with generally accepted auditing standards and in compliance with audit requirements as prescribed by the division of Local Government Services, Department of Community Affairs, State of New Jersey, and, accordingly, included such tests of the accounting records and such other auditing procedures as we considered necessary in the circumstances. We made a similar examination of the financial statements for the year ended December 31, 1982.

As described in Note A, the County of Morris prepares its financial statements in conformity with accounting principles prescribed by the Division of Local Government Services, Department of Community Affairs, State of New Jersey, which are designed primarily for determining compliance with legal provisions and budgetary restrictions and as a means of reporting on the stewardship of public officials with respect to public funds. Accordingly, the accompanying financial statements are not intended to present financial position or results of operations in conformity with generally accepted accounting principles applicable to local government units.

In our opinion, the financial statements referred to above present fairly the financial position of the various funds of the County of Morris at December 31, 1983, and the results of operations of such funds for

the year then ended, in accordance with accounting principles and practices prescribed by the Division of Local Government Services, Department of Community Affairs, State of New Jersey, applied on a basis consistent with that of the preceding year.

Our examination was made for purposes of forming an opinion on the financial statements taken as a whole. The information included in the supplementary schedules, including the Schedule of Currently Active Federal Assistance Programs through December 31, 1983, is presented for purposes of additional analysis and is not a required part of the financial statements. The accompanying supplemental schedules and information presented in the "Supplementary Data" section are not necessary for a fair presentation of the financial statements, but are presented as additional analytical data, as required by the Division of Local Government Services. This information has been subjected to the tests and other auditing procedures applied in the examination of the financial statements mentioned above and, in our opinion, is fairly stated in all material respects in relation to the combined financial statements taken as a whole.

[Registered Municipal Accountant]
[Certified Public Accountants]

To Mayor Stephen J. Alfred
    and
The City Council
City of Shaker Heights

We have examined the Combined Statements of Cash, Investments and Fund Balances of the various funds of the City of Shaker Heights as listed in the accompanying Index of Funds as of December 31, 1983 and 1982, and the related Combined Statements of Cash Receipts, Disbursements and Changes in Fund Balances; Statements of Receipts—Estimated and Actual; and Statements of Disbursements and Encumbrances Compared with Expenditure Authority for the years then ended. Our examinations were made in accordance with generally accepted auditing standards and, accordingly, included such tests of the accounting records and such other auditing procedures as we considered necessary in the circumstances.

As described in Note 1 of Notes to Financial Statements, the City prepares its financial statements on the basis of cash receipts and disbursements. As a result, revenue is recognized when received rather than when earned, and certain expenses are recognized when paid rather than when incurred. Accordingly, the accompanying financial statements are not intended to present and, in our opinion, do not present financial position and results of operations in conformity with generally accepted accounting principles.

In our opinion, the financial statements referred to above present fairly the combined cash, investments and fund balances of the various funds of the City of Shaker Heights as of December 31, 1983 and 1982, the related combined cash receipts, disbursements and changes in fund balances and the related budgetary information included in Statements 4 and 5, for the years then ended, on the basis of accounting described in Note 1 applied on a consistent basis.

[Certified Public Accountants]
Cleveland, Ohio
April 27, 1984

Honorable Mayor and City Council
City of Muskogee, Oklahoma

We have examined the statements of assets, liabilities, reserves and fund equity arising from cash transactions of the various funds and account group of the City of Muskogee, Oklahoma, as of June 30, 1984, and the related statements of revenues, expenditures, claims and contracts pending, transfers and changes in fund equity for the year then ended. Our examination was made in accordance with generally accepted auditing standards and accordingly, included such tests of the accounting records and such other auditing procedures as we considered necessary in the circumstances.

The aforementioned financial statements are prepared on the basis of cash receipts and disbursements; consequently, certain revenues and the related assets are recognized when paid rather than when the obligation is incurred. The City has not maintained a record of its general fixed assets and a statement of general fixed assets is not included in the financial report. Accordingly, the accompanying financial statements are not intended to present financial position and results of operations in conformity with generally accepted accounting principles.

In our opinion, the financial statements referred to above present fairly the assets and liabilities arising from cash transactions of the various funds and account groups of the City of Muskogee, Oklahoma, as of June 30, 1984, and its revenues collected and expenditures paid during the year then ended, which basis has been applied in a consistent manner.

Our examination was made for the purpose of forming an opinion on the combined financial statements taken as a whole. The supplementary information is presented for purposes of additional analysis and is not a required part of the basic financial statements. Such information has been subjected to the auditing procedures applied in the examination of the basis financial statements and, in our opinion, is fairly stated in all material respects in relation to the combined financial statements taken as a whole.

[Certified Public Accountants]
Muskogee, Oklahoma
September 30, 1984

EXHIBIT 13-7. OPINIONS BY TWO OR MORE AUDITORS

To the Honorable County Commissioners and
 Constitutional Officers
Alachua County, Florida

We have examined the combined financial statements of Alachua County, Florida, and the combining financial statements of Alachua County as of and for the year ended September 30, 1983, as listed in the table of contents. Our examination was made in accordance with generally accepted auditing standards and, accordingly, included such tests of the accounting records and such other auditing procedures as we considered necessary in the circumstances.

In our opinion, the combined financial statements referred to above present fairly the financial position of Alachua County, Florida, at September 30, 1983, and the results of its operations and changes in financial position of its proprietary fund types and similar trust fund for the year then ended, in conformity with generally accepted accounting principles applied on a basis consistent with that of the preceding year. Also, in our opinion, the combining financial statements referred to above present fairly the financial position of the individual funds of Alachua County, Florida, at September 30, 1983, and the results of operations of such funds and the changes in financial position of individual proprietary funds and similar trust fund for the year then ended, in conformity with generally accepted accounting principles applied on a basis consistent with that of the preceding year.

Our examination was made for the purpose of forming an opinion on the combined financial statements taken as a whole and on the combining financial statements. The accompanying statistical section listed in the table of contents on Pages 158 through 171 is presented for purposes of additional analysis and are not a required part of the combined financial statements of Alachua County, Florida. The information has not been subjected to the auditing procedures applied in the examination of the combined and combining financial statements and, accordingly, we express no opinion.

[Firm A, Certified Public Accountants]
[Firm B, Certified Public Accountants]
January 4, 1984

To the Honorable Mayor and Members of City Council,
City of Atlanta, Georgia

We have examined the general purpose financial statements of the City of Atlanta (a Georgia municipal corporation) as of December 31, 1983, and for the year then ended, shown on Pages 2 through 19 in the accompanying table of contents. Our examination was made in accordance with generally accepted auditing standards and, accordingly, included such tests of the accounting records and such other auditing procedures as we considered necessary in the circumstances.

In our opinion, the general purpose financial statements referred to above present fairly the financial position of the City of Atlanta as of December 31, 1983, and the results of its operations and the changes in financial position of the Proprietary and Similar Trust Funds for the year then ended, in conformity with generally accepted accounting principles, which, except for the change (with which we concur) in method of recording revenues of the Water and Sewerage System (as explained in Note 1), and after giving retroactive effect to the changes (with which we concur) in the methods of accounting for current maturities of debt and noncurrent receivables (as explained in Note 1 to the financial statements) have been applied on a basis consistent with that of the preceding year.

Our examination was made for the purpose of forming an opinion on the general purpose financial statements taken as a whole. The combining and individual fund and account groups financial statements as of December 31, 1983, and for the year then ended, shown on Pages 20 through 70 in the accompanying table of contents, are presented for purposes of additional analysis and are not a required part of the general purpose financial statements. Such information has been subjected to the auditing procedures applied in the examination of the general purpose financial statements; however, we did not examine the financial statements of the City of Atlanta and Fulton County Recreation Authority, shown on Pages 54 through 56 in the accompanying table of contents. These statements were examined by other auditors whose report thereon has been furnished to us, and our opinion expressed herein, insofar as it relates to the amounts included for the City of Atlanta and Fulton County Recreation Authority, is based solely upon the report of the other auditors. In our opinion, based upon our examination and report of other auditors referred to above, such information is fairly stated in all material respects in relation to the combined financial statements taken as a whole.

[Firm A, Certified Public Accountants]
[Firm B, Certified Public Accountants]
March 9, 1984

To the Mayor and Members of the Council of the District of Columbia

We have examined the general purpose financial statements of the District of Columbia as of September 30, 1983, and for the year then ended, listed as Exhibits 1 through 5 in the table of contents of this report. Our examination was made in accordance with generally accepted auditing standards and, accordingly, included such tests of the accounting records and such other auditing procedures as we considered necessary in the circumstances.

In our opinion, the general purpose financial statements referred to above present fairly the financial position of the various funds and account groups of the District of Columbia as of September 30, 1983, and the results of their operations, changes in their retained earnings/fund balances and, for the proprietary fund types, changes in their financial position for the year then ended, in conformity with generally accepted accounting principles applied on a basis consistent with that of the preceding year.

Our examination was made for the purpose of forming an opinion on the general purpose financial statements taken as a whole. The combining and individual fund statements listed in the table of contents as Exhibits A-1 through F-3 are presented for purposes of additional analysis and are not a required part of the general purpose financial statements of the District of Columbia. Such information has been subjected to the auditing procedures applied in the examination of general purpose financial statements and, in our opinion, is fairly stated in all material respects in relation to the general purpose financial statements taken as a whole.

[Firm A, Certified Public Accountants]
[Firm B, Certified Public Accountants]
January 27, 1984

To the Honorable Members of the Board of County Commissioners and Constitutional Officers
Seminole County, Florida

We have examined the combined financial statements of Seminole County, Florida, as of and for the year ended September 30, 1983, as listed in the table of contents. Our examination was made in accordance with generally accepted auditing standards and, accordingly, included such tests of the accounting records and such other auditing procedures as we considered necessary in the circumstances.

In our opinion, the combined financial statements referred to above present fairly the financial position of Seminole County, Florida at September 30, 1983, and the results of its operations and changes in financial position of its Proprietary Fund Types for the year then ended, in conformity with generally accepted accounting principles applied on a basis consistent with that of the preceding year.

Our examination was made for the purpose of forming an opinion on the combined financial statements taken as a whole. The financial statements and schedules listed in the table of contents on Pages 82 through

143 are presented for purposes of additional analysis and are not a required part of the combined financial statements of Seminole County, Florida. The information has been subjected to the auditing procedures applied in the examination of the combined financial statements and, in our opinion, is fairly stated in all material respects in relation to the combined financial statements taken as a whole.

The accompanying financial information listed under the statistical section of the table of contents is presented for purposes of additional analysis and is not a required part of the combined financial statements of Seminole County, Florida. Such information has not been subjected to the auditing procedures applied in the examination of the combined financial statements and, accordingly, we express no opinion.

[Firm A, Certified Public Accountants]
[Firm B, Certified Public Accountants]
[Firm C, Certified Public Accountants]
February 28, 1984

EXHIBIT 13-8. AUDIT OPINIONS BY A GOVERNMENT AUDITOR

The Honorable Warren W. Schaber, Chairman
Board of County Commissioners
Room 316, Ramsey County Courthouse
Saint Paul, Minnesota 55102

We have examined the combined financial statements of Ramsey County, Minnesota, and the combining and individual fund financial statements of the County as of and for the year ended December 31, 1983, as listed in the table of contents. Our examination was made in accordance with generally accepted auditing standards and, accordingly, included such tests of the accounting records and such other auditing procedures as we considered necessary in the circumstances.

In our opinion, the combined financial statements referred to above present fairly the financial position of Ramsey County, Minnesota, at December 31, 1983, and the results of its operations and the changes in financial position of its proprietary fund types for the year then ended, in conformity with generally accepted accounting principles applied on a basis consistent with that of the preceding year—after giving retroactive effect to the changes, with which we concur, in the method of accounting for compensated absences and minor trusts as described in Note 2 and the reclassification of funds as described in Note 3 to the financial statements. Also, in our opinion, the combining and individual fund financial statements referred to above present fairly the financial position of the individual funds of Ramsey County, Minnesota, at December 31, 1983, and the results of operations of

such funds and the changes in financial position of the individual proprietary funds for the year then ended, in conformity with generally accepted accounting principles applied on a basis consistent with that of the preceding year—after giving retroactive effect to the changes, with which we concur, in the method of accounting for compensated absences and minor trusts as described in Note 2, and the reclassification of funds described in Note 3 to the financial statements.

Our examination was made for the purpose of forming an opinion on the combined financial statements taken as a whole and on the combining and individual fund financial statements. The accompanying financial information listed as supplementary information in the table of contents is presented for purposes of additional analysis and is not a required part of the combined financial statements of Ramsey County, Minnesota. The information has been subjected to the auditing procedures applied in the examination of the combined, combining, and individual fund financial statements and, in our opinion, is fairly stated in all material respects in relation to the combined financial statements taken as a whole.

The statistical information presented in Tables I through XXI is not necessary for a fair presentation of the financial statements, but is presented as additional analytical data. This information has not been subjected to any audit procedures and, accordingly, we do not express an opinion on it.

[State Auditor]
May 14, 1984

Honorable City Commission
City of Dayton, Ohio
101 West Third Street
Dayton, Ohio 45402

We have examined the combined financial statements of the City of Dayton, Ohio, as of and for the years ended December 31, 1983 & 1982, as listed in the accompanying table of contents. Our examination was made in accordance with generally accepted auditing standards and the standards of the Auditor of State and, accordingly, included such tests of the accounting records and such other auditing procedures as we considered necessary in the circumstances.

In our opinion, the aforementioned combined financial statements present fairly the financial position of the City of Dayton, Ohio, at December 31, 1983 and 1982, and the results of its operations and the changes in financial position of the proprietary fund types for the years then ended, in conformity with generally accepted accounting principles.

Our examination was made for the purpose of forming an opinion on the combined financial statements taken as a whole. The combining financial statements and schedules listed in the table of contents are presented for purposes of additional analysis rather than to present the financial position and results of operations of its individual funds or account groups, or the changes in financial position of its individual proprietary funds. This information has been subjected to the auditing procedures applied in the examination of the combined financial statements, and in our opinion, is stated fairly in all material respects in relation to the combined financial statements taken as a whole.

[Auditor of State]
June 1, 1984

Honorable Donna Owens, Mayor
David Boston, City Manager
City of Toledo
One Government Center
Toledo, Ohio 43604

We have examined the combined financial statements of the City of Toledo, Ohio, as of December 31, 1983, and for the year then ended, as listed in the Table of Contents. Our examination was made in accordance with generally accepted auditing standards and the standards of the Auditor of State and, accordingly, included such tests of the accounting records and such other auditing procedures as we considered necessary in the circumstances.

In our opinion, the aforementioned combined financial statements present fairly the financial position of the City of Toledo, Ohio, at December 31, 1983, and the results of its operations and the changes in financial position of the proprietary fund types for the year then ended, in conformity with generally accepted accounting principles applied on a basis consistent with that of the preceding year.

Our examination was made for the purpose of forming an opinion on the combined financial statements taken as a whole. The combining, individual fund and account group financial statements and schedules listed in the Table of Contents are presented for purposes of additional analysis and are not a required part of the combined financial statements of the City of Toledo, Ohio. The information has been subjected to the auditing procedures applied in the examination of the combined financial statements and, in our opinion, is fairly stated in all material respects in relation to the combined financial statements taken as a whole.

We did not examine the statistical data included in the statistical section of this report and, therefore, express no opinion thereon.

[Auditor of State]
June 18, 1984

TABLE 13-3. NATURE OF THE AUDITOR'S OPINION FOR SURVEYED FINANCIAL STATEMENTS

Nature of Auditor's Opinion for Surveyed Financial Statements That Contained an Audit Report	Instances Observed (%)
Unqualified	66
Qualified	34
Qualifications related to*	
departure from GAAP	81
accounting principles not being consistently applied	33
litigation	14
scope limitation	12
contingent liabilities, other than litigation	4
other	<1

* Observations for units having qualified auditor's opinions.

TABLE 13-4. ANALYSIS OF QUALIFICATIONS WITH REFERENCE TO DEPARTURES FROM GAAP

Basis of Departures*	Instances Observed (%)
Fixed asset accounting	73
Method of accruing revenues and expenditures	13
Pension liability	9
Cash basis of accounting	9
Incomplete financial statements	8
Fixed asset valuation	7
Compensated absences	6
Entities reported	4
Reporting entity	4
Inventory valuation accounting	4
Interest capitalization	2
Internal control limitation	2
Inadequacy of records/inability to obtain sufficient evidential material	2
Other reasons	<1

* Observations for the 81% of the units with qualified audit opinions for departures from GAAP.

EXHIBIT 13-9. EXCERPTS FROM QUALIFIED AUDIT OPINIONS

[QUALIFICATION: FIXED ASSET VALUATION]
[Example 1]

General fixed assets are stated principally at appraisal values as of June 30, 1979, which is not in conformity with generally accepted accounting principles. The appraisal values were determined by the [Appraisal] Company and the Budget and Finance Officer.

In our opinion, except for the effects on the combined financial statements of the matter discussed in the preceding paragraph, the combined financial statements referred to above present fairly the financial position of [the] County at June 30, 1984, and the results of its operations and the changes in financial position of its proprietary fund type for the year then ended, in conformity with generally accepted accounting principles applied on a basis consistent with that of the preceding year.

[Example 2]

As more fully described in Note 1 to the financial statements, the City has stated Inventories and Property and Equipment at values other than cost. In our opinion, generally accepted accounting principles require that such assets be stated at cost.

In our opinion, except for the effects of not stating Inventories and Property and Equipment at cost, the accompanying financial statements present fairly the financial position of each of the several funds of the City at December 31, 1983, and the results of their operations for the year then ended, in conformity with generally accepted accounting principles applied on a basis consistent with that of the preceding year.

[Example 3]

As discussed in Note 1 to the financial statements, [the Authority] has not provided depreciation on its buildings and equipment. In the opinion of the auditors, generally accepted accounting principles require that depreciation be provided on such assets. If depreciation had been provided, retained earnings and the carrying value of the assets would have been decreased by $920,634 at December 31, 1983, and the excess of operating expense over operating revenue would have been increased by $323,000 for the year then ended.

In our opinion, based upon our examination and the reports of other auditors referred to in paragraph 1 above, except for the effect on the financial statements of the enterprise fund of [the Authority] not providing depreciation on its buildings and equipment as discussed in paragraph 2 above, and except that the omission of the general fixed asset account group results in an incomplete presentation as explained in paragraph 3 above, the financial statements referred to above present fairly the financial position of the various fund types and account group of the City at December 31, 1983, and the results of operations of such fund types and the changes in financial position of its proprietary fund types for the year then ended, in conformity with generally accepted accounting principles applied on a basis consistent with that of the preceding year.

[Example 4]

No provision has ever been made for depreciation of the property, plant and equipment of the proprietary fund types. Generally accepted accounting principles require the depreciation of these assets.

In our opinion, except for the failure to provide for depreciation on the depreciable property, plant and equipment of the proprietary fund types, the combined financial statements referred to above present fairly the financial position of the City at September 30, 1983, and the results of its operations and the changes in financial position of its proprietary fund types for the year then ended, in conformity with generally accepted accounting principles applied on a basis consistent with that of the preceding year.

[Example 5]

The County did not maintain adequate records of the general fixed assets in the general fixed asset group of accounts, stated at $36,005,210 in the accompanying combined financial statements. In addition, the values included for land and buildings are appraised values and not historical cost, as required by generally accepted accounting principles. Because the County's records do not permit the application of adequate audit procedures, we are unable to and do not express an opinion on the general fixed asset group of accounts as included in the combined financial statements.

In our opinion, the combined financial statements referred to above, other than the general fixed asset group of accounts, as discussed in the preceding paragraph, present fairly the financial position of [the] County, at September 30, 1983, the results of its operations, and the changes in financial position of its Enterprise Fund for the year then ended, in conformity with generally acepted accounting principles applied on a basis consistent with that of the preceding year.

[Example 6]

As disclosed in Note 2 to the financial statements, generally accepted accounting principles require that fixed assets be recorded at historical cost or a reasonable estimation thereof. Management has elected to state various items of fixed assets at estimated value at June 30, 1979. The effects of this departure from generally accepted accounting principles on the financial position of the General Fixed Asset Group of Accounts have not been determined.

In our opinion, except for the effects of the matter discussed in the preceding paragraph on the financial statements of the General Fixed Asset Group of Accounts, the combined financial statements referred to above present fairly the financial position of [the] County, at June 30, 1984, and the results of its operations and the changes in financial position of the Vehicle Maintenance Fund for the year then ended; and the combining, individual fund and account group financial statements referred to above, which we examined, present fairly the financial position of the individual funds and account groups of [the] County, at June 30, 1984, and the results of operations of such funds for the year then ended, all in conformity with generally accepted accounting principles applied on a basis consistent with that of the preceding year after giving retroactive effect to the change, with which we concur, in the method of recording delinquent tax revenue as explained in Note 8 of the Notes to Financial Statements.

[Example 7]

The City has not maintained historical cost records relative to the general fixed asset group of accounts, the fixed assets of the enterprise funds, or the fixed assets of the internal service funds. Our examination was restricted to tests of asset cost additions for the current period only. Accordingly, we do not express an opinion as to the general fixed asset group of accounts and the related investment therein, which are stated in the accompanying balance sheet at June 30, 1984, in the amount of $35,413,950. Further, as more fully described in note six to the financial statements, historical costs of fixed assets of the enterprise and internal service funds were not maintained prior to 1972 and the related depreciation expense has not been included in these financial statements. These should be included to fully conform with generally accepted accounting principles.

In our opinion, except for the limitation stated in the foregoing paragraph relating to fixed assets, the combined financial statements referred to above present fairly the financial position of the City at June 30, 1984, and the results of its operations and the changes in financial position of its proprietary fund types for the year ended, in conformity with generally accepted accounting principles applied on a consistent basis after restatement for the changes, with which we concur, resulting from the application of Statement 3 of the National Council of Governmental Accounting as described in Note 1 to the financial statements.

[QUALIFICATION: FIXED ASSET ACCOUNTING]

[Example 1]

As discussed in Note 1 to the financial statements, "Fixed Assets," certain significant accounting procedures with respect to past accounting for fixed assets did not comply with generally accepted accounting principles, resulting in outdated and unsupported fixed asset records. However, the amounts reported as additions and retirements for the current period are reasonable.

In our opinion, except for the effects of not following generally accepted accounting principles for the general fixed assets mentioned in the preceding paragraph, the combined financial statements referred to above present fairly the financial position of [the] County, at December 31, 1983, and the results of its operations and the changes in financial position of its proprietary fund types for the year then ended in conformity with generally accepted accounting principles, applied on a basis consistent with that of the preceding year, except for the changes in accounting principles, with which we concur, as described in Note 2 to the financial statements.

[Example 2]

[The] County has not maintained a record of its fixed assets; consequently the financial statements do not include a general fixed asset group of accounts required by generally accepted accounting principles.

In my opinion, except for the omission of the general fixed asset group of accounts referenced in the preceding paragraph, the financial statements referred to above present fairly the financial position of [the] County, at June 30, 1984, and the results of its operations for the year then ended, in conformity with generally accepted accounting principles applied on a basis consistent with that of the preceding year.

[Example 3]

The County has not maintained a record of its general fixed assets and their cost. Accordingly, the general fixed asset accounts group, required by generally accepted accounting principles, is not included in the combined financial statements.

In our opinion, except for the omission of the general fixed asset account group explained in the preceding paragraph, which results in an incomplete presentation, the combined financial statements referred to above present fairly the financial position of [the]

County, at November 30, 1983, and the results of its operations for the year then ended and the results of operations and changes in financial position of the proprietary fund type for the year ended November 30, 1983, in conformity with generally accepted accounting principles applied on a basis consistent with that of the preceding year.

[Example 4]

The City has not maintained a complete updated record of its general fixed assets, and accordingly, a statement of general fixed assets, required by generally accepted accounting principles, is not included in the combined financial statements.

In our opinion, the combined financial statements referred to in the first paragraph present fairly the combined financial position of the funds and the General Long-Term Debt Account Group of the City at December 31, 1983, and the combined results of operations of such funds and the combined changes in financial position for the year then ended, in conformity with generally accepted accounting principles applied on a basis consistent with that of the prior year after giving retroactive effect to the changes, with which we concur, in the method of accounting for retirement liabilities and bond anticipation notes as described in Note 9 of the combined financial statements.

[Example 5]

The City has not maintained a record of its general fixed assets, and accordingly, a statement of general fixed assets and property, plant and equipment for certain enterprise funds, which is required by generally accepted accounting principles, is not included in the financial report. The actuarial present value of non-vested accumulated plan benefits for the Employees Retirement System has not been disclosed as it was not available.

In our opinion, except for the omission of the financial statement data cited in the preceding paragraph, the combined financial statements referred to above present fairly the financial position of the City, at June 30, 1984, and the results of its operations, and the changes in financial position of its proprietary fund types for the year then ended, in conformity with generally accepted accounting principles which, except for the changes described in Note 11, C., with which we concur, have been applied on a basis consistent with that of the preceeding year.

[Example 6]

The City has not maintained a record of its general fixed assets and, accordingly, a general fixed asset account group, required by generally accepted accounting principles, is not included in the accompanying combined balance sheet.

In our opinion, the combined financial statements referred to above present fairly the financial position of the various funds and the general long-term debt account group of the City, as of September 30, 1983, and the results of operations of such funds and the changes in financial position of the Proprietary Fund for the year then ended, in conformity with generally accepted accounting principles which, except for the changes, with which we concur, in the methods of accounting described in Note 2 to the financial statements, have been applied on a basis consistent with that of the preceding year.

[Example 7]

The City has not recorded its general fixed assets in the accompanying combined financial statements. Accordingly, a statement of the general fixed asset account group required by generally accepted accounting principles is not included in the financial statements. In addition, records of certain fixed assets of the Enterprise Funds (Sewer Service and Golf Funds) have not been maintained and, accordingly, these assets and the related depreciation are not included in the financial statements of the Enterprise Funds as required by generally accepted accounting principles (see note 4 to combined financial statements).

In our opinion, except that the omission of the general fixed asset account group results in an incomplete presentation as explained in the preceding paragraph and except for the effect on the financial statements of the Enterprise Funds of not recording certain fixed assets and the related depreciation, the aforementioned combined financial statements present fairly the financial position of the City at June 30, 1984, and the results of its operations and the changes in financial position of its Enterprise Funds for the year then ended, in conformity with generally accepted accounting principles which, except for the change, with which we concur, in the method of accounting for claims and judgments and compensated absences in accordance with Statement 4 of the National Council on Governmental Accounting as described in Note 7 to the combined financial statements, have been applied on a basis consistent with that of the preceding year.

[Example 8]

The County has not maintained a record of general fixed assets and accordingly a statement of general fixed assets required by generally accepted accounting principles is not included in the accompanying financial report.

In our opinion, except as noted in the preceding paragraph, the combined financial statements referred to above present fairly the financial position of the County at December 31, 1983, and the results of its operations for the year then ended, in conformity with generally accepted accounting principles applied on a basis consistent with that of the preceding year. Also, in our opinion, the combining and individual fund financial statements referred to above present fairly the financial position of the individual funds of the County at December 31, 1983, and their results of operations, for the year then ended, in conformity with generally accepted accounting principles applied on a basis consistent with that of the preceding year.

[Example 9]

As described in Note 4 to the financial statements, except for the addition of capitalized lease-purchase agreements in 1982, the amounts presented in the general fixed asset account group have not been updated since 1976. The amount of change in the general fixed asset account group since 1976 cannot be readily determined at this time; accordingly, we do not express an opinion on this account group.

In our opinion, except for the general fixed asset account group, the combined financial statements referred to above present fairly the financial position of the City at December 31, 1983, and the results of its operations for the year then ended in conformity with generally accepted accounting principles applied on a basis consistent with that of the preceding year.

[Example 10]

The Town does not maintain a record of its General Fixed Asset Account Group as required by generally accepted accounting principles.

In our opinion, except for the lack of a General Fixed Asset Account Group, the combined financial statements mentioned above present fairly the financial position of the Town at June 30, 1984, and its results of operations and changes in financial position of its pension and nonexpendable trust funds for the year then ended, in conformity with generally accepted accounting principles applied on a basis consistent with that of the preceding year.

[Example 11]

A record of general fixed assets is not maintained and, accordingly, a statement of general fixed assets, required by generally accepted accounting principles, is not included in this report.

In our opinion, except that the general fixed asset group is not maintained as explained in the preceding paragraph, the combined financial statements referred to above present fairly the financial position of [the] County, at December 31, 1983 and 1982, and the results of its operations for the years then ended, in conformity with generally accepted accounting principles. Also, in our opinion, the combining and individual fund financial statements referred to above present fairly the financial position of the individual funds of [the] County, at December 31, 1983 and 1982, and their results of operations for the years then ended, in conformity with generally accepted accounting principles.

[QUALIFICATION: COMPENSATED ABSENCES]

[Example 1]

In our opinion, the aforementioned financial statements present fairly the financial position of the various funds and account groups of the City, as of April 30, 1984, and the results of its operations for the year then ended, in conformity with generally accepted accounting principles which, except for the change, with which we concur, in the method of recognizing compensated absences as described in Note 14 to the financial statements, have been applied on a basis consistent with that of the preceding year.

[Example 2]

In our opinion, the financial statements referred to above present fairly the financial position of the City, as of September 30, 1983, and the results of its operations and the changes in financial position of its proprietary fund types and nonexpendable trust fund for the year then ended, in conformity with generally accepted accounting principles applied on a basis consistent with that of the preceding year, except for the change, with which we concur, in the method of accounting for compensated absences, as described in Note 2 to the financial statements.

[Example 3]

In our opinion, the aforementioned combined financial statements present fairly the financial position of the various fund types and account groups of the City, at June 30, 1984, and the results of operations of such fund types for the year then ended and the changes in financial position of the proprietary fund types for the year then ended, in conformity with generally accepted accounting principles applied on a basis consistent with that of the preceding year except for the change after restatement of the General Long-Term Debt Account Group, with which we concur, in the method of accounting for compensated absences as described in note 14 of the notes to the combined financial statements.

[Example 4]

Material vested amounts of employees' accumulated vacation as of June 30, 1984, are required by generally accepted accounting principles to be disclosed. However, records maintained by the city do not reflect the total amount of such employee benefits as of June 30, 1984.

In our opinion, except for the effect on the financial statements of the preceding paragraph, the general purpose financial statements referred to above present fairly the financial position of the City, at June 30, 1984, and the results of its operations and the changes in financial position of its proprietary fund types for the year then ended, in conformity with generally accepted accounting principles applied on a basis consistent with that of the preceding year. Also, in our opinion, the combining, individual fund and account group financial statements referred to above present fairly the financial position of the individual funds and account groups of the City, at June 30, 1984, and the results of operations of such funds and the changes in financial position of individual proprietary funds for the year then ended, in conformity with generally accepted accounting principles applied on a basis consistent with that of the preceding year.

[Example 5]

In our opinion, based upon our examination and the reports of other auditors, the aforementioned combined financial statements present fairly the financial position of the City and County, at June 30, 1984, and the results of its operations and changes in the financial position of its proprietary fund types and similar trust funds for the year then ended, in conformity with generally accepted accounting principles which, except for the change, with which we concur, in accounting for accrued vacation and sick leave pay as described in note 2k, to the combined financial statements, have been applied on a basis consistent with that of the preceding year.

[Example 6]

In our opinion, the financial statements referred to above present fairly, the financial position of the City, at June 30, 1984, and the results of its operations and the changes in financial position of its proprietary fund types for the year then ended, in conformity with generally accepted accounting principles consistently applied during the period except for the change, with which we concur, made as of July 1, 1983, in the method of accounting for compensated absences as described in Note 1(g).

[Example 7]

In our opinion, the combined financial statements referred to above present fairly the financial position of the City, at December 31, 1983, and the results of its operations and the changes in financial position of its proprietary fund types for the year then ended, in conformity with generally accepted accounting principles applied on a consistent basis except for the change, with which we concur, in the method of accounting for compensated absences as described in Note 11 to the financial statements.

[Example 8]

In our opinion, the combined financial statements referred to above present fairly the financial position of [the] County, at December 31, 1983, and the results of its operations and changes in financial position of its proprietary fund types for the year then ended in conformity with generally accepted accounting principles which, except for the change, with which we concur, in recording liabilities for compensated absences as described in Note 3, had been applied on a basis consistent with that of the preceding year. Also, in our opinion, the combining, individual fund and account group financial statements referred to above present fairly the financial position of the individual funds and account groups of [the] County, at December 31, 1983, and the results of operations of such funds and changes in financial position of individual proprietary funds for the year then ended, in conformity with generally accepted accounting principles which, except for the change, with which we concur, in recording liabilities for compensated absences as described in Note 3, have been applied on a basis consistent with that of the preceding year.

[Example 9]

In our opinion, the combined financial statements referred to above, present fairly the financial position of the City at September 30, 1983, the results of its operations, and the changes in financial position of its proprietary funds for the year then ended, in conformity with generally accepted accounting principles applied on a consistent basis, except for a change, in which we concur, in the method of accounting for compensated absences as described in Note 3.

Also, in our opinion, the combining, individual fund and account group financial statements referred to above, present fairly the financial position of the individual funds and account groups of the City, at September 30, 1983, and the results of operations of such funds and the changes in financial position of individual proprietary funds for the year then ended, in conformity with generally accepted accounting principles applied on a consistent basis, except for a change, in which we concur, in the method of accounting for compensated absences as described in Note 3.

[QUALIFICATION: CHANGES IN ACCOUNTING]

[Example 1]

In our opinion, the combined financial statements referred to above present fairly the financial position of the City at September 30, 1983, and the results of its operations and the changes in financial position of the proprietary fund types for the year then ended, in conformity with generally accepted accounting principles that, except for the change, with which we concur, in the method of computing depreciation as described in note P to the financial statements, have been applied on a basis consistent with that of the preceding year. Also, in our opinion, the combining, individual fund and account group financial statements referred to above present fairly the financial position of the individual funds and account groups of the City, at September 30, 1983, and the results of operations of such funds and the changes in financial position of the proprietary fund types for the year then ended, in conformity with generally accepted accounting principles that except for the change, with which we concur, in the method of computing depreciation as described in note P to the financial statements, have been applied on a basis consistent with that of the preceding year.

[Example 2]

In our opinion, based on our examination and the reports of other auditors referred to above, the combined financial statements referred to above present fairly the financial position of the City at June 30, 1984, and the results of its operations and the changes in financial position of the proprietary fund types and similar trust

funds for the year then ended, in conformity with generally accepted accounting principles which, except for the change, with which we concur, in the method of applying the City's capitalization policy as described in Note 4 to the combined financial statements have been applied on a basis consistent with that of the preceeding year after giving retroactive effect to the change, with which we concur, resulting from implementation of National Council on Governmental Accounting Statement 4, "Accounting and Financial Reporting Principles for Claims and Judgments and Compensated Absences," described in Note 11 to the combined financial statements.

[Example 3]

In our opinion, the combined financial statements referred to above present fairly the financial position of the City, at December 31, 1983, and the results of its operations and the changes in financial position of its proprietary fund types and similar trust funds for the year then ended, in conformity with generally accepted accounting principles. Also, in our opinion, the combining, individual fund and account group financial statements referred to above present fairly the financial position of the individual funds and account groups of the City, at December 31, 1983, and the results of operations of such funds and the changes in financial position of the individual proprietary funds and similar trust funds for the year then ended, in conformity with generally accepted accounting principles. In our opinion, the accounting principles have been applied on a basis consistent with that of the preceding year except for the change in the application of these principles to some of the City's activities and after restatement for the changes in capitalization of interest cost, compensated absences and account group adjustments and related changes. We concur with these changes, which are described in Note 4 under establishment of new funds and Note 8 to the financial statements.

[Example 4]

In our opinion, the aforementioned combined financial statements present fairly the financial position of the various fund types and account groups of the City, at June 30, 1984, and the results of operations of such fund types for the year then ended and the changes in financial position of the proprietary fund types for the year then ended, in conformity with generally accepted accounting principles applied on a basis consistent with that of the preceding year except for the change after restatement of the General Long-Term Debt Account Group, with which we concur, in the method of accounting for compensated absences as described in note 14 of the notes to the combined financial statements.

[Example 5]

In our opinion, the combined financial statements referred to above present fairly the financial position of the City, at December 31, 1983, and the results of its operations and the changes in financial position of the proprietary fund types for the year then ended, in conformity with generally accepted accounting principles applied on a basis consistent with that of the preceding year, except for the inclusion of the Housing Authority, with which we concur, as described in note 1(N) to the financial statements.

[Example 6]

In our opinion, the aforementioned combined financial statements present fairly the financial position of the City at December 31, 1983, and the results of its operations and the changes in financial position of its proprietary fund types for the year then ended, in conformity with generally accepted accounting principles which, except for the changes, with which we concur, in the methods of accounting for income tax and special assessment revenues as described in notes 2 and 3 to the financial statements, have been applied on a basis consistent with that of the preceding year. Also, in our opinion, the combining financial statements referred to above present fairly the financial positions of the Water, Sewer, Electricity and Airport Enterprise Funds of the City, at December 31, 1983, and the results of their operations and changes in their financial position for the year then ended, in conformity with generally accepted accounting principles applied on a basis consistent with that of the preceding year.

[Example 7]

As described more fully in Note A-14, certain grant and solid waste activities have been accounted for in different funds in 1983 as compared to prior years.

In our opinion, the combined financial statements referred to above present fairly the financial position of the City, at September 30, 1983, and the results of its operations and the changes in financial position of its proprietary fund types and nonexpendable trust funds for the year then ended, in conformity with generally accepted accounting principles which, except for the change (with which we concur) in the presentation of certain activities described above, have been

applied on a basis consistent with that of the preceding year.

[Example 8]

In our opinion, the combined financial statements referred to above present fairly the financial position of the City, at June 30, 1984, and the results of its operations and the changes in financial position of its proprietary fund types for the year then ended, in conformity with generally accepted accounting principles which, except for the change, with which we concur, in reportable funds as described in Note O to the financial statements, have been applied on a basis consistent with that of the preceding year.

[Example 9]

In our opinion, the combined financial statements referred to above present fairly the financial position of [the] County at June 30, 1984, and results of its operations and the changes in financial position of its Proprietary Fund for the year then ended, in conformity with generally accepted accounting principles which, except for the change, with which we concur, in the method of accounting for accrued vacation pay and the Special School District Fund, as described in Note 12 to the financial statements, have been applied on a basis consistent with that of the preceding year.

[Example 10]

In our opinion, the combined financial statements mentioned above present fairly the financial position of the City at June 30, 1984, and the results of operations and the changes in financial position of its proprietary fund types for the year then ended, in conformity with generally accepted accounting principles applied on a basis consistent with that of the preceding year, except for the change, with which we concur, in the reporting entity described in Note 1 to the combined financial statements.

Our examination was made for the purpose of forming an opinion on the combined financial statements taken as a whole. The combining, individual fund and account group financial statements and other schedules listed as additional financial information in the table of contents are presented for purposes of additional analysis and are not a required part of the combined financial statements of the City. Such additional financial information has been subjected to the auditing procedures applied in our examination of the combined financial statements and, in our opinion, is fairly stated in all material respects in relation to the combined financial statements taken as a whole.

[Example 11]

In our opinion, based upon our examination and the report of other auditors, the accompanying combined financial statements referred to above present fairly the financial position of the City, at September 30, 1983, and the results of its operations and the changes in financial position of its proprietary fund types and similar trust funds for the year then ended; and the combining, individual fund and account group financial statements referred to above present fairly the financial position of the individual funds and account groups of the City, at September 30, 1983, and the results of operations of such funds and the changes in financial position of individual proprietary funds and similar trust funds for the year then ended. The combined, combining, individual fund and account group financial statements are presented in conformity with generally accepted accounting principles applied on a basis consistent with that of the preceding year except for the change, with which we concur, to conform to generally accepted accounting principles, as described in Note 14 to the financial statements.

[QUALIFICATION: OTHER BASIS OF ACCOUNTING]

[Example 1]

As described in note 1, the consolidated financial statements were prepared on a basis that differs from the fund basis of accounting required by generally accepted accounting principles. Accordingly, the accompanying consolidated financial statements are not intended to present financial position and results of operations in conformity with generally accepted accounting principles.

In our opinion, the aforementioned consolidated financial statements of [the] County present fairly the consolidated assets, liabilities and equity at December 31, 1983 and 1982, and the consolidated revenues, expenses and changes in equity, changes in cash and investments and the consolidated financial activity for the two years then ended, on the basis of accounting described in note 1, applied on a consistent basis after restatement for the changes, with which we concur, in the methods of accounting as described in note 7 to the financial statements.

[Example 2]

The aforementioned financial statements are prepared on the basis of cash receipts and disbursements; consequently, certain revenues and the related assets are

recognized when paid rather than when the obligation is incurred. The City has not maintained a record of its general fixed assets and a statement of general fixed assets is not included in the financial report. Accordingly, the accompanying financial statements are not intended to present financial position and results of operations in conformity with generally accepted accounting principles.

[Example 3]

These financial statements have been prepared in conformity with accounting practices prescribed by the Division of Local Government Services, which are designed primarily for determining compliance with legal provisions and budgetary restrictions and as a means of reporting on the stewardship of public officials with respect to public funds. These practices differ in certain respects, which in some instances may be material, from generally accepted accounting principles applicable to local government units. The more significant of these practices are described in Note 1 to the financial statements.

[Example 4]

As described more fully in Note 2, the statements referred to above have been prepared on the basis of cash receipts and disbursements, except for the City's Proprietary Fund Types, which are prepared on the accrual basis. The cash basis of accounting omits recognition of accounts receivable, accounts payable, and other accrued items (see exception in Note 2 relating to property taxes receivable). Accordingly, the statements for the Governmental and Fiduciary Fund Types are not intended to, and do not present financial position, results of their operations, or changes in their fund equity in conformity with generally accepted accounting principles.

[Example 5]

The policy of [the] Community College is to prepare its financial statements on the basis of regulatory accounting practices prescribed or permitted by the State. As described in note 1(b) to the combined financial statements, these practices differ in some respects from generally accepted accounting principles.

In our opinion, except for the effect on the combined financial statements of the matters described in the two preceding paragraphs, based upon our examination and the report of other auditors, the aforementioned combined financial statements present fairly the financial position of the County, at December 31, 1983, and the results of its operations, the changes in its fund balances and the changes in financial position of its proprietary fund type for the year then ended, in conformity with generally accepted accounting principles applied on a basis consistent with that of the preceding year after giving retroactive effect to the changes, with which we concur, in the reporting entity as described in note 1(a) and in the method of accounting for compensated absences as described in note 1(i).

[Example 6]

The statements of the capital projects funds are presented on the cash basis. Consequently, certain revenue and the related assets are recognized when received rather than when earned, and certain expenses are recognized when paid rather than when the obligation is incurred. Accordingly, the statements do not present financial position and results of operations in conformity with generally accepted accounting principles.

In our opinion, the financial statements of the funds referred to above present fairly the assets and liabilities arising from cash transactions of the Capital Project Funds as of June 30, 1984, and the revenue collected and expenses paid during the year then ended, on a basis of accounting described in Note 1 applied on a basis consistent with that of the preceding year.

[Example 7]

As described in Note A, the County prepares its financial statements in conformity with accounting principles prescribed by the Division of Local Government Services, Department of Community Affairs, which are designed primarily for determining compliance with legal provisions and budgetary restrictions and as a means of reporting on the stewardship of public officials with respect to public funds. Accordingly, the accompanying financial statements are not intended to present financial position or results of operations in conformity with generally accepted accounting principles applicable to local government units.

In our opinion, the financial statements referred to above present fairly the financial position of the various funds of the County at December 31, 1983, and the results of operations of such funds for the year then ended, in accordance with accounting principles and practices prescribed by the Division of Local Government Services, Department of Community Affairs, applied on a basis consistent with that of the preceding year.

[QUALIFICATION: PENSION LIABILITY]

[Example 1]

As described in Note 9, the 1982 contributions to the pension plans of the General and Enterprise Funds were as required by actuarial studies but were not in amounts sufficient to provide pension expense as required by generally accepted accounting principles.

In our opinion, except for the effects on the 1982 General Fund and Enterprise Fund financial statements of the matters referred to in the third paragraph, the combined financial statements referred to above present fairly the financial position of the City at September 30, 1983 and 1982, and the results of its operations and the changes in financial position of the proprietary fund types and similar trust funds for the years then ended, in conformity with generally accepted accounting principles applied on a consistent basis after giving cumulative effect to the change, with which we concur, in the method of accounting for compensated absences as described in the second paragraph. Also, in our opinion, except for the effects on the 1982 General Fund and Enterprise Fund financial statements of the matters referred to in the third paragraph, the combining, individual fund and account group financial statements referred to above present fairly the financial position of the individual funds of the City at September 30, 1983 and 1982, their results of operations, and the changes in financial position of the individual proprietary funds for the years then ended, in conformity with generally accepted accounting principles applied on a consistent basis after giving cumulative effect to the change, with which we concur, in the method of accounting for compensated absences as described in the second paragraph.

[Example 2]

We have examined the financial statements of the City as of June 30, 1984, and for the year then ended, as listed in the accompanying table of contents. Our examination was made in accordance with generally accepted auditing standards and, accordingly, included such tests of the accounting records and such other auditing procedures as we considered necessary in the circumstances.

The City is required by Section 5 of the City's pension ordinance to provide a pension supplement, as more fully described in Note 4 to the financial statements. This supplement is funded using a "pay-as-you-go" method, which is not an acceptable method of determining pension costs under generally accepted accounting principles. The unfunded liability attributable to the pension supplement at July 1, 1981, the date of the last actuarial valuation, was $30,202,286.00.

In our opinion, except for the effects of not following generally accepted accounting principles as indicated in the two preceding paragraphs, the financial statements listed in the accompanying table of contents present fairly the financial position of the City at June 30, 1984, and the results of its operations and the changes in its financial position for the year then ended, in conformity with generally accepted accounting principles applied on a basis consistent with that of the preceding year.

[QUALIFICATION: RECOVERABILITY OF ASSETS]

[Example 1]

The accounts receivable for Sewerage Fund treatment charges were not confirmed by direct correspondence with the debtors and no provision has been made for uncollectible accounts. Accounts receivable billing is on a cyclical basis and we have verified through examination of individual accounts that their total agrees with the control total. Inventories shown in the balance sheet were obtained from City employees and no verification by actual physical count or inspection was made. We do not consider the inventories to be a material item.

In our opinion, except for the effects of such adjustments, if any, as might have been determined to be necessary had we been able to confirm accounts receivable and observe the physical inventories, the aforementioned financial statements of the Proprietary Fund Types of the City present fairly their financial position at April 30, 1984, and the results of their operations and changes in financial position for the year then ended in conformity with generally accepted accounting principles applied on a basis consistent with that of the preceding year. It is also our opinion, except for the omission of depreciation described above, that the statements of the City's Governmental and Fiduciary Fund Types and General Fixed Asset and General Long-Term Debt Account Groups present fairly the assets and liabilities resulting from cash transactions at April 30, 1984, and the cash receipts and disbursements for the year ended. The use of the cash basis for these fund types is consistent with that of the preceding year.

[Example 2]

As discussed in Note 8 to the financial statements, in October 1983, [a State] Appellate Court ruled unconstitutional [a State] Statute permitting counties to uti-

lize, for general County purposes, interest earned on County Collection trust and agency funds. The Appellate Court decision specified that such interest be distributed to the appropriate taxing bodies, retroactive to October 1976. The [State] Supreme Court has agreed to review the Appellate Court decision. While management believes the [State] Supreme Court will likely uphold the unconstitutionality finding of the Appellate Court, it is not clear that the requirement for retroactive distribution of interest will be upheld. As the ultimate outcome of this matter cannot presently be determined, no provision for any liability that may result has been made in the financial statements.

In our opinion, subject to the effects of such adjustments, if any, as might have been required had the outcome of the uncertainty referred to in the preceding paragraph been known, the financial statements referred to above present fairly the financial position of [the] County, at November 30, 1983, the results of its operations and changes in financial position of the Nonexpendable Trust Fund for the year then ended in conformity with generally accepted accounting principles applied on a basis consistent with that of the preceding year.

[Example 3]

As discussed more fully in note 5 to the combined financial statements, the County has a long-term note receivable from the Economic Development Corporation of the City, substantially all of which is held jointly by the Capital Projects and Internal Service Funds in the amounts of $800,000 and $200,000, respectively. The note is collateralized by a second mortgage on certain real estate located in the City Mall and by the assignment of the related leases. The Economic Development Corporation of the City has not had profitable operations since its inception and the County has not been recording interest income on its note receivable. Realization of the investment in the long-term note receivable is dependent upon either (1) the success of future operations of the Economic Development Corporation of the City and the related Mall or (2) the sale or other disposition of the Mall property for an amount at least equivalent to repay the related debt of the holder of the first mortgage on the Mall property and the note held by the County.

In our opinion, based upon our examination and the aforementioned reports of other auditors, subject to the realization of the investment in the long-term note receivable recorded in the capital projects and internal service funds discussed in the preceding paragraph, the general purpose financial statements referred to above present fairly the financial position of such fund types and account groups of the County as of December 31, 1983 (September 30, 1983, for certain special revenue funds), and the results of operations of such funds and the changes in financial position of the proprietary fund types and similar trust funds for the year then ended, in conformity with generally accepted accounting principles applied on a basis consistent with that of the preceding year, after giving retroactive effect to the change, with which we concur, in the method of accounting for accrued vacation and sick pay as described in note 14 to the financial statements.

[QUALIFICATION: INCOMPLETE FINANCIAL STATEMENTS]

[Example 1]

As described more fully in note 7, the financial statements referred to above do not include the financial statements of the General Fixed Asset Account Group of Accounts, which should be included to conform with generally accepted accounting principles.

In our opinion, except that the omission of the financial statements described above results in an incomplete presentation, the financial statements referred to above present fairly the financial position of the County at December 31, 1983, and the results of its operations for the year then ended, in conformity with generally accepted accounting principles applied on a basis consistent with that of the preceding year after giving retroactive effect to the change, with which we concur, in the method of accounting for accrued sick leave benefits as described in note 9 to the financial statements.

[Example 2]

The combined financial statements referred to above do not include financial statements of the general fixed asset group, which should be included to conform with generally accepted accounting principles.

In our opinion, except that the omission of the financial statements described above results in an incomplete presentation, as explained in the preceding paragraph, the combined financial statements referred to above present fairly the financial position of the City, at September 30, 1983, and the results of its operations and the changes in financial position of its proprietary fund types for the year then ended, in conformity with generally accepted accounting principles applied on a basis consistent with that of the preceding year.

[Example 3]

As described more fully in note O, the financial statements referred to above do not include financial statements of the general fixed asset account group, which should be included to conform with generally accepted accounting principles.

In our opinion, except that the omission of the financial statements described above results in an incomplete presentation, as explained in the preceding paragraph, the combined financial statements referred to above present fairly the financial position of the City, at September 30, 1983, and the results of its operations and the changes in financial position of its proprietary fund types for the year then ended, in conformity with generally accepted accounting principles applied on a basis consistent with that of the preceding year.

[Example 4]

As described more fully in note 1, the general purpose financial statements referred to above do not include financial statements of the General Fixed Asset Account Group, which should be included to conform with generally accepted accounting principles.

In our opinion, except that the omission of the financial statements of the General Fixed Asset Account Group results in an incomplete presentation as explained in the preceding paragraph, the aforementioned general purpose financial statements present fairly the financial position of the County at June 30, 1984, and the results of its operations of such funds and the changes in financial position of the proprietary fund type and similar trust fund for the year then ended in conformity with generally accepted accounting principles which, except for the changes, with which we concur, as described in note 2 to the financial statements, have been applied on a basis consistent with that of the preceding year.

[Example 5]

As discussed in Note 1, the County has not included in its combined financial statements all organizations, functions and activities of its government required by application of the criteria of NCGA Statement 3, "Defining the Governmental Reporting Entity."

As discussed in Note 2, the operations of the County Nursing Home for 1983 have been accounted for in an Enterprise Fund. Such operations were previously accounted for within the County's General Fund. In addition, the operations of Human Service Agencies, previously accounted for within the General Fund, are reported in separate Special Revenue Funds for 1983.

In our opinion, except for the omission of organizations as discussed above, the combined financial statements referred to above present fairly the financial position of the County at December 31, 1983, and the results of its operations and the changes in financial position of its Proprietary Fund and Pension Trust Fund for the year then ended, in conformity with generally accepted accounting principles applied on a basis consistent with that of the preceding year, except for the changes, with which we concur, in accounting and reporting the operations of the County Nursing Home and Human Service Agencies, and the method of accounting for compensated absences.

[Example 6]

As described more fully in Note 1, the combined financial statements designated above do not include financial statements of the Department of Utilities, the Hospital, or the Housing Authority, which should be included to conform with generally accepted accounting principles.

In my opinion, except that the omission of the financial statements referred to in the preceding paragraph results in an incomplete presentation, the combined financial statements designated above present fairly the financial position of the City at December 31, 1983, and the results of its operations and the changes in financial position of its proprietary fund types and similar Trust Funds for the year then ended, in conformity with generally accepted accounting principles applied on a basis consistent with that of the preceding year.

[Example 7]

As described in Note 1, the County does not maintain accounting records relating to the cost of general fixed assets it owns and, accordingly, a balance sheet for the general fixed asset account group, required by generally accepted accounting principles, is not included in the general purpose financial statements. Also as described in Note 1, the County has not included all of the financial activities of the Airport Authority in its general purpose financial statements in accordance with the provisions of Statement 3 of the National Council on Governmental Accounting. In our opinion, generally accepted accounting principles require that the financial activities of the Airport Authority be included in the accompanying general purpose financial statements of the County.

In our opinion, based upon our examination and the report of other auditors referred to above, except that the omission of the balance sheet of the general fixed asset account group results in an incomplete financial presentation, and except for the noninclusion of all of the financial activities of the Airport Authority, the accompanying general purpose financial statements present fairly the financial position of the County at December 31, 1983, and the results of its operations and the changes in financial position of its Enterprise Funds and Employees' Retirement Fund for the year then ended, in conformity with generally accepted accounting principles applied on a basis consistent with that of the preceding year.

[QUALIFICATION: METHOD OF ACCRUING REVENUES AND EXPENDITURES]

[Example 1]

As more fully explained in Note A–Property Taxes to the combined financial statements, the City has recognized property tax revenue and has included tax anticipation notes payable in the general, special revenue, and capital projects funds, and the collection/payment of these items is anticipated to be at least 60 days after September 30, 1983. In our opinion, generally accepted accounting principles require that such revenues be deferred and that such debt be classified as long-term debt.

In our opinion, except for the effects on the general, special revenue, and capital projects funds' financial statements of not deferring property tax revenue and of not classifying the debt as long-term, as discussed in the preceding paragraph, the combined financial statements referred to above present fairly the financial position of the City, at September 30, 1983, and the results of its operations and the changes in financial position of its proprietary fund types and similar trust funds for the year then ended, in conformity with generally accepted accounting principles applied on a basis consistent with that of the preceding year after giving retroactive effect to the changes, with which we concur, in the treatment of operating subsidies in certain funds and defining the reporting entity in enterprise fund type and general fixed assets account group as described in Note I.

[QUALIFICATION: LITIGATION]

[Example 1]

As discussed in Note 6 to the financial statements, the City, through its Board of Public Utilities, is involved in litigation concerning an alleged breach of a coal contract. No decision as to the amount of any damages has yet been rendered and, accordingly, the ultimate outcome of this litigation cannot presently be determined.

In our opinion, subject to the effect of the outcome of the matter referred to in the preceding paragraph, the combined financial statements referred to above present fairly the financial position of the City, as of June 30, 1984, and the results of its operations and the changes in the financial position of its proprietary and certain fiduciary fund types for the year then ended, in conformity with generally accepted accounting principles applied on a basis consistent with that of the preceding year after giving retroactive effect to the change (with which we concur) in accounting for compensated absences and claims and judgments, as discussed in Note 3 to the combined financial statements.

[Example 2]

The City is currently defendant in a number of claims and lawsuits as described in note J to the financial statements. The final outcome of such claims and lawsuits, described by the City Attorney as "reasonably possible" loss contingencies, is not presently determinable, and no provision has been made in the financial statements for the effect, if any, of such litigation.

In our opinion, based upon our examination and the reports of other auditors, subject to the effects of such adjustments, if any, as might have been required had the ultimate outcome of the matter discussed in the preceding paragraph been known, the aforementioned combined financial statements present fairly the financial position of the City at December 31, 1983, and the results of its operations and the changes in financial position of its proprietary fund types for the year then ended, in conformity with generally accepted accounting principles which, except for the change, with which we concur, in the method of recognizing amusement tax revenue as described in note B to the financial statements, have been applied on a basis consistent with that of the preceding year.

[Example 3]

The City is currently defendant in certain lawsuits as described in note 19. The final outcome of these suits is not presently determinable and, accordingly, no provision has been made in the financial statements for the effect, if any, of such litigation.

In our opinion, subject to the effects on the combined financial statements of such adjustments, if any, as might have been required had the outcome of the uncertainties discussed in the preceding paragraph been known, the aforementioned combined financial statements present fairly the financial position of the City at June 30, 1984, and the results of its operations

and the changes in financial position of its proprietary and certain fiduciary funds for the year then ended, in conformity with generally accepted accounting principles applied on a basis consistent with that of the preceding year after giving retroactive effect to the changes, with which we concur, in the methods of accounting for accrued vacation and special assessments revenue as described in note 2. Also, subject to the effects on the combining, individual fund and account group financial statements of such adjustments, if any, as might have been required had the outcome of the uncertainties discussed in the preceding paragraph been known, in our opinion the aforementioned combining, individual fund, and account group financial statements present fairly the financial position of the individual funds and account groups of the City at June 30, 1984, and the results of operations of such funds and the changes in financial position of the individual proprietary and certain fiduciary funds for the year then ended, in conformity with generally accepted accounting principles applied on a basis consistent with that of the preceding year after giving retroactive effect to the changes, with which we concur, in the methods of accounting for accrued vacation and special assessments revenue as described in note 2.

[Example 4]

As discussed in Note 9C to the financial statements, a disputed arbitration award and resulting litigation is pending between the City and the Fire Fighters Local 731. The ultimate outcome of this action cannot presently be determined.

In our opinion, subject to the effects on the financial statements of such adjustments, if any, as might have been required had the outcome of the uncertainty referred to in the preceding paragraph been known, the combined financial statements referred to above present fairly the financial position of the City at June 30, 1984, and the results of its operations and the changes in financial position of its proprietary fund types for the years then ended, in conformity with generally accepted accounting principles which have been applied on a basis consistent with that of the preceding year. Also, in our opinion, the combining, individual fund and account group financial statements referred to above, present fairly the financial position of the individual funds and account groups of the City at June 30, 1984, and the results of operations of such funds and the changes in financial position of the individual proprietary funds for the year then ended, in conformity with generally accepted accounting principles which have been applied on a basis consistent with that of the preceding year.

[Example 5]

In our report dated October 28, 1983, our opinion on the above financial statements was unqualified. As discussed in Note "O", the City is subject to a class action lawsuit which was filed in 1983 and decided against the City in 1984 for refund of parking citations paid during the period 1976 to 1980. The ultimate outcome of this lawsuit cannot presently be determined, and no provision for any liability that may result has been made in the financial statements of the Parking Enterprise Fund. Accordingly, our present opinion concerning the financial statements of the Parking Enterprise Fund, as expressed herein, is different from that expressed in our previous report.

In our opinion, the combined financial statements referred to above present fairly the financial position of the City, as of September 30, 1984, and the results of its operations and the changes in financial position of its proprietary, nonexpendable trust and pension trust funds for the year then ended, in conformity with generally accepted accounting principles applied on a consistent basis. Also, in our opinion, subject to the effects on the financial statements of the Parking Enterprise Fund of such adjustments, if any, as might have been required had the outcome of the uncertainty referred to in the preceding paragraph been known, the combining, individual fund and account group financial statements referred to above present fairly the financial position of the individual funds and account groups of the City, as of September 30, 1984 and 1983, and the results of operations of such funds and the changes in financial position of the individual proprietary, nonexpendable trust and pension trust funds for the years then ended, in conformity with generally accepted accounting principles applied on a consistent basis.

[Example 6]

As discussed in the first paragraph of Note 8, the City is involved in litigation which alleges that it inaccurately represented the capacity of its ocean outfall line in its contract with [the] County. The City has counterclaimed for damages.

In our opinion, subject to the effect of such adjustments, if any, as might have been required had the outcome of the litigation referred to in the preceding paragraph been known, the combined financial statements referred to above present fairly the financial position of the City at September 30, 1983, and the results of its operations and the changes in financial position of its proprietary fund types for the year then ended, in conformity with generally accepted accounting prin-

ciples applied on a basis consistent with that of the preceding year.

[QUALIFICATION: INTERNAL CONTROL LIMITATION]

[Example 1]

Because of the inadequacy of accounting records and controls in the Proprietary Fund type—Enterprise Fund (Bureau of Sewage)—I was unable to form an opinion regarding the amount of accounts receivable at December 31, 1983. The 1982 financial statements were examined by other auditors who, for similar reasons, did not express an opinion on the Proprietary Fund Type—Enterprise Fund (Bureau of Sewage).

In my opinion, except for the departure from generally accepted accounting principles discussed in the second paragraph, and subject to the effects of such adjustments, if any, as might have been determined to be necessary if the Bureau of Sewage records were adequate, the combined financial statements referred to in the first paragraph present fairly the financial position of the City at December 31, 1983, and the results of its operations and the changes in financial position of its proprietary fund type for the year then ended, in conformity with generally accepted accounting principles. Also, in my opinion, the combining and individual fund financial statements referred to above, except for the statements of the Proprietary Fund Type–Enterprise Fund (Bureau of Sewage), present fairly the financial position of the individual funds of the City at December 31, 1983, and their results of operations for the year then ended, in conformity with generally accepted accounting principles. I do not express an opinion on the financial statements of the Proprietary Fund Type–Enterprise Fund (Bureau of Sewage) at December 31, 1983, or for the year then ended.

[QUALIFICATION: OTHER]

[Example 1]

In our opinion, except for the accounts of [The] Economic Development Corporation, the general purpose financial statements referred to above present fairly the financial position of the fund types and account groups of the City at December 31, 1983, and the results of operations of such funds types the changes in financial position of all Proprietary and certain Fiduciary fund types for the year then ended, in conformity with generally accepted accounting principles applied on a basis consistent with that of the preceding year, after restatement for the change in accounting for vacation pay and the change in composition of the entity, with which we concur, as more fully described in Note C to the general purpose financial statements.

[Example 2]

As described in Note 7 to the financial statements, the City funds and provides for medical claims of covered employees in the Health and Medical Benefits Fund, an expendable trust fund, as claims are reported, which is the City's budgetary policy. Accordingly, claims which have been incurred but not reported have not been funded or provided for as required by generally accepted accounting principles.

In our opinion, except for the item discussed in the preceding paragraph, the general purpose financial statements referred to above present fairly the financial position of the City, at June 30, 1984, and the results of its operations and changes in financial position of its proprietary fund and similar funds for the year then ended. Also, in our opinion, except for the item discussed in the second paragraph, the combining, individual fund and account group financial statements referred to above present fairly the financial position of the individual proprietary fund and similar funds for the year then ended. Also, in our opinion, except for the item discussed in the preceding paragraph, all of the financial statements referred to above have been prepared in conformity with generally accepted accounting principles applied on a consistent basis after restatement for the change, with which we concur, in the method of accounting for Special Assessment Fund revenues and expenditures as explained in Notes 1J and 8 to the financial statements.

[MULTIPLE QUALIFICATION: VARIOUS]

[Example 1]

A) The County has not maintained complete and adequate records of historical cost of its general fixed assets (stated at $237,134,054) and, accordingly, we were unable to satisfy ourselves as to the carrying amount of general fixed assets. The scope of our work was not sufficient to enable us to express, and we do not express, an opinion on the general fixed asset account group. In addition, substantial general fixed assets acquired prior to 1972 are carried at appraised values, a practice that is at variance with generally accepted accounting principles.

B) As more fully discussed in the first two paragraphs of Note 23 to the combined financial statements, the County is the defendant in two lawsuits. The ultimate outcome of the lawsuits cannot presently be determined, and no provision for liability, if any, that may result has been made in the financial statements.

In our opinion, subject to the effects of such adjustments, if any, on the financial statements of the Combined–General Funds and Combined–Special Revenue Funds, as might have been required had the outcome of the uncertainty referred to in paragraph B) above been known, the combined financial statements, other than the general fixed asset account group, as listed in the Table of Contents on Page II-1, present fairly the financial position of [the] County, at September 30, 1983, and the results of its operations and the changes in financial position of its proprietary fund types for the year then ended, in conformity with generally accepted accounting principles applied on a basis consistent with that of the preceding year after giving retroactive effect to the change, with which we concur, in the method of accounting for the operations of the Public Building Corporation as described in Note 13 to the financial statements.

[Example 2]

As described more fully in Note 1, the combined financial statements referred to above do not include financial statements of the Health Facilities Fund. The financial statements of the Health Facilities are the subject of a separate audit by the County Auditor; the audit of the Health Facilities Fund for the fiscal year ended December 4, 1983, has not been completed as of this date.

As explained in Note 1, the combined financial statements mentioned above do not include financial statements of the General Fixed Asset Account Group, which should be included to conform with generally accepted accounting principles.

As described in Note 8 to the combined financial statements, the County provides for pension costs in accordance with State Statutes; this provision is less than the amount required by generally accepted accounting principles.

In our opinion, except for the omission of financial statements of the Health Facilities Fund and the General Fixed Asset Account Group, and the provision for pension costs, as noted in paragraphs 2, 3 and 4 above, the combined financial statements referred to above present fairly the financial position of [the] County, at December 4, 1983, and the results of its operations for the year then ended, in conformity with generally accepted accounting principles applied on a basis consistent with that of the preceding year.

[Example 3]

The combined financial statements referred to above do not include financial statements for the general fixed asset group of accounts, which should be included to conform with generally accepted accounting principles.

In our opinion, except for the effects of the omission of the general fixed asset group of accounts and the inclusion of tax titles as currently available assets, the aforementioned combined financial statements present fairly the financial position of the City as of June 30, 1984, and the results of operations and changes in financial position for the year then ended, in conformity with generally accepted accounting principles applied on a basis consistent with that of the preceding year.

[Example 4]

As described in Note 1, the records of the general fixed assets group of accounts were incomplete as to details concerning the various properties and equipment. We were unable to satisfy ourselves by appropriate audit tests or by other means as a result of such incomplete records and, therefore, we are unable to express an opinion on the accompanying financial statements of the general fixed asset group of accounts.

Our opinion expressed elsewhere herein is qualified concerning the enterprise funds, Board of Water Supply and Parking Authority, as follows: (i) A substantial portion of the revenues of the Parking Authority consists of coin collections from meters and accordingly, it was not practicable to extend our audit with respect to such revenues beyond the amounts received. (ii) As discussed in Note 3 to the financial statements, the Parking Authority is a defendant in lawsuits alleging personal injuries due to negligence. The Authority's counsel is unable to evaluate the ultimate outcome and no provision for any liability that may result has been made in the financial statements of the Parking Authority. (iii) As described in Note 1, the Board of Water Supply does not follow generally accepted accounting principles concerning the recording of property and equipment and related depreciation.

In our report dated May 10, 1983, relating to the financial statements for the year ended December 31, 1982, our opinion was qualified as to the method of recording the city-wide retirement liabilities. Under the latest conventions regarding generally accepted accounting principles, this method (described in Note 2) is now acceptable. Accordingly, our present opinion on the 1982 financial statements, as presented herein, is different from that expressed in our previous report.

In our opinion, the general purpose financial statements referred to above present fairly the financial position of each of the fund types and general long-term debt group of accounts of the City at December 31, 1983 and 1982, and the results of operations of such

fund types and the changes in financial position of the proprietary fund types for the years then ended; and the combining, individual fund and long-term debt group of accounts financial statements referred to above present fairly the financial position of the individual funds and the general long-term debt group of accounts of the City at December 31, 1983 and 1982, the results of operations of such funds and the changes in financial position of the individual proprietary funds for the years then ended, all in conformity with generally accepted accounting principles applied on a consistent basis, after considering the following qualifications concerning the enterprise funds, Board of Water Supply and Parking Authority: (i) except for the effect of the method of recording Board of Water Supply property and equipment and related depreciation; (ii) except for the effects of any adjustments had the coin collection of the Parking Authority been susceptible to audit; and (iii) subject to the effects of such adjustments, if any, as might have been determined to be necessary had the outcome of uncertainties described above been known.

[Example 5]

As described more fully in Note 1, the combined financial statements referred to above do not include financial statements of the Special Assessment Fund, which should be included to conform with generally accepted accounting principles.

The City has not maintained a complete record of its general fixed assets or the historical cost thereof. The City's records are not such as to permit us to apply adequate alternative procedures to satisfy ourselves regarding the general fixed assets or the costs thereof.

In our opinion, except that the omission of the Special Assessment Funds financial statements described in the second preceding paragraph results in an incomplete presentation, the combined financial statements referred to above present fairly the financial position of the fund types and general long-term debt account group of City at April 30, 1984, and the results of its operations and as to the proprietary fund types and pension and nonexpendable trust funds, the changes in their financial positions for the year ended, in conformity with generally accepted accounting principles applied on a basis consistent with that of the preceding year. Since, as discussed in the preceding paragraph, we were unable to satisfy ourselves as to the general fixed assets, the scope of our work was not sufficient to enable us to express, and we do not express, an opinion on the general fixed assets account group included in the combined balance sheet. Also, in our opinion, the combining and individual fund financial statements referred to above present fairly the financial position of the individual funds of the City at April 30, 1984, and the results of operations of such funds and the changes in the financial position of individual proprietary and pension and nonexpendable trust funds for the year then ended, in conformity with generally accepted accounting principles applied on a basis consistent with that of the preceding year.

[Example 6]

The City utilizes the *Uniform System of Accounts for Cities,* as mandated by the State for financial record-keeping and reporting. These accounting principles differ in some degree from generally accepted accounting principles. Accordingly, the accompanying financial statements do not present either financial position or results of operations in conformity with generally accepted accounting principles to the extent disclosed in Note 2 of the Notes to Financial Statements.

The Uniform System of Accounts for Cities has been amended by the State in certain areas in order to comply with generally accepted accounting principles with respect to the accounting and reporting for general fixed assets, bond anticipation notes, compensated absences, and retirement. The City has not adopted the required changes. Accordingly, the accompanying financial statements do not fully present either financial position or results of operations in conformity with the *Uniform System of Accounts for Cities* to the extent described in Note 3 of the Notes to Financial Statements.

Revenues and expenditures of the Hospital Fund are understated by $20,000 for the year ended December 31, 1982. The amount represents a deposit for a lease of a former Hospital. The deposit was from monies not recorded as revenues and the disbursement was not made in accordance with the requirements of Article VII, Section 93, of the City Charter.

In our opinion, based on our examination and the report of other auditors, except for the matters discussed in Notes 2 and 3, the financial statements present fairly the financial position of the various funds and account groups of the City at December 31, 1983 and 1982, and the results of operations of such funds for the years then ended in conformity with generally accepted accounting principles, the *Uniform System of Accounts for Cities,* grant agreements, and *OMB Circular A-87* applied on a consistent basis, except for the change, with which we concur, in the method of providing accruals of salaries and wages and social security as described in Note 4 of the Notes to Financial Statements.

[Example 7]

As described in Note 10, the City changed its accounting for compensated absences in 1983 to include the accrual whereas previously no accrual was made.

As described in Note 9, the 1982 contributions to the pension plans of the General and Enterprise Funds were as required by actuarial studies but were not in amounts sufficient to provide pension expense as required by generally accepted accounting principles.

In our opinion, except for the effects on the 1982 General Fund and Enterprise Fund financial statements of the matters referred to in the third paragraph, the combined financial statements referred to above present fairly the financial position of the City at September 30, 1983 and 1982, and the results of its operations and the changes in financial position of its proprietary fund types and similar trust funds for the years then ended, in conformity with generally accepted accounting principles applied on a consistent basis after giving cumulative effect to the change, with which we concur, in the method of accounting for compensated absences as described in the second paragraph. Also, in our opinion, except for the effects on the 1982 General Fund and Enterprise Fund financial statements of the matters referred to in the third paragraph, the combining, individual fund and account group financial statements referred to above present fairly the financial position of the individual funds of the City at September 30, 1983 and 1982, their results of operations, and the changes in financial position of individual proprietary funds for the years then ended, in conformity with generally accepted accounting principles applied on a consistent basis after giving cumulative effect to the change, with which we concur, in the method of accounting for compensated absences as described in the second paragraph.

[Example 8]

As described more fully in Notes 2 and 3 to the financial statements, the combined statements referred to above do not include the financial statements of the Firemen's and Police Pension Funds, the operations of the Civic Center and the group of accounts for general fixed assets, which should be included to conform with generally accepted accounting principles.

The City prepares its annual budget and makes expenditures on the basis of the current-year property tax levy. Accordingly, it is the City's policy to recognize property tax revenues in the year in which they are levied. National Council on Governmental Accounting Interpretation 3, "Revenue Recognition—Property Taxes," requires property tax levies be recognized as revenue only to the extent they are available to pay liabilities of the current period. As described more fully in Note 5 to the financial statements, the City's noncompliance with generally accepted accounting principles results in an overstatement of total fund equity at December 31, 1983 of $17,570,130 ($12,371,326 in the Corporate Fund) and an overstatement of total 1983 general property tax revenues of $495,207 ($137,946 in the Corporate Fund).

As described more fully in Note 14 to the financial statements, it is the City's policy to recognize revenue from special assessments in the year in which the assessments are levied. National Council on Governmental Accounting Statement 1, "Governmental Accounting and Financial Reporting Principles," requires revenues be recognized when they become available to finance expenditures of the current period. The City's noncompliance with generally accepted accounting principles results in an overstatement of Special Assessment Fund equity at December 31, 1983, of approximately $1,484,000 and an overstatement of 1983 special assessment revenues of approximately $144,000.

In our opinion, except for the incomplete presentation resulting from the omission of those financial statements described in the second paragraph and the effects of not accounting for the recognition of general property tax revenues and special assessment revenues in accordance with generally accepted accounting principles as described in the third and fourth paragraph, the combined financial statements referred to above present fairly the financial position of the City at December 31, 1983, and the results of its operations for the year then ended, in conformity with generally accepted accounting principles, which, except for the change, with which we concur, in the method of accounting for compensated absences as required by National Council on Governmental Accounting Statement 4 as explained in Note 8 to the financial statements, have been applied on a basis consistent with that of the preceding year.

[Example 9]

The financial statements of the Response Incorporated Fund and Parking Authority Revenue Fund have not been included. The financial statements of these funds were examined by other independent auditors.

The City has not maintained a record of its general fixed assets and accordingly a statement of general fixed assets, required by generally accepted accounting principles, is not included in the financial report.

Also, the City has excluded from property and debt in the accompanying Combined Balance Sheets certain

lease obligations, discussed in Note 2 to the financial statements, which in our opinion are material and should be capitalized in order to conform with generally accepted accounting principles. In accordance with the City's decision not to capitalize these leases, the extensive calculations needed to determine the effect on property, debt and income were not performed.

As more fully described in Note 3 to the financial statements, the City has underprovided for the cost of certain pension plans. In our opinion, generally accepted accounting principles require provision of at least the minimum amounts prescribed by Accounting Principles Board Opinion No. 8.

In addition, as more fully described in Note 4 to the financial statements, the City at December 31, 1983, reflected advances to the Parking Authority of the City of $1,789,000. The ultimate recoverability of the advances cannot presently be determined.

In our opinion, except for the effects of not capitalizing lease obligations, the absence of a Statement of General Fixed Assets, and underproviding pension costs, as stated previously, and subject to the effects, if any, resulting from the ultimate resolution of the uncertainty as to the recoverability of the advances, as discussed in the preceding paragraph, the financial statements listed in the aforementioned index present fairly the financial position of the fund types and account groups of the City as of December 31, 1983, and the results of their operations, the changes in fund balances of such fund types and changes in financial position of proprietary fund types and similar trust funds for the year then ended in conformity with generally accepted accounting principles applied on a basis consistent with that of the preceding year. The other financial information appearing on Pages 17 to 24 has been subjected to the same auditing procedures and, in our opinion, is stated fairly in all material respects when considered in conjunction with the basic financial statements taken as a whole.

[Example 10]

The County Comptroller's report dated February 24, 1984, on the other combined financial statements (Exhibits X-2 to X-5) and applicable notes (Exhibit X-6) is on page 13. We did not perform auditing procedures related to these combined financial statements.

As more fully described in Note 1G to the combined financial statements, the County does not have complete financial records to support the amounts included in its General Fixed Assets Account Group. Accordingly, we were unable to examine sufficient evidential matter to support such amounts.

As described in Note 3 to the combined financial statements, the County has reported $26,397,000 in the General Fund as "due from towns and cities" and revenue in 1983 and prior years related to excess sales tax credits given by the County against real property taxes due from taxpayers in certain towns and cities. The County expects to recover this amount from future property taxes. In our opinion, under generally accepted accounting principles, this amount should not be recognized at December 31, 1983, since it will not be available as revenue until 1984 or later.

As more fully discussed in Note 14A to the combined financial statements, there are significant claims pending and other claims may be asserted related to (i) matters brought before the State Human Rights Commission by certain labor unions and others based on the theory of "comparable worth," and (ii) alleged malpractice and other matters occurring at the County Medical Center (Medical Center), which is part of the County's Enterprise Funds. The ultimate outcome of these matters cannot be determined at this time.

In our opinion, except for the effect of recognizing excess sales tax credits in 1983 and prior years in the General Fund Balance Sheet, as discussed in the fourth paragraph, and subject to the effects of such adjustments, if any, as might have been required had the outcome of the uncertainties discussed in the fifth paragraph been known, the combined balance sheets referred to above present fairly the financial position of the fund types and General Long-Term Obligations Account Group of the County at December 31, 1983, in conformity with generally accepted accounting principles applied on a basis consistent with that of the preceding year except for the changes (applied retroactively for Enterprise Funds), with which we concur, in accounting for bond anticipation notes, compensated absences liabilities, and pension liabilities as described in Note 2. For the reason discussed in the third paragraph, we do not express an opinion on the General Fixed Assets Account Group.

[Example 11]

2. The County does not maintain sufficient records of its general fixed assets and, accordingly, a statement of general fixed assets, required by generally accepted accounting principles, is not included in the accompanying financial statements.

3. Revenues and expenditures in the Hotel/Motel Tax, Veterans' Trust and Industrial Center Fund were not budgeted for in 1983 and certain Special Revenue Funds are budgeted on a fiscal year to coincide with the fiscal year of the State. Therefore, the accompanying financial statements for the Special Revenue Funds do not include a comparison with a formal budget, as required by generally accepted accounting principles.

4. The report of other auditors disclosed that the Community Hospital is contesting certain settlements proposed by third-party payors. The collectibility of certain accounts receivable related to these contested settlements cannot be determined at this time.

5. In our opinion, based upon our examination and the aforementioned reports of other independent auditors, except for the effects of such adjustments and disclosures as might have been required had we been able to obtain sufficient competent evidential matter with respect to the items mentioned in paragraphs 2 and 3 above and subject to the effects, if any, of such adjustments as might have been required had the ultimate resolution of the matter referred to in paragraph 4 been known, the General Purpose Financial Statements referred to above present fairly the financial position of the various fund types and account group of the County as of December 31, 1983, and results of their operations and the changes in financial position of the proprietary fund types and similar trust funds, for the year then ended, in conformity with generally accepted accounting principles, applied on a consistent basis after giving effect to the changes in the method of accounting for compensated absences, with which we concur.

[Example 12]

The City has maintained only a partial record of its general fixed assets and, accordingly, a Statement of General Fixed Assets, required by generally accepted accounting principles, is not included in the accompanying combined financial statements.

As described in Note 1(C), the City does not accrue revenue currently for sales taxes collected by the state, property taxes collected by the county and payments in lieu of taxes to which the City is legally entitled but does not receive in cash in the current fiscal year. Had such revenues been recognized currently, as required by generally accepted accounting principles, the fund balance in the General Fund would have been increased $3,982,000 at December 31, 1983. Fund revenue in the General Fund would have been increased $42,000 for the year then ended December 31, 1983.

As described in Note 10, the accrual of pension costs with respect to the Police and Firemen's Pension Trust Fund is not in accordance with generally accepted accounting principles.

As described in Note 1(G), capital outlays prior to 1981 in Internal Service Funds were recorded as expenditures. Under generally accepted accounting principles such outlays should have been capitalized and depreciated over their estimated useful lives. It is not practical to determine the amount of such assets which should be recorded as of December 31, 1983, or the related depreciation expense for the year then ended.

As described in Note 1(C), encumbrances are recorded as expenditures or expenses at the time the commitment is made in all funds of the City. Such practice is not in accordance with generally accepted accounting principles, which require that such items be recorded as expenditures or expenses in the period in which the related benefit is realized. Beginning in 1983, the General Fund changed its methods of accounting for encumbrances to conform with generally accepted accounting principles (Note 2). However, the financial statements have not been restated to reflect the change in the method of accounting on the General Fund as the effect is not readily determinable.

In our opinion, except for the effect of the matters discussed in paragraphs two through six above, the combined financial statements referred to above present fairly the financial position of the City at December 31, 1983, and the results of its operations and the changes in financial position of its proprietary fund types and Pension Trust Funds for the year then ended, in conformity with generally accepted accounting principles applied on a basis consistent with that of the preceding year, except for the change in the method of accounting for encumbrances in the General Fund and after restatement for the change, with which we concur, in the method of accounting for compensated absences as described in Note 2 to the financial statements.

[Example 13]

The County does not maintain sufficient records of its general fixed assets to allow for the preparation of financial statements for the account group. Inclusion of such financial statements in the County's financial statements is, in our opinion, required by generally accepted accounting principles and the omission of such information results in an incomplete presentation of the County's financial statements.

As discussed in Note H to the financial statements, significant accounts receivable balances in the Revolving Water Fund remain uncollected and the municipalities that owe these amounts have questioned the validity of such obligations. The ultimate outcome of this matter and, accordingly, the collectibility of such balances and the recoverability of the County's investment cannot presently be determined, and no al-

lowance for any loss that may result has been made in the financial statements of the Revolving Water Fund.

Because of the possible material effect on the financial statements of the Revolving Water Fund of the matter referred to in the third paragraph, we express no opinion on the financial statements of the Revolving Water Fund.

In our opinion, based on our examination and the report of other auditors referred to in the first paragraph, except for the omission of the financial statements referred to in the second paragraph, the general purpose financial statements referred to above other than those of the Revolving Water Fund present fairly the financial position of the fund types and the general long-term debt account group of the County at December 31, 1983, and the results of operations of such fund types and the changes in financial position of the Proprietary Fund Types for the year then ended, in conformity with generally accepted accounting principles applied on a basis consistent with that of the preceding year after giving retroactive effect to the change, with which we concur, in the recognition of compensated absences as described in Note M to the financial statements.

[Example 14]

As described in Note 1 to the notes to financial statements, two accounting policies followed in the Municipal Water and Sewer Systems differ from generally accepted accounting principles. Depreciation expense has been recorded on the basis of a required percentage of revenues rather than on the basis of the cost of the water plan and sewer plant in service. The amount and the effect on the financial statements of this departure from generally accepted accounting principles are not reasonably determinable. In addition, the annual provision for principal redemptions of the Waterworks Refunding Revenue Bonds and the Sewer Refunding Revenue Bonds, required by the related City ordinance, is presented in the combining statement of revenues, expenses and changes in retained earnings for all enterprise funds as a direct charge against income rather than a direct appropriation of retained earnings. If such provision had been presented as a direct appropriation of retained earnings, net income for 1983 for the Water and Sewer Systems would have been increased by $206,058 and $219,623, respectively.

As described in Note 9, the Advertising and Tourist Promotion Commission has pledged the proceeds from the first 2% of the 3% Hotel and Restaurant Gross Receipts Tax as security on the City Taxable Revenue Bond Series 1982. On May 1, 1984, the Commission was informed that the guarantee on the bond issue will be exercised, wholly or in part, for the payment due on May 1, 1984. The Commission has evaluated the criteria for accruing contingent liabilities and has accrued the bond payment due May 1, 1984, as a current liability on its balance sheet as reflected at Statement F-1. The amount accrued of $344,693 has been reflected as a deferred expense and will be charged to income in 1984. As further discussed in Note 9, the Commission has a contingent liability for the interest due November 1, 1984, of approximately $140,000 plus bond principal in 1985 and thereafter totaling $2,800,000. The interest due in 1985 through 1998 is not determinable at present due to a fluctuating interest rate.

In our opinion, except for the effects of the departures from generally accepted accounting principles, as described in the second paragraph of this report, and subject to the effects, if any, of the eventual outcome of the material contingent liability discussed in the preceding paragraph, the combined financial statements referred to above present fairly the financial position of the City at December 31, 1983, and the results of its operations and changes in financial position of its proprietary fund types and similar trustee funds for the year then ended, in conformity with generally accepted accounting principles applied on a basis consistent with that of the preceding year. Also, in our opinion, except for the effects of the departures from generally accepted accounting principles, as described in the second paragraph and subject to the effects, if any, of the eventual outcome of the material contingent liability discussed in the preceding paragraph, the combining and individual fund financial statements referred to above present fairly the financial position of the individual fund of the City, at December 31, 1983, their results of operations and changes in financial position of the individual proprietary and trustee funds for the year then ended, in conformity with generally accepted accounting prinicples applied on a basis consistent with that of the preceding year.

equipment suppliers, who have filed counter-suit against the Authority and its engineers. The ultimate outcome of this litigation cannot presently be determined, and no provision for any settlement has been made in the financial statements at June 30, 1984. In addition, no provision has been made for any amount payable to or receivable from the U.S. Environmental Protection Agency in connection with grants for construction cost and related expenses. The ultimate amount payable to or receivable from the U.S. Environmental Protection Agency cannot presently be determined.

As more fully explained in Note N, the County Public Service Authority has entered into contracts with major users which require that certain costs be recovered through additional user charges. The Authority is involved in litigation to recover $1,655,655 of these charges. The collectibility of these charges is not determinable at this time and such charges are not included in these financial statements. In addition, other charges have not been recorded because the basis for the calculation has not been determined.

In our opinion, subject to the effects on the financial statements of such adjustments, if any, as might have been required had the outcome of the uncertainties referred to in the two immediately preceding paragraphs been known, and except that the omission of financial information described in the second paragraph of this report results in an incomplete presentation, the combined financial statements listed in the Table of Contents present fairly the financial position of the County at June 30, 1984, and the results of its operations and the changes in financial position of its proprietary fund types and nonexpendable trust funds for the year then ended, in conformity with generally accepted accounting principles applied on a basis consistent with that of the preceding year, after giving retroactive effect to several changes in accounting principles as described in Note B to the combined financial statements.

[Example 15]

The County has not maintained adequate records of its general fixed assets, and therefore information regarding general fixed assets and changes in general fixed assets required by generally accepted accounting principles, is not included in the accompanying financial statements.

As discussed in Note N, the County Public Service Authority is a plaintiff in a lawsuit relating to the construction of certain plant equipment and facilities. The Authority has filed suit against the contractor and

[Example 16]

The combined financial statements do not include financial statements of the General Fixed Asset Account Group, which should be included to conform with generally accepted accounting principles.

As discussed in note K to the financial statements, the County Road Commission has been named as defendant in several lawsuits in which the amount of damages claimed exceeds, or could exceed, insurance coverage by a material amount. The likelihood of a loss to the Road Commission resulting from these lawsuits cannot presently be determined. Accordingly, the Road Commission's independent auditors have qualified their opinion subject to the outcome of the lawsuits.

In our opinion, based upon our examination and the reports of other auditors, except that the omission of the financial statements described above results in an incomplete presentation, and subject to the effects on the financial statements of the Road Commission of the ultimate resolution of the matter discussed in the previous paragraph, the financial statements referred to above present fairly the financial position of the County at December 31, 1983, and the results of its operations and the changes in financial position of all proprietary and selected fiduciary fund types for the year then ended, in conformity with generally accepted accounting principles applied on a basis consistent with that of the preceding year except for the change, with which we concur, in the reporting entity as described in note B to the financial statements.

[Example 17]

The policy of Community College is to prepare its financial statements on the basis of regulatory accounting practices prescribed or permitted by the State. As described in note 1(b) to the combined financial statements, these practices differ in some respects from generally accepted accounting principles.

As described more fully in notes 10 and 13, no provision has been made in the accompanying combined financial statements for certain liabilities associated with current and prior periods' employees' compensation, and the County's self-insurance programs, as required by generally accepted accounting principles. The effect on the combined financial statements of not providing for such liabilities is not reasonably determinable.

In our opinion, except for the effect on the combined financial statements of the matters described in the two preceding paragraphs, based upon our examination and the report of other auditors, the aforementioned combined financial statements present fairly the financial position of the County at December 31, 1983, and the results of its operations, the changes in its fund balances and the changes in financial position of its proprietary fund type for the year then ended, in conformity with generally accepted accounting principles on a basis consistent with that of the preceding year after giving retroactive effect to the changes, with which we concur, in the reporting entity as described in note 1(a) and in the method of accounting for compensated absences as described in note 1(i).

TABLE 13-5. TIME ELAPSED BETWEEN THE CLOSE OF THE FISCAL YEAR AND THE DATE OF THE AUDITOR'S REPORT

Elapsed Time* (months)	Instances Observed (%)	Elapsed Time* (months)	Instances Observed (%)
1	2	7	1
2	19	8	1
3	31	9	1
4	23	10	1
5	13		
6	7	More than 10	<1

* Observations for those units having an auditor's report.

Chapter 14
Governmental Financial Statements

INTERIM AND ANNUAL FINANCIAL STATEMENTS

Governmental units have generally conformed to the pronouncements of the NCGA with respect to financial reporting. The NCGA has presecribed the following types of reports as appropriate for governmental units:

a. Interim financial statements and reports of financial position, operating results, and other pertinent information that are used to facilitate management control of financial operations, legislative oversight, and where necessary or desired, for external reporting purposes.
b. A comprehensive annual financial report (CAFR), covering all funds and account groups of the governmental unit, should include the general purpose financial statements (see 3 below); combining and individual fund statements; schedules to present greater detail for reported information and to demonstrate compliance with finance-related legal and contractual provisions; narrative explanations; and statistical tables.
c. General purpose financial statements (GPFS), including the basic five combined financial statements and the notes to the financial statements, are essential to fair presentation of financial position and operating results (and changes in financial position of proprietary funds and similar trust funds).

HIERARCHY OF FINANCIAL INFORMATION

The reporting systems of government are structured in a hierarchical pattern similar to those of commercial organizations. Supporting all reporting and financial statements must be a system for coding economic events having financial consequences and having consistent transaction relationships. Transactions must then be recorded in accounts to aggregate related information for analysis and reporting. The heirarchical structure of governmental reports includes, from the more detailed to the more general, (1) schedules, (2) individual fund and account group statements, (3) com-

bining statements, (4) combined statements, and (5) condensed and consolidated statements.

Schedules

Schedules are used to demonstrate compliance with finance-related legal requirements, to present other types of useful data, and to give details on the data summarized in higher-level financial statements. Schedules are not necessary in the annual financial report to meet the requirements for fair presentation in accordance with generally accepted accounting principles. However, when the financial statements make reference to the supporting schedules, these schedules should be included as part of the total report.

Table 14-1 highlights some of the supplementary data that were included by governmental units in the surveyed financial statements.

Individual Fund and Account Group Statements

For compliance with NCGA Statement 1, statements for individual funds and the two account groups (general fixed assets and general long-term debt) are required under two conditions: (1) A government unit has only one fund of a specific type, or (2) the combining financial statements do not present enough detail to ensure disclosure sufficient to meet CAFR reporting objectives.

Combining Statements

Combining statements refer to balance sheets; statements of fund revenues, expenditures (or expenses), and changes in fund balances (or retained earnings); and statements of changes in financial position. Combining statements are used to show the accounts of two or more individual funds of a given fund type.

The total columns of combining statements should agree with the amounts presented in the general purpose financial statements. The NCGA views combining statements as the link between the general purpose financial statements and the individual fund statements.

The governments surveyed frequently included combining financial statements for several fund types in the annual report, as shown in the following table.

Use of Combining Financial Statements by Surveyed Units	Instances Observed (%)
Special revenue funds	74
Capital projects funds	54
Enterprise funds	53
Trust and agency funds	40
Debt service funds	33
Internal service funds	32
Trust funds only	30
Agency funds only	30
Special assessment funds	25

Combined Statements: The Overview

Five basic combined financial statements are usually required to present the financial position and results of operations of the governmental unit. The details of a combined statement show the totals of the various fund types (a fund type may comprise several individual funds) and account groups. The combined statements may include balance sheets; statements of revenues, expenditures (or expenses), and changes in fund balances (or retained earnings or equity); and statements of changes in financial position.

The combined statements show the overall summary financial information for all fund types and account groups and are supported or more fully described by the subordinate combining statements, individual fund and account group statements, and schedules.

CAFR AND GPFS

Governmental units prepare a comprehensive annual financial report, which provides for an accounting of all funds and account groups and includes

general purpose financial statements containing financial information for all fund types and the two recommended account groups, along with related footnotes;

combining financial statements by fund type; and

individual fund and account group financial statements.

The CAFR is the all-inclusive financial report of governmental units and includes introductory, supplementary, and statistical information and other supporting schedules to provide background information to demonstrate compliance with finance-related legal and contractual provisions. Exhibit 14-1 lists the NCGA-suggested content statements of the CAFR.

As mentioned in Chapter 1 and referred to in other chapters, the information reported in this survey was obtained principally from an analysis of the combined financial statements—the five financial statements and related footnotes that constitute the GPFS. These five statements are

the combined balance sheet;

the combined statement of revenues, expenditures, and changes in fund balances—governmental fund types;

the combined statement of revenues, expenditures, and changes in fund balances—budget and actual—governmental fund types;

the combined statement of revenues, expenses, and changes in retained earnings—proprietary fund types;

the combined statement of changes in financial position—proprietary fund types.

TOTAL COLUMNS

On combined statements there may be columns, referred to as *total columns,* that are stated to be for memorandum purposes only. These columns merely sum the columnar information by fund type and account group and may not have been adjusted for interfund and similar eliminations.

The AICPA, in its Statement of Position 80-2, is quite specific in its guidance concerning the use of these total columns in the combined statements for governmental units:

> If a total column is shown, it should be captioned "Memorandum" because a total column of a combined financial statement is not comparable to a consolidation. A note to the financial statement should disclose the nature of the column and should explain that it does not present consolidated financial information.

It should also be noted that the totals appearing in the memorandum columns do not appear in any of the accounts of the governmental unit. These amounts appear only on the combined financial statements.

Table 14-2 outlines the usage of "memorandum" total columns for the various combined financial statements included in the survey. Exhibit 14-2 contains excerpts from selected governmental financial statements relating to the purpose of such columns appearing in the government's financial statements.

CONSOLIDATED FINANCIAL STATEMENTS

Combined statements merely sum the data of the fund types and account groups and do not conform with the applicable corporate consolidated accounting practices, even when certain interfund eliminations are made. Although a few governments have experimented with consolidated and condensed financial statements, such methods of presentation are not presently considered to be in accordance with generally accepted accounting principles for governmental units.

The NCGA has encouraged research and experimentation with other forms of financial reporting. In this connection, some governmental units have published statements with financial data appearing in a highly condensed or consolidated format, significantly abbreviating or summarizing the information appearing in the CAFR for that particular government.

COMPONENT UNIT FINANCIAL STATEMENTS

The NCGA intended to limit the use of the CAFR and GPFS to financial statement presentations of the reporting entity as defined in NCGA Statement 3, "Defining the Governmental Reporting Entity." However, there may be a need for separate financial statements for a part of the reporting entity or a component unit. Statement 7, "Financial Reporting for Component Units Within the Governmental Reporting Entity," states that component unit financial statements (CUFS) require adequate disclosure that the unit or units presented is a part of a larger reporting entity.

Statement 7 also includes specific guidance related to the presentation of component unit data in a governmental unit's CAFR and GPFS. Statement 7 is to be applied to financial statements for fiscal years ending after June 30, 1984.

REPORTING FOR UNITS RECEIVING FEDERAL ASSISTANCE

Attachment P to Office of Management and Budget (OMB) Circular A-102 requires organization-wide ("single audit") audits of certain governmental units that received financial assistance and grants in excess of a threshold amount. The objective of organization-wide audits is to eliminate the need for the various federal agencies to conduct separate audits of their grants and contracts with an individual state or local governmental unit.

In the fall of 1984 the Single Audit legislation, which embraced the organization-wide audit concept of Attachment P, was enacted. The Single Audit Act and Attachment P require three different reports:

1. an auditor's report on the general purpose (or component unit) financial statements and on supplementary schedules of federal assistance, the basic financial statement, and a schedule of federal assistance showing the total receipts and expenditures for each federal assistance program;

2. an auditor's letter commenting on the study and evaluation of internal control performed as part of the financial and compliance audit, any material weaknesses noted, and other conditions identified, including the underlying causes for these weaknesses and, where appropriate, management responses to these comments;

3. an auditor's compliance letter containing (1) a statement of positive assurance for items tested with respect to compliance with applicable laws and grant regulations and negative assurance for untested items; (2) material instances and underlying reason for noncompliance, fraud abuse, or illegal acts found in connection with the compliance audit, including identification of total amounts questioned, if any; and (3) pertinent views of responsible government officials concerning audit findings, conclusions, and recommendations.

Exhibit 14-3 contains selected illustrations of three types of reports made under Attachment P of OMB Circular A-102.

STUDY OBSERVATIONS

Almost all the units surveyed prepared combined financial statements, although it appears that the nature of activities dictated the specific combined statements used by individual governments, as shown in the following table.

Type of Combined Financial Statements	Instances Observed (%)
Combined balance sheet	88
Combined statement of revenues, expenditures, and changes in fund balances—governmental fund types	85
Combined statement of revenues, expenditures, and changes in fund balances—budget and actual—governmental fund types	83
Combined statement of revenues, expenses, and changes in retained earnings—proprietary fund types	72
Combined statement of changes in financial position—proprietary fund types	70

A compilation was made of the types of supplementary schedules and other information included in the CAFR. Table 14-1 is a summary of the type of information provided to the public by many governments.

The total or memorandum column is unique to governmental and nonprofit financial statements. While the combined financial statements of many governments contained these total columns, not all the governments surveyed used this method of reporting, and there was a variance between governments as to whether the total column was included for one or two fiscal years. Table 14-2 contains details on those financial statements that displayed total columns.

Certain governments published other types of reports directed toward different users. Exhibit 14-2 contains selected excerpts from consolidated governmental financial statements. Exhibit 14-3 contains selected excerpts of reports of audits made in connection with OMB Circular A-102, Attachment P.

EXHIBITS AND TABLES FOR CHAPTER 14

Table 14-1. Information Included by Governmental Units Surveyed in Supplementary Data to Annual Financial Statements

Exhibit 14-1. Minimum Contents of a Comprehensive Annual Financial Report

Table 14-2. Use of Total or Memorandum Columns in Financial Statements

Exhibit 14-2. Illustrations of Consolidated Financial Statements

Exhibit 14-3. Illustrations of Reports under OMB Circular A-102, Attachment P

TABLE 14-1. INFORMATION INCLUDED BY GOVERNMENTAL UNITS SURVEYED IN SUPPLEMENTARY DATA TO ANNUAL FINANCIAL STATEMENTS

Nature of Subject Matter	Instances Observed (%)	Nature of Subject Matter	Instances Observed (%)
Miscellaneous statistics	45	Property tax rates, all overlapping governments, last ten fiscal years	33
Ratio of net general bonded debt of assessed value and net bonded debt for capital, last ten fiscal years	42	Property value, construction, and bank deposits, last ten fiscal years	27
Assessed and estimated actual values of taxable property, last ten fiscal years	41	Special assessments collection, last ten fiscal years	15
Property tax levies and collections, last ten fiscal years	41	Schedule of insurance in force	14
General government expenditures by function, last ten fiscal years	40	Tax revenues by source	11
Ratio of annual debt services for general bonded debt to total expenditures	39	Salaries and surety bonds of principal officials	10
		Debt service requirements to maturity	7
General revenues by sources, last ten fiscal years	39	Summary of debt service requirements to maturity	5
Computation of overlapping debt	38	Schedule of insurance coverage	4
Demographic statistics	36	Schedule of cash and investment balances	4
Principal taxpayers	36	Insurance in force	3
Computation of legal debt margin	34	Insurance coverage	3
		Schedule of interfund receivables and payables/transfers	3
		Analysis of current tax levy	3

EXHIBIT 14-1. MINIMUM CONTENTS OF A COMPREHENSIVE ANNUAL FINANCIAL REPORT

Introduction Section
Tables of contents, letter(s) of transmittal, and other material deemed appropriate by management.

Financial Section
A. Auditor's report
B. General purpose financial statements (combined statements—overview)
　1. Combined balance sheet—all fund types and account groups
　2. Combined statement of revenues, expenditures, and changes in fund balances—all governmental fund types
　3. Combined statement of revenues, expenditures, and changes in fund balances—budget and actual—general and special revenue fund types (and similar governmental fund types for which annual budgets have been legally adopted)
　4. Combined statement of revenues, expenses, and changes in retained earnings (or equity)—all proprietary fund types
　5. Combined statements of changes in financial position—all proprietary fund types
　6. Notes to the financial statements (Trust Fund operations may be reported in 2–5 above, as appropriate, or separately.)
C. Combining and individual fund and account group statements and schedules
　1. Combining statements, by fund type—where a governmental unit has more than one fund of a given fund type
　2. Individual fund and account group statements—where a governmental unit has only one fund of a given type and for account groups and/or where necessary to present prior year and budgetary comparisons
　3. Schedules
　　a. Schedules necessary to demonstrate compliance with finance-related legal and contractual provisions

　　b. Schedules to present information spread throughout the statements that can be brought together and shown in greater detail (e.g., taxes receivable—including delinquent taxes; long-term debt; investments; and cash receipts, disbursements, and balances)
　　c. Schedules to present greater detail for information reported in the statements (e.g., additional revenue sources detail and object of expenditure data by departments)

Statistical Section
A. General statistical information
　1. General governmental expenditures by function—last ten fiscal years
　2. General revenues by source—last ten fiscal years
　3. Property tax levies and collections—last ten fiscal years
　4. Assessed and estimated actual value of taxable property—last ten fiscal years
　5. Property tax rates—all overlapping governments—last ten fiscal years
　6. Special assessment collections—last ten fiscal years
　7. Ratio of net general bonded debt to assessed value and net bonded debt per capita—last ten fiscal years
　8. Computation of legal debt margin (if not presented in the GPFS)
　9. Computation of overlapping debt (if not presented in the GPFS)
　10. Ratio of annual debt service for general bonded debt total general expenditures—last ten fiscal years
　11. Revenue bond coverage—last ten fiscal years
　12. Demographic statistics
　13. Property value, construction, and bank deposits—last ten fiscal years
　14. Principal taxpayers
　15. Miscellaneous statistics

Source: Statement 1, "Governmental Accounting and Financial Reporting Principles," National Council on Governmental Accounting, Chicago, Illinois, March 1979.

TABLE 14-2. USE OF TOTAL OR MEMORANDUM COLUMNS IN FINANCIAL STATEMENTS

Statements Containing Memorandum Columns	Instances Observed (%) of Units with Totals	for Current and Past Year	for Current Year Only	Statements Containing Memorandum Columns	Instances Observed (%) of Units with Totals	for Current and Past Year	for Current Year Only
Combined balance sheet	73	59	41	Combined statement of revenues, expenses, and changes in retained earnings—proprietary fund types	46	64	36
Combined statement of revenues, expenditures, and changes in fund balances—governmental fund types	73	59	41	Combined statement of changes in financial position—proprietary fund types	47	65	35
Combined statement of revenues, expenditures, and changes in fund balances—budget and actual—governmental fund types	40	92	8				

EXHIBIT 14-2. ILLUSTRATIONS OF CONSOLIDATED FINANCIAL STATEMENTS

[CITY OF DALLAS, TEXAS]
REPORT OF CERTIFIED PUBLIC ACCOUNTANTS

The City Council
Dallas, Texas

Under the dates of January 27, 1984, and January 14, 1983, we have reported on the combined financial statements of the City of Dallas, Texas as of and for the years ended September 30, 1983 and 1982, respectively, and rendered our qualified opinions thereon. Our examinations were made in accordance with generally accepted auditing standards and, accordingly, included such tests of the accounting records and such other auditing procedures as we considered necessary in the circumstances.

Our examinations were made for the purpose of forming an opinion on the combined financial statements taken as a whole. The accompanying consolidated financial statements, which are presented for purposes of additional analysis, have been prepared on the basis of accounting practices, as more fully described in note 1, which differ from generally accepted accounting principles. Accordingly, the accompanying consolidated financial statements are not intended to present the financial position, results of operations and changes in financial position of the City of Dallas in conformity with generally accepted accounting principles.

As more fully described in note 5 to the combined financial statements, the City has not provided sufficient pension expense for certain pension plans as required by generally accepted accounting principles.

In our opinion, except for the effect of the matter referred to in the preceding paragraph, the accompanying consolidated financial statements, which have been subject to auditing procedures applied in the examinations of the combined financial statements, are presented fairly on the basis of accounting described in note 1, which basis has been applied consistently.

[Certified Public Accountants]
January 27, 1984
Dallas, Texas

Consolidated Balance Sheets (September 30, 1983 and 1982) [in thousands]

	1983	1982 Restated
Assets		
Current assets		
Cash and cash investments	$ 254,815	$ 182,172
Receivables (net of estimated uncollectible accounts)	58,291	56,202
Other current assets (principally current portion of cash and cash investments restricted for construction and debt service)	148,277	113,834
Total current assets	461,383	352,208
Restricted assets		
Cash, cash investments and other investments (principally for debt service requirements)	25,447	20,380
Customer deposits	2,563	6,560
Total restricted assets	28,010	26,940
Property, plant and equipment— Net of accumulated depreciation of $538,971 in 1983 and $495,290 in 1982	1,856,761	1,724,315
Other assets	9,155	5,748
Total assets	$2,355,309	$2,109,211
Liabilities and Municipal Equity		
Current liabilities		
Accounts payable and other accrued liabilities	$ 33,202	$ 29,552
Accrued vacation and sick leave	30,577	29,806
Total current liabilities	63,779	59,358
Current liabilities payable from restricted assets	49,650	55,828
Long-term bonded debt, contractual obligations, unfunded pension contributions and unfunded claims	919,572	716,244
Other liabilities	37,013	37,825
Total liabilities	1,070,014	869,255
Municipal equity		
Contributed equity	264,963	248,358
Retained earnings	544,332	508,238
Fund balance		
Reserved	105,502	76,745
Unreserved	370,798	406,615
Total municipal equity	1,285,295	1,239,956
Total liabilities and municipal equity	$2,355,309	$2,109,211

Consolidated Statements of Financial Activity (for the Years Ended September 30, 1983 and 1982) [in thousands]

	1983				1982 Restated
		Related Revenues			
	Total Costs	Intergovern- mental	Customer Charges and Other	Net Costs	Net Costs
General Government					
Mayor and Council	$ 474	$ —	$ —	$ 474	$ 429
City Manager	954	—	—	954	836
Support activities	95,669	19,104	26,261	50,334	40,559
General obligation debt service— interest	29,289	15,261	—	14,028	9,096
Public Safety					
Police	135,930	840	149	134,941	86,935
Fire	87,455	—	1,148	86,307	53,046
Other	10,755	208	1,195	9,352	5,633
Public Works					
Public Works	4,626	—	—	4,626	6,535
Streets and Sanitation	67,293	—	21,856	45,437	38,674
Human Resources					
Public Health	8,428	93	1,120	7,215	7,247
Human Services	8,078	7,796	—	282	(314)
Culture and Recreation					
Parks and Recreation	36,116	5	4,076	32,035	31,201
Library	13,731	1,101	238	12,392	12,098
Convention Center	15,283	—	12,557	2,726	5,845
Radio	792	—	1,043	(251)	(129)
Urban Development					
Housing	4,292	—	—	4,292	3,382
Public Utilities					
Water Utilities	107,782	—	133,799	(26,017)	(23,336)
Transportation					
Aviation	6,946	—	16,003	(9,057)	(6,881)
Transit	43,760	9,610	23,493	10,657	8,128
Surtran	4,380	33	3,727	620	780
Total	$682,063	$54,051	$246,665	$ 381,347	$ 279,764
Financed by:					
Taxes					
Ad valorem				178,818	157,202
Sales				83,529	77,647
Hotel occupancy				7,756	7,791
Other				52,725	48,213
Total taxes				322,828	290,853
Licenses and permits				1,395	1,160
Fines and forfeitures				18,242	15,405
Interest—unallocated				37,096	31,007
Intergovernmental revenues— unallocated				607	1,002
Other				22,612	17,320
Total financing				402,780	356,747
Excess of revenues over costs of operations				21,433	76,983
Municipal equity, October 1, as restated				1,239,956	1,149,259
Increase in contributions				23,906	13,714
Municipal equity, September 30				$1,285,295	$1,239,956

Consolidated Statements of Changes in Current Cash and Cash Investments (for the Years Ended September 30, 1983 and 1982) [in thousands]

	1983	1982 Restated
Resources Provided by Operations		
Excess of revenues over costs of operations	$ 21,433	$ 76,983
Add operating costs not requiring current resources—depreciation	49,861	54,491
Resources from operations	71,294	131,474
Other sources		
Bond proceeds	175,950	14,915
Increase in water supply and wastewater treatment obligations	339	119,356
Decrease in other assets	—	9,447
Increase in current liabilities	—	20,047
Increase in long-term bonded debt, contractual obligations, unfunded pension contributions, and unfunded claims	27,039	—
Increase in other liabilities	—	9,026
Increase in contributed capital	23,906	13,714
Total resources provided	298,528	317,979
Decrease in current liabilities	1,757	—
Decrease in other liabilities	812	—
Acquisition of property, plant and equipment	182,307	265,989
Decrease in long-term bonded debt and contractual obligations	—	42,021
Increase in restricted assets	1,070	2,036
Increase in other assets	3,407	—
Increase in receivables and other current assets	36,532	8,989
Total resources used	225,885	319,035
Increase (decrease) in current cash and cash investments	72,643	(1,056)
Cash and cash investments, October 1	182,172	183,228
Cash and cash investments, September 30	$254,815	$182,172

[SALT LAKE CITY, UTAH]
REPORT OF CERTIFIED PUBLIC ACCOUNTANTS

The Honorable Mayor and
  Members of the City Council
Salt Lake City Corporation

We have examined the general purpose financial statements of Salt Lake City Corporation at June 30, 1984 and 1983, and for each of the years then ended appearing in the City's Comprehensive Annual Financial Reports (not presented herein). In our reports, dated November 2, 1984, and October 28, 1983, we expressed our opinions that the general purpose financial statements mentioned above present fairly the financial position of Salt Lake City Corporation at June 30, 1984 and 1983, respectively, and the results of its operations and changes in financial position of its proprietary fund types for each of the years then ended, in conformity with generally accepted accounting principles applied on a basis consistent with that of preceding years.

The accompanying condensed statements of financial position of Salt Lake City Corporation at June 30, 1984 and 1983, and the related condensed statements of source and application of financial resources and net current operating expenditures for the years then ended have been derived from the general purpose financial statements on the basis described in Note 1 to these condensed financial statements. In order to summarize the overall financial position and results of operations of the City, these statements omit the classification of assets and liabilities into fund types and account groups and also reflect elimination of interfund and account group balances. Accordingly, the accompanying condensed financial statements are not intended to present financial position or results of operations in conformity with generally accepted accounting principles. In our opinion, the information set forth in the accompanying condensed financial statements is fairly stated in all material respects in relation to the general purpose financial statements from which it has been derived.

[Certified Public Accountants]
November 2, 1984
Salt Lake City, Utah

Condensed Statements of Financial Position (June 30, 1984 and 1983) [in thousands]

Assets	1984	1983	Liabilities and Municipal Equity	1984	1983
Current assets:			Current liabilities:		
Cash and temporary cash			Cash overdraft	$ —	$ 1,653
investments	$ 44,907	$ 36,377	Accounts payable	10,122	6,782
Receivables:			Accrued liabilities	8,639	13,548
Taxes	2,552	2,030	Total current liabilities	18,761	32,983
Airport, water and sewer service,			Liabilities payable from capital		
less allowance for losses of $378			restricted assets:		
($214 in 1983)	8,647	6,967	Cash overdraft	—	1,000
Loans for redevelopment activities	2,697	—	Accounts payable	1,608	412
Due from other governments	2,596	4,550	Unearned special assessments	4,380	4,977
Other	974	2,816	Total liabilities payable from capital		
Inventories of supplies	1,771	1,545	restricted assets	5,988	6,389
Other current assets, principally			Long-term liabilities (Note 3):		
temporary investment in land held			General obligation bonds	18,985	19,885
for resale	3,696	1,454	Redevelopment tax allocation bonds	10,000	11,500
Total current assets	67,840	55,739	Obligations under capital leases	3,910	3,350
Capital restricted assets, principally			Revenue bonds	93,418	90,533
under revenue bond agreements:			Accrued compensation (Note 1)	7,538	7;795
Cash and temporary cash			Other	817	1,300
investments	34,850	52,910	Total long-term liabilities	134,668	134,363
Receivables	4,648	889	Deferred contributions	2,115	1,229
Total capital restricted assets	39,498	53,799	Commitments and contingencies		
Property, plant and equipment at cost:			(Note 5)		
General fixed assets	45,784	44,693	Municipal equity (Note 2):		
Net enterprise fixed assets	230,507	210,117	For current operations	49,079	33,756
Net internal service fixed assets	10,756	10,143	For capital restricted operations	33,510	47,410
Total property, plant and equipment	287,047	264,953	Equity in property, plant and		
Other assets	1,698	1,734	equipment and other assets, less		
TOTAL ASSETS	$396,083	$376,225	related long-term liabilities and		
			deferred contributions	151,962	131,095
			Total municipal equity	234,551	212,261
			TOTAL LIABILITIES AND		
			MUNICIPAL EQUITY	$396,083	$376,225

Condensed Statements of Source and Application of Financial Resources (June 30, 1984 and 1983) [in thousands]

Current Operations	1984	1983
Revenues:		
Taxes (property, sales and franchise)	$ 57,888	$ 47,703
Charges for services	53,955	44,330
Intergovernmental revenues	15,466	10,387
Interest	9,928	8,012
Licenses, fines and forfeitures	4,651	5,635
Other	6,482	4,017
Total revenues	148,370	120,084
Expenditures and other uses:		
Current services:		
Payroll and fringe benefits (Note 4)	63,157	63,683
Contract services	29,247	19,501
Supplies and materials	9,948	9,234
Other	5,041	3,883
Debt service:		
Principal (Note 3)	6,488	4,256
Interest	8,703	7,949
Total operating expenditures	122,584	108,506
Transfer to capital-restricted operations	10,463	8,804
Total expenditures and other uses	133,047	117,310
Excess of revenues over expenditures and other uses, before extraordinary items	15,323	2,774
Extraordinary items (Note 6)	—	(4,241)
Excess of revenues over (under) expenditures and other uses	15,323	(1,467)
Net financial resources available for current operations:		
Beginning of the fiscal year	33,756	35,223
End of the fiscal year	49,079	33,756

Capital Restricted Operations	1984	1983
Financing and other sources:		
Proceeds of bonds and other long-term debt (Note 3)	$ 7,551	$ 37,190
Grants and conditions	11,536	8,783
Other	1,948	2,476
Total financing sources	21,035	48,449
Transfer from current operations	10,463	8,804
Total financing and other sources	31,498	57,253
Expenditures:		
Capital outlay	44,598	36,334
Other	800	910
Total expenditures	45,398	37,244
Excess of financing and other sources over (under) expenditures	(13,900)	20,009
Capital restricted operations resources:		
Beginning of fiscal year	47,410	27,401
End of fiscal year	33,510	47,410
EQUITY IN PROPERTY, PLANT AND EQUIPMENT AND OTHER ASSETS, LESS RELATED LONG-TERM LIABILITIES AND DEFERRED CONTRIBUTIONS	151,962	131,095
Total Municipal Equity, end of fiscal year	$234,551	$212,261

Net Current Operating Expenditures (June 30, 1984 and 1983) [in thousands]

	1984 Total Operating Expenditures	Charges for Services	Intergovernmental Revenues	Net Expenditures (Revenues)
Related Revenues—1984				
1984 Net Current Operating Expenditures:				
General government	$ 22,507	$ 2,733	$ 1,017	$18,757
Development services	18,442	522	7,708	10,212
Fire	12,653	83		12,570
Police	15,760	295	4,425	11,040
Parks	3,859	388	106	3,365
Highways and streets	10,894	54	2,125	8,715
Library	3,544		85	3,459
Water and sewer, including debt service	16,963	25,179		(8,216)
Airport, including debt service	16,375	22,932		(6,557)
Golf courses	1,587	1,769		(182)
	$122,584	$53,955	$15,466	$53,163

(continued)

[SALT LAKE CITY, UTAH] (Continued)

	Related Revenues—1983			
	1983 Total Operating Expenditures	Charges for Services	Intergovernmental Revenues	Net Expenditures (Revenues)
1983 Net Current Operating Expenditures:				
General government	$ 20,787	$ 738	$ 831	$19,218
Development services	10,511		2,945	7,566
Fire	12,841	41	34	12,766
Police	15,962	217	4,587	11,158
Parks	3,634	517	482	2,635
Highways and streets	10,188	44	1,508	8,636
Library	2,989			2,989
Water and sewer, including debt service	16,522	20,160		(3,638)
Airport, including debt service	13,788	21,003		(7,215)
Golf courses	1,284	1,610		(326)
	$108,506	$44,330	$10,387	$53,789

	1984	1983
Net Current Operating Expenditures	$53,163	$53,789
Sources of Support:		
Taxes	57,888	47,703
Other current operations revenue	21,061	17,664
Transfer to capital-restricted operations	(10,463)	(8,804)
Total sources of support	68,486	56,563
Excess of revenues over expenditures and other uses before extraordinary items (sources of support over net current operating expenditures)	$15,323	$ 2,774

[HENNEPIN COUNTY, MINNESOTA]
REPORT OF CERTIFIED PUBLIC ACCOUNTANTS

The Board of County Commissioners
Hennepin County, Minnesota:

We have examined the consolidated financial statements of Hennepin County, Minnesota, as of and for the years ended December 31, 1983 and 1982, as listed in the accompanying table of contents. Our examination were made in accordance with generally accepted auditing standards and, accordingly, included such tests of the accounting records and such other auditing procedures as we considered necessary in the circumstances.

As described in note 1, the consolidated financial statements were prepared on a basis that differs from the fund basis of accounting required by generally accepted accounting principles. Accordingly, the accompanying consolidated financial statements are not intended to present financial position and results of operations in conformity with generally accepted accounting principles.

In our opinion, the aforementioned consolidated financial statements of Hennepin County, Minnesota, present fairly the consolidated assets, liabilities and equity at December 31, 1983 and 1982, and the consolidated revenues, expenses and changes in equity, changes in cash and investments and the consolidated financial activity for the two years then ended, on the basis of accounting described in note 1, applied on a consistent basis after restatement for the changes, with which we concur, in the methods of accounting as described in note 7 to the financial statements.

[Certified Public Accountants]
May 4, 1984
Minneapolis, Minnesota

Consolidated Balance Sheets, December 31, 1983 and 1982

	1983	1982 (Restated— Note 7)		1983	1982 (Restated— Note 7)
ASSETS			*LIABILITIES AND EQUITY*		
Current Assets:			Current Liabilities:		
Unrestricted:			Payable from unrestricted assets:		
Cash and investments (note 1D)	$ 82,161,880	$ 81,967,697	Warrants and accounts payable	$ 37,432,879	$ 35,501,502
Current real estate taxes receivable (note 3A)	212,774,000	201,046,000	Accrued expenses	6,042,619	6,226,710
Current installment agreements receivable	615,800	807,100	Current portion of capital lease (note 5)	455,000	427,500
Receivables, net of allowance of $12,621,049 in 1983 and $8,797,000 in 1982 (note 3B)	44,275,909	38,132,010		43,930,498	42,155,712
Inventories (note 1E)	2,210,177	2,298,801	Payable from restricted assets:		
	342,037,766	324,251,608	Current maturities on general obligation debt	7,333,789	5,370,237
Restricted:			Warrants and accounts payable	59,680,428	46,229,185
Cash and investments (note 1D)	101,255,609	62,309,162		67,014,217	51,599,422
Accounts receivable	868,968	1,374,113	Total Current Liabilities	110,944,715	93,755,134
	102,124,577	63,683,275	Long-term Debt, less current portion:		
Total Current Assets	444,162,343	387,934,883	General obligation debt (note 6)	41,376,959	30,582,168
Property and Equipment:			Capital lease (note 5)	14,955,000	15,410,000
General fixed assets (note 1F)	205,992,613	190,707,698	Accrued vacation and sick leave	29,192,622	27,916,153
Proprietary fund fixed assets (note 5)	90,630,781	86,157,967		85,524,581	73,908,321
	296,623,394	276,865,665	Deferred Revenue	214,217,252	204,054,272
Less accumulated depreciation and amortization	81,267,788	70,970,376	Total Liabilities	410,686,548	371,717,727
Net Property and Equipment	215,355,606	205,895,289	Equity (note 2)	283,362,873	253,957,617
Other Assets:			Total Liabilities and Equity	$694,049,421	$625,675,344
Delinquent taxes receivable, net of allowances of $15,508,000 in 1983 and $12,837,000 in 1982 (note 3A)	28,395,000	23,987,000			
Installment agreements receivable	5,542,200	7,263,900			
Prepaid lease	594,272	594,272			
Total Other Assets	34,531,472	31,845,172			
Total Assets	$694,049,421	$625,675,344			

Consolidated Statement of Operations
and Changes in Equity

	1983	1982 (Restated— Note 7)
Revenues:		
Property taxes	$162,807,646	$148,748,614
Other taxes	352,901	293,217
Intergovernmental	193,670,351	165,086,550
Investment earnings	16,509,066	15,078,950
Charges for services	103,245,245	101,164,333
Fines and forfeits	1,153,769	1,070,949
Licenses and permits	1,490,953	1,430,369
Other	9,300,295	12,955,745
Total Revenues	488,530,226	445,828,727
Expenses:		
General government	31,796,416	33,592,477
Social services	203,948,856	182,034,112
Health	111,365,999	101,329,073
Public safety and judiciary	63,093,906	60,037,660
Public service	25,685,171	29,511,895
Education	13,786,846	11,540,189
Capital projects	7,120,571	3,214,257
Interest	3,196,847	1,799,722
Total Expenses	459,994,612	423,059,385
Excess of Revenues over Expenses	28,535,614	22,769,342
Equity at Beginning of Year	253,957,617	231,141,111
Increase in Contributed Capital	869,642	47,164
Equity at End of Year	$283,362,873	$253,957,617

Consolidated Statement of Changes
in Financial Position

	1983	1982 (Restated— Note 7)
Cash Provided From Operations:		
Excess of revenues over expenses	$ 28,535,614	$ 22,769,342
Item not affected cash— depreciation and amortization	11,912,760	11,123,683
	40,448,374	33,893,025
(Increase) decrease in:		
Receivables	(17,175,454)	(2,674,586)
Inventories	88,624	59,685
Other assets	(2,686,300)	(5,948,900)
Increase (decrease) in:		
Warrants and accounts payable	15,382,620	15,465,054
Accrued expenses	(184,091)	2,254,685
Current portion of capital lease	27,500	(21,505)
Current maturities on general obligation debt	1,963,552	(1,254,763)
Contributed capital	869,642	47,164
Accrued vacation and sick leave	1,276,469	2,065,889
Deferred revenues	10,162,980	9,737,557
Cash Provided from Operations	50,173,916	53,623,305
Cash Provided From Financing—General obligation borrowings	17,650,000	8,300,000
Total Cash Provided	67,823,916	61,923,305
Cash Applied:		
General obligation debt payments	7,310,209	5,345,332
Additions to fixed assets	21,373,077	20,826,490
Total Cash Applied	28,683,286	26,171,822
Increase in Cash and Investments	39,140,630	35,751,483
Cash and Investments at Beginning of Year	144,276,859	108,525,376
Cash and Investments at End of Year	$183,417,489	$144,276,859

Consolidated Statement of Financial Activity

	Total Cost	Intergovern-mental	Services*	Other	1983 Net Cost	1982 Net Cost (Restated— Note 7)
Cost of Services:						
General government	$ 31,796,416	$ 376,201	$ 374,356	$ 30,162	$ 31,015,697	$ 32,869,014
Social services	203,948,856	127,633,633	3,229,852	4,508,558	68,576,813	63,462,741
Health	111,365,999	3,384,342	90,354,529	165,644	17,461,484	7,660,180
Public safety and judiciary	63,093,906	4,347,147	6,851,251	65,848	51,829,660	48,884,511
Public service	25,685,171	3,338,929	3,814,115	49,455	18,482,672	23,438,699
Education	13,786,846	255,844	112,095	—	13,418,907	11,186,528
Capital projects	7,120,571	6,174,130	—	—	946,441	(1,547,685)
Debt service	3,196,847	—	—	—	3,196,847	1,799,722
Total	$459,994,612	$145,510,226	$104,736,198	$4,819,667	$204,928,521	$187,753,710
Sources of Financing:						
Taxes:						
Property					162,807,646	148,748,614
Other					352,901	293,217
					163,160,547	149,041,831
Intergovernmental					48,160,125	39,139,043
Investment earnings					16,509,066	15,078,950
Fines and forfeits					1,153,769	1,070,949
Other					4,480,628	6,192,279
Total Sources of Financing					233,464,135	210,523,052
Sources of Financing Over Net Cost of Services					28,535,614	22,769,342
Increase in Contributed Capital					869,642	47,164
Equity at Beginning of Year					253,957,617	231,141,111
Equity at End of Year					$283,362,873	$253,957,617

* Includes revenue from licenses and permits.

EXHIBIT 14-3. ILLUSTRATIONS OF REPORTS UNDER OMB CIRCULAR A-102, ATTACHMENT P [Example 1]

FINANCIAL AUDIT REPORT:

Board of City Commissioners

Gentlemen:

We have examined the combined financial statements of the City and its combining and individual fund financial statements as of and for the year ended December 31, 1983, as listed in the table of contents. Our examination was made in accordance with generally accepted auditing standards and the Minimum Standard Audit Program approved by the State Municipal Accounting Board, and accordingly included such tests of the accounting records as we considered necessary in the circumstances.

In our opinion, the combined financial statements referred to above present fairly the financial position of the City as of December 31, 1983, and the results of its operations and the changes in financial position of its proprietary fund types and similar trust funds for the year then ended, in conformity with generally accepted accounting principles applied on a basis consistent with that of the preceding year. Also, in our opinion, the combining and individual fund financial statements referred to above present fairly the financial position of the individual funds of the City at December 31, 1983, and their results of operations, and the changes in financial position of the individual proprietary funds for the year then ended, in conformity with generally accepted accounting principles applied on a basis consistent with that of the preceding year.

Our examination was made for the purpose of forming an opinion on the combined financial statements taken as a whole and on the combining and individual fund financial statements. The accompanying financial information listed as supplemental information in the table of contents is presented for purposes of additional analysis and is not a required part of the combined financial statements of the City. The information has been subjected to the auditing procedures applied in the examination of the combined, combining, and individual fund financial statements and, in our opinion, is fairly stated in all material respects in relation to the combined financial statements taken as a whole.

[Certified Public Accountants Firm]
July 25, 1984

[CPA in charge of and actively engaged in this audit]

COMPLIANCE COMMENTS:

Mayor and City Commission

We have examined the financial statements of the City, for the year ended December 31, 1983, and have issued our report thereon dated July 25, 1984. Our examination was made in accordance with generally accepted auditing standards; the provisions of the *Standards for Audit of Governmental Organizations, Programs, Activities and Functions,* promulgated by the U.S. Comptroller General, as they pertain to financial and compliance audits; the provisions of *Guidelines for Financial and Compliance Audits of Federally Assisted Programs,* promulgated by the General Accounting Office; the provisions of the Office of Management and Budget's (OMB) *Compliance Supplement—Uniform Requirements of Programs for Grants to State and Local Governments* (the compliance supplement); the provisions of OMB's Circular A-102, *Uniform Administrative Requirements for Grants-in-Aid to State and Local Governments,* Attachment P, *Audit Requirements,* and, accordingly, included such tests of the accounting records and such other auditing procedures as we considered necessary in the circumstances.

Based on our examination, we found that, for the items tested, the City complied with the material terms and conditions of the federal award agreements, except as described in the Schedule of Findings and Questioned Costs. Further, based on our examination and the procedures referred to above, nothing came to our attention to indicate that the City had not complied with the significant compliance terms and conditions of the awards referred to above.

This report is intended solely for the purpose of the management, the cognizant federal agency, and other federal audit agencies and should not be used for any other purpose.

[Certified Public Accountant]
July 25, 1984

INTERNAL CONTROL COMMENTS:

Mayor and City Commission

We have examined the financial statements of the City, for the year ended December 31, 1983, and have issued our report thereon dated July 25, 1984. As part of our examination, we made a study and evaluation of the system of internal accounting control of the City, to the extent we considered necessary to evaluate the system as required by generally accepted auditing standards and the standards for financial and compliance audits contained in the U.S. General Accounting Office's *Standards for Audit of Governmental Organizations, Programs, Activities and Functions.* For the purpose of this report, we have classified the significant internal accounting controls in the following categories: Petty Cash, Bank Accounts, Cash Receipts, Cash Disbursements, Investments, Inventories, Purchasing-Receiving and Payables, Bonded Indebtedness, Payrolls, Budget, Fixed Assets, Other Revenue and Receivables.

Our study included all of the control categories listed above. The purpose of our study and evaluation was to determine the nature, timing and extent of performing the auditing procedures necessary for expressing an opinion on the entity's financial statements. Our study and evaluation was more limited than would be necessary to express an opinion on the system of internal accounting control taken as a whole on any of the categories of controls identified above.

The Management of the City is responsible for establishing and maintaining a system of internal accounting control. In fulfilling this responsibility, estimates and judgments by management are required to assess the expected benefits and related costs of control procedures. The objectives of a system are to provide management with reasonable, but not absolute, assurance that assets are safeguarded against loss from unauthorized use or disposition, and that transactions are executed in accordance with management's authorization and recorded properly to permit the preparation of financial statements in accordance with generally accepted accounting principles.

Because of inherent limitations in any system of internal accounting control errors or irregularities may nevertheless occur and not be detected. Also, projection of any evaluation of the system to future periods is subject to the risk that procedures may become inadequate because of changes in conditions or that the degree of compliance with the procedures may deteriorate.

Our study and evaluation made for the limited purpose described in the first paragraph would not necessarily disclose all material weaknesses in the system. Accordingly, we do not express an opinion on the system of internal accounting control of the City taken as a whole or on any of the categories of controls identified in the first paragraph. Our study and evaluation disclosed no conditions that we believe to be material weaknesses.

This report is intended solely for the use of management, the U.S. Department of Transportation, the cognizant federal agency, and other federal audit agencies and should not be used for any other purpose.

[Certified Public Accountant]
July 25, 1984

[Example 2]
FINANCIAL AUDIT REPORT, INTERNAL CONTROL COMMENTS, AND COMPLIANCE COMMENTS:

The Honorable Members of the Board of Supervisors

We have examined the combined financial statements of the County, and the combining and individual fund financial statements of County as of and for the year ended June 30, 1984, as listed in the Table of Contents. Our examination was made in accordance with generally accepted auditing standards, *Standards for Audit of Governmental Organizations, Programs, Activities and Functions* (1981 Revision) issued by the Comptroller General of the United States as related to financial and compliance audits and *Specifications for Audit of Counties, Cities and Towns* (1983) issued by the Auditor of Public Accounts, and, accordingly, included such tests of the accounting records and such other auditing procedures as we considered necessary in the circumstances.

The County is not required by the Auditor of Public Accounts to maintain a general fixed asset account group and, accordingly, such account group required by generally accepted accounting principles is not included in the accompanying financial statements.

In our opinion, except for the omission of the general fixed asset account group, the combined financial statements referred to above present fairly the financial position of the County, at June 30, 1984, and the results of its operations and changes in financial position of its proprietary fund types and similar trust funds for the year then ended, in conformity with generally accepted accounting principles applied on a basis consistent with that of the preceding year. Also, in our opinion, the combining and individual fund financial statements referred to above present fairly the financial position of the individual funds of the County at June 30, 1984, and the results of operations of such funds and changes in financial position of individual proprietary funds for the year then ended, in conformity with generally accepted accounting principles applied on a basis consistent with that of the preceding year.

Our examination was made for the purpose of forming an opinion on the combined financial statements taken as a whole and on the combining and individual fund financial statements. The accompanying financial information listed as supplementary schedules in the Table of Contents is presented for purposes of additional analysis and is not a required part of the combined financial statements of the County. The information has been subjected to the auditing procedures applied in the examination of the combined, combining and individual fund financial statements and, in our opinion, is fairly stated in all material respects in relation to the combined financial statements taken as a whole.

AUDITOR'S REPORT ON INTERNAL ACCOUNTING CONTROLS

As part of our examination of the County's financial statements, we made a study and evaluation of the system of internal accounting control of the County to the extent we considered necessary to evaluate the system as required by generally accepted auditing standards, the standards for financial and compliance audits contained in the U.S. General Accounting Office's *Standards for Audit of Governmental Organizations, Programs, Activities and Functions* (1981 Revision), Office of Management and Budget Circular A-102, *Uniform Requirements for Assistance to State and Local Governments*, Attachment P, *Audit Requirements*, and the *Specifications for Audit of Counties, Cities, and Towns* (1983) issued by the Auditor of Public Accounts. For the purpose of this report, we have classified the significant internal accounting controls in the following categories: Budget, Receivables, Cash receipts/revenues, Purchasing and receiving, Accounts payable, Cash disbursements, Payroll, General ledger (cash and cash equivalents, investments, bonded and other formal indebtedness, other liabilities).

Our study included all of the control categories listed above. The purpose of our study and evaluation was to determine the nature, timing and extent of performing the auditing procedures necessary for expressing an opinion on the entity's financial statements. Our study and evaluation was more limited than would be necessary to express an opinion on the system of internal accounting control taken as a whole or on any of the categories of controls identified in the preceding paragraph.

The management of the County is responsible for establishing and maintaining a system of internal accounting control. In fulfilling this responsibility, estimates and judgments by management are required to assess the expected benefits and related costs of control procedures. The objective of a system are to provide management with reasonable, but not absolute, assurance that assets are safeguarded against loss from unauthorized use or disposition, and that transactions are executed in accordance with management's authorization and recorded properly to permit the preparation of financial statements in accordance with generally accepted accounting principles.

Because of inherent limitations in any system of internal accounting control, errors or irregularities may nevertheless occur and not be detected. Also, projection of any evaluation of the system to future periods is subject to the risk that procedures may become inadequate because of changes in conditions or that the degree of compliance with the procedures may deteriorate.

Our study and evaluation made for the limited purpose described in the first paragraph would not necessarily disclose all material weaknesses in the system. Accordingly, we do not express an opinion on the system of internal accounting control of the County taken as a whole or on any of the categories of controls identified in the first paragraph. However, while our study and evaulation disclosed no condition that we believe to be a material weakness, it did disclose conditions requiring the attention of management. These conditions are discussed under the heading "Recommendations for Improvements in Internal Accounting Controls."

AUDITOR'S REPORT ON COMPLIANCE
The examination of the County's financial statements reported on under the heading Auditor's Report on Financial Statements and Supplementary Schedules was also made in accordance with the provisions of the Office of Management and Budget's (OMB) *Compli-*

ance Supplement—Uniform Requirements for Grants to State and Local Governments, the provisions for OMB's Circular A-102, *Uniform Administrative Requirements for Grants-in-Aid to State and Local Governments,* Attachment P, *Audit Requirements, Guidelines for Financial and Compliance Audits of Federally Assisted Programs,* and accordingly, included such tests of the accounting records and such other auditing procedures as we considered necessary in the circumstances.

These tests included the selection of a representative number of charges to federal awards to determine if (1) federal funds are being expended in accordance with the terms of applicable agreements and those provisions of federal law or regulations that could have a material effect on the financial statements or on the awards tested and (2) federal financial reports accurately present the underlying financial data of the federal grants of the County. The results of our tests indicate that, for the items tested, the County complied with the material terms and conditions of the federal award agreements and that federal financial reports accurately present the underlying financial data of the federal grants of the County. Further, for the items not tested, based on our examination and the procedures referred to above, nothing came to our attention to indicate that the County had not complied with the significant compliance terms and conditions of the awards referred to above.

[Auditor of Public Accounts]

Chapter 15
Accounting and Reporting Practices for Selected Topics

This chapter considers a variety of topics related to the nature of accounting or reporting disclosures made by various governmental units. The topics have been selected to illustrate alternative ways of reporting on similar issues; some have been briefly discussed in earlier chapters. Neither priority ranking nor significance is intended from the order of discussion.

CAPITALIZATION OF INTEREST

Many governmental units provided footnote disclosures of their procedures relating to capitalization of interest. FASB Statement 34, "Capitalization of Interest Cost," established the standards of financial accounting and reporting for capitalizing interest cost as a part of the historical cost of acquiring certain assets. Statement 34 defined *interest cost* as including interest recognized on obligations having explicit interest rates; interest imputed on certain types of payables in accordance with APB Opinion 21, "Interest on Receivables and Payables"; and interest related to a capital lease determined in accordance with FASB Statement 13, "Accounting for Leases." By FASB Statement 34, the amount of interest cost to be capitalized for qualifying assets is intended to be that portion of the interest cost incurred during the assets' acquisition periods that theoretically could have been avoided (for example, by avoiding additional borrowings or by using the funds expended for the assets to repay existing borrowings) if expenditures for the assets had not been made.

Later, FASB Statement 62 amended FASB Statement 34, "Capitalization of Interest Cost," (a) to require capitalization of the interest cost of restricted tax-exempt borrowings, less any interest earned on temporary investment of the proceeds of those borrowings from the date of borrowing until the specified qualifying assets acquired with those borrowings are ready for their intended use, and (b) to prescribe capitalization of the interest cost on qualifying assets acquired using gifts or grants that are restricted by the donor or grantor to acquisition of those assets.

Exhibit 15-1 contains descriptive illustrations of the capitalization procedures for several of the surveyed units.

COMMITMENTS AND CONTINGENCIES

Many governments, in the footnotes of their financial statements, provided disclosure of a reasonable possibility of future liability with respect to commitments and contingencies. *Commitments* are obligations, generally under contracts not yet completed, for which the financial liability is reasonably determinable. *Contingencies* are defined as conditions, situations, or circumstances that will ultimately be resolved when one or more future events occur or fail to occur. Commitments or contingent liabilities were disclosed in the footnotes of many of the financial statements surveyed.

The reporting of commitments and contingencies varied. Where the amount of the obligation was known, some governments recorded the commitment or contingency as a liability; in other instances disclosures were made in the footnotes to the financial statements. In many instances, no dollar amount was cited in the financial statements, but a caption may have been included in the body of the combined balance sheet. When this latter format was used, the caption appeared in one of three places: (1) between the liabilities and equity sections of the balance sheet, (2) after the equity section of the combined balance sheet but before the total balances of the liability and equity section, or (3) following the total balances of the liability and equity section of the combined balance sheet. Table 15-1 summarizes the various methods used by the surveyed governments to report contingencies and commitments.

Excerpts from selected footnote disclosures and balance sheet formats appearing in the financial statements surveyed appear in Exhibit 15-2 and 15-3, respectively. These exhibits contain examples of footnotes relating to both commitments and contingencies, since a distinction was not always maintained by the governmental units between these two types of liabilities.

COMPLIANCE, STEWARDSHIP, AND ACCOUNTABILITY

Several of the surveyed governments provided a grouping of footnote disclosures under the heading "compliance, stewardship, and accountability." This footnote may have been included as part of the note titled "summary of significant accounting policies" or separately. Generally, subjects such as fund deficits, grants from other governments, budget compliance and adjustments, and debt were discussed.

Exhibit 15-4 contains excerpts from selected financial statements on this type of footnote.

ENCUMBRANCES

Many of the governmental units provided information concerning the status of outstanding encumbrances at the end of the fiscal year. The accounting for encumbrances was described in the footnotes to the financial statements by about 61% of the governments surveyed. Exhibit 15-5 contains several examples of footnotes related to encumbrances.

JOINT VENTURES

Governmental units commonly have joint agreements with other units to provide services to their respective constituents. These arrangements might include nongovernmental units, authorities, or regional quasi-governmental entities, for example.

Exhibit 15-6 contains excerpts from several financial statements relating to joint ventures.

INVESTMENTS

Most of the governments surveyed provided footnote disclosure of their investment policy and accounting and valuation procedures. In 58% of the financial statements there were references to investments. Excerpts of footnotes related to the reporting of investments appear in Exhibit 9-4.

NEW FUNDS

Some governmental units found it necessary to establish new funds and provided that disclosure in the footnotes to the financial statements. Exhibit 15-7 illustrates excerpts from the footnotes of several surveyed financial statements.

OPERATING LEASES

Chapters 3 and 4 contain information and illustrations of the accounting and reporting made by governmental units for capital, nonoperating, and noncancellable leases. However, many communities also had significant operating-type leases for which disclosure was made in the footnotes to the financial statements. Exhibit 15-8 illustrates several examples of these disclosures.

RELATED PARTY TRANSACTIONS

Many of the surveyed governmental units had operations that involved agreements and arrangements that were termed to be related party transactions by the reporting governments. These transactions involved a wide variety of transactions between funds and organizations.

Exhibit 15-9 contains excerpts from the footnotes to the statements of some of the surveyed governmental units of related party transactions.

SELF-INSURANCE

Many of the surveyed governments self-insured certain risks. The areas of self-insurance varied and included risks related to workers compensation, property liabilities, medical claims, and, in some cases, general liability. In several instances, governments provided self-insurance up to a specified maximum; in other instances deductible-type insurance programs were used. Examples of footnotes related to some of the reported self-insurance programs appear in Exhibit 15-10.

SPECIAL ASSESSMENT ACCOUNTING

As shown in earlier chapters, special assessment funds are among the less frequently used fund types. Many of the surveyed governmental units provided footnote disclosures relating to special assessment accounting. Typically, the footnotes related to the basis for recognizing revenues in special assessment funds. Some governments elected to discontinue this type of funds.

Exhibit 15-11 contains excerpts of footnotes from several financial statements illustrating the reporting for special assessments.

SUBSEQUENT EVENTS

In certain instances events affecting the financial data disclosed by governments, most often related to debt, occurred subsequent to the close of the fiscal year of the surveyed financial statements. Because these events affect the financial data reported, disclosure of significant events is required. Excerpts of footnotes related to subsequent events have been included in Exhibit 15-12.

EXHIBITS AND TABLES FOR CHAPTER 15

Exhibit 15-1. Excerpts of Footnotes Relating to Capitalization of Interest

Table 15-1. Reporting of Commitments and Contingencies in Combined Balance Sheets

Exhibit 15-2. Excerpts of Footnotes Relating to Commitments and Contingencies

Exhibit 15-3. Excerpts of Balance Sheet Formats for Commitments and Contingencies

Exhibit 15-4. Excerpts of Footnotes Relating to Compliance, Stewardship, and Accountability

Exhibit 15-5. Excerpts of Footnotes Relating to Governmental Encumbrances

Exhibit 15-6. Excerpts of Footnotes Relating to Joint Ventures

Exhibit 15-7. Excerpts of Footnotes Relating to Establishment of New Funds

Exhibit 15-8. Excerpts of Footnotes Relating to Operating Leases

Exhibit 15-9. Excerpts of Footnotes Relating to Related Party Transactions

Exhibit 15-10. Excerpts of Footnotes Relating to Governmental Self-Insurance Programs

Exhibit 15-11. Excerpts of Footnotes Relating to Special Assessments

Exhibit 15-12. Excerpts of Footnotes Relating to Events Subsequent to the Balance Sheet Date

EXHIBIT 15-1. EXCERPTS OF FOOTNOTES RELATING TO CAPITALIZATION OF INTEREST

[CITY OF AURORA, COLORADO (DECEMBER 31, 1983), NOTES TO FINANCIAL STATEMENTS (IN PART)]

Note 12. Capitalization of Interest

The City has adopted the provisions of Statements No. 34 and 62 of the Financial Accounting Standards Board which, in general, require that interest costs be capitalized for those assets that are constructed or acquired for an entity's own use and that interest earned on investments acquired with the proceeds of the tax-exempt borrowing entered into after August 31, 1982, be offset against related constructed assets until completed for use. The provisions of this statement only apply to the Enterprise Funds. The net amount of interest capitalized during 1983 is as follows:

Water Fund	
Interest cost capitalized	$3,710,575
Sewer Fund	
Interest cost capitalized	1,120,217
Interest earnings on related borrowings	(669,191)
	451,026
Net	$4,161,601

[CITY OF DAYTONA BEACH, FLORIDA (SEPTEMBER 30, 1983), NOTES TO FINANCIAL STATEMENTS (IN PART)]

Note 12. Capitalized Interest

Construction in progress for the Water and Sewer System fund at September 30, 1983 and 1982, consisted of extensions and improvements to the water and sewer system. During the 1977 fiscal year, the City began construction on a new wastewater treatment plant. This Regional Wastewater Treatment Plant was constructed from funds provided by the federal government and The City of Daytona Beach.

The capitalized interest during construction of the new regional wastewater treatment facility is as follows:

	As of September 30	
	1983	1982
Capitalized Interest	$ —	$610,980

In the 1981 fiscal year, the new regional wastewater treatment facility (plant and force main) became operational and was recorded in fixed assets for $22,576,142, including capitalized interest of $1,610,239. The remaining sludge dewatering facility under construction has capitalized interest accumulating to $226,716 through September 30, 1981.

Construction relating to the $8,400,000 Water and Sewer Revenue Bonds, Series 1979, for various improvements and additions to the existing water and sewer system resulted in an additional capitalized interest amount of $241,155 for the 1982 year and $175,600 for 1983.

[BERKELEY COUNTY, SOUTH CAROLINA (JUNE 30, 1984), NOTES TO FINANCIAL STATEMENTS (IN PART)]

Note 1 [in part]—Summary of Significant Accounting Policies

Capitalization of Interest

Effective July 1, 1980, the Enterprise Fund adopted Statement of Financial Accounting Standards No. 34, whereby interest costs related to certain long-term construction projects are capitalized rather than charged directly to expense. Accordingly, of total interest costs of $1,528,900 incurred during the year ended June 30, 1984, $331,110 was capitalized.

[CITY OF ENID, OKLAHOMA (JUNE 30, 1984), NOTES TO FINANCIAL STATEMENTS (IN PART)]

Note G [in part]

The City capitalizes interest cost in its enterprise funds on bonds used for capital construction net of interest income earned on interest-bearing investments. The investments are acquired with proceeds of tax exempt borrowings that are restricted for either the acquisition of fixed assets or to service debt. Interest costs of $1,061,881 were capitalized during the fiscal year.

[CITY OF FORT COLLINS, COLORADO (DECEMBER 31, 1983), NOTES TO FINANCIAL STATEMENTS (IN PART)]

Note 8 [in part]. Changes in Accounting Principles, Correction of Errors, and Restatements

Capitalization of Interest Cost

1982 statements for the Southridge Green Golf Course Fund have been restated to comply with provisions of FASB Statement No. 62. The statement amends FASB Statement No. 34, *Capitalization of Interest Cost,* to require "capitalization of interest cost of restricted tax-exempt borrowings less any interest earned on temporary investment of the proceeds. . .from the date of borrowing until the specified qualifying assets acquired with those borrowings are ready for their intended use." 1982 interest income of $64,351 has been offset against interest expense, which when capitalized, resulted in a restated Work in Progress of $257,440. 1982 Reserve from Interest Earnings has been eliminated pending completion of construction of the Golf Course, at which time future interest earnings will be reserved for debt service.

[CITY OF JACKSONVILLE, FLORIDA (SEPTEMBER 30, 1983), NOTES TO FINANCIAL STATEMENTS (IN PART)]

Note D. Interest Capitalization

In 1982, the Financial Accounting Standards Board issued FASB Statement No. 62 amending FASB Statement No. 34, Capitalization of Interest Costs, to require capitalization of interest costs of restricted tax-exempt borrowings less any interest earned on temporary investments of the proceeds of those borrowings during the acquisition period of certain qualifying assets. The city has adopted this policy to material items.

The resultant net interest capitalization for the year ended September 30, 1983, is $3,221,265, and $325,400 for the year ended September 30, 1982.

[MARTIN COUNTY, FLORIDA (SEPTEMBER 30, 1983), NOTES TO FINANCIAL STATEMENTS (IN PART)]

Note J. Interest Costs—Enterprise Fund

For the year ended September 30, 1983, the Enterprise Fund incurred total interest costs (including amortization of debt insurance costs) amounting to $458,305, of which $273,946 was capitalized as part of fixed asset construction costs. Interest earned on the proceeds of long-term borrowings held in the construction trust account, which amounted to $39,329 for the year, was recorded as a reduction of construction costs capitalized.

[CITY OF McALLEN, TEXAS (SEPTEMBER 30, 1983), NOTES TO FINANCIAL STATEMENTS (IN PART)]

Note 8. Construction Period Interest

The McAllen International Toll Bridge (an Enterprise Fund) has capitalized interest cost during the construction period of the Bridge's new crossing facilities. The capitalized interest is recorded as part of the cost of the facility and will be depreciated over the asset's estimated useful life. Interest expense capitalized during the year totaled $67,888.

[PALM BEACH COUNTY, FLORIDA (SEPTEMBER 30, 1983), NOTES TO FINANCIAL STATEMENTS (IN PART)]

Note 16. Interest Costs

Total interest costs related to the County's proprietary funds are summarized below:

	Total Interest Costs Expensed	Total Interest Costs Capitalized
Enterprise funds:		
Water and Sewer	$5,341,353	$1,678,473
Internal Service Funds:		
Property Appraiser—		
Data Processing	100,430	—
	$5,441,783	$1,678,473

[CITY OF OKLAHOMA CITY, OKLAHOMA (JUNE 30, 1984), NOTES TO FINANCIAL STATEMENTS (IN PART)]

Note 8. Interest Capitalization

Interest costs incurred by proprietary funds on tax-exempt bonds whose proceeds were used to finance the construction of assets are capitalized. Interest earned on proceeds of tax-exempt borrowing arrangements restricted to the acquisition of qualifying assets shall be offset against interest costs in determining the amount to be capitalized. During 1984, the interest revenue which was used to offset interest costs in the Transportation and Parking Fund, the Airports Fund, and the Myriad Gardens Fund were $98,033, $1,139,218, and $87,353, respectively. Total interest costs incurred in the respective funds were $3,378,119, $5,521,017, and $105,000, of which $302,088, $881,773, and $17,647 have been capitalized.

[TULSA, OKLAHOMA (JUNE 30, 1984), NOTES TO FINANCIAL STATEMENTS (IN PART)]

Note I. Interest Capitalization

The City capitalizes interest cost in its enterprise funds on bonds used for capital construction net of interest income earned on interest-bearing investments. These investments are acquired with proceeds of tax exempt borrowings that are restricted for either the acquisition of fixed assets or to service the debt. Interest costs incurred during 1984 were $19,110,870, of which $1,363,017 has been capitalized.

TABLE 15-1. REPORTING OF COMMITMENTS AND CONTINGENCIES IN COMBINED BALANCE SHEETS

Nature of Disclosure	Instances Observed (%)
No captions in balance sheet—footnote only	58
Caption between liabilities and equity section	8
Reservation of fund balance/retained earnings	6
Caption between equity total and total liability and equity	5
Caption following total liability and equity	4
Liability caption	<1

EXHIBIT 15-2. EXCERPTS OF FOOTNOTES RELATING TO COMMITMENTS AND CONTINGENCIES

[BIBB COUNTY, GEORGIA (SEPTEMBER 30, 1983), NOTES TO FINANCIAL STATEMENTS (IN PART)]

Note 11. Contingent Liabilities

Litigation

The County Attorney reports numerous lawsuits have been filed against the County, but in his opinion, based upon the facts of these lawsuits and the amount of claimed damages in these cases, the potential liabilities will not impair the County's financial position.

Asserted Claims

All local banks have made demands upon the County for refund of Georgia bank shares based upon a ruling by the U.S. Supreme Court in a Texas case prohibiting the use of the values of federal obligations in imposing state or local taxes. The County feels the refund of such taxes will be limited to 10% of the amount collected over the three previous years and such amount will not impair the County's financial position.

Unasserted Claims

Due to a recent Georgia Supreme Court decision which struck down a local ordinance of a Georgia County taxing insurance companies on their property and casualty premiums and other litigation of the same nature against a municipality, it is possible claims will be made upon the County for a refund of similar taxes collected by the County for three prior years. A full determination of the impact on the County cannot be reached until other litigation noted above is settled.

Subsequent to the above litigation, the State of Georgia has amended Chapter 8 of Title 33 of the Official Code of Georgia, which will provide for collection of these taxes by the State. The State will in turn remit the insurance premiums tax to the local government units based upon a set formula.

Federal Grants

The County participates in a number of federally assisted grant programs, principal of which is the General Revenue Sharing program. These programs are subject to program compliance audits by the grantors or their representatives, and the audits of these programs for or including the year ended September 30, 1983, have not yet been conducted. Accordingly, the County's compliance with applicable grant requirements will be established at some future date. The amount, if any, of expenditures which may be disallowed by the granting agencies cannot be determined at this time although the County expects such amounts, if any, to be immaterial.

Workmen's Compensation

Workmen's compensation benefits as defined by state statute are paid from the Fiduciary Fund (Workmen's Compensation Fund). The funding is provided by transfers from the General Fund based upon the anticipated claims for the year.

Unemployment Compensation

Unemployment compensation is paid quarterly as the state assesses the County based upon actual claims. The claims are paid from the Fiduciary Funds (Unemployment Compensation Fund).

[CUMBERLAND COUNTY, NORTH CAROLINA (JUNE 30, 1984), NOTES TO FINANCIAL STATEMENTS (IN PART)]

Note 8. Contingent Liabilities

The County attorney has advised that, except for the cases referred to below, there are no suits pending against Cumberland County and no claims being made which, in his opinion, could result in a material liability on the part of Cumberland County at June 30, 1984.

Department of Labor vs. Cumberland County CETA

This litigation arises out of disallowed costs in connection with operation of several CETA programs during the period 1974–1978. Direct monetary recovery of $75,893 could be asserted against the County in this matter.

Workman's Compensation

This is a workman's compensation case where the employee was injured in an automobile accident caused by the negligence of a third party. The County's maximum liability as of June 30, 1984, in this matter was $3,006.

Department of Social Services

This is a claim of racial discrimination asserted by a former employee of the department. The claim may result in litigation. The County's maximum liability at June 30, 1984, in this matter was approximately $10,000.

Cumberland County

This is a workman's compensation case where the employee was allegedly injured in the course of employment. The County's probable liability in this matter at June 30, 1984, was $3,310.

Department of Social Services

This case involves a claim of racial discrimination and has been filed with EEOC, which is currently investigating the matter. No direct monetary liability to Cumberland County will result from this claim.

Cumberland County

This is a claim for $35,000 against the County due to an injury incurred in an elevator accident in one of the County's public buildings. The claim is covered by insurance and is being defended by the County's insurance carrier.

Sheriff's Department, et al.

This lawsuit involves the County through its Sheriff's department. The plaintiff alleges civil rights violations and that the County's sheriff, O. F. Jones, was negligent in supervising an investigation, which resulted in the violation of civil rights. The plaintiff is seeking damages in excess of $23,000,000; however, counsel for the County expects that the lawsuit will be dismissed by the court.

Accident

This is a claim filed against an employee of the County related to an automobile accident. Damages are sought in excess of insurance coverage by $25,000. the insurance company is defending the claim.

Contingent Liabilities Under Grants

Cumberland County conducts many public programs which are funded by various Federal and State grants and entitlements. Many of these programs are subject to audit for compliance with applicable Federal and State regulations. In certain cases disallowed costs could result in a payback of Federal or State grant money. Preliminary review of Mental Health grant activities indicates that a potential liability for payback of grant funds exists. This liability may be as much as $100,000. No other material liabilities are anticipated in any other Federal or State grant funded programs.

[CITY OF GALVESTON, TEXAS (SEPTEMBER 30, 1983), NOTES TO FINANCIAL STATEMENTS (IN PART)]

Note 6. Litigation

The City Attorney estimates that the potential claims against the City not covered by insurance resulting from such litigation would not materially affect the financial statements of the City.

Note 7. Significant Commitments Under Noncapitalized Leases and Contracts

General Fund

Through management agreement with Galveston City Coach Lines, Inc., the City paid a management fee of $7,515 per month for the management and operation of the City's public transportation system during the fiscal year ended September 30, 1983. In addition, the City paid operating expenses of the transit system less passenger fares amounting to $424,665.

Management fees for the third through the fifth years of the contract, beginning October 1, 1982, are to be negotiated at the beginning of each year. In addition, the City will reimburse the management company for net operating losses.

The City leased a bus depot and repair facility through agreement with Kelso Industries, Inc., at a cost of $2,875.00 per month. This lease agreement was terminated upon completion of construction of the City's new bus facility, which was placed in service on October 31, 1982.

As of September 30, 1983, an operating assistance grant from Urban Mass Transit Administration totaling $244,214, for the fiscal year 1981–82, had been recorded as Due from Other Governments and as revenue realized in fiscal year 1982–83 (prior year expense refund). $257,686 has been applied for as reimbursement for operating expenses during the 1982–83 fiscal year. This amount has been recorded as Due from Other Governments and as an expense reimbursement of transportation system expenses.

Waterworks System Fund

By contract with the Galveston County Water Authority, as approved by election on March 11, 1969, the City purchases surface water from the Authority. The City agreed to purchase, whether taken or not, the following quantities of water:

1-1-76 to 12-31-80	8 million gallons per day
1-1-81 to 12-31-85	10 million gallons per day
1-1-86 to 12-31-90	12 million gallons per day
1-1-91 to 12-31-08	15 million gallons per day

The City has exercised its option to purchase water in excess of the minimum. Purchases during the current year averaged over 10 million gallons per day. The price of water increases periodically based on the actual cost of water to the Authority.

In addition to water purchase payments the City agreed to pay its proportionate share (89.87%) of the Authority's debt service requirements on the revenue bonds issued to finance construction of the water conveyance facilities. The fixed debt service charge is paid monthly and is based upon the amount of the Authority's debt currently maturing. Annual debt requirements to be paid by the City will increase from $245,016 in the fiscal year ending September 30, 1984, to $264,421 in the year ending September 30, 2001. Upon the Authority's debt being paid in full this fixed charge to the City will cease. At September 30, 1983, the total principal payable on the Authority's bonds was $3,060,000, of which the City's proportionate share was $2,753,015.

The Authority is paid an operating charge as reimbursement for actual maintenance and operating expenses incurred in providing water to the City.

[CITY OF LANCASTER, PENNSYLVANIA (DECEMBER 31, 1983), NOTES TO FINANCIAL STATEMENTS (IN PART)]

Note 4. Contingent Liability

The City of Lancaster is contingently liable under lease agreements between the Parking Authority Revenue Fund and the Parking Authority of the City of Lancaster until the year 2012. The aggregate remaining rental at December 31, 1983, was $27,699,640. Total lease payments made in 1983 were $1,008,200.

The City has advanced $1,789,000 to the Parking Authority to enable the Authority to meet current debt service payments required under its bond indentures. The Authority has agreed to repay the advance to the City. City officials believe that, based on present projections of future increased revenue, the Authority will be able to repay all advances by 1995.

However, as of December 31, 1983, the Authority had an accumulated deficit of $6,878,164, including accumulated depreciation of $3,921,606. The accumulated deficit does not include reserves under bond indentures of $1,068,815. In 1983, the Authority reflected net income of $67,831.

[CITY OF LARGO, FLORIDA (SEPTEMBER 30, 1983), NOTES TO FINANCIAL STATEMENTS (IN PART)]

Note L. Commitments and Contingencies

The City has an unused line of credit with a local bank for borrowings of up to $2,000,000. If utilized, this line of credit includes agreements with the bank for compensating balances. As of September 30, 1983, no borrowings had been made against this line.

As of September 30, 1983, construction contract commitments amounted to $1,748,200 for Phase II construction. Construction is being funded by proceeds from both the 1982 and 1983 Public Improvement Revenue Bonds.

As of September 30, 1983, enterprise fund (sewer fund) construction contracts amounted to $1,794,000 for the 126th Avenue West interceptor sewer line.

[CITY OF WAUKESHA, WISCONSIN (DECEMBER 31, 1983), NOTES TO FINANCIAL STATEMENTS (IN PART)]

Note K. Litigation

There are several pending lawsuits in which the City is involved. The City Attorney estimates that the potential claims against the City not covered by insurance resulting from such litigation would not materially affect the financial statements of the City.

EXHIBIT 15-3. EXCERPTS OF BALANCE SHEET FORMATS FOR COMMITMENTS AND CONTINGENCIES

[CITY OF ALBUQUERQUE]

Combined Balance Sheet [in part]—All Fund Types and Account Groups, June 30, 1984 [in thousands]

| | Governmental Funds | | | | | Proprietary Funds | | Fiduciary Funds | Account Groups | |
	General	Special Revenue	Debt Service	Capital Projects	Special Assessments	Enterprise	Internal Service	Trust and Agency	General Fixed Assets	General Long Term Debt
LIABILITIES AND FUND EQUITY										
Liabilities:					* * *					
Fund equity:					* * *					
				* * *						
Total fund equity (deficit)	(15,031)	13,636	32,721	81,833	(3,885)	257,943	(3,701)	18,326	269,616	—
TOTAL LIABILITIES AND FUND EQUITY	$23,135	$16,013	$61,107	$85,445	$8,804	$402,244	$10,212	$42,444	$269,616	$185,392

Commitments and contingent liabilities (Notes 18, 19).

Note 18. Commitments

The City of Albuquerque and Bernalillo County have entered into a joint powers agreement to construct a joint city/county building. Construction of the building commenced in October 1983. The County has issued $9,160,000 of general obligation bonds, the proceeds of which, including interest earned, will be used to cover the first portion of the costs. The City has issued $15 million of gross receipts tax revenue bonds to finance the remaining costs.

At June 30, 1984, uncompleted construction and other contracts totaled $14.6 million for water and sewer projects and $3 million for airport projects. The payment of these contracts will be made from assets restricted for construction, improvements and replacements in the enterprise funds.

Lease commitments other than the capital lease described in Note 10 at June 30, 1984, are not material.

Note 19. Contingent Liabilities

During 1984, the City's user fee which funded the vehicle emission inspection program was found by the courts to be unlawful. The City Council has been unable to establish an alternative method of funding the program and, accordingly, terminated its agreement with the private contractor providing the inspection services. The contractor has brought suit against the City for damages of approximately $2.3 million arising from termination of the agreement. The City admin-istration maintains, based upon consultation with legal counsel, that no amounts are due the contractor because the agreement was not entered into pursuant to an ordinance levying a tax to pay the contractor and was not approved by the voters. Under the New Mexico Constitution, a proper ordinance and voter approval are necessary in order for such agreements to be binding.

Two anti-trust suits have been filed against the City regarding the collection and disposal of refuse. The suits seek unspecified treble damages, costs and attorney's fees, and injunctive relief. During 1984, for one of the suits, the City obtained a favorable ruling in federal district court that the City's ordinance prohibiting private refuse disposal derived its authority from state statutes and, accordingly, was included in the exemption of states from federal anti-trust laws. The ruling is being appealed.

No amounts have been recorded for possible losses, if any, arising from the matters discussed in the two preceding paragraphs. Legal counsel has indicated the outcome of these matters is not determinable.

The City has received a number of Federal and State grants for specific purposes. These grants are subject to audit, which may result in requests for reimbursements to granting agencies for expenditures disallowed under the terms of the grants. Based on prior experience, City administration believes that such disallowances, if any, will not be material.

[COUNTY OF NASSAU, NEW YORK]

All Fund Types and Account Groups Combined Balance Sheet [in part]
December 31, 1983 [in thousands]

| | Governmental Fund Types | | | Proprietary Fund Type | Fiduciary Fund Type | Account Groups | |
	General	Special Revenue	Capital Projects	Enterprise	Trust and Agency	General Fixed Assets	General Long Term Obligations
LIABILITIES AND FUND EQUITY							
Liabilities:			* * *				
Fund Equity:			* * *				
Total Fund Equity	$(10,950)	$42,539	$147,339	$ 41,421		$2,151,711	
Contingencies (Note 14)							
TOTAL LIABILITIES AND FUND EQUITY	$255,924	$76,564	$211,336	$163,794	$33,621	$2,151,711	$1,380,500

Note 14. Contingencies

A. Claims and Litigation. The County is a defendant in numerous claims and lawsuits, including medical malpractice actions pertaining to Nassau County Medical Center (Medical Center). The County is uninsured for such matters. In the opinion of the County Attorney and Medical Center management, the amounts claimed in these suits and actions are overstated and are not fair estimates of ultimate settlements, if any. The County intends to defend itself vigorously against all claims.

Liabilities of $22 million have been reported in the General Long-Term Obligations Account group for settlement of litigation and claims other than malpractice claims and unasserted claims. The County Attorney is of the opinion that the ultimate settlement of such claims and litigation outstanding at December 31, 1983, will not result in a material adverse effect on the County's financial position.

Approximately $2.75 million has been accrued as a liability at December 31, 1983, related to malpractice claims where the County Attorney and Medical Center management can reasonably estimate the ultimate outcome.

The County Attorney and Medical Center management are unable, however, to determine the ultimate outcome of a significant number of medical malpractice claims, unasserted claims, and litigation outstanding at December 31, 1983.

Certain labor unions have filed an official complaint with the State Human Rights Commission based on the theory of "comparable worth." This complaint has been augmented by several individual complaints concerning specific matters. These steps are required procedural steps prior to instituting suit in the United States District Court. The theory of "comparable worth" is relatively new and undoubtedly will be litigated through the Federal courts until there is a final determination made in the Supreme Court of the United States. The ultimate outcome of these complaints cannot be determined at this time.

Appropriations and actual expenditures in all funds for the settlement of such claims and litigation have been as follows for the past five years (dollars in thousands):

Year	Appropriation	Expenditure
1983	$6,531	$5,503
1982	2,398	2,370
1981	1,350	1,130
1980	1,350	948
1979	1,560	1,464

B. Tax Certioraris. At December 31, 1983, there were over 5,000 taxpayers' claims pending for the redetermination of assessed valuation (certiorari proceedings) for assessments through 1983. Since January 1, 1978, the County has either negotiated settlements or had judgments against it for certiorari claims totaling approximately $106 million ($23 million in 1983). Additionally, an amount estimated for future settlements and judgments of $120 million has been reported in the General Long-Term Obligations Account group.

The law provides that the County may issue bonds for up to $50 million in each year in which proceedings are settled. During 1983, the County has issued such bonds in the amount of approximately $17 million, bringing the total amount of such bonds issued for all years through December 31, 1983, to approximately $78 million.

C. Contingencies Under Grant Programs. The County participates in a number of Federal and State assisted grant programs. These programs are subject to financial and compliance audits by the grantors or their representatives. As of December 31, 1983, the audits of certain programs have not been completed. Accordingly, the County's compliance with applicable grant requirements will be established at some future date. Provisions for certain expected disallowances where considered necessary have been made as of December 31, 1983.

D. Certain Third Party Reimbursement Matters. Net patient service revenue of the Nassau County Medical Center and the A. Holly Patterson Home includes amounts estimated to be reimbursable by third party payor programs. Such amounts are subject to revision based on changes in a variety of factors as set forth in the applicable regulations. It is the opinion of management that adjustments, if any, would not have a material effect on the financial statements.

The Medical Center and Patterson Home have filed appeals related to certain third party rates for the years 1977 through 1983. The additional revenue to be received as a result of these appeals has been accrued only to the extent it is reasonably assured of being received. In the opinion of management, any additional revenue which may be received would not have a material effect on the financial statements.

E. Insurance. The County is generally self-insured. Certain insurance is carried to cover fire or other property loss in excess of $100,000. No material property losses occurred during 1983.

[COUNTY OF NORTHAMPTON, PENNSYLVANIA]

Combined Balance Sheet [in part]—All Fund Types and Account Groups, December 31, 1983

	Governmental Fund Types			Fiduciary Fund Types	Account Groups	
	General	Special Revenue	Capital Project	Trust and Agency	General Fixed Assets	General Long-Term Debt
			* * *			
Liabilities and Fund Equity						
Liabilities:			* * *			
Total Liabilities	$2,150,737	$5,617,841	$64,832	$2,973,760	—	$17,168,282
Commitments and contingent liabilities (notes 12, 13 and 14)						
Fund equity:						
Contributed capital (note 6)	—	—	—	954,413	—	—
Investment in general fixed assets (note 6)	—	—	—	—	42,236,047	—
Fund balances:						
Reserved for:			* * *			

Note 12. Contingencies

The County receives Federal and State funding under a number of programs. Payments made by these sources under contractual agreements are provisional and subject to redetermination based on the filing of reports and audits of those reports. Final settlements due from or to these sources are recorded in the year in which the related services are performed. Any adjustments resulting from subsequent examinations are recognized in the year in which the results of such examinations become known. County officials do not expect any significant adjustments as a result of these examinations.

Based on an audit by the Commonwealth of Pennsylvania, Office of the Auditor General for the year ended December 31, 1981, of a program administered by the County's skilled nursing facility (Graceland), certain interest expenses aggregating approximately $1,300,000 as of December 31, 1983, are disallowed reimbursement because of the County's alleged failure to reduce interest expense by program investment income. The County has appealed the audit finding to the Commonwealth Department of Public Welfare. In the opinion of County officials and the County Solicitor, the County will prevail.

Note 13. Commitments for Construction Contracts

At the end of fiscal 1983, the County had contractual agreements with ten (10) different vendors for construction to be performed as part of the prison expansion and improvement project. The amount remaining to be paid for work which will be completed in future periods was $450,540 as of December 31, 1983.

Note 14. Litigation

The County is involved in various actions related to construction costs, tax billings, assessment valuations, property damages and other matters. In the opinion of County officials and the County Solicitor, the ultimate outcome of these actions will not have a material adverse effect on the County's financial statements.

EXHIBIT 15-4. EXCERPTS OF FOOTNOTES RELATING TO COMPLIANCE, STEWARDSHIP, AND ACCOUNTABILITY

[CLAYTON COUNTY, GEORGIA (JUNE 30, 1984), NOTES TO FINANCIAL STATEMENTS (IN PART)]

Note 2. Stewardship, Compliance and Accountabilty

A. Bond Indenture

There were no material violations of bond indenture provisions.

B. Fire District Special Revenue Fund

The Fire District Special Revenue Fund had deficit fund balances of $317,431 and $524,354 at June 30, 1984 and 1983, respectively. There was a 1 mill increase in the fire district tax rate effective during the year ended June 30, 1984. The resulting increase in tax revenue contributed to the decrease in fund deficit. Also contributing to the decrease was use of long term financing of the purchase of some capital equipments.

C. Street Lights Special Revenue Fund

The Street Lights Special Revenue Fund had deficit fund balances of $70,259 and $45,499 at June 30, 1984 and 1983, respectively. Loans to this fund from the General Fund have been used to finance the deficits.

The Street Lights Special Revenue Fund had expenditures in excess of revenues of $24,760 and $15,920 for the years ended June 30, 1984 and 1983, respectively.

The Street Lights Special Revenue Fund expenditures of $24,760 in excess of revenues were in excess of appropriations. Therefore, the county is not in compliance with statutes of the State of Georgia.

Management's review of street light operations has resulted in an approximate doubling of revenue each year for the past several years and plans include accelerated billing following installation of new lighting. Utility costs during the periods have been increasing. However, the balances involved are not material relative to the revenues, expenditures and unreserved fund balances of the General Fund, from which contributions may be made to the Street Light Special Revenue Fund.

D. Capital Projects Fund

While the Capital Project Fund has fund balance of $7,278,387, there are contracts payable of $8,387,774 which constitute a reservation of the fund balance. This results in a deficit or an overencumbered balance of $1,109,387. Management believes interest earnings will offset most of this encumbrance, and they are seeking opportunities for efficient cost reductions in the construction contracts.

[CITY OF ENID, OKLAHOMA (JUNE 30, 1984), NOTES TO FINANCIAL STATEMENTS (IN PART)]

Note 2. Stewardship, Compliance and Accountability

A. Budget Reconciliations

Items required to adjust budget funds' actual revenues, expenditures, and fund balances reported on the budgetary basis to those reported on the GAAP basis are as follows.

	General Fund	Special Revenue Funds	Capital Projects Funds
Fund balances, June 30, 1984 (Non-GAAP budgetary basis)	$4,854,843	$ 558,279	$2,848,656
Current year encumbrances included in expenditures	36,827	459,457	127,222
Reservations of fund balance for inventory	178,749	—	—
Effect of functional blending reclassifications:			
Central Fire Station	—	—	29,157
Airport	—	(140,767)	—
Revenue accruals	752,874	295,837	46,268
Expenditure accruals	(90,992)	(38,145)	(2,030)
Fund balances, June 30, 1985	$5,732,301	$1,134,661	$3,049,273

B. Retained Earnings or Fund Balance Deficits

The retained earnings (deficit) of the Airport Fund results from the recording of Airport Fund liabilities for improvements and hangar construction while the corresponding assets have not been recorded.

The deficit in the retained earnings for the Gold Course Fund resulted from the application of generally accepted accounting principles to the financial reporting for the fund. The deficit does not indicate that expenditures in excess of budgeted amounts have been made.

C. Prior Period Adjustments

The changes in fund balance/retained earnings (deficit) are as follows:

1. To accrue the following revenues previously recorded on cash basis.
   Sales taxes
   Interest on investments
   Revenue sharing funds
   Intergovernmental grant revenues for expenditures made before year end on expenditure driven grants
   Accounts receivable
2. To accrue expenses previously recorded on cash basis.
3. In order to comply with NCGA *Statement 3,* various adjustments have been made to restate fund balances and include the following activities in the accompanying financial statements:
   The General Fund has been restated to include the Central Fire Station Fund.

The Capital Projects Fund has been restated to include the Convention Center Fund.

The Enterprise Funds have been restated to include the assets and operations of trash collection, golf course operations, and airport operations. Trash collection and golf course operations were previously included in the General Fund, while the Airport Fund was reported as a Special Revenue Fund.

The Public Transportation Fund was created in 1984 to account for the EPTA assets and the results of the management and operations of those assets.

4. In accordance with NCGA *Statement 4,* a liability has been recorded for accrued vacation and sick pay benefits previously recorded when paid. In the governmental funds only the portion of the liability to be liquidated with expendable available financial resources is reported. The remaining liability has been recorded in the General Long-term Debt Group. Adjustments have been made to restate proprietary fund balances to correctly reflect the liability on an accrual basis.

[CITY OF EVANSTON, ILLINOIS (FEBRUARY 29, 1984), NOTES TO FINANCIAL STATEMENTS (IN PART)]

Note 2. Stewardship, Compliance, and Accountability

A. Deficit Fund Balances/Retained Earnings of Individual Funds

The following funds had deficits in fund balances/retained earnings at February 29, 1984:

Special Assessment Warrants	
#1317	$17,094
#1336	2,465
#1337	5,964
#1339	139
#1345	1,016
#1348	41,979
#1349	3,247
#1353	99,347
#1354	59

B. Excess of Actual Expenditures/Expenses over Budget in Individual Fund

The following funds had an excess of actual expenditures/expenses (exclusive of depreciation and amortization) over budget for the year ended February 29, 1984:

Fund	Excess
Funds That Have Legally Adopted Budgets	
Mental Health	$ 976
Playground and Recreation	59,167
Mass Transit	68,762
Community Development Block Grant	41,852
Federal Revenue Sharing	59,998
Insurance	92,641
Debt Service	7,291,433
Other Funds Disclosing Budgetary Information	
Water	$ 115,914
Sewer	12,573

[NEW HANOVER COUNTY, NORTH CAROLINA (JUNE 30, 1984), NOTES TO FINANCIAL STATEMENTS (IN PART)]

Note 2. Stewardship, Compliance and Accountability

A. Deficit Retained Earnings of Individual Fund

The deficit balance of the County's Airport Enterprise Fund ($9,134,017) at June 30, 1984, was caused primarily by depreciation of fixed assets acquired with contributed capital.

B. Excess of Expenditures over Appropriations in Individual Fund

Expenditures exceeded appropriations in the County's Special Revenue Fund. As previously discussed in Note 1, this resulted from the retroactive establishment of this fund made necessary by State legislation approved June 26, 1984. The County has budgeted for this fund's operations in its 1984–85 fiscal year.

[SHREVEPORT, LOUISIANA (DECEMBER 31, 1983), NOTES TO FINANCIAL STATEMENTS (IN PART)]

Note (2). Compliance, Stewardship, and Accountability

A. Material Violations of Finance Related Legal and Contractual Provisions

There are a number of limitations and restrictions contained in the various bond indentures. The City is in compliance with all significant limitations and restrictions. No material violations of finance-related legal and contractual provisions occurred during 1983.

B. Fund Deficits

During 1980 the State Fair Stadium Commission Fund was dissolved and combined with the Parks and Recreation Fund, which resulted in a residual equity transfer of a deficit in the amount of $262,966. The City Council has approved an appropriation which will eliminate this deficit over a five year period. Transfers were made during the year which totaled $100,000.

The Shreveport Area Transit System Fund has a deficit in the amount of $315,559, which will be funded in future periods by subsidies from the General Fund.

The deficit of $84,315 in the Municipal and Regional Airports Fund results from the transfers to the General Fund including amounts for debt service payments.

The Firemen's Pension and Relief Fund had a deficit of $300,817 at December 31, 1983; however, when combined with the Fire Escrow Trust, net assets available for benefits amounted to $523,815.

The deficit of $536,547 in the Special Assessment Fund is due to the application of generally accepted accounting principles to the financial reporting for such funds. Bond proceeds used to finance construction of special assessment projects are not recognized as an "other financing source." Liabilities for special assessment bonds payable are accounted for in the Special Assessment Fund. Special assessments are recognized as revenue only to the extent that individual installments are considered current assets. The deficit of the fund will be reduced and eliminated as deferred special assessment installments become current assets.

C. Excess of Expenditures over Appropriations

During 1983, no individual fund had an excess of expenditures over appropriations.

[CITY OF RALEIGH, NORTH CAROLINA (JUNE 30, 1984), NOTES TO FINANCIAL STATEMENTS (IN PART)]

Note 2. Stewardship, Compliance and Accountability

Excess of Expenditures over Appropriations

Any excesses of expenditures over appropriations result from either the accrual of amounts at year-end for which budget provision had not been made or result from operating conditions near year-end for which a subsequent budget amendment was made. These excesses are not considered material and do not reflect control at the level of budget ordinance appropriation but, rather, at the management control line item level.

[CITY OF SAN ANGELO, TEXAS (SEPTEMBER 30, 1983), NOTES TO FINANCIAL STATEMENTS (IN PART)]

Note 2. Stewardship, Compliance and Accountability

In the comparison of data reported on Bureau of the Census Forms RS-9 and F-21A with audited records of the City for fiscal year ended September 30, 1982, the following substantial differences were noted:

Intergovernmental Revenue (Part II) on Form RS-9 was reported on the cash basis while the City's records reported revenue on the accrual basis. Use of the two reporting methods resulted in a total difference in revenues reported of $90,759.

Budgeted Revenue Sharing Expenditures (Part V, Column A) on Form F-21A were reported as being the same as actual expenditures.

At September 30, 1983, the following funds had deficit total equity balances:

Special Revenue Fund	
Ft. Concho Debt Retirement	$ 38,527
Capital Project Funds	
Foster Street—Loop 306	8,427
East-West Throughway	10,494
Flood Control	17,965
Museum Restoration	4,121
Enterprise Funds	
Ambulance	12,394
Transit	219,880
Airport	1,442,989

The following funds have expenses or expenditures (after adjustment to budgetary basis) in excess of appropriations for the year ended September 30, 1983:

Coliseum, Auditorium, and Convention	$12,654
Nutrition	5,496
Ambulance	898
Shop and Garage	1,527

[CITY OF SEATTLE, WASHINGTON (DECEMBER 31, 1983), NOTES TO FINANCIAL STATEMENTS (IN PART)]

Note 2. Stewardship, Compliance and Accountability

Budgetary Compliance

The City does not budget all Special Revenue Funds on an annual basis. A reconciliation of actual results for budgeted and unbudgeted Special Revenue Funds follows:

	Revenues	Expenditures	Other Financing Sources (Uses)	Fund Balance, December 31
Annually budgeted fund—Exhibit 3	$ 72,391,374	$100,500,436	$29,010,986	$11,279,306
Budgeted on basis other than annual:				
Seattle Center Maintenance and Repair	(3,665)	—	—	3,993
Cumulative Reserve	3,737,160	1,559,396	1,436,511	11,959,443
Emergency	167,583	595,459	3,674,331	6,831,769
Arterial City	5,942,520	5,818,664	86,647	8,761,262
Transit	493,136	64,110	(357,094)	1,271,803
Housing and Abatement Revolving	28,507	15,195	—	251,354
Economic Development Grant	13,259	13,259	—	—
Vanpool	777,421	551,071	—	787,600
Housing Replacement	—	—	—	78,802
Housing and Community Development Revenue Sharing	16,731,559	18,127,611	1,510,354	1,232,176
TOTALS—SPECIAL REVENUE FUNDS	$100,278,854	$127,245,201	$35,361,735	$42,457,508

Fund Deficits

Special Revenue Funds. Actual revenues were less than anticipated in the Seattle Center Fund and a transfer of $227,847 in revenues to deferred was required when certain receivables were renegotiated as promissory notes due in one to ten years. This resulted in the following deficit:

Fund balance deficit reported	$600,680
Unrecorded reserves for:	
Encumbrances	19,513
Continuing appropriations	29,496
Bumbershoot operations	73,181
Total Deficit	$722,870

On April 23, 1984, Council Bill 104235 was introduced to provide $456,000 from the Emergency Fund to reduce the part of the deficit caused by the revenue shortfall. The portion of the deficit caused by the revenue deferral will be reduced as the notes become current.

Special Assessment Funds. The deficits of the local improvement districts result from the application of generally accepted accounting principles to the financial reporting for such funds. Bond proceeds used to finance construction of special assessment projects are not recognized as "other financing sources" but liabilities for special assessment bonds payable are recorded. Special assessments are recognized as revenue only to the extent that individual installments are considered current assets. The fund deficits will be reduced and eliminated as deferred special assessment installments totaling $5,079,463 become current assets. The Business Improvement Area Fund commenced operations in 1983 and its first assessments, which are based on sales by businesses located in the district, will be collected in early 1984.

Internal Service Funds. The Industrial Insurance Fund's deficit of $1,064,526 resulted from accrual of estimated claim settlements for claims filed and pending.

Available Fund Balance—General Fund

The Executive Department, Office of Management and Budget (OMB), annually prepares an estimate of available General Fund fund balance for the new budget year. To ensure sufficient cash balances at December 31, 1983, OMB has determined that the amount of fund balance needed to be reserved is the sum of desired cash reserve plus the portion of fund balance at year-end attributable to the excess of non-cash assets over liabilities. The following table compares the actual 1983 results with OMB's estimate of available fund balance as presented in the 1984 Budget.

	Budget	Actual	Variance Favorable (Unfavorable)
Unreserved Fund Balance—12/31/82 (accrual basis)	$ 15,725,705	$ 15,725,705	$ —
Revenues and Other Financing Sources:			
1983 Adopted Budget $ 194,911,469			
Decrease in Revenue Estimate (1,459,750)	193,451,719	197,114,120	3,662,401
	209,177,424	212,839,825	3,662,401
Expenditures and Other Financing Uses:			
1983 Adopted Budget $(194,911,469)			
Underexpenditure of Finance—General 3,102,917			
1983 DAS Rate Adjustment 839,499			
Transfer to Cumulative Reserve Fund (876,305)			
Transfer to Emergency Fund (1,931,611)	(193,776,969)	(191,223,993)	2,552,976
Decrease in Reserved Fund Balance over 12/31/82	—	562,941	562,941
Residual Equity Transfers:			
Pre-1927 Local Improvement Districts	—	155,456	155,456
Design Commission Fund	18,545	33,443	14,898
Unreserved Fund Balance—12/31/83 (accrual basis)	15,419,000	22,367,672	6,948,672
Net Non-cash Asset Balance—12/31/83	(8,021,693)	(5,059,923)	2,961,770
Unreserved Fund Balance—12/31/83 (cash basis)	7,397,307	17,307,749	9,910,442
Cash Reserve (Not Formally Recorded)	(6,700,000)	(9,116,747)*	(2,416,747)
AVAILABLE FUND BALANCE FOR 1984	$ 697,307	$ 8,191,002	$ 7,493,695

* Furnished by the Office of Management and Budget.

Following is a reconciliation of the total unreserved and reserved fund balance (cash basis) with the cash balance of the General Fund at December 31, 1983:

Unreserved Fund Balance—(cash basis)	$17,307,749
Reserved Fund Balance	1,522,080
CASH AND EQUITY IN POOLED INVESTMENTS	$18,829,829

[CITY OF YAKIMA, WASHINGTON (DECEMBER 31, 1983), NOTES TO FINANCIAL STATEMENTS (IN PART)]

Note 3—Compliance and Accountability

a. Debt Limit

The State law provides that debt cannot be incurred in excess of the following percentages of the value of the taxable property of the City.

General Purpose (A maximum of .75% can be levied without the vote of the people)	2.50%
Utilities Purpose	2.50%
Open Space and Park Facilities	2.50%
TOTAL	7.50%

As of December 31, 1983, the debt limits for the City were as follows:

	Legal Limit	Outstanding Indebtedness	Margin Available
General Purpose (Non-voted legal limit is $9,578,544)	$31,928,480	$2,873,194	$28,848,107
Utilities Purpose	31,928,480	—	31,928,480
Open Space and Park Facilities	31,928,480	—	31,928,480
	$95,785,439	$2,873,194	$92,912,245

b. Individual Fund Deficits

The following table depicts all individual fund deficits at December 31, 1983.

Fund	Deficit Fund Balance
Community Development	$47,174
Cumulative Reserve	5,210

The deficit in the Community Development Fund is a result of the normal lag in receipt of Federal Grant reimbursements and the Cumulative Reserve deficit is due to non-timely receipt of funds due. Both deficits were subsequently cleared.

c. Excess Expenditures over Appropriations

Expenditures of the General Fund and individual funds within the Special Revenue Funds did not exceed appropriations for the year ended December 31, 1983.

EXHIBIT 15-5. EXCERPTS OF FOOTNOTES RELATING TO GOVERNMENTAL ENCUMBRANCES

[BIRMINGHAM, ALABAMA (JUNE 30, 1984), NOTES TO FINANCIAL STATEMENTS (IN PART)]

Note 1 [in part]. Encumbrances

Encumbrances outstanding at year end are reported in the general purpose financial statements as a reservation of fund balance since they do not constitute expenditures or liabilities. The following table reconciles excess of revenues and other sources over expenditures and other uses of the General Fund on a budgetary basis using encumbrance accounting in the Combining Statement of Revenues, Expenditures and Changes in Fund Balances–Budget and Actual to the amount reported on a GAAP basis:

As reported, budgetary basis:	
Encumbrances at beginning of the year	$ 701,864
Less:	
Encumbrances at end of the year	(1,864,085)
Excess of revenues and other sources over expenditures and other uses	1,291,633
Excess of revenues and other sources over expenditures and other uses	$ 129,412

[CITY OF BROWNSVILLE, TEXAS (SEPTEMBER 30, 1983), NOTES TO FINANCIAL STATEMENTS (IN PART)]

Note 1 [in part]. Encumbrances Outstanding

Encumbrances outstanding for the governmental fund types as of September 30, 1983, are as follows:

General Fund			Housing Assistance program		
Police cars	$ 97,070		contracts	174,230	
Other materials and supplies	32,058	$ 129,128	Other contracts	18,000	
Special Revenue Funds			Other materials and supplies	75,569	
Community Development				267,799	2,096,253
Housing assistance program contracts	1,557,212		Capital Project Funds		
Sewer improvement contracts	213,526		Fire Station Construction		
Other contracts and supplies	55,992		Construction contract	3,660	
	1,826,730		Police Station Construction		
Convention and Tourism			Construction and engineering contracts	22,950	
Supplies	32		Equipment	22,922	
Brownsville Community Health Clinic				45,872	49,532
Supplies	1,692		Total (memo only)		$2,274,913
Jobs Development					

[CITY OF GLENDALE, CALIFORNIA (JUNE 30, 1984), NOTES TO FINANCIAL STATEMENTS (IN PART)]

Note (1) [in part]. Appropriations and Encumbrances

Budgetary control is an essential element in governmental accounting and reporting. The City adopts a non-GAAP annual budget and utilizes an "encumbrance system." Under this procedure, commitments such as purchase orders and uncompleted contracts are recorded as reservations of fund balance. The budget is adopted on a modified accrual basis for Governmental Funds and a full accrual basis for Proprietary Funds.

The City takes into consideration encumbered amounts when comparing actual results of operations against its annual budget. Exhibit C shows our non-GAAP budget and the results of the year. This activity is then converted to a GAAP basis by eliminating encumbrances of $144,177 in the General Fund and $1,615,530 in the Special Revenue Funds.

[CITY OF GREENSBORO, NORTH CAROLINA (JUNE 30, 1984), NOTES TO FINANCIAL STATEMENTS (IN PART)]

Note 1 [in part]. Encumbrances

Appropriations in governmental funds are encumbered upon issuance of purchase orders, contracts or other forms of legal commitments. Even though goods and services have not been received, the transactions are accounted for as a reservation of fund balances in the year that the commitment is made. While appropriations lapse at the end of the fiscal year, the succeeding year's budget ordinance specifically provides for the reappropriation of year end encumbrances.

[COUNTY OF HANOVER, VIRGINIA (JUNE 30, 1984), NOTES TO FINANCIAL STATEMENTS (IN PART)]

Note 1 [in part]. Encumbrances

Encumbrance accounting, under which purchase orders, contracts and other commitments for the expenditure of funds are recorded in order to reserve that portion of the applicable appropriations, is employed in the governmental funds. Encumbrances are not the equivalent of expenditures; therefore, the reserve for encumbrances is reported as part of the fund balance.

[HILLSBOROUGH COUNTY, FLORIDA (SEPTEMBER 30, 1983), NOTES TO FINANCIAL STATEMENTS (IN PART)]

Encumbrances

Encumbrances outstanding at year-end represent the estimated amounts of expenditures ultimately to be paid on unperformed contracts in process at year-end. Because appropriations lapse at year-end, it is the County's policy to close encumbrances at year-end to the reserve account and to reencumber those amounts at the beginning of the next budget cycle. Encumbrances outstanding at September 30, 1983, totaled $11,089,269.

[INDIANAPOLIS, INDIANA (DECEMBER 31, 1983 AND 1982), NOTES TO FINANCIAL STATEMENTS (IN PART)]

Note 1 [in part]. Encumbrances

Encumbrance accounting, under which purchase orders, contracts, and other commitments for the expenditure of monies are recorded in order to reserve that portion of the applicable appropriation, is employed as an extension of formal budgetary integration in the General Fund, Special Revenue Funds, Capital Projects Funds, and Expendable and Pension Trust Funds. Encumbrances do not lapse with the expiration of the budget period. Encumbrances to be financed from future revenues other than approved grant revenues are recorded in their entirety as a reservation of fund balance since they do not constitute expenditures and may result in reporting an overreservation of fund balances. Encumbrances to be financed from approved grants (see Note 4) are not reflected in the financial statements and are as follows:

Generic Fund Type	1983	1982
General Fund	$8,470,258	$9,108,816
Special Revenue Funds	23,401	49,444
Capital Projects Funds	2,278,775	5,299,437

[MECKLENBURG COUNTY, NORTH CAROLINA (JUNE 30, 1984), NOTES TO FINANCIAL STATEMENTS (IN PART)]

Note 1 [in part]. Encumbrances

Encumbrance accounting, under which purchase orders, contracts, and other commitments for the expenditure of funds are recorded in order to reserve that portion of the applicable appropriation, is employed in the governmental funds. At year-end, open encumbrances are reported as reservations of fund balances since those commitments are accommodated through subsequent years' budget appropriations. Encumbrances do not constitute expenditures or liabilities.

[CITY OF NEW ROCHELLE, NEW HAMPSHIRE (DECEMBER 31, 1983), NOTES TO FINANCIAL STATEMENTS (IN PART)]

Note 1 [in part]. Encumbrances

Encumbrance accounting, under which purchase orders, contracts, and other commitments for the expenditure of monies are recorded in order to reserve applicable appropriations, is employed as an extension of formal budgetary integration in the General and Special Revenue Funds. Encumbrances outstanding at year-end are reported as reservations of fund balance since they do not constitute expenditures or liabilities.

[PRINCE GEORGE'S COUNTY, MARYLAND (JUNE 30, 1984), NOTES TO FINANCIAL STATEMENTS (IN PART)]

Note 1 [in part]

(e) Encumbrances

Encumbrance accounting, under which purchase orders, contracts, and other commitments for the expenditure of funds are recorded in order to reserve that portion of the applicable appropriation, is employed in the General, Special Revenue, and Capital Projects Funds. Encumbrances are reported as reservations of fund balances since they do not constitute expenditures or liabilities under the GAAP basis of accounting.

[CITY OF SAVANNAH, GEORGIA (DECEMBER 31, 1983), NOTES TO FINANCIAL STATEMENTS (IN PART)]

Note 1 [in part]

(G) Encumbrances

Encumbrances, if material, are reported as a reservation of the fund balance. However, for the current year, it was determined that the total encumbrances outstanding were not material except for the Capital Projects Fund.

[CITY OF VIRGINIA BEACH, VIRGINIA (JUNE 30, 1984), NOTES TO FINANCIAL STATEMENTS (IN PART)]

Note 1 [in part]

F. Encumbrances

Encumbrance accounting, in which purchase orders, contracts, and other commitments for the expenditures of monies are recorded (reduces the applicable appropriation), is followed in the General, Special Revenue, and Capital Projects Funds (except as reported in Note 6A). Encumbrances outstanding do not constitute expenditures until expended or accrued as liabilities. Fund balances have been reserved equal to the unliquidated encumbrances at June 30 in the governmental funds.

EXHIBIT 15-6. EXCERPTS OF FOOTNOTES RELATING TO JOINT VENTURES

[ATLANTA, GEORGIA (DECEMBER 31, 1983), NOTES TO FINANCIAL STATEMENTS (IN PART)]

Note 8. Joint Venture

City of Atlanta and Fulton County Recreation Authority

The Authority was created in 1961 with powers, among other things, to acquire, construct, equip, maintain and operate an athletic stadium (the ''Stadium'') and an athletic coliseum (the ''Omni'') and to authorize the issuance of revenue bonds.

The City and Fulton County, Georgia, participate in a joint venture relationship with the Authority. Each party has contracted with the Authority to make prin-

cipal and interest payments on the applicable revenue bonds issued for construction of the Stadium and the Omni. Such payments are to be reduced by any amounts in the Authority's sinking funds available for current debt service at the beginning of each sinking fund year. These debt service deficiencies are shared two-thirds by the City and one-third by Fulton County. When these revenue bonds have been fully paid, the authority will convey fee simple title to the Stadium and the Omni to each party based on their proportionate shares noted above.

As described above, the City has responsibility in the financing of debt and is entitled to an interest in the Authority's property. Also, the Mayor appoints a majority of the governing body of the Authority. Accordingly, the Authority is a part of the City's reporting entity and is an Enterprise Fund. The assets, liabilities and income accounts of the Authority are stated at their full amount. Fulton County's minority interest (one-third) is reflected as a separate line item in the accompanying financial statements.

The Authority's financial statements have been examined by other auditors. Certain reclassifications have been applied to such audited financial statements for inclusion herein to conform their presentation to the other Enterprise Funds of the City.

[CITY OF CHESAPEAKE, VIRGINIA (JUNE 30, 1984), NOTES TO FINANCIAL STATEMENTS (IN PART)]

Note 12 [in part]. Joint Venture

The City has guaranteed approximately $5,980,000 in bonds and the interest thereon, issued by the Southeastern Public Service Authority (SPSA). The purpose of the SPSA is to provide and operate a regional system for the reception, transfer, processing and disposal of solid waste. Under the guaranty agreement, the City has agreed to make payments to the trustee for deposit in a reserve account, as necessary, to maintain in such account the sum of the amount of interest due on the next succeeding interest payment date for the bonds and the amount required to pay principal of all the bonds maturing on the next July 1. The City's allocable portion of the amount that may be due is 23%, with the remaining balance being due from neighboring localities which are also members of the SPSA. No payments were made under the provisions of the guaranty agreement to the reserve account during the year ended June 30, 1984.

Additionally, should SPSA perform any act that constitutes default under the bond indebture, the entire bond principal could be considered due, of which the City would be liable for its allocable portion.

The full faith and credit of the City is pledged to redeem its allocable portion of the interest and bonds if SPSA revenues are insufficient to meet the obligations.

Summary financial information of SPSA for the year ended June 30, 1984, is as follows:

Assets	$32,095,794
Liabilities	31,240,811
Equity	854,983
Debt payable from operating revenues:	
Current portion of long-term debt	—
Long-term debt	29,840,000

Since SPSA is in the development stage of operations, it had no operations (revenues or expenses) for the year end June 30, 1984.

[CITY OF FORT WORTH, TEXAS (SEPTEMBER 30, 1983), NOTES TO FINANCIAL STATEMENTS (IN PART)]

Note K: Joint Ventures

A. Dallas–Fort Worth Regional Airport

The Dallas–Fort Worth Regional Airport (Airport) is owned jointly by the cities of Fort Worth (4/11) and Dallas (7/11) and operated by an eleven member board comprised of the mayor of each City, three members from Fort Worth and six members from Dallas as appointed by the respective City Councils. Financial statements of this entity are not included since this organization is not operated under the sole control of the Fort Worth City Council.

The cities have executed an agreement with the Airport which provides for the Airport to pay $30,000,000 over a maximum of fifteen (15) years to reduce the cities' initial capital investment in land. Fort Worth's share of this amount is reflected as a receivable and deferred revenue in the Capital Projects Fund. Approximately $900,000 was collected in fiscal 1983. The City's remaining investment in the Airport is recorded in the General Fixed Asset Account Group.

The cities issued Joint Revenue Bonds and Special Facility Revenue Bonds to construct the Airport. The Joint Revenue Bonds are payable from and secured by Airport gross revenues. The Special Facility Revenue Bonds are payable from and secured by the net lease rentals derived from the special facilities. The outstanding debt and related debt service are accounted for by the Dallas–Fort Worth Regional Airport.

The cities have executed covenants individually, by ordinance, to levy a maintenance tax if necessary to assure that the Airport will be efficiently operated and maintained. The amount of such tax is limited for each city in its respective ratio to the lesser of 5 cents per $100 of assessed valuation of the property in each city or the amount of the maintenance tax required. For fiscal 1983, a 5 cent maintenance tax would have been $3,571,000 for the City of Fort Worth. The obligation of the City to pay the maintenance tax is junior and subordinate to a prior pledge for the benefit of the holders of City of Fort Worth Airports Revenue Bonds, Series 1960, 1960A and 1961. The Airport Board has entered into agreements with air carriers utilizing the Airport which provide for adjustments to rentals, fees and other charges which management believes would preclude losses from being incurred. To date, no maintenance tax has been levied by the cities.

B. SURTRAN

The City participates with the City of Dallas in a joint venture for operation of the Dallas–Fort Worth SURTRAN system to provide ground transportation to the Dallas–Fort Worth Regional Airport. The City makes annual operating subsidies to SURTRAN as required. The City's equity ownership is based on the 15% capital contribution provided in the year of organization. All operations are reported by the City of Dallas.

C. Railroad Line

In January, 1984, the cities of Fort Worth and Dallas jointly purchased approximately thirty-four miles of rail line and right-of-way extending between the two cities. The purchase price of $18,000,000 for property and right-of-way has been 80% and 13% financed through Urban Mass Transportation Administration and State Department of Highways and Public Transportation grants, respectively. The remaining portion has been provided equally by the cities.

In addition, it is anticipated that the cities of Fort Worth and Dallas will purchase a local easement on the same property from the Missouri-Kansas-Texas Railroad Company. The expected purchase price of $15,000,000 will be financed in the same manner as described above. In fiscal 1983, the City of Fort Worth issued $1,000,000 in Certificates of Obligation for such purposes.

[CITY OF LAKEWOOD, CALIFORNIA (JUNE 30, 1984), NOTES TO FINANCIAL STATEMENTS (IN PART)]

Note 13. Joint Venture

The City is a member of the Southern California Joint Powers Insurance Authority (Authority). The Authority has been evaluated under the criteria set forth in

NCGA Statement 3 and it does not fall within the definition of the City's reporting entity.

The Authority is comprised of 43 Southern California member cities and is organized under a Joint Powers Agreement pursuant to the California Government Code. The purpose of the Authority is to arrange and administer programs of insurance for the pooling of self-insured losses and to purchase excess insurance coverage.

Each member city has a representative on the Board of Directors. Officers of the Agency are elected annually by the Board members.

A. Self-insurance Programs of the Authority

General Liability Insurance. Annual deposits are paid by member cities and are adjusted retrospectively to cover costs. Each member city, including Lakewood, self-insures for the first $10,000 of each loss. Participating cities then share in the next $10,000 to $500,000 per loss occurrence. Excess insurance has been purchased to a limit of $9.5 million. Specific coverage includes comprehensive and general automotive liability, personal injury, contractual liability, errors and omissions and certain other coverage.

Worker's Compensation. Periodic deposits are paid by member cities and are adjusted retrospectively to cover costs. Each member city has a specific retention level. The City of Lakewood has a retention level of $50,000 and pays 100% of all losses incurred under $50,000. The City does not share or pay for losses of other cities under $50,000. Losses of $50,000 to $250,000 are prorated among all participating cities on a payroll basis. Losses in excess of $250,000 are covered by excess insurance purchased by the participating cities, as a part of the pool, to a limit of $10 million.

Property Protection. The City of Lakewood participates in the All Risks Property Protection Program, which is primarily underwritten by a casualty insurance company. The annual deposits paid by participating member cities are based upon deductibility levels and are not subject to retroactive adjustments.

B. Condensed Financial Information of the Authority

At June 30, 1984, the Authority had assets of $16,467,345, current liabilities of $4,515,581 and fund equity of $11,951,764 which is reserved for losses and claims. As a result of operations, reserves increased during the year $1,375,852.

The amount of the City's share of Authority equity at June 30, 1984, is not available.

[CITY OF PUEBLO, COLORADO (DECEMBER 31, 1983), NOTES TO FINANCIAL STATEMENTS (IN PART)]

Note 10. Joint Ventures

The City is a participant in two joint ventures consisting of the Regional Building Department and the Pueblo City-County Health Department. A summary of the activities of these joint ventures is as follows:

Regional Building Department

The Pueblo Regional Building Department was created by the governments of the City of Pueblo, Colorado, and the County of Pueblo, Colorado, to promote the public health, safety and welfare through the enforcement of building codes and licensing of contractors. The governing body of the Department consists of seven members, three of which are appointed by the City, three are appointed by the County and one member is jointly appointed. The governing body of the Department has authority for the appointment of management. The joint venture agreement requires that the annual operating budget of the Department be submitted to the City and County for approval prior to adoption. The agreement also stipulates that the Department provide an accounting of actual revenues and expenses to the City and County on a monthly basis. In addition, the fees charged for the issuance of permits and licenses are subject to the approval of the City and County. To the extent feasible, expenses of the Department are allocated to the participants based on the proportion of the value of construction work performed within the participant's jurisdiction compared to the total value of construction work performed in the entire area. If allocated expenses to any participant exceed revenues generated in that participant's jurisdiction, the governing body of the Department may charge the participant for the deficiency subject to appropriation and the conformity of the expenses incurred to the annual budget approved by the City and County.

Summary financial information of the Regional Building Department as of and for the year ended December 31, 1983, is as follows:

Pueblo Regional Building Department Balance Sheet, December 31, 1983

Assets	
TOTAL ASSETS	$91,732
Liabilities and Fund Equity	
TOTAL LIABILITIES	$10,810
FUND EQUITY	80,922
TOTAL LIABILITIES AND FUND EQUITY	$91,732

Pueblo Regional Building Department, Statement of Revenues, Expenses and Changes in Retained Earnings, Year Ended December 31, 1983

Operating revenues	$ 195,695
Operating expenses	386,949
Operating income (loss)	(191,254)
Other financing sources (uses)	
City of Pueblo subsidy	158,000
County of Pueblo subsidy	30,000
Other	556
NET INCOME (LOSS)	(2,698)
Retained earnings, January 1	56,417
Retained earnings, December 31	$ 53,719

In as much as the purpose of the Department is to be self-supporting through user fees, the Department has adopted accounting principles which correspond to those used by proprietary funds. Thus, the investment in the joint venture is accounted for using the equity method of accounting. Additionally, the joint venture has no debt which would necessitate the pledging of Department assets as collateral.

Pueblo City-County Health Department

The Pueblo City-County Health Department was created by the governments of the City of Pueblo, Colorado, and the County of Pueblo, Colorado, in 1952. The purpose of the Department is to provide public health services to the residents of the city and county. The governing body of the Department consists of five members, two of which are appointed by the City, two are appointed by the County and one member is jointly appointed by the City and County. The governing body of the Department appoints the administrator and the administrator appoints all other personnel. The joint venture agreement requires that the governing body of the Department submit a proposed annual operating budget to the City and County for their approval. Based upon the proposed budget, the City and County individually determine the amount of their respective annual subsidies for the Department. The joint venture agreement also stipulates that the participants' shall endeavor to appropriate funds to the Department that are reasonable, fair and equitable to all parties.

Summary financial information of the Pueblo City-County Health Department as of and for the year ended December 31, 1983, is as follows:

Pueblo City-County Health Department, Combined Balance Sheet—All Fund Types and Account Groups, December 31, 1983

	General Fund	General Fixed Assets	Total (Memorandum Only)
ASSETS			
TOTAL ASSETS	$361,965	$320,099	$682,064
LIABILITIES AND FUND EQUITY			
TOTAL LIABILITIES	$ 85,877	$	$ 85,877
TOTAL FUND EQUITY	276,088	320,099	596,187
TOTAL LIABILITIES AND FUND EQUITY	$361,965	$320,099	$682,064

Pueblo City-County Health Department, Statement of Revenues, Expenditures and Changes in Fund Balance, Year Ended December 31, 1983

Total revenues	$ 932,691	EXCESS (DEFICIENCY) OF REVENUES AND OTHER FINANCING SOURCES OVER EXPENDITURES	(10,929)
Total expenditures	1,859,400		
Excess (deficiency) of revenues over expenditures	(926,709)	Fund balance, January 1	287,017
Other financing sources		Fund balance, December 31	$ 276,088
City of Pueblo	471,390		
County of Pueblo	444,390		

In as much as the accounting principles used by the Department correspond to those used by governmental-type funds, no investment in the joint venture has been recorded in the accompanying financial statements. In addition, the joint venture has no debt which would necessitate the pledging of Department assets as collateral.

[ROANOKE, VIRGINIA (JUNE 30, 1984), NOTES TO FINANCIAL STATEMENTS (IN PART)]

Note 12. Joint Venture

The City of Roanoke, Town of Vinton, and Roanoke County jointly own a regional sanitary landfill operated by the Roanoke Valley Regional Solid Waste Management Board. The Board is composed of six members, three of whom are appointed by the Roanoke City Council. The remaining three members are appointed by the joint owners. The City of Roanoke has control over budget and financing of the venture only to the extent of representation by the three board members appointed.

Roanoke Valley Regional Solid Waste Management Board	June 30, 1984
Operating Revenues	$1,259,740
Operating Expenses	988,912
Operating Income	270,828
Non-operating Income	59,295
Net Income	330,123
Total Fund Balance, July 1, 1983	$3,091,667
Net Income	330,123
Contributed Capital	168,145
Total Fund Balance, June 30, 1984	$3,589,935
Total Assets	$3,959,717
Total Liabilities	$ 369,782
Total Equity	$3,589,935
City of Roanoke Equity, June 30, 1983	$1,694,887
Increase in Equity	107,593
City of Roanoke Equity, June 30, 1984	$1,802,480

[TULSA, OKLAHOMA (JUNE 30, 1984), NOTES TO FINANCIAL STATEMENTS (IN PART)]

Note V. Joint Ventures

The City of Tulsa has entered into several joint ventures with other governmental units to provide services to their respective constituents. These joint ventures are considered to be separate reporting entities and, with the exception of the River Parks Authority, the Regional Metropolitan Utility Authority and the City-County Electrical Board, for which the City maintains the accounting records and certain assets, have not been included within the financial statements of the City. These joint ventures are as follows:

City of Tulsa–Rogers County Port Authority

The City of Tulsa–Rogers County Port Authority was formed on October 4, 1963, by joint resolution of the City of Tulsa and Rogers County pursuant to Oklahoma state law providing for the establishment and operation of intergovernmental water ports. The Authority, also known as the Tulsa Port of Catoosa, is managed by a nine member board of directors, each serving four year terms. The City of Tulsa appoints six of the directors and the Rogers County Commission appoints the remaining three directors.

The Authority operates the terminal and storage facilities related to shipping activities and has general oversight responsibility for the use and development of an industrial park located adjacent to the port. In 1967, the voters of the City of Tulsa approved a $20 million General Obligation Bond issue to acquire approximately 2,000 acres of land, construct facilities and acquire equipment for the operation of the Port. The City has leased the land to the Port Authority until the year 2075. The operating budget for the Port Authority through June 30, 1984, was $1,444,449. Through fees, charges and lease income, the Port Authority is a self-sustaining operation.

Indian Nation Council of Governments

Created on July 1, 1967, the Indian Nation Council of Governments (INCOG) is a voluntary association of municipal and county governments surrounding the City which provides a forum for regional cooperation and provides coordination of public projects and activities that are mutually beneficial to participating members. Such members include Tulsa, Creek and Osage counties and the cities of Tulsa, Broken Arrow, Sand Springs, Sapulpa, Bristow, Bixby, Jenks, Owasso and Drumright.

Membership in INCOG is represented by a General Assembly consisting of one delegate from each participating member who must be an elected official from the county or municipality represented.

The operating budget for INCOG in FY 1983–84 was $2,112,810, of which the City contributed $648,805. In addition, the City provides computer support for INCOG and leases vehicles for INCOG staff.

Joint City-County Electrical Examining and Appeals Board

Established by joint resolution of the City of Tulsa and Tulsa County in December, 1955, to administer examinations to candidates for electrician's licenses, to issue such licenses, to hear appeals on violations of the City's electrical code and to interpret the application of the electrical code upon request.

The Board consists of seven members who serve two year terms. Two members are appointed by the City of Tulsa, two members are appointed by Tulsa County and the remaining three members are jointly appointed by the City and County.

Through examination fees and other charges, the Board is able to cover its annual budget. All revenues in excess of the Board's expenses are split equally between the City and County. On June 30, 1984, the City's portion of this excess was $9,723. In addition, the City provides office space and equipment maintenance for the Board's staff and certain administrative assistance.

Regional Metropolitan Utility Authority

A public trust created under Oklahoma law on October 10, 1972, to provide, operate and maintain waste water, pollution control and sewage treatment facilities for the City of Tulsa and the other beneficiaries of this public trust, which include the cities of Broken Arrow, Claremore, Jenks, Owasso, Sapulpa, Sperry, Bixby and Catoosa.

The management of RMUA is vested in a Board of Trustees, five of whom are also members of Tulsa's Utility Board. This board has responsibility for its Haikey Creek Sewage Treatment plant, located between the City of Tulsa and Broken Arrow on the Arkansas River, and also administers study programs, funded with federal grants and local contributions, which focus on regional sewage treatment planning involving the City and other beneficiaries of the trust.

Located on a site of approximately 320 acres leased from the City, RMUA's Haikey Creek plant is operated by the City under contract which provides that the City receive its actual cost plus 5%. In turn, RMUA bills the City and Broken Arrow, prime users of the facility, at its cost plus 15%. In addition to this revenue source, RMUA subleases land and storage or processing facilities for private enterprises and sells sand from the Arkansas River.

The City of Tulsa maintains the books and records of RMUA and accounts for it as a non-expendable trust fund.

River Parks Authority

A public trust created under Oklahoma law on April 9, 1974, by the City of Tulsa and Tulsa County as co-beneficiaries. Seven trustees comprise the board of the River Parks Authority, three are appointed by the City of Tulsa, three are appointed by Tulsa County and one is appointed by the Tulsa Metropolitan Area Planning Commission. Each trustee serves a three year term.

The Authority is responsible for the planning, financing, implemention and maintenance of the economic and recreational development of the Arkansas River and its banks within Tulsa County.

The City and County contribute equally to the annual operating budget of the Authority. Through June 30, 1984, the City has contributed $250,069 in operating grants and $167,642 in capital grants. In addition, the City provides administrative services including legal, accounting, purchasing and personnel services. The City records the Authority in its financial report as an expendable trust fund.

Tulsa City-County Civil Defense Administration

Formed by joint resolution of the City and County commissions in January, 1961, the Tulsa City-County Civil Defense Administration currently operates under the provisions of the Oklahoma Civil Defense and Emergency Resources Management Act.

Funding for the Civil Defense Administration is provided by the City of Tulsa (25%), Tulsa County (25%) and the Federal Emergency Management Agency (50%) via the Oklahoma Civil Defense Office. With an FY 1983–84 operating budget of $246,817, the City of Tulsa had contributed, through June 30, 1984, $48,027 in operating funds and $53,000 in capital funds for equipment purchases.

Tulsa City-County Health Department

The Department was created in 1950 by joint resolution of the City of Tulsa and Tulsa County. In 1963, the Health Department was reorganized under state law providing for City-County Health Departments. The nine member Tulsa City-County Board of Health oversees the operation of the Department. The City appoints five of the members, all of whom must be licensed physicians. Tulsa County appoints the remaining four members with no restrictions on qualifications except that they be registered voters.

The Health Department administers the health laws of the State of Oklahoma, applicable federal statutes regarding environmental protection and City ordinances for public health.

Although most of the Health Department's $7,924,306 budget for FY 1983–84 was funded by state and federal grants, the City of Tulsa contributed $211,535 through June 30, 1984, for various programs including Nuisance Abatement, Code Enforcement and the Area Agency on Aging.

Tulsa City-County Library

Formed by joint resolution of the City of Tulsa and Tulsa County on July 1, 1982, the Tulsa City-County Library system operates the Central Library and twenty-two branches in Tulsa County. Management of the Library is vested in a Library Commission consisting of nine members, each serving a term of three years. Six members are appointed by the City Commission and the remaining three are appointed by the County commission.

With an annual budget of $6,951,558 for fiscal 1983–84, the Library is funded by State and Federal grants, user charges, contributions, an ad valorem tax levy and proceeds from two County bond issues.

[CITY OF YAKIMA, WASHINGTON (DECEMBER 31, 1983), NOTES TO FINANCIAL STATEMENTS (IN PART)]

Note 7. Joint Ventures

The City and the County of Yakima entered into a joint venture for the operation of the Yakima Air Terminal on July 1, 1982. The City and the County have contributed equally to the joint venture and will share all profits and losses equally. The 1974 Airport General Obligation Bonds are a liability of the Joint Fund. Operating revenues and expenditures are under the control of the Air Terminal Board. The Enterprise Fund statements usually include the Airport Financial Statements. However, the 1983 Airport Financial Statements are not available and are not included in the 1982 Comparative Totals.

EXHIBIT 15-7. EXCERPTS OF FOOTNOTES RELATING TO ESTABLISHMENT OF NEW FUNDS

[CITY OF ALBUQUERQUE, NEW MEXICO (JUNE 30, 1984), NOTES TO FINANCIAL STATEMENTS (IN PART)]

Note 3—New Funds

During 1984, the City established seven new funds. Those activities previously accounted for in the General Fund are as follows:

Lodgers Tax (Special Revenue) Fund

This fund was established to account for lodgers tax revenues, which are restricted by state statute to specific uses.

Corrections and Detention (Special Revenue) Fund

This fund was established to account for the operations of the City/County Corrections and Detention Center, which is operated by the City under a joint powers agreement with Bernalillo County. Revenues of the fund are legally restricted for operations of the Center.

Fleet Management (Internal Service) Fund

The Fleet Management Fund was established to account for the City's motor pool and vehicle maintenance activities.

The following tables present the effect of excluding these activities from the 1983 revenues and expenditures of the General Fund.

	As Presented	Excluded Activities	Net
Revenues:			
Taxes	$ 31,146,685	$1,558,612	$29,588,073
Licenses and permits	2,444,621	—	2,444,621
Intergovernmental	66,819,616	—	66,819,616
Charges for services	16,179,038	5,362,817	10,816,221
Fines and forfeits	43,705	—	43,705
Miscellaneous	4,901,729	—	4,901,729
Total Revenues	$121,535,394	$6,921,429	$114,613,965
Expenditures:			
General government	$ 21,357,412	$3,880,006	$ 17,477,406
Public safety	46,234,158	5,023,806	41,210,352
Culture and recreation	19,283,623	—	19,283,623
Public works	6,729,572	—	6,729,572
Highways and streets	7,590,412	—	7,590,412
Health	3,102,950	—	3,102,950
Human services	2,383,771	—	2,383,771
Total Expenditures	$106,681,898	$8,903,812	$ 97,778,086

Other new funds are as follows:

City/County Building Construction (Capital Projects) Fund

A joint City/County office building is being constructed under a joint powers agreement between the City and the County. This fund was established to account for the City's portion of the costs of construction.

City/County Building Debt Service Fund

The City has issued $15 million of gross receipts tax revenue bonds to finance its share of the costs of the

City/County office building. This fund was established to account for the debt service of the bonds.

Urban Enhancement Principal and Income Trust (Fiduciary) Funds

These funds were established to account for the transactions of the City's urban enhancement trust, the earnings of which are to be used to finance the design, implementation, and construction of urban enhancement improvement projects.

[BIBB COUNTY, GEORGIA (SEPTEMBER 30, 1983), NOTES TO FINANCIAL STATEMENTS (IN PART)]

Note (12) Funds Added and Deleted

Special Revenue Funds

The L.E.A.A. Fund was deleted during the 1982–83 fiscal year due to termination of Law Enforcement Assistance grants.

Fiduciary Funds

The following expendable trust funds were established during the current fiscal year to account for items which had previously been recorded in the General Fund as restrictions of Fund Balance:

Workmen's Compensation Fund

Employee Group Insurance Fund

Unemployment Compensation Fund

Commissary Trust Fund

Law Library Fund

Prior period financial information presented in these statements has been restated to insure comparability with the current period.

[CITY OF DALY CITY, CALIFORNIA (JUNE 30, 1984), NOTES TO FINANCIAL STATEMENTS (IN PART)]

Note 4

Funds Established or Closed During the Year

On July 1, 1982, the City retired the last of its general obligation bonded indebtedness. These bonds legally required the maintenance of a debt service fund. Ef-

fective July 1, 1983, the City discontinued the use of its Debt Service Fund. The City currently provides for the payment of long-term debt through the General Fund and (where applicable) proprietary funds. Prior year balances have been restated to reflect this change.

As of July 1, 1983, the City created the Facility Maintenance/P.B.X. Internal Service Fund for the purpose of controlling and allocating the costs of facility maintenance and telephone operations (P.B.X.). For the year ended June 30, 1984, the City reflected $857,000 of costs for facility maintenance and P.B.X. in the General Fund. Prior to the creation of this fund, these charges were not billed to user departments and other funds. Prior year balances have not been restated to reflect this change.

The City Council authorized separate assessments for improvements of streets in the Carter-Martin district, and for improvements of water facilities in the Bayshore Community. These special assessment districts are reported in the Carter-Martin Streets Assessment District fund and the Improvement District No. 1 Special Assessment Fund respectively. The City intends to issue special assessment bonds to finance these improvements and to levy assessments against properties which benefit from them. Assessment levies will be used to retire the bonds. No Special Assessment bonds have been legally authorized or issued to date.

[CITY OF SAVANNAH, GEORGIA (DECEMBER 31, 1983), NOTES TO FINANCIAL STATEMENTS (IN PART)]

Note 19 Establishment of New Funds

Two new funds were established in 1983.

The Old Pension Fund was established to account for assets dedicated to pay future benefits owed by the City to pensioners who retired prior to 1972 under plans which were terminated in 1972. The assets of the fund are invested in a dedicated bond portfolio which will provide a flow of income and maturing principal sufficient to pay future old pensions benefits.

The Investment Fund was established to account for pooled cash and investments of the City, except for those funds whose cash and investments must remain segregated because of bond resolution or federal regulation requirements.

EXHIBIT 15-8. EXCERPTS OF FOOTNOTES RELATING TO OPERATING LEASES

[COUNTY OF CONTRA COSTA, CALIFORNIA (JUNE 30, 1984), NOTES TO FINANCIAL STATEMENTS (IN PART)]

Note (7) Lease Commitments [in part]

Operating Leases

Total rental expense for the year ended June 30, 1984, for all operating leases and month-to-month lease arrangements amounted to $5,139,845 for the General Fund, $408,096 for the Special Revenue Funds, and $1,272,747 for the Hospital Enterprise Fund.

At June 30, 1984, the future minimum rental payments required under operating leases for buildings and equipment, other than month-to-month lease arrangements, are as follows:

Fiscal Year Ending June 30	General Fund	Hospital Enterprise Fund
1985	$2,482,510	563,836
1986	1,477,381	544,452
1987	1,062,309	515,782
1988	806,044	332,290
1989	373,756	86,225
Thereafter	706,855	44,990
	$6,908,855	2,087,575

[CUMBERLAND COUNTY, NORTH CAROLINA (JUNE 30, 1984), NOTES TO FINANCIAL STATEMENTS (IN PART)]

Note 7 Lease Commitments

The County had the following lease commitments in effect at June 30, 1984.

Company	Equipment	Monthly Rate	Months Remaining	Total Amount Remaining
3M Corp	Copier	$ 234	28	$ 6,552
Pitney Bowes	Tax Meter	39	12	471
Xerox	Copier	240	6	14,380
Xerox	Copier	40	38	1,520
Xerox	Copier	1,512	22	33,268
Xerox	Copier	433	5	2,165
Xerox	Copier	163	3	489
Xerox	Copier	235	35	8,225
IBM Corp	Copier	336	12	4,032
IBM Corp Telephone	Copier	358	5	1,790

The lease payments are appropriated annually from the General Funds. No liability is reflected in the financial statements for the above comments.

[RICHMOND, VIRGINIA (JUNE 30, 1984), NOTES TO FINANCIAL STATEMENTS (IN PART)]

Note 14 Leases

The City leases office space, business machines and vehicles under operating lease agreements. Lease agreements are generally for one-year terms or allow cancellation if funds are not appropriated for each year's payments. One lease for office space is non-cancellable for an original five-year term. GRTC leases tires and tubes based on mileage driven; RMA leases expressway toll-collecting equipment.

At June 30, 1984, the approximate annual long-term operating lease commitments subject to appropriation of funds, except for the office space lease also include below, were as follows:

Fiscal Year	City	RMA
1985	$2,131,928	$369,000
1986	755,741	369,000
1987	707,234	—
1988	105,488	—
1989	—	—
Total	$3,700,391	$738,000

Rent expense for the City during fiscal 1984 aggregated approximately $2,446,143. For GRTC and RMA it aggregated $166,870 and $369,000, respectively.

[SHREVEPORT, LOUISIANA (DECEMBER 31, 1983), NOTES TO FINANCIAL STATEMENTS (IN PART)]

Note 12 Lease Commitments

The City has commitments under operating lease agreements for various facilities and equipment used in the City's operations. Generally, these lease agreements provide for cancellation in the event the City Council does not appropriate funding in subsequent fiscal years. Therefore, the City is not obligated beyond the end of each fiscal year. However, management expects that in the normal course of business, leases that expire for data processing and duplicating equipment will be renewed or replaced by other leases. Total rent expense under operating leases was approximately $122,500 and $290,000 for 1983 and 1982, respectively.

The City has entered into long-term leases for facilities used in water operations. These lease agreements have been classified as capital leases for financial reporting purposes. The following information summarizes future value of the net minimum lease payments as of December 31, 1983:

Year ending December 31:	
1984	$ 121,867
1985	119,783
1986	120,659
1987	118,223
1988	118,758
Later years	344,494
Total minimum lease payments	943,794
Less: Amount representing interest	(164,794)
Present Value of net minimum lease payments	$ 779,000

[SIOUX FALLS, SOUTH DAKOTA (DECEMBER 31, 1983), NOTES TO FINANCIAL STATEMENTS (IN PART)]

Note 8 Operating Leases

The City has entered into a lease with Robert Bruns for the purpose of providing a sanitary landfill site. The lease is to be terminated upon the filling of the site and the restoration of the surface area. The consideration for the leased site is 6% of the gross receipts from disposal at the site and is payable quarterly. The rent expense for 1983 under this lease was $8,990.

The City is also a party to several leases for equipment and office space that are on an annual basis.

The total rent expense for the City, including the above amount, for the year ended December 31, 1983, was $266,918.

[CITY OF WICHITA FALLS, TEXAS (SEPTEMBER 30, 1983), NOTES TO FINANCIAL STATEMENTS (IN PART)]

Note 13 [in part] Description of Leasing Arrangements

Computer and other equipment leases expiring in 1986 and 1987, a vehicle lease expiring in 1988, and a lease of land expiring in 1991 are classified as capital leases and are included in the General Fixed Asset account group and General Long Term Debt account group.

The majority of operating leases contain the option for annual renewal at the end of the initial lease term. In most cases, leases will be removed or replaced by other leases. The City leases certain equipment and data processing software under operating leases expiring in 1984–1989.

* * *

Operating Leases

The following is a schedule by years of future minimum rental payments required under operating leases that have initial or remaining noncancelable lease terms in excess of one year as of September 30, 1983:

Year ending September 30:	
1984	$ 47,313
1985	28,659
1986	20,581
1987	16,945
1988	16,945
Later years	9,986
Total minimum payments required*	$140,429

* Minimum payments do not include contingent rentals which may be paid under the airport lease based on the number of scheduled landings.

The following schedule shows the composition of total rental expense for all operating leases:

	Year Ending September 30	
	1983	1982
Minimum rentals	$115,421	$149,640
Contingent rentals	8,992	20,538
	$124,413	$170,178

[WINNEBAGO COUNTY, WISCONSIN (DECEMBER 31, 1983), NOTES TO FINANCIAL STATEMENTS (IN PART)]

Note 9. Airport Leases

The County is the lessor of hangar, parking, office, and related building space at its airport under various operating leases for periods ranging from 1984 through

2010. Revenues and related expenses for these leases are recorded in the Airport enterprise fund.

Non-cancellable operating leases at December 31, 1983, provide for the following future minimum lease payments (excluding any contingent rentals):

1984	$217,000
1985	86,000
1986	40,000
1987	39,000
1988	39,000
Thereafter	240,000
	$661,000

Contingent rentals for the year ended December 31, 1983, were not significant.

EXHIBIT 15-9. EXCERPTS OF FOOTNOTES RELATING TO RELATED PARTY TRANSACTIONS

[COUNTY OF ALLEGHENY, PENNSYLVANIA (DECEMBER 31, 1983), NOTES TO FINANCIAL STATEMENT (IN PART)]

Note (12) Related Party Transactions

Several public authorities and a college have been created within the County under the laws of the Commonwealth of Pennsylvania. Those entities are separate and distinct bodies, corporate and politic, from the County. They publish separate, audited financial statements annually. The nature and function of those entities with which the County has significant transactions are described below. Those entities do not meet the component unit criteria of NCGA Statement No. 3—Defining the Governmental Reporting Entity.

Port Authority of Allegheny County

Port Authority of Allegheny County (the Port Authority) was created by an act of the Pennsylvania General Assembly in 1956 pursuant to the Second Class County Port Authority Act, as amended. The Port Authority is responsible for the management and operation of certain public transit facilities for the County and portions of adjacent counties.

The twelve members of the Board of the Port Authority are appointed by the Board of County Commissioners.

The County is authorized to issue its own general obligation bonds for the purpose of providing funds for the acquisition, construction or improvement of the County's transportation system. In addition, the County has the power to make grants or loans to the

Port Authority from either current revenues or from the proceeds of general obligation bonds to assist in defraying costs relating to the transportaion system. As of December 31, 1983, the County had general obligation bonds outstanding in the amount of $76,616,000 to finance such activities; those bonds are included in the County's General Long-Term Debt Account Group. The County, the United States Department of Transportation and the Commonwealth of Pennsylvania assist in financing Port Authority capital improvement projects. County Capital Projects Fund expenditures in 1983 include $5,500,000 for this purpose and $4,600,000 has been included in the capital budget for 1984. Presently, the capital funding proprotions are: 80%—Federal, 16⅔—Commonwealth of Pennsylvania; and 3⅓—County.

The County has historically participated with the Commonwealth of Pennsylvania and the Federal government in funding the gross operating deficit of the Port Authority. General Fund expenditures in 1983 include $13,300,000 for this purpose and $15,200,000 has been budgeted for 1984.

[CITY OF BOCA RATON, FLORIDA (SEPTEMBER 30, 1983), NOTES TO FINANCIAL STATEMENTS (IN PART)]

Note 9 [in part]. Related Party Transactions

Related party transactions include charges by the City to the Water and Sewer Fund for administrative functions and internal services, such as in-house legal costs and the use of central purchasing departments. The charges for administrative functions have been included in the statement of revenues and expenses.The costs of other internal services have not been determined, but their omission is not believed to have a material effect upon the results of operations.

[COUNTY OF KANE, ILLINOIS (NOVEMBER 30, 1983), NOTES TO FINANCIAL STATEMENTS (IN PART)]

Note 4 [in part]. Long-Term Debt

Capital Leases with Related Party

The County has entered into four noncancelable capital lease agreements with the Kane County Public Building Commission (Commission), a related party through common control. The Commission issued $750,000, $3,200,000, and $1,040,000 of revenue bonds to finance the cost of constructing improvements to the courthouse, the courthouse project and public safety building, and jail addition and courthouse annex, respectively.

The County is responsible for maintenance, operation, upkeep, and safekeeping of the public safety building, jail addition, courthouse project and the courthouse annex. The County signed an agreement with the Commission whereby the Commission pays the County to operate and maintain the Courthouse through October 31, 1984.

The following is a schedule by years of future minimum lease payments under the capital leases together with the present value of the net minimum lease payments as of November 30, 1983:

* * *

The present value of net minimum lease payments is recorded in the General Long-term Debt Account Group.

Under provisions of the lease agreements, the County is entitled to reimbursement from the Commission at the expiration of each lease for any amounts not required to pay outstanding bonds and expenses of the Commission for the related project. It is management's policy to record the reimbursement at the time the lease expires and funds are received in that actual reimbursement is contingent upon future events.

At November 30, 1983, the estimated amounts that would be reimbursable, by fiscal year, are as follows:

Fiscal Year	
1984	$ 855,000
1987	3,000
1988	9,000
1995	1,317,000

Under the agreements, the County transferred the deed for land and facilities of the courthouse, public safety building, jail addition, and courthouse annex to the Commission. Ownership will revert to the County upon termination of the leases. Accordingly, the original cost of the assets transferred and the $4,990,000 cost of the additions and improvements are included in the General Fixed Assets Account Group.

Future aggregate maturities of long-term debt are as follows:

1984	$ 464,403
1985	726,967
1986	755,192
1987	633,918
1988	582,093
After 1988	2,055,000
	$5,217,573

[NEWPORT NEWS, VIRGINIA (JUNE 30, 1984), NOTES TO FINANCIAL STATEMENTS (IN PART)]

Note 11. Related Party Transactions

Not included in the City's financial statements are certain public commissions and authorities created as separate governments under the laws of the State of Virginia. These agencies are separate legal entities having governmental character and sufficient autonomy in the management of their own affairs to distinguish them as separate from the administrative organization of the City; however, certain members of their governing bodies are appointed by Council. Specific information on the nature of the individual agencies and a description of their financial transactions affecting the City are provided in the following paragraphs:

Newport News Redevelopment and Housing Authority (NNRHA)

The NNRHA is a public corporation that administers urban development projects and operates all public housing in the City. City Council selects the members of the Authority's board; however, the board designates its own management and has the responsibility for budget adoption and revision. The Authority's operating and capital expenditures, including debt service, are financed principally with Federal funds and rentals.

Office of Human Affairs (OHA)

The OHA was established by City Council resolution for the purpose of conducting anti-poverty programs. OHA designates its own management and adopts its own budget. Its operations are financed principally by Federal funds.

Other

Certain agencies and commissions service the City and surrounding localities. Board membership is allocated among and appointed by the various localities. These agencies include: Peninsula Transportation Commission (PENTRAN), Peninsula Airport Commission (PAC), Peninsula Planning District Commision (PPDC), the Regional Redevelopment and Housing Authority (RRHA), and the Virginia Peninsula Economic Development Council (VPEDC). The PAC's operating and capital expenditures, including debt service, are financed by its operations and contributions from participating localities. Expenditures of the other agencies are financed by Federal and State grants, fees, and contributions. During the year ended June 30, 1984, the City provided operating and capital support to PPDC in the amount of $29,260, and to VPEDC of $200,000.

[PALM BEACH COUNTY, FLORIDA (SEPTEMBER 30, 1983), NOTES TO FINANCIAL STATEMENTS (IN PART)]

Note 22. Related Party Transactions

The County allocates certain support department costs, which include legal, fiscal, purchasing, personnel, internal audit and communication costs. Certain funds are also charged for the cost of services provided by the Motor Pool, Casualty Self-Insurance, Employee Health Insurance, Workers' Compensation and Data Processing internal service funds.

Costs of approximately $14,000,000 for the above services were charged to expenditures (expense) for the year ended September 30, 1983.

On December 14, 1982, the Department of Airports entered into a sales contract with the Board of County Commissioners, a related party, in which a parcel of land was sold for $3,650,000. The Department received a 10% interest-bearing note for the full purchase price. The note provides for amortization of principal over a ten year period beginning January 1985.

[CITY OF RICHMOND, VIRGINIA (JUNE 30, 1984), NOTES TO FINANCIAL STATEMENTS (IN PART)]

Note 10. Related Party Transactions

Capital Region Airport Commission

During fiscal 1984 the Commission reimbursed the City $585,532 for debt service. Certain Commission employees are covered under the Richmond Supplemental Retirement System. Also see Note 1A, "Capital Region Airport Commission."

Richmond Redevelopment and Housing Authority

During the year ended June 30, 1984, the City provided approximately $3,500,000 in Community Development Block Grant monies (accounted for in the Special Revenue Funds) to the RRHA for specific projects. Also the City was party to a certain lease agreement recorded with the RRHA.

During fiscal 1983 the City granted to RRHA $24,000,000 to be made available by the RRHA to the Marriott Corporation for the development of a hotel, convention facility and exhibition hall. Any unexpended balance and any interest earned by RRHA from investment of the unexpended balance ($3,157,550 (unaudited) interest earned through August 31, 1984) is to be returned by RRHA to the City by December 31, 1985.

At August 31, 1984, $16,131,924 (unaudited) of the $24,000,000 had been loaned to the Marriott Corporation by RRHA under an $18,000,000 note in con-

nection with the hotel and convention facility. The note is secured by a second deed of trust on the improvements and other property of the hotel and convention facility project. The note bears interest at 8% per annum on the unpaid balance and is payable annually beginning January 1, 1986, only if available cash flow, as defined in the deed of trust agreement, is sufficient to provide for payment of such interest. Principal is payable in forty installments ranging from $125,000 due January 1, 1986, to $9,000,000 due January 1, 2026. Future principal repayments received by the RRHA from the Marriott are to be returned to the City.

In addition, in connection with the settlement of certain lawsuits (see note 14, "Litigation Settlement") from the amount earned from investment of the unexpended balance through August 31, 1984 (presented on an unaudited basis), at the direction of City management:

a. $2,500,000 was loaned to certain plaintiffs;
b. $75,000 principal and $75,000 interest was paid to certain plaintiffs; and
c. $300,000 was paid to certain plaintiffs on July 2, 1984, for exterior site improvements required under terms of a lease agreement.

Also see Note 14, "Sixth Street Festival Marketplace."

[ST. LOUIS COUNTY, MISSOURI (DECEMBER 31, 1983), NOTES TO FINANCIAL STATEMENTS (IN PART)]

Note 13—Related Party Transaction

In accordance with a contract, effective July 14, 1981, the County has agreed to advance funds, not to exceed $4.5 million, to the Missouri Highway and Transportation Commission for improvements of State maintained highways in St. Louis County. The State has agreed to pay back the advances within five years of the completion of the improvements. Through December 31, 1983, the State has reimbursed the County for $1,000,000 of the advances. The County has accounted for the advances and reimbursements as expenditures and revenues of the Transportation Trust Fund. At December 31, 1983, the County had net unreimbursed advances to the Commission of $1,900,588.

[CITY OF SANTA ANA, CALIFORNIA (JUNE 30, 1984), NOTES TO FINANCIAL STATEMENTS (IN PART)]

Note 5. Related Party Transactions

As explained in Note 1, this report includes the accounts of the Redevelopment Agency, the Housing

Authority, the Economic Development Corporation, and the Industrial Development Authority, all of which are considered component units of the oversight unit, the City, since they meet the criteria of NCGA Statement No. 3. Each of these units has a common governing body (or a board over which this body has oversight responsibility) and is operated by City employees some of which provide services for or exert management influence over more than one of these units. Charges to these units for labor, materials and overhead are made directly at the City's standard rate per formal agreements with the City. Real property transfers are executed at appraised value usually net of cost incurred by the acquiring unit. Projects performed by the City on behalf of the Redevelopment Agency are charged at cost, for which this agency assumes a long-term obligation to pay from future tax increment revenues. During the year ended June 30, 1984, obligations for project costs totalling $5,638,095 and for land acquisitions totalling $3,028,375 were assumed by the Redevelopment Agency.

EXHIBIT 15-10. EXCERPTS OF FOOTNOTES RELATING TO GOVERNMENTAL SELF-INSURANCE PROGRAMS

[CITY OF BELLEVUE, WASHINGTON (DECEMBER 31, 1983), NOTES TO FINANCIAL STATEMENTS (IN PART)]

Note II E (in part)

Effective in 1983, *NCGA Statement 4* required that all payments made from an uninsured fund to a *self-insurance* fund be accounted for as an operating transfer rather than as an expenditure. The City has three self-insurance internal service funds for which this accounting treatment has been implemented for 1983. However following statement preparation, the City was notified that the effective date of the change had been delayed until further notice. Since 1983 conversions had already been implemented by the City, financial statements report such payments as operating transfers for 1983. For 1982 this conversion of accounts was not made due to the unavailability of historical information or the resources required to determine the values. All such values are considered as not material and have no impact on 1982 values for total income, fund balance or fund equity.

[BIRMINGHAM, ALABAMA (JUNE 30, 1984), NOTES TO FINANCIAL STATEMENTS (IN PART)]

Note 1 [in part] Self-Insurance

The City is self-insured for general liability coverages (excluding vehicle liability insurance and certain other catastrophes). Expenditures for these liabilities are measured in accordance with Financial Accounting Standards Board (FASB) Statement No. 5 and are recognized when incurred in the appropriate fund. Corresponding revenues are recognized in the Expendable Trust Fund from which payment of these liabilities is made. Expenditures and liabilities for these claims are recognized in the Expendable Trust Fund when incurred.

The City is also self-insured for employees medical coverage. Expenditures are recognized in the General Fund and other applicable funds for the amount determined to fund claims presented for payment. Corresponding revenues are recognized in the Expendable Trust Fund from which payment of these claims is made. Expenditures and liabilities for these claims are recognized in the Expendable Trust Fund when reported for payment (see Note 7).

[CITY OF DAYTONA BEACH, FLORIDA (SEPTEMBER 30, 1983), NOTES TO FINANCIAL STATEMENTS (IN PART)]

Note 14. Self-Insurance Program

Effective October 1, 1975, the City, in an effort to combat the rising cost of insurance premiums, initiated self-insurance workers' compensation and liability programs. The objective was not only to reduce insurance costs, but to provide a means of controlling workers' compensation and liability claims. The current program effectively interrelates between an internal risk manager, a loss adjuster, an excess insurer and City management.

Effective October 1, 1980, the City became self-insured for workers' compensation coverage. Since that date, the City has not had any primary or excess insurance for workers' compensation coverage.

For general liability, the City has umbrella liability insurance with coverage up to $10,000,000 of liability per occurrence with a $500,000 deductible per occurrence and a $1,000,000 policy year aggregate deductible. This means the City's maximum exposure for all claims occurring in 1983 is $1,000,000 except for any claim which is in excess of the $10,000,000 umbrella limit.

The City periodically evaluates the insurance market to determine the feasibility of obtaining insurance coverage.

[ELGIN, ILLINOIS (DECEMBER 31, 1983), NOTES TO FINANCIAL STATEMENTS (IN PART)]

Note 7 [in part]

Risk Management Fund

The City accounts for its self-insurance program through the Risk Management Fund (an Internal Service Fund). Under this program, the City is self-insured up to a maximum of $514,000 for claims under the Workers' Compensation Act for the period of October 1, 1983, through September 30, 1985. For general liability matters and each property damage occurrence, the City is self-insured for $125,000 and $5,000 respectively, for the period of October 1, 1983, through September 30, 1984. Claims in excess of these amounts are fully insured. The program is administered by Gallagher-Bassett Insurance Service. Fund revenues are primarily contributions from other fund groups and are planned to match expenses of insurance premiums, claim payments and operating expenses.

Effective March 1, 1983, the City began a self-insurance program for medical claims. The purpose of the program is to pay medical claims of the City of Elgin employees and their covered dependents and minimize the total cost of annual medical insurance to the municipality. The medical insurance program is administered by Washington National Insurance Company. The medical costs are limited to a maximum liability of 105% of a projected cost factor determined by Washington National Insurance Company and agreed upon by the City. This projected cost factor was $720,657, for the period of March 1, 1983, through February 29, 1984. The projected cost factor will be $760,673 for the period of March 1, 1984, through February 28, 1985. Total claims in excess of 105% of this amount are fully insured by Washington National Insurance Company.

[COUNTY OF LANCASTER, PENNSYLVANIA (DECEMBER 31, 1983), NOTES TO FINANCIAL STATEMENTS (IN PART)]

Note 1 [in part] Self-Insurance

The County is self-insured for unemployment and workmen's compensation. The liability for unemployment compensation claims is estimated at two times the average of the benefits paid for the three highest claim years. The liability for workmen's compensation is recorded as estimated by the plan administrator. The County is also required to maintain a reserve for workmen's compensation, which has been accrued as a liability of the General Fund.

CITY OF OKLAHOMA CITY, OKLAHOMA (JUNE 30, 1984), NOTES TO FINANCIAL STATEMENTS (IN PART)]

Note 13. Risk Management

The City's Risk Management Division is accounted for in the General Fund. Insurance Programs administered through this Division are employee health, property and liability, and workers' compensation. The estimated liability for insurance claims includes the estimated future liability on a case-by-case basis for all pending claims and an actuarially determined amount for claims incurred but not reported. As of June 30, 1984, the General Fund recorded an estimated liability of approximately $5,000,000 that was substantially funded and recorded as a restricted asset.

Employee health insurance is administered through two private carriers. Employees may choose a health maintenance organization for which a premium is paid and the City retains no more liability. Alternatively, employees may choose a traditional insurance program under which the City is self-insured. The estimated liability for pending and incurred but not reported employee health insurance claims at June 30, 1984, was approximately $2,020,000.

Property and liability insurance is acquired as required by bond indentures and as considered prudent. Property insurance policies generally have a $5,000 deductible. Liability insurance is purchased in limited areas. In those areas where property and liability insurance is not purchased the City is self-insured and an estimate of liability on a case-by-case basis are established. State law limits a City's liability for an incident to $1,000,000, with a maximum of $100,000 per person. However, there is no such limitation under Federal law. The estimated liability for property and liability insurance claims at June 30, 1984, was approximately $2,100,000.

Workers' compensation claims are administered by a private contractor and are totally funded by an annual General Fund appropriation. This self-insurance agreement is approved by the State. The estimated liability for pending and incurred but not reported workers' compensation claims at June 30, 1984, was approximately $890,000.

[PINELLAS COUNTY, FLORIDA (SEPTEMBER 30, 1983), NOTES TO FINANCIAL STATEMENTS (IN PART)]

Note D [in part]

Self-Insurance Program

Pinellas County is self-insured for its auto and general liability losses pursuant to Section 768.28, Florida

Statutes. It is also self-insured for its workers' compensation and auto physical damage. The following table summarizes the insurance coverages in force:

Area Covered	Limits of Outside Liability Coverage	Deductible Amount
Property	$106,917,168 for scheduled valuations for buildings and contents	$100,000
Property—Difference and Conditions	Blanket—Buildings and contents $15,000,000 per occurrence 7,500,000 flood 7,500,000 earthquake	$100,000 each occurrence
Windstorm/Restaurant Ft. Desoto Park	$217,384	90% of the amount of loss in excess of $500
Boiler and Machinery	$500,000 per accident	$250
Bridge Property Damage	$9,600,000 property damage $1,500,000 use and occupancy	
Crime insurance	$600,000 Faithful Performance Blanket Bond Coverage $4,000,000 Securities and Physical damage all premises $4,000,000 Securities and Physical damage all messengers	
Crime Insurance/Tax Collector	$200,000 Faithful Performance Public Official Bond	
Sheriff's AD&D	$20,000 per person	
Inland Marine	$184,000	$500
Airport Liability	$10,000,000 CSL	—
Airport Excess Liability	$25,000,000	—
Aviation Liability	$25,000,000	—
Watercraft Liability	$125,000,000	$500,000
Physician's Professional	$1,500,000	—
Professional Liability	$1,000,000 each person	—
Juvenile Welfare Board	$3,000,000 total limit	—
Signal Maintenance Liability	$500,000 each occurrence $500,000 aggregate	$500 per occurrence
Vehicle Terminal Coverage	$5,600,000	$250,000 per occurrence
E.M.S./General Liability	$1,000,000 CSL BI	$1,000 per claim (damage only)
E.M.S./Medical Malpractice	$1,000,000 per claim $5,000,000 aggregate	$1,000
E.M.S./Auto Liability	$5,000 BI or PD $10,000 PI $500 comprehensive $3,000 collision	$3,000

[CITY OF SARASOTA, FLORIDA (SEPTEMBER 30, 1983), NOTES TO FINANCIAL STATEMENTS (IN PART)]

Note 1 [in part] Self-Insurance

The City of Sarasota's self-insurance programs are accounted for in the Insurance Trust Funds. The City is self-insured for the following types of risk exposures:

Automotive Liability. Funding is provided by charges to the various funds of the City based on vehicle use. Individual claims for property damage or liability claims of others arising from vehicular accidents are charged to this fund. Each department is responsible for repairs to its own property from its operating accounts.

Worker's Compensation. Worker's Compensation benefits as defined by State Statute are paid from a separate trust fund. This fund was established during the fiscal year ended September 30, 1976. The funding is provided by charges to the various funds of the City based upon payroll exposure.

Unemployment Compensation. Unemployment compensation is charged quarterly to the various departments. The State assesses the City quarterly based upon actual claims.

Group Medical. Group medical benefits are paid from a self-insurance plan with an annually negotiated stop loss provision, which was established during the fiscal year ended September 30, 1981. The plan is funded by the City contributing the costs for its employees and charged to the various funds of the City based upon projected claims expense. Employee dependent coverage is paid by the employee through payroll deductions.

Public Liability. This is a non-funded program. Individual claims are charged to the appropriate operating funds. Effective October 1, 1981, State Statutes limited municipal liability under certain circumstances to $100,000 per claim and $200,000 per incident.

[CITY OF STOCKTON, CALIFORNIA (JUNE 30, 1984), NOTES TO FINANCIAL STATEMENTS (IN PART)]

Note 11—Self-Insurance

Effective August 1, 1978, the City adopted a self-insured group health insurance program, which is administered by a service agent. The City is also self-insured for workers' compensation insurance, unemployment insurance and for the first $500,000 per claim of general liability insurance (for general liability insurance the maximum liability per year is limited to $1,000,000). All these self-insurance plans are administered by a service agent.

The City is self-insured for the first $500,000 of casualty liability losses and $250,000 for worker's compensation losses. The City has excess casualty insurance for losses from $500,000 to $10,000,000 and $250,000 to $1,000,000 for workers' compensation losses.

The City believes that the self-insurance reserves recorded in the Internal Service Fund of $5,369,000 at June 30, 1984 are adequate to cover losses for which the City may be liable.

EXHIBIT 15-11. EXCERPTS OF FOOTNOTES RELATING TO SPECIAL ASSESSMENTS

[CITY OF ALBUQUERQUE, NEW MEXICO (JUNE 30, 1984), NOTES TO FINANCIAL STATEMENTS (IN PART)]

Note 2 [in part] Accounting Changes

Prior to fiscal year 1984, the City recorded as revenues the total amount of special assessments levied at the time the assessment rolls were approved by the City Council. Effective July 1, 1984, the policy for recording special assessment revenues was changed to the modified accrual basis in conformity with GASB Statement 1. The comparative information included in the financial statements for 1983 has been restated to reflect this change as follows:

	As Previously Reported	Restatement	As Restated
Total revenues	$ 3,205,171	$ 425,326	$ 3,630,497
Deferred revenues	2,167	3,159,062	3,161,229
Unreserved fund balance (deficit)	$(1,940,197)	$(3,159,062)	$(5,099,259)

[BIRMINGHAM, ALABAMA (JUNE 30, 1984), NOTES TO FINANCIAL STATEMENTS (IN PART)]

Note 8 [in part] Accounting Changes

A. Special Assessment Fund—Revenue and Expenditure Recognition

During 1984, the City changed its method of accounting for revenues and expenditures of the Special Assessment Fund. In prior years, construction costs of public improvements were capitalized as assets until the completion of the improvement projects. Upon completion of the projects, assessments were levied and charged against the capitalized construction cost. As a result of this accounting method, assessment revenues and capital outlay expenditures were not reflected and resulted in an overstatement of the 1984 fund balance. The effect of the change in 1984 was to increase excess of revenues over expenditures by $3,956,544 and deferred revenues have been recognized for 1984 as $2,993,067. The adjustment of $3,956,544 to apply retroactively the new method is included in revenues and expenditures of 1984.

[CITY OF FARMINGTON HILLS, MICHIGAN (JUNE 30, 1984), NOTES TO FINANCIAL STATEMENTS (IN PART)]

Note 1 [in part]—Summary of Significant Accounting Policies

Special Assessment Revenue

Currently, there exists a difference between governmental industry officials regarding the proper method of recognizing revenue for special assessment levies. The major alternative policies advocated are as follows:

a. When the levy is both measurable and available (modified-accrual approach).
b. When the assessment becomes an enforceable lien against the benefiting properties.
c. Eliminate Special Assessments Funds by reporting the related debt service payments and construction costs in Debt Service and Capital Project Funds. Under this approach, long-term debt previously reported in the Special Assessments Funds would be reflected in the General Long-term Debt Group of Accounts.

The City cannot predict which method described above, if any, will become generally accepted. Consequently, the City has decided to remain consistent with prior years and continues to recognize revenue on special assessment levies on the date they become enforceable liens against the benefiting properties.

[CITY OF FREMONT, CALIFORNIA (JUNE 30, 1984), NOTES TO FINANCIAL STATEMENTS (IN PART)]

Note 1 [in part] Accounting Policies

Change in Accounting

Special assessments receivable are recognized as revenue as they become available to fund current debt service requirements. The portion of total special assessments receivable due beyond one year is recorded as both an asset and deferred revenue on the balance sheet of the special assessment funds. Bond proceeds used to finance construction of special assessment projects are not recognized as revenues from other financing sources. In previous years, the proceeds of special assessment bonds were recorded as revenue when the related capital expenditures were incurred and special assessments receivable due beyond one year were not deferred. The change in accounting was made to present special assessment fund activity in a manner consistent with general practice, and the retroactive effect at July 1, 1983, has been recorded as a

restatement of the previously reported special assessment fund balances as follows:

As previously reported	$ 3,734,090
Deferred revenue to be received in future years from special assessment levies	(30,247,216)
Record the deferred proceeds of special assessment bond sale	9,723,659
As restated	$(16,789,467)

[WASHTENAW COUNTY, MICHIGAN (DECEMBER 31, 1983), NOTES TO FINANCIAL STATEMENTS (IN PART)]

Note 12. Accounting Change

During 1983, the County changed their method of accounting for deferred special assessments receivable in order to conform to the recommended methodology per the National Council on Governmental Accounting Statement 1. This new method results in a deficit fund balance because revenue from special assessment levies is recorded when available. The deficit will be eliminated as revenue is recognized over the assessment period. The County also has changed their method of recognizing state funding for Special Revenue Funds to the modified accrual basis, earned when expended, which is the recommended methodology.

[CITY OF ROCHESTER, MINNESOTA (DECEMBER 31, 1983), NOTES TO FINANCIAL STATEMENTS (IN PART)]

Note 15. Elimination of the Special Assessment Fund

Prior to 1983 the City accounted for projects principally related to street, sewer and water improvement construction and financed with improvement bonds in the Special Assessments Fund. Improvement bonds were recorded as a liability in the fund.

Revenues used to repay improvement bonds are generated from assessments against benefited property owners and tax levies. These revenues are generally reported only in the year of collection. Under the Special Assessments Fund accounting this normally results in deficit fund equity in the early years of a project.

Because only a portion of these projects are assessed, and since the bonds are general obligation debts backed by the full faith, credit and taxing power of the City, the City has determined that it is preferable to report improvement construction in the Capital Project Funds beginning in 1983. Improvement bonds are now shown as other financing sources in the operations of the Capital Project Funds and the debt repayment is reported in the Debt Service Funds, supported by revenues from assessments and tax levies. The outstanding debt is reported in the General Long-term Debt Account Group.

The reclassification of the activity related to these improvement projects has been applied retroactively in the accompanying financial statements. The effect of the change on opening fund equity balances at January 1, 1983, is as follows:

January 1, 1983, Fund Balances	Debt Service Funds	Capital Project Funds	Special Assessments Funds
Previously stated	$ 693,547	$10,760,727	$ 484,553
Record improvement bonds in the General Long-term Debt Account Group			8,175,000
Record deferred assessments receivable as deferred revenue			(5,198,565)
Elimination of Special Assessments Funds	1,244,803	2,216,185	(3,460,988)
Restated Balances	$1,938,350	$12,967,912	$ —

The effect on this change applied retroactively to 1982 operations would result in an increase of $487,670 in financing sources over uses in the Capital Project Funds and a decrease of $1,859,485 in the Debt Service Funds.

EXHIBIT 15-12. EXCERPTS OF FOOTNOTES RELATING TO EVENTS SUBSEQUENT TO THE BALANCE SHEET DATE

[BALTIMORE, MARYLAND (JUNE 30, 1984), NOTES TO FINANCIAL STATEMENTS (IN PART)]

Note 18. Subsequent Events

On July 1, 1984, a Parking Enterprise Fund was established to account for operations of City constructed public parking garages, and on July 6, 1984, the City issued $22,650,000 in Parking System Facilities Series 1984A Commercial Paper Notes. The notes mature from 1 to 270 days from issuance but not after June 29, 1987. The Notes are collateralized by certain pledged revenues and certain amounts held in accounts by the Trustee. The Notes bear interest at a market rate of interest.

On September 5, 1984, the City issued $35,450,000 in Parking System Facilities Series 1984B Commercial Paper Notes. The Notes mature from 143 to 152 days from issuance but not after February 18, 1985. The Notes are collateralized by certain pledged revenues and certain amounts held in accounts by the Trustee. From the proceeds, $500,000 was used to defease Series 1984A Parking System Facilities Commercial Paper Notes. The Notes bear interest at a market rate of interest.

On December 1, 1984, the City borrowed $8,000,000 from the State of Maryland for highway construction purposes. The loan bears interest at rates varying $6\frac{3}{4}\%$ to $9\frac{3}{4}\%$ and matures serially from 1986 to 1999. The principal and interest payments will be deducted by the State from the City's share of highway user revenues.

The City issued $22,000,000 of Highway User Revenue Anticipation Notes on July 3, 1984. The Notes bear interest at 50% of the prime rate and are due June 10, 1985.

[CITY OF CHICAGO, ILLINOIS (DECEMBER 31, 1983), NOTES TO FINANCIAL STATEMENTS (IN PART)]

Note 11. Subsequent Events

Certain revenues anticipated and appropriated in 1983 were not realized by the end of the year. Such revenues from the sale of City owned garages and cable television franchise fees amounting to $14,216,000 and $13,610,000, respectively, have been realized in 1984. These revenues were not reappropriated as part of the 1984 budget.

In April 1984, the City issued $259,200,000 General Obligation Daily Tender Notes in three series with stated maturities of December 31, 1984, October 31, 1985, and October 31, 1988. Interest is payable monthly at a rate to be determined weekly by the City Comptroller. Note holders have the option at any time to tender the notes for payment at par. Any notes paid in this manner are to be resold at par on a best efforts basis. The City obtained a $264,200,000 irrevocable letter of credit to provide for payment of the notes upon maturity or tender.

The notes were issued to (1) replace the $100 million line of credit, (2) anticipate the receipt of $112 million of property taxes and (3) purchase $47,200,000 of capital equipment.

[CITY OF OMAHA, NEBRASKA (DECEMBER 31, 1983), NOTES TO FINANCIAL STATEMENTS (IN PART)]

Note 12. Subsequent Events

(a) Litigation

In 1981 Peter J. McGinn filed suit in the District Court of Douglas County seeking damages for injuries sustained when a large tree on City right-of-way fell on his auto during a violent storm, severing his spinal column. In April 1983, the Douglas County District Court returned a verdict in favor of the plaintiff, assessing damages of $5,000,000. The City contested this decision through an appeal to the Nebraska Supreme Court. In June 1984, the Nebraska Supreme Court reversed the District Court verdict relieving the City of any liability for damage suffered by the plaintiff.

(b) Issuance of Bonds

In accordance with the provisions of the Downtown Redevelopment Project No. 1 bond covenants, the City is currently negotiating the sale of refunding bonds to retire all of the existing outstanding Parking Revenue Bonds. The City anticipates the sale to be consummated by July 15, 1984. The principal debt service requirements of the refunding bonds to be retired over ten years would be as follows:

1984	$ —
1985	110,000
1986	115,000
1987	125,000
1988	135,000
Later years	1,115,000
	$1,600,000

In addition, it is anticipated the refunding bonds will bear interest at 9.36% and be payable semi-annually.

In the event the refunding bonds are not sold by October 1, 1984, the original bond ordinance provides for the purchase of the refunding bonds by the present bondholders. These refunding bonds would mature October 1, 1986, and bear interest at 70% of Norwest Bank's prime rate, payable semi-annually.

[PINELLAS COUNTY, FLORIDA (SEPTEMBER 30, 1983), NOTES TO FINANCIAL STATEMENTS (IN PART)]

Note 5—Subsequent Events

On December 28, 1983, Pinellas County issued the Solid Waste and Electric Revenue Bonds, Series 1983 totalling $83,375,000 to finance a portion of the cost of acquiring and constructing a third boiler, a second electric generator and certain real estate as an addition to existing solid waste disposal and electric generating facility. These bonds were issued on a parity with the $160 million Solid Waste and Electric Revenue Bonds, Series 1980, and will be equally secured by and payable from a prior lien upon and pledge of the net operating revenues of the project. As further security for the payment of the bonds, the County covenants to pay from non–ad valorem revenues such amounts as necessary to restore any deficiencies as required in the indenture.

The County also entered into an irrevocable loan agreement for $12.5 million for the purpose of providing funds for the design, acquisition and construction of portions of the 1983 project, which could not be financed on a tax exempt basis. Repayment of the monies borrowed by the County pursuant to this loan agreement is to be made from pledged revenues, but is expressly subordinated to the obligation of the County to pay principal and interest on the 1983 and 1980 bonds. The ad valorem taxing power of the County is not pledged to the payment of the 1983 bonds or the loan.

In October 1983, the Water System issued additional Junior Lien Water Revenue Certificates, Issue of 1983, totalling $2.6 million to acquire real property to be used for water supply purposes by the County. These certificates are junior and subordinate to the outstanding Water Revenue Certificates of the County; thus debt service will be payable and secured by a lien upon the net revenues derived from the operation of the facility after satisfying debt service requirements of the Water Revenue Certificates.

On December 20, 1983, the Pinellas County Board of County Commissioners passed a resolution pledging a portion of the Tourist Development tax to the payment of a portion of revenue notes and bonds to be issued by the Pinellas Sports Authority which will provide the financing for the cost of a multipurpose stadium facility to be located in the City of St. Petersburg.

Both the City of St. Petersburg and Pinellas County are obligated for payments of debt service as set out in the Interlocal Agreement between the City, the County and Pinellas Sports Authority.

In December, 1983, the Pinellas Sports Authority issued $61 million, 7.25% Revenue Bond Anticipation Notes due June 1, 1985, to fund the construction of a $59.5 million sports stadium and the interest during the construction period.

[CITY OF RICHMOND, VIRGINIA (JUNE 30, 1984), NOTES TO FINANCIAL STATEMENTS (IN PART)]

Note 15. Subsequent Events

Revenue Anticipation Notes

On September 5, 1984, the City issued $70,000,000 of Revenue Anticipation Notes (the "Notes"). The Notes were issued in anticipation of the collection of revenue during fiscal 1985. The Notes bear interest at 6.9% per annum and will mature January 8, 1985.

Money Center Loan Agreement

In accordance with the terms of the Agreement discussed in Note 5, the City on August 17, 1984, received an additional advance of $600,000.

RMA Bonds and Notes (Unaudited)

On July 5, 1984, the City transferred ownership of a parcel of land containing a baseball stadium facility to the Richmond Metropolitan Authority to enable the RMA to finance the construction and assume responsibility for the maintenance and operation of a new stadium. The aggregate cost of the assets transferred is $390,319 and is included in the General Fixed Assets Account Group in the Accompanying financial statements. In this connection the Richmond Metropolitan Authority on September 1, 1984, issued Richmond Metropolitan Authority Stadium Bonds Series of 1984 ("RMA Bonds") and Richmond Metropolitan Authority Stadium Notes Series of 1984 ("RMA Notes") which aggregated $3,810,000 and $3,400,000, respectively, bearing interest rates of 6.75% to 10.25% as to the RMA Bonds and 6.75% to 7.75% as to the RMA Notes. The RMA Bonds mature beginning September 1, 1985 through 2004, and the RMA Notes mature beginning July 15, 1985 through 1987. The RMA also, at the date of the issuance of the RMA Bonds and RMA Notes, entered into reimbursement agreements with United Virginia Bank to provide letters of credit over the life of the RMA Bonds and the RMA Notes in amounts sufficient to pay the principal and interest on both instruments at their respective due dates. The reimbursement agreements will only be used in the event the RMA is unable to pay the principal and interest on the RMA Bonds and RMA Notes.

In addition to the reimbursement agreements, the RMA Bonds and RMA Notes are secured by the revenues of the stadium facility and do not pledge other revenues of the RMA.

In connection with the aforementioned stadium transaction, the City of Richmond and the Counties of Henrico and Chesterfield entered into a nonbinding but moral obligation agreement to assist the RMA with respect to its ownership, operation, maintenance and improvement of the stadium. Under this agreement, the RMA may request from each jurisdiction, on or before February 1 of each year, an appropriation equal to one-third of the amount budgeted for the stadium for:

(i) debt service on the RMA Bonds,
(ii) capital improvements,
(iii) operating loss, and
(iv) contingency requirement (as defined by the agreement).

The RMA may, in addition to the items identified in the preceding paragraph, request from the City the budgeted amount of local admissions or similar taxes and the estimated real estate taxes expected to be paid by the RMA to the City during the calendar year.

In connection with the aforementioned stadium transactions, on August 31, 1984 the RMA had entered into contractual commitments of $6,695,000 for demolition of the old baseball stadium and construction of the new stadium facility.

Richmond Redevelopment and Housing Authority

See Note 10, "Related Party Transactions," subparagraph "Richmond Redevelopment and Housing Authority."

[SALT LAKE CITY CORPORATION, UTAH (JUNE 30, 1984), NOTES TO FINANCIAL STATEMENTS (IN PART)]

Note 17. Subsequent Events

Subsequent to June 30, 1984, the following commitments for major construction projects were made:

General Fund	$ 67,000
Special Revenue Funds	26,000
Capital Projects Fund	3,098,000
Special Assessment Funds	848,000
Enterprise Funds	7,842,000
	$11,881,000

Subsequent to June 30, 1984, the City issued $92,000 of curb and gutter special assessment bonds dated September 1, 1984, and maturing September 1, 1985 through 1994.

Subsequent to June 30, 1984, the City issued $24,000,000 of tax anticipation notes dated July 2, 1984, and maturing September 1, 1985 through 1994.

Subsequent to June 30, 1984, the City issued $24,000,000 of tax anticipation notes dated July 2, 1984, maturing June 28, 1985 at a variable interest rate per annum with an option to convert to a fixed rate. On October 12, 1984, the City exercised the option at a fixed rate of 6.5%.

[SHREVEPORT, LOUISIANA (DECEMBER 31, 1983), NOTES TO FINANCIAL STATEMENTS (IN PART)]

Note 14. Subsequent Events

Sales Tax Election

On November 19, 1983, a majority of the voters of the City of Shreveport approved a one-half cent sales tax increase which went into effect January 3, 1984. This should provide additional revenue of approximately $9,000,000 annually to the General Fund. The City Council adopted Resolution No. 252 of 1983, which outlined the general uses of the proceeds derived from the propositions as follows:

To provide additional funding for the merger of the Firemen's and Policemen's Pension and Relief-Funds with the respective State retirement systems.

To provide money to acquire additional firefighters and police officers along with the necessary equipment, provide cost-of-living increases for all City employees, and provide funding for various other street maintenance and improvement work.

To provide money to be utilized in constructing, acquiring, improving, and extending capital facilities and improvements.

Proposed Bond Sale

The City is scheduled to issue general obligation bonds with a face value of $29,000,000 during May of 1984. The bonds are payable from ad valorem tax revenues and the proceeds from the bonds will be used for capital improvements.

Firefighters Longevity Pay Settlement

During August of 1978 a law suit was brought against the City by a group of firefighters for an increase in longevity pay. On January 27, 1984, a judgment was rendered in favor of the firefighters. The total award granted was for $152,000, which amount was accrued for in 1983. The individual longevity payments were increased by various amounts based on service time with the City.

Chapter 16
General Study Observations and Other Matters

This chapter contains several general observations on selected reporting topics. Neither priority ranking nor significance is intended from the order of topics discussed.

TRANSMITTAL LETTERS IN ANNUAL REPORTS

Often an annual report contained two transmittal letters: one from the chief executive or administrative officer and a second from the chief or senior financial officer of the governmental unit. Each letter had a slightly different focus.

Of the reports analyzed, 20% contained letters of transmittal from the chief executive or administrative officer or from the financial officers (in 41% of these cases), either to the Mayor or to the Mayor and members of the City Council. In general, this letter described the content of the annual financial report and provided a general economic and operating summary of the governmental unit. Thirty-five percent of the letters contained a reference to the unit's concern with the Certificate of Conformance of the Government Finance Officer's Association of the United States and Canada. In some instances (31%), a copy of the Certificate for the preceding fiscal year was included in the report.

Table 16-1 summarizes the transmittors of annual financial reports. Table 16-2 summarizes the various addressees to whom annual financial reports were transmitted.

The topics discussed in the transmittal letters varied. The letters from the chief executive officers were generally not as detailed as those from the financial officers. Exhibit 16-1 illustrates a letter from a chief executive officer; Exhibit 16-2 is an example of a transmittal letter from a financial official.

THE NATURE OF ANALYSIS IN TRANSMITTAL LETTERS

Some of the transmittal letters contained a financial analysis or explanation of the information provided in the financial report. Communities made an effort to present the data in a variety of forms to facilitate analysis. Some of the topics discussed in these letters are listed on Table 16-3. The information in transmittal letters was presented in different formats (in addition to narrative), as shown in the following table.

Data Format or Presentation Techniques*	Letters by Chief Elected or Appointed Officials	Letters by Financial Officers
	Instances Observed(%)	
Numerical analysis; references to specific dollar amounts	75	92
Percentages and ratios	66	87
Year-to-year comparisons	61	74
Charts	31	45
Trend tables	15	15
Graphic presentations	5	8

* Observations for those units having a letter of transmittal.

SELECTION OF FISCAL YEARS

Unlike some private sector corporations, governmental units do not have a natural business year, which, from an accounting standpoint, is the most appropriate way to report the cycle of business activities for an organization. The month in which the surveyed governmental units ended their fiscal year varied. Table 16-4 contains a summary of the fiscal years adopted.

The surveyed financial statements contained footnotes on a wide variety of subjects. Footnotes related to accounting practices were usually summarized in the first footnote of a financial statement and entitled, "Summary of Significant Accounting Policies." (See Table 2-1 for the subjects included in these summary footnotes.) A partial listing of topics discussed in the other footnotes to the surveyed financial statements is contained in Table 16-5. It should be noted that the distinction between the two groupings of footnotes was not totally uniform across all surveyed statements.

EXHIBITS AND TABLES FOR CHAPTER 16

TABLE 16-1. TRANSMITTOR OF TRANSMITTAL LETTERS

	Chief Elected or Appointed Official (%)	Financial Officer (%)
Letters in financial reports	79	41
Letters sent by		
finance director		60
city or county manager	19	
city manager and director of finance	38	
mayor	7	
county executive	5	
county administrators	3	
mayor and director of finance	5	
county auditor	5	
chief accountant		14
treasurer		4

TABLE 16-2. RECIPIENTS OF TRANSMITTAL LETTERS

	Chief Elected or Appointed Official (%)	Financial Officer (%)
Letters in financial reports	79	41
Letters addressed to		
mayor	5	21
city council	14	16
mayor and council	47	36
county executive	3	3
county council	5	2
executive and council	12	2
citizens of city or county	1	7
residents	3	
city manager		22
board of directors/ supervisors/commissioners		20

EXHIBIT 16-1. SAMPLE TRANSMITTAL LETTER FROM A CHIEF EXECUTIVE OFFICER

[City of Indianapolis, Indiana]
April 25, 1984

To the Members of the City-County Council:

This report on the 1983 financial condition of the City of Indianapolis has been prepared following the guidelines set by the Municipal Finance Officers Association of the United States and Canada. Like our past practice, this report will be submitted to the Municipal Finance Officers Association for review.

The City ended the year on solid financial footing and has new operations for income to meet future necessities. Our lengthy efforts for Local Option Tax legislation were rewarded when the Indiana General Assembly passed House Bill 1217, which gives local governments some flexibility to meet obligations, such as the pensions of retired police officers and firefighters.

As you know, 1983 was a year of recovery for our nation's economy, and a year of continued growth, vitality and positive signs for the future in our City. A survey by the Indianapolis Growth Project included interviews with more than 120 businesses and found that 73 percent of them have decided to expand or are considering an expansion, and 100 projected increased employment within five years. I regret that a large Western Electric Co. operation could not be retained in the wake of the telecommunications industry deregulation. But other major manufacturing operations in our City are rebounding very well from the national recession. Recently, the 100,000th 6.9 liter diesel engine was produced at the International Harvester plant here, which is partly equipped and operated with loan and grant assistance from the City and State. That is gratifying because 1,400 jobs were saved and about 900 laid-off workers are back on the job. This Administration continues to actively work to help companies to bring new products on-line, like the Harvester engine, and encourages new technologies in our manufacturing plants. Our City's industrial foundation is being strengthened while we continue efforts to create more jobs in small businesses and to diversify our local economy in the sunrise industries.

The dreams and plans we hold for neighborhoods and the redevelopment, restoration and new construction in downtown moved steadily closer to reality in 1983. The timely assistance of the City will prevent the former Sears, Roebuck & Co. store downtown from standing vacant too long before a coordinated renaissance transforms that landmark structure into a health spa, retail space and other adaptive reuses. Land acquisition and progress continued on the 150 acre White

River State Park project. The design plans for a $160 million downtown retail mall also moved ahead. Recent approval of a $4.8 million Federal Urban Development Action Grant will trigger $30 million in loans from the three largest local banks to a developer in a public-private partnership to restore and rejuvenate historic Union Station.

The eyes of the nation which were not already opened to this new Indianapolis surely could see that our City is on the move when a National Football League team franchise recently moved here. The Indianapolis Colts will play in the new Hoosier Dome beginning this fall. The direct economic impact of the team on our city is at least $22 million this year, but the indirect benefits of big league sports publicity and community spirit are immeasurable.

Indianapolis is not just holding our own in the war for jobs, population, and recognition that the northern "rust belt" wages with the southern "sun belt." Our City is winning!

The preparation of this annual report could not have been successful without the dedicated efforts of the Audit Committee, the City Controller and his staff and many others. Their efforts in recent years toward upgrading the accounting and financial reporting systems of the City have led substantially to the improved quality of information being reported to the City-County Council and to our citizens.

Sincerely yours,
[Signature]

EXHIBIT 16-2. SAMPLE TRANSMITTAL LETTER FROM A FINANCIAL OFFICER

City of Atlanta, Georgia
April 10, 1984

Honorable Mayor and Council
The Comprehensive Annual Financial Report of the City of Atlanta, Georgia, for the fiscal year ended December 31, 1983, is submitted herewith. The report has been prepared in accordance with Section 6-308 of the Charter of the City of Atlanta, Georgia, and complies with all applicable generally accepted accounting principles.

FINANCIAL REPORTING STANDARDS

This report, together with the exhibits and statistical data contained herein, has been prepared in conformity with current accounting and financial reporting principles as promulgated by the National Council on Governmental Accounting and the Municipal Finance Officers Association of the United States and Canada.

REPORTING ENTITY

The financial statements, schedules, and statistical tables included in this report pertain to all functions and funds directly under the control of the Mayor and Council of the City of Atlanta, including trust and agency funds administered and controlled by various elected or appointed officials which are not reported upon by any other entity. To comply with Statement No. 3 issued by the National Council on Governmental Accounting, financial statements for the City's Pension Trust Funds, Group Life Insurance Fund, and the City of Atlanta and Fulton County Recreation Authority have been included as part of the City's reporting entity. Certain entities are not included within the scope of this report since they are established by the Constitution of the State of Georgia or State Laws and are administered by separate boards which act independent of the City of Atlanta, including the Atlanta Board of Education and the Atlanta Housing Authority.

The City of Atlanta is a major municipal government providing a full range of services to some 425,000 citizens. Included in these services are traditional city functions such as police and fire protection, sanitation, road and traffic signal maintenance, water and sewer operations, parks, recreation and cultural affairs, courts, and inherent support activities as well as an international airport which serves as the air transportation hub of the southeast. Selected demographic information is provided within the statistical section of this report.

BASIS OF ACCOUNTING

Governmental and Expendable Trust Funds' statements are prepared on the modified accrual basis of accounting in accordance with current accounting standards for governmental units. However, due to legal requirements, statements for these governmental funds for which an annual budget is adopted are also presented on a modified cash basis for budgetary comparison. The primary difference in the two bases is that revenues, notably taxes, are recognized on an actual collection basis, and grants in aid are recognized on an authorization basis, rather than when they become susceptible to accrual under generally accepted accounting principles. Due to the multi-year program nature of the Proprietary funds, no budgetary comparison is presented for these funds. Proprietary Fund statements are prepared on the accrual basis of accounting. Fiduciary Funds statements are prepared as appropriate in accordance with generally accepted accounting principles. Further explanation of the basis of accounting for all fund types and the City's budgetary controls are furnished in the accompanying Notes to the Financial Statements.

1983 FINANCIAL OVERVIEW

GOVERNMENTAL FUNDS

The City of Atlanta maintains a General Fund, three Special Revenue Funds, two Debt Service Funds, five Capital Projects Funds, and a Special Assessment Fund. All funds ended the 1983 year in sound financial condition. The General Fund balance at December 31, 1983, available for appropriation (budget basis) in 1984 was $31,649,477. This makes the 47th consecutive year in which a cash surplus has been available for the ensuing year's budget appropriations.

The Special Revenue Funds group includes three funds primarily designated to account for Federal grants-in-aid, including: the Comprehensive Employment Training Act Fund, the Community Development Fund, and the Intergovernmental Grant Fund. These funds were established to account for grants from outside agencies which are designated by law or policy for specific purposes. The 1983 financial results for these funds, which are principally dependent on non-City funding, were favorable.

The Debt Service Fund (remaining at December 31, 1983) consists of the General Obligation Bond Sinking Fund and accounts for the accumulation and subsequent disbursement of principal and interest on long-term municipal debt. The Sanitary Department Revenue Fund was closed during 1983 with sufficient balances transferred to an escrow account to defease outstanding Sanitary Department Revenue Certificates, resulting in a gain of $232,000. All remaining funds in this debt service account were transferred to the General Fund.

The Capital Projects grouping consists of five funds whose resources are accumulated primarily from bond proceeds and restricted for governmental purposes except for the Park Improvement Fund, whose resources accrue primarily from a special tax levy restricted to capital improvements of park facilities. All Capital Projects Funds are used for the acquisition, development, and improvement of major governmental fixed assets.

The Special Assessment Fund accounts for the accumulation and expenditures of resources for various public improvements such as sidewalks, curbs, and gutters which are financed through assessments to individual property owners.

PROPRIETARY FUNDS

Included in this group are four Enterprise Funds and an Internal Service Fund. The Water and Sewerage System, which is financed primarily by user charges for water and sewer services, ended 1983 with accrual basis net income of $19,632,000 compared to $25,389,000 in 1982.

This decrease results from a reduction of $5.7 million in investment income due primarily to significant declines in interest rates from 1982 to 1983. To a lesser extent, increased operating expenses as well as adjusted depreciation on The Flint River Plant contributed to this decline in net income. The Flint River Plant will be abandoned and retired upon completion next year of the Three Rivers Water Quality Management Program. Rate increases, effective March 1, 1984, and more fully discussed in the following section on capital financing, should improve net income flows for future years.

Construction continued during 1983 on the Three Rivers Water Quality Management Program, a water pollution control project designed to re-route sewerage discharge now flowing into the Flint River, South River, and Intrenchment Creek back into the Chattahoochee River, from which all water intake for the system is derived. The majority of the Project is expected to be operational in 1984 at an estimated total cost of $188 million (of which $125 million was incurred through December 31, 1983). This project is being financed 75% by U.S. Environmental Protection Agency grants and 25% by the City of Atlanta and five other municipalities in the surrounding area. In December 1983 the Water Works Revenue Fund was closed through escrow and defeasance of outstanding bonds which resulted in a net gain to the Water and Sewerage System of $171,000.

The Cyclorama Restoration Project is accounted for in the Parks and Recreational Facilities Fund, which was created in 1979 and became operational in July 1982.

As required by the National Council on Governmental Accounting Statement 3, the City of Atlanta and Fulton County Recreation Authority financial statements are included in the Comprehensive Annual Financial Report as an Enterprise Fund.

The Hartsfield Atlanta International Airport is the primary aviation facility in the State of Georgia and the southeastern United States and is the second busiest airport in the world in terms of total enplaned passengers. Income for this fund is derived primarily from use agreements with major airlines, a principal concessionaire for the terminal facility, and a parking operations concessionaire. The City of Atlanta completed construction of the world's largest air terminal facility in 1981. During 1983, the City purchased and installed seven additional cars to the Automated Guideway Transit System (AGTS). In addition, the City issued $85,230,000 of revenue bonds to fund, in part, the construction of a fourth parallel runway and the extension of an existing runway. Completion of the runway projects (in 1985) should make the Airport the busiest in the world.

Although operating income increased from $35.1 million in 1982 to $39 million, the Airport experienced a net loss of $7,380,000 in 1983 compared to net income of $16,060,000 for 1982. This net loss is attributable primarily to the retirement of the old terminal facilities ($16.8 million) in order to construct the new fourth parallel runway and secondarily to the reduction in investment income ($6.9 million) due to significant declines in interest rates from 1982 to 1983.

The Internal Service Funds is comprised of the activities of the Office of Motor Transport Services, Duplicating Division, and the Office of Management Systems.

FIDUCIARY FUNDS
Contained in this group are the City's Pension Trust Funds as well as the City's Non-expendable Trust Fund, Expendable Trust Funds, and Agency Fund.

OUTLOOK FOR THE FUTURE
The City of Atlanta's overall financial posture, as well as its prospect for the immediate future, is favorable. Atlanta, as hub of the southeast, demonstrates its economic vitality by such statistics for 1983 as a 8.6% unemployment rate (which compares favorably with the state and national averages). Atlanta's cost-of-living is one of the lowest in the nation for a major metropolitan area. Strong emphasis on responsible economic development has produced healthy growth during 1983. The City of Atlanta issued building permits valued at $373,373,299 million in 1983 and registered 1.3 million convention delegates with estimated spending of $544,000,000.

ECONOMIC VITALITY
As the principal city in one of the nation's most vibrant economic regions, Atlanta has reaped both the benefits and the costs of national and regional migratory trends. While Atlanta's surrounding suburbs are both growing and competing with the central city, the well-planned transportation infrastructure, diversified economic base, and rapidly increasing international image places Atlanta in an enviable posture for the decade of the 1980s and the years beyond. The City's rapid transit authority, MARTA, opened new stations on the critical north-south line in 1983. This transportation system, which represents an investment of over $1.5 billion, provides a direct linkage between downtown and other areas of the city.

Although disruptive to the short-term, the State is spending approximately $1.2 billion over the next three years on the complete reconstruction of the downtown expressways. This will give downtown Atlanta one of the best surface transportation systems within the nation. The City also operates Hartsfield Atlanta International Airport, the second busiest airport in the world, which provides vital direct links to domestic and international points and is only 7.2 miles from downtown. Atlanta also boasts one of the largest and finest convention facilities in the nation, the Atlanta World Congress Center, with 350,000 square feet of exhibit space, 200,000 square feet of meeting space, and a 2,000 seat auditorium. An expansion of over 300,000 square feet of exhibit space is presently under construction. Of the 30,000 hotel rooms located in the metropolitan region, approximately 7,250 rooms are in the downtown area with 6,300 of these rooms located within an eight block walking radius. Over the next several years, as this capacity increases by approximately 3,000 rooms, the convention potential will be unmatched anywhere else in the nation.

Atlanta is currently the third largest convention center in the nation. With the completion of the proposed "new" Underground Atlanta entertainment district and the expansions mentioned earlier, it is expected that Atlanta could easily become the major convention center in the nation.

Atlanta is not only a place to visit, but, according to a Rand McNally study of 277 metropolitan areas in the nation, it was rated, on the average, as the #1 place to live in the Places Rated Almanac. The sum of this "chamber-of-commerce-type" dialogue is that Atlanta is the centerpiece to a very vibrant economic region, all of which portends well for the basic financial health of the city.

BUDGETARY PROSPECTIVE
From a financial viewpoint, the City of Atlanta, like many local governmental units, has faced for the last several years the unpleasant realities of high inflation rates coupled with a distinctly limited ability to broaden its revenue base. The 1982 General Fund Budget required an increase in the millage rate as well as substantial upward revisions in the sanitary service charge. Because of these adjustments and tightened expenditure controls, the 1983 budget process was less traumatic; however, pressure in the near term for similar adjustment or decrease in service will be experienced unless Atlanta continues to find new ways of diversifying its revenue base and places strong emphasis on productivity in basic governmental services.

Late in fiscal year 1982, Atlanta was successful in enacting a local option sales tax. Although certainly not a panacea to the City's financial concerns, passage of the sales tax could be the single most significant stabilizing influence on basic government finances in the decade of the 1980s. Even with its strong economy, Atlanta has experienced increasing costs and service demands and has depended upon the property tax as its largest single revenue source. Implementation of the sales tax will allow Atlanta to diversify and increase its revenue base. Since a rollback in property taxes is mandated there will be a decrease in the property tax levy, thereby improving Atlanta's competitive position with the outlaying suburbs. The sales tax is more elastic than the traditional property tax and, in Atlanta's case, should be exportable by at least 40% to 50% to tourists, conventioneers, and commuters.

Since the State enabling legislation requires a continuing dollar-for-dollar property tax rollback in the first full year after implementation, the first year's sales tax collections will, in essence, become a "windfall" to the City and will be utilized for a number of one-time, high-priority public projects, many of which will be related to the City's economic development. During 1983 the City received $19,314,418 (cash basis) in "windfall" sales tax revenues representing seven months' cash collections.

Total "windfall" sales tax revenues expected from the first full year of collection are anticipated to be $35,500,000. Such revenues are to be prorated among the following projects up to the amount anticipated:

Reserve for Underground Atlanta	$10,000,000
Atlanta Convention and Visitors Bureau	5,000,000
Construction of Municipal Court Building	6,500,000
City Hall Renovation, Expansion, and Parking	14,000,000
Total	$35,500,000

Atlanta has operated and will continue to operate on a highly conservative financial plan (the 1937 Budget Law). This process, an outgrowth of the Depression, requires that the City anticipate not more than 99% of what it actually collected in the prior year from recurring revenue sources and also make a five-member Budget commission personally liable for overanticipations. Atlanta's financial challenge in the intermediate term will be to make a careful transition from the typical property tax-dependent municipality to one with a more diversified revenue base.

CAPITAL FINANCING

Perhaps the most important within the multitude of capital projects currently funded or proposed within Atlanta's Capital Improvement Program are those related to the City's largest enterprise operations—Hartsfield Atlanta International Airport and the Water and Sewerage System. During the latter portion of 1982, the City was successful in refunding the outstanding 4th and 5th Lien Airport Revenue Bonds, thus

clearing the way for future project funding under 3rd Lien status. During 1983, $85,230,000 of revenue bonds were sold and construction is in progress on a 4th parallel runway and extension of the existing southern-most runway. The completion of this project will fulfill all major elements of the airport layout plan as envisioned during the late 1960s.

In terms of the water-sewer infrastructure, the Three Rivers Water Quality Management Program is nearing completion and should be totally operational by early 1985. For the foreseeable future, it is expected that this project will mark the end of major Federal participation in Atlanta's wastewater treatment capital financing. A Capital Improvement Program for the period 1983–1986 totalling $176 million was adopted in December 1983. Major components include modernization of the City's existing water treatment facilities, as well as a new water treatment plant in North Fulton County. In addition major upgrades are planned for Atlanta's Clayton and Utoy Wastewater Treatment Plants. The Water and Sewerage rate study was completed in September 1983. On December 19, 1983, the City Council adopted rate increases averaging 44% for customers inside the City and 30% for customers outside the City. The new rates are effective for service on and after March 1, 1984.

In addition to the City's normal capital improvements programming for basic government purposes, including the Annual Bond Fund and the Park Improvement Fund, funds have been set aside for much needed municipal building structures, including a municipal court and a renovated/expanded City Hall, utilizing existing annual bond funds and proceeds from the sales tax "windfall" discussed previously.

Additionally, it is anticipated that the City will approve commencement of the Underground Atlanta Project, which will provide major specialty shopping, entertainment, and dining facilities in a central downtown location with significant open public space. The project is estimated to cost $124,570,000 and will be financed with a combination of Atlanta Downtown Development Authority Revenue Bonds, sales tax "windfall" proceeds, UDAG grant, general funds of the City, and privately raised capital.

FEDERAL AND STATE LEGISLATURE ISSUES

Although there is a myriad of Federal and State legislative decisions or pending issues which have major import for the City of Atlanta, several are worthy of note in this transmittal. On the State level, legislation enacted by the General Assembly affecting Atlanta's Library System was ratified in late 1982 in a general referendum. This law transfers the responsibility for provision of library services from the City of Atlanta to Fulton County effective July 1, 1983. This transfer has been effected and will result in a required roll back in City ad valorem taxes coupled with an increase in County taxation. However, the broader tax base of the County should result in a slight net tax reduction for most City tax payers.

With the passage of a new State Constitution by referendum in late 1982, a number of legal changes will ultimately affect to the City of Atlanta. One major adjustment resulted from the transfer of all legislative authority over the City's existing pension plans from the State General Assembly to the Atlanta City Council effective July 1, 1983. Local legislation has been adopted to define the parameters by which home rule functions may be exercised including appropriate safeguards relating to the actuarial soundness of the pension plans.

With the passage of the local option sales tax, Atlanta was faced with the prospect of having exceeded the State cumulative sales tax cap. Since this would have effectively reduced the existing Hotel/Motel Tax from 3% to 2%, the City was successful in obtaining an increase in the cap. Concurrently, it was agreed that a major portion of this tax would be utilized in direct support of the Atlanta Convention and Visitors' Bureau and the Georgia World Congress Center in order to stimulate and improve the convention and tourism industry in Atlanta. On the negative side of the ledger, State legislation was also enacted requiring statewide uniform insurance premium taxes with revenues being collected by the State for distribution in cities and counties on a population basis. At current underwriting levels, this action is expected to result in an ultimate annual revenue loss of $6.76 million phased over three years beginning in 1984. During the 1984 session of the Georgia General Assembly, no legislation was enacted which has a significant impact on the financial resources of the City.

On the Federal front, the City is pleased by the reenactment of the Federal Revenue Sharing Program. Currently these funds are utilized to pay for a large segment of firemen's salaries. The only apparent alternative would be ad valorem taxation. With respect to many of the other "Reagan" cutbacks or proposed cutbacks, most effect this City in an indirect sense, as Atlanta is not the primary service provider. Although the ultimate direct impact (particularly in the social service area) is difficult to forecast, it appears obvious that pressure to replace Federal funding with local money will mount from civic groups, non-profit organizations, and citizens-at-large. Atlanta's most immediate direct Federal losses will be in water treatment, water resource construction, urban development, public service employment, arts, humanities, and recreation. In the short-term, it appears

that Atlanta may actually benefit significantly in transportation-related funding at the Airport and indirectly through MARTA, as well as through jobs bill programs.

SUMMARY

In summary, the City of Atlanta has entered the decade of the 1980s on a foundation of stable economic vitality. As the centerpiece in a major metropolitan region, it cannot be denied that Atlanta has many of the problems generally associated with an inner city; however, its vibrant economy, well-planned basic infrastructure, and conservative financial underpinning should continue to support Atlanta's strong financial posture. In an era of increasing demands for governmental services with perhaps even greater cries for decreased taxation, Atlanta's greatest financial challenge is one of continuing to diminish its dependence upon the property tax, to oppose State intrusion on its basic revenue-producing authority, and to emphasize increased productivity in government.

LONG TERM DEBT ADMINISTRATION

Atlanta's financial condition is demonstrated by the following ratings of its bonds:

	Moody's Investor Service	Standard and Poor's
General Obligation	Aa	AA
Sanitation Certificates	Aa	AA
Water and Sewerage System Revenue		
First Lien Revenue Certificates	Aa	AA
Second Lien Revenue Bonds	A-1	AA
Airport Revenue		
First Lien, Series 1956–66	A-1	AA
Second Lien, Series 1967–75	A-1	A
Third Lien, Series 1977–83	Baa-1	A
Refunded Series 1980	Aaa	AAA

During 1983, the City retired principal in the amount of $12,273,000 on general obligation bonds. Outstanding principal, less debt service funds available for general obligation debt on a cash basis at December 31, 1983, was $123,329,000.

The Constitutional limit on general obligation bonds is 8% of the assessed property value for general government purposes and 4% for school purposes. Based on 1983 assessed property values, the city had a legal debt margin exceeding $375.1 million available at December 31, 1983, of which $270.8 million is available for general government purposes and $104.3 million for school purposes. During the past ten years, the City's ratio of net general obligation bond debt to assessed value has decreased from a high of 6.01% to 2.82% in 1983 and net general obligation bond debt per capita has decreased from a high of $394 in 1976 to $292 in 1983.

Details of direct and overlapping debt and legal debt margin are contained in the Statistical Section of this report, together with information on revenue bonds for the Water and Sewerage System and the Department of Aviation Funds.

INTERNAL AUDIT

In accordance with Part 7, Chapter 5, Article C, Section 7-5021, the Internal Audit Division is established as a separate and independent division of the Finance Department. This division has the responsibility to examine and audit accounts and financial transactions of all City departments, offices, and agencies, as well as grantees, subgrantees, and other agencies which have entered into contractual agreements with the City. Examinations are conducted by the Internal Audit Division to insure that records and reports fairly and accurately reflect actual operations, that established controls are effectively maintained to safeguard City assets, and that each department, agency, or grantee is performing in accordance with the plans, policies, and procedures for which it is responsible. The Internal Audit Division provided assistance, to a limited extent, in the preparation of this report, most notably in the inventory testing for the Water and Sewerage System and Internal Service Fund, reviewing the property tax digest, and performing payroll tests. However, since the Internal Audit Division reports organizationally to the Commissioner of Finance, and thus cannot be considered independent, the City's contract with the independent auditor requires them to complete a financial audit of all information contained in the financial section of this report.

ANNUAL INDEPENDENT AUDIT

Section 6-308 of the Charter of the City of Atlanta requires an annual independent audit of City financial records by a certified public accountant or certified public accounting firm, and the audit shall be completed not later than six months after the end of the fiscal year being audited. This requirement has been met, and a copy of the auditor's opinion is included in this report. The Finance Department is responsible for the preparation and fair presentation of the financial statements, schedules, and statistical tables contained in this report.

Management of the Finance Department and officials of the City have made appropriate representations to the independent auditors regarding availability of records, validity of data, and other matters regarding proper financial disclosure.

CERTIFICATE OF CONFORMANCE

The Municipal Finance Officers Association of the United States and Canada (MFOA) awarded a Certificate of Conformance in Financial Reporting to the City of Atlanta for its comprehensive annual financial report for the fiscal year ended December 31, 1982.

In order to be awarded a Certificate of Conformance, a governmental unit must publish an easily readable and efficiently organized comprehensive annual financial report, whose contents conform to program standards. Such reports must satisfy both generally accepted accounting principles and applicable legal requirements.

A Certificate of Conformance is valid for a period of one year only. We believe our current report continues to conform to Certificate of Conformance Program requirements, and we are submitting it to MFOA to determine its eligibility for another certificate.

ACKNOWLEDGEMENTS

The preparation of this report could not have been accomplished without the efficient and dedicated efforts of the entire staff of the Finance Department and cooperation of the various elected officials. I wish to express my appreciation to everyone who contributed to its preparation.

Respectfully submitted,
[Commissioner of Finance]

TABLE 16-3. SELECTED TOPICS DISCUSSED IN TRANSMITTAL LETTERS OF GOVERNMENTAL FINANCIAL STATEMENTS*

Topic	Chief Elected or Appointed Official	Financial Officer	Topic	Chief Elected or Appointed Official	Financial Officer
	Instances Observed (%)			Instances Observed (%)	
Accounting system and budgetary control	53	68	Water and sewer	12	13
Independent audit	60	59	Expenditures	10	10
Debt administration	58	57	Fiduciary funds	9	8
General fixed assets	53	56	Pensions/compensation	9	8
Certificate of conformance	52	52	Outlook/prospects/future	9	9
Cash management	49	56	Financial highlights	8	8
Capital projects	45	47	Proprietary funds	8	8
Reporting entity and services	38	52	Debt service	7	12
General government functions	37	52	Revenues	6	10
Enterprise funds	27	40	Investments	5	<5
General fund	18	19	Accounting system and reports	<5	8
Reporting entity	17	15	General government funds	<5	7
Special revenue funds	17	20	Long-term debt	<5	7
Special assessment funds	13	12	Trust funds	<5	6
Internal service funds	13	21	Fund balances	<5	5

* Observations for those units having a transmittal letter.

TABLE 16-4. FISCAL YEARS OF THE GOVERNMENTAL UNITS SURVEYED

End of Fiscal Year*	Instances Observed (%)	End of Fiscal Year*	Instances Observed (%)
January 31	0	August 31	<1
February 28 (or 29)	<1	September 30	15
March 31	<1	October 31	<1
April 30	4	November 30	1
May 31	0	December 31	40
June 30	38	Other	<1
July 31	0		

* Observations for those units having a transmittal letter.

TABLE 16-5. PARTIAL LISTING OF TOPICS DISCUSSED IN OTHER FOOTNOTES TO THE FINANCIAL STATEMENTS OF GOVERNMENTAL UNITS*

Topic	Instances Observed (%)	Topic	Instances Observed (%)
Commitments/contingencies	73	Fund balance information	7
Long-term debt	70	Budgetary basis of accounting	7
Fixed assets	62	Excess of expenditures	6
Employee benefits/plan/retirement/pension	46	Fund equity	6
Litigation	40	Detail notes on all funds/account groups	6
Property taxes	37	Compensated absences	6
Pensions	30	Deferred revenues	6
Interfund accounts/balances/commitments	30	Special assessments	6
Segment information/enterprise funds	22	Proprietary fund	5
Subsequent events	22	General obligation bonds	5
Changes in accounting principles	20	Bonds payable	5
Lease agreements/balances/commitments	18	Debt service fund	5
Fund deficits	17	Contributed capital	5
Cash and investments	16	Capitalized lease obligations	5
Self-insurance	14	Individual fund disclosures	5
Enterprise funds	13	General fund	5
Restricted assets	11	Governmental funds	4
Due from governments	10	Due to/from other funds	4
Property, plant, and equipment	10	Police pension	4
Prior period adjustment	10	Internal service funds	4
Notes payable/receivable	8	Fireman's pension fund	3
Capital projects	8	Account groups	3
Other required individual fund disclosures	8	Other descriptors	<3
Deferred compensation plan	7		

* See Table 2-1 for observations of those units having a summary of significant accounting policies.

Chapter 17
Special Analyses of Recent Governmental Accounting Standards

Chapter 19 contains a list of the several statements of governmental accounting approved by the National Council on Governmental Accounting. The following statements have been issued in recent years:

NCGA Statement	Accounting Subject	Effective Date
3	"Defining the Governmental Reporting Entity"	Fiscal years ending after December 31, 1982
4	"Accounting and Financial Reporting Principles for Claims and Judgments and Compensated Absences"	Fiscal years beginning after December 31, 1982
5	"Accounting and Financial Reporting Principles for Lease Agreements of State and Local Governments"	Fiscal years beginning after June 30, 1983
6	"Pension Accounting and Financial Reporting: Public Employee Retirement Systems and State and Local Government Employers"	Postponed indefinitely
7	"Financial Reporting for Component Units Within the Governmental Reporting Entity"	Fiscal years ending after June 30, 1984

Survey data are included in this chapter for NCGA Statements 3, 4, 5, and 7. Statement 6 is discussed and related survey data are presented in Chapter 18.

THE GOVERNMENTAL REPORTING ENTITY

Background

In 1981 the NCGA issued its Statement 3, "Defining the Governmental Reporting Entity," to be effective for fiscal years ending after December 31, 1982. The purpose of NCGA Statement 3 was to provide criteria related to the financial data that should be included in governmental financial statements relating to separate agencies of government, such as public authorities, whose officials are appointed rather than elected.

In developing its reporting entity definition criteria, the NCGA assumed that all functions of government are responsible to elected officials at the federal, state, or local level. Therefore, all functions of government must be a part of either federal, state, or local government. The NCGA concluded that a function (which could be a governmental department, agency, institution, commission, public authority, or other governmental organization) should be reported at the lowest level of legislative authority consistent with the criteria of Statement 3. Initially, three criteria were cited by the NCGA as a basis for deciding whether to include a function in the governmental unit's financial statements:

1. the exercise of oversight authority;
2. where there may be only partial oversight, the scope of public service rendered by the function; and
3. where there is no oversight, the existence of any special financing relationships.

Statement 3 also contains specific guidance to governmental units for implementing these criteria.

Although Statement 3 established the criteria for defining the governmental entity, it was necessary for the NCGA to issue additional guidance on this matter. In 1983 the NCGA published its Interpretation 7, "Clarification of the Application of the Criteria of NCGA Statement 3 Defining the Governmental Reporting Entity." In 1984 the NCGA approved and published Statement 7, "Financial Reporting for Component Units Within the Governmental Reporting Entity."

In Statement 7 the NCGA defined a component unit as a separate governmental unit, agency, or nonprofit corporation that, pursuant to the criteria in NCGA Statement 3, is combined with other component units to constitute the reporting entity. Statement 7 provides guidance on the "discrete presentation" of such organizations in a governmental financial statement (possibly as a separate column in the financial statements, with footnote descriptions of the accounting policies and the relationships of the unit to the oversight governmental unit).

Statement 7 provides that

> those instances in which a component unit has adopted accounting principles which are not consistent with NCGA pronouncements but those principles are considered to be generally accepted, and where the inclusion of the component unit would distort a fund type of the reporting entity, the component unit may be presented in a separate column on the financial statements of the reporting entity. The accompanying notes to the financial statements should clearly disclose the accounting policies of the component unit and the relationship of the component unit to the oversight unit.

Additionally, guidance is also given for combining the financial statements of the component unit by fund within fund types of the oversight entity.

Statement 7 was to be applied to financial statements for fiscal years ending after June 30, 1984.

Survey Information

The entities being reported in a governmental unit's financial statements may have been discussed in one or more parts of the unit's financial report. Examples are shown in the accompanying table.

Section of Report Containing Disclosure of Reporting Entities	Instances Observed (%)
Footnote concerning significant accounting policies	79
Letter of transmittal	78
Separate-entity footnote	26
Other sections of the report	1
Auditor's report	<1
No mention of reporting entities	36

In 63% of the reports examined for this topic, there was discussion of the specific component units or functions that were included or excluded from the entity being reported on in the financial statements.

Joint ventures were discussed in 7% of the surveyed financial statements. In 47% of these instances the joint venture was a governmental-type operation; in 25% of the instances the venture was more of a proprietary-type operation.

Where functions were excluded from the reporting entity in the financial statements, several reasons were noted. Table 17-1 summarizes the more frequently cited bases for excluding certain governmental functions from the reported entity. Exhibit 17-1 contains

examples of the types of footnote disclosures relating to the entity issue that were included in the surveyed financial statements.

CLAIMS, JUDGMENTS, AND COMPENSATED ABSENCES

Background

Statement 4, "Accounting and Financial Reporting Principles for Claims and Judgments and Compensated Absences," was adopted by the NCGA in May 1982, to be effective for fiscal years beginning after December 31, 1982. The purpose of this statement was to provide additional guidance with respect to its two subjects.

First, with respect to claims and judgments, the NCGA required adherence with FASB Statement 5, "Accounting for Contingencies," which required the liability for contingencies to be recognized in the financial statements. In its Statement 4 the NCGA concluded that claims should be recognized as governmental fund liabilities when they normally would be liquidated with expendable available financial resources. Otherwise, the NCGA requires that the claims be reported in the general long-term debt account group if the probable loss is estimable, whether the loss is asserted or not. Proprietary funds should follow the procedures in FASB Statement 5. (Additional information and survey observations relating to contingencies also appear in Chapter 15.)

Second, for compensated absences, the NCGA requires adherence to AICPA Statement of Position 75-3, "Accrual of Revenues and Expenditures by State and Local Governmental Units." The AICPA stated that, for accumulated unused vacation and sick leave in governmental funds, the commitment for the estimated amount should be disclosed in a footnote if material, rather than recorded as an expenditure at the time leave is accumulated. If the accumulated unused vacation and sick pay at fiscal year end does not exceed a normal year's accumulation, a footnote disclosure is not required by the AICPA statement of position.

Statement 43 of the FASB requires that under certain conditions employers accrue liability for future vacation, sick leave, and other leave benefits. These criteria were adopted by the NCGA; its Statement 4 requires that liabilities for compensated absences be inventoried at the end of each year and adjusted to current salary costs. If all the conditions of FASB Statement 43 are met, the amount of compensated absences recorded as an expenditure in governmental funds is the amount accrued during the year that would normally be liquidated with expendable available resources. The current portion of this liability should be reported in the appropriate governmental fund; the remainder of the liability should be reported in the general long-term debt account group.

Proprietary funds should follow FASB Statement 43 without modification. (Additional information and survey observations relating to the accounting and reporting of amounts due to employees for vacations, sick time, and other compensated absences appear in Chapter 10.)

Survey Information

Most of the governmental financial statements included in this special analysis contained some reference to claims or judgments. Table 17-2 lists the most frequently cited origins of liabilities for claims or judgments referred to in the footnotes to the financial statements.

Exhibit 15-2 contains examples of the types of footnotes used to disclose liabilities related to commitments and contingencies. Table 15-1 describes the reporting of commitments and contingencies.

Many statements provided footnote disclosures in connection with compensated absences. In some instances specific references were made to governmental accounting requirements.

Liabilities for compensated absences for the reporting units, were shown in the fund types and account group noted in the accompanying table. In other instances, the accounting was not discernible from the report. Exhibit 17-2 contains examples of footnote disclosures related to the liabilities for compensated absences.

Fund Type/Account Group	Instances Observed (%)
General fund	16
Special revenue funds	8
Capital projects funds	1
Special assessment funds	<1
Enterprise funds	29
Internal service funds	12
General long-term debt account group	48

LEASE AGREEMENTS

Background

Statement 5, "Accounting and Financial Reporting Principles for Lease Agreements of State and Local

Governments," was adopted by the NCGA on December 7, 1982, for fiscal years beginning after the effective date June 30, 1983. The purpose of this statement was to provide specific accounting and financial reporting guidance for lease agreements. The NCGA concluded that the criteria of FASB Statement 13 ("Accounting for Leases") should apply to governments and that if an agreement is a capital lease pursuant to the criteria of FASB Statement 13, the lease agreement should be capitalized. According to the NCGA, general fixed assets acquired by lease agreements should be capitalized in the general fixed asset account group at the inception of the agreement, in an amount determined by the criteria of FASB 13. A liability in the same amount should be recorded simultaneously in the general long-term debt account group. If the lease is an acquisition or construction lease, the general fixed asset should be shown as an expenditure and the lease should be shown as an other financing source, consistent with the accounting applicable to general-obligation bonded debt.

Proprietary funds, according to the NCGA, should follow FASB Statement 13, without modification.

Survey Information

Of the units whose financial statements were surveyed, 47% provided a footnote disclosure relating to capital or noncancellable leases. Twenty-seven percent accounted for the related lease liability in the general long-term debt account group of their financial statements.

Chapter 3, which discusses general fixed assets, and Chapter 4, relating to long-term liabilities, illustrate the manner in which some governments reported these assets and liabilities. These chapters also include excerpts from footnotes related to capital and noncancellable leases.

EXHIBITS AND TABLES FOR CHAPTER 17

Table 17-1. Reasons Cited for Excluding Governmental Functions and Organizations from Disclosures Related to Entities Reported in Financial Statements

Exhibit 17-1. Excerpts of Footnotes Relating to Functions and Organizations Included in the Financial Statements

Table 17-2. Origins of Liabilities for Claims and Contingent Liabilities

Exhibit 17-2. Excerpts of Footnotes Relating to the Disclosure of Liability for Compensated Absences

TABLE 17-1. REASONS CITED FOR EXCLUDING
GOVERNMENTAL FUNCTIONS AND ORGANIZATIONS
FROM DISCLOSURES RELATED TO ENTITIES
REPORTED IN FINANCIAL STATEMENTS

Reasons Cited*	Instances Observed (%)
Not controlled by the reporting entity	45
Management not appointed or controlled by the reporting entity	36
Discrete government entity apart from the reporting entity	27
Budgets not approved by the reporting entity	25
Not funded by the reporting entity	21
Not a significant influence on operations	10
Not accountable for fiscal matters	10
No oversight authority	9
Not administered by oversight authority	9
Not financially interdependent	6
Not part of taxing authority	6
Not within scope of public service entity	5
Joint venture	4
Privately owned	2
Other reasons	<1

* Observations for the 66% of the units in the special analysis that cited such reasons.

EXHIBIT 17-1. EXCERPTS OF FOOTNOTES RELATING
TO FUNCTIONS AND ORGANIZATIONS INCLUDED IN
THE FINANCIAL STATEMENTS

[BREVARD COUNTY, FLORIDA (SEPTEMBER 30, 1983), NOTES TO FINANCIAL STATEMENTS (IN PART)]

Note 1. Statements and Reporting Entity

The reporting entity has been defined to include all constitutional offices of Brevard County, Florida: the Clerk of the Circuit and County Courts, Tax Collector, Sheriff, Property Appraiser, Supervisor of Elections and the Board of County Commissioners. In addition, other entities included in the reporting entity are the Brevard County Mosquito Control District, Brevard County Free Public Library District, Brevard County Special Improvement Districts, A. Max Brewer Memorial Law Library, North Brevard County Library District and the South Brevard Water Authority. All of these entities except the North Brevard County Library District and the South Brevard Water Authority were included in the financial statements for the fiscal year ended September 30, 1982. The South Brevard Water Authority was created during fiscal year 1983. The inclusion of the North Brevard County Library District resulted in an adjustment to the be-

ginning fund balance of the Special Revenue Funds as follows:

Fund Balance, September 30, 1982	$11,530,414
Add Beginning Fund Balance, North Brevard County Library District	12,586
Fund Balance, October 1, 1982	$11,543,000

[CHICAGO, ILLINOIS (DECEMBER 31, 1983), NOTES TO FINANCIAL STATEMENTS (IN PART)]

Note (1) Summary of Significant Accounting Policies [in part]

The City of Chicago was incorporated in 1837. It is a "home rule" unit under the Illinois Constitution. The City has a mayor-council form of government.

The Mayor is the Chief Executive Officer of the City and is elected by general election to a four-year term. The City Council is the legislative body of Chicago and consists of 50 members who each represent one of the City's 50 wards. The members of the Council are elected through popular vote by ward for four year terms.

Other than the City of Chicago, there are seven major Chicago area units of local government, each of which (i) is separately incorporated under laws of the State of Illinois, (ii) derives its power and authority under laws of the State, (iii) has an independent tax levy, and (iv) maintains its own financial records and accounts. These are the Chicago Board of Education, the Chicago Park District, Community College District No. 508, Cook County, the Forest Preserve District of Cook County, the Chicago School Finance Authority, and the Metropolitan Sanitary District of Greater Chicago.

Under National Council on Governmental Accounting (NCGA) Statement No. 3, the basic criterion for including a governmental department, agency, institution, commission, public authority, or other governmental organization in the City's general purpose financial reports is the exercise of oversight responsibility over such agencies by the City's elected officials. Oversight responsibility is derived from the City's power and includes but is not limited to:

financial interdependency;

selection of governing authority;

designation of management;

ability to significantly influence operations; and

accountability for fiscal matters.

The City has made a study and evaluation of potential oversight responsibility and concluded that it would be inappropriate to include the seven governmental units referred to above or any other governmental unit within the City's reporting entity (see Note 2).

Note (2) Accounting Changes [in part]

NCGA Statement No. 3—Financial Reporting Entity

This Statement defines the criteria to be used in assessing whether certain entities, funds, or accounts should be considered a part of a governmental reporting entity. The basic criterion is the exercise of oversight responsibility as described in Note 1. Certain trust and agency funds have therefore been included in the financial statements.

[FULTON COUNTY, GEORGIA (DECEMBER 31, 1983), NOTES TO FINANCIAL STATEMENTS (IN PART)]

Note B. Accounting Changes [in part]

3) Reporting Entity

National Council on Governmental Accounting Statement 3, effective for years beginning after December 31, 1982, requires inclusion of entities in the reporting entity's financial statements if the reporting entity can: 1) select the governing authority; 2) designate management; 3) significantly influence operations; or 4) have accountability for fiscal matters.

During 1983, the County adopted the provisions of NCGA Statement 3, the effect of which was to include the Fulton-DeKalb Hospital Authority in the County's financial statements for the first time as discussed in Note C.

Note C. The Reporting Entity

NCGA Statement 3, "Defining the Reporting Entity," which is effective for years ending after December 31, 1982, defines the reporting entity and requires inclusion of certain entities and organizations in a reporting entity's financial statements which previously might not have been included.

1) Entities Not Included

The following entities are excluded from the County's financial statements because the County does not have the ability to significantly influence operations, appoint Board members or have responsibility over budgets. The specific reasons for exclusion are indicated:

Hospital Authority of Fulton County (Northside). Fulton County currently provides no funding for Northside Hospital. The County does have the right to appoint Board members and is guarantor on the Authority's debt. The County has never had to make any payments under its guarantee since Northside Hospital has traditionally been highly profitable. Hospital Authority Board members are approved by the County.

Atlanta–Fulton County Recreation Authority. The County is a joint venture partner in the Atlanta–Fulton County Recreation Authority and guarantees one-third of the revenue bonds of the authority. Therefore, in the event the Authority is unable to retire the principal and interest on the outstanding debt, the County would have to fund one-third of the shortfall.

See Note M for a discussion of the county's commitment to the Authority.

The Georgia Plaza Project. Fulton County is a one-third joint venture partner the Georgia Plaza Project. Under the terms of this joint venture agreement the County guarantees one-third of the bonds outstanding. As a result of its one-third interest, the County does not control operations or the budget. The County's obligation to the project is discussed in Note M.

Fulton County Board of Education. The Fulton County Board of Education is completely independent of Fulton County. The Board is appointed by the Grand Jury and the budget is substantially funded through property tax revenues.

Housing Authority of Fulton County. The Housing Authority of Fulton County receives no funding from the County, and the County cannot influence operations of the Authority.

2) Additions to the Reporting Entity

A description of the entities that are included in the County's financial statements for the first time in 1983 and the reasons for their inclusion are discussed below:

Fulton-DeKalb Hospital Authority. Fulton and DeKalb Counties entered into a contract in 1953 to jointly fund operating deficits of the Fulton-DeKalb Hospital Authority (The Authority). Fulton County currently provides approximately $36 million annually to fund operating deficits of the Fulton-DeKalb Hospital Authority.

Fulton County's contribution represents a substantial portion of the County's annual operating budget as well as the budget of the Authority. As a result, the County does have the authority to appoint Board members, influence operations and review the budget of the Authority. DeKalb County's minority interest in the Authority has not been eliminated from the financial statements presented for the Authority.

As the Hospital Authority does not operate as a enterprise with its primary objective being to generate sufficient revenues to cover its cost, it is inappropriate to include the Hospital Authority as an Enterprise Fund of the County. The Hospital Authority is included in the County's financial statements as a discrete presentation as discussed in NCGA Statement 7.

The Authority's financial statements have been examined by other auditors, whose report thereon was qualified. Certain reclassifications have been made to the audited financial statements for inclusion in the county's general purpose financial statements to conform their presentation to the other funds and account groups of the County.

Building Authority of Fulton County. The Building Authority of Fulton County was established by the County to provide funding for the construction of fire stations. The County guarantees all the debt of the Authority and has a lease agreement whereby it currently pays the Authority lease payments equivalent to the principal and interest on the Authority's outstanding debt.

[GREEN BAY, WISCONSIN (DECEMBER 31, 1983), NOTES TO FINANCIAL STATEMENTS (IN PART)]

Note B—Reporting Entity

Several other governmental entities have operations within the City but are not included in the financial report because they are separate legal entities. The entities are described below:

Green Bay Area School District

Green Bay Area Public Schools operate as a unified school district with separate taxing power providing elementary and secondary education within the school district boundaries, which includes the City and several surrounding townships.

As of July 1, 1982, a change in state statute allowed for the School District to own real property and become totally independent. Therefore, the City is in the process of transferring all real property and debt obligations to the School District. General long-term debt payable includes $5,543,222 and $7,475,591 at December 31, 1983 and 1982 respectively, incurred for school purposes. General Fixed Assets in the amount of $41,398,958 are used as school facilities.

All financial activity of the School District prior to July 1, 1982, was handled by the City in an agency capacity and reflected in the accompanying financial statements in the Green Bay Area School District Agency Fund. Also, title to real property used by the School System was vested, by State statute, in the City of Green Bay. Likewise the City of Green Bay was obligated by statute to provide financing for the acquistion of real property and has done so customarily by the issuance of general obligation debt.

Green Bay Housing Authority. Although members of the Authority are appointed by the Common Council, the Housing Authority is a separate legal entity. The City exercises no budgetary control over the Authority and its long-term debt is funded by the Federal government.

[KANSAS CITY, MISSOURI (APRIL 30, 1984), NOTES TO FINANCIAL STATEMENTS (IN PART)]

Note (2) Reporting Entity

Statement 3, "Defining the Governmental Reporting Entity," provides the criteria for defining the reporting entity of a governmental unit for financial reporting. This statement provides for the inclusion in the financial statements of a reporting entity of financial data of separate governmental organizations if certain criteria are met. In evaluating which governmental organizations were to be included as part of the reporting entity, management of the City considered factors such as manifestation of oversight of the City, scope of public service and special financial relationships. In assessing the City's oversight responsibility over separate governmental organizations, consideration was given to factors such as financial interdependency, selection of governing authority, designation of management, ability to significantly influence operations and accountability for fiscal matters. As a result, the following governmental organizations have been identified as part of the report entity:

Metropolitan Ambulance Services Trust and Subsidiary (MAST): a public trust primarily engaged in providing ambulance transportation services within the city limits of Kansas City, Missouri.

Land Clearance for Redevelopment Authority (LCRA): a not-for-profit corporation designed to undertake clearing and redevelopment activities within designated areas of the City.

Rehabilitation Loan Corporation (RLC): a corporation engaged primarily in administering a rehabilitation loan program funded by certain Community Development Block Grant Funds in Kansas City, Missouri.

Maintenance Reserve Corporation (MRC): a corporation engaged in administering a maintenance reserve program designed to encouage maintenance of homes over the period of time loans made by RLC are repaid.

Kansas City Public Building Authority (PBA): a not-for-profit corporation incorporated in October 1983 to acquire or construct facilities for the benefit of the City.

The financial statements of MAST and LCRA as of and for the years ended April 30, 1984 and 1983, are included in the accompanying financial statements as part of the Enterprise Funds and Trust and Agency Funds, respectively. Financial statements for the PBA are combined with those of the Auditorium Plaza Garage Fund, an Enterprise Fund, in accordance with NCGA Statement 5, "Accounting and Financial Reporting Principles for Lease Agreements of State and Local Governments." This statement provides for the reporting of a public authority's debt and assets as a form of a local government's debt and assets for financial reporting purposes when the public authority is created to provide financing for construction of fixed assets for the local government. Financial statements for RLC and MRC from the accompanying financial statements do not materially affect the fairness of presentation of these financial statements.

As a result of the review described above, management of the City has determined that a number of agencies and organizations should not be included as part of the accompanying financial statements in accordance with NCGA Statement 3 due to the inability of the City's elected officials to exercise oversight responsibility, the more notable of which are the Kansas City, Missouri, Police Department, the Boards of Election Commissioners and the School District of Kansas City, Missouri.

The Kansas City, Missouri, Police Department and the Boards of Election Commissioners are administered by independent boards appointed by the Governor of the State of Missouri. The annual operating budgets of these entities, which are approved by their respective boards, are substantially financed by general City revenues. Expenditures made by the City on their behalf are included in the financial statements of the General Fund. The School District of Kansas City, Missouri, is administered by an independent board elected by the general public. The annual operating budget of this entity is approved by its board, and financial support from the City is limited to revenues received as a result of a one-half percent sales tax. Since the City does not exercise control or have oversight responsibilities over the financial activities of the Kansas City, Missouri, Police Department, the Boards of Election Commissioners or the School District of Kansas City, Missouri, financial statements of these entities are not included in the accompanying financial statements.

[ROCKFORD, ILLINOIS (DECEMBER 31, 1983), NOTES TO FINANCIAL STATEMENTS (IN PART)]

Note 2. Financial Reporting Entity

The funds, account groups, agencies, boards and commissions included in the comprehaensive annual financial report are controlled by or dependent on the City. Determination of "controlled by or dependent on" is based on criteria set forth in Statement 3 and Interpretation 7 by the National Council on Governmental Accounting. As a result of these accounting pronouncements, this comprehensive annual financial report includes as enterprise funds the operations of the Rockford Mass Transit District and the Rockford Metropolitan Exposition, Auditorium and Office Building Authority (Metro Authority).

Both of these entities maintain separate accounting and financial reporting systems and report independently based on their June 30 fiscal years. Therefore this report includes these entity's financial statements according to their respective fiscal years of June 30, 1983. As a result certain items included in this report, such as operating transfers, involve different reporting periods and will not coincide with the comparable information of the City.

A reconciliation of the combined enterprise funds' municipal equity accounts as of December 31, 1982, as previously reported, with the beginning combined municipal equity of these funds, as presented in this report, is as follows:

	Contributed Capital	Retained Earnings	Total
Balance, December 31, 1982, as previously reported	$ 1,556,352	$23,415,197	$24,971,549
Rockford Mass Transit District	1,442,396	(4,824)	1,437,572
Rockford Metropolitan Exposition, Auditorium and Office Building Authority	21,721,920	(834,270)	20,887,650
Balance, beginning, as restated	$24,720,668	$22,576,103	$47,296,771

[SAINT PAUL, MINNESOTA (DECEMBER 31, 1983), NOTES TO FINANCIAL STATEMENT (IN PART)]

Note II (in part). Financial Reporting Entity

For financial reporting purposes, in conformance with National Council on Governmental Accounting Statement No. 3, *Defining the Governmental Reporting Entity*, the City of Saint Paul includes all funds, account groups, departments agencies, boards, commissions, and other organizations over which City officials exercise oversight responsibility.

Oversight responsibility includes such aspects as appointment of governing body members, budget review, approval of property tax levies, outstanding debt secured by City full faith and credit or revenues, responsibility for funding deficits, and others.

As a result of applying the criteria of Statement No. 3, certain organizations have been included or excluded from the City's financial statements, as follows:

Included

Civic Center Authority of the City of St. Paul

City of St. Paul Board of Water Commissioners

Housing and Redevelopment Authority of the City of Saint Paul (HRA). Formerly the Housing and Redevelopment Authority was considered a separate unit of government and was not included in the City of Saint Paul's Comprehensive Annual Financial Report (CAFR). However, it has been determined that, as a result of application of the criteria of Statement No. 3, HRA is a component unit of the City of Saint Paul and thus its financial statements have been included in the City's 1983 CAFR. The beginning January 1, 1982, and January 1, 1983, fund balances have been restated to reflect the inclusion of HRA. See Note VI.C.vi.

Excluded

Independent School District No. 625. Independent School District No. 625 is an organized governmental agency empowered by the State Legislature to perform the duties of educating children of the City of Saint Paul. The Minnesota Supreme Court has stated that the School District is not subservient to the City in its performance of its duties. Independent School District No. 625 has an independently elected board of directors, adopts and controls its own budget, and virtually has no significant financial interrelationships with the City.

Port Authority of the City of Saint Paul. The Port Authority of the City of Saint Paul was established as a "Public body corporate and politic" pursuant to Minnesota Statute Section 458. As an industrial development corporation its specific purpose is to promote and develop commercial, industrial and manufacturing enterprises and encourage employment within the City. The law authorizes the corporation to issue industrial development bonds. The bonds do not constitute indebtedness of the City and are secured solely by revenues from the commercial organizations on whose behalf the bonds are issued. The City assumes no responsibility for the day-to-day operating expenses, nor is it responsible for financing deficits. Based upon the Port Authority's financial independence, the City does not exercise oversight responsibility.

Public Housing Agency of the City of Saint Paul. The Public Housing Agency of the City of Saint Paul was established pursuant to Laws of Minnesota 1977, Chapter 228. The agency owns and operates 4,400 housing projects for low income, elderly and handicapped families. It administers Section 8 existing and moderate housing rehabilitation programs for eligible participants. The City has no responsibility for financing any deficits, nor is it responsible for its debt. The Public Housing Agency can sue or be sued, has perpetual succession and is solely accountable for its fiscal matters.

Saint Paul Police Relief Association; Saint Paul Fire Department Relief Association. These associations are organized as non-profit organizations by their members to provide pension and other benefits to such members in accordance with Minnesota statutes. Their boards or directors are appointed by the membership of the organization. All funding is conducted in accordance with Minnesota statutes, whereby state aids flow to the associations, tax levies are determined by the association and are only reviewed by the City and the associations pay benefits directly to their members. (See Note VI.B.x. for disclosures relating to the pension plans operated by the associations.)

[SAVANNAH, GEORGIA (DECEMBER 31, 1983), NOTES TO FINANCIAL STATEMENTS (IN PART)]

Note 3—Reporting Entity

In accordance with NCGA Statement 3, "Defining the Governmental Reporting Entity," the City has reviewed and evaluated its relationship with various boards, commissions, and agencies to determine if these agencies should be included in the annual financial statements of the City. The agencies evaluated were the Savannah Transit Authority, the Savannah Port Authority, the Savannah Airport Commission, the Chatham-Savannah Metropolitan Planning Commission, and the Housing Authority of Savannah.

The criteria used to determine whether or not to include these agencies in the financial statements were: (1) the selection of governing authority, (2) designation of management, (3) ability to significantly influence operations, and (4) accountability for fiscal matters. In several cases, the Mayor and Aldermen appoint the governing authority (or a portion of the governing authority) of the agency, but these appointees have little continuing relationships to the Mayor and Aldermen and can only be removed for cause. These appointments are therefore not authoritative as defined in Statement 3.

There were no situations where the City designates the management of an agency or where the City was able to significantly influence operations (there is no control over agency budget, ability to sign contracts, approve hiring of key personnel, etc.). Also, the City has no accountability for fiscal matters for any agency. The City does not fund deficits or receive the surplus funds, there is no outstanding debt that is an obligation of the City, and the City does not contribute a significant part of any agencies' revenues.

Based on the above criteria, the City has not included any of the above agencies in the annual financial statements.

TABLE 17-2. ORIGINS OF LIABILITIES FOR CLAIMS AND CONTINGENT LIABILITIES

Cited Origin of Claims and Contingent Liabilities*	Instances Observed (%)
Possible disallowance or dispute related to federal contract or grant	50
Discrimination/civil rights	29
Action of governmental personnel (e.g., accident by government driver, malpractice by government doctor, or improper arrest)	19
Claim for property damage	13
Disputes—tax levies or assessed valuations	11
Contract dispute	10
Lawsuits:	
Specified	6
Unspecified	20
Compensation claim	6
Unemployment liability	1
Other descriptors	<1

* Observations for the 74% of the units in the special analysis that had a note discussing claims or contingencies.

EXHIBIT 17-2. EXCERPTS OF FOOTNOTES RELATING TO THE DISCLOSURE OF LIABILITY FOR COMPENSATED ABSENCES

[COUNTY OF ALLEGHENY, PENNSYLVANIA (DECEMBER 31, 1983), NOTES TO FINANCIAL STATEMENTS (IN PART)]

Vacation and Sick Leave

The County's vacation policy for union and non-union employees provides that such employees are to take vacation within the year it is earned, with no carry-forward provisions. Thus, there is no County Liability for unused vacation at December 31, 1983.

Certain County police and Airport System firefighters earn vested sick benefits that are paid at termination or retirement based on then current rates of compensation. The Liability for benefits applicable to Airport System firefighters is accrued in the Enterprise Fund at current rates of compensation (see note 13). The Liability for benefits applicable to County police has been established in the General Long-term Debt Account Group, also at current rates of compensation (see note 7). Personnel of all other County departments may generally accumulate up to 60 days of sick leave; these future benefits do not vest and, accordingly, have not been recognized in the accompanying financial statements.

[COOK COUNTY, ILLINOIS (DECEMBER 4, 1983), NOTES TO FINANCIAL STATEMENTS (IN PART)]

Vacation and Sick Leave

Employees can earn from ten to twenty vacation days per year, depending on their length of employment with the County. An employee can accumulate no more than two years' vacation allotment. Accumulated vacation leave is due to the employee, or employee's beneficiary, at the time of termination or death. Accrued vacation leave is recorded as a liability when incurred.

Salaried employees can accumulate sick leave at the rate of one day for each month worked, up to a maximum of 175 days. Accumulated sick leave is forfeited at the termination of employment; therefore, sick leave pay is not accrued, it is charged as an expenditure when paid.

[CITY OF DALLAS, TEXAS (SEPTEMBER 30, 1983), NOTES TO FINANCIAL STATEMENTS (IN PART)]

Note 1.

K. Vacation and Sick Leave

The City's employees earn vacation which may either be taken or accumulated until paid upon retirement or termination. Unused sick leave may be accumulated up to certain limits which are subject to specified reduction if paid in cash upon retirement or death. Beginning in fiscal year 1983, the City accrued vacation and sick leave based on the criteria set forth in National Council on Governmental Accounting Statement Number 4, "Accounting and Financial Reporting Principles for Claims and Judgements and Compensated Absences." For all funds this liability has been restated to reflect amounts attributable to employees services already rendered, cumulative, probable for payment and reasonably estimated. The governmental and fiduciary type funds liability is recorded in the general long-term debt account group as payment of this liability will not be made with expendable available financial resources. In 1982 the appropriate vacation and sick expense was charged to income and, accordingly, there is no effect on 1982 net income of the proprietary funds for the restatement. The retained earnings in the proprietary funds and the general long-term debt account group have been restated as follows:

	Balance Before Restatement	Restatement	Balance as Restated
Surtran	$ (1,305)	$ 204	$ (1,101)
Public Transit	(2,489)	2,798	309
Water Utilities	409,474	3,700	413,174
Convention Center	4,943	214	5,157
Municipal Radio	558	50	608
Airport Revenue	72,041	168	72,209
Equipment Services	14,683	824	15,507
Communication Services	1,116	180	1,296
Office Services	1,043	36	1,079
Total Proprietary Funds	$500,064	$ 8,174	$508,238
General Long-Term Debt (Amount to be provided for retirement of general long-term debt)	$363,679	$23,457	$387,136

[CITY OF ELGIN, ILLINOIS (DECEMBER 31, 1983), NOTES TO FINANCIAL STATEMENTS (IN PART)]

Note 11. Change in the Method of Accounting for Compensated Absences

In 1983, the City of Elgin changed its method of accounting for compensated absences to comply with the provisions of Statement No. 43 of the Financial Accounting Standards Board. The Statement requires employers to accrue a liability, with a corresponding charge to current operations, for employees' rights to receive compensation for future absences when certain conditions are met. Previously, the City of Elgin recognized compensated absences when paid. It was not practical to determine the amount of restatement for the year ended December 31, 1982. The effect of this change for the year ended December 31, 1983, was to reduce the excess of revenue over expenses as follows:

Enterprise Funds	$ 16,695
Internal Service funds	1,668
	$ 18,363

The adjustment necessary to apply the new method retroactively is included as a reduction of revenue over expenses in the year ended December 31, 1983, as follows:

Enterprise Funds	$103,760
Internal Service Funds	15,903
	$119,663

[HILLSBOROUGH COUNTY, FLORIDA (SEPTEMBER 30, 1983), NOTES TO FINANCIAL STATEMENTS (IN PART)]

Compensated Absences

It is the County's policy to allow employees to accumulate unused sick leave and vacation benefits. For the fiscal year ended September 30, 1983, for all governmental fund types, the liability relating to such unused vacation and sick leave to the extent of certain vested maximum hours is recorded in the accompanying financial statements. In compliance with NCGA Statement 4, expenditures for compensated absences in governmental funds are those paid during the current fiscal year and the amount unpaid at the end of the reporting period that normally would be liquidated with expendable available financial resources. The remainder of the liability is reported in the General Long-Term Debt Account Group. The amounts shown in the "Additions" column in the Statement of Changes in General Long-Term Debt for compensated absences represents the current year liability for compensated absences. The beginning balance reflected in the accompanying Statement of Changes in General Long-Term Debt represents restatement of the liability for compensated absences as of October 1, 1982.

For Proprietary Funds, the liability relating to vested sick leave and vacation is recorded in the accompanying financial statements as long-term debt.

[CITY OF JACKSONVILLE, FLORIDA
(SEPTEMBER 30, 1983), NOTES TO FINANCIAL
STATEMENTS (IN PART)]

Note P. [in part]: Compensated Absences

In August, 1982, the NCGA issued Statement 4, "Accounting and Financial Reporting for Claims and Judgements and Compensated Absences," which in part, adopts the criteria of Statement of Financial Accounting Standards No. 43, "Compensated Absences," to be the guidelines for recognizing a liability for compensated absences for state and local government. In recognizing this liability, Statement 4 gives consideration to the distinction between the governmental fund and proprietary fund types. For governmental funds, Statement 4 requires "the amount of compensated absences recorded as expenditures. . .shall be the amount accrued during the year that would normally be liquidated with expendable available financial resource. . . . The remainder of the liability should be reported in the General Long-Term Debt Account Group. Proprietary funds should follow SFAS 43 without modifications."

Statement 4 is effective for fiscal years beginning after December 31, 1982, and, accordingly, City management will adopt Statement 4 for the 1983–84 fiscal year.

At September 30, 1983, the compensated absences (accumulated annual personal leave) earned by employees of the City of Jacksonville approximate $17,671,000 based on the assumption that all employees would end their terms of employment at that date and would be payable at current salary rates. Such amount is not reflected in the accompanying financial statements.

[CITY OF NEW ORLEANS, LOUISIANA
(DECEMBER 31, 1983), NOTES TO FINANCIAL
STATEMENTS (IN PART)]

Note 14. Vacation and Sick Leave

All full-time classified employees of the City hired prior to January 1, 1979, are permitted to accumulate a maximum of 90 days of accrued vacation (annual leave) and an unlimited number of days of accrued sick leave (accumulated at a maximum of 24 pays per year). Employees hired after December 31, 1978, can accrue a maximum of 45 days of annual leave and an unlimited number of days of accrued sick leave. Upon termination of employment an employee is paid for his accumulated annual leave based on his current hourly rate of pay and for his accumulated sick leave on a formula basis. If termination is the result of retirement,

the employee has the option of converting his accrued sick leave to additional years of service.

Annual leave and sick leave liabilities are accrued when incurred in the proprietary funds. In the governmental funds, only that portion which would normally be liquidated within one year with expendable available financial resources is accrued. The remainder of the liability is reported in the General Long-Term Debt Account Group. The amount of accumulated annual and sick leave at December 31, 1983, applicable to governmental fund operations was $36,883,307, all of which is reported in the General Long-Term Debt Account Group.

[PINELLAS COUNTY, FLORIDA (SEPTEMBER 30,
1983), NOTES TO FINANCIAL STATEMENTS
(IN PART)]

Note D [in part]—Commitments, Contingencies
and Guarantees

Accrued Vacation and Sick Leave

All full time employees of the County are entitled to annual vacation and sick leave with pay. The employees are generally allowed to accumulate vacation leave of 30 to 60 days depending on length of service. Sick leave may be accumulated with no maximum; however, upon termination, the employee is paid for one-third of accumulated sick leave. Vacation pay and sick leave payments are included in operating costs, for Governmental and Fiduciary Fund Types, when the payments are made to the employees. The estimated commitment for vacation and sick leave for governmental and fiduciary fund types, at September 30, 1983, was approximately $5 million.

Pursuant to the requirements of Financial Accounting Standards Board Statement No. 43, Accounting for Compensated Absences, it is the County's policy in its Proprietary Funds to reflect on an accrual basis the amounts of earned but unused vacation leave and that portion of earned but unused sick leave estimated to be payable upon retirement.

[CITY OF PUEBLO, COLORADO (DECEMBER 31,
1983), NOTES TO FINANCIAL STATEMENTS
(IN PART)]

Note 12. Accrued Compensated Absences

In accordance with NCGA Statement 4, the City has recognized as an expenditure and a liability in the general fund the accrued vacation and sick pay that is expected to be liquidated with available spendable resources. The remaining amount of the unpaid vacation and sick pay attributable to governmental funds has been recognized in the general long-term debt account group. The unpaid vacation and sick pay attributable to proprietary funds has been accrued in its entirety. The following is a summary of the prior period adjustment to reflect recognition of this liability for the general fund:

Fund balance, January 1, 1983, as previously reported	$10,032,270
Prior period adjustment to record accrued compensated absences expected to be liquidated with available spendable resources	(176,402)
Fund balance, January 1, 1983, as restated	$ 9,855,868

The following is a summary of the toal unpaid vacation and sick pay that existed at December 31, 1983:

General fund	$ 150,000
Enterprise funds	
Memorial Airport	48,895
Sewer User	88,625
Internal Service Funds	
City Shops	25,989
General long-term debt account group	1,896,280
Total	$ 2,209,789

The total amount of $2,209,789 consists of $1,003,184 vacation pay and $1,206,605 sick pay.

[CITY AND COUNTY OF SAN FRANCISCO, CALIFORNIA (JUNE 30, 1984), NOTES TO FINANCIAL STATEMENTS (IN PART)]

Note K: Accrued Vacation and Sick Leave Pay

Vacation pay, which may be accumulated up to six weeks, is payable upon termination.

Sick leave may be accumulated up to six months. Unused amounts accumulated prior to December 6, 1978, are vested and are payable upon termination of employment by retirement, or death or disability caused by industrial accident. Sick leave earned subsequent to that date is nonvesting.

Vested vacation and sick leave pay are accrued for all fund types. Such accruals were recorded for the first time in 1984 in the governmental fund types and the General Long-Term Obligations Account Group, in accordance with National Council on Governmental Accounting Statement 4, "Accounting and Financial Reporting Principles for Claims and Judgments and Compensated Absences." Amounts expected to be paid in the ensuing year, which are estimated based on historical information, are accrued in the governmental fund types and the remainder is recorded in the General Long-Term Obligations Account Group.

The effect of implementing Statement 4 was to reduce the General Fund fund balance by $14.3 million as of July 1, 1983, to record accrued vacation and sick leave pay expected to be paid within the ensuing year. In addition, a long-term obligation of $18.7 million was recorded in the General Long-Term Obligations Account Group as of July 1, 1983, for vacation and sick leave pay expected to be paid after one year. Prior periods were not restated because information was not available.

Chapter 18
Pension Accounting and Reporting for Public Employee Retirement Systems

In July 1984 the Governmental Accounting Standards Board (GASB) issued its first statement (GAS-1). Relative to pension reporting, pending issuance by the GASB of a statement or statements concerning pension accounting and reporting, the GASB considers the following pronouncements as acceptable accounting and reporting principles for public employee retirement systems (PERS) and state and local government employers:

NCGA Statement 1, "Governmental Accounting and Financial Reporting Principles";

NCGA Statement 6, "Pension Accounting and Financial Reporting: Public Employee Retirement Systems and State and Local Government Employers"; and

FASB Statement 35, "Accounting and Reporting by Defined Benefit Plans."

NCGA Statement 6 differs from FASB Statement 35 in two important ways: (1) the valuation of investments (at cost or amortized cost under NCGA 6, at "fair" or market value under FASB Statement 35) and (2) the consideration given to future changes in compensation in computing the actuarial present value of accumulated pension benefits. (The changes are taken into account under NCGA Statement 6, but not under FASB Statement 35.)

Because the accounting standards-setting pronouncements of the FASB and NCGA differ, the GASB is considering a new standard that will reconcile these differences. As of March 1985, the effective date of NCGA Statement 6 has been extended indefinitely. The FASB has also indefinitely deferred the effective date of FASB Statement 35 insofar as it applies to pension plans of state and local governmental units.

A SPECIAL ANALYSIS ON PENSION REPORTING

An analysis was made of the financial statements of 489 cities and counties. Eighty-four percent of these statements contained a footnote describing the existence of or providing other details on pension or retirement plans. This analysis was made to identify the various types of pension presentations and disclosures found in the financial statements.

Types of Pension Plans Disclosed in Footnotes to Governmental Financial Statements

Many governmental units belong to multiple-employer pension plans, which are often legislated by a higher level of government. A multiple-employer pension plan is a plan where more than one employer contributes to the plan for the benefit of all covered employees for each of the governmental units. Single-employer plans cover only the employees, or a specific group of employees, of one governmental unit and are generally administered by that governmental unit. Some organizations have a combination of multiple-employer and single-employer pension plans. For example, a city could have a single-employer pension plan for its general employees and belong to two separate statewide multiple-employer plans for the employees of the fire department and police department.

Pension plans can also be classified by nature as defined-contribution plans and defined-benefit plans. In defined-contribution plans, the employer typically contributes funds based upon a formula. The benefits available for the employee are based directly upon the contributed amounts. Earnings on the contributions and the risk and rewards pertaining thereto generally belong to the employees. Defined-benefit plans specify a determinable pension benefit, usually based upon such factors as age, years of service, and salary. Generally, employer contributions for defined-benefit plans are actuarially computed and periodically adjusted to enable such stated benefits to be maintained. Certain plans were not clearly described as defined-benefit or defined-contribution. Employers may have defined both the contribution and the benefit but may not have specified whether the contribution will be adjusted to meet the stated benefits or the benefits will be adjusted to conform to the amounts accumulated from the stated contributions.

The study disclosed the following types of plans for the surveyed units. Multiple responses were possible, since many governmental units had more than one pension plan.

Entries Having Certain Types of Pension Plans	Instances Observed (%)
Single employer	40
Multiple employers	61
Not determinable	13
Average number of plans per financial statement	1.37

Nature of Pension Plans	Instances Observed (%)
Defined benefit	88
Defined contribution	13
Other (not disclosed or unclear)	15

The 40% of single-employer plans were included in the financial statements surveyed in one of three ways:

a. The plan was incorporated as a part of or as a separate column in 84% of the financial statements
b. The plan was not incorporated in the financial statements but separate pension financial statements were attached in 2% of the financial statements
c. In the remaining 14% of the cases the plan was not incorporated and separate statements were not attached; the plan was described in the footnotes to these statements.

Information Provided by Governments on Pension Plans

Numerous types of disclosures were made in the 411 financial statements having the pension plan footnotes. The following table lists several of these disclosures.

Information Disclosed for Pension Plans	Instances Observed (%)
Number and type of plan beneficiaries	98
Description of the terms of the plan	88
Funding requirements or actual contributions	74
Date of latest actuarial valuation	48
Significant assumptions used in actuarial valuation	33
Employers' legal obligations to the plan	28
Actuarial cost method used for funding purposes	13
Significant changes affecting reporting comparability	10
Major investments of the plan	6
Explanation of actuarial changes and values	4
Historical statistical summary data	1
Actuarial cost method used for reporting	<1

An actuarial valuation is the process by which an actuary reviews the terms of a pension plan, the demographics of the workforce covered by the plan, the investment results of the plan, etc. and thus estimates the present value of benefits to be paid under the plan and calculates the amount of employer contributions and accounting charges for the period. Actuarial valuations normally are only conducted for defined-benefit plans, since for defined-contribution plans both the current period contribution and expense are already known and the benefits to be paid are determined by the funds available. However, for some defined-contribution plans actuarial studies may be performed for other reasons.

Relationship of Actuarial Valuation Date and Fiscal Year End of Financial Statements

In many of the governmental statements the notes stated that an actuarial study was performed, and the date of the latest actuarial valuation was mentioned. The time elapsed between the date this valuation was performed and the end of the fiscal year of the reporting entities varied, as shown in the following table:

Time from Actuarial Valuations to the End of the Fiscal Year	Instances Observed (%)
1 year	55
2 years	13
3 years	4
4 years	1
More than 4 years	3
Not disclosed	24

Assumed Rates of Return on Pension Plan Investments

A significant assumption in the actuarial valuations is the assumed rate of return on pension plan investments. The various cited rates of return are summarized in the accompanying table for those 411 survey units that had pension plan footnotes.

Assumed Rate of Return on Pension Plan Investment*	Instances Observed (%)
Less than 4%	1
4% but less than 6%	5
6% but less than 8%	30
8% but less than 10%	11
10% or greater	1
Not disclosed	58

* Many statements contained multiple plans.

The actuarial cost method used for funding and/or expensing purposes is also an essential element in pension plan accounting. The following types of actuarial cost methods were disclosed for the 411 units surveyed having pension plan footnotes.

Actuarial Cost Method for Funding Purposes*	Instances Observed (%)
Entry age normal cost method	6
Entry age actuarial cost method	5
Aggregate actuarial cost method	2
Frozen entry age actuarial cost method	2
Projection of actuarial cost	<1
Unit credit actuarial cost	<1
Individual-level actuarial cost	<1
Others	6
Not disclosed	77

* Many statements contained multiple plans.

For those 411 financial statements containing a pension footnote, the basis of the pension plan investment assets was disclosed in many instances. Further, there were circumstances where different bases were used for different types of investment assets within the same governmental unit. Those cited could be categorized as shown in the following table.

Basis of Investment Assets	Instances Observed (%)
Cost, which approximates market value	17
Cost	12
Market value	9
Other basis	7
Lower of cost or market value	3
Cost based (equity securities at cost; fixed-income securities at amortized cost)	1
Not disclosed	51

Reference to FASB Statement 35 and NCGA Statements

Few of the 411 governmental units with footnotes specifically made reference to the FASB Statement of Financial Accounting Standards 35 in the footnotes. However, there was evidence of at least partial compliance with FASB Statement 35 noted in many financial statements. This disclosure pertained to the actuarial present value of vested accumulated plan benefits, the actuarial present value of nonvested accumulated plan benefits, and the plan net assets available for benefits. The following data illustrate the extent to which each one of these items was observed:

Benefits and Net Assets Disclosure*	Instances Observed (%)
Plan net assets available for benefits	30
Actuarial present value of vested accumulated plan benefits	30
Actuarial present value of nonvested accumulated plan benefits	26
Actuarial present value of both vested and nonvested accumulated plan benefits	26

* Instances observed related to the 411 governmental units that have pension plan footnotes.

The footnotes for a few (less than ten) of the surveyed financial statements contained references to NCGA Statement 6. In these instances the following disclosure requirements of NCGA Statement 6 were presented: (1) the actuarial present value of projected benefits payable to current retirants and beneficiaries, (2) the actuarial present value of projected benefits payable to terminated vested participants who have not yet reached the eligibility requirements, and (3) the actuarial present value of credited projected benefits payable to active participants.

References to Pensions in Auditors' Reports

In 10 of the 489 financial statements surveyed, the auditors' reports made reference to the pension area and contained qualifications related to pension accounting and reporting. In 34% of the cases the auditors' opinion included the pension financial statements by virtue of the fact such statements were part of the agency and trust fund types in the government's financial report. In these instances, the auditors' opinion was unqualified as to such fund types.

Where the auditors' reports contained a qualified opinion on the financial statements owing to pension circumstances, such qualifications included instances where the pay-as-you-go method was utilized for pension expense and funding and instances where the recorded pension expense was less than the actuarially calculated amount. Neither of these conditions is consistent with generally accepted accounting principles.

OTHER STUDY OBSERVATIONS

Other types of pension disclosures included such data as the following:

Four governmental units disclosed their policy of reporting gains or losses when there is an exchange of fixed-income securities (bonds or notes). In these four cases the gains or losses would be recognizable at the time of the exchange.

For those entities where there are multiple-employer pension plans not incorporated in the financial statements, a net pension liability was shown as a separate line item in the balance sheet on 24 occasions. A net pension prepaid asset was shown for 12 entities, and in 13 other entities a net pension liability was disclosed in the footnotes.

ILLUSTRATIONS OF PENSION FOOTNOTE DISCLOSURES

The format, content, and detail of the discussions contained in the footnotes to the surveyed financial statements varied considerably. The length of the explanations was from a paragraph or two to several pages. Exhibits 18-1 to 18-5 contain selected illustrations of footnotes for several of the topics mentioned earlier in this chapter.

EXHIBITS FOR CHAPTER 18

Exhibit 18-1. Excerpt of a Single-Employer Pension Plan Footnote

Exhibit 18-2. Excerpt of a Multiple-Employer Pension Plan Footnote

Exhibit 18-3. Excerpt of a Pension Footnote with Both Single-Employer and Multiple-Employer Pension Plans

Exhibit 18-4. Excerpt of Pension Financial Statements Not Part of the CAFR, but to which Separate Financial Statements were Attached

Exhibit 18-5. Excerpts from Selected Combining Financial Statements Containing Pension Plans

EXHIBIT 18-1. EXCERPT OF A SINGLE-EMPLOYER PENSION PLAN FOOTNOTE

[CITY OF JACKSONVILLE, FLORIDA (SEPTEMBER 30, 1983), NOTES TO FINANCIAL STATEMENTS (IN PART)]

Note H. Pension Funds

The City has two single employer contributory pension plans covering substantially all general employees of the City and members of the Police and Fire Departments of the City who meet defined age and service requirements. Additionally certain other employees are covered by the State of Florida Retirement System state-wide plan. These are employees that were covered by the Florida Retirement System prior to consolidation and elected continued coverage by the State's Retirement System.

The group covered under the General Employees' pension fund is in one of five plans and the group covered under the Police and Fire pension fund is in one of four plans. The specific plan an employee is covered

under is determined by hire date and age at date of hire.

The percentages of compensation to be contributed by plan members and the City are as follows:

	General Employees Pension Fund	Policemen's and Firemen's Pension Fund
Employee contributions	4% of earnings	4% of earnings
City contributions	27.3% of base pay	19.5% of base pay plus 30% of traffic parking fines plus Chapter 175 and 185 State contributions

A summary of selected data for these plans as of the most recent actuarial valuation date (October 1, 1982) is as follows:

	General Employees Pension Fund	Policemen's and Firemen's Pension Fund
Total Actuarial Present Value of Accumulated Plan Benefits as defined in FASB Statement Number 35:		
Vested benefits of participants and beneficiaries currently receiving payments	$149,440,000	$ 43,519,000
Other vested benefits	95,211,000	55,419,000
Non-vested benefits	9,868,000	3,442,000
Total Actuarial Present Value of Accumulated Benefits	$254,519,000	$102,380,000
Total Actuarial Present Value of Accumulated Benefits with salary increase assumptions	$306,232,000	$136,079,000
Unfunded Past Service Costs	$197,751,000	$ 55,291,000
Net Assets Available for Plan Benefits:		
At the Market Value of Plan Assets	$ 81,491,000	$ 72,684,000
At the Statement Value of Plan Assets	$ 83,460,000	$ 75,481,000
Total Employer's Contribution for the fiscal year ended September 30, 1982	$ 22,340,000	$ 7,106,000
Total minimum annual contribution based on the October 1, 1980, actuarial contribution for plan year beginning October 1982:		
Amounts	$ 25,186,000	$ 10,068,000
As a Percent of Payroll	31.3%	29.8%

The assumed rate of return used in determining the actuarial computations was 7.5% per year.

No significant changes in the nature of the plans or amendments to the plans occurred during the year.

The City's policy is to fund pension cost as determined by actuarial valuation. It is the opinion of the City General Counsel that any liability for actuarially sound funding of the pension funds is that of the General Fund.

Pension cost is determined based on an actuarial valuation using the attained age normal cost method. This valuation is performed every two years as of the beginning of the fiscal year and is used to determine the pension funding required during the next two budget years. Pension cost includes normal cost and amortization of prior service cost over a forty year period.

EXHIBIT 18-2. EXCERPT OF A MULTIPLE-EMPLOYER PENSION PLAN FOOTNOTE

[CITY OF DALY CITY, CALIFORNIA (JUNE 30, 1984), NOTES TO FINANCIAL STATEMENTS (IN PART)]

Note 10. Retirement Plan

City employees are members of the Public Employees' Retirement System (PERS) of the State of California.

PERS is a multi-employer pension plan administered as an Agency of the State. PERS calculates benefits and contributions separately for each participating employer and each plan. All City employees are covered by either the PERS plan for local safety employees (police and fire) or the plan for local miscellaneous employees (all other employees). Significant information regarding these two PERS plans is summarized as follows:

	Local Safety	Local Miscellaneous
Benefits	Retirement, death and survivor benefits under a defined benefit plan	Same
Minimum Retirement Age:	50	Same
Vesting:	5 years of credited service	Same
Benefit Formula:	"2% at 50"	"2% at 60"
	Under which employees earn 2% of final compensation per year of credited service when retiring at age 50. This percentage increases quarterly with the employee's retirement age. An employee may earn up to a maximum 75% of final compensation.	Under which employees earn 2% of final compensation per year of credited service when retiring at age 60. This percentage increases quarterly with the employee's retirement age.
Actuarial Cost Method:	Entry age normal cost method, a projected benefit cost method assuming an interest factor of $8\frac{1}{2}\%$.	Same
Contribution rates: (effective 7-1-83)		
Employee	9%	7%
Employer	20.4%	12.2%
Participation (at 7-1-84)	166 employees	206 employees
Unfunded liability will be funded by	2011	2000
City Funding Policy	The City pays and charges to expense each year the full amount of contributions for both normal cost and unfunded liability as determined by the PERS actuary.	Same
Costs (year ended June 30, 1984)	$1,152,000	$587,000
Unfunded liability (at 6-30-83) as allocated by PERS to the City	$6,081,000	$4,102,000
Net Assets available (at 6-30-83) as allocated by PERS to the City	$15,240,000	$9,840,000
Actuarial present value of credited projected benefits (at 6-30-83)	$34,606,000	$20,535,000

The above figures are based on financial statements of the PERS at June 30, 1983, which are the most recent statements available to the City.

During the year ended June 30, 1983, the City contributed a total of $1,203,000 to the PERS. This contribution reflected a one-time credit of $476,000 as calculated by the PERS.

EXHIBIT 18-3. EXCERPT OF A PENSION FOOTNOTE WITH BOTH SINGLE-EMPLOYER AND MULTIPLE-EMPLOYER PENSION PLANS

[CITY OF ALLENTOWN, PENNSYLVANIA (DECEMBER 31, 1983), NOTES TO FINANCIAL STATEMENTS (IN PART)]

Note B—Summary of Significant Accounting Policies [in part]

Pension

All full-time employees of the City are covered by either a state administered plan (PMRS) or the City's local plans (Officers and Employees, Firemen and Police). Contributions to the PMRS Plan are made by the City in amounts sufficient to fund current service costs and to fund prior and past service costs over a thirty-year period. Member employees contribute amounts to the Plan based on salary levels. The City computes pension expense on the basis of normal cost plus the amortization of prior service cost over forty years. Contributions are made to the City plans by active participants based on a formula, by the City in varying amounts based upon appropriations and by the state to the fire and police plans. The excess of pension expense over the current pension contributions recorded in the governmental funds is reflected in the general long-term obligation account group.

Note G—Pensions

The City of Allentown makes contributions to the Pennsylvania Municipal Retirement System (PMRS), a statewide plan, the Policemen's Pension Fund, the Firemen's Pension Fund, the Officers and Employees Pension Fund, all local plans. Each of these funds managed by an Association separate and distinct from the City.

City pension expenditures/expense for all plans consists of the following:

General Fund	$1,607,448
Water Fund	412,422
Sewer Fund	284,282
Pennsylvania Motor Fund	66,880
Trexler Park Fund	19,031
CDBG	28,960
	$2,419,023

For governmental funds, pension expense (normal cost plus amortization of past service cost over 40 years) related to City plans exceeded contributions by $1,029,793. This amount is recorded in the General Long-Term Debt Group.

The City and employee contributions to the state plan equal the normal cost of these benefits plus amortization of past service cost over 30 years.

Contributions to and expenditure/expense for the City plans for the year ended December 31, 1983, are as follows:

	Officers and Employees	Policemen's	Firemen's
City contributions	$3,228,448	$105,877	$518,559
Other contributions	269,303	600,666	372,095
TOTAL CONTRIBUTIONS	$3,497,751	$706,543	$890,654
City pension expenditure/expense	$1,290,483	$105,877	$518,559

Included in city contributions was $2,200,000 transferred from the Allentown Authority Water Project excess funds.

The actuarially-computed present value of vested benefits of the City plans which exceeded plan assets at December 31, 1983, the most recent valuation date, follows:

	Officers and Employees	Policemen's	Firemen's
Actuarial present value of accumulated plan benefits:			
Vested benefits:			
Participants currently receiving payments	$12,812,498	$ 7,171,525	$ 5,495,130
Other participants	9,020,915	3,747,218	4,629,563
	21,833,413	10,918,743	10,124,693
Nonvested benefits	7,640,475	8,203,797	7,657,559
	$29,473,888	$19,122,540	$17,782,252
Net assets available for plan benefits	$ 8,246,564	$ 7,952,049	$ 4,855,263

Investments of the City pension funds consist of the following at December 31, 1983:

	Officers and Employees		Policemen's		Firemen's	
	Market	Cost	Market	Cost	Market	Cost
Common Stock	$3,373,725	$2,854,817	$3,021,750	$2,732,592	$ 195,700	$ 128,611
Bonds	4,196,426	4,016,270	4,047,105	3,880,156	4,319,440	4,117,292
Other	1,083,249	1,083,249	802,316	802,316	239,271	239,271
	$8,653,400	$7,954,336	$7,871,171	$7,415,064	$4,754,411	$4,485,174

The City plans cover City employees hired prior to June 8, 1976. Effective June 8, 1976, membership into the three existing City pension funds was closed. During 1981 over 100 employees transferred membership from the City's Officers and Employees Plan to the PMRS Plan. The total obligation for past service cost for these employees was $1,900,984, of which $912,015 was funded. The remaining obligation is due in 21 equal annual installments beginning in 1991. In order to meet this obligation, the Plan segregated an asset with an original cost of $365,625, the future value of which is equal to this obligation. All other employees hired after June 8, 1976, are enrolled in one of the three pension funds established under the Pennsylvania Municipal Retirement Law, Act 15, 1974, as amended. City and member contributions are payable directly to the Commonwealth of Pennsylvania, which serves as Administrator for the plans. During 1981, the City upgraded the benefits of the PMRS plan. This charge increased unfunded past service cost by $717,180, which will be funded over the thirty years in annual payments of $23,906. The City contributed $504,103 to the state during 1983. At December 31, 1983, the unfunded past service cost for all participants in the PMRS Plan was $1,762,146. PMRS does not capture any other data related to the Plan at the municipal level.

The actuarial valuations of the various plans are based on the following factors.

	Officers and Employees	Policemen's	Firemen's	PMRS
Mortality	1970 group	1970 group	1970 group	1971 group annuity table (male with female ages set back 6 years)
Interest	8%	8%	8%	6½%
Retirement age	62 with 12 years service	57 with 20 years service	60 with 20 years service	Uniformed members: members eligible at ages 56 will retire at 59, members eligible at ages 57–60 will retire at 60. Nonuniformed members: rates indicated are adjusted by adding 5% for the year in which the member is first eligible for normal retirement
Annuity form	Joint and 50–70% survivorship	Joint and 100% survivorship	Joint and 100% survivorship	Not available
Turnover	0–17.5%	None Assumed	None Assumed	An empirical rate based on actuarial studies of actual experience using rates related to years of service and number of members
Salary scale	6% per year	6% per year	6% per year	5% per year

The fair value of individual investments that represent 5% or more of plan at December 31 are as follows:

	Officers & Employees		Policemen's		Firemen's	
	1983	1982	1983	1982	1983	1982
Federated Auto Cash Management Money Market Fund	$1,083,249	$	$802,316	$697,828	$	$256,829
Federal Home Loan Bank, 12.5%, due 9-25-90, face $300,000		321,375			308,250	
Federal National Mortgage Association, 14.3%, due 4-10-87, face $250,000		276,718			276,813	
U.S. Treasury Note, 14.375%, due 4-15-89, face $250,000		289,530				
U.S. Treasury Bonds, 10.375%, due 11-15-12, face $500,000			442,185			
Federal National Mortgage Association, 13.75%, due 4-10-85, face $250,000					259,298	
Federal National Mortgage Association, 13%, due 1-10-86, face $200,000						212,750
AVCO Financial Services, Inc. Subordinated Debentures Zero Coupon, 14.733%, due 11-24-90, face $1,250,000						443,750
Key Pharmaceuticals, Inc. Common Stock, 6,750 shares						210,938

EXHIBIT 18-4. EXCERPT OF PENSION FINANCIAL STATEMENTS NOT PART OF THE CAFR, BUT TO WHICH SEPARATE FINANCIAL STATEMENTS WERE ATTACHED

[CITY OF SYRACUSE, NEW YORK]

Firemen's Pension Fund Cash Receipts and Disbursements for the Year Ended December 31, 1983

RECEIPTS		
City of Syracuse Budget Appropriation		$365,000.00
Foreign Insurance Tax		170,591.34
Refund of Unearned Pension, Prior Year		1,738.66
TOTAL RECEIPTS		$537,330.00
Cash Balance, January 1, 1983		$ (4,939.99)
TOTAL RECEIPTS AND BALANCE		$532,390.01
DISBURSEMENTS		
Firemen's Regular Pension	$130,087.48	
Firemen's Supplemental Pensions	124,292.39	
Firemen's Widows' Regular Pensions	69,022.00	
Firemen's Widows' Supplemental Pensions	204,020.00	
TOTAL DISBURSEMENTS		$527,421.87
Cash Balance, December 31, 1983		$ 4,968.14
Total Disbursements		$532,390.01

Firemen's Pension Fund

This Fund was established by the Legislature June 1, 1905, and closed to new entrants on May 1, 1934. Since that time all employees must join the New York State Employees' Retirement System. The Fund is administered by a Board of Trustees consisting of the Mayor, Chief of Fire and the Commissioner of Finance.

Police Pension Fund Cash Receipts and Disbursements for the Year Ended December 31, 1983

RECEIPTS		
City of Syracuse Budget Appropriation		$400,000.00
Bail Bonds—Police Court		1,326.00
Police Disciplinary Fines		210.00
Refund of Unearned Pension, Prior Year		461.00
TOTAL RECEIPTS		$401,997.00
Cash Balance, January 1, 1983		$ 11,089.31
TOTAL RECEIPTS AND BALANCE		$413,086.31
DISBURSEMENTS		
Policemen's Regular Pension	$ 85,789.98	
Policemen's Supplemental Pensions	96,683.23	
Police Widows' Regular Pensions	60,962.00	
Police Widows' Supplemental Pensions	151,492.00	
TOTAL DISBURSEMENTS		$394,927.21
Cash Balance, December 31, 1983		$ 18,159.10
TOTAL DISBURSEMENTS AND BALANCE		$413,086.31

Police Pension Fund

This Fund was established by the Legislature June 1, 1905, and closed to new entrants on May 1, 1934. Since that time all employees must join the New York State Employees' Retirement System. There are 23 Police Pensioners and 67 Police Widows. The Fund is administered by a Board of Trustees consisting of the Mayor, Chief of Police and the Commissioner of Finance.

EXHIBIT 18-5. EXCERPTS FROM SELECTED COMBINING FINANCIAL STATEMENTS CONTAINING PENSION PLANS

[CITY OF TOLEDO, OHIO]

Fiduciary Funds, Combining Balance Sheet [in part], December 31, 1983 [in thousands]

	Expendable Trust Funds				Expendable Trust Funds		
	Expendable Trust	Police Pension	Fire Pension		Expendable Trust	Police Pension	Fire Pension
Assets				*Liabilities and Fund Balances*			
Equity in pooled cash	$865	$35	$ —	Liabilities:			
Other cash	—	—	—	Due to pooled cash	$ —	$—	$ —
Accounts receivable (net of allowances for uncollectibles)	40	—	—	Accounts payable	8	—	—
				Escrow	—	—	—
Prepaid expenditures	—	—	—	Due to other governments	—	—	—
Total Assets	$905	$35	$ —	Other current liabilities	—	—	—
				Total liabilities	8	—	—
				Fund Balances:			
				Unreserved, Undesignated	897	35	—
				Accumulated deficit	—	—	—
				Total fund balances	897	35	—
				Total liabilities and fund balances	$905	$35	$ —

Expendable Trust Funds, Combining Statement of Revenues, Expenditures and Changes in Fund Balances, for the Year Ended December 31, 1983 [in thousands]

	Expendable Trusts	Police Pension	Fire Pension	Totals 1983	Totals 1982
Revenues:					
Property taxes	$ —	$787	$787	$ 1,574	$ 1,478
Intergovernmental revenues	177	—	—	177	379
Charges for services	286	—	—	286	195
Investment earnings	13	—	—	13	191
Other revenue	633	—	37	670	582
Total revenues	1,109	787	824	2,720	2,825
Expenditures:					
Current					
General government	1,222	—	—	1,222	2,230
Public service	203	—	—	203	17
Public safety	30	764	781	1,575	1,740
Community environment	351	—	—	351	2
Parks and recreation	305	—	—	305	154
Total expenditures	2,111	764	781	3,656	4,143
Excess (deficiency) of revenues over expenditures	(1,002)	23	43	(936)	(1,318)
Other financing (uses):					
Operating transfers (out)	(168)	—	—	(168)	(238)
Total other financing (uses)	(168)	—	—	(168)	(238)
Excess (deficiency) of revenues over expenditures and other uses	1,170	23	43	(1,104)	(1,556)
Fund balances at beginning of year	2,067	12	(43)	2,036	3,593
Fund balances at end of year	$ 897	$ 35	$ —	$ 932	$ 2,037

[CITY OF DELRAY BEACH, FLORIDA]

Combining Balance Sheet—Fiduciary Funds, September 30, 1983

	General Employees' Pension Fund	Police and Firemen's Pension Fund	Special Projects Fund	Cemetery Perpetual Care Fund	Total
ASSETS					
Cash and cash equivalents	$ 7,534	$	$	$	$ 7,534
Investments (at market)	6,651,804	5,676,690			12,328,494
Accounts receivable, net	39,634	7,279			46,913
Accrued interest receivable	73,434	75,563			148,997
Due from other funds			50,273	66,415	116,688
Prepaid expenses		3,614			3,614
	$6,772,406	$5,763,146	$50,273	$66,415	$12,652,240
LIABILITIES AND FUND BALANCES					
LIABILITIES					
Accounts payable	$	$ 309	$18,419	$	$ 18,728
Due to other funds	35,292	5,238			40,530
	35,292	5,547	18,419		59,258
FUND BALANCES					
Reserved for special projects			31,854		31,854
Reserved for retirement benefits and refund of employee contributions	6,737,114	5,757,599			12,494,713
Unreserved					
Undesignated				66,415	66,415
	6,737,114	5,757,599	31,854	66,415	12,592,982
	$6,772,406	$5,763,146	$50,273	$66,415	$12,652,240

Combining Statement of Revenue, Expenses and Changes in Fund Balance—Pension Trust Funds, Year Ended September 30, 1983

	General Employees' Pension Fund	Police and Firemen's Pension Fund	Total
Operating revenue			
Contributions			
Employees	$ 252,034	$ 213,668	$ 465,702
Employer	623,267	509,214	1,132,481
State		213,594	213,594
	875,301	936,476	1,811,777
Earnings on investments			
Interest on investments	275,150	364,368	639,518
Dividends on stock	112,056	94,884	206,940
Gain on sale of investments	224,056	12,663	236,719
Net appreciation in fair value of investments	491,057	332,015	823,072
	1,102,319	803,930	1,906,249
TOTAL OPERATING REVENUE	1,977,620	1,740,406	3,718,026
Operating expense			
Benefit payments	211,706	233,582	445,288
Refunds	155,103	34,347	189,450
Other operating expenses	39,148	14,425	53,573
	405,957	282,354	688,311
NET INCOME	1,571,663	1,458,052	3,029,715
Fund balance, October 1, 1982	5,165,451	4,299,547	9,464,998
FUND BALANCE, SEPTEMBER 30, 1983	$6,737,114	$5,757,599	$12,494,713

Combining Statement of Changes in Financial Position—Pension Trust Funds, Year Ended September 30, 1983

	General Employees' Pension Fund	Police and Firemen's Pension Fund	Total
SOURCE OF FUNDS			
Net income	$1,571,663	$1,458,052	$3,029,715
APPLICATION OF FUNDS			
Increase in investments	1,571,186	1,501,618	3,072,804
INCREASE (DECREASE) IN WORKING CAPITAL	$ 477	$ (43,566)	$ (43,089)
CHANGES IN COMPONENTS OF WORKING CAPITAL			
Increase (decrease) in current assets			
Cash	$ 369	$ (35,546)	$ (35,177)
Accounts receivable	1,586	6,838	8,424
Accrued interest receivable	1,132	(1,387)	(255)
Due from other funds		(14,078)	(14,078)
Prepaid expenses		3,614	3,614
	3,087	(40,559)	(37,472)
Increase (decrease) in current liabilities			
Accounts payable	(140)	169	29
Due to other funds	2,750	2,838	5,588
	2,610	3,007	5,617
INCREASE (DECREASE) IN WORKING CAPITAL	$ 477	$ (43,566)	$ (43,089)

Chapter 19
Status of Governmental Accounting Standards

Chapter 1 provided background information on the organizations involved in setting accounting standards for governmental organizations. Until 1984 the principal originators of guidance affecting the accounting and reporting and the auditing involved with local government financial statements were the National Council on Governmental Accounting (and its predecessor, the National Committee on Governmental Accounting) and the American Institute of Certified Public Accountants (AICPA), respectively. The roles of these organizations have been assumed by a newly established Governmental Accounting Standards Board (GASB).

PRONOUNCEMENTS BY THE NCGA

Throughout the study extensive reference was made to NCGA Statement 1. The Council has issued six additional statements, as well as other guidance to the profession. Statement 1 is of particular significance, however, for this publication sets forth, in a single document, the several desired accounting principles and reporting practices for governmental units. The NCGA issuances have taken several forms:*

Statements reflect the conclusions of at least a majority plus one of the council as to governing principles and explain and illustrate their application, including alternative applications where such alternatives are deemed appropriate.

Interpretations are issued by a majority plus one vote of the council to clarify, elaborate upon, or explain a council statement, a principle or illustration, or related matters.

Exposure drafts, proposed statements, background papers, working drafts, and discussion memoranda may be issued by the council as necessary to solicit comments and assist in resolving issues.

Table 19-1 lists several statements and other publications issued by the NCGA through March 31, 1984.

---

* James S. Remis, "An Historical Perspective on Setting Governmental Accounting Standards," in *Governmental Finance,* Municipal Finance Officer's Association, Chicago, Illinois, 1982.

PRONOUNCEMENTS BY THE AICPA

Since 1974 audits of governmental units and the form of financial reporting have been significantly influenced by the AICPA. In that year the AICPA published an industry audit guide, *Audits of State and Local Governmental Units.* An exposure draft of a proposed revised and updated audit and accounting guide for state and local government units was issued by the AICPA in October 1984. When published in final form this newer guide will supersede the 1974 audit guide. At the present time this AICPA industry audit guide is under revision. A revised and updated audit guide is expected to be published by the AICPA during 1985. As shown in Table 19-2, the AICPA has issued statements of positions since 1974 to revise or clarify certain of the practices outlined in the audit guide.

PRONOUNCEMENTS BY THE GASB

Shortly after its formation the Governmental Accounting Standards Board issued its Statement 1, "Authoritative Status of NCGA Pronouncements and AICPA Industry Audit Guide." This statement continues in force the pronouncements of the NCGA and the AICPA, which until they are changed or superseded by GASB, are considered as representing generally accepted accounting principles.

Table 19-3 is a partial listing of GASB publications through March 1, 1985.

TABLES FOR CHAPTER 19

Table 19-1. Partial Listing of Publications by the NCGA and Its Predecessors (as of March 1985)

Table 19-2. Partial Listing of Publications by the AICPA on Governmental Auditing (as of March 1985)

Table 19-3. Partial Listing of Publications by the GASB on Governmental Accounting (as of March 1985)

TABLE 19-1. PARTIAL LISTING OF PUBLICATIONS BY THE NCGA AND ITS PREDECESSORS (AS OF MARCH 1985)

Publication	Title	Year Issued	Publication	Title	Year Issued
	National Council on Municipal Accounting			*Statements*	
1	"Principles of Municipal Accounting"	1934	3	"Defining the Governmental Reporting Entity"	1981
2	"Suggested Procedure for a Detailed Municipal Audit"	1934	4	"Accounting and Financial Reporting Principles for Claims and Judgments and Compensated Absences"	1982
3	"A Bibliography of Municipal Accounting"	1934	5	"Accounting and Financial Reporting Principles for Lease Agreements of State and Local Governments"	1983
4	"Municipal Accounting Terminology"	1935			
5	"Municipal Funds and Their Balance Sheets" (replaced No. 1)	1935	6	"Pension Accounting and Financial Reporting: Public Employee Retirement Systems and State and Local Government Employers"	1983
6	"Municipal Accounting Statements"	1936			
7	"Bibliography of Municipal and State Accounting" (replaced No. 3)	1937	7	"Financial Reporting for Component Units Within the Governmental Reporting Entity"	1984
8	"Municipal Audit Procedure" (replaced No. 2)	1938			
9	"A Standard Classification of Municipal Revenues and Expenditures"	1939		*Interpretations*	
10	"A Report of Progress"	1940	1	"GAAFR and the AICPA Audit Guide" (superseded by Statement 1)	1976
11	"Municipal Accounting Terminology for State, Municipal, and Other Local Governments" (replaced No. 4)	1941	2	"Segment Information for Enterprise Funds"	1980
12	"Municipal Accounting Statements" (replaced No. 6)	1941	3	"Review Recognition—Property Taxes"	1981
13	"Governmental Accounting Bibliography" (replaced No. 7)	1941	4	"Accounting and Financial Reporting for Public Employee Retirement Systems and Pension Trust Funds"	1981
	National Committee on Governmental Accounting		5	"Authoritative Status of Governmental Accounting, Auditing, and Financial Reporting" (1968)	1982
14	"Municipal Accounting and Auditing" (replaced Nos. 5 and 12)	1951	6	"Notes to the Financial Statements Disclosure"	1982
15	"Municipal Audit Procedure" (replaced No. 8)	1951	7	"Clarification as to the Application of the Criteria in NCGA Statement 3 Defining the governmental Reporting Entity"	1983
16	"Municipal Accounting Terminology" (replaced No. 11)	1951			
17	"A Standard Classification of Municipal Accounts" (replaced No. 9)	1953	8	"Certain Pension Matters"	1983
	"Governmental Accounting, Auditing and Financial Reporting" (codified Nos. 14–17)	1968	9	"Certain Fund Classifications and Balance Sheet Accounts"	1984
			10	"State and Local Government Budgeting Reporting"	1984
	National Council on Governmental Accounting Statements		11	"Claim and Judgment Transactions for Governmental Funds"	1984
1	"Governmental Accounting and Financial Reporting Principles" (replaced 1968 GAAFR and Interpretation 1)	1979		*Concepts Statements*	
2	"Grant, Entitlement, and Shared Revenue Accounting and Reporting by State and Local Governments"	1979	1	"Objectives of Accounting and Financial Reporting for Governmental Units"	1981

Source: Technical Agenda National Council on Governmental Accounting, Chicago, Illinois, March 1, 1983, updated to March 1985.

TABLE 19-2. PARTIAL LISTING OF PUBLICATIONS BY THE AICPA ON GOVERNMENTAL AUDITING (AS OF MARCH 1985)

Publication	Title	Year Issued
Industry Audit Guide	"Audits of State and Local Governmental Units"	1974
Statement of Position 75-3	"Accrual of Revenues and Expenditures by State and Local Governmental Units"	1975
Statement of Position 77-2	"Accounting for Interfund Transfers of State and Local Governmental Units"	1977
Statement of Position 78-5	"Accounting for Advance Refunding of Tax-Exempt Debt"	1978
Statement of Position 78-7	"Financial Accounting and Reporting by Hospitals Operated by a Governmental Unit"	1978
Statement of Position 78-10	"Accounting Principles and Reporting Practices for Certain Nonprofit Organizations"	1978
Statement of Position 79-1	"Accounting for Municipal Bond Funds"	1979
Statement of Position 80-2	"Accounting and Financial Reporting by Governmental Units"	1980
Exposure draft, Industry Audit Guide (revision)	"Proposed Audit and Accounting Guide—Audits of State and Local Governmental Units	1984

TABLE 19-3. PARTIAL LISTING OF PUBLICATIONS BY THE GASB ON GOVERNMENTAL ACCOUNTING (AS OF MARCH 1985)

Publication	Title	Year Issued
Statement 1	"Authoritative Status of NCGA Pronouncements and AICPA Industry Audit Guide"	1984
Technical Bulletin 84-1	"Purpose and Scope of GASB Technical Bulletins and Procedures for Issuance"	1984
Interpretation 1	"Demand Bonds Issued by State and Local Governmental Entities"	1984

Appendix
Cities and Counties Whose Financial Statements
Were Included in The Survey

State	Fiscal Year End	Cities and Counties	State	Fiscal Year End	Cities and Counties
ALABAMA	9/30/83	Bessemer		6/30/84	Riverside
	6/30/84	Birmingham		6/30/84	Rosemead
	9/30/83	Decatur		6/30/84	San Buena Ventura
	9/30/83	Dothan		6/30/84	San Francisco
	4/30/84	Florence		6/30/84	San Leandro
	9/30/83	Huntsville		6/30/84	San Mateo
	9/30/83	Mobile		6/30/84	Santa Ana
	9/30/83	Montgomery		6/30/84	Santa Barbara
	9/30/83	Prichard		6/30/84	Santa Clara
	9/30/83	Tuscaloosa		6/30/84	Santa Cruz
	9/30/84	Clarke County		6/30/84	Santa Monica
	9/30/83	Colbert County		6/30/84	Stockton
	9/30/83	Escambra County		6/30/84	Thousand Oaks
	9/30/84	Madison County		6/30/84	Upland
				6/30/84	Vacaville
ARKANSAS	12/31/83	Fayetteville		6/30/84	Visalia
	12/31/83	Hot Springs		6/30/84	Vista
	12/31/83	Pine Bluff		6/30/84	W. Covina
				6/30/84	Westminster
ALASKA	12/31/83	Anchorage County		6/30/84	Whittier
				6/30/84	Contra Costa County
ARIZONA	6/30/84	Flagstaff		6/30/84	Orange County
	6/30/84	Glendale		6/30/84	San Luis Obispo County
	6/30/84	Mesa			
	6/30/84	Phoenix	COLORADO	12/31/83	Arvada
	6/30/84	Scottsdale		12/31/83	Aurora
	6/30/84	Tempe		12/31/83	Boulder
	6/30/84	Tucson		12/31/83	Colorado Springs
				12/31/83	Ft. Collins
CALIFORNIA	6/30/84	Alhambra		12/31/83	Grand County
	6/30/84	Anaheim		12/31/83	Greeley
	6/30/84	Bellflower		12/31/83	Lakewood
	6/30/84	Buena Park		12/31/83	Longmont
	6/30/84	BuenaVentura		12/31/83	Pueblo
	6/30/84	Chula Vista		12/31/83	Thornton
	6/30/84	Covina		12/31/83	Westminster
	6/30/84	Daly City		12/31/83	Denver County
	6/30/84	Fountain Valley		12/31/83	Jefferson County
	6/30/84	Fremont		12/31/83	Pitkin County
	6/30/84	Fullerton			
	6/30/84	Garden Grove	CONNECTICUT	6/30/84	East Hartford
	6/30/84	Gardena		6/30/84	Enfield
	6/30/84	Glendale		9/30/83	Greenwich
	6/30/84	Huntington Beach		6/30/84	Guilford
	6/30/84	Irvine		6/30/84	Hartford
	6/30/84	Lakewood		6/30/84	Milford
	6/30/84	Modesto		6/30/84	Norwalk
	6/30/84	Placentia		6/30/84	Stamford
	6/30/84	Rialton		6/30/84	Trumbull

State	Fiscal Year End	Cities and Counties	State	Fiscal Year End	Cities and Counties
DELAWARE	6/30/84	New Castle County		12/31/83	Floyd County
				12/31/83	Fulton County
DISTRICT OF COLUMBIA	9/30/83	Washington		12/31/83	Gwinnet County
				6/30/84	Houston County
FLORIDA	9/30/83	Baco Raton		12/31/83	Monroe County
	9/30/83	Clearwater		12/31/83	Richmond County
	9/30/83	Coral Springs		6/30/84	Warren County
	9/30/83	Daytona Beach			
	9/30/83	Delray Beach	HAWAII	6/30/84	Hawaii County
	9/30/83	Dunedin			
	9/30/83	Ft. Lauderdale	IOWA	6/30/84	Cherokee County
	9/30/83	Ft. Meyers		6/30/84	Chicksaw County
	9/30/83	Ft. Pierce		6/30/84	Dallas County
	9/30/84	Hollywood		6/30/84	Greene County
	9/30/83	Jacksonville		6/30/84	Howard County
	9/30/83	Lakeland		6/30/84	Humboldt County
	9/30/83	Largo		6/30/84	Jerrerson County
	9/30/83	Lauderhill		6/30/84	Linn County
	9/30/83	Melbourne		6/30/84	Mahaska County
	9/30/83	Miami		6/30/84	O'Brien County
	9/30/83	Miramar		6/30/84	Shelby County
	9/30/84	North Miami		6/30/84	Stony County
	9/30/83	Orlando			
	9/30/83	Pensacola			
	9/30/83	Plantation	IDAHO	9/30/83	Boise City
	9/30/83	Sarasota			
	9/30/83	St. Petersburg			
	9/30/83	Tallahassee	ILLINOIS	3/31/84	Alton
	9/30/83	Tampa		4/30/84	Belleville
	9/30/83	Titusville		12/31/83	Bolingbrook
	9/30/83	Alacua County		4/30/84	Calumet City
	9/30/83	Brevard County		4/30/84	Carbondale
	9/30/83	Charlotte County		6/30/84	Champaign
	9/30/83	Dade County		12/31/83	Chicago
	9/30/83	DeSoto County		4/30/84	Danville
	9/30/83	Hillsborough County		6/30/84	DeKalb
	9/30/84	Indian River County		9/30/83	Decatur
	9/30/84	Lake County		12/31/83	Des Plaines
	9/30/84	Martin County		12/31/83	Downers Grove
	9/30/83	Orange County		12/31/83	Elgin
	9/30/83	Palm Beach County		4/30/84	Elmhurst
	9/30/83	Pinellas County		2/29/84	Evanston
	11/30/83	Santa Rose County		12/31/83	Evansville
	9/30/83	Seminole County		3/31/84	Galesburg
	9/30/83	Volusia County		4/30/84	Highland Park
				4/30/84	Hoffman Estates
GEORGIA	6/30/84	Albany		12/31/83	Joliet
	6/30/84	Athens		4/30/84	Kankakee
	12/31/83	Atlanta		4/30/84	Mount Prospect
	6/30/84	Catersville		9/30/84	Naperville
	6/30/84	Columbus		4/30/84	Niles
	6/30/84	Macon		3/31/84	Normal
	12/31/83	Savannah		12/31/83	Oak Park
	6/30/84	Taunton		4/30/84	Park Ridge
	6/30/84	Valdosta		12/31/83	Peoria
	9/30/84	Bibb County		12/31/83	Rockford
	12/31/83	Bleckley County		4/30/84	Skokie
	12/31/83	Chatham County		2/29/84	Springfield
	6/30/84	Clayton County		4/30/84	Waukegan
	9/30/84	Cobb County		4/30/84	Wheaton
	6/30/84	Colquitt County		12/4/83	Cook County
	12/31/83	DeKalb County		11/30/83	Dekalb County
	6/30/84	Dougherty County		11/30/83	Kane County

State	Fiscal Year End	Cities and Counties	State	Fiscal Year End	Cities and Counties
	11/30/83	Madison County		12/31/83	Oakland County
	11/30/83	Rock Island County		12/31/83	Monroe County
INDIANA	12/31/83	Indianapolis	MINNESOTA	12/31/83	Bloomington
	12/31/83	Marion		12/31/83	Brooklyn Center
	12/31/83	South Bend		12/31/83	Brooklyn Park
	12/31/83	Terre Haute		12/31/83	Coon Rapids
				12/31/83	Fridley
KANSAS	12/31/84	Lawrence		12/31/83	Minnetonka
	12/31/83	Manhattan		12/31/83	Plymouth
	12/31/83	Overland Park		12/31/83	Richfield
	12/31/83	Topeka		12/31/83	Rochester
	12/31/83	Wichita		12/31/83	St. Paul
	12/31/83	Johnson County		12/31/83	Anoka County
	12/31/83	Riley County		12/31/83	Blue Earth County
	12/31/83	Saline County		12/31/83	Brenton County
	12/31/83	Sedgwich County		12/31/83	Brown County
	12/31/83	Shawnee County		12/31/83	Clay County
				12/31/83	Farrbault County
LOUISIANA	12/31/83	Bossier City		12/31/83	Hennepin County
	12/31/83	Houma		12/31/83	Houston County
	10/31/83	Lafayette		12/31/83	Itasca County
	4/30/84	Monroe		12/31/83	Murray County
	12/31/83	New Orleans		12/31/83	Olmstead County
	12/31/83	Shreveport		12/31/83	Pennington County
	12/31/83	St. James Parish County		12/31/83	Ramsey County
				12/31/83	Washington County
MASSACHUSETTS	6/30/84	Everett			
	6/30/84	Leominster	MISSISSIPPI	9/30/83	Hattiesburg
	6/30/84	Malden		9/30/83	Jackson
	6/30/84	Salem			
			MISSOURI	4/30/84	Kansas City
MAINE	6/30/84	Bangor		6/30/84	Springfield
	12/31/83	Penebscot		6/30/84	University City
	12/31/83	Cumberland County		12/31/83	Greene County
				12/31/83	Jackson County
MARYLAND	6/30/84	Annapolis		12/31/83	Randolph County
	6/30/84	Baltimore		12/31/83	St. Louis County
	6/30/84	Bowie			
	6/30/84	Anne Arundel County	NEBRASKA	12/31/83	Omaha
	6/30/84	Caroline County			
	6/30/84	Carroll County	NEW HAMPSHIRE	12/31/83	Concorde
	6/30/84	Charles County		12/31/83	Nashua
	6/30/84	Frederick County		12/31/83	Cheshire County
	6/30/84	Harford County		12/31/83	Merrimach County
	6/30/84	Howard County			
	6/30/84	Montgomery County	NEW MEXICO	6/30/84	Albuquerque
	6/30/84	Prince George's County		6/30/84	Clovis
	6/30/84	Talbot County		6/30/84	Farmington
	6/30/84	Wicomico County		6/30/84	Roswell
MICHIGAN	6/30/84	Farmington Hills	NEW JERSEY	12/31/83	East Brunswick
	12/31/83	Kalamazoo		12/31/83	Elizabeth
	6/30/84	Port Huron		12/31/83	Linden
	12/31/83	Genesee County		12/31/83	Middletown
	12/31/83	Ingham County		12/31/83	Montclair
	12/31/83	Kent County		12/31/83	Pennsauken
	12/31/83	Midland County		12/31/83	Piscataway
	12/31/83	Muskegan County		12/31/83	Teaneck
	12/31/83	Ottawa County		12/31/83	Camden County
	12/31/83	Saginaw County		12/31/83	Gloucester County
	12/31/83	St. Clair County		12/31/83	Mercer County
	12/31/83	Washtenaw County		12/31/83	Middlesex County

State	Fiscal Year End	Cities and Counties	State	Fiscal Year End	Cities and Counties
	12/31/83	Monmouth County		6/30/84	New Hanover County
	12/31/83	Morris County		6/30/84	Orange County
	12/31/83	Passaic County		6/30/84	Pamlico County
	12/31/83	Somerset County		6/30/84	Person County
	12/31/83	Union County		6/30/84	Pitt County
				6/30/84	Randolph County
NEW YORK	6/30/84	Auburn		6/30/84	Stokes County
	12/31/84	Binghampton		6/30/84	Transylvannia County
	12/31/83	Mount Vernon		6/30/84	Troy County
	12/31/83	N. Tonawanda		6/30/84	Warren County
	12/31/83	New Rochelle		6/30/84	Washington County
	6/30/84	New York		6/30/84	Wayne County
	6/30/84	Rochester		6/30/84	Wilkes County
	12/31/83	Rome			
	12/31/84	Schenectady	NORTH DAKOTA	12/31/83	Grand Forks
	12/31/83	Syracuse			
	12/31/83	Broome County	OHIO	12/31/83	Akron
	12/31/83	Chautaqua County		12/31/83	Cleveland
	12/31/83	Chemung County		12/31/83	Columbus
	12/31/83	Clinton County		12/31/83	Cuyahoga Falls
	12/31/83	Dutchess County		12/31/83	Dayton
	12/31/83	Erie County		12/31/83	Euclid
	12/31/83	Herkimer County		9/30/83	Idaho Falls
	12/31/83	Livingston County		12/31/83	Kettering
	12/31/83	Madison County		12/31/84	Lakewood
	12/31/83	Monroe County		12/31/83	Lorrain
	12/31/83	Nassau County		12/31/83	Mentor
	12/31/83	Niagara County		12/31/83	Sandusky
	12/31/83	Oconodaga County		12/31/83	Shaker Heights
	12/31/83	Ontario County		12/31/84	Springfield
	12/31/83	Rensselaer County		12/31/83	Toledo
	12/31/83	Rockland County		6/30/84	Cuyahoga County
	12/31/83	Saratoga County		12/31/83	Greene County
	12/31/83	Steuben County		12/31/83	Hamilton County
	12/31/83	Suffolk County		12/31/83	Hardin County
	12/31/83	Ulster County			
			OKLAHOMA	6/30/84	Enid
NORTH CAROLINA	6/30/84	Burlington		6/30/84	Lawton
	6/30/84	Durham		6/30/84	Midwest City
	6/30/84	Goldsboro		6/30/84	Muskogee
	6/30/84	Greensboro		6/30/84	Oklahoma City
	6/30/84	Raleigh		6/30/84	Stillwater
	6/30/84	Wilmington		9/30/84	Tulsa
	6/30/84	Alamance County			
	6/30/84	Bertie County			
	6/30/84	Bladen County	OREGON	6/30/84	Eugene
	6/30/84	Buncombe County		6/30/84	Portland
	6/30/84	Burke County			
	6/30/84	Camden County			
	6/30/84	Catawba County	PENNSYLVANIA	12/31/83	Allentown
	6/30/84	Chatham County		12/31/83	Altoona
	6/30/84	Cumberland County		8/31/84	Bethlehem
	6/30/84	Davidson County		12/31/83	Johnston
	6/30/84	Durham County		12/31/84	Lancaster
	6/30/84	Granville County		12/31/83	Mount Lebannon
	6/30/84	Guilford County		12/31/84	Pittsburgh
	6/30/84	Halifax County		12/31/83	Wilkes Barre
	6/30/84	Harnet County		12/31/83	Williamsport
	6/30/84	Johnston County		12/31/83	Allegheny County
	6/30/84	Lee County		12/31/83	Bradford County
	6/30/84	Macon County		12/31/83	Chester County
	6/30/84	Mecklenberg County		12/31/83	Delaware County

State	Fiscal Year End	Cities and Counties	State	Fiscal Year End	Cities and Counties
	12/31/83	Erie County	VIRGINIA	6/30/84	Alexandria
	12/31/83	Lancaster County		6/30/84	Chesapeake
	12/31/83	LeHigh County		6/30/84	Newport News
	12/31/83	Lebannon County		6/30/84	Norfolk
	12/31/83	Lycoming County		6/30/84	Petersburg
	12/31/83	Northampton County		6/30/84	Portsmouth
	12/31/83	Somerset County		6/30/84	Richmond
	12/31/83	Westmoreland County		6/30/84	Roanoke
				6/30/84	Suffolk
RHODE ISLAND	12/31/83	East Providence		6/30/84	Virginia Beach
	6/30/84	Woonsocket		6/30/84	Albemarle County
				6/30/84	Amherst County
SOUTH CAROLINA	12/31/84	Greenville		6/30/84	Goochland County
	12/31/83	Rock Hill		6/30/84	Hanover County
	6/30/84	Spartanburg		6/30/84	James County
	6/30/84	Aiken County		6/30/84	Loudoun County
	6/30/84	Berkeley County		6/30/84	Montgomery County
	6/30/84	Clarendon County		6/30/84	Prince William County
	6/30/84	Greenville County		6/30/84	Roanoke County
	6/30/84	Greenwood County		6/30/84	Rockingham County
	6/30/84	Lancaster County			
	6/30/84	Richland County	WASHINGTON	12/31/83	Bellevue
	6/30/84	Spartanburg County		12/31/83	Bellingham
	6/30/84	Sumter County		12/31/83	Richland
	12/31/83	Ulster County		12/31/83	Seattle
				12/31/83	Spokane
SOUTH DAKOTA	12/31/83	Rapid City		12/31/83	Takoma
	12/31/84	Sioux Falls		12/31/83	Vancouver
				12/31/83	Yakima
TENNESSEE	6/30/84	Jackson		12/31/83	Shohomis County
	6/30/84	Oak Ridge			
			WISCONSIN	12/31/84	Appleton
TEXAS	9/30/83	Baytown		9/30/84	Beloit
	9/30/84	Beaumont		12/31/83	Eau Claire
	9/30/83	Brownsville		12/31/83	Fon duLac
	6/30/84	College Station		12/31/83	Green Bay
	9/30/83	Dallas		12/31/83	Greenfield
	9/30/83	Denton		12/31/83	LaCrosse
	9/30/83	Ft. Worth		12/31/83	Madison
	9/30/83	Galveston		12/31/83	Manitowoc
	9/30/83	Grand Prarie		12/31/83	New Berlin
	9/30/83	Harlingen		12/31/83	Oskosh
	9/30/83	Irving		12/31/83	Plymouth
	9/30/83	Killeen		12/31/83	Waukesha
	9/30/83	Lubbock		12/31/83	Ashland County
	9/30/83	McAllen		12/31/83	Dane County
	9/30/83	Odessa		6/30/84	Manitowoc County
	9/30/83	Plano		12/31/83	Milwaukee County
	9/30/83	San Angelo		12/31/83	Monroe County
	9/30/83	San Antonio		12/31/83	Outgamie County
	9/30/83	Temple		12/31/83	Pepin County
	9/30/83	Texarkana		12/31/83	Rock County
	6/30/84	Texas City		12/31/83	Washington County
	9/30/83	Tyler		12/31/83	Winnebago County
	9/30/83	Waco			
	9/30/83	Wichita Falls	WEST VIRGINIA	6/30/84	Charleston
	9/30/83	Montgomery County		6/30/84	Cabell County
				6/30/84	Mercer County
UTAH	6/30/84	Brigham City		6/30/84	Mongolia County
	6/30/84	Ogden			
	6/30/84	Salt Lake City	WYOMING	6/30/84	Cheyenne
	6/30/84	Sandy City		12/31/83	Wailesja County

Index